NECTAR GAZE AND POISON BREATH

An Analysis and Translation of the Rajasthani Oral Narrative of Devnārāyaṇ

ADITYA MALIK

Śrī Hukamārām Bhopā, the singer of the narrative.

OXFORD
UNIVERSITY PRESS

2005

OXFORD
UNIVERSITY PRESS

Oxford University Press, Inc., publishes works that further
Oxford University's objective of excellence
in research, scholarship, and education.

Oxford New York
Auckland Cape Town Dar es Salaam Hong Kong Karachi
Kuala Lumpur Madrid Melbourne Mexico City Nairobi
New Delhi Shanghai Taipei Toronto

With offices in
Argentina Austria Brazil Chile Czech Republic France Greece
Guatemala Hungary Italy Japan Poland Portugal Singapore
South Korea Switzerland Thailand Turkey Ukraine Vietnam

Published by Oxford University Press, Inc.
198 Madison Avenue, New York, New York 10016

www.oup.com

Library of Congress Cataloging-in-Publication Data
Malik, Aditya.
Nectar gaze and poison breath : an analysis and translation of the Rajasthani oral
narrative of Devnārāyaṇ / Aditya Malik.
p. cm.—(South Asia research)
In English; includes translation from Marwari.
Includes bibliographical references and index.
ISBN-13 978-0-19-515019-3
ISBN 0-19-515019-8
1. Folk poetry, Indic—India—Rajasthan—History and criticism.
2. Epic poetry, Rajasthani—History and criticism. 3. Devanārāyaṇ
(Hindu diety)—Cult—India—Rajasthan. 4. Devanārāyaṇ (Hindu deity)—
Poetry. I. Title. II. South Asia research (New York, N.Y.)
PK2708.2.M35 2004
398.2'0954'401—dc22 2004050140

2 4 6 8 9 7 5 3 1

Printed in the United States of America
on acid-free paper

NECTAR GAZE AND POISON BREATH

SOUTH ASIA RESEARCH

SERIES EDITOR
Patrick Olivelle

A Publication Series of
The University of Texas Center for Asian Studies
and
Oxford University Press

The Early Upanisads
Annotated Text and Translation
Patrick Olivelle

Indian Epigraphy
A Guide to the Study of Inscriptions in Sanskrit, Prakrit, and the Other Indo-Aryan Languages
Richard Salomon

A Dictionary of Old Marathi
S. G. Tulpule and Anne Feldhaus

Donors, Devotees, and Daughters of God
Temple Women in Medieval Tamilnadu
Leslie C. Orr

Jimutavahana's Dayabhaga
The Hindu Law of Inheritance in Bengal
Edited and Translated with an Introduction and Notes by Ludo Rocher

Nectar Gaze and Poison Breath
An Analysis and Translation of the Rajasthani Oral Narrative of Devnārāyaṇ
Aditya Malik

For Bele

and for Renuka and Ambika

Preface

My interest in the narrative of Devnārāyaṇ began when I was doing fieldwork for my Ph.D. dissertation on the pilgrimage center of Puṣkar in Rajasthan. During 1984 and 1985 I spent several months consecutively in Puṣkar and a number of villages surrounding it. My visits to villages around Puṣkar were focused on details of the villages' history, and their relationship—if any—to Puṣkar or more specifically to what was defined as the *Puṣkara-kṣetra* (sacred field of Puṣkara). One of the larger villages I spent most time in was Pisāṅgan, about 20 kilometer west of Puṣkar. It was here that I became acquainted with Pusā Nāth Dāṅgī, who then must have been in his late forties. Pusā Nāth belonged to the caste of Damāmīs, or drummer-genealogists, for Rajput (warrior or aristocratic caste) families. He and his ancestors had been in the service of the rājā of Pisāṅgan. Pusā Nāth was well known in Pisāṅgan and in many villages in the surrounding area. My meeting with him was quite unplanned, as were many acquaintances and friendships I made during field trips. On one of my first trips to Pisāṅgan I visited the old dilapidated *gaṛh* (fort) of the rājā of Pisāṅgan. While I was walking along the ramparts of the outer wall—rather lost—I was spoken to by Lakṣman Singh, the purohit (chaplain) of the rājā of Pisāṅgan, who was accompanied by the rājā's son. I told him that I was doing research on Puṣkar and the villages surrounding it. I asked him whether he knew of anyone who might be able to assist and accompany me in my work. Lakṣman Singh suggested I get in touch with Pusā Nāth Dāṅgī, whom he then personally introduced me to. Pusā Nāth had married a second time after his first wife died. He had two grown-up daughters who were married a few years later, and a son who was then about 10 years old. Pusā Nāth's second wife was quite open in telling me (in front of Pusā Nāth) that she had salvaged ("saved") Pusā Nāth's life: "If it hadn't been for me this fellow would have been a wreck!" Pusā Nāth didn't argue with this statement, although he didn't find it very flattering. His sole comment was that his son was the anchor in his life, who'd saved his "head being eaten up" by the three women in his home! It came as no surprise then that all the men left their homes as early as possible to gather among themselves at tea stores and under trees, safe from the imagined domestic dominance of their wives, where stories of manliness and heroism could flow freely and be believed in.

One of the villages we visited was Pagārā, which was about 4 kilometers away from Pisāṅgan. It was here that Pusā Nāth introduced me to Bhopā Haridās Mahārāj, who was the keeper of the Devnārāyaṇ temple in Pagārā. Bhopā Haridās was a temple-bhopā, in contrast to *paṛ*-bhopās, who sang the narrative of Devnārāyaṇ professionally. At that time I had not heard of Devnārāyaṇ. My real interest was in (oral) stories or legends about Puṣkar. I was specifically interested in narratives about Gāyatrī, the second wife of Brahmā (the chief deity of Puṣkar), since Gāyatrī—so the legend goes—belonged to the Gujar community. Before Bhopā Haridās actually told me a story about Gāyatrī and Brahmā, he, and also some other Gujar men who would meet at the temple, began singing sections of the Bagaṛāvat,[1] mostly for "recreational" and not exactly ritual purposes. Later Pusā Nāth took me to another village much further away in the district of Pali, where he introduced me to another acquaintance of his, Bhopā Lābū Rām. Bhopā Lābū Rām was both temple and paṛ-bhopā. He belonged to the Kumhār or potter community. He must have been in his early forties then. I recorded a number of hours of the narrative from him, which he sang in a loud and powerful way, accompanied by the stringed double-gourd instrument called *bīṇ*. Although I didn't follow the words completely, I was deeply impressed by the strength of the melody and Bhopā Lābū Rām's sincerity. Back in Heidelberg, I would listen to the tapes, bringing back the powerful spirit and atmosphere of the song. I then decided to go back to Rajasthan, after my dissertation, on a research project focused on the narrative of Devnārāyaṇ.

After completing all my Ph.D. dissertation formalities in April 1990, I applied for a research project on Devnārāyaṇ to be financed by the Deutsche Forschungs Gemeinschaft (German Research Council). The project was sponsored and supported by Günther-Dietz Sontheimer, who had also supervised my dissertation work. The funding was granted in early 1991, and I left for Rajasthan for a six-month field trip in March 1991. Since I had already recorded some hours of the narrative from Bhopā Lābū Rām, my plan was to continue work with him. I visited Pusā Nāth in Pisāṅgan, and we set out on a local bus to Dhaneriyā, the village where Lābū Rām lived. Bhopā Lābū Rām was out on tour then, and no one knew exactly where he was. We decided to find him, with the help of his elder brother, who also sang sections of the narrative, though in the role of the second singer, "answering" the lead singer's lines.

After some bumpy, dusty, and hot bus rides we arrived in a village where we were told that the bhopā was performing in the next small village called Āsarlāī, which was about 10–12 kilometers away. There being no transport to this village, the only option we had was to walk the sandy tract in the company of thorny babul trees. Midway we halted at the hut of a Gujar farmer who knew Lābū Rām. After a midday meal we continued on our way to Āsarlāī. In Āsarlāī we finally met Bhopā Lābū Rām, who was sitting with a group of men at the *hathāī*, a raised platform with a thatched roof that functioned as the community meeting place. It was late afternoon. Lābū Rām had performed the narrative two nights earlier in another part of the village. A second performance was scheduled for the same evening. Bhopā Lābū Rām was accompanied by his elder brother Parburām on this occasion. On the earlier occasion it had been his nephew.

Śrī Lābū Rām Bhopā pointing to a scene on the paṛ during a night-time performance.

During the performance members of the audience were curious to know why I was recording the narrative. Was it to make commercial cassettes? Was I doing this for a living (*dhandhā*)? Where did I come from? And what community did I belong to? All these questions were actually not specific to the situation I was in in Āsarlāī but were common to many encounters I had with people during my field trips. People wanted to know two things: my village and my "caste." Answering the first question was not all that difficult: my "village" was Delhi. But once I said "Delhi," the next question was always "Originally from Delhi?" Then I'd have to spin out my family history—my grandparents, who come from a region in Pakistan, and my relatives, who had settled in Kashmir. I didn't go into details about my mother's family, who were from Bombay, because I thought it would just be complicating matters. But the second question about my "caste" (*jāt, dūd*, etc.) wasn't always easy to answer. All I knew was that my family "belonged" to the kṣatriya "caste." But this didn't help much in terms of clan and lineage specifications. Early on during field work for my Ph.D. dissertation

Śrī Lābū Rām Bhopā during a night-time performance.

I wrote to my father in Delhi asking which *gotra* we had. He wrote back saying we belonged to the *kaśyap* gotra, which I presumed was subsumed under the Suryavaṃśī lineage. But this was wrong; as the mahant (who himself was of Rajput origin) of the Brahmā temple where I was staying then told me that the kaśyap gotra was subsumed under the Raghuvaṃśī lineage, which traced its history back to Rāma and his immediate ancestors. After my conversation with the Mahant Lahirpurī I realized that I "belonged" to the Rajput Raghuvaṃśī lineage, and this became my new social identity, for the period of fieldwork at any rate; and sometimes even for times after fieldwork was over and I was back in Delhi or Heidelberg. However, masquerading as a kṣatriya, which in local parlance meant I was a Rajput, didn't always suffice to establish a sense of credibility among people I met. Often there were long discussions of Rajput lineages and clans, about who could intermarry among whom and so on. To all these discussions I was often a mute witness, feigning social ignorance and general linguistic incompetence. The discussions and frequent crossquestionings were not always comfortable for me. How could this quasi-fictional social identity of mine be maintained if I told my questioners that my mother was a Parsi, my maternal great-grandmother was a German, and my father, who was from Punjab, had a particular physical syndrome found otherwise only in scant numbers of Macedonians?[2] How could I even make sense out of my "real" identity within this world of lineages and clans without which social existence itself became improbable? Why was I not wearing a sacred thread like other higher caste initiates wore? What about property and land? Above all, it was very questionable that I didn't attach the title *Singh* to my first or family name. *Malik* was understood to be a title but not sufficient for Rajput identity. Moreover, my first name, Aditya, was "strange" and hardly known in the villages I visited. The situation was not unlike to the one in Germany, where people would either say "What was that?" when I introduced myself as "Aditya" or simply nodded politely without understanding what I had muttered. Pusā Nāth came up with the brilliant solution of dropping my first name and giving me the name Malik Singh—a doubly strong appellative. So now I was Malik Singh, or simply Kanwarjī (princeling), implying that my father, the *ṭhākur* (Rajput headman), was still alive. The other term of endearment and respect was *banā*, or "bridegroom," which is used for Rajputs who are not yet ṭhākurs or rājās.

I found this new identity as a Rajput from distant Delhi often uncomfortable, first because I felt I was being dishonest to the people I made contact with and second because it required a particular kind of lifestyle and attitude from me. It was difficult to turn down offerings of extremely strong country liquor, which I was not used to consuming, and extremely pungent, nonvegetarian meals specially prepared by my hosts for their "Rajput" guest. This new social identity, and the expectations attached to it from the point of view of people from other communities and Rajputs themselves, colored my interactions strongly. Being a Rajput drew a lot of immediate respect and attention—much more than being a Brahman or other "high caste" would have. As a Rajput I was expected to sit, talk, and mix freely with members of other, often lower castes. There were less restrictions regarding with whom I could eat and drink. In fact one Gujar woman who wanted me to stay over for meal, at a time I couldn't, strengthened her invitation and argument by saying "We—Gujars and Rajputs—are not like these Brahmans, are we? We don't have to worry about all those restrictions. Warriors [and warrior pastoralists like Gujars] have mutual respect for one another." In most instances, however, my behavior was not quite the same as that of Dilip Singh, who later drove the jeep I rented from Shyam Singh of Fort Kharwa. There was not all that much tolerance between "real" Rajputs and Gujars, and in some ways I was disrupting the normal hierarchy.

In recent years there has been a growing critical awareness that the goal of cultural studies (anthropology, Indology, sociology) is not and has never been about the production of "objective" knowledge. Knowledge, and especially such knowledge about "other" cultures elicited through the endeavors of European and American scholars, has itself now come to be situated in cultural, historical, and political contexts. In colonial and even postcolonial contexts the content of knowledge production was and is determined by the strivings of power.[3] However, self-reflection has now led us to speak not of "objectivity" but of "interpretations," "constructions," "images," and "representations."[4] Because knowledge about others is constructed within culturally and historically specific epistemic frames, we no longer have direct access to the "object" of our research, but to representations of it. The representations are what we then present to the academic community and the social community. But the active enterprise of investigating, interpreting, constructing, and representing occurs within a framework of self and other, whereby the self is either European or American and the "other" Indian, African or "non-Western." But what if the "self" and "other" are both from the same culture? What epistemic frame is required for representing encounters between "self" and "self," so to speak? Or, as Veena Das (1995:25) puts it—the "otherness" within the "self" in which the researcher occupies a liminal status and identity? As she points out,

> there is a peculiar double bind which traps the non-western anthropologist who wishes to relate experience and representation gained through membership in her own society, when constructing the anthropological text . . . a frank engagement with the problem is necessary if the inventories of our subject are to include modes of knowing that are different from those within classic models of studying "other" societies.[5]

Although Das raises a number of important issues here, she does not provide solutions to the dilemmas proposed. It remains for the reader herself/himself (and in this case the researcher) to address these questions and to grapple with the challenge posed by them. The double bind, as I see it, is one of having been formed intellectually by Western conceptual modes while living in and knowing the cultural idiom of the society one has lived in and wants to "study." This knowledge is not inferred and analytic but direct, as in understanding the point of a joke or a tale. Thus many customs and modes of behavior do not appear themselves as "strange" or even "worthy" of "understanding," as they would perhaps for a researcher from another culture. However, the intellectual training received both in India and in the West always arises like a parental voice that reminds me of the "real" questions and debates. Being in the field and being at the writing table becomes an exercise in remembering and imagining: remembering what the issues are, although the experience of fieldwork itself may not underscore the "otherness" of a social encounter; and imagining what the issues would be for a researcher from another culture, what he or she would consider worthy of representation, and what I should in fact pay attention to. The "postcolonial predicament," as Carol Breckenridge and Peter van der Veer (1993) call it, is thus first that

> the colonial period has given us both the evidence and the theories that select and connect them; and, second, that decolonization does not entail immediate escape from colonial discourse. Despite all the recent talk of "third-world voices," this predicament defines both the ex-colonizer and the ex-colonized . . . in the Indian subcontinent—

and the study thereof—we cannot escape from a history characterized by a particular discursive formation that can be called "orientalism."[6]

There is, it appears, no return to some imagined pristine mode of experiencing, knowing, and representing one's own culture. The deed, so to speak, has already been done.

After the tiresome and dusty experience of traveling either by bicycle or by bus I decided that it would make sense to either buy a motorcycle or rent a jeep. Not knowing how or where I should go about doing this, I contacted Aditi Mehta, who was district commissioner of Ajmer district. She and her husband were both very open and sympathetic toward my research plans. It was their suggestion that I contact Shyam Singh Rathor of Kharwa. Kharwa had been a small but powerful principality. Shyam Singh and his four brothers lived alternatively in Fort Kharwa, which was near Ajmer on the southern route to Bhilwara, or in their *haveli* (manor house) in Ajmer. Shyam Singh and his brothers had all been educated at Mayo College in Ajmer. Their parents were still alive and lived in the fort. Each brother had in his possession at least one or two jeeps that were used for everyday transport or for regular "hunting" sessions in the countryside. Shyam Singh advised me against buying a motorcycle, which would have involved all kinds of risks, besides exposing myself to the dust and heat of the desert sun. Instead he suggested I should hire out one of his jeeps, an olive green World War II jeep that had been overhauled and refitted with a new powerful Mahendra motor. The canvas roof and windshield were both collapsible, making it possible to drive an open vehicle—as long as the sun and temperature permitted. In front on the bonnet there was a golden-colored falcon, symbol of autocracy and warriorhood. Sometimes while driving through small villages, people on the roadside would bow toward us. Pusā Nāth corrected my assumption by saying it was the jeep with its martial symbol on the bonnet that people were paying their respects to, not to the persons in the jeep. Shyam Singh requested his younger cousin Dilip Singh, who lived in Bhawanipura, a village on the opposite side of the railway tracks running parallel to Kharwa, to drive the jeep. This ensured that the jeep would be well looked after, cleaned, and returned safely to its owner. In fact the jeep was maintained and nurtured by Dilip Singh—who even preferred at times to sleep in the jeep—like a living being. Like a horse, I thought. Jeeps had replaced horses, but people's perception of Rajput jeeps and their drivers' relationship to them hadn't altered all that much. Besides the winged image on the bonnet, the jeep was equipped with jerry cans for fuel or water, a stout log for purposes not quite clear to me, a pickaxe, and a shovel. These instruments, I was told, were in case there was a breakdown somewhere far from repair shops and tea stalls. Other people told me that the instruments had very little to do with their original purpose. In reality they enhanced the awe and respect for the vehicle of passers-by.

Whereas Shyam Singh and his brothers were about the same age as me, Dilip Singh was maybe five to six years younger. He had been married recently, but their first child hadn't survived long. I had never seen his wife, or for that matter any other women in the house where he lived. He was proud about the fact that the women of his family always stayed indoors and were never seen in public, unlike the college-educated wives of Shyam Singh and his brothers, and of course unlike the other lower caste women who went about their daily chores in broad daylight. Dilip Singh had bloodshot eyes, which spoke of his consumption of hard liquor in the evenings, and sometimes also during the day. He was generally soft-spoken but could also be quite firm and impulsive. Dilip Singh rarely introduced himself as the son of his father, but as the grandson of Lachman Singh, his father's father. Lachman Singh had been till his death in the 1970s one of the most famous dacoits of Mewar. Almost everyone knew of him, and mentioning his name brought forth both fear and true respect among many people we encountered. "I am Lachman Singh's grandson," Dilip Singh would say. Lachman Singh was forced to abandon home and family after a feud in which he shot and killed his opponent. For many years he hid out in forests with his band of men, dodging both the British and later Indian authorities. Dilip Singh would proudly tell me how his grandfather together with a handful of faithful men, slaughtered a train full of 1,500 Muslims during the partition years. On one of our trips to a village in the district of Nagaur, an old woman who had heard of Dilip Singh's ancestry came up to the jeep and told us in a reverential tone how many years ago either she or her mother had gone looking for Lachman Singh to ask for money for her wedding. On the outskirts of a jungle she met a man who asked her whom she was looking for. When she replied that it was Lachman Singh she was looking for, he told her to follow him. They walked deeper and deeper into the jungle, the woman repeatedly asking where Lachman Singh was, and the man telling her to follow. Then in the middle of the forest they abruptly stopped. Once again the woman asked for Lachman Singh, and the man replied, saying "I am Lachman Singh!" After she told him her story, Lachman Singh then gave her all the wealth she required for the wedding. At some point Lachman Singh and his men were killed in an ambush by the police, but before that even SPs[7] held him in awe.

On my trips to villages in which Gujars lived, Dilip Singh did not always approve of my friendliness toward them. He would often remain sitting in the jeep, would eat his meals elsewhere, and would also sleep in the home of local Rajputs. Although he did develop respect for Hukamārām Bhopā from whom I recorded the narrative, he generally considered Gujars to be "dirty" (*gaṇde*) This sentiment was corroborated also by Shyman Singh, who also added that at some earlier point in history "these people were quite powerful." On the whole, however, Dilip Singh tolerated the fact that I was interested in their narratives and religious ideas. The worst encounter I experienced was in 1994, when I decided to pay Dilip Singh's father-in-law, the ṭhākur of Jītiyā, a village in southern Bhilwara, a visit. Dilip and I were accompanied by Hukamārām Bhopā and his nephew Kishnārām. On the very first evening a cat-and-mouse questioning game ensued between the ṭhākur and Hukamārām Bhopā. The ṭhākur persisting in asking insinuating questions like "Isn't there a Gujar clan called Thug?" The underlying implications were that Gujars were not to be trusted, and that they were exploiting my good faith and naivete. The next day Kishnārām complained

Śrī Hukamārām Bhopā (center), his nephew Śrī Kiṣnārām (left), and me (right).

to me that Hukamārām Bhopā had never been treated this badly in his life. He had not been given a cot to sleep on like the rest of us but had to lie on the hard floor of a mud platform built along the inner walls of the entrance to the courtyard. My attempts to record sections of the Bagaṛāvat were also unsuccessful, since the ṭhākur insisted that I listen and work with a semicommercial recording of the narrative song by a Brahman devotee. On the second day Hukamārām Bhopā whispered to me that the place reeked of death ("jam kā bū āve") and that it was not possible for him to work under these conditions. Proper inspiration was only possible in the serene and holy atmosphere of the Savāī Bhoj temple in Puṣkar, where we had spent the days prior to our visit to Jītiyā. However, it wasn't all that easy to leave Jītiyā before the date we had said we would. But after visiting the fort of Chittorgarh, which lay south of Jītiyā, we drove back to Puṣkar after about three days and three nights. In the evenings the ṭhākur spent hours telling me tales about his lineage ancestors and the brave acts they had committed. There had, for example, been the case of two front line soldiers who sacrificed themselves in different ways so us to beat the other into entering the enemy fort first. In one case the warrior had himself tied to the forehead of the ramming elephant so the iron spikes from the fort's gate would pierce him and not the elephant. When the other warrior saw this as he was attempting to climb up a ladder along the fort's tall walls, he beheaded himself and threw his head over the wall into the compound. In this way the second soldier claimed his place as front line soldier ahead of the first who had tied himself to the elephant. After I had finished with my research on Devnārāyaṇ, the ṭhākur suggested, I should turn to writing on the history and narratives of Rajput warriors, which in any case was a much more fitting topic than being interested in Gujars. Thus once again the rivalries and tensions that the narrative of Devnārāyaṇ expresses were to be found in the ordinary, everyday encounters between Rajputs and Gujars. My Gujar acquaintances did not acknowledge the superiority of the Rajputs, and the Rajputs did not refrain from expressing their disdain and simultaneous rivalry in terms of power.

Thus if there is no going back or unentangling oneself from the diverse and complex features of oneself, there can at least be both a sharing and a difference. A sharing of some conceptual frames and critical attitudes and a differing in the ethnographic description of meetings and encounters between people—in this case from the "same" culture. Since the ethnographic encounter is in a sense that which determines or elicits anthropological/Indological knowledge, I cannot write something about Devnārāyaṇ and his Gujar devotees without realizing that answers I received were somehow linked to my acquaintances' perception of myself. Thus my identity as a "Rajput" had a bearing on my interactions with people, since "caste" was of crucial importance as an identity mark. I could not overlook the fact that the narrative of Devnārāyaṇ is in many ways a discourse about the overlapping identities of Gujars and Rajput, their rivalries, kinship, and conflicts. While many singers were Gujars, the tale they told me was about interrelationships between Gujars and Rajputs. Had I been a Brahman or Banyā perhaps their response would have been different, which in turn would have elicited a different sense of the narrative and cult for me. Thus, although I was not born and brought up in a village in Rajasthan but in faraway cosmopolitan cities, I still shared a set of assumptions common (though not in a deterministic sense) to Indian culture. My experience therefore could not be the same as that of foreign researchers "who set out from the 'first world' to speak of 'others.' "[8] Was it possible for me to describe my work as a discovery/rediscovery of aspects of my own culture rather than an investigation into an "alien" culture? But then again, while writing in English and having research funds from the German Research Council, was I—at least in external terms—doing anything different from "privileged" first-world researchers?

Nevertheless it seems to me that there is a difference, and that this difference lies in the context created about the work I am involved in—which for all purposes looks the same as anything a European or American scholar might also do. This context, which then frames the particular activity—of research—is for me both one of appreciation and of representation. Through my research I am engaged in an appreciation of—which includes a revealing and reentering into—that which constitutes my own larger cultural self. The motivation is thus radically different from wanting to discover the "other" from which to then construct the self; it is about constructing the self for the "other" in order to then discover the self. The production of knowledge is not aimed at wielding power or at establishing differences or even similarities between cultures. But the nonhegemonic context of such a study can only be achieved by first asserting the hegemonic context of cultural studies and adopting a critical stance toward this context. It can only be achieved by being frank about the problems and issues facing the enterprise of representing one's own culture to oneself through a conceptual framework learned from the "other" and experience gained from belonging to the culture under investigation. Where does all this lead us in the study of oral narratives like those of Devnārāyaṇ and "folk" cults?

After I had sat through two nights listening and taping Bhopā Lābū Rām's performances, I asked him whether I could record the "whole" story from him. He informed me that his knowledge of the narrative only went up to certain point. He did not, for example, know the story following the Bagaṛāvat's deaths and Devnārāyaṇ's birth. He suggested we visit his uncle, a well-known elderly singer in a village in Nagaur District. His name was Nārāyanjī Bhopā, and he must have already been in his seventies. We drove to his village in Shyam Singh's jeep with Dilip Singh as the driver. After spending a night talking to Nārāyanjī, he promised to sing the entire narrative to us, although he was quite feeble. But then suddenly the next day he decided against singing, the reason being it would cost him too much effort and energy. He did however narrate other stories, some connected to the main narrative and some not connected to it. So even after this very

Śrī Nārāyaṇjī Bhopā and Śrī Lābū Rām Bhopā.

rewarding encounter with Nārāyanjī Bhopā, I was still without a "complete" recording of the narrative. Back in Pisāṅgan, Pusā Nāth and I asked several Gujars whom they considered to be good singers. Some names were fairly well known among the Gujar community, but there was also a lot of difference of opinion. Thus, for example, one name that cropped up again and again was associated with embellishments (*mirc-masālā*) sprinkled in the narrative to entertain audiences. Other singers were understood to be more earnest and knowledgeable. Singer lineages were mentioned to establish their credentials, and so on. But the question still remained on how I was going to contact these singers. The big question was, also, who would assist me in transcribing the stories and statements I had already and would be recording. Pusā Nāth could read and write a little bit, but not enough to transcribe the tapes—besides which he was not interested in spending his time on a job like that.

In Puṣkar I would hang about in the temple of Savāī Bhoj, which was located beyond the Brahmā temple in the western edge of the town. One day while I was playing a recording to a young Gujar whom I thought could perhaps assist me, a man about my age walked up to me. He was returning from the "field" fairly late in the morning, and the temple lay on the way home. His name was Nāthu Lāl Solaṅki, and coincidentally he also belonged to the Damāmī community, as did Pusā Nāth. Nāthu Lāl immediately guessed that I was not one of the many tourists who visit Puṣkar. I told him about my work, and asked him whether he could help me transcribe the tapes. He agreed to do this, saying that he had already been research assistant to an American scholar working on folk music in Rajasthan. He had been recommended by Komal Kothari, the well-known expert on Rajasthani society and culture. Nāthu Lāl's elder brother was an award-winning drummer himself, and Nāthu Lāl too played the *nagāṛā* (kettle drums) excellently. Nathu Lal had heard of some bhopās with good reputations. We decided to travel to a small village north of Puṣkar in the district of Nagaur almost at the border of Churu District—hoping to meet the well-known singer Hukamārām Bhopā. However, when we arrived in the village, which consisted of maybe 20 to 30 thatched huts surrounded by a sandy barren landscape, we were told that Hukamārām had left for Sujangarh, the district capital of Churu. He would not be returning until the next day or maybe the day after, no one was sure. Hukamārām Bhopā had a number of friends and advisers in Sujangarh. He would visit and stay in the Devnārāyaṇ temple over there, which was frequented by town-dwelling Gujar devotees. We then returned again to the *ḍhāni* (settlement) after a day to enquire whether Hukamārām Bhopā was back from Sujangarh. He had not yet returned, so we decided to drive to Sujangarh and meet him personally in the Devnārāyaṇ temple. I was very fortunate to meet Hukamārām Bhopā, who then must have been in his late fifties or early sixties. He agreed to sing me the narrative together with his assistant Moṭārām Gūjar, who lived in Sujangarh. We began the recordings in the Devnārāyaṇ temple in Sujangarh in a tiny room that had a fan that blew the hot muggy air round round the room. Dilip and I slept in the room too. Hukamārām chose to sleep outside on the temple veranda, which was much cooler.

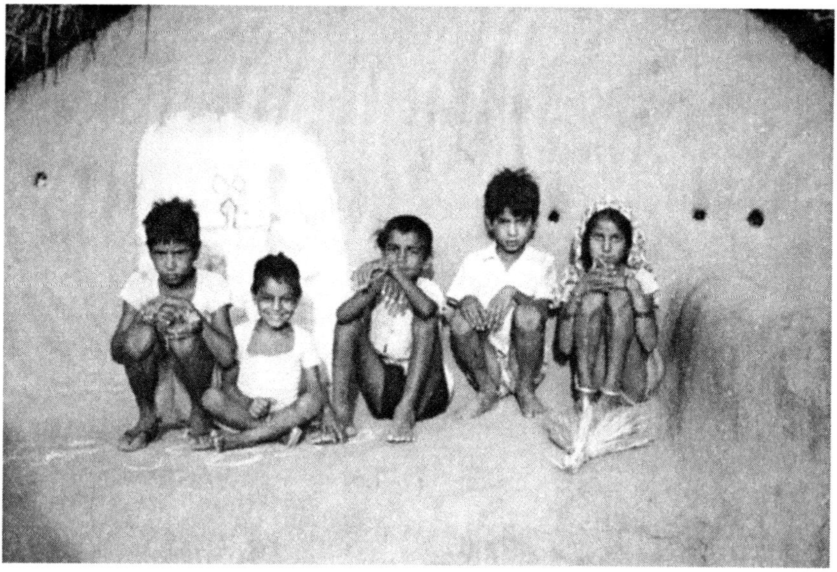

Śrī Hukamārām Bhopā's youngest son (second from left) and younger daughter.

Where can I begin to disengage from colonial discourse, and where can I begin to participate in a discourse derived from being a member of Indian culture? Two things seem apparent: one is of course to engage in the academic discourse/debate on the study of oral narratives and folk cults and thereby point out the cultural specificity and unexamined assumptions of that discourse. The other is to reintroduce a notion that knowledge is the result of interactions and relationships between people and not just "sources." Thus, as I mentioned earlier, it should be possible to observe that the knowledge I elicit in the field is the result of a social interaction that itself is the result of the perceived identities of both myself and the people I met. The point I want to make here is that it may not be possible for a researcher to elicit objective knowledge about a community, cult, or other cultural phenomena by gathering together different kinds of information derived from different kinds of "texts": spoken, written, oral, and so on. It will always be the cultural specificity of the researcher, the interactions that flow from this, and the imagined action of completeness that will determine the representation of the so-called object of study. To put it another way, the presence of the researcher necessarily alters the interactive situation he or she is in, thereby creating individual and unique components of knowledge. A thoroughly efficient yet neutral field researcher is a fiction in itself.

Ultimately Hukamārām Bhopā found me to be a person worthy of telling the narrative to. He considered me to be sincerely interested in Devnārāyaṇ and in what he himself had to say. Our recordings, which began at the temple in Sujangarh, continued after interruptions again at Hukamārām's own house or hut in the village where I had previously encountered another singer, Bhopā Rām

Lāl. Between the recordings, Hukamārām was invited to perform at a *savāmaṇi* (see later in paragraph) that had been sponsored by one individual as an answer to a vow that had been fulfilled. There were perhaps about 60 to 100 guests, who were invited for a meal in the evening, after which Hukamārām and some others performed sections of the narrative. The name *savāmaṇi* derived from the fact that the first offerings of prasād made by the sponsor were all in quantities of one and a quarter *maṇ* (or 75 kilograms). Hukamārām did not sing all through the night because of his age and bad health. There was a lot of talking and commenting from the audience. At times during pauses many men from the audience would get up and sing episodes as best as they could. Sometimes members of the audience called out to Hukamārām to sing a particular section of the narrative that they liked. After the long night, we returned to Hukamārām's village. I had begun to feel somewhat exasperated by the fact that the recording had breaks in between, and I never felt sure whether it was going to continue or not. In the end it did continue, and over a period of about 10 days I recorded the entire narrative on Devnārāyaṇ, with the exclusion of the first part on his ancestors, the Bagaṛāvats. The recording took up 16 cassettes, each 90 minutes long, or 24 hours. Although I would sit and listen attentively to Hukamārām and his cosinger Moṭārām sing, there were many, many things I didn't follow, both because of the language and the way the passages were sung. It was only a year later after I had transcribed and typed the narrative in *devanāgari* script, that I could ask Hukamārām what particular words and different scenes meant and who the characters were. The questions and their answers resulted in some 20 hours of further recording. All together over 120 hours of recordings were made of the story, substories, and other relevant information. Often an explanation would be in terms of another story that had taken place prior to the event in the narrative. I had the feeling that the entire narrative was not a single continuous whole but a crisscross and branching of different narratives that you could pull out of the main narrative, like a pull-out picture book that offered different options; or, to use an analogy from computers, the narrative and its subnarratives functioned similarly to a hyper-text. Thus there was not only the *bhārat* (story/narrative) of the Bagaṛāvats but also the bhārat of individual brothers like Nevā who were particularly brave and who fought for particularly long periods during the final bloody battle. Or there was the story of Bhūṇāji's journey to Bhināy in Afghanistan. Or the story about Sāḍū Mātā's birth and marriage to Savāī Bhoj. Hukamārām told me that the narrative was in fact "untellable" because of its length and complexity. The whole story would take six months to tell, and not even that would suffice. At any rate I was fortunate enough to have recorded the "entire" narrative,[9] which came to about 46 hours, as well as the other questions and talks I had with him. Hukamārām was very patient in answering my questions, which at times didn't make sense to him (especially when I enquired about phonological details—was it ḍ or ḍh?). As if teaching a child, he would sometimes repeat what he had said in a slow and deliberate manner that was also very funny. He was very particular about timings, and was not interested in anything else but "getting the job done."

The next year he came to Puṣkar and resided in the Savāī Bhoj temple, where I would visit him early in the mornings and in the afternoons. I had fixed a time of 7:30 a.m. for our meeting. After a day or two he told me that this was too late, he'd be up at 5 a.m. and had nothing productive to do till 7:30 a.m. So I started being at the temple at 7 a.m. which was suitable for him, and in fact also to me. Given that people in Indian villages and places like Puṣkar rose very early in the morning, even 7 a.m. seemed a bit late in the day. We would work till about 11–11:30 a.m., when I would return to my room at the Tourist Bungalow. I would visit him, walking from one end of Puṣkar to the other, at 3 p.m., and we would again work for about two or three hours. At times I would also eat my midday meal in the temple, which was run by a bhopā of the *jamaat* (religious association) of Savāī Bhoj, a celibate ochre-clad order of priests. Jamaat Bhopās carried the title of Nāth or Dās. In outward appearance they could hardly be distinguished from ascetics of the Śaivite Nāth Sampradāya. Once we were joined by another bhopā, who was also a bit surprised at the number of questions I was asking. Then he told me and Hukamārām that I would only understand the narrative after going through it a full seven times. Dumb listeners like me needed that kind of extensive repetition before they could learn something. And coming to think of it now, the bhopā wasn't all that wrong at all. It has taken at least seven readings and listenings for me to even begin to understand the ideas, themes, events, and characters of which the story is made up. On the whole I still get the feeling of trying to carry a pile of loose papers from which every now and then some fall out. When I try picking those up, the pile shifts around again, and some others fall down, and so the entire meaning of the narrative resists being fixed and pinned down once and for all. Meanings emerge and disappear and reemerge. As Barthes once remarked, "the text is open *ad infinitum*: no reader, no subject, no science can exhaust the text."[10]

The analysis I offer in the following pages is first and foremost a product of the relationship and trust placed in me by the people I met, most of all by Hukamārām Bhopā. He himself was very keen to see that the narrative was published in book form. At one point when I was reading the transcription aloud with him, a large group of Gujar men traveling in a tractor carriage came to the temple of Savāī Bhoj after having cremated a member of their community in Puṣkar. Hukamārām told them of the undertaking we were involved in. Finally the Gujars too would have a "book" of their own—like the Bhagavad Gītā. He urged the men to read aloud from my transcription. But none of the fifteen to twenty men could read or write. Instead they reverently touched the cover of the transcription with their hands, as if touching a holy object.

Acknowledgments

The process of writing this book since its inception in 1991, when I undertook my first field trip to Rajasthan for this project, has accompanied many important events in my life: the birth of my two daughters, the deaths of my teacher and the singer from whom I recorded the narrative, changes in jobs, applying for research funds, moving between three countries (India, Germany, and now New Zealand). All these movements beneath the surface—certainly not specific to my situation—usually remain invisible in the pages of a printed book. Equally invisible sometimes is the tremendous support, appreciation, and encouragement that accompanies the writing of a book, intertwined as it is with various life events.

One person who has persistently believed in the possibility of this book and the value of my work is Bele, my wife, who has, at times, expressed more commitment to its completion than I myself have shown. Her constant encouragement for accomplishing more than one believes is possible has made writing this book an exercise in fullness and joy that is superseded only by being in the presence of our daughters Renuka-Maria and Ambika-Diana.

The fact that I undertook this project at all is a reflection of the inspiration and guidance provided by my teacher, Günther-Dietz Sontheimer, who opened my eyes to the richness of the subject. When he died unexpectedly in 1992, a year after I began the project, I did not think I would ever continue with my research, but the foundation laid by him has been stronger than I imagined. I am extremely fortunate to have received all the academic training I did from him at Heidelberg.

Another source of inspiration has been Shri Hukamaram Bhopa, the singer of the narrative, whose wit, brilliance, and sincerity as one of the foremost singers of the tradition opened up the myriad dimensions of the narrative, while making my stay in Rajasthan so worthwhile. He too died before this book was completed. Its publication is the fulfilment of a promise, one that I gave him and one that he saw in the spread of the story of his deity, Lord Devnārāyaṇ.

I was very fortunate to be welcomed and assisted by many people in Rajasthan, especially Pusa Nath Dangi and his family in Pisangan; Nathu Lal Solanki in Pushkar; Bhopa Labu Ram and his family in Dhaneriya; Shyam Singh Rathor of Kharwa and Dilip Singh Rathor of Bhawanipura; the mahants of the Brahmā temple and the temples of Devnārāyaṇ and Savāī Bhoj in Pushkar, as well as various acquaintances I made in the villages and towns I visited. The painter of the paṛ or scroll of Lord Devnārāyaṇ, Shri Shrilal Joshi of Bhilwara, was particularly generous in unselfishly providing his great expertise on each and every detail of the scroll.

In Heidelberg I received the support of my teachers, colleagues, and friends at the South Asia Institute. Monika Horstmann has over many years and in many ways been a most patient and committed support. I owe it to her that the thesis that grew out of this research was accepted in fulfilment of my Habilitation degree by the Faculty of Oriental and Classical Studies at the University of Heidelberg in 1998; Hermann Berger graciously sponsored the project with the German Research Council after its being initially sponsored by Günther-Dietz Sontheimer. For stimulating and frank discussions on various aspects of this project I am grateful to Martin Fuchs, Antje Linkenbach-Fuchs, Ulli Demmer, Elizabeth Schoembucher, Claus Peter Zoller, Martin Gaenszle, Joerg Gengnagel, Thomas Lehmann, Michael Martinec, Srilata Müller, Birgit Mayer-Koenig, Ulla and Sadashiva Rao, Sonja Stark-Wild, and Alexander Henn.

Heidrun Brückner and Anne Feldhaus have provided ongoing support and encouragement. I am grateful for their comments and suggestions, and for all that I have learnt from them. David Shulman, Peter Claus, Saskia Kersenboom, Alf Hiltebeitel, Axel Michaels, John Smith, Komal Kothari, Bahadur Singh, Joan Erdman, Ann Gold, and Joseph Miller have enriched this work or previous lives of it through many insightful readings.

Financial assistance for research and writing was provided through generous grants of the *Deutsche Forschungsgemeinschaft* (German Research Council) over a period of more than five years between 1991 and 1993 and 1996 and 1998, for which I am extremely grateful.

At the University of Canterbury, not only for their comments and appreciation but for making me feel welcome and at home "down under," I am grateful to my colleagues in the School of Philosophy and Religious Studies, particularly Paul Harrison, Mike Grimshaw, Ghazala Anwar, Phil Catton, Dorothy McMenamin, Cynthia and Graham Macdonald, and Carol Hiller. I also thank Bruce Penno of the IT Department for his friendly support and advice in preparing the manuscript.

Kalima, Henni, Claudia, Ronald, and Ursula provided the space for thought and inspiration each time I visited their home in Engelskirchen. Katharina, Gabi, Henrik, Elke, Sigrid, and Markus provided friendship in Erlangen and Dossenheim. Brigitte gave her valuable time for last-minute discussions and corrections in Christchurch.

The support of my parents, Subhash Chandra Malik and Zarine Malik, began well before this project, and continues in many forms after its completion. It was through them that I first experienced how enduring knowledge is transmitted through spoken words, and other fleeting means. Both of them took time to read the manuscript meticulously and offer valuable suggestions, as did Keshiji, Ushaji, and Kapilaji, who have, as persons and through their work, brought poetry, dance, and inspiration to my own life. My brother Sushant Malik and his wife, Ruksher, and daughters, Alaiqa and Aarya, have sent a constant supply of affection through e-mails across continents; as have Leila Moushie, Ashok, Ayesha, Vinayak, and Aditya. My wife's parents, Fritz (who is no longer with us) and Erna Ohm, provided the warmth of their home on many winter (and summer) visits to Krefeld. I thank them, as well as Barbara and Wolfgang, Ursula, Jochen, and Lukas for providing comforts reserved only for family.

Finally, I am grateful to Oxford University Press, particularly Cynthia Read, Theo Calderara, and Bob Milks, and to the Center for Asian Studies at the University of Texas, Austin, for choosing to publish this volume in the South Asia Research series.

May the nectar gaze of Lord Devnārāyaṇ fall on them all!

Contents

ANALYSIS

1
Introduction 3

2
Verbal Narrative 10

3
Visual Narrative 37

4
Textual Narrative 55

5
Historical Narrative 92

6
Social Narrative 117

7
Divine Testimony 136

TRANSLATION 173

Line Drawing of Paṛ 497

Notes 505

Glossary 533

Bibliography 539

Index 545

NECTAR GAZE AND POISON BREATH

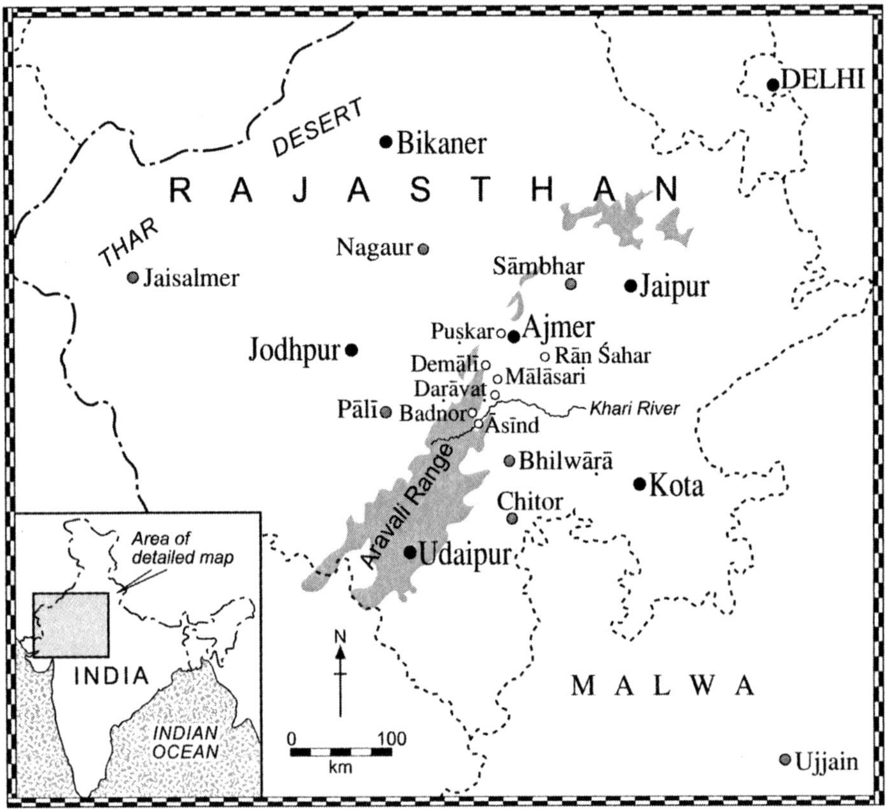
DELHI
THAR DESERT
Bikaner
R A J A S T H A N
Nagaur
Jaisalmer
Sāmbhar
Jaipur
Puṣkar
Ajmer
Jodhpur
Rān Śahar
Demāli
Mālāsari
Darāvat
Pālī
Badnor
Khari River
Āsīnd
Aravali Range
Bhilwāṛā
Kota
Chitor
Udaipur
Area of detailed map
INDIA
INDIAN OCEAN
N
0
100
km
M A L W A
Ujjain

❁ I ❁
Introduction

❁ Word and World ❁

Human beings are persistently engaged in exploring ways of relating to themselves, to other individuals, and to the world about them. Human societies are thus a dynamic reflection of a vast assortment of concerns and connections. But these interrelationships can be said to be "experimental" in the sense that they are created, reformulated, changed, dismantled, improvised, and re-created again and again by people in different situations and times. Usually our relationship to other human beings and to what we perceive the world about us to be is not only articulated in but also constructed through language, which is constituted not simply by words or sentences but by a variety of verbal and written genres ranging from spoken conversation, songs, ballads, epics, novels, poems, academic works, and philosophical treatises. We could even go so far as to say that it is through language that we know the world, and that it is through different verbal and written discourses in language that our knowledge of ourselves and the world is produced, sustained, broken down, transmitted, and established.[1] Language is thus not simply a symbolic representation of things or linguistic discourses simply a "description" of the world, they are, in fact, the media through which we perceive, experience, and construct our "reality." To concur with the words of Paul Ricoeur, language and its expression in literature is thus not limited to describing the world; rather it is about "redescribing" or *reinterpreting* it.[2]

Despite the vast proliferation of verbal *and* nonverbal literary forms, in most circles "literature" has come to be connected primarily with written examples such as novels, dramas, short stories, poems, essays, and so on. As Ong (1982:8) has aptly remarked,

> oral expression can exist and mostly has existed without any writing at all, writing never without orality . . . despite the oral roots of all verbalization, the scientific and literary study of language and literature has for centuries, until quite recent years, shied away from orality. Texts have clamoured for attention so peremptorily that oral

> creations have tended to be regarded generally as variants of written productions or, if not this, as beneath serious scholarly attention.[3]

Yet many "non-Western" cultures have produced a staggering array of verbal, nonwritten "literary" works. India is a case in point of a culture that in particular emphasizes the primacy of the oral and "aural." Thus, regardless of having "formal" skills of reading and writing, people have developed a rich and complex "literary" response to the diverse aspects of human life such as aesthetics, ethics, social organization, religion, politics, nature, art, life, and death. Although oral expressive forms are often stamped as "traditional," they do not—given the entire range of human concerns they deal with—cease to have relevance in contemporary times.

Devnārāyaṇ

This study deals with the oral narrative of Devnārāyaṇ. It attempts to explore the world or worlds that are articulated and created within and through the narrative. As such it is primarily an exercise in textual exegesis, being concerned with a text and its meaning. But the meaning of the narrative emerges on two distinct levels. One level or domain of meaning is the configuration of meaning given to it by the community of people who actually listen, tell, and know the text. The other domain of meaning is created about the text through the exercise of connecting it to a body of academic knowledge that is not necessarily present within the first domain. Owing to the fact that both domains of meaning are the result of *interpretations* offered through the mediality of different kinds of texts ("oral/folk" and "academic") this study is both about the "construction" and the "reconstruction" of knowledge in the broadest sense. As author of an academic study of the meaning(s) a narrative has for the community of people who primarily relate to the text, I am, therefore, dealing here with the reconstruction of a particular construction of knowledge about the world. But this endeavor is also about the "deconstruction" of academic conceptualizations that tend to place limits on the possible meanings of the narrative. Thus, as Valdés (1991:16) points out,

> the task of hermeneutic interpretation must be focused at the intersection of the two directions of language, that is, neither exclusively with the writer's text nor with the reader, but in the encounter between the two. . . . The task of interpretation is never completed, for the aim cannot be to deplete the text of its dynamism. The aim must be to arrive at a temporary statement that participates in a tradition of commentary of texts.

Ideally speaking, thus, construction, deconstruction and reconstruction overlap at some point, resulting in a common domain of meaning that nevertheless does not exhaust the range of possible meanings and interpretations of the narrative. But the task of interpretation is particularly complex in the case of an oral narrative, since one significant, but almost ephemeral, field of meaning emerges in the telling of the narrative and its reception by listeners. As in conversational dialogue, meanings emerge and vanish here with the appearance and disappearance of *sound* in different instances of the narrative's recitation. The oral "text" is marked for performance and therefore does not fall within the parameters of "writer" and "reader." It is part of an entire event that itself is geared toward engendering an equally tenuous quantity, namely "divine presence" (*prakāś*). By taking recourse to one telling of the narrative, as well as commentaries on it in the form of answers to questions put to singers and listeners, I am admittedly limiting its scope, and treating it almost as a written text.

The narrative of Devnārāyaṇ—which has frequently been classified as an "epic"[4]—is one of the most well-known folk narratives in Rajasthan.[5] The narrative and Devnārāyaṇ's cult covers a large area extending over most of Rajasthan and Malwa, the northwestern region of Madhya Pradesh. Together with the "epic" narratives of Pābūjī, Gūgājī, Tejājī, Rāmdevjī, and Gopi Cand and Bharthari, it belongs to a rich and significant corpus of oral narratives current in Rajasthan today.[6] The current work is based on a recorded version of the narrative that Śrī Hukamārām Bhopā and his companions Śrī Moṭārām Gūjar and Śrī Kiṣnārām Gūjar sang over a period of days on different occasions in 1991 and 1994.[7] The recordings of the two parts of the narrative were done alternatively in the town of Sujangarh (Churu District), in the villages of Agunta and Kharesh (Nagaur District), and in the pilgrimage town of Pushkar (Ajmer District). The total number of hours of recording time came to about 46 hours: the first part of the narrative, dealing with the lives and deeds of Devnārāyaṇ's ancestors, the Bagaṛāvats, spanned some 22 hours; the second part, which focuses on Devnārāyaṇ, resulted in 24 hours of recitation. In addition, roughly another 100 hours of recordings were made. These consisted of interviews with other singers and devotees of Devnārāyaṇ, shorter narratives related to the main narrative, and various details regarding the content of the narrative as well as its visual counterpart, the paṛ (painted cloth scroll).[8] Altogether approximately 12 months were spent in Rajasthan collecting materials on the narrative on three different occasions between 1991 and 1994.

The task of transcribing and translating the 24-hour-long part of the narrative dealing with Devnārāyaṇ that forms the centerpiece of this study was completed in the spring of 1996, resulting in around 700 pages of Marwari text and English translation. Apart from recordings of the narrative, field trips were also conducted to the important centers of the cult of Devnārāyaṇ in the districts of Ajmer, Bhilwara, and Chitor. Many of the shrines and temples that were visited are mentioned in the narrative and are connected to specific events and actions related either to the Bagaṛāvats or to Devnārāyaṇ. Thus, for instance, the hilltop shrine of Demālī is considered to be the very first place of worship that was founded by Devnārāyaṇ himself; the temple of Savāī Bhoj commemorates the battlefield on which the Bagaṛāvats lost their lives in the "mahābhārat" against their arch-enemy, the rāṇā of Rāṇ City; and the hill of Mālāsarī, where Devnārāyaṇ was born to his mother Sāḍū Mātā, and so on.[9]

❁ Aims ❁

In studying the oral narrative of Devnārāyaṇ, one is confronted with a number of questions at the outset. Most immediate among these are: How is it recited or performed? Who are the performers? How is the oral recitation structured? What is the relationship between verbal narrative and visual narrative? However, beyond these questions the concern here is also with the ways the categories of "text," "performance," "performer," "visual narrative," "orality," "communicative event," and so on are defined from within the tradition itself. For example, are there categories that correspond to these conceptual terms? If this be the case, then what kind of understanding of the narrative do they represent? Does this understanding perhaps warrant a revision of our own conceptual categories? Moreover, does the tradition represent a coherent "system" of communication? And, if so, is there a specific framework in which the arrangement of terms and components can be placed?

Another set of questions that arises is concerned both with the classification of the narrative, and above all with its content: How is the narrative to be defined and classified? What interpretative frameworks are "thrown up," or made to emerge, so to speak, by particular categorizations and not by others?[10] Is it possible to avoid a rigid classification? Moreover, what does the content of the narrative (both verbal and visual) actually deal with? What are the themes or discourses present within the narrative? Do these themes relate to the self-representations of the community of devotees of Devnārāyaṇ?

The answer to the question of definition, in previous studies of Devnārāyaṇ, has been, of course, that the narrative belongs to the class of narratives called "epics."[11] However, in giving the narrative the label "epic"—even though it may approximate to the notion of an epic—we may in some respects be limiting both the meaning of the text and our approach to understanding its meaning. What other labels might be appropriate? For example, could it be termed a "caste purāṇa"? What possibilities open up with the latter label?[12] On the other hand one might ask whether it is at all appropriate to label it in terms of specific genres. Supposing we were to loosely call it a "religious narrative"; what implications would emerge here? Is an epic necessarily "religious," or conversely can a religious narrative be an epic? If we take the examples of the *Rāmāyaṇa* and *Mahābhārata,* of course, the answer to the latter question is "yes." However, not all epics are "religious." On the other hand are "caste purāṇas" religious texts or are they "social texts"? Is it possible to locate the boundary between social, religious, or for that matter historical "texts"?[13]

One advantage of calling the narrative of Devnārāyaṇ a "religious narrative" lies in the fact that we may begin then to examine a whole range of meanings that would perhaps be of secondary importance were we to only emphasize the "epic" character of the narrative. By calling it an epic we might focus more on a set of questions related to the narrative's formal, structural, and even performative aspects, sometimes forgetting that the narrative is an integral part of a religious cult. Thus as a central component of a religious cult, the narrative plays a singular role in the construction of a number of categories that may be termed religious: "sacred territory," "divine testimony," "forms of worship," "sacrifice," "devotion," "sacred power," and so on.[14] As a text the narrative then embodies a discourse on these issues of religious importance for the community of worshippers within the framework of the cult of Devnārāyaṇ. But again it is obvious that the narrative must be "more" than a religious text: of necessity it also embodies a statement about the community of worshippers as a social group both in the present as well as in the past. Not only this, it also entails a discourse about the community of worshipers and groups who are defined as being outside of that community, or in some cases as being specifically in conflict with them. Thus, to sum up on the different discourses of meaning broadly embedded in the text, one could maintain that it deals with (1) "items" of religious significance, (2) with interrelationships between groups and individuals either belonging to or not belonging to the community of worshipers, and (3) with a "history" of both these categories of groups. Although (1) and (2) are relatively easy to understand, it may be useful to briefly clarify what is meant by "history." First of all, I do not mean "oral" history, in the sense that the narrative may or should be used as a source to reconstruct the history of a social group or of a region. Second—already implied in the foregoing—I do not mean that the text involves an attempt to inscribe the "actual" or "real" history of the community. What I mean is that the text articulates an "imagined" or "constructed" history of the community.[15] But this "imagined" history is, however, no less important or, in fact, "objective" or "subjective" than the "concrete," linear chronologies and histories of historians. Thus I am concerned with the way the community of worshippers perceive their past and how this perception is manifest in the narrative.

The narrative thus carries different discourses within itself. Each of these discourses is, however, related to the other. Thus the discourse on interrelationships between the community of worshippers is intimately connected to a discourse on their "history." The discourse on community history is again closely connected to the discourse on sacred power, worship, devotion, and so on. Different discourses thus converge within the text as part of a continuous arena of meaning.[16] My concern is, therefore, with how these three topics define, sustain, and create each other within the discursive framework of the narrative.

Having said this, a number of more specific questions may be asked with regard to each discourse. To provide an example of questions relating to "religious discourse," one could ask: How is the notion of sacred territory and divine power perceived and established? How are different religious currents within Hinduism redefined and integrated into the narrative? How is this reflected in the cult? What is the role, for example, of devotion (*bhakti*), divine testimony (*parcyo*), bodily sacrifice (*balidāna*), or divine incarnation (*avatāra*) in constituting the religious fabric of the narrative? Regarding the discourse on interrelationships between individuals and groups within the community of worshippers, one could ask how those interrelationships are constructed. Do they, for example, issue from clear-cut notions of social identity, or are they constructed in an ambivalent manner? In other words, does the narrative substantiate a relatively bounded notion of sociality or does it conjure up notions of indeterminate, flexible social identities? However, since the interrelationships within groups are marked not solely by "co-operation" and "solidarity," but also by conflict, we might ask to what extent the narrative succeeds in constructing a discourse (or even paradigm?) for social cohesion and conflict. What models, if any, are offered for relationships of both discord and harmony? And, once again, how do these models operate within (and through) a discourse about sacred power? Finally, regarding the discourse about history, one could ask the question about how history is "imagined." What are the conceptual categories or "cultural schemas"[17] within which it is imagined? In what manner does the particular history represented in the narrative relate to other "histories" within Rajasthan? Given the "peripheral" status of the narrative's bearers, along with the resulting social as well the historical perspective offered in the narrative, to what extent is it fruitful or even legitimate to call it a "subaltern" history? In this respect, how far does the narrative attempt to provide a "counterhistory" of dominant groups such as the Rajputs, who themselves have more or less "established" histories? In other words, how does the history provided in the narrative exist on the boundaries of other "histories" prevalent in the region? Finally, it should be reiterated that the three areas of enquiry just outlined can only be artificially separated from one another: in reality they form an inseparable, continuous whole.

This study is thus divided into two main parts. In the first, I deal with questions relating to the verbal and the visual narrative. Specifically, I look at how performance is defined; how the oral narrative structure of the text is shaped; how the communicative context of the narrative is composed of epistemological categories such as "remembrance" on the one hand and aspects of "speech genres" such as "repetition," "dialogue," and "reported speech" on the other; how the visual narrative or paṛ is perceived, and how it relates to the verbal narrative; how the imagery of the scroll is organized; and, finally what the religious and symbolic meaning of particular sets of images on the scroll entails. In the second part, I focus on a series of questions related to the content of the narrative. In particular, I first attempt to establish an "intertextual" framework in which to understand important features of the narrative such as the notion of Devnārāyan's status as an avatāra, or the occurrence of epic and puranic motifs and patterns in the narrative. Then I look at the meanings of the narrative in terms of the three areas ("sacred power," "sociality," "history") outlined earlier. Within this framework I also focus on the significance of particular events; for example, the release of Devnārāyan's cows into the Rāṇā's fields, or the role(s) played by particular characters in the narrative, by Devnārāyaṇ's mother Sāḍū Mātā or by his genealogist Chochū Bhāṭ, whereby each brings to the surface certain fundamental concerns and tensions of the narrative.

What links the subject matter of the first half of the study to the second is the essentially *communicative* character of the narrative as a "conversational" or "dialogic" production of both structure and meaning.[18] While on the one hand the narrative is composed of a series of exchanges between different voices (and between the singers themselves), on the other hand the statement(s) being made in the narrative as a whole is (are) forged out of a convergence of different perspectives and interests and contending ideologies. For example, Devnārāyaṇ's divinity is something that is almost continuously doubted and needs to be "proven" or "established" in the context of various encounters between him or his representatives and others who do not perceive his true nature immediately. The notion of "proof" or "verification" (parcyo) used here itself suggests the contentional nature of the itinerary of the god through various physical, social, and religious regions laid out in the narrative.

Finally, it is perhaps the latter feature, namely the issue of "divine testimony" (parcyo)[19] that is the most central theme of the narrative, on which perhaps all other meanings hinge. While universally speaking kings always embark on conquests, in India so do gods. The narrative of Devnārāyaṇ is an allegory of such a conquest. It is a journey of the god's conquest not only of physical spaces but of different realms—over realms of power issuing from asceticism, divine healing, warriorhood, and the authority of kings. It is a chronicle of miraculous and sometimes martial victories within the world inhabited by his devotees. It is the story of the establishment of his cult, which is never taken for granted: it is always something that has to be achieved, founded, and "proven" by him. The narrative is thus fashioned out of a series of incidents through which he provides us with "divine testimony." And it is through these acts of testimony that Devnārayaṇ demonstrates his divinity and establishes his own religious following and cult.

Since the idea of a narrative is to hear it, to know it, and to be immersed in its idea, the last chapter of this study pursues a path provided by the story of Devnārāyaṇ itself. The sections are organized according to the structure of the narrative: parcyo follows parcyo, beginning with Devnārāyaṇ's birth and ending with his departure to Baikuṇṭh. Here, as well as elsewhere, the interpretation offered is interspersed with other tales, excerpts of interviews, texts, and observations that collectively invoke the texture of meaning.

2
Verbal Narrative

One of the chief concerns of this study of a folk narrative is not only to understand the structure and content of the narrative and the context in which it is performed but also to understand in depth and take seriously the notion of text and performance that is offered from within the cultural framework of the narrative. How are text and performance defined and perceived? Are there distinct and articulate notions of what constitutes a text and performance? How do these notions depart from a notion of text and performance derived from the researcher's own cultural framework? Thus, as Ricoeur (1981: 51),[1] writing on the goal of hermeneutics, points out:

> hermeneutics comprises something specific; it seeks to reproduce an interconnection, a structured totality by drawing support from a category of signs which have been fixed by writing, or by any other process of inscription equivalent to writing. So it is no longer possible to grasp the mental life of others in its immediate expressions; rather it is necessary to reproduce it, by interpreting objectified signs. This *Nachbilden* (reproducing) requires distinct rules since the expressions are embedded in objects of particular nature. . . . [I]t is philology—the explanation of texts—which provides the scientific stage of understanding.

But as Kersenboom (1995: 5), writing with reference to the "Tamil text," points out, this notion of the hermeneutic goal outlined by Ricoeur (and others) is seriously questionable, since

> in moments of actual encounter with alien textual activity, this agenda proved to be a hidden one: phenomena were not studied in order to detect their individual coherence and autonomy, but rather for the sake of something hidden behind them: a *universal-validity-of-interpretation-upon-which-all-certainty-in-history-rests.* This cascade of concepts was bewilderingly strange to Tamil experts. . . . [S]tructured totality, fixation, *Nachbildung, Auslegung* and *Interpretation*, produced constructs that had no physical shape or presence, but were never-

theless there, influencing the quality of life. Orientalism developed a life of its own, reigning supreme in the West and as an obnoxious reminder of difference in the East. The agenda of Tamil experts was a straightforward one: their language, and *eo ipso* their literature, were of divine origin, or divine substance and directed at a divine aim.

If, as in Kersenboom's study of the "Tamil text," the very notion of text and its relationship to the actual world within the so-called alien cultural context of research diverges from the scholar's own point of reference, would it not be necessary to set up an entirely different framework within which to ask questions? Would it not indeed be necessary to explore a whole new set of questions that may not tally with the researcher's well-treaded paths of analysis and explanation? As Piatigorsky (1985: 215), with regard to the analysis of Indian religion, notes:

> it is therefore of great importance to identify the main conditions under which terms corresponding to 'religion,' or 'ritual,' or 'cult'—where such exist—are used in a religion investigated as meta-concepts for its objective understanding of itself. . . . In the Indian case these terms of reflexive understanding developed within speculative structures of consciousness which neither codified the religion (as in theology) nor existed separately from it (as in philosophy) but analysed the religion from within the religion itself.

Following Piatigorsky's observation on Indian religion, we could analogously ask whether there are corresponding terms such as *verbal narrative, visual narrative, performance, performer,* and so on found within the narrative (and religious) tradition of Devnārāyaṇ. Although these may not be codified into a "theory" of the text or of performance, they nevertheless do exist as metalevel concepts used and transmitted by the community of devotees for whom the narrative is of fundamental importance. And it is as metalevel concepts used to describe the narrative and its performance that such terms and concepts need to be taken seriously.

In the following chapter I successively examine the categories of performance, remembrance and memory, song and declamatory chant, repetition, dialogue, and reported speech. All of these features individually and collectively build the context for the communicative act of telling and listening to the oral narrative. Taken together they also form the framework for the "reason" why the narrative is told, which is to elicit the *presence* of Devnārāyaṇ.[2] Thus the notion of "text" (both oral and visual) is bound to a larger context. As is not the case of the written text, neither the oral nor the visual narrative exist as self-contained objects.[3]

Performance

The narrative of Devnārāyaṇ—or more precisely, sections from the narrative—is performed in religiously determined contexts. Most usually a performance is part

Devnārāyaṇ's paṛ at dawn after a night-time performance by Śrī Hukamārām Bhopā.

of a *jāgraṇ* or "night-wake."[4] The purpose of a jāgraṇ is to evoke the presence (prakāś) of Devnārāyaṇ.[5] Performances are called paṛ *vā̃cṇo* ("speaking/reading the paṛ"), implying the use of an elaborately structured painted scroll, 1½ meters wide and 8½ meters long, on which characters and scenes of the narrative are depicted. Performances of this kind take place in three distinct places: (1) the home of a devotee; (2) in front of a Devnārāyaṇ or Savāī Bhoj temple; or (3) in front of the community meeting place (hathāī). Performances can take place any time of the year except for the period called *caumāsā*, the rainy season. During this time Devnārāyaṇ (and other Hindu deities) are supposed to be asleep. Performances begin on the eleventh day of the bright half of the month of Kārttik, which falls in October–November. During the caumāsā period the painted scroll, called paṛ, which is a central element in performances, is never unrolled. Narratives and songs may be sung, but in the so-called seated posture (*baiṭho gāṇo*) without the use of the paṛ and other dance techniques that are operative during "regular" performances. Thus, as Śrī Hukamārām Bhopā pointed out,

> the fact of the matter is this—now either the temple of Bhagavān—some people recite praises of him in front of the temple. And, some [people] who worship and honor Bhagavān, what does Bhagavān do for them? He is beneficial to them. So such a [person] is understood to be a *bhagat* of Dev. In his home, *jātīs*—pure *jātīs*—would receive water from his hand. So, in some of their homes it is recited. At our village, it is recited in the [homes] of Jāṭs; And even [in the homes] of Rajpūts it is recited—even now. There is the Khātī community—it is recited [in their homes]. So, Brahmans, Paṇḍits, they too have

> it recited even today. And, whoever honors Bhagavān is his favorite. And, in his home Bhagavāṇ's story is recited. There's nothing wrong with that. But, in lanes and alleys, in such places it is not recited. When the full-moon night of Kārttik arrives—when Dev awakes on the eleventh—from that time on, in the evening of the eleventh, [the recitation] begins. During [the month of] Āṣāḍh, Dev sleeps. For four months all the *devatās* go to the place of Rājā Baḷ. In earlier times there was this powerful king, who would give the gods strength. They go there to work. We say the gods have gone to sleep. But what should gods sleep for? They don't sleep! They go abroad to Rājā Baḷ's place to do "duty" for four months. Thus the work of Chatrīs and gods is stopped. It is wrong to open Bhagavān's door for four months. If the door is not opened, and only a jāgraṇ is done just sitting, then it is possible to tell the story. The paṛ can't be opened. Then after that on the eleventh day of the bright half of Kārttik open it and start [recitations]—there's no harm or hindrance in that.

The space marked by the scroll when it is unfolded and stood up is "sacred." The scroll itself is considered to be a "portable" temple, in the center of which there is the life-size figure of Devnarayaṇ seated together with his four brothers in his royal court (*darbār*). A makeshift altar is set up in front of his image. Here incense sticks are burnt and offerings of grain and money are made. Each time an offering from a member of the audience is made, the bhopā or his cosinger blows a conch (*saṅkh*) and proclaims the devotee's name and the quantity

Devnārāyaṇ in his court together with his four brothers, Medu, Bhuṇo, Madno, and Bhāṇgī.

The altar in front of Devnārāyaṇ's image on the paṛ.

and item offered by him. The performance is interrupted here. Besides such interruptions there are other pauses during which the singers are offered tea or tobacco and are asked to be seated. Such pauses can be relatively frequent, so that out of a total time of about nine hours, six are spent in narrating and performing the story. The singers wear a particular costume (*bāgā*) and use a stringed instrument called *bīṇ* or *jantar*. This double-gourd instrument is worn by the main singer, who plays on it while singing the narrative and pointing to corresponding sections of the scroll. His partner carries an oil lamp that illuminates the scroll during the performance, which involves a series of movements back and forth along the length of the scroll and between the two singers. The main singer may also undertake a series of pirouette-like steps at specific moments during the recitation. There is a great deal of interaction between singers and the audience. The audience members often comment on the episode concerned or the singers' performance itself. The singers are also apt to comment on the audience's degree of attentiveness and wakefulness. Audience members may also claim to know more than the singer, who must claim and reclaim his authority as a "specialist" by successfully answering "critical" questions. At times, during pauses, members of the audience may also entertain the audience by performing a few lines themselves.

The sequence such a performance follows can be summarized as follows:

1. Purificatory rites
2. Setting up the paṛ
3. Wearing the costume by the bhopā
4. A sevā for consecrating the paṛ
5. Invocations of many deities
6. Prosimetric narration of the story
7. Donation during frequent pauses
8. An āratī for deities and characters on the paṛ
9. A sevā at the end of the performance when the paṛ is rolled together again[6]

The first term that provides us with a correspondence to "performance" is paṛ vā̃cṇo Thus, the external description of song, narrative, dance, pointing to the paṛ, audience participation, and so on is—for bhopās and bhaktas alike—simply called "speaking/reading the paṛ." Thus the performance is not—as one might expect from a textual perspective—described as "narrating or telling Devnārāyaṇ's story." The focus here is not on the "text" as such but on the scroll, which is an icon of the deity, and of the text. However, the scroll is not self-explanatory: it needs to be "spoken" or "read," that is, it needs to be "decoded" and rendered meaningful by a specialist, namely the singer. Each performance thus involves a deconstruction of the entirety of images on the paṛ and a simultaneous reconstruction of its meaning. The meaning of the images becomes distinct, or rather emerges through the juxtaposition of spoken and sung narrative, together with visual images located on the paṛ. The paṛ, therefore, is not spoken or read like a picture book; it is read, on the contrary, through a narrative that manifests on account of its own recitation. The bhopa does not decode the images on the paṛ according to his own interpretation, as an art historian may do; he is bound by the interpretation of the images encoded in the narrative. The paṛ, according to the definition provided by the term paṛ vā̃cṇo, is not, therefore, simply an illustration of verbal, narrative content. It is, in fact, that which gets revealed through the interpretative framework provided by the narration. It would appear then that the imagery and iconicity of the paṛ is much more central to a performance than is the narration itself. This iconical emphasis can also be traced in phrases such as "paṛā̃ kā lekh," meaning "writing of the paṛ," that the singer Śrī Hukamārām Bhopā used to prove the existence and authenticity of specific passages and episodes from the narrative. Thus the paṛ was "proof" of the oral text and not vice versa. Visual imagery and iconicity are thus considered primary to verbal expression. But without verbal expression, the meaning(s) of the images do not reveal themselves.[7]

Before moving further, one point needs to be clarified here, and that is the use of the term *image*. This again is an external category used to describe the pictures on the scroll. The term *image* suggests a static visual representation or symbol of a real or imagined object. However, the "images" on the paṛ are, as I have mentioned, "icons" in a special sense of the term. Once again, they are not icons in the sense of only being traditionally conceived visual representations of religious themes;[8] they are, in fact, the iconic or visual *presence* of characters and scenes from the narrative. A term often used by singers when pointing to deities, persons, animals on the *paṛ* is that they are *birājmān*, that is, they are "present," "seated," or "manifest." The images of deities, persons, animals, and so on, therefore, *are* those deities, persons, animals, and so on.[9] There is no distance created between the symbol and thing. While this correlation undoubtedly results from the sacred nature of the scroll, it is to also a product of the "oral" and "aural" culture built into the tradition of Devnārāyaṇ. As Jardine (1996: 6) observes:

> An oral culture can hardly conceive of words as labels of some sort, as literate people tend to do, since spoken words are not "things" that can be picked up and "attached" to other things; a word must be an event or an action. Further, sound for oral peoples is dynamic also in the sense that it is linked to power: it must be driven by power from a source of some kind, which is why words (i.e., dynamic actions, events) themselves are understood to have great, even magical power. . . . Since oral cultures communicate mainly through sound, which is irreducibly dynamic, they lack the capacity to "stop" the dynamism of the lifeworld and subject it to abstract analysis. Oral thought processes, in other words, are always highly contextual.[10]

This correlation of word or image and thing is also evident in the case of the visual narrative that, as I have already pointed out, is also conceived in terms of the metaphor of "written text" or "script" (*lekh*). Thus it is not as though the paṛ is simply a picture book spread out to accompany the narration. The paṛ and its imagery is a concrete expression of the presence of the content of that imagery. This is particularly evident in the case of Devnārāyaṇ himself, who is seated on his "python throne" in the center of the paṛ. The presence of Devnārāyaṇ in the two-dimensional image is as real as the presence of a deity in *mūrtis* in Hindu temples.[11] There is no contradiction in the fact that there may be simultaneous performances of the narrative of Devnārāyaṇ, done by different bhopās using different paṛs, because the presence of Devnārāyaṇ—like that of other deities—is manifest in both a universal and localized form.[12] The presence of Devnārāyaṇ and other deities or persons on the paṛ is of central importance because the entire performance is focused on manifesting Devnārāyaṇ's *prakāś* ("presence," "radiance," "light," "splendor"). Thus on another level the activity of "speaking/reading the paṛ," which also involves not only the narration of the text but also dancing, musical instrumentation, and so on, occurs within the larger framework of "presencing" Devnārāyaṇ. The narration does not stop at revealing or decoding the meaning of the paṛ. The decoding in reality continues further than the semantic and cultural meanings into the domain of experiencing "presence" (prakāś). The culturally specific sense of both "speaking/reading" (vā̃cṇo) and "the written" (lekh) in terms of visual images of the paṛ (and not the verbal

Devnārāyaṇ sitting on his "python throne" casts his nectar gaze while faced by the serpent king Rājā Basak who emits his poison breath.

expression of the narrative) thus extends into the realm of *presencing* the divine.[13] Thus the meanings of the images ultimately make sense within the context of the manifestation of divine power.

❁ Remembrance ❁

In this section I briefly examine the meaning of the act of *remembering* with which a recitation always begins. Rather than regard this preliminary segment of the narrative situation as a "formulaic" and therefore an insignificant, recurrent beginning, my intention is to relocate it as a primary source of knowledge. My contention is that this source, which is almost unintelligible or unimaginable to the rationalized users of the printed word, is of prime importance to a wide variety of expressive traditions in India, ranging from story-telling to dance, theatre, and music. Similarly, the efforts of scholars—who themselves no longer cognize through the oral and aural—to understand oral narratives in terms of "mental texts," "memorization," "formulaic language," and so on are drastic attempts at making orality intelligible. Nevertheless, by virtue of being cut off ourselves from the source of creative inspiration as it is perceived of in different expressive traditions, we tend to gloss over its validity and authenticity.

Typically, the narration of Devnārāyaṇ begins with an invocation of different benevolent and auspicious deities that are also present on the paṛ. In the invocation, the deities are revered and remembered. The verb used here is *siṃvarṇo*, which is cognate with the Hindi *sumiraṇ* or *smaraṇ* and means "remembering," "recollecting," "calling to mind," "memory."[14] The deities invoked during the invocatory section are Devī Śāradā, Gaṇeṣ, Devnārāyaṇ, Bhairū̃nāth, Sarasvatī, and one's guru. The deities are invoked in order to provide protection, learning, and wisdom. Thus, for example, two lines tell us that without one's guru there is no "knowledge," and without Mother Sarasvatī there is no song or voice. By remembering Śāradā (a name of Sarasvatī or Durgā), the singer begins by saying she will always reside in the heart. The goddess Sarasvatī also resides in the singer's voice (*kaṇṭh*; literally: "throat"), inspiring him to sing. By remembering Gaṇpat or Bināyak one gains happiness and satisfaction. And, again, whoever reveres Devnārāyaṇ, the god worshipped in the form of bricks (*ī̃ṭh*),[15] will never have a scarcity of milk or cereals. The important point here is not only of course that the protective and inspirational qualities of different deities are being invoked but also that they are being "remembered." There is an invitation to remember. In other words, the singer is "re-membering" or "re-attaching" himself to the source from which the recitation flows.

In fact the reference to remembrance at the beginning of the narrative marks out the very nature of the work of narrating, which is an exercise in bringing something forth from an epistemological domain presided over by the goddess of learning, creativity, and wisdom. It is not, from the point of view of the singer, an exercise in bringing forth from memory, in the sense of an internalized, "mental" act of the retrieval of knowledge. The domain of knowledge and inspiration from which a singer draws out the song is in a sense *external* to him. It is an "objectified," phenomenological sphere that grants him knowledge. This understanding of oral narration is, from an epistemological point of view, contrary to the understanding that oral narration is the result of complex processes of learning and memorization. Thus, for example, Finnegan (1992: 114–117) in her chapter on composition, transmission, and memory, points out that in earlier models narratives were "pictured as coming down automatically irrespective of human agency" but that later critical studies move "away from the idea of storing verbatim memories to one of people reconstructing and organizing on the basis of what they know and do, so that remembering means not drawing on rote memory but a *creative* and organizational activity by the user." The emphasis in more recent work is, thus, on "memory as a social process." Some of the questions that are put in this context are as follows (116):

> What kinds of processes and ideologies are recognized for the preservation of records and memories without writing, and how are they

> valued and sanctioned? Are there recognized ways in which people are explicitly or implicitly trained to remember or to forget? What kinds of mechanisms are involved, and memory of what? Are such devices—and the content of what is remembered—necessarily all verbal or are there other media, images, and/or active performances additionally or alternatively involved, and if so what is the interaction between these?

This set of questions in the context of Devnārāyaṇ relates to how bhopās learn and transmit their knowledge, and how this knowledge is culturally sanctioned. To begin with it is important to point out that the office of a bhopā is not necessarily hereditary. An apprentice may or may not learn the trade from his father. Of fundamental importance is the "call" (or attitude) that an individual feels toward Devnārāyaṇ and learning the narrative. Many individuals may, in fact, function as an assistant to a bhopā, but not all finally become bhopās. Those who do become Bhopās do not receive any formal training. On the contrary, they "pick up" their trade by listening to the bhopā at performances and by occasionally joining in the performance. The text is thus learnt in a process analogous to the learning of natural language. Besides "picking up" the text itself through instructional prose narratives, the apprentice pays attention to other features of the performance such as *nāc* (dance), *vāṇo* (pointing out pictures), *gāv* (verse), *arthāv* (explanation), and *muskarī* (jokes). The performance itself, therefore, involves a wide range of "transmission media": the paṛ, dance, narration, song, jokes, gestures, instrumental music, costumes, riddles, lighting, and so on. Above all, of course, it should not be forgotten that the performance is a religiously determined event that serves in the worship of Devnārāyaṇ, the deity of the majority of audience members.[16]

But while the foregoing questions posed by Finnegan are important from the researcher's perspective, they nevertheless tend to overlook the cultural categories used by singers and performers to describe their own activity. Thus

> the Indian notions of *smara* (Sanskrit) and *marapu* (Tamil) combine love, memory, tradition and worship. They refer to reverential acts of ritual attendance, and also to the passionate longing of love. . . .*Smara*, 'memory,' 'love,' 'worship,' constitute 'tradition,' that which is handed down from one generation to the next (Skt. *parampara*). The heritage one receives from the elders is kept alive and fostered in love, for its beauty, value and concrete "indexicality."[17]

Moreover, the Sanskrit category of *smṛti* refers to the remembrance of revealed knowledge, *śruti*. Marwari *siṃvarṇo*, Hindi *sumiraṇ*, and Sanskrit *smara*, in the context of oral narratives and written texts, thus all refer to the *source* of religious literature. In the case of Devnārāyaṇ it is also this source that allows the oral narrative to manifest itself. The invocation of deities at the beginning of a recitation need not, therefore, be reduced to a matter of "formula" or ritual prescription of some kind. It is a matter of becoming "re-connected" to a sphere of inspiration and knowledge.

❁ Song and Declamatory Chant ❁

I shall now turn to the formal structure of the narrative, while keeping in mind that the formal structure, by virtue of also being a reflection of what the singers do, provides us with an insight into the larger communicative framework of the narrative. As mentioned earlier, the bhopā begins the narrative with an invocation (remembrance) of various deities, most notably Śāradā and Sarasvatī, the goddesses of learning, music, wisdom, speech, and creative inspiration. Following this he begins with the narrative per se. The narrative itself is a weave of verse and prose on the one hand and song and declaimed speech on the other. In addition to the interaction between these textual forms and delivery modes, there is the interaction between the main singer and his partner. The dialogic form of the delivery is furthermore also to be found in the narrative itself, which proceeds through a series of dialogues between different characters or voices. Before turning to this central element of the narrative, I shall first deal with the verse and prose sections.

Gāv and Arthāv

The verse sections of the text, which incidentally are also called "gāv,"[18] on account of their being sung, consist of four lines and a refrain. In some cases the sung sections have more than four lines. These exceptions will be discussed later. The "gāv" is sung by both singers simultaneously. In many instances they begin with an extended vowel "on-line": *e . . .* The first line ends with an extended *auvū̃ rai* or simply *rai*. The last words in the second and fourth lines invariably rhyme, but not the first and third lines. The refrain usually consists of "Bhalā̃ jī bhalā̃. Dev bhalā̃" ("Very good, sir. Very good, Dev"). When not referred to in terms of song (i.e., gāv), the verse sections are called *kaṛī*, which literally means link in a chain, "connection," or "sequence." Thus the verse sections are understood to be links in the narrative chain. And, in fact, the narrative moves from one set of kaṛīs to the next. Each set of kaṛīs contains a short, compressed monologue spoken by a particular character. In the prose section following a verse, this "monologue" is repeated almost verbatim. The difference of course lies in the form of delivery, which is now "declamatory." The prose sections that are declaimed are called *arthāv*, literally meaning "explanation" or "meaning" (Hindi: *arth*). In contrast to the verse sections, here there is a definite spacing of the singers' voices. While the lead singer begins the sentences, his partner may rejoin in a number of alternate ways: (1) he may complete a sentence ended halfway by the lead singer; (2) he may simply repeat the lead singer's text; (3) he may add a line of his own; and (4) he may simply acknowledge the lead singer's text with remarks such as "mhe" or "vāh vāh."

After the lines of the verse section have been faithfully repeated in the declaimed prose section, the singer and his partner continue the narrative in the dialogic manner already mentioned, until it is time to sing another kaṛī. The declaimed section invariably ends with lines such as "*Let's see what news x has to say / says*" and "*By saying it, know it, let's see.*" These lines denote (1) that a person is about to speak and (2) that whatever is to be *known* is to be revealed by saying it or by speaking it. The word used for "news" is *samcār.*[19] Thus X always begins his speech to Y in the form of first-person sung "news." Logically, then, that which is to be known through X's speech, and by implication the continuation of the narrative, becomes apparent in telling it/saying it/speaking it aloud. The emphasis on the connection between speaking and knowing is significant because it underlines the oral nature of the narrative. The singers do not say, for example, "Know it by reading it" or "know it by understanding what is written." The reference throughout is to speaking and telling. This aspect importantly underscores the emergent nature of *knowledge* for this particular oral tradition. Since there is no knowing before someone speaks, we cannot take recourse to "frozen" receptacles of knowledge such as scriptures, inscriptions, palm leaves, books, and so on to preserve and reveal knowledge.

Conversational Discourse

The dialogic interaction between the lead singer and his partner is matched on an internal level by the dialogical structure of the narrative. By this I mean very specifically that the narrative is fundamentally nothing more than a series of conversations or dialogues between different voices.[20] There are hardly any extended third-person descriptions of events or scenes offered by the singers themselves. Whatever happens in the narrative takes place through the voices of various characters. Thus the narrative both in its internal structure as well as external expression comes closest to the speech genre of *conversation.* The analysis offered here and in the subsequent sections on repetition, dialogue, and reported speech, therefore, focuses primarily on the nature and occurrence of *utterances* as a fundamental unit of *speech,* rather than on linguistic features such as grammar, or even "formulaic" language, in order to understand the oral composition of the narrative.

While describing the features of conversational discourse in everyday situations,[21] Tannen (1994: 25) points out that

> conversational discourse frequently represents what others have said ("reported speech") as dialogue ("direct speech" or "direct quotation") rather than third-person report ("indirect speech"), and that "direct speech" is more vivid, more effective. But why is dialogue more vivid? I believe it is because the creation of voices occasions the imagination of a scene in which characters speak in those voices, and that these scenes occasion the imagination of alternative, distant,

or familiar worlds, much as does artistic creation. Finally, the casting of ideas as the speech of others is an important source of emotion in discourse.[22]

Whereas the conversations in the narrative are situated in the present, giving us a scene of a current event, the commentary offered by the singers is situated in the past. For example, such a commentary may be inserted between dialogues to spell out time and place:

So when they arrived in Sindhbāḍā—*mhe*—both Bhairũnāths
caught hold of the tree trunk—*vāh vāh*—
After catching hold of the tree trunk they shook it. There were
Jogīṇīs sitting on each leaf. Crack, crack, crack, crack they all
came and fell down, sir said.
By God's grace there was a well close by—*mhe*—
They went and fell into the well
Bhairũnāth said: "Śrī Mahārāj we threw them down with difficulty—
the whores have gone and fallen into the well."

Verbs involving saying or telling are most frequently used. These are almost always in the present tense, facilitating the usage of direct speech. One example has already been given, the line preceding a verse section ("*Let's see what news X has to say/says*"). Other examples are to be found in sentences preceding actual "direct speech." Thus "Bhairavnath said," "Dev Mahārāj said," "He or she said." Sometimes simply "said" is used. In such cases the speaker can be determined by the preceding sentences. In addition to these usages of the verb "said" at the beginning of a spoken sentence, the second singer makes use of "said" to end his lines: "*'came and fell down,' sir said.*" Thus while the lead singer introduces a character's speech by saying "X said," the second singer ends his version of the text also by saying "he or she said." The second singer's usage of "he or she said" in fact facilitates the repetitive nature of his delivery. Not only is the content thus repeated but also the fact of the direct speech being spoken by X is reemphasized and repeated. Repetition and dialogicity thus together form a fundamental aspect of both narrative delivery and narrative style.

Repetition

Finnegan (1977: 90) notes that "the most marked feature of poetry is surely repetition."[23] Furthermore, (129), she observes that

> repetition in some form is a characteristic of oral poetic style: repetition of phrases, lines or verses; the use of parallelisms; recurrent formulae. Oral poetry is necessarily ephemeral. Repetition has a real point in such circumstances. It makes it easier for the audience to grasp what has been said and gives the speaker/singer confidence that it has understood the message he is trying to communicate. In antiphonal forms, refrains, choruses or the direct repetition of a leader's

lines, repetition offers an opportunity for an audience to take part with ease in the act of performance, to a degree not possible without some measure of repetition.[24]

The oral style of Devnārāyaṇ's narrative is repetitive on many levels. One obvious form of repetition is the verbatim declamation of sung sections. Then there is the refrain at the end of each verse section, and the use of certain stock descriptions to mark "battle scenes." In addition there is repetition in the case of certain passages where a specific action is repeated by different people. Thus, for example, in the search for Bhūṇā, each family member, in consecutive sung sections, entrusts Chochū Bhāṭ with a letter for Bhūṇā. Here we find a degree of repetition in the phrases used, which describe, as mentioned, the same act carried out by different persons. The use of repetition here adds to the emotional and poetic quality of the moment, which in terms of the narrative bears the promise of a reunion with a family member. Whereas these examples relate to the poetic structure of the narrative, the kind of repetition mentioned earlier involving the singers can be said to relate to the style of delivery. In this case it is not that lines from the sung sections are repeated in the declaimed section but that lines in declaimed sections are repeated by the lead singer's partner. "Internal" repetition is thus paralleled by "external" repetition. And the "internal" dialogue of the narrative as a series of spoken encounters between different characters is paralleled by the "external" dialogue of the singers.

But repetition even in this case is quite varied and may involve a wide range of possibilities. However, given the nature of repetition itself as something that is not necessarily produced but "reproduced," this would mean that even though there may be many options available to the singer, the ultimate choice of utterance is determined by the first singer's speech. Creativity on the part of the second singer then lies in choosing from a range of given responsive modes. But the second singer's response is not limited to repetition. He also may bring in his own text, which is either a commentary on the preceding line or an addition that propels the narrative forward.

Examples of Repetition

In the context of conversational discourse Tannen (1994: 54) distinguishes between different forms of repetition:

> First, one may distinguish self-repetition and allo-repetition (repetition of others). Second, instances of repetition may be placed along a scale of fixity in form, ranging from exact repetition (the same words uttered in the same rhythmic pattern) to paraphrase (similar ideas in different words). Midway on the scale . . . is repetition with variation, such as questions transformed into statements, statements changed into questions, repetition with a single word or phrase changed, and repetition with change of person or tense . . . patterned rhythm, in which completely different words are uttered in the same syntactic and rhythmic paradigm as a preceding utterance.

Before turning to the function of repetition in the narrative, I would like to first present some examples of different forms of repetition as a subcategory of rejoinders offered by the second singer. In discussing the repetition involved in the second singer's utterances, I am primarily focusing on what Tannen calls "allo-repetition" or the repetition of others (in this case of the first singer).

Example 1: Exact repetition. In the cases of exact repetition, most frequently only a part of the phrase is repeated verbatim by the second singer.[25] It is apparent that the second singer uses verbatim repetition almost always to emphasize the last one, two, or even three words spoken by the lead singer. Rarely is a whole line repeated unless this itself is fairly short. Once the words are repeated by the second singer, he may extend the phrase on his own, thereby either adding new information, or again, reemphasizing the preceding line through a reformulation.

> kīyo: Hā̃ śrī mahārāj *mharai kannai hī hai*
> (hā̃ "*mharai kannai hai*" kīyo)
> Aurū̃ māvo *baṭhai hi karā̃*
> (hā̃ "*baṭhai hī karā̃* cālo sāge hī cālū̃)
> *syāl tū̃ hviyo*
> ("*syāl tū̃ hai*" kīyo)
> paḍihār ko nā̃v liyo jarā̃ bhāṭ ke eḍī kī cāṭī jaḷ *lāgī* jī jāḷā
> (hā̃ "*lāgī*" kīyo)
> ābā dey bhai dev kā ghar kī bajarśilā māthā par *āḍi hai*
> ("*āḍi hai*" kīyo)
> jiyān jūjaḷo nai marai jatī ṭaim hi koni lagāvai *hāthi nai mārtā̃*
> ("*i hāthi nai mārtā̃*" kīyo)
> tanai *cir āvai* kā̃i
> (hā̃ "*cir āvai*" kīyo "o bābā bhāṭ")
> āpanai darbār ke mā̃yanai ek *sūṇi rahavai*
> (hā̃ "*sūṇī rahavai*" kīyo)

Example 2. In the following examples there is a transposition of words while the meaning of the phrase is retained. In some cases words have been replaced by their synonyms, producing a different phrase with the same semantic content. In this case, where the second singer does not just identically repeat the lead singer's lines, the phrases are longer, spanning more than only a few words as in the preceding examples. Apparently the freedom the second singer has in reproducing the lines in "his own words" also facilitates the production of more text than does a faithful reproduction.

> Darbār kā hukamū̃ bagaṛāvatā̃ ko bhāṭ *manavār ko hi liyoḍo kadai koni ho*
> (hā̃ "*manavār ko kadai hi liyo koni ho*")
> *Kanai* to pisiyo lagābā *nai eka hi*
> ("*i mhārai kanai hai koni*")
> darbār kā hukamū̃ lāl mē̃ to nīmā *thārai jaṇā āyo bhai*
> (hā̃ "*i vāstai āyoḍā hū̃*")
> jaṇā *kā̃i dorā hai* bhai

(hā̃ "*kī̃ dorā koni* bā mē̃ to")
kiyo dhūliyo ekānai hojā bhai *kā̃var khāṇḍerāv kī asavāri ab kī āri hai*
(hā̃ "*kā̃var khaṇḍerāvjī padhār riyā hai*" kīyo)
bhūṇojī o kīyo bhāṭ man mē̃ dekhiyo thārā dhaṇī nai *surgyāṇī suṇayo*
("paṇ *surgyāṇī jarūr hi hai*" kīyo)
Mhānā bāp dādā ko nā̃v *jāṇai koni*
(hā̃ "tū̃ *jaṇai koy nī* kā̃ī" kīyo)
man mē̃ dekhiyo kā̃i bāt hui *māthā nai kāmaṇāvū̃ bā̃dh lyo*
(hā̃ "*māthā nai* kāṭ *bā̃dh liyo*" kīyo "*jādūvū̃*")
tanai ṭhā hviyo koni hviyo
(hā̃ "*tanai ṭhā paḍiyo koni paḍiyo*")

Monosyllabic Rejoinders

In addition to the two recurrent kinds of repetition just mentioned, there is the repetition of particular monosyllabic words or interjections that the second singer uses as a response. These words are repeated extensively during a recitation at those intervals where the second singer does not repeat, reformulate, or add phrases or words to the first singer's lines. In a sense they amount to an almost formless or meaningless kind of response. Śrī Moṭārām, the second singer, uses "vāh vāh" and "mhe" as a "formless" response. It is difficult to determine a structure in the instrumentation of this kind of response. "Mhe," which is much shorter than "vāh vāh," is used at times like an exclamation mark or interjection or even for the kind of spacing provided by the use of a comma. Thus for example:

Nīmde kīyo "re Mū̃gtā" (mhe)
"Jagīśyā" (mhe)
kīyo "Dhūliyā" (mhe)
darbār kā hukamū̃ kīyo "Bhāṭ" (mhe)
nīgevān siradārā̃ kīyo "Śrī Mahārāj" (mhe)
kīyo "Nimā" (mhe)
kīyo "Bhairavanāth" (mhe)
kanāt ke mā̃yanai baḍ siradār kīyo "Śrī Mahārāj" (mhe)
muṇḍ agalā sirdār kīyo "re bhāī Dhūliyā" (mhe)
"are Jagīśyā" (mhe)
"are Siradārā̃" (mhe)

In these examples we can see that "mhe" appears regularly after a person's name has been spoken out at the beginning of direct speech. It functions as a form of punctuation used after one person has been addressed by another. But this is not the only placement of "*mhe*". The other placements are varied, and a pattern is difficult to discern. Some examples are given below to illustrate its varying usages:

"are amaldār ādamī hū̃" (mhe)
"ke koy jamānā mē̃ bagaṛāvat hviyā" (mhe)

to bhaṭ man mẽ dekhiyo "ke moharā̃ to ladhī" (mhe)
dev ko nā̃v ley (mhe)
dev ko nā̃v lay ar dhūl mẽ bhar ḍhāl nai (mhe)
kīyo "bhāī ghaṇā din hviyā suṇiyā ī nai" (mhe)

In these examples we see that "mhe" is used interchangeably at the end of a section of direct speech or even at the end of a section that does not involve direct speech.

I shall now examine some extended examples of the narrative to determine where "mhe" and "vāh vāh" are used:

"are amaldār ādmī hū̃ (mhe)
mẽ suṇayoḍi bāt hai bhāī Nimā re (hā̃ "dekhyoḍī konī" kīyo)
ke koy jamānā mẽ bagaṛāvat hviyā (mhe)
pācatolī moharā̃ kācā tārā̃ mẽ poy poy (ar) aṭīkar ghoṛā ke galai
("mẽ rāḷ rāḷ dapaṭāyā batāve hai" kīyo)
kah batāvai bai moharā̃ bhāī re ṭūṭ ṭūṭ ar (hā̃ "paḍī bajār mẽ")
mẽ dekhū̃ (mhe)
ek hi mhanāī mohar ("āj lādh jāve")
āj āj ko amal pāṇī ("mhāre ho jāve" kīyo)
mẽ dekhū̃ bhagavān kharco de mhanai (vāh vāh)
Nimde kīyo "re Mū̃gtā (mhe)
kuṇa deś ko hāī bol" ("kuṇso deś ko ayo tū̃" kīyo)
kīyo "sāt samandrā pār ko hū̃ (hā̃ "sāt samandrā pār kā hū̃")
"kuṇ log hai" ("jaki batā")
kīyo "rājāvõ ko baī ko bhāṭ hū̃" (vāh vāh)
"Nā̃v" "sẽsārī duniyā jagīśyo kah ar batalāvai" (hā̃ "jagīśyo kah ar
batalāyā karai" kīyo)[26]

The passage cited here involves a conversation between Chochū Bhaṭ and Rājā Nīmde, the Rāṇā's younger brother. Chochū Bhāṭ begins the dialogue with "*are amaldār ādamī hū̃.*" This is followed by "mhe," which is followed by a further remark spoken by Chochū Bhāṭ. Chochū Bhaṭ's speech continues till "*mẽ dekhū̃ bhagavān kharco de mhanai.*" The end of his speech is marked by "*vāh vāh.*" With the exception of one instance where "*mhe*" is used (*mẽ dekhū̃* [*mhe*]), Chochū Bhāṭ's speech is not punctuated by Śrī Moṭārām. On the contrary, the lines spoken by Śrī Hukamārām are supplemented and extended by Śrī Moṭārām in his response. After the first occurrence of "vāh vāh" Nīmde begins his section of the dialogue. Here again "mhe" is used as a punctuation mark after Nīmde addresses Chochū Bhāṭ: "*re mū̃gtā (mhe).*" "Vāh vāh" is inserted after Chochū Bhāṭ has ended his speech "*rājāvõ ko baī ko bhāṭ hū̃*" (*vāh vāh*).

In the passage just quoted we find that "mhe" is used as a form of punctuation within a single character's speech. "Vāh vāh" on the other hand is used to mark the end of one character's speech and the beginning of another character's speech. "Mhe" and "vāh vāh" in these examples thus mark off elements of speech belonging to one character and the speech of different characters. However, while this description may give the impression of a patterned usage, there are also examples in which "vāh vāh" is used internally within a series of spoken lines belonging to one character in the same way "mhe" is. In such examples we find that "vāh vāh" is placed as a punctuation within a particular character's speech. Conversely, "mhe" is placed at the end of a character's speech. On the whole, however, there is a greater frequency with which "mhe" is used within speech and "vāh vāh" to mark its end. In addition, "vāh vāh" is used regularly at the end of the sentence introducing the person who speaks a gāv section. Thus for example:

> darbār kā hukamū̃ bhūṇojī bole (vāh vāh) / kā̃ī samcār kahavai dekhā̃ . . .
> to bhāṭ bole (vāh vāh) / kā̃ī ghoḍīmātā nai samcār kahavai dekhā̃ . . .
> mīr bole (vāh vāh) / kā̃ī samcār kā̃ī bhāṭ nai kahavai dekhā̃ . . .
> kalāḷī bole (vāh vāh) / kā̃i samcār kahavai dekhā̃ . . .

Here it is apparent that "vāh vāh" is not being used to induce a pause in speech but as an interjection involving the original sense of the word *vāh*, which may be translated as "great," "wonderful," or "splendid."

Samcār

The foregoing lines also make it clear that the gāv passages always consist of "packets" of direct speech spoken by a particular character, usually in response to another character's speech. These "packets" of direct speech are referred to as *samcār*—a word translatable as "news, message, report, or information." It can also have the sense of "dialogue" (*saṃvād*). In the content of the narrative tradition of Devnārāyaṇ, samcār has an almost "technical" status as a dialogue marker within the narrative. Thus singers or listeners may inquire of a given passage "Whose samcār is it?" or simply "Which samcār is it?" in order to determine up to which point the narrative has progressed or from which point it should be taken up. Sometimes the singer may also ask "Who said this samcār?" immediately after he has sung the samcār. This sort of question (and its answer) reinforces the samcār speaker's identity in the singer's and audience's minds. Thus the narrative progresses not only through interchanges between song (gāv) and declamatory prose (arthāv) but also through a series of "messages," "reports," "newses," or "dialogues" which constitute the content of the sung passages. The meaning of the term samcār as a concept used to describe fundamental units of the narrative once again highlights the "dialogic" conception of the narrative. Not only is the narrative in its declaimed sections built up of dialogues between characters, the sung sections too are understood as being units of direct speech that constitute a "reply" within the parameters of a foregoing dialogue.

In addition to the concept of samcār, which is most frequently used before beginning the four-lined verse section of the gāv, the singer Śrī Hukamārām also variously uses the term *vārtā*, which means "story," "conversation," "occurrence/truth/reality/fact," "speech," "talk," "short tale," "narration," "report." The preverse line in this case is usually "kā̃ī vārtā ban jāvai dekhā̃." This does not, as in the case of *samcār*, imply that someone is speaking but rather that an event or a scene is about to be described in the following song sections. The song sections that fall under the category of vārtā are considerably longer than the sections described as samcār. Thus a vārtā may contain nine lines (of which the last words of the second and third lines rhyme). Each line itself also contains more syllables than the line belonging to the samcār sections. Besides the nine-line vārtās, there are also long sung sections describing a preparation for battle or a clash between two parties. These descriptions are fairly standardized and contain 10 or 18 sung lines. Here too each individual line contains more syllables than the verse sections characterized as samcār.

The Function of Repetition

Tannen (1994: 47), while analyzing repetition in conversation, asks the following fundamental question:

> Why is there repetition in conversation? Why do we waste our breath saying the same thing over and over? The various purposes simultaneously served by repetition can be subsumed under the categories of production, comprehension, connection, and interaction. The congruence of these functions of discourse provides a fourth and overarching function in the establishment of coherence and interpersonal involvement.

In the case of production, she points out that "repetition enables a speaker to produce language in a more efficient, less energy-draining way. It facilitates more language, more fluently" (48). Comprehension is facilitated by repetition "by providing semantically less dense discourse. If some of the words are repetitions, comparatively less new information is communicated than if all words uttered carried new information" (49). Connection is established through repetition because "it serves a referential and tying function. Repetition of sentences, phrases, and words show how new utterances are linked to earlier discourse, and how ideas presented in the discourse are related to each other" (50). Tannen goes on to point out that the function of repetition in relation to production, comprehension, and connection "refer(s) to the creation of meaning in conversation. But repetition also functions on the interactional level of talk: accomplishing social goals, or simply managing the business of conversation" (51).

Having so far discussed the various possibilities of repetition within the narrative, I will now turn to the function and role of repetition under the four headings given earlier. The first category is that of "production." Repetition in this case facilitates "more language, more fluently." Certainly this feature is apparent in the arthāv sections, where the second singer repeats parts of the first singer's lines. Undoubtedly "more language" is created here by using more of the same words while providing information. As a whole the narrative is enlarged and extended through repetition, and the production of "more language" does actually also contribute to its lengthy "epic" dimension. However, the production of more language here is closely linked to the second category, namely comprehension. Thus the repetition of the gāv passages in the arthāv sections facilitates a better understanding of the sung verses. In fact the term arthāv, which means "explanation," "meaning," "commentary," itself implies that the repetition of verse in declaimed prose is meant to provide a clearer comprehension of the former.

Here again we find that a term is used that suggests a conceptual, metalevel perception of the narrative and its narration from within the tradition. Thus the passages following the gāv sections are not called "prose" as against "song" but, significantly, "meaning" or "explanation." This distinction enables us to again visualize how the narrative is conceptualized. According to the terms used, the narrative of Devnārāyaṇ in this case consists of sung sections that are then laid out and "explained."[27] Of course this form of "explanation" does not involve answers to "how and why" questions. It does not "explain" the sung sections in different words. Rather it explains by repeating the same words in a different mode of delivery. It is repetition itself, as Tannen observes, that lays bare the meaning of the words and sentences, since in the initial lines of the arthāv practically no new information is supplied. New information is supplied in subsequent lines. But here too there is repetition, as a consequence of which it is easier to comprehend the import of the first singer's utterance. But more than facilitating simple semantic comprehension, repetition within the arthāv—which often involves only some select words—functions as an instrument of emphasis. Thus the few words that are repeated (sometimes the whole line in transposed form) carry within them the core of what the first singer intended to mean in his speech. Thus, repetition involving the arthāv and sections within it, facilitates and serves not only comprehension but also emphasis.[28]

Tannen's third category is "connection": "Repetition of sentences, phrases, and words show how new utterances are linked to earlier discourse, and how ideas presented in the discourse are related to each other." (1994: 50). This category, it would appear, is more linked to everyday conversation than to the situation of the narration of Devnārāyaṇ, in which it is not so much ideas as scenes and events that are presented and linked with one another. The linkage of scenes and events is, of course, partially created through repetition but even more so is afforded by the structure of plots and subplots in the narrative.

As Tannen points out, theses three functions ultimately relate "to the creation of meaning in conversation [and] accomplishing social goals, or simply managing the business of conversation" (1994: 52). It is quite evident that repetition in the special case of the narrative also relates to the production of meaning. The creation of meaning is guided in this case not toward the singers themselves, but toward the audience that listens to the performance of the narrative. However, meaning does not emerge only at a purely linguistic or semantic level. It emerges here also at an "experiential" level through the "bringing-forth" of the content of the narrative that revolves about the life and deeds of Devnārāyaṇ, and the devotees' participation in the evocation of his power. Thus the various forms of repetition inherent to the narrative and its telling are transformed from being literary features to partaking in the realm of praxis. Together with the various other aspects of the whole performance they too take on a causal character in the production of meaning as an interplay of semantic, sensory, cultural, and religious elements.

❁ Dialogue ❁

As pointed out earlier, the narrative is "repetitive" on (at least) two levels: the level of form (verse and prose, etc.) and the level of delivery (lead singer and second singer). Furthermore, it became clear to me that the narrative is also "dialogic" in two senses: the sense in which dialogue between characters occupies a central position as a narrative strategy and the sense in which the singers are engaged in a dialogue with one another (and of course also with the audience, producing a third sense of dialogue). Thus, as indicated previously, a full understanding of the narrative as a communicative event would involve not only an understanding of its language but also an understanding of the nature and relationship of *utterances* to one another as a vehicle for constructing oral narrative structure,[29] and, as will be shown in the second half of the study, also for the dialogic structure of the *world* represented in the narrative.

Given the centrality of the fact that the narrative delivery of Devnārāyaṇ is essentially constituted by two voices who spin out the narrative content through an exchange of utterances, it is worthwhile to examine the nature of this dialogue. As already pointed out, it is possible to locate this form of dialogue within the umbrella category of speech genres we call *conversation*. Naturally, the kind of conversational dialogue that occurs during a narration of Devnārāyaṇ is contextually distinct from the kind of conversational dialogue that may occur in "everyday life." Whereas conversations of everyday life are centered around a variety of subjects and may develop in a variety of forms, the conversation occurring during a narrative of Devnārāyaṇ is focused and determined by the content of the narrative. In addition, the form of the conversation or exchange between the singers is quite regularized. It is to be limited to a set of options (which have already been discussed).[30] Above all, however, the conversational nature of the exchange between the singers has a distinguishing feature that "everyday" conversation (fortunately) does not possess. Whereas in everyday conversation there is always the possibility that the respondent will become the speaker and the speaker take the place of the respondent, in the case of the narrative, the identity of the respondent is always fixed. The second singer is the one who provides the rejoinder to the first singer's utterances and not vice versa. The role of listener and speaker is, therefore, predetermined by the narrative style. Although the dialogue between the singers thereby involves a certain level of inflexibility, it also provides a set of options in terms of which the second singer's rejoinder may be expressed.

At this point it should be noted that the narrative tradition of Devnārāyaṇ itself has a notion of "rejoinder." This is called *hũkāro* (*hũkāriyo* is the person) and means a verbal expression of assent or of comprehension and agreement, of urging the narrator to carry on speaking. Thus there is conceptual awareness here of the fact that a speaker always requires a listener. In other words human communication is considered to be essentially "dialogic" rather than monologic. The speaker or singer cannot express himself in a vacuum. It is the active comprehension of the listener expressed through the hũkāro that draws out the singer's lines and ultimately facilitates the progress of the narrative. This notion of the active listener or respondent comes close to Bakhtin's (1987: 68–69) understanding of speech communication:

> when the listener perceives and understands the meaning (the language meaning) of speech, he simultaneously takes an active, responsive attitude toward it. He either agrees or disagrees with it . . . augments it, applies it, prepares it for execution, and so on. Any understanding of live speech, a live utterance, is inherently responsive, although the degree of this activity varies extremely. Thus all real and integral understanding is actively responsive, and constitutes nothing other than the initial preparatory stage of a response (in whatever form it may be actualized).

Given the importance of a response for all "live speech," it is not surprising that the narrative tradition of Devnārāyaṇ with its focus on orality should involve a lead singer and his respondent. It is remarkable that such a notion should in fact be formalized (institutionalized) to such a degree.[31]

So far I have pointed out the role of the dialogue, and of speaker and respondent, in relation to the actual narration of the narrative. But what implications, if any, does such a narrative form have on the structure of the text? How is a text constructed through a series of utterances (and not "sentences")? What kind of text emerges in this way? Thus, given the spoken nature of the narration as a series of utterances, the text is composed of a body of sometimes complete and sometimes only partially complete sentences (in the case of arthāv), of exclamations, of monosyllabic rejoinders, and so on. The text as a whole is thus made up of grammatically fragmented linguistic units (such as the sentence). These broken units only make sense due to the fact that they are utterances in an oral narrative and not written sentences in prose. The oral nature of the narrative allows for the *incompleteness* of the grammatical structure of the text. And, as has been pointed out earlier, within the chain of "incomplete" sentences there is a chain of grammatically incomplete repetitive utterances created through the second singer's response to the lead singer's words. Thus the text contains within itself a repetition of itself. As a series of dialogic utterances, it responds to and imitates itself. Thus the "text" created by the second singer does not give importance to being "autonomous" or "original." It is caught up in a perfect "intertextual" flow with the text of the first singer. In other words, it exists on the boundaries of the lead singer's text by referring to and in fact reproducing it.[32]

Reported Speech

It was mentioned earlier that the delivery of the narrative and the narrative itself are dialogic in two different senses. The first sense is that in which the recitation proceeds on the basis of an interchange between the two singers. This interchange—a communicative event situated in a performance setting—is directed at setting up and establishing a corpus of meaning for the audience who listens (and also interacts) with the singers. The second sense of dialogue involves the construction of the narrative in terms of dialogues between characters of the story. Thus it was shown that the central sections of the story (gāv) are units of speech or conversation uttered by one character and directed toward another character. Given these two senses of dialogue, one could say that the "inner" dialogue of the narrative occurs within the "outer" dialogue of the singers, which in fact provides the frame for the narration. But in what sense are we to understand the relationship between the "outer" and "inner" dialogues? How is the inner dialogue part of or built into the outer dialogue? Once again the line of inquiry I will take up here rests on the assumption that the recitation of the narrative is a particular speech genre that comes closest to that of "everyday" conversation following an interchange between two speakers. But before proceeding with this inquiry, I shall refer to an understanding of what in linguistic terms can be called a dialogue. A dialogue, in the sense Bakhtin refers to, arises from the fact that all utterances are in fact *polyphonic* in nature: "Utterances are not indifferent to one another, and are not self-sufficient; they are aware of and mutually reflect one another. . . . Each utterance is filled with echoes and reverberations of other utterances" (1986: 91). A special form of dialogic utterance is an interchange that involves the reporting of another's speech. "Reported speech" can have two forms:[33] one that involves a direct quotation such as "He/she said: 'I did that' "; another that involves an indirect quotation such as "He/she said that he/she did that/had done that." The assumption behind reported speech as "direct quotations" is that the utterance of one person can be faithfully repeated by someone else in a content other than the original one in which the utterance was spoken. Thus there is the belief that the utterance and its meaning content can remain untouched regardless of speaker and spoken content.

However, as Tannen (1994: 133) points out,

> "reported speech" is a misnomer, an abstraction with no basis in the reality of interaction. When speakers cast the words of others in dialogue, they are not reporting so much as constructing dialogue. . . . Dialogue is not a general report; it is particular, and the particular enables listeners (or readers) to create their understanding by drawing on their own history of associations. . . . The constructing of dialogue for framing as reported speech reflects the dual nature of language, like all human behavior, as repetitive and novel, fixed and free, transforming rather than transmitting what comes its way.

From the point of view of the narrative of Devnārāyaṇ, we find that what the singers are doing—at least on the surface—is to continuously "report" what characters in the narrative said (to one another). By inserting the name of the person who speaks before each dialogue the singer identifies his or her voice. The singers do not, for example, personify characters or speak in the first person as characters might do in theatre. On the contrary, they are involved in reporting to the audience or listeners what went on or what was spoken. In this sense it is the singer who claims access to the scenes and events of the narrative, just like a third person who witnesses a conversation between two people and then reports the conversation to a fourth. However, as Tannen points out, "reported speech" is not just repetition but also construction. How does the singer's activity of reporting dialogue involve construction? If it does involve construction, is this the same as saying that the singers "improvise" while narrating? What consequences follow if we begin to view the "constructed" nature of the narrative rather than its "improvisational" nature? Supposing we were to perceive the singers' task not as "recitation" but as "reporting"? How would our understanding of the communicative event alter from this perspective? Would our search for fixity (formula, repetition) and free play ("creativity/improvisation") be altered? Thus, for example, as Tannen argues, "the construction of dialogue represents an active, creative, transforming move which expresses the relationship not between the quoted party and the topic of talk but rather the quoting party and the audience to which the quotation is delivered." In other words, it is the context in which the act of reporting is done that determines the sense the "quoted" speech is to have. If reported speech does involve the creative and transforming aspect Tannen refers to, then it would seem obvious that singers alter what they say according to who they perceive the audience to be and what relationship they have to the audience. A simple example of this alteration or, in fact, choice in telling, can be seen in terms of the episode a singer "reports" to the audience. He "reports" not only episodes of his own choice but also those wished for by the audience. By placing the communicative act of singer and audience within the framework of "reported speech," we can conceptualize the process of selectivity being involved in a different way. Selectivity in reporting is not just a question of desires or wants but also of being in rapport with the "listening" of the audience, just as a speaker reports what he or she has heard selectively depending on the intention he or she has in "reproducing" an utterance in a specific social or interpersonal context. But what exactly is meant by "listening"? How is listening different from verbal response? Listening, we may say, is an internal state of the listener that provides the context for the speaker's utterence to unfold and make sense. Therefore, it is a nonverbal *activity* that engenders speech.[34] Thus, the activity of singing and speaking is bound not solely to the singers' agency but also to the audience's particular agency evoked through listening. Thus, depending on this interrelationship between audience and singer, the singer would tend to "report" the narrative in varying ways. This would explain why performances are never exactly the same. However, it would also shift the emphasis from "improvisation," that is, an explanation of variation in terms of a singer's individual capability, to "construction," or the creative building up of narrated dialogue in a specifically interactive situation in which listening plays a vital role. In such a situation it would be natural that there is a movement between fixity, that is, the use of "formula," and "free play" (or creativity). Thus the problem of formulaic language and improvisation during a performance need not refer solely to the phenomenon of "memorization," and "improvisation," and so on but to the question of "construction," and the "interaction" based on listening.

By viewing a performance or recital of the narrative as an example of extended "reported" speech, we can also begin to appreciate the nature of the singer's work. The singer's work is thus not simply to sing, recite, or perform the narrative; rather it is to mediate or report what happened and what was said to the audience. Thus implicit in the singer's work is a knowledge of past events that are then passed on as dialogue in the present to the audience. It is the singer's privilege then to have "overheard" or gained knowledge about Devnārāyaṇ that is then communicated to his devotees.

Examples of Reported Speech

The phenomenon of reported speech is found in a number of other textual examples. Among written genres, the most common use of reported speech is in epics and purāṇas. In many purāṇas (and *māhātmyas*) it is the bard or *sūta* who reports what has happened to group of interested listeners (mostly *ṛṣis*). The bard's reporting of what has happened invariably follows questions that have been put to him from the "audience." Thus, in puranic (and epic) texts, the bard is very explicitly asked to narrate or report on what he has seen or knows. In a sense by inserting the voice of the bard and the audience into the text, the text in fact describes both the "performance" (narrational) situation and that which is narrated or reported. The text is thus a "report" on both: the setting and that which is being reported. Both levels are in a sense inscribed into the written text. In the oral narrative situation of Devnārāyaṇ, the first level of "reporting", that is, about the setting itself, is nonexistent. This is because the setting involves an event that occurs in the present. The reporting is, as in the case of purāṇas and epics, of events or dialogues that have occurred in the past. However, there are other basic differences in the construction of dialogue between written texts and the narrative of Devnārāyaṇ. For example, the dialogues contained in epic and puranic texts are frequently quite lengthy, bordering on monologues. Moreover, they are placed within the parameters of Sanskrit poetic conventions, appearing in verse form. The dialogues reported in the narrative of Devnārāyaṇ, are, on the other hand, short. Except for the gāv sections, they are formulated in the language of everyday situations, lacking poetic or literary embellishments. Their shortness, coupled with the frequency with which voices change, gives the overall impression of a dialogue as we may encounter it in everyday conversation. The simplicity of language and the rapidness of exchange all heighten the sense of an actual dialogue with its dramatic overtones:

> The Bhāṭ said: "Hey, Śrī Mahārāj when did I ever quarrel?" *Yes, I'm frightened of frightening a lion*
> Dev Mahārāj said: "Then come close Bhāṭ!"—*vāh vāh*—
> "I'll protect you!"—*vāh vāh*—
> The Bhāṭ said: "How are you going to do that, Śrī Mahārāj?" *Yes, tell me that!*
> Dev Mahārāj said: "Bābā Bhāṭ, I'll tie you down on top of this rock." *Yes, keep sitting up there*
> The Bhāṭ said: "Great, great, hey, my lord, you thought good!"—*vāh vāh*—

Dev Mahārāj said: "Pāliyā,—*mhe*—
protect the Bhāṭ up there!" *Yes, tie his arms firmly to the rock and come back!*
"By God's command, tie the Bhāṭ up on to the branch"—*mhe*—
He took the sash, wrapped it around the branch—*vāh vāh*—
and gave it a knot.

In this short example there are two main voices: Chochū Bhāṭ and Devnārāyaṇ. The interchanges are rapid, one person's part not lasting more than a maximum of two sentences. Often the speaker's name is not even explicitly referred to. The speaker's identity is deduced from the context. Sometimes only "said" is used to convey that one of the persons is about to speak. Otherwise one utterence follows the other without being interrupted by any markers from which to judge the speaker's identity. A vivid sense conveyed is of the Bhaṭ's fear of the lion and the irony and skeptical tone of his response to Devnārāyaṇ. The singer himself adds only a single line at the end of the passage that steps out of the dialogic situation (a descriptive sentence in his own voice). The dramatic character of the interchange in the oral delivery is, however, watered down, for example, in the printed version of the narrative. In one case of the printed text, the narrative begins to assume a form similar to a puranic text. The major difference, is of course, that the dialogues are now composed of grammatically "complete" sentences rather than simply utterances that may or may not entail complete sentences. The dialogues are longer and have the form of spoken passages rather than spoken lines. Besides this, the element of repetition, so crucial to the oral rendering, is virtually absent from the printed text:[35]

> Many eons went by. Because of their great *sat* Brahmā, Viṣṇu and Śiva's thrones began quivering. The three gods rode on their celestial chariots and arrived at Mount Meru. But even after the three gods arrived there, those two didn't come out of *samādhi*. The gods spoke to them: "Oh Suvāī Manu, oh Satarūpā, you've done heaps of flawless penance. Termites have crawled all over you. Your blood and flesh have been eaten away. Only bones remain. And still you haven't stopped uttering Rām's name. We're extremely pleased with you. We want to grant you all your desires: a kingdom, unending wealth or even a place in Vaikuṇṭh." Hearing this Suvāī Manu and Satarūpā replied: "Go home Brahmā, go home Viṣṇu, go home Śaṅkar! There's nothing we want from any of you!" Perplexed Śaṅkar asked: "Whose name are you repeating anyway?" Suvāī Manu replied: "We're repeating Rām's name." Then Śaṅkar exclaimed: "Well, who's this other Rām besides us? Isn't it good enough that the three gods have appeared in front of you?" "Well, none of you are Rām," they said, "It's true that you're the three substances contained in Rām (*satoguṇ, rajoguṇ* and *tamoguṇ*), but we're worshipping that Rām who gave birth to the three of you. Now that Rām is Pārbṛhm Parameśvar!"

In this passage there are a number of evident differences from the oral rendering. First, there are longer sections inserted in the narrator's voice that describe a situation leading up to the actual dialogue between characters. The dialogues themselves are on the whole relatively long, giving one more of the sense of an idea being expressed in the form of a dialogue than of an exchange between two parties as in everyday life. Second, the speakers are introduced with a comment, for example, "Hearing this ——— replied" or "Perplexed Śaṅkar said" or "Then Śaṅkar exclaimed." In the oral rendering we simply learn whose voice it is, without a comment on the inner state of the speaker. The inner state of the speaker is left wholly to the utterance he speaks and not to a comment on part of the singer. Later on in the written text we also encounter passages that have the character of prophecies:

> "Oh Lord, oh Rām! Tell us at least when you'll appear as an *avatār*? When will our desire be fulfilled?" "Look, Suvāī Manu, there'll come a time when Rāvaṇa will appear. He'll be so mighty that Indra will fetch water for him, Baimātā will feed his horses, and Pavan will sweep the rubbish. Listen, Suvāī Manu, there'll be a town called Ayodhya on the banks of the Sarju River where a king named Raghu from the Solar dynasty will rule. Suvāī Manu you'll be born in Raghu's clan. In that birth you'll have to split yourself into two bodies. Through one you'll become a king called Daśarath. Your wife Satarūpā will be Kauśalya. Listen, oh Suvāī Manu it's then that I will manifest myself as your child!"

This form of a long dialogue embodying a prophecy is virtually absent from the oral rendering. In fact the idea of different time cycles coupled with the birth of mythic-religious figures like Rāma and Rāvaṇa does not arise. The only exception is in the prose beginning of the narrative in which the circumstances of the rebirth of 24 sages in the form of the 24 Bagaṛāvats is described. Once again, in the "reported" speech of the written text, the dialogue tends to convey the sense of an idea being expressed rather than a living conversational interchange. The reported speech of the oral rendering, through its short, simple dialogues similar to those of everyday situations, heightens a sense of being present at the actual event for the audience. Whereas the singers might engage in presenting what they know or have "overheard," the audience experiences "hearing" the event in the present.

3
Visual Narrative

The focus in this chapter shifts from an examination of the verbal narrative to the meanings of the visual narrative encompassed by the paṛ. In chapter 2 I pointed out that the paṛ, or rather "speaking/reading the paṛ" occupies a central position within the ritual and performative tradition of Devnārāyaṇ. Thus, the term paṛ vā̃cṇo places the focus of a performance on the visual imagery of the paṛ. Then, the paṛ by definition is composed of sets of images. But first we need to clarify what is meant by the word *image*. The commonplace understanding of image is that of a *picture*, a *reflection*, or a *likeness*. While the first two meanings are applicable to a variety of examples, the last meaning of the word image as "likeness" has an overt religious connotation and is directly derived from an idea expressed in Judeo-Christian theistic traditions:

> This is the tradition which begins, of course, with the account of man's creation "in the image and likeness" of God. The words we now translate as "image" (the Hebrew *tselem*, the Greek *eikon*, and the Latin *imago*) are properly understood, as the commentators never tire of telling us, not as any material picture, but as an abstract, general, spiritual "likeness". . . . "[I]mage" is to be understood not as "picture" but as "likeness," a matter of spiritual similarity.[1]

But as I noted in chapter 2, the images on the paṛ are neither reflections nor representations of objects; on the contrary, they signify the "presence" of deities, people, animals, and so on. The images are thus a concrete manifestation of Devnārāyaṇ and of other characters as well as objects portrayed on the paṛ. Thus even an understanding of image as *spiritual similarity* does not quite concur with the meaning of image suggested by the paṛ, which, as I have already pointed out, refers to the tangible existence of God and not only to a similarity or likeness. The painted picture of Devnārāyaṇ is, therefore, the equivalent of a "true image," in a very literal sense, whose radiance is revealed by the act of worship that includes the verbal text.[2]

Thus the images on the paṛ are not a spiritual "likeness," nor are they a reflection of something, nor are they simply pictures. It is only through the entire context of the religious cult of Devnārāyaṇ that the meaning of the images is revealed to us. To substitute what Mitchell (1986: 28) writes on the idea of the petroglyph[3] with reference to the paṛ, we could similarly claim that

> the meaning of the picture does not declare itself by a simple and direct reference to the object it depicts. It may depict an idea, a person, a "sound image" . . . or a thing. In order to know how to read it, we must know how it speaks, what is proper to say about it and on its behalf. The idea of the "speaking picture" which is often invoked to describe certain kinds of poetic presence or vividness on the one hand, and pictorial eloquence on the other hand, is not merely a figure for special effects in the arts, but lies at the common origin of writing and painting.

In this chapter I broaden the scope of this enquiry by asking in what other ways the paṛ is conceptualized by bhopās and devotees; where it derives its central position from in terms of their understanding; and how it fits into the extensive and complex reservoir of meaning that is acquired and sustained from the main narrative and other stories the Bhopās tell. In addition to this, I also examine the scroll's organizational features and the symbolic and religious significance of certain relevant images and scenes.

The Signs of Persistence

To begin with, the literal meaning of the word paṛ is simply "cloth."[4] As a religious object it is understood to be a *calato devaro* or *calato mandir*, that is, a "moveable" or "moving" shrine or temple.[5] This is in contrast to the "fixed" or "immovable" shrine or temple of Devnārāyaṇ, in which the deity, together with the attendants Kālā and Gorā Bhēru, and his brothers[6] or ancestors[7] are worshipped in the form of aniconic bricks (*ī̃ṭh*).[8]

This section focuses on three stories. The first deals with the origins of the two principal objects of worship, namely bricks (ī̃ṭh) and the scroll (paṛ). The second deals with the origin of the two lineages of priests in the cult of Devnārāyaṇ. The third story, which deals with the erection of an important temple, is a variation on the theme of cloth occurring in the first story. Here it is not cloth that is worshipped directly but cloth that is instrumental in building a place where the objects of worship (namely bricks) can be installed. It also brings out the role of the weaver community of the Bhā̃bhīs in the cult. Taken together, these three stories widen our understanding of the context in which the sacred object of the scroll is embedded. Furthermore, in these examples we also see that items of religious significance for the cult derive a large share of meaning from the main narrative or stories related to it. Thus the narrative and the cult build a self-referential whole: while the cult promotes the emergence and reemergence of the narrative through ritual performance, the narrative explains and legitimizes the emergence and establishment of the cult. Similarly, meaning emerges as a kind of epiphenomenon out of the plethora of individual details, formal characteristics, organizational rules, and minute segments of verbal and visual expres-

Row of bricks representing Devnārāyaṇ.

sion in fluctuating contexts. To draw an analogy from an hypothesis on the nature of consciousness itself,

> the explanations of "emergent" phenomena in our brains—for instance, ideas, hopes, images, analogies, and finally consciousness and free will—are based on a kind of Strange Loop, an interaction between levels in which the top level reaches back down towards the bottom level and influences it, while at the same being itself determined by the bottom level. In other words, a self-reinforcing "resonance" between different levels. . . . The self comes into being at the moment it has the power to reflect itself.[9]

Bricks and Cloth

The following account deals with the creation of bricks, the scroll, and the "science of singing." The short episode belongs to the last sections of the narrative, when Devnārāyaṇ is about to depart to Baikuṇṭh after having completed his "mission."

> Now about the science of singing [*gāṇo bidyā*].[10] It's like this. The day Bhagavān went to Indrāsan—[when] he returned after 11 years [had passed][11]—after that, on that day Devnārāyaṇ's wife [Rāṇī Pīpalde], she said: "Maharāj, you've departed to Indrāsan. What about me? What's going to happen to me?" So, Devnārāyaṇ said: "Rāṇī Sāhab, now in my temples—the worship *pūjā* will be for you, the name will be mine." So, in all the big temples there are, Rāṇī Pipalde

is worshipped in [the form of] bricks [*ĩṭh*].[12] Now when we go into a temple we say, "Oh, *ĩṭhā kā śyām*."[13] So, we make Devnārāyaṇ Śyām, and, for Pīpalde Rāṇī there is the worship of bricks. We say: "Let's go to Demālī's devarā."[14] After going inside the temple, the worship is done to bricks. So, the worship [*pūjā*] is Pipalde's, and the name is Dev's.

So, Bhagavān gave that promise to Pīpade: "Go, the worship [*pūjā*] is [for] you. The world will worship you." [But Pipalde said:] "Well, Mahārāj, I'm alone. I don't feel good like this." [So,] he created Bīlā and Bīlī, two children [for her].[15] Even then, Pīpalde said: "I won't let you go now!" So, when Devnārāyaṇ departed he wore a bāgā.[16] So, Rāṇī Pīpalde caught hold of the bāgā—of the cloth: "I won't let you go!" Darbār[17] gave a jerk. So, Bhagavān sat down in the celestial chariot [*biyān*]. And, from that bāgā a long piece of cloth was made. On that [piece of cloth], by Bhagavān's command—Bhagavān thought: "I'm going to Indrāsan—what sign will the world have?"—on its own—because of Devnārāyaṇ—on that cloth "mūrtīs" appeared—a map [*nakṣo*] was created. So, on that day [on] the cloth of that "bāgā" the paṛ originated. And, these Paṇḍits called Jośī in Bhilwara, the design was appropriated by them. At no other place is there Dev's map [*nakṣo*]. [People] can of course make false images, but the real thing is over there. The real thing is not available anywhere else but in Bhilwara. Some say Brāhmaṇ or Paṇḍit—only they do the writing of the paṛ.[18] Only they have the old plan [*nakṣo*] of the paṛ. And, from that day onwards there has been a paṛ—and it came to belong to Bhopās. And, the Bhāṭ's[19] baī[20]—by looking at it—everyone by looking at the Bhāṭ's—Nārad Bhāṭ's[21] "baīs" began the song. From then on the song originated, and the recitation of Bhagavān's story began. There you are sir!

Although the row of bricks in shrines and temples is usually considered to be a manifestation of Devnārāyaṇ, this narrative above also connects them specifically to Devnārāyaṇ's wife, Rāṇī Pīpalde. Similarly, the creation of the paṛ is also indirectly caused by Rāṇī Pīpalde, who holds onto Devnārāyaṇ's knee-length coat. In addition to this, two other important constituents of worship in shrines are related to Devnārāyaṇ's first two wives (Rāṇī Pīpalde being the third): seat/throne or *pāṭ* to his wife Cā̃vṭī, the daughter of a Dait (Skt.: *daitya*); and flame/light or *jot* to his wife Nāgkanyā, the daughter of a Nāga king.[22] Furthermore, in this account we find that two potent signs of continuity are being given shape: the one hard and indelible (brick), the other soft and fragile (cloth).[23] The story also expresses a notion of continuity in a very literal sense: the cloth of Devnārāyaṇ's coat is *extended* to accommodate the size and dimensions of a paṛ. Each individual paṛ is thus, at least figuratively if not literally speaking, for devotees, an extension of that first length of cloth. Thus, as in to the case of the verbal narrative being transmitted from generation to generation after Chochū Bhāṭ's recording of the events he has witnessed, the visual narrative in the appearance of the paṛ too is an "unbroken" roll of sacred image and cloth.[24] It is "complete" in its form by being connected to Devnārāyaṇ's apparel. Moreover, the appearance of mūrtis on the scroll also substantiates the idea that it is a concrete manifestation of divine presence. Thus, the paṛ is, in terms of the foregoing story, an enduring replica of the past in the present. Not only this, it is also, like the components of a bhopā's costume, a re-creation of Devnārāyaṇ's regal body through items of his dress.

The creation of the paṛ and individual elements of a bhopā's costume, as well as forms of worship in shrines, is not limited to Devnārāyaṇ's immediate self but includes the social extensions of it in the form of marriage bonds and kin relationships. Thus, for example, the costume worn by bhopās is composed of signs or emblems of the god and his wives: the coat (bāgā) and turban (*sāphā*) represents the god himself; the wrap of thin cloth worn around the coat represents Pīpalde; the ornament attached to the front of the turban Devnārāyaṇ's first wife, Nāgkanyā; the peacock feather pointer used for referring to the paṛ his second wife, Cā̃vṭī. This feature of the god's signs is also repeated in the items occurring in shrines mentioned earlier. Thus the name (of temples) is the god's, while the bricks, seat, and flame are signs of his wives. Moreover, the double-gourd stringed instrument (bīṇ/jantar) played by bhopās is considered identical to the one played by Chochū Bhāṭ. Finally, as the next story recounted shows, bhopās themselves are in the direct descendancy of Devnārāyaṇ's son, Bīlā. Almost each and every important facet of the worship is defined in terms of the god or through an extension of his own self in the person of his wives, children, or genealogist. By identifying these different features with the god or his wives, children, or genealogist, his devotees not only keep their memory alive, but also participate in the re-creation and reconstruction of the god's "extended" self expressed through these different relationships.

Bhopās: Ochre-Clad and Scroll-Bearing

The following account relates the origin of two kinds of priests in the cult of Devnārāyaṇ: the ochre-clad temple priests and the scroll-bearing itinerant singer-priests.[25] The story of the creation of the institutions of the ochre-clad (bhekdhārī) and the scroll-bearing (paṛdhārī) bhopās, like the story of the paṛ, is consigned to an episode occurring at the tail end of the narrative. The story that is told by Śrī Hukamārām bhopā, a scroll-bearing bhopā himself, also opens a window into the perceptions and evaluations of scroll-bearing bhopās and of their ochre-clad, celibate counterparts, who control not only the administration of shrines and temples but ultimately also the activities of the former. The context for the story is provided by a "competition" between a famous physician, Baidnāth Bābā, and Devnārāyaṇ. After curing hundreds of individuals who have been afflicted by leprosy, Devnārāyaṇ challenges the physician to do the same or at least to cure his son, Bīlā of the disease. In this manner the story also highlights Devnārāyaṇ's sovereignity over matters relating to physical healing.

> Look, there are two kinds of Bhopās of Devnārāyaṇ. Understood!
> What happened? Now, the day Bhagavān cured Bīlā of leprosy—

healed his body—in Demālī—it happened then. So, Baidnāth Bāba—Dev and Baidnāth reflected—Devmahārāj said: "Thousands of lepers. Their leprosy was cured in one moment." Baidnāth Bābā said: "In one moment. I can't do that. I'm a physician. I give visible [things] like herbs and so on. If it's someone's *karam*—good [*karam*]—then he'll be cured in one month. It could take two months. It could also take six months." Devmahārāj said: "Cure it immediately." Baidnāth Bābā said: "There's no medicine in my science [*baid*] to cure it immediately!" Then Devmahārāj cast his "nectar gaze" [ammī kī nazar]. Thousands of lepers' bodies were made pure. Baidnāth Bābā said: "Mahārāj, I don't have this [kind] of knowledge." Devmahārāj brought his own son. "I've cured thousands. You cure one!" [Baidnāth Bābā] said: "Devmahārāj, I admit defeat! I can't cure leprosy in one moment. I join my hands in reverence to you. Here's my pouch, my flag, my conch, and my science. I hand it over to you." The bhopās of that "panth" they live in big temples—in Puṣkar Rāj—even today. They have ochre clothes. With these clothes, they keep to the form [*rūp*] of Baidnāth Bābā.

Now, [for] the paṛdhārī bhopās who tell the tale of Devjī in different villages, [the ones] who set up the paṛ. So, afterwards Bhagavān came on his own to Demālī, and healed Bīlā's body. At that time he said: "Bīlā, you become Bhagavān's—become my Bhopā, and perform service [sevā]," So Bhagavān healed Bīlā's body. He started the service and worship. And Bhagavān told Bīlā: "You become a bhopā." [Was Bīlā the first bhopā?] "No! Before Bīlā there was neither temple nor bhopā. The day Bhagavān made a temple [*devaro*] on his own in Demālī, the time he cured Bīlā's body—that time. Understood?" [Yes] "That devaro is still existent. It's there today. So, the time he cured Bīlā's body, there was no mandir, masjid, and Bhagavān created the devaro of Demalī by himself. After that all these big temples—having seen it [Demālī]—sprouted up everywhere. So, look, from Bīlā the title of bhopā originated. From Demālī the devaro came into existence. Bīlā—he performed service didn't he—then all the following bhopās also did service for Bhagavān and sang songs for him [*bhajan kartā*], and told the story."

In this account we see that the scroll-bearing bhopās to which the narrator himself belongs, are the followers of a tradition of worship founded by Devnārāyaṇ's son, Bīlā. The circumstances of the narrative thereby bring scroll-bearing bhopās much closer in kinship terms to Devnārāyaṇ than the bhekdhārī bhopās, who—at least in Śrī Hukamārām's account—are somewhat removed from the central characters of the story. The bhekdhārī bhopās are followers of Baidnāth Bābā, the physician who submits to the superior healing abilities of Devnārāyaṇ.[26] Baidnāth Bābā and Devnārāyaṇ are thus involved in a clash of powers whose outcome is decided when the physician has been utterly "defeated" by Devnārāyaṇ, who heals thousands of lepers in an instant. After his recognition of the god's miraculous powers, Baidnāth Bābā hands over the symbols of his profession to Devnārāyaṇ in acknowledgment of his lesser, human abilities.[27]

A Temple from Cloth

In the third and last account provided here, it is a member of the Bhā̃bhī community who becomes the first priest of an important temple of Devnārāyaṇ. Revealingly, the construction of the temple is financed through the sale of *cloth*. The story thus underscores a further connection Devnārāyaṇ has to cloth, and to the community of weavers. It provides a variation on the themes highlighted in the first narrative related in this section regarding the significance of bricks and the scroll.

> "I've heard that the Bhā̃bhī *jāt* first began serving Devjī." "They still do that—but that's not counted in the parvāṛo." "No, no not in the parvāṛo . . . but . . ." "Well, let me tell you how it was. Like, Bhagavān, here was a Bhā̃bhī called Lālo—he used to weave *bejo*." "What was that?" "Like, you know "cloth," this was called "bejo" in earlier times. [He] wove cloth, when Devnārāyaṇ called out. [He] said: "Lālā, you weave cloth, now all my mūrtis—you should worship and serve them, brother." Now, he [Lālo] said: "What's that sound?" "Where did this happen?" "This is about Dā̃tā, the devaro of Dā̃tā. I told you about this place yesterday didn't I?" "Yes, in fact this morning [you] were talking about it." "It's about that place, didn't Bhopājī say so? So, the next day the voice spoke again. [Lālo] said: "Who is it Mahārāj?" "I'm Dev, who took incarnation after Savāī Bhoj. [I want you to] serve in my shrines." [Lālo] said: "I'll do it Mahārāj. I'll be of some use to you." He started serving [Devmahārāj]. Everyday he'd produce a yard or a yard and a half of cloth, sell it, feed his children, and make do in this way. Again the voice said: "Lālā, build a temple for me! A superb one!" [Lālo] said: "Mahārāj, what should I make the devaro from? I work just enough to rear my children, that's all the labor I do. So, I don't even save this much. And . . ." "What do you do?" "I make a piece of cloth, one and a quarter hands, and sell it to the Mahājan; I produce one and a quarter hands a day. The devaro will be built with those one and a quarter hands." "It'll get it done with that. Keep it under your arm—don't let go of it. Tell him to measure it!" [Lālo] said: "All right, then I'll go tomorrow!"
>
> He took the cloth, put it under his arm, and told the mahājan: "Measure it, sir." [The mahājan] said: "Brother, you bring it all measured everyday. I have trust [in you]. Put it in the shop, and take your money!" [Lālo] said: "No, Mahārāj. I won't place it [in the shop] like that. I don't have Bhagavān's permission today! Today I'll have it measured, and give it to you." [The Mahājan] said: "Okay, Lālā, come over here we'll measure it out!" The seth [merchant]

started measuring it. [He] went on measuring it and measuring it and measuring it—it didn't fit into the house [shop]. Now, when it didn't fit into the shop, the māhājan said: "Lālā, I can't take anymore. I'm satisfied. Take away [the rest]." He took a pair of scissors and cut it. Those one and a quarter hand—that's all that remained in the end—the one and a quarter hand that the Bhā̃bhī had measured at home, that's what remained under his arm. And, through miraculous powers it was increased such a lot. Money was obtained from that. From that money Lālo made a devaro for Dev. Worship and service began.

In the meantime, the Bādshāh launched an assault—Aurangdīb [*sic*]—from Delhi. He came from Delhi. On the road from Delhi, Dā̃tojī came on the way [Where is Dā̃tojī?—It's beyond Jaypur]. So, he arrived there and reflected: "It's very late, so let's go and have a meal." They had a meal—ate well—ate different good things. The leading Sirdār said: "It's a nice devaro. It has a parcyo too! But, there's one thing missing." "What?" "Well, like the priest [*pujāro*], he's a Bhā̃bhī. It's a low [*halkī*] jāt. So, we'll have to accept the cirṇāmṛt from his hands." The Bādshāh thought about this. He said, "Sister—, then he's fouled us ("It's like when a Bhā̃bhī would give us to drink—we say we won't drink your water!")—get the pujārī out of the temple—get him out!" He got in a rage and went back in. [They] told Lālā: "Lālā your time's up, the Bādshāh's coming." [He] said: "Where should I go now?" He told Dev: "Mahārāj, I made the temple and did the service. That Bādshāh's going to skin me alive!" He started trembling. Devnārāyaṇ said: "Don't tremble! Don't be afraid! Lālā don't run away, don't you run away, don't run. There's a Nīm [tree] in front of the temple." So, when the Bādshāh came, Lālo grasped hold of the Nīm. When he caught hold [of it], the body of the Bhā̃bhī stayed there—on the branch (trunk?). [He] got out of that body, [was born again] he went and sat down in the temple. Devmahārāj removed the body. Then the Bādshāh accepted the parcyo at that place. He said:

dhin dātā, dhin devarā
dhin pujārī lāl
are pārbṛhm nai sī̃vatā
Lālā Bhā̃bhī kī Udojī kholiyo
paltī khāl.[28]

He made the Camār's body "uttam [pure, high]." No, no he didn't change his jāt, he stayed a Bhā̃bhī, but he made an uttam jāt with that body [*kholiyo*]. That's the parcyo given to the Bhā̃bhī. ["So, when did this happen?"—This happened after Devnārāyaṇ went to Indrāsan. It's not the first devaro. Demālī is the [first one]. The first devarā began from Demālī. There wasn't a masīd [*sic*] in Dev's name, nor was there a devarā, nor dhūp, nor dhyān, nothing at all."]

In this story we find a recurrence of the motif of cloth being "extended" as it is done in the case of Devnārāyaṇ's coat when it is held onto by his wife as he is about to depart to Baikuṇṭh. While in temporal terms the incident related here occurs after the god has left the earth, it nevertheless expresses the value of cloth as an item not only for the representation of sacred images but also for the construction of a place of worship. As I pointed out earlier, it also stresses the role of the weaver community in the cult of Devnārāyaṇ. Importantly, it also deals with the transformation of the weaver's "impure" body into a "pure" one. Although the weaver's life is saved in this way, the motif also suggests an ambivalent attitude toward the community of Bhā̃bhīs. This attitude is also revealed, for example, in the story of Devnārāyaṇ's grandfather, Bāgh Siṃh, who, while marrying 12 women from different castes, does not marry a woman belonging to the Bhā̃bhī caste. She is married to his Brahman caretaker.[29]

In chapter 2, and at the beginning of this chapter I pointed out that the paṛ rather than the narrative is considered crucial to a performance because the images on it were not simply pictures, or icons, or even spiritual likenesses but the *presence* of the god and various other persons and objects. In the preceding section it has also become clear that the paṛ is a *sign*. It shares this status of a sign together with a range of other objects relevant to the cult. But what kind of a sign is the paṛ (and the other items mentioned earlier)? Obviously it is not a sign in the commonsense understanding of a symbol that stands for something else.[30] The paṛ is a sign that generates persistence and continuity while at the same time evoking presence. In terms of the narrative just retold, and its actual employment in performances, the paṛ is, therefore, a sign[31] that ties together the past and the present in a particular unfolding of radiance and splendor. Together with the other objects mentioned earlier, the paṛ creates a matrix of signs that replicates the "core" of the cult defined by Devnārāyaṇ, his wives, son, and genealogist. By invoking these signs, devotees recreate the presence of the past in each performance, and in each service conducted in a temple. Thereby commemorating the presence of the past, they also celebrate the presence of Devnārāyaṇ in the present.

Organizational Features

Nothing, I suppose, seems more intuitively obvious than the claim that literature is an art of time, painting an art of space.
—W. J. T. Mitchell, *Iconology: Image, Text, Ideology*

In this section the organizational features of the paṛ before moving on to an appreciation of the religious and symbolic content of sets of select images are examined. The analysis of organizational features is begun by reviewing the work of scholars on paṛ-painting traditions. The perspective of the scholars presented here focuses primarily on an understanding of the paṛ as a specific arrangement of *space*.[32] While the analysis offered by the scholars under consideration admirably brings out the abstract principles of spatial organization (such as scenes, scale, or space), they do not always deal with the ritual, symbolic, and religious meanings underlying characters, scenes, and images. For example, questions regarding the organization of space in terms of auspiciousness and inauspiciousness (life and death), or kinship, or temporality (past and present) are left in abeyance. But it would appear that it is these concerns that bind the content of the paṛ to the larger context of the religious cult of Devnārāyaṇ, and to the issues that are of relevance to its devotees. Moreover, the preoccupation with space as the fundamental feature of the paṛ, as the epigraph suggests, perhaps unconsciously reflects the general limitations we place on the media of painting.[33] Thus, as Mitchell (1986: 98), discussing the influential work of Gotthold Ephraim Lessing, asks,

> just what does it mean to say that literature is a temporal art, painting a spatial art? Literary critics usually follow Lessing's lead by unpacking this expression with parallel accounts of the reception, medium, and content of literary works. Reading occurs in time; the signs which are read are uttered or inscribed in a temporal sequence; and the events represented or narrated occur in time. There is thus a kind of homology, or what Lessing calls a "convenient relation" (*bequemes Verhältnis*) between medium, message, and the mental process of decoding. A similar homology operates in accounts of visual art; these forms represent bodies and their relationships in space; and the perception of both medium and message is instantaneous, taking no appreciable time.

Of course, the paṛ is a special case of visual art. It is more than a painting—it is a visual *narrative*.[34] Its meaning does not unfold instantaneously but in the time taken to tell the verbal narrative.[35] Thus while the message of the paṛ reveals itself in *time*, the message of the verbal narrative reveals itself in *space*, that is, in the space of the unrolled scroll and its images. Both verbal and visual art thereby transgress their apparent "natural" boundaries by being dependant on each other for their full expression. In fact both narratives, like other aspects of the cult, form a seamless whole that again is deeply informed by the language of presence. Strictly speaking, we ought to refer—perhaps a little inelegantly—to an "oral-visual" narrative art. In the case of Devnārāyaṇ, this involves the fragmented utterances of the verbal narrative proceeding dialogically between the singers, interlocked with the nonlinear sequence of pictorial images. The description of the scroll and story as parts of a composite oral-visual art leads naturally to the conclusion that both have a spatial *and* a temporal dimension. In a similar vein, Mitchell (1986: 103) offers a critique of Lessing's divide between space and time:

> Our beginning premise would be that works of art, like all other objects of human experience, are structured in space-time, and that the interesting problem is to comprehend a particular spatial-temporal construction, not to label it as temporal *or* spatial. A poem is not literally temporal and figuratively spatial: it is literally a spatial-

temporal construction. The terms "space" and "time" only become figurative or improper when they are abstracted from one another as independant, antithetical essences that define the nature of an object. The use of these terms is, strictly speaking, a concealed synecdoche, a reduction of the whole to a part.

While the visual image is framed by the space of the paṛ, its meaning unfolds within the temporal parameters of the verbal narrative. Similarly, the verbal narrative, which is framed by the time taken to recount its contents, gains complete expression within the spatial dimensions of the paṛ. As I pointed out earlier, by mutually participating in both realms of space and time, the visual image and verbal narrative produce a composite spatial-temporal, oral-visual object that oversteps the borders of each individual component. But how is this composite object to be described? How is an object that is neither wholly composed of words nor wholly of pictures to be portrayed in terms of only one medium, namely that of language (and its temporal dimension) alone? What are the limits of representation posed here?

One obvious limitation that arises in *writing* about an "oral-visual" composition, is, of course that not only the aural but also the visual dimension is lost. We cannot switch over here from one medium to the other. The written description can only operate within the framework of linguistic pointers such as analogies, metaphors, and models to reveal what an oral-visual composition looks like.[36] I nevertheless attempt here to briefly outline what the representation of an oral-visual composition might entail.

The spatial-temporal framework of the composition is not static but dynamic. In other words, the interplay between the spatial and the temporal in any given performance has to be seen as a *simultaneous* interchange between space and time, or between visual image and verbal narrative. We cannot thus talk of a linear beginning with its inception in the verbal narrative (i.e, in time) that then shifts to the visual image (i.e. to space) and then back again. Verbal narrative and visual image are held in a constant balance.

The time taken to sing and declaim a given episode, say the birth of Devnārāyaṇ and the circumstances immediately following it, would, for example, be roughly 30 to 40 minutes.[37] In contrast to the time taken to relate these events in narrative form, the corresponding images on the paṛ number perhaps five or six, taking up relatively little space. Each individual image is therefore accompanied by a proliferation of details in the verbal narrative. Therefore, the images are highly concentrated units of communication that, like the gāv sections of the verbal narrative, need to be "explained" or, as previously mentioned, "spoken" or "read." To emerge at the end of the story, while simultaneously revealing the meaning of the images, we need to "jump" back and forth between the visual image and the verbal narrative. An analogy may be drawn here to the concept of recursion. In its simplest sense, the oral-visual narrative is recursive because its components refer to one another in a very essential manner. In other words, the visual image is entailed in the verbal narrative, and vice versa. But the idea of recursion can also suggest different levels or kinds of "nesting" or "stacking" of information.[38] Supposing we were to take this notion and apply it to the paṛ and the verbal narrative, what kind of description of an oral-visual narrative would we arrive at? For instance, if, for the sake of convenience, we took a particular visual image as the starting point of any given series, the visual image would precipitate a specific insertion or "stack" of verbal narrative information, which itself causes a new visual image to be introduced at the end, and so on. So for any given episode we would have to show a sequence composed of compressed units of space that trigger longer units of time that themselves again lead to compressed units of space. Any satisfactory representation of the oral-visual composition would, therefore, have to simultaneously combine these twofold dimensions.

Thus, the paṛ, in terms of its actualization during a performance, is located both in space and time. Similarly, its contents are also situated in space and time, being concerned with a narrative and its locations. But as I shall show hereafter, the paṛ not only is embedded *in* space and time but also thematizes or creates a discourse *about* different kinds of spaces and times. This discourse transcends its formal organizational elements. Its larger concerns such as historical time and present time, ancestry and kinship, and the bonds of social cohesion or political conflict are all built into the spatial-temporal organization of the paṛ.

"Picture Story-Telling" in the Past

According to Mair (1988) the tradition of "picture story-telling"[39] and the related forms of "shadow" theatre probably goes back more than two thousand years. The most crucial reference is to be found in Pātāñjali's grammatical treatise, the *Mahābhāṣya*. Composed between 160 and 140 BCE, it refers to *śaubhikas* (illusionists) and *granthikas* (reciters) who perform that which has happened in the past in the present in front of audiences. For Lüders *śaubhika* referred to picture showmen or shadow players. Its cognates in Pali (*sobhiya*) and Buddhist Hybrid Sanskrit suggest a similar profession: "magician, trickster, clown, shadow-playman, juggler, actor." *Śaubhika* and its cognates derive from the root *śubh*: "to appear; flash; flit; shine; look like; adorn." A further cognate, *sobhanagarakam*, is found in the Pali text *Brahma-jāla-sutta*. The text classifies sobhanagarakam (picture story-telling) along with other performances such as instrumental music, ballad recitations, acrobatics, bardic chants, nautch dances, and so on. Otto Franke links sobhanagarakam to *paṭibhānacittam* by way of a Pāli commentary, pointing out the latter term's relationship to "pictures on cloth to be used in connection with recitation" (Mair 1988: 21). Mair cites a number of passages to show that there is textual evidence for this tradition up to the fourteenth century CE.

Contemporary Traditions

In the contemporary period the specific use of a cloth scroll in the performances of Devnārāyaṇ is matched by many other traditions in South Asia.[40] Most notable of these is the narrative scroll tradition of the epic of Pābūjī, which both in terms of the scroll, as well as actual performances, corresponds closely with those of

Devnārāyaṇ.[41] According to Smith (1991) the paṛ in the epic tradition of Pābūjī functions as a kind of "epic map" or representation of an "epic geography." Thus individual scenes on the paṛ are not arranged according to the linear sequence of the narrative but in terms of their relative spatial positioning. Pābujī's court, for example, is in the center of the paṛ, whereas two other regions called Laṅkā and Umarkoṭ appear to the left of the court. The towns of Puṣkar and Sāmbhar, on the other hand, appear to the right of Koḷū, Pābūjī's capital city, where his court is located. Such a positioning of towns and regions is determined by their real geographical location either to the west or to the east of Koḷū. Furthermore, Smith discusses the important question of what constitutes a "scene" on the paṛ. The conclusion is not a clear-cut answer, since a number of "scenes" may represent a simple episode and vice versa—a "single scene" may consist of a number of individual elements that are temporaly distinct from each other. In addition, "space" may be considered "expandable" in the sense that certain scenes are "enlarged" and others are "deflated." Not only scenes but characters also are represented on either a large or a small scale. Finally, Smith notes that particular scenes can be ambiguous in their meaning because of their multiple usage to illustrate different narrative elements. These observations can be summarized (1991: 62) in terms of five principles that determine the visual structure of the paṛ:

> 1) The paṛ is highly directional: the orientation of the characters within one scene very likely depends on the relative position of other scenes.
>
> 2) Scenes depicted on the paṛ may well be ambiguous: the same scene, or the same item within a scene, may stand for different narrative elements at different points in time.
>
> 3) Conversely, there may be a multiple occurrence of items within a scene.
>
> 4) The disposition of scenes and figures aim to fill all available space.
>
> 5) Space, like scale, is elastic, and can shrink or stretch as desired.[42]

In the important studies of Smith, Miller (1994), and Singh (1995), these scholars have each attempted to analyze the pictorial structure of the paṛ. Whereas Smith arrives at the conclusions just outlined regarding the notion of "space" on the paṛ of Pābūjī, Miller and Singh outline the organizational features of Devnārāyaṇ's paṛ. According to Miller (1994: ch. 3(c)) there are six levels of organization:

level 1: Programme
level 2: Location
level 3: Scenes and Iconography
level 4: Characters, Objects and Backgrounds
level 5: Features
level 6: Compositional elements

Following Smith, Miller (193–194) in his discussion of level 2 (locations) points out that:

> the placement of the courts and their connected scenes creates an epic map which relies first and foremost on a kind of spatial logic. The temporal sequence of narrated events does not organize the layout. . . . What is the spatial logic for putting the courts where they occur? An approximation of a real geographic map is out of the question. The crux of the organization is the placement of the courts around the large central figure of Devnārāyaṇ. Devnārāyaṇ is the cosmological center of the painting. The center is the commanding space.

Singh (1995: 433) carries the analysis further:

> The scroll may be composed of a number of locales, but it is more than the sum of its parts. It is not a list of places but an organic space whose parts interrelate. Firstly, the positioning of the locales is governed by an approximate geography where relation between places is psychologically, if not cartographically, acceptable. . . . Secondly, links are maintained between the different areas by the continuity of action; a continuity which is both spatial (linking different parts of the scroll) as well as temporal (encompassing a span of time).

Since Miller and Singh have already done extensive research on the (formal) organizational features of the paṛ, I shall not repeat their analysis here. Instead, I will extend the enquiry in the direction suggested earlier, that is, toward the discursive organization and meaning of the paṛ.[43]

The Cosmology of the Paṛ

The paṛ not only represents scenes, locations, and characters from the narrative, it represents—on closer examination—an entire cosmology, albeit a cosmology describing not the cosmos in general but the cosmos of the narrative framed by the topography of a specific region in Rajasthan and Malwa. This topography is contained within the extraterrestrial domains of *svarg* (heaven) and *patāl* (underworld) depicted at the top and bottom center of the paṛ. But it would be wrong to assume that the cosmology of the narrative is composed only of locales within the topography of that region. The cosmology is suffused with the signs and symbols of a natural and human environment: animals, humans, gods, trees, mountains, stones, water sources, musical instruments, workman's tools, weapons, palaces, forts, and courts.[44] Events do not simply take place and characters are not simply depicted. Each is shown in connection with markers of the natural environment, for example, with particular kinds of trees, or with water sources such as wells, ponds, and rivers, or with animals such as horses, elephants, snakes, dogs, scorpions, crows, owls, and tigers. Events and characters cannot be thought of as being without these markers. The visual imagery, in unanimity with the verbal narrative, thus places itself within what may be termed a "holistic" field in which events, places, characters, and the "natural" environment are intrinsically connected. The one does not occur without the other.[45]

A Map of Kinship, Time, and Religious Power

Although Devnārāyaṇ undoubtedly occupies the physical and cosmological center of the paṛ, the scenes and figures surrounding him are juxtaposed in terms of (1) kinship and (2) temporality, that is, the past (Devnārāyaṇ's ancestors) and the present (Devnārāyaṇ's life). The closer a character is to Devnārāyaṇ in terms of kin relationships, the closer the character is to the center of the paṛ. The less a character is related to Devnārāyaṇ in terms of kinship, the further away he or she may be shown on the paṛ. Similarly, events and scenes closely connected to Devnārāyaṇ's ancestors are depicted on the left of the paṛ, and those connected to his own adult life are shown on the right.[46] The logic of kinship and temporality (albeit not the temporality of narrative sequence) followed here, is, thus, one of generations spanning time past and time present. This is a different logic from a spatial logic or the logic of narrative continuity. The "spatial" organization of the paṛ can thus be said to be based on social, and by extension, also temporal concerns crucial to the inner structure of the narrative. Kinship and ancestry both play a fundamental part in the narrative as themes. It is within the circumference of these themes that the individual episodes are spun out that in turn provide the narrative with continuity.

The "epic map" both Smith and Miller talk of is thus a map not only of physically visible locations such as courts, palaces, lakes, rivers, and so on but also of physically "invisible" and yet socially concrete relationships determined by lineage, marriage, and kinship. The organization of images on the paṛ within these parameters also provides a significant link between visual imagery and the construction of a social and historical discourse through the narrative. By placing kin in the proximity of the hero, Devnārāyaṇ, and nonkin or even "enemies" on the peripheries of the scroll, the paṛ too expresses the openings and closures articulated in the narrative. It also follows the pattern of reaching into the past and of creating a present that is fundamentally connected to that past.

However, the pictorial representation of the past on one half of the paṛ is itself differentiated.[47] This differentiation is again based on a scale determined by the immediacy of (1) past events and (2) kinship. Thus, for example, Devnārāyaṇ's birth on the Hill of Mālāsarī (L 9, 18)—an event in the god's "immediate" past—is located very close to the central figure. Similarly, Devnārāyaṇ's affinal and agnate kin are situated adjacent to him. The figures of his ancestors, the Bagarāvats, and scenes involving them are, following the preceding schema, situated further away from the center since they do not play a role in Devnārāyaṇ's "immediate" past. Nevertheless, since they fulfil the criteria of kinship and temporality as the god's ancestors, they too are placed in the middle and in the far left half of the paṛ.

The right half of the paṛ, toward which Devnārāyaṇ is shown facing in profile, is reserved for the "present," that is, the present constituted by the events occurring in Devnārāyaṇ's life as an adult in fulfilment of his quest. The right half of the paṛ is also, significantly, set aside for the depiction of Devnārāyaṇ's enemies (who are the enemies of his ancestors, the Bagaṛāvats). Major battle scenes that constitute an important part of Devnārāyaṇ's earthly itinerary are depicted in the area of the paṛ that is earmarked for the "present." Yet again, by falling in the right half of the paṛ, which is to Devnārāyaṇ's *left*, his enemies occupy a less auspicious space than his kin and ancestors to his *right*. Indeed, the notion of auspicious and inauspicious halves of the paṛ is reminiscent of Devnārāyaṇ's gaze, which can be either merciful or destructive. Whereas the merciful or compassionate gaze[48] is granted to persons who seek Devnārāyaṇ's protection and help, his destructive gaze[49] is aimed at his opponents and foes, who dare to underestimate his divine power. From the direction in which he is seated on his "python throne" it would appear as though it is his destructive gaze that is focused on his enemies collected at the far right end of the paṛ in the Rāṇā's territory of Rāṇ. But his gaze is, more immediately, also directed toward Rājā Basak (R 6, 15), the serpent king of the underworld who faces him. While it is the Nāga king's poison breath that envelopes the lotus blossom the god holds in his hand, it is the god's "nectar gaze" that restores it to freshness and life. Thus there is an interplay of "gazes" that symbolize the poles of life and death, violence and healing, auspiciousness and inauspiciousness that the paṛ intricately plays out.

I will now look in more detail at the cluster of figures and places located closest to the central character of Devnārāyaṇ (0, 15). Immediately surrounding Devnārāyaṇ to his right are a number of places associated with his birth, the events following his birth, the events associated with his marriage to Pīpalde, and those connected to his "return journey" from his mother's home in Malwa. Finally, a large area of this section of the paṛ represents three places at once: Goṭhā, Daṛāvat, and Kheḍā Causlā (L 3–R 25, 1–18) (and Mekhlā Parvat).[50] Of the approximately 25 places located to the right of Devnārāyaṇ on the paṛ, some 14 places are directly connected to the events just mentioned. The first place in this context is Devnārāyaṇ's birthplace on the Hill of Mālāsarī. This is depicted on the upper part of the paṛ just to the left of Devnārāyaṇ. Facing this is "svarg" (L 4, 18), which is occupied by Viṣṇu Bhagavān, beneath whom is the "milk ocean" (*kṣīr sāgar*). Subsequent to this on the lower middle of the paṛ we have Pāṇḍal (L 12, 2). At Pāṇḍal Devnārāyaṇ was briefly abandoned by his carriers on the way to Malwa. A lioness gave him shelter here. Then there is the region of Malwa, which is Saḍū Mātā's natal home. The places depicted after Devnārāyaṇ's residence in Malwa are all connected to his journey back from Malwa, up to the point where he reestablishes the capital of Kheḍā Causlā. Ujjinī Dhār and Gaḍgājanā are connected to his marriage to Rānī Pipalde, the daughter of the king of Dhār, and to the daughter of a demon king (Dait Rāj). Before he is able to marry Rānī Pipalde, the king of Dhār devises a test for him that consists in recapturing a doorway made of seven metals that has been stolen by the demon king of Gaḍgājanā (L 44, 14). Although Dhār is situated close to Kheḍā Causlā, Gaḍgājanā, perhaps because of the relatively minor role played by Devnārāyaṇ's wife Rāṇī Cā̃vṭī, is represented much further away, above the court of Ajmer (L 42–55, 9–13) in the far left of the paṛ. Other places connected to Devnārāyaṇ's journey back from Malwa are: Soniyānā kī Baṛ, Devdā̃, Tīmkyā Talāv, and Maṅgrop. Geographically speaking each of these places is between the cities of Cittor and Bhilwara in southeastern Rajasthan. At Soniyānā kī Baṛ, Devnārāyaṇ is supposed to have slept for six months. At Devdā̃ he struck his spear into the ground, causing a stream of water to gush out. At Maṅgrop he brought out the milk he had drunk from Sāḍū Mātā as an infant; the milk turned into a lime quarry. At Tīmkyā Talāv he vanquished Sokhīyo Pīr (L 27, 2), who had dried up the Siprā river's waters, causing the waters to flow again.

Whereas the places just mentioned are related to events beginning with Devnārāyaṇ's birth and ending with the establishment of Kheḍā Causlā, the other places occurring on this half of the paṛ are associated with Devnārāyaṇ's ancestors and/or their foes.[51] The list of Devnārāyaṇ's ancestors goes back to King Bisaldev of Ajmer, who is his great-great-grandfather. King Bisaldev (L 54, 12) is shown seated together with other Sirdārs, the generals Dīyājī Jodhkā (L 51, 12) and Kālū Mīr Paṭhān (L 44, 12) in the court of Ajmer in the extreme left of the paṛ. Devnārāyaṇ's great-grandfather, Hari Rām (L 52, 7), is shown riding with a lion's head perched on the point of his spear on the banks of Puṣkar, where he encounters Līlā Sevrī, his future wife. Devnārāyaṇ's grandfather, Bāgh Siṃh, is shown in his garden, called "Bāghbaṛ" (L 39, 1–5). Swings hang low from the banyan tree in the garden; on them are the girls who later become Bāgh Siṃh's 12 wives, from whom Devnārāyaṇ's immediate ancestors, the 24 Bagaṛāvats, are born. In addition to these locations there are courts that are related to events and people connected with the 24 Bagaṛāvats. There is the court of Sāvar (L 28–35, 8–12), which is ruled by Dīyajī Jodkhā. He is shown here together with other Sirdārs, Kālū Mīr Paṭhān, and Savāī Bhoj's mare, Bāvlī Ghoḍī, in captivity. In the lower section of the paṛ there is the court of Pīlodā (L 15–23, 1–3), ruled by the Kumhār king of Pilodā. He is depicted here with Devnārāyaṇ's brother Bhūṇājī, other Sirdārs, and the Bagaṛāvats' elephant, Jaymaṅgalā Hāthī, in captivity. Above this there is the court of the Bhīl King Dhundhu (L 21–23, 6–8), who is shown seated together with Bhūṇājī, and Nevājī's[52] mare, Bor Ghoḍī, in captivity. Located in the upper part of the left half of the paṛ is the court of the king of Bhūā̃l (L 12–19, 10–15), whose daughter is Rāṇī Jaimatī. Scenes around the court show Rāṇī Jaimatī conducting marriage rites with Savāī Bhoj's sword, marrying the Rāṇā in public, and Savāī Bhoj striking down the marriage emblem (*toraṇ*) (L 9, 16) hung over the gateway to Bhūā̃l. The places located in the lower middle section of the paṛ beneath Devnārāyaṇ and his brother's court, are once again closely related to Devnārāyaṇ's life. However, here it is not the past that is being represented but the present, and in fact a time after Devnārāyaṇ has left the earth and departed to Baikuṇṭh. The places depicted in this area are Devnārāyaṇ's palace, Kheḍā Causlā, and, most important, Demālī (R 1–4, 3–4). Demālī is represented in terms of two upright slabs of brick flanked by Devnārāyaṇ's children, Bīlā and Bīlī. As I pointed out earlier, the bricks are the signs left behind by Devnārāyaṇ. It is through these that he and his wife Pīpalde are worshipped in shrines and temples. The other places in this area are the *rāvlā* (landlord's mansion) of Devnārāyaṇ's elder brother Medūji, Sāḍū Mātā's palace, and the town of Cāmpānehrī. Toward the right of the lower middle section we have Rāṭhorā kī Talāv and Gudalīyā Talāv (R 25–29, 1–3). Gudalīyā Talāv's significance lies in its being situated on the border between Kheḍā Causlā and Rāṇ. This provides us with the transition to the right half of the paṛ, which, as I have mentioned, is occupied by Devnārāyaṇ's enemies, the rāṇā and his generals.

The far right of the paṛ is reserved for Rāṇ City (R 46–55, 8–12) which consists of Nolkhā Bāg (R 46–55, 4–8), the Aradu bazaar (R 42, 7), Pātū Kaḷālī's brewery (R 48–53, 1–4), the queen's palaces (R 46–55, 12–14), and Rātā Koṭ, the red fort (R 46–55, 14–17). Interspersed between Kheḍā Causlā and Rāṇ are the kingdom of Kharnār, the Khārī river (R 35–40, 1–2), Rātā Devrā, Rāyalā, Nekdiyā Gā̃v, Rupāylī, Cāndārūn, and Bagaṛāvatā̃ kī Bāvḍī. These are locations that primarily concern events in the lives of the Bagaṛāvats. On the right side of the paṛ—which again is to Devnārāyaṇ's left—is, as already mentioned, a concentration of places and events connected with his enemies Rāvjī and his generals. Many of the events depicted here involve violent encounters of one kind or another. There are outright battle scenes: warriors' heads are shown severed or about to be severed; pieces of human bodies—arms, hands, legs, heads, torsos—are shown scattered on the banks of the Khārī river; and, last but not least, Queen Jaimatī is shown revealing her awesome form as Bhavānī (R 25–29, 13–19). Squatting on the grounds of the final bloody battle between the Bagaṛāvats and the Rāṇā, she wears a necklace of the brothers' heads. The right half of the paṛ is thus concerned with violence, with confrontation, and with sacred power issuing from particular acts of violence. This is the religious power that manifests through the acts of *jhū̃jhārs* (warriors) and *satīs* in the sacrificial arena of battle. This half of the paṛ thus powerfully articulates one of the two ways in which sacred power is constructed in the narrative.[53]

While the middle of the paṛ is reserved for the paramount figure of divine power, the right half is concerned with the depiction of the central place of political power in the narrative, namely the city of Rāṇ, and Rātākoṭ, or the red fort that is the headquarter of the Rāṇā. A large area is devoted to the many components of the Rāṇā's territory, like those mentioned earlier: the garden of Nolkhā, the brewery of Pātū, the queen's palaces, and the main marketplace. Apart from these "secular" locations, on the right side of the paṛ battles are lost while at the same time revenge is taken and ancestors redeemed. If anything, the right side of the paṛ is dominated by the various acts, the various associates, and the various enemies of the Bagaṛāvats. It is the region where heroes meet as allies only to break up as enemies. It is the place where violence is celebrated; where death, war, and dismemberment are "sacred." Here the visual narrative of the paṛ does not concern itself with the establishment of a divine itinerary, as in the sections directly adjacent to Devnārāyaṇ on the left half of the paṛ. The visual narrative here focuses on geographically and, therefore, spatially distinct sites connected by the language of conflict and "sacrifice."

❁ 4 ❁
Textual Narrative

The concluding section of the previous chapter, an examination of the religious and symbolic meaning of the images of the paṛ, provides a transition to the second half of this study, which is chiefly devoted to an interpretation of the contents of the narrative—or *text*, as I shall call it now. This interpretation of the contents, while drawing heavily from the oral narrative, will also rely on the visual narrative that may, in some cases, literally tell a different story. In addition to the materials provided by the oral narrative and the paṛ, reference will also be made (in chapters) to passages from a printed version of the story. The printed text is particularly important, not only with regard to the kind of "historical discourse" it creates but also in terms of the contrast it provides to the oral narrative. Before moving on to the questions relevant to the current chapter, I will give a synopsis of the narrative.

❁ Synopsis of the Narrative ❁

The narrative is composed of two main parts. These are recognized by singers as being distinct halves, and are called *Bagaṛāvat* or *Bagaṛāvat Bhārat* and the *Śrī Devnārāyaṇ Kathā*. The first half deals, as its title suggests, with the Bagaṛāvats, or the Twenty-Four Brothers, who are the ancestors of Devnārāyaṇ. The second half, as is also clear from its title, deals with Śrī Ḍevnārāyaṇ. While both halves of the narrative extoll the heroic deeds of the Bagaṛāvats and Devnārāyaṇ, they also articulate different sets of values. Above all, this is apparent in the sources of sacred power that each gives prominence to. In the first half, sacred power flows from the devotional, self-sacrificial deeds of the 24 brothers. In the second half, it issues directly from the divine acts of Devnārāyaṇ, an avatāra of Bhagavān.

Bagaṛāvat Bhārat

The first half of the narrative, called the Bagaṛāvat, has a time frame spanning two world-ages. The beginning of the narrative is situated in the *satya yuga*, at a time when Brahmā is performing a Vedic sacrifice (Rajasthani: *jug*) in Pushkar, the famous pilgrim town in Rajasthan.[1]

> Brahmā invites all the gods and ṛṣis to his sacrifice in Pushkar. Among them is a group of 24 ṛṣis living in the Nāg Pahāḍ (Serpent Mountain), a mountain chain running parallel to Pushkar. These ṛṣis are disciples of Śaṅkar. When Śaṅkar hears of the invitation, he forbids them to attend the sacrifice. But they insist on going because they have been called by Brahmā. All of a sudden Śaṅkar grows ravenously hungry. The ṛṣis suggest he eat the fruits growing in the forest in which they live. But Śaṅkar claims this will not satisfy his hunger. He requires more than plain fruit. But what else is available in the forest? There is no cereal or grain either. So what does Śaṅkar do? He turns to his disciples and demands they offer their bodies to him. He commences consuming them one after another.[2] After he has eaten them and satiated his hunger, he then takes it upon himself to visit Brahmā's sacrifice. The sacrifice comes to a halt because of the misdeed Śaṅkar has commited.[3] He asks Brahmā how he should atone for his misconduct. Brahmā lets him know that the only means would be to offer the ṛṣis his own body in a future existence, in which the ṛṣis are to be born as the 24 sons of a single father.

After this relatively brief spoken (not sung) prelude, the temporal frame of the narrative abruptly shifts to the *kali yuga*. The geographical location has not changed. It is the reign of the legendary medieval king Rājā Bisaldev of Ajmer.

> The populace in the kingdom of Rājā Bisaldev is being terrorized by a lion. In order to curb rampant killings, the king orders that one person offer himself as food for the lion every night. On one particular night, a Rajput called Hari Rām,[4] who is traveling through the ill-fated kingdom, offers to take the place of a boy from the Kumhār community whose turn it is to be eaten by the lion. He tricks the lion by placing a figure made of dough at the place where it feeds. When the lion attacks the figure of dough, Hari Rām comes out of his hideaway and beheads it. Then in order to wash the blood off his sword and to cleanse himself of the impurity of slaughter, he goes to the holy lake of Pushkar, carrying the lion's head on his shoulder.[5] It is a full moon night (*pūnam*). Exactly at the same time on the opposite bank a Brahman girl called Līlā Sevrī, who has taken a vow never to look at a man, is performing ablutions and bathing in the lake. While bathing, she sees the reflection of a man's body with the head of a lion on the surface of the lake. Not only is her vow broken; she also conceives upon seeing the image on the water surface. She insists that Hari Ram marry her now, but he vacillates, saying that such a marriage is not possible because she is a Brahman and he a Kṣatriya. Finally, they receive permission from King Bisaldev, who wants to reward Hari Rām in any way that he wishes.

Hari Rām and Līlā Sevrī at Pushkar.

After nine months a son is born to Hari Rām and Līlā Sevrī. He has the head of a lion and the body of a man, and he is named Bāgh Siṃh or Bāgh Rāvat. Bāgh Siṃh is abandonded at birth. But the trees in the grove where he has been begin to turn green and blossom, signaling that he has a godly nature. The king adopts him. But because of his frightening appearance he is placed in a garden under the care of a Brahman teacher and cook. Later when he grows up, his unusual features stand in the way of his finding a bride. He continues to live his solitary existence in the garden, attended by his Brahman cook. One day, on the festival of swings (*sāvan tīj*), a number of young girls of various castes come to the garden, attracted by Bāgh Siṃh's silken swing. The Brahman allows them to use the swing on the condition that each of them circumambulate Bāgh Siṃh. While they are doing this, he performs the necessary engagement rites. Thus, unknowingly, they are all engaged to Bāgh Siṃh. Later Bāgh Siṃh marries 12 of them. Each of his wives gives birth to two sons, they are collectively called the Bagaṛāvats.

The Bagaṛāvats, whose mothers belong to different castes, are all married to Gujar women. Of the 24 Bagaṛavats, Savāī Bhoj is the most well-known and courageous. Each day Savāī Bhoj takes the Bagaṛavats' cattle herds to graze on the slopes of Nāg Pahāḍ. One of the cows regularly leaves the herd and returns on its own in the evening. One day Savāī Bhoj follows the cow and discovers that it is being milked by the ascetic Rūpnāth. As compensation for milking

Young girls swinging on Bāgh Siṃh's silken swing(s).

the Bagaṛavats' cow, Rūpnāth gives Savāī Bhoj a sack full of grain. But the brothers have no use for the small quantity of grain, so they feed it to birds. The next morning, they discover that the few grains left sticking to the seam of the sack have turned into gems.[6] They realize their folly. Savāī Bhoj returns to the ascetic to become his disciple. One day Rūpnāth has Savāī Bhoj heat a cauldron of oil. When the oil is boiling he asks Savāī Bhoj to go around the cauldron, while he himself follows. While they are encircling the cauldron, the ascetic tries to push Savāī Bhoj into the boiling oil, but Savāī Bhoj—who has been forewarned of Rūpnāth's intentions—leaps over it with the help of his cowherd's staff.[7] In the next round, Savāī Bhoj follows the ascetic and pushes him into the cauldron. Not so agile, the ascetic falls into the boiling oil. Instantly his body turns into solid gold. While Savāī Bhoj stands there repenting his crime, the ascetic reappears in the hermitage as though nothing had taken place. He explains that the golden image is a gift that will grant the Bagaṛāvats unending wealth for a period of 12 years, after which both wealth and life (*māyā-kāyā*) shall come to an end. He also gives Savāī Bhoj the gifts of a mare, a cow, and an elephant, all of which have special powers.[8] Savāī Bhoj returns to his home. The brothers ask Tejājī, the eldest among them, what they should do with their newly acquired wealth. Tejājī, whose mother is a Banyā, advises them to bury the money in the ground and hoard it.[9] Nevājī, one of the youngest brothers, counters this idea by suggesting that they do good deeds with the money, that is, build wells and temples, distribute the wealth, and make a name for themselves, because both the wealth and their lives are to end after 12 years. The brothers choose the latter alternative. Soon their fame spreads far and wide. In due course they meet their future enemy, the Rajput chieftain of Rāṇ City whose name is Rāvjī and is called the Rāṇā. The Rāṇā and the Bagaṛāvats become *dharam* (oath) brothers. In one extended drinking session, they overturn jars laden with alcohol onto a hillside, flooding the earth to such an extent that the alcohol actually flows down into the kingdom of Bāsak Nāg, the serpent lord of the underworld. Angered, Rājā Bāsak deposits the Earth temporarily on a bull's horns

The image of Savāī Bhoj receiving an offering of alcohol from the temple's abbot.

Sāḍū Mātā, covered only by her tresses, receiving Bhagavān.

Rāṇī Jaimatī circumambulating Savāī Bhoj's sword.

The battle at the Khārī river.

and goes to Bhagavān's court to complain about the Bagaṛāvats. But neither Bāsak nor Hanumān nor Bhagavān can do anything to remedy the situation, not only because the Bagaṛāvats are so powerful but more so because they are fervently devotional toward the gods. Finally, Bhagavān assumes the form of a mendicant (*jogī*) and visits Sāḍū Mātā, the wife of Savāī Bhoj, begging for alms. Sāḍū, who has just finished performing ablutions and bathing, appears in front of the mendicant covered only by her long tresses.[10] Struck by her devotion, Bhagavān grants her a boon. Sāḍū Mātā desires that Bhagavān be born as her son. Bhagavān promises to be born as her son on the thirteenth day after the Bagaṛāvats have been killed.

After his return, Bhagavān requests Śakti, who agrees, to go to Earth to fulfill the task of destroying the Bagaṛavāts. She manifests herself as an infant girl in a forest, where she is discovered by the king of Bhūāl, who adopts her. Exactly at the time of her birth, her maidservant, Hīrā Dāsī, is born in the house of a Mahājan. Śakti grows up unusually fast, and soon Brahmans are sent out to find a suitable bridegroom for her. She insists that they find someone belonging to a family in which one father has 24 sons. After a long and frustrating search the Brahmans find the Bagaṛāvats. They arrange to have the queen married to Savāī Bhoj. But because they are already married, the Bagaṛāvats suggest that the queen be married to their dharam-brother, the Rāṇā.[11] Thus arrangements are made for the Rāṇā to marry Rāṇī Jaimatī, as the queen is called. When the marriage procession sets out, Savāī Bhoj, instead of the Rāṇā, leads it. Meanwhile, Rāṇī Jaimatī orders the marriage emblem (toran) to be hung in a high place that the Rāṇā, who is old and feeble,[12] cannot reach up to. Instead of the Rāṇā, Savāī Bhoj strikes down the emblem.[13] When the marriage procession arrives, the queen pretends she has a high fever. She asks her maidservant to fetch Savāī Bhoj's sword, which is supposed to have healing powers. In the inner cham-

The image of the goddess Bhavānī at the temple of Savāī Bhoj.

The goddess Bhavānī with a necklace of the 24 brothers' heads.

bers of the palace she then circumambulates the sword, thereby secretly marrying Savāī Bhoj. In public, however, she marries the Rāṇā. At the end of the ceremonies, when she is to accompany the Rāṇā to her new home, she insists on staying with the Bagaṛāvats. The Bagaṛāvats coax her into going with the Rāṇā, promising to fetch her after a period of six months. Upon arriving in the Rāṇā's palace, however, the queen says she will not play dice with the Rāṇā till he has constructed a new palace for her.[14] The construction of the palace, of course, takes a long time, and six months are soon over. Meanwhile, the Bagaṛāvats—against the advice of their wives—prepare to fetch the queen. The queen elopes with the Bagaṛāvats. The Rāṇā is patient, advising the Bagaṛāvats in a brotherly manner to send the queen back to him. But the Bagaṛāvats stick to their decision. Finally, the Rāṇā gathers together the armies of 52 forts on the banks of the Khārī river.[15] Rāṇī Jaimatī, who now has assumed her true form as Bhavānī, promises to accompany the Bagaṛāvats only on the condition that they fight the Rāṇā's army one at a time. She also demands that the brothers offer their heads to her. The Bagaṛāvats willingly agree to her grotesque demands. A great war (mahābhārat) is fought on account of Rāṇī Jaimatī (or Bhavānī). In the battle, some of the brothers continue fighting even after their heads have been severed by the goddess's discus. In the end all of them are slain, and the Rāṇā is victorious. The Goddess assumes her awesome, terrifying form. Amid the corpses of slain warriors, she squats on the battleground, dripping with blood, stringing a necklace of the Bagaṛavāts' heads.[16] After their deaths, the heroes' wives, with the exception of Savāī Bhoj's wife, Sāḍū Mātā, commit satī. Four infants survive the carnage. These are Bhāṅgījī, Medūjī, Madnājī, and Bhūṇājī, each of whom is raised by stepparents.

Śrī Devnārāyaṇ Kathā

The part of the narrative concerned with the life of Devnārāyaṇ is, in terms of time frames, also situated in the kali yuga. While the first part climaxes in the great bloody battle, the second part begins in the aftermath of the war. In the midst of this cataclysmic setting, the birth of Devnārāyaṇ ushers in a new era of renewal and well-being.

Sāḍū Mātā practices severe *tapas* (asceticism) on a hill near the battlefield. After 11 days, when her honor and life are about to be threatened by the Rāṇā, she calls out to Bhagavān, who has promised to be born as her son. Devnārāyaṇ, who is playing a game of dice at the time with Rājā Bāsak, lord of the underworld, rises up on a stream of water that splits apart the rock on which Sāḍū is seated. Carried on that jet of water in a lotus blossom, the infant Devnarayan falls into Sāḍū Mātā's lap.[17]

Threatened by the Rāṇā again, Sāḍū Mātā decides to flee to her natal home in Malwa. Devnārāyaṇ spends his childhood there without any knowledge of past events. One day Chochū Bhāṭ, the bard and genealogist of the 24 Bagaṛāvat brothers, comes to Malwa in search of Devnārāyaṇ. Sāḍū Mātā, who knows of his intentions, tries to get him killed, but Devnārāyaṇ revives him. Chochū Bhāṭ then informs him of the battle between the Bagaṛāvats and the Rāṇā. Devnārāyaṇ then decides, against his mother's will, to return to his father's ancestral land and take revenge on the Rāṇā. While returning to the region of Bhilwara and his capital town of Causlā Kheḍā, Devnārāyaṇ marries three princesses—first, the daughter of a demon king (*dait rāj*); second, the niece of an underworld serpent king; and third, the daughter of the Rajput ruler of Ujjain. The latter is Queen Pīpalde, who plays a greater role than the other queens in the cult and narrative. While returning, Devnārāyaṇ also meets with his four cousins Medū, Madno, Bhāṅgī, Bhūṇā, who likewise have grown up unaware of each others' existence. Whereas Medū and Madno have been adopted by the Rāṇā's ally, the king of Ajmer, Bhāṅgī has grown up as a Nāth Jogī in the company of the Bagaṛāvats' guru Bābā Rūpnāth. Bhūnā, whose name has been changed to Khāṇḍerāv, has been adopted by the Rāṇā himself. But once the cousins realize their true origins, they join Devnārāyaṇ to launch an assault against the Rāṇā. Before the final encounter takes place, Devnārāyaṇ releases his herd of 980,000 cows and buffaloes into the royal fields in order to destroy the Rāṇā's crops. In the end the cousins catch up with

The temple on Mālāsar Hill (Ajmer District) marking the site where Devnārāyaṇ was born.

the Rāṇā, who is trying to escape. He is beheaded by Devnārāyaṇ's bowstring. But when Devnārāyaṇ sees that Bhūṇā is sad over the death of his foster father, he revives the Rāṇā—only after Chochū Bhāṭ has extracted the Bagaṛāvats' revenge from the Rāṇā's stomach. Devnārāyaṇ then retracts the title "Rāṇā," giving him the title of Sisodia. Thereafter Devnārāyaṇ instructs the revived Rāṇā to establish the city of Udaipur, which, according to the narrative takes its name from one of Devnārāyaṇ's names, Ud.

After Devnārāyaṇ has taken revenge on the Rāṇā, he decides to depart to heaven. But his queen, Pīpalde, requests him not to leave her childless. A boy, Bīlā, and a girl, Bīlī, are born to her. Bīlī is quick to realize her father's divinity. But Bīlā is stubborn and refuses to acknowledge his father's authority. After many unhappy incidents, including having leprosy befall him, Bīlā begins to realize the divine power of his father. He then agrees to look after Devnārāyaṇ's very first shrine and become Devnārāyaṇ's first priest, from which the lineage of priests follows. Then, having established a place of worship, a lineage of priests, and a community of devotees, Devnārāyaṇ finally returns in his celestial chariot to Baikuṇṭh.

❁ Imagining a Text ❁

After my discussion of verbal and visual narratives, even an "oral-visual" narrative, the use of the word *text* in the heading of this chapter may come as a surprise. After all, the oral-visual narrative is not a *text* in the strict sense of the term: its meanings emerge only in the interactive contexts of different oral renderings and are, therefore, not bound by the apparent limitations of the written or printed word.[18] The oral-visual narrative is not, like the printed text or written word, held within the physical constraints of letters and pages that give the interpreter of texts the feeling of being able to dispassionately examine a motionless, well-defined object. By choosing the medium of the written word to represent an oral-visual narrative, I am involved in transforming it precisely into a *text*.[19] The presentation of the narrative in transcription and translation is, on one level, an attempt to render it "manageable," to "catch" its runaway meaning. Thereby the emergent and ephemeral nature of an oral recitation is locked into lines, passages, and pages—into a book. Simultaneity, spontaneity, and nonlinearity are reshaped into a controlled, linear discourse. However, it is not my aim here to delve into the limitations and politics of scholarly representation. The purpose of this brief exercise in self-reflection is to remind the reader (and the writer!) that the interpretations that are to follow are not intended to be binding and final. They are offered as a particular way of imagining the narrative of Devnārāyaṇ.

To *imagine a text* is not only to perceive it in a distinct manner but also to think of it as something unbounded and open, as a series of perspectives caught within an "ocean of interpretations." As Barthes (1987a: 135), in his very original reading of a story by Edgar Allan Poe, has remarked:

> We are then going to take a narrative text, and we're going to read it, as slowly as necessary, stopping as often as we have to (being at ease is an essential dimension of our work), and try to locate and classify without rigour, not all the meanings of the text (which would be impossible because the text is open to infinity: no reader, no subject, no science can arrest the text) but the forms and codes according to which meanings are possible. We are going to locate avenues of meaning. Our aim is not to find *the* meaning, nor even *a* meaning of the text. . . . Our aim is to manage to conceive, to imagine, to live the plurality of the text, the opening of its "signifiance."[20]

Definitions

One of the challenges facing the kind of approach to texts suggested here is that of definitions. To define is to outline, to make clear, but also to bind and limit. Definitions, like words, "throw up" associations, qualities, ways of seeing things. Although in the normal course of events we can hardly avoid classifications and definitions, it is still worthwhile to critically reflect on some of the issues at hand. In the subsections that follow, I discuss certain questions relevant to one's understanding of the narrative of Devnārāyaṇ as a *text*: What kind of text is it? Is it to be named in terms of a particular genre? For example, is it right to call it an epic? What are some of the problems that beset such a definition? What if it was not called an epic or legend or myth, and so on? Supposing that instead of attempting to define it, we were to concentrate on listening to the kinds of discourses that are expressed through it? What if, instead of searching for its "origins" in the historical past—as scholars of epic texts tend to do—we were to place it within a network of texts with no real beginning or end, except for a series of interrelationships? What if it is the quality of these interrelationships, and the discourses articulated through the narrative, that actually *define* and characterize it—define not as belonging to a *class* of texts but in a particular sense of revealing its "signifiance" and meaning?

If there is one thing that can be said in certain terms about the text of Devnārāyaṇ, then it is this: it is a *narrative*. In other words, it has a beginning, a middle, and an end. Moreover, the end and the middle are entailed in the beginning. The beginning contains a prefiguration of things to come. The unfolding of this prefiguration provides the narrative with a plot, or rather a number of subplots, that finally culminate in the completion of the narrative's objective. However, to move beyond this tautologous-sounding description and to specify or determine the exact genre the narrative belongs to is to tread uncertain grounds. The reason for this uncertainty does not lie in the complex nature of the narrative or in a lack of discussion on the question of genres and their definitions. As I have already pointed out, the reason lies in the deliberate avoidance of rigid classifications and typologies that often narrow down the ways a text can speak to us. Barthes (1987b: 45):

> We are not *subtle* enough to perceive the probably absolute *flow* of *becoming*; the *permanent* exsists only thanks to our coarse organs which summarize things and reduce them to common levels, when in fact nothing exists in that form. The tree is at each instant a new thing; we assert *form* because we do not grasp the subtlety of an absolute movement.[21]
>
> The text is likewise this tree to which we can (provisionally) give a name only because of the coarseness of our organs.

Of course the problem of definitions could be easily solved by saying—as has been frequently done—that the narrative of Devnārāyaṇ is an epic narrative.[22] But by labeling it an epic we would conjure up a set of questions considered relevant to what we understand to be the content, structure, and significance of narratives classified as *epic*. The same issue would arise were we to call it a myth, legend, historical account, or ballad and so on. While the use of each of these labels would naturally open up certain areas of enquiry, at the same time they would also conceal aspects of the narrative. For example, while the term *epic*, broadly speaking, brings to mind the "heroic," the term *myth* would suggest the divine or the supernatural. *Legend* on the other hand would suggest a concrete historical context. For as Hiltebeitel (1990: 31–32) points out:

> Epic, whatever its stylistic features and its origins as a narrative and poetic genre, should be regarded, in terms of context as falling under the heading of legend. And legend, with epic as a subcategory, should be distinguished from myth. . . .
>
> Myths are stories which take place in the fullest expanses of time and space (they articulate a cosmology); they deal with the

> origin, nature, and destiny of the cosmos, and their most prominent characters are gods. . . .
>
> Legends are stories which take place at a specific time and on a specific terrain; they deal with the origins, nature and destiny of men, and their most prominent characters are heroes.

He adds that in the context of Indo-European epic and mythic tradition "only in a few cases is there a sustained interaction between the figures of myth and epic: for instance, in Rome, Greece, and India" (30). But he concludes by saying that "only in India, then, are the epic poets not only fully aware of, but deeply involved in, a living mythology" (31). There are, thus, overlappings, borrowings, and transfers between the mythic and the epic. This is particularly the case in the examples of the two great epics the *Mahābhārata* and the *Rāmāyaṇa* but is also strongly characteristic of the narrative text of Devnārāyaṇ. On the one hand the narrative is firmly situated in a particular epochal and historical time, as well as regional geography and landscape; on the other hand themes, characters, and events in the narrative are permeated with mythological personages and structures also found in the *Purāṇās*, the *Mahābhārata*, and the *Rāmāyaṇa.* In fact, the temporal and spatial locale of the narrative cannot be understood without the mythological framework that accompanies it. However, to limit the narrative's scope to the mythic and epic would be to undermine its significance as a living text in association with a cult. Although *mythic* may suggest a religious connotation, it does not fully bring out the contextual meaning of the narrative. As part of the cult of Devnārāyaṇ, the narrative thus has an important religious significance. This does not mean that its performance is only connected to the worship of Devnārāyaṇ; to the fulfilment of vows; or to the concrete involvement of Devnārāyaṇ in his devotees' lives. The narrative in itself creates a discourse about things "religious": divine testimony, sacred territory, divine power, sacrifice, devotion, and so on. The narrative, therefore, articulates and constructs a world in which the sources, objects, and subjects of religious power are defined and identified. This fundamental concern of the narrative is what provides a linkage between the "mythic" and the "epic" elements of the narrative. But in fact, in terms of the devotees' own perception of the narrative, no such distinction between mythic and epic is maintained. The borders between the "asituated" (divine) and the "situated" (heroic) are blurred. The narrative is "simply" about *dharam. Dharam* is, thus, the overarching concern that spans the mythic and the epic. It is the same as the Sankrit "dharma": moral conduct, religious life, right action, and so on.

Myth, Legend, or History?

Given the connections *and* the distinctions postulated among epic, legend, and myth, one of the questions repeatedly asked by scholars of epics[23]—both written and oral—has been about "historical origins": What are the historically "testifiable" events that underly the formation of an epic narrative? Who are the historically "real" characters the epic narrative takes up and weaves into its heroic and divine web? How is physical, social, and historical "reality" transformed and represented through the edifice of an epic?[24] In short, how do epics *evolve* from concrete events located in time and space to the grand narratives that they are, incorporating both the legendary and the mythical? This historically oriented, evolutionistic approach to our understanding of epics—whether in India or elsewhere—has, as I mentioned earlier, also permeated our understanding of oral epics. The strongest case for this has been articulated in S. H. Blackburn's work on oral epics in India. Blackburn (1985: 259) suggests a scheme in which the divine hero or heroine of an epic regularly originates from a "real" person who has suffered a premature or violent death:

> To the well-known Hindu perspectives on death, the cults of the deified dead add something new. In the *Purāṇas* (and in ancient Tamil poetry) death is deified, but in these [folk] cults it is the dead themselves who are deified . . . not just any death has this effect; only a special kind makes the dead hero an object of worship. First, the death must be premature, an end that cuts short a person's normal life span. Second, and more important, the death must be violent, an act of aggression or a sudden blow from nature. . . . Lastly, the death that deifies is undeserved; the person killed is an innocent (if often ill-fated) victim.

Blackburn arrives at this threefold criteria from his reading of narratives in South India, particularly those belonging to the *Bow Song* tradition. Whereas these particular elements surrounding the death of a victim or hero lie, according to Blackburn (271), at the core of such folk cults, the stories themselves reveal a pattern that seems to conceal the human origins of the hero or heroine:

> Stories (especially epics) about folk heroes/gods in India seem to develop in a particular pattern by adding two primary motifs: a supernatural birth and then an identification with a pan-Indian god or hero. The effect of this pattern is that the human history of the deified hero is gradually absorbed into a divine pedigree; often his birth and his death are forgotten or simply explained away as a consequence of a prior curse, vow, or boon from Kailāsa. . . . Even the stories of Śakyamuni Buddha, Mahāvīra, and Śaṅkara were constructed to establish the prior divinity of these "historical" figures, to show that they were, from the very beginning, manifestations of a transcendental reality.

This developmental hypothesis of Blackburn has been further elaborated in the introduction and first chapter of his book *Oral Epics in India.* Moreover, his developmental understanding of oral epics has been taken up in studies conducted in other regions of India.[25] In the case of Rajasthan, it is J. D. Smith who applies the hypothesis most stringently to his study of the epic of Pābūjī (1991). Chapters 4 and 5 of his book on Pābūjī are entitled: "Pabujī: The Man" and "Pabūjī: The God." The chapter headings themselves suggest a division between the "historical" and the "mythical" or "legendary" Pābūjī. In the chapter entitled

"Pābūji: The man," Smith attempts to sift out historical evidence for the existence of Pābūjī from various sources, literary and other. The centerpiece of this analysis is the comparison of a seventeenth-century chronicle (*Khyāta*) in which the story of Pābūjī is recounted by the chronicler, Naiṇasī, with present-day versions of the epic. He writes (1991: 72):

> Naiṇasī's version of it [the epic] bears important and deep seated similarities to that of the modern epic singers. The possibility of a direct connexion between the two is further enhanced by the near certainty that Naiṇasī's own story was oral in origin . . . it seems likely that these two forms of the story are earlier and later versions from the same tradition, or perhaps from two closely connected traditions.

Smith suggests that divergences between Naiṇasī's and present-day epic singers' versions of the story, hinges on the effects of "a single process," which he characterizes as "the inflation of history" (1991: 73). Smith warns us, while concurring with Henige (1974: 52–3, 78–81, 201–6), of "the unreliability (in terms of 'our' history) of traditional orally transmitted history in general, and of the treatment of early material in the Rajasthani chronicles in particular" (Smith 1991: 73). Then, after reviewing historical sources and the evidence from topology, he finally concludes (82):

> In the end, then, we can say that the likelihood is that Pābūjī did exist, probably in the early fourteenth century A.D., and that some parts of Naiṇasī's account of him . . . may well approximate to the truth . . . what we are told of him corresponds closely with what we should expect of a small Rajpūt chief in early medieval times: he was a brigand who lived by his wits and his weapons. What, exactly led to his deification we shall never know . . . it is important to remember that traditional orally transmitted history and conventional history are informed by two very different conceptions of what history is . . . Traditional history is not concerned with facts as such; it is concerned not with the *right* story but with the *best* story.

In his next chapter, entitled "Pābūjī: The God," Smith, following the general hypothesis that (oral) epic narratives must have a historical core, attempts to explain how the figure of Pābūjī develops from that of a "noble brigand" (or bandit) to an avatāra or manifestation and incarnation of God (or a god; in this case Pābūjī is considered to be a reincarnation of Rāma's brother, Lakṣmaṇa). According to Smith (and Kothari 1989), Pābūjī belongs to a category of minor deities in Rajasthan called *bhomiyos*, "local heroes who are venerated after their death, the classical case being the hero who dies in the act of rescuing stolen cows" (1991: 90). Not only Pābūjī's narrative is similar to those of bhomiyos but also his iconography, which, on memorial stones, depicts him on a horse carrying a spear "with the sun and moon at the top as witness to his glory" (90). But in contrast to narratives centering around bhomiyos, Pābūjī's epic is steeped in "background mythology." In other words, the characters in the epic, including

Pābūjī, are incarnations (avatāra) or reincarnations of deities of "classical" mythology. Thus, for example, Pābūjī is an avatāra of Lakṣmaṇa, his faithful companion Dhẽbo an avatāra of Hanumān, and his bride Phulvanti an avatāra of Rāvaṇa's sister, Śūrpaṇakhā, his brother-in-law and enemy Jindrāv Khĩcī an avatāra of Rāvaṇa; his horse Kesar Kāḷamī an avatāra of the Goddess; and Lady Devāḷ, the Cāraṇ woman whose cows he protects, also an incarnation of the Goddess. Not only are a number of characters informed by a notion of avatāra, but many events too have a "cosmic significance": "The existence of this mythological background to the epic of Pābūjī is crucial. . . . A 'drama' of cosmic importance is being played out on earth, and human actions are now doubly accountable: they must simultaneously further both human aspiration and the cosmic plan" (p. 94). This double accountability is expressed in a tension "between free will and determination" (95). This tension—one between *daiva* and *pauruṣa*—is also well known in the Sanskrit epics.[26] In the concluding section of the chapter, Smith is explicit (91) about the "evolutionary" nature of the mythological background in relation to the events and characters of Pābūjī's epic:

> There can be little doubt that the provision of a mythological background to the story of Pābūjī—with all its consequences for the meaning of that story—was originally motivated by the desire to secure a higher status for the god by linking him to the gods of the "Great Tradition." I am not . . . suggesting that once a particularly cunning and devious *bhopo* consciously invented the account of the incarnation-system . . . no doubt the idea evolved slowly and unconciously. But evolution is generally purposeful, whether conscious or not. The priests of Pābūjī have used their epic as a medium for the theophany of their god.

Smith thus endorses Blackburn's view that oral epics evolve from historical events and historical figures, which are then gradually nourished with epic and puranic mythologies, invariably to raise the status of their respective heroes and cults.

The approach just outlined appears to me to assume the inevitability of historical processes underlying the formation of complex folk narratives, which at a final stage of development assimilate or "borrow" the notion of the avatāra from "classical" sources. Folk epics, according to this view, are therefore not generated in an environment that *already always knows* of avatāras and so-called classical mythology but in a supposedly isolated or rarefied literary and religious environment in which the corporeal existence of heroes and heroines is foremost in the minds of hypothetical story-makers. Rather than propose that the idea of the avatāra may in fact be a key concept reworked and applied by different religious and literary streams, Smith and Blackburn suggest that the notion is "grafted" onto folk narratives in order to provide legitimacy in the context of the so-called Great Tradition. Beneath this conjecture there appears to be a desire not only to sift fact from fiction and history from myth but also to view the growth of texts in a linear manner, moving from simpler to complex, local to regional, regional to transregional, and so on, along the analogy of evolutionary theories found in both the natural sciences and anthropology: literary and cultural traditions are thus implicitly represented in a teleological fashion.

In terms of a general theory of texts, the position formulated by Smith and Blackburn also seems to unreflectingly draw on an epistemology that is at home in Judeo-Christian theological traditions, which in turn has given philology its theoretical underpinnings. As Hiltebeitel (1995: 27) aptly points out, there have been two important influences on the study of (oral and) "classical" epics. The first concerns A. B. Lord's (1960) oral-formulaic theory, which has been applied to Homeric studies, the other which has been

> drawn from the higher criticism of nineteenth-century scholarship on sources, strata, and interpolations, [and] has prevailed as critical orthodoxy in modern biblical studies . . . these methods . . . grew organically from within scholarly traditions that were addressed to questions raised about distinctive features of Homer and the Bible, but not of Indian epics. *Yet they have become virtually axiomatic in scholarship on Indian epics, and have served as vehicles for imagining them in terms that globalize the methods without addressing the distinctiveness of the texts.* (Emphasis added.)

According to Hiltebeitel, "the same historically effected conciousness" ("wirkungsgeschichtliches Bewusstsein") [27] that drives and permeates the interpretation of classical epics also affects scholarship on India's oral epics. Hiltebeitel's observations raise critical questions regarding the appropriateness of approaches generally adopted for the analysis of folk epics: Are the linkages between "classical" and "folk" epics only limited to "borrowing" and "legitimizing" on the part of the latter? Are folk epics always about heroes and heroines who were historically "real"? Do folk epics necessarily deal with the death of a single ("real") hero or heroine? Is it at all relevant (or even possible) to determine a "real," historical core for complex literary objects such as folk epics? Moreover, if such narratives are about formulating different discourses, then are we not missing the point by searching for underlying historical reality? Finally, since in Indian cultural thought there is no cleavage between "history," "legend," "story," and so on—all being subsumed under one conceptual category, namely *itihāsa* ("so it has been")—is it not critically important to develop an interpretative framework informed by an "Indian" instead of a "Western" historiography and ideas about texts? As Shulman (1989: 9) points out:

> We can continue to cling to the path of Herodotus, categorically sifting fact from fable, myth, or legend, but with rather unsatisfactory results. At some point our understanding of Hinduism should incorporate an Indian epistemology as well—a sensitivity to the inner world of the actors. . . . If India blurs the boundary between "history" and "myth" (all *itihāsa*) . . . do we not distort by drawing in sharp contours?

Clearly, then, the meaning of a folk narrative cannot be appreciated by disengaging a historical core from a mythic or legendary overlay. Nor can its construction be understood in terms of textual implantations and amplifications. Thus, the very notion of "text," especially in the Indian folk (and classical) context, needs to be restated.[28] This is more than necessary since there has been a general criticism carried out in literary studies against the notion of a pure, self-existent, well-defined, "authentically" created text. Texts are considered as being heavily saturated with the language of other texts, as being links in a network of texts, and as being nothing more and nothing less than *intertexts* in "an ever-flowing river" (Vatsyayan 1995: 5). Thus if, according to this view, no texts exist in isolation, then folk narratives too, even at their very inception, could not have arisen in a literary and cultural vacuum. The implication is that the mythologies that are supposed to have been added on later actually form a part of the fundamental matrix in which folk narratives are conceived right from the very beginning. And basic to this matrix are the ideas of birth, rebirth, death, avatāra, "sacrifice," bhakti, warriorhood, asceticism, and so on.[29] These ideas, along with a universe of narrative motifs, constitute something of a *common pool* of the culture(s), from which both "folk narratives" and "classical texts" draw for their sustainance.

Text and Intertext

> The vast variety of Indian literature, oral and written, over the centuries, in hundreds of languages and dialects, offers an intricate but open network of such relations, producing families of texts as well as texts that are utterly individual in their effect, detail, and temporal/regional niches. But these relations are perceived by native commentators and by readers. To them, texts do not come in historical stages but form a "simultaneous order," where every new text within a series alters the whole order ever so slightly, and not always so slightly.
>
> —A. K. Ramanujan, *Where Mirrors Are Windows*

Rather than examining the narrative text of Devnārāyaṇ in terms of the distinction between history, legend, or myth, I suggest that we view it as a part of a network of texts that mutually reflect and define each other in different ways. The idea on which this approach primarily rests is that of intertextuality.

The basic idea behind the notion of the intertext or intertextuality[30] is that any communicative situation in language, be it verbal, written or visual is primarily, *interactive* or *dialogic*:[31] dialogic not only in the sense of invoking an interchange between two parties, as in a conversation, but in the sense in which all "utterances" can, in fact, be considered to be polyphonic in nature, that is, "they 'echo' and 'reverberate' other utterances." As Bakhtin (1986: 192), in his radical understanding of language and textuality, points out:

> Any concrete utterance is a link in the chain of speech communication of a particular sphere. . . . Utterances are not indifferent to one another, and are not self-sufficient; they are aware of and mutually

> reflect one another. These mutual reflections determine their character. Each utterance is filled with echoes and reverberations of other utterances. . . . Every utterance must be regarded primarily as a *response* to preceding utterances of the given sphere. . . . Each utterance repeats, affirms, supplements, and relies on the others, presupposes them to be known, and somehow takes them into account. . . . Therefore, each utterance is filled with various kinds of responsive reactions to other utterances. Both whole utterances and individual words can retain their alien expression, but they can also be reaccentuated. Other's utterances can be repeated with varying degrees of reinterpretation. . . . The utterance is filled with dialogic overtones.

Although Bakhtin in this passage focuses on "speech events" one can use his notion of an "utterance" as a metaphor for the individual elements of an intertextual field or matrix of narratives. There are, however, at least two possible senses in which the intertextual elements of any given text can be envisioned and investigated. The first sense is that in which intertextuality manifests in the form of "unconscious quotation marks" (Barthes 1987b: 39):

> Intertexuality, the condition of any text whatsoever, cannot, of course, be reduced to a problem of sources or influences; the intertext is a general field of anonymous formulae whose origin can scarcely ever be located; of unconscious or automatic quotations, given without quotation-marks. Epistemologically, the concept of intertext is what . . . makes sure the text has the status not of a reproduction but of a productivity.

In other words, the occurrence of semantic units from other texts in any given text arises from the fact that the text belongs to and exists along the intersection of a semantic field that permeates each utterance. This could be called a "grammar" of intertextuality, in which questions related to the quantity, quality, distribution, and frequency of intertextual elements in any given text can be investigated. The second sense of intertextuality takes us closer to the communicative situation involving "sender, receiver, code, place, time, medium, function etc" (Plett 1991: 12). Here we become concerned less with "unconscious quotation marks" as with the "agency" of producers and receptors of texts; of "authors," speakers, listeners, and readers. By turning to this dimension of intertextuality, namely the *pragmatics* of intertextuality, we can begin to place the phenomenon of text production within its appropriate literary, cultural, and historical context. The task of understanding the "intertext" is, therefore, to investigate "the specificity of different textual arrangements by placing them within the general text (culture) of which they are a part and which is in turn, part of them."[32] The production of texts or narratives thus embraces both a specific time and place, a specific literary and cultural context, as well as a more general shared, ideational "pool" of motifs, narrative elements and images, and so on.

Clearly, then, the production of folk narratives need not necessarily be grasped in terms of a "vertical" path of textual augmentation but can be conceived, as A. K. Ramanujan astutely observes, in terms of a "simultaneous order." The hub around which this simultaneous order revolves is built up of the many manifestations of reflexivity

> of self and other, mirroring, distorted mirroring, parody, family resemblances and rebels, dialectic, anti-structure, utopias and dystopias, the many ironies connected with these responses and so on. . . . Reflexive elements may occur in various sizes: one part of the text may reflect on another; a whole tradition may invert, negate, rework, and revalue another . . . encompassment, mimicry, criticism and conflict, and other power relations are expressed by such reflexivities.[33]

In the course of this study it will become evident that the narrative of Devnārāyaṇ creates a tradition within itself by reflecting on and reworking parts of puranic and epic traditions. While at times there is a conscious reference to puranic, "folk," and epic motifs and characters, there is also a wide range of motifs that occur in a seemingly fragmented arrangement if one takes the puranic and epic motifs to be the "original" models.[34] These motifs, which are closer to a "grammar" of intertextuality than a "pragmatics," make sense, however, within the overall structure and purpose of the narrative. As a brief example of what is meant by this, consider two incidents that occur toward the end of the narrative. In the first a patel sent by the Rāṇā to Devnārāyaṇ's capital of Causlā gets to take a look into Devnārāyaṇ's mouth:

> He saw all the three worlds!—*vāh vāh*—
> The patel thought to himself: "Hey, how can your master defeat
> him? *Yes, how can he defeat him? He's sitting there with all the three worlds in his mouth*
> He can't win!—*vāh vāh*—."

In the second incident there is a dialogue between a cowherd (*Guāl*) and Suremātā, a divine cow in Devnārāyaṇ's herd of a 980,000 cows. The cowherd refuses to believe in Suremātā's claims of divinity:

> What did Suremātā do? She took the "five-faces" form and gave darśan to the Guāl.—*vāh vāh*—
> One face she took on of the mare.—*mhe*—
> One of the Udaṇmerī.[35]
> One of Suremātā—of the cow—was there anyway.—*mhe*—
> One she took on of Śakti.
> "By god's grace, look inside the mouth of Śakti, Guāl! See, what play there is!" *Yes, look*
> So, over there, in Śakti's mouth the discus was whirling.—*vāh vāh*—
> He looked inside the cow's mouth.
> The way the entire world is created. *Yes, everything was visible*
> All the three worlds she showed in the cow's mouth.

The horses and riders were all there. The cow was standing near
Dev Māhārāj.—*vāh vāh*—. The Guāl folded his hands together—*mhe*—
And stood in front of her: "Mother, I didn't know.
Yes, all these days I didn't know that you were like this. I thought you were a cow among cows!"

Both these scenes are strongly reminiscent of a well-known scene from the *Bhāgavata Purāṇa* in which Kṛṣṇa's mother looks into the boy's mouth:

> One day when Rāma and the other little sons of the cowherds were playing, they reported to his mother, "Kṛṣṇa has eaten dirt." Yaṣodā took Kṛṣṇa by the hand and scolded him, for his own good, and she said to him, naughty boy, why have you secretly eaten dirt? . . . Kṛṣṇa said: "Mother, I have not eaten. They are all lying. If you think they speak the truth, look at my mouth yourself." "If that is the case, then open your mouth," she said to the Lord Hari. . . . She then saw in his mouth the whole eternal universe, and heaven, and the regions of the sky, and the orb of the earth with its mountains, islands, and oceans; she saw the wind, and lightening, and the moon and the stars, and the zodiac; and water and fire and air and space itself; she saw the vacillating senses, the mind, the elements, and the three strands of matter. She saw within the body of her son, in his gaping mouth, the whole universe with all its variety, with all the forms of life and time and nature and action and hopes, and her own village, and herself. Then she became afraid and confused.[36]

Admittedly, the passages in the oral narrative are not as detailed and breathtaking in their description of the cosmos as the written passage from the *Bhāgavata Purāṇa* is, but they are equally powerful in terms of an "embedded cosmology" that brings out the concern of the narrative in providing testimony to Devnārāyaṇ's presence.[37] Furthermore, their importance lies in their appearance in the oral narrative and the place where they occur. In the first instance the emissary (the patel) of Devnārāyaṇ's arch-enemy, the Rāṇā, is allowed to look inside the god's mouth. Seeing the triple world resting in the mouth of what he took to be a young, naive boy of eleven, he realizes that Devnārāyaṇ is a manifestation of divinity and that his royal master, the Rāṇā, cannot in any way match him in terms of strength and power. Proving one's divinity is again the theme of the second instance, in which the divine cow Suremātā manifests her fivefold countenance to the disbelieving cowherd.[38] Here it is not Devnārāyaṇ but a manifestation of Śakti who is shown as containing the universe within her. The symbolism is decidedly "martial": "horses and riders," "the discus whirling." In addition to this, there is the self-reflexive vision of Suremātā positioned next to Devnārāyaṇ, which explains both her status and the reason for her manifestation along with Devnārāyaṇ. Given the strong bond between Śakti and Devnārāyaṇ,[39] there is no contradiction felt in depicting both of them as receptacles of the cosmos. The form, content, and purpose of the two passages are undoubtedly far simpler than the passage from the puranic text. Whereas the former are concerned with providing a message, as well as proving Devnārāyaṇ's and Suremātā's divinity to two relatively unimportant figures in the narrative, the latter brings about a deep transformation in the self-perception of Kṛṣṇa's own mother Yaśodā: "he through whose power of delusion there arise in me such false beliefs as 'I,' 'This is my husband,' 'This is my son,' 'I am the wife of the village chieftain and all this wealth is mine, including these cow-herds and their wives and their wealth of cattle.' "[40]

In the oral narrative there are no explicit allusions to Devnārāyaṇ's greatness in terms of other texts: "She considered Hari—whose greatness is extolled by the three Vedas and the Upaniṣads and the philosophies of Sāṅkhya and Yoga and all the Sātvata texts—she considered him to be her son" (Bhāgavata Purāṇa, 10.8.45).[41] The vision of the triple world does not result in any groundbreaking, metaphysical awakening on the part of either the Patel or the Guāl. In keeping with the directness and simplicity of the narrative, both merely acknowledge the presence of Devnārāyaṇ's and Suremātā's divinity. Divinity is thus directly perceived and felt without the philosophical distinctions drawn in Sāṃkhya and Yoga.[42]

Of Kings, Queens, and Avatāras

Although motifs such as the foregoing[43] constitute a significant portion of the entire intertextual field of the narrative, the crux of intertextuality can be said to rest on the notion of the avatāra. Moreover, it is through different avatāras and distinct "avatāric strands" that the religious ideology of the narrative fully unfolds. Although certain avatāras in the narrative seem to belong to a "background mythology,"[44] others (such as Bhavānī and Devnārāyaṇ) relate to the "foreground" mythology of the narrative, being the product of actions and events occurring during the course of the narrative and not those belonging to past lives or time cycles. What is meant by this will become evident in the passages that follow. Thus the idea of the avatāra is responsible for providing the narrative of Devnārāyaṇ with its *literary and religious* design. First, the idea of the avatāra is a vehicle for establishing an "outer" linkage with other narratives and narrative figures. Second, it provides an "inner" linkage between the seemingly distinct religious ideologies (Śaivite/Śāktā and Vaiṣṇavite) of the two halves of the narrative. And, last of all, together with the idea of bhakti, it provides the narrative with its deeper, overall religious structure. Before coming to the examples offered by the narrative of Devnārāyaṇ I will give a brief overview of the notion of the avatāra as it is found in "classical" texts.

It is a well-known fact that the idea of the avatāra, which occupies a vital place in the religious ideology of Hinduism, is firmly connected to the function, manifestation, and mythology of Viṣṇu, who, in order to free the earth from the burden of evil and degeneration, frequently incarnates himself in order to restore the balance of order in the world. Conventionally, Vaiṣṇava texts speak of 10 avatāras, although there is also mention of 24 or 39 incarnations. In the "conventional" list of 10 avatāras, there is a succession of divine manifestations leading from the aqueous to the animal, half animal half human, and human.[45] Notwithstanding the apparent "canonicity" of the 10 avatāras (*daśāvatāra*) of Viṣṇu, the idea of the avatāra is found in non-Vaiṣṇava contexts in many "folk-cults." Thus, for example, Khaṇḍobā in the Maharashtrain cult is considered an avatāra of Śiva; Vaiṣṇo Devī in Himachal Pradesh an avatāra of Devī; Rāmdevjī in Rajasthan an avatāra of Kṛṣṇa; and Brahma Nāyūḍū in the Telugu epic of Paḷnāḍu an avatāra of Viṣṇu.[46] Thus there is a wide application of the idea of the avatāra in contexts other than those of Vaiṣṇava theological texts, and this again suggests that the idea cannot be understood as the cultural or religious "property" of one filament of Hinduism. Again, it would be more appropriate to consider the notion as belonging to the *common pool* of ideas, values, motifs, concepts, and so on from which different cultural and religious constellations are formed.

D. A. Soifer (1991) in her study of the Narasiṃha and Vāmana avatāras sets up a motif checklist for examining the avatāra myths. Since the list is based on a reading of classical (puranic, vedic, brahmanic, and epic) sources, it will be worthwhile to mention it here, so as to subsequently compare the manner in which the avataric figures have been redrawn in our narrative text. Soifer (8) outlines five basic motifs that represent a diverse group of statements of relationships, context, action, and position:

1. *A special relationship with Indra*: The avatāra continues an alliance with Indra that began as early as the Vedic literature, which often united the two gods in battle against demons, portraying Indra as a kṣatriya par excellence, possessor of physical strength, and Viṣṇu as his aid, his subordinate, who nevertheless possessed a higher, superior power.
2. *Invocation of a cosmogonic scenario*: The avatāra invokes the quality of the interstitial period of pralaya (destruction) and recreation through the use of cosmological language describing his appearance and the events surrounding it.
3. *Mediating power and activity*: The avatāra amasses power by positioning himself "betwixt and between" two opposing groups, gaining the role of mediator.
4. *Action through trickery*: The avatāra often encloses deceit, guile, or trickery to win a victory for the gods (or protagonists) over the demons (or antagonists).
5. *The loophole in the law*: Faced with what appears to be an airtight situation that threatens to imperil the gods (or protagonists), the avatāra finds a chink, a loophole that provides a solution to the conflict without direct violation of the pact or law.

Soifer continues (a) by suggesting that

> the overriding emphasis . . . of these motifs was the concept of liminality . . . That is, the avatāra brought with him, clothed himself in, an "interstructural" period, via the pralaya imagery appearing as a figure of pure potency, oftentimes an unlikely hero, the "underling

made uppermost," an amoral trickster, the very principle of ambivalence.

Avatāras in the Narrative of Devnārāyaṇ

At the very outset the narrative text of Devnārāyaṇ displays a series of avatāras, together with other "reincarnations" or "rebirths." To begin with we have, of course, Devnārāyaṇ himself, who, as his very name suggests, is an avatāra of Bhagavān/Viṣṇu/Nārāyaṇa. Then there is the powerful figure of Queen Jaimati, an incarnation of the goddess Bhavānī or Durgā (or simply Śakti). Similarly, Devnārāyaṇ's elder cousin brothers are reincarnations of Lakṣmana, Bhārata, and Śatrughna.[47] Devnārāyaṇ's father and his 23 brothers, the Bagaṛāvats, are reincarnations of 24 ṛṣis who have lived (and died) in the satya yuga; their genealogist and bard, Chochū Bhāṭ, who later accompanies Devnārāyaṇ on his journeys, is often called Nāradī Bhāṭ, suggesting not only his trickster-like character but also connections to Nārada. Again this connection echoes the relationships between Viṣṇu/Nārāyaṇa and Nārada Muni.

However, the list of avatāras and reincarnations is not exhausted by this. The incarnational intertwinings continue to include other major and minor characters of the narrative. These incarnational features broaden the intertextual spread of the narrative. For example, Devnārāyaṇ's enemy, the Rāṇā, is held to be an incarnation of Rāvaṇa; one of his generals, Dīyājī Jodhkā, is an incarnation of Kaṃsa; Savāī Bhoj (at least in the visual narrative of the paṛ) is shown to be an avatāra of Śeṣa;[48] and the three gifts Savāī Bhoj receives during his encounter with the ascetic Rūpnāth, namely a horse (Bāvlī Ghoḍī), a cow (Suremātā), and an elephant, (Jaymaṅgalo Hāthī) are all manifestations of Śakti.[49] While there is an obvious incarnational scheme provided by Rāma's or Bhagavān's avatāra as Devnārāyaṇ and Rāvaṇa's avatāra as the Rāṇā, there is a secondary but nevertheless much more potent scheme provided by Kṛṣṇa/Devnārāyaṇ and Kaṃsa/Dīyājī Jodhkā. Whereas the Rāṇā is portrayed both as enemy and also as "grandfather," conjuring up complex interrelationships between the Rāṇā, the Bagaṛāvats, and Devnārāyaṇ, Dīyājī Jodhkā is definitely more the arch-fiend. The encounters between Devnārāyaṇ, his four cousins, and Dīyājī are much more dramatic and violent than those between the former and the Rāṇā, even though it is the Rāṇā's defeat that has an important place in the final trajectory of the narrative.

Thus it is evident from the foregoing inventory that the narrative forms a series of interlockings with other texts. These interlockings and the layers produced thereof, within the narrative itself, are woven about the notion of the avatāra in general and avatāras specific to the narrative. Even the central avataric figure of Devnārāyaṇ does not exist in isolation. He is backed by an ancestry of avatāras, a lineage or succession similar to that visible in the "classical" daśāvatāra sequence. Therefore, not only is his father Savāī Bhoj an incarnation of Śeṣa but his grandfather Bāgh Siṃh is half man, half lion and is referred to as an *autārī puruṣ* (divine or incarnational person/man). Bāgh Siṃh's father Hari Rām marries Līlā Sevrī, who is known to be a devotee of Varāha, whom she regularly worships on the banks of the sacred lake of Puṣkara.[50] The imagery here is predominantly *Vaiṣṇavite*, beginning with Varāha (and his association with water), then with Bāgh Siṃh or Narasiṃha (and his transgressive/transitional nature), Śeṣa, and finally with Devnārāyaṇ or Kṛṣṇa/Rāma/Bhagavān. While the sequence put together here from the verbal narrative may seem arbitrary, the paṛ is quite explicit in its representation of the different avatāras of Viṣṇu. A long section of the uppermost left part of the scroll is reserved for a series of deities, beginning with Ganeṣa and Sarasvatī, who are invoked at the start of each recitation. Subsequent to these two deities there is Matsya-Avatāra, followed by Kūrma-Avatāra. The latter is shown in a scene depicting the churning of the ocean. After this follow Varāha-Avatāra, Narasiṃha-Avatāra, and Paraśurāma fighting with an axe. Between these two figures is the minute figure of Vāmana-Avatāra. Subsequent to this there are a number of scenes portraying events from the lives of Kṛṣṇa and Rāmā. Kṛṣṇa is shown playing the flute and subduing Kaṃsa. Rāma, Lakṣmaṇa, and Sītā are attended by Hanumān during their exile in the forest. Sītā is abducted by Rāvaṇā; Hanumān delivers Rāma's ring to Sītā in Aśokavāṭika; and Rāvaṇā does battle with Rāmā, Lakṣmaṇa, and Hanumān across the ocean.[51] Thus, the religious imagination of the paṛ as well as the verbal narrative is strongly determined by *Vaiṣṇavite* themes. But even this is not the complete picture.

Thus, for example, Savāī Bhoj, notwithstanding being an avatāra of Śeṣa, is a disciple of Rūpnāth, who in turn is identical with Śaṅkar. In keeping with his Śaivite leanings, Savāī Bhoj is also a devotee/lover of the goddess Bhavānī in her incarnation as Queen Jaimatī. Even Devnārāyaṇ does not escape such admixtures: he is attended to and accompanied by Kālā and Gorā Bherū̃, who, at least in puranic texts, with the appellation of Bhairava, are manifestations of Śiva. Similar to the sequence of avatāras, the paṛ also has its share of Śaivite and Śāktā images. Rūpnāth is shown in the cauldron of oil beneath the figure of Narasiṃha-Avatāra on the upper left of the paṛ. Kālā and Gorā Bherū̃, armed with swords, stand beneath Devnārāyaṇ's court. Adjacent to the court on the upper middle section of the paṛ (R 25–29, 14–18), Queen Jaimatī reveals her true form as Bhavānī, or Durgā. To her immediate right, riding on a donkey is Śītalā Mātā, followed by Pārvatī riding a tiger, and Śiva seated on Nandi.

The religious imagery of the visual and verbal narrative is, therefore, neither exclusively Vaiṣṇavite nor Śaivite/Śāktā. Rather, it represents a fusion or linking together of typically discrete religious currents: Śaivite and Śāktā on the one hand and Vaiṣṇavite on the other. But how is this fusion maintained and sustained? What allows a successful synthesis to exist without being a contradiction or anomaly? What is the cementing force of coexistence, or of "interculturality" and "interreligiosity"? As I shall explain here, it is the idea of the avatāra in two different yet interconnected expressions in the forms of the Goddess and Kṛṣṇa that give the different religious currents a cohesion.

Before going into the details of how this synthesis is maintained, it needs to be mentioned that while a crossing of Śaivite and Vaiṣṇavite ideologies is not so readily found in classical texts, the notion of the avatāra operating in the narrative corresponds closely to "classical" Śāktā and Vaiṣṇava traditions. Thus it is both the Goddess *and* Viṣṇu who in the narrative fulfill their respective *avatāric* functions found in "classical" texts extolling their powers and deeds. This in turn provides the narrative with its deeper structure.

As Gonda (1954: 124) in the case of Viṣṇu's avatāras writes:

> The phenomenon of the god's multiformity, metamorphosis and reincarnation in itself is no matter of great surprise, as similar adventures were also attributed to other gods. . . . The god is born each time for a specific purpose . . . for the rescue of the good, for the preservation of the world and its culture, for the destruction of the evil-doers and the establishment of *dharma* (see *BhG.* 4.7ff.).

While the fact that Viṣṇu may take on different forms and manifestations is not something unique, the purpose of his sojourn on earth is regular, well-defined, and unique. Furthermore, his function as a deity and as an avatāra is closely interlinked, if not identical, with that of the king whose primary duty is to protect the world and to defend the dharma. But beyond the identity of function, the body of Viṣṇu and the body of earthly kings are identical. Not only is Viṣṇu "the supreme ruler and protector of the universe," represented as king, occupying a royal throne, but the earthly king's body is "entered" upon by Viṣṇu (Gonda 1954: 164):

> King Pṛthu Vainya was his favourite. It was Viṣṇu himself who crowned him and confirmed his power. He even entered his body, for which reason the entire universe bows to the king as to a god (*Mahābhārata* 12, 59, 127ff.). The king is really, the text adds, endowed with Viṣṇu's greatness on earth (*mahattvena ca saṃyukto Vaiṣṇavena naro bhuvi* . . .). Thus the god entered all kings . . . in the *TB.* 1, 7, 44 it is observed that by identifying himself with Viṣṇu the king is able to conquer the worlds: *viṣṇur eva bhūtvemāṃl lokān abhijayati.* . . . All *cakravartins* . . . bear a portion of Viṣṇu's personality which is sometimes more precisely stated to consist of *tejas* "fiery energy."

This corporeal identity of Viṣṇu and earthly kings is complemented by their association with vegetation and fertility, and their concern for the welfare of people through the enhancement of vegetative production (Gonda 1954: 165):

> It was the essential part of the king's duty to make rain and to cause the crops to be good. It was he who by his conduct made the sun to shine, or drought to vex mankind. . . . The same functions are attributed to Viṣṇu who is always concerned with generation and fertility, whether he is believed to be active in the atmosphere or in other provinces of the universe.

From the foregoing it becomes clear that not only is there a connection/identity between Viṣṇu and kingship (both cosmic and earthly) but that there is an essential overlap between the qualities and function of kingship and those of the avatāra: both the king and the avatāra are primarily concerned with the preservation and protection of the earth's inhabitants and the dharma.

Besides the verbal narrative itself, to which I will come later, the richest and most explicit indication of Devnārāyaṇ's royal identity is expressed in his portrayal on the paṛ. Devnārāyaṇ's figure occupies the center of the paṛ. He is faced by his four brothers, each depicted in a smaller size than him. The entire unit, including Devnārāyaṇ, his four brothers, and certain other scenes adjacent to them, shows Devnārāyaṇ's *darbār* or court. Devnārāyaṇ, and his brothers as well, wears full regal dress. In his right hand Devnārāyaṇ bears a sword that is placed upright against his shoulder. In his left hand he holds a lotus blossom. He squats on a "python-throne" and is faced by the upright figure of the serpent king of the underworld, Rājā Basak. In the vicinity of his feet there is the (relatively) minute figure of Chochū Bhāṭ, who faces him in a reverential posture. At the level of his right shoulder there are two figures waving fly whisks. Directly above him there are figures of two *paris* (fairies, "angels") along with two peacocks facing each other. At the lower end of the middle section of the paṛ depicting Devnārāyaṇ and his brothers are his two assistants, Kālā and Gorā Bherū̃, riding (as Bhairava does) on dogs.[52] Next to them is Devnārāyaṇ's steed, Līlāgar, whose reigns are held onto by his stable attendant. In addition to the depiction of Devnārāyaṇ's royalty on the paṛ, there are also lithographs of him available in major temples (for example, in Pushkar). On these he is again shown in a regal costume riding his horse Līlāgar, accompanied by Kālā and Gorā Bherū̃. Above him there is an ornate parasol, or *chattri*, which is usually reserved for kings.

The evidence from the visual/iconic representations of Devnārāyaṇ is further enhanced by the use of various epithets that occur both in his narrative and in worship. Thus, for example, a term of reverence/reference used for Devnārāyaṇ throughout the narrative is *darbār*, which is the Persian term for "royal

Kālā and Gorā Bherū̃.

Devnārāyaṇ's horse, Līlāgar. The horse's eye is unfinished because the paṛ has not been consecrated yet.

court" or "royal audience." In the narrative it is used to refer to the holder of the royal court, which in this case is Devnārāyaṇ. Similarly Devnārāyaṇ is also spoken of as Ṭhākur Dev or "Lord" Dev.[53] The narrative (as well as the paṛ) also speaks of his "capital" city, Causlā Kheḍā, where his court is held, and from where he "rules" over his territory. Thus the visual and verbal representation of Devnārāyaṇ both point toward a perception of the deity as a king ruling over a geographical territory and over his devotees. In fact, as will become clear in subsequent chapters, the narrative is essentially an itinerary of his "conquest" over geographical and other realms. This perception is substantiated by the fact that Devnārāyaṇ, like the traditional king (and Viṣṇu), is a source of welfare for his devotees, whom he protects and shelters.[54]

In addition to Devnārāyaṇ's *avatāric* ancestry as described earlier, he also belongs to a lineage of kings. The genealogy of this lineage is pronounced by Chochū Bhāṭ on several different occasions. The first name in the genealogical list is Ād Rājā, which from the etymology of *ād* or *ādi* suggests that it is the very first or "ur" king whom Chochū Bhāṭ is referring to. The sequence is as follows:

> Ād Rājā, from Ād Rājā came Jugāj,[55] from Jugāj came Kācchap, from Kācchap came Raṃdhol, from Raṃdhol came Kajali, from Kajali came Harirāmjī. Harirāmjī had Bāgh, Bāgh had Bhoj. Bhoj had Dev. Arisen from the fire pit, the great lineage of the Cauhān.

The last four names, that is, Harirām, Bāgh, Bhoj, and Dev feature actively in the narrative. The other names refer to ancestors from the deep past. The final line establishes Devnārāyaṇ and his ancestors as members of the famous Kṣatriya clan of the Rajputs,[56] the Cahamānas (Cauhāns).[57]

In the preceding passages Devnārāyaṇ is envisioned both as an avatāra and as a king. He also fulfills the functions of the avatāra and the king, thereby corroborating the identification between the two suggested in early textual sources as well as other historical examples.

Devī as Avatāra

The other avatāra that has close parallels with epic and puranic examples is that of the Goddess. Bhavānī or Durgā plays a major role in the first part of the narrative. She incarnates herself in the form of a local king's daughter in order to fulfil the mandate of destroying Devnārāyaṇ's father, Sāvāī Bhoj, and his 23 brothers. The circumstances of her incarnation are particularly reminiscent of Devī's manifestation on the earth to annihilate demons and other evil doers. In the *Devī-Māhātmya* of the *Mārkaṇḍeya Purāṇa*, the Goddess is born out of the combined energies of the gods, who are unable to destroy the great demon Mahiṣa.[58] The text then continues to describe how the various gods supply the Goddess with different parts of her body, her apparel, and her weapons and lion-mount. Armed with the powers of the gods, she is able to slay the nearly invincible buffalo-demon, restoring to the gods their position in heaven and reestablishing the world order. Moreover, as T. Coburn points out, the particular aspect of the Goddess as restorer of the dharma and salvific presence for terrestrial creatures is again strongly reflected in the classical model of the king described in *Manu*:

> when these creatures, being without a king, through fear dispersed in all directions, the Lord created a king for the protection of this abode (creation),
>
> Taking (for that purpose) eternal particles of Indra, of the Wind, of Yama, of the Sun, of Fire, of Varuṇa, of the Moon and of the Lord of wealth (Kubera).
>
> Because a king has been formed of particles of those lords of the gods, he therefore surpasses all created beings in lustre [*tejas*];
>
> And, like the sun, he burns eyes and hearts; nor can anyone on earth gaze on him. . . .
>
> Having fully considered the purpose, (his) powers, and the place and time, he assumes by turns many (different) shapes for the complete attainment of justice.
>
> He, in whose favour resides Padmā, the goddess of fortune, in whose valour dwells victory, in whose anger abides death, is formed of the lustre of all (gods).[59]

Coburn goes on to point out (1982: 160) that this description of "secular power" also

> underlies the *Devī-Māhātmya*'s vision of Devī's earthly origins . . . for only one who is of unrivaled power on the world's own terms can

> cope with the great disturber of the mundane equilibrium, Mahiṣa. What the *Devī-Māhātmya* thus affirms is that the effective agent on earth, as in the cosmos, is not masculine but feminine, not King but Queen.

This vision of the Goddess as an "unrivaled power" and "effective agent on earth" is reproduced in the narrative's understanding of Bhavānī or Durgā, who takes avatāra in order to slay the 24 Bagaṛāvats. Interestingly, she responds to a plea of Viṣṇu, who has pronounced the Bagaṛāvats' destruction on account of a request by Rājā Basak, the serpent king of the underworld. Prior to summoning the Goddess, Viṣṇu calls various other gods and asks them to destroy the Bagaṛāvats. However, each of the gods declines Viṣṇu's request. The reason they give for not wanting or being unable to destroy the Bagaṛāvats is *not*, as it is in the case of the demons in epic and puranic texts, because of the Bagaṛāvats' invincibility but because of their flawless devotion and pure character. The Bagaṛāvats, even though they have committed the impurity of pouring jars of alcohol onto a hillside that seeps down into Rājā Basak's kingdom, are not considered to be worthy of the gods' wrath. It is only then that Viṣṇu calls the Goddess and bestows on her the task of destroying the brothers. But the Goddess realizes that the Bagaṛavats cannot be slain in an open encounter, so she resorts to tricking them into a conflict with the Rāṇā that results in their deaths. Before sending the Goddess on her mission, Viṣṇu himself visits the brothers in disguise in order to test them. However, the brothers see through Viṣṇu's disguise and treat him with the honor, respect, and devotion deemed appropriate for a visitation by Bhagavān himself. Viṣṇu, too, can find no excuse to slay them on that occasion:

> Is there any god who is so great who can slay the Bagaṛāvats? Everyone looked down. [Only] Śakti took up the challenge [saying:] "I'm the greatest. I'm the greatest. I'm the greatest of all!" "What are you going to do?" "The Bagaṛāvats can't be destroyed without me!" [she said] "But I won't be able to kill them off straight—I'll have to trick them to kill them. They can't be killed just like that!" Then Bhagavān said: "All right, this time. But, I'm going now, right now, to their door. If anyone [of them] slips up and gets into my control, I'll finish them [all] off. If not, then I'll send you! Pay heed to what I've said!" So Bhagavān assumed the form of a leper. Well, sir, blood and pus were oozing out of his body. Nevājī[60] said: "The old man himself is coming to test us. He's taken on such a form. What should we do? We should fill up jugs with milk and *ghī*. Cow's milk. Some of us should pour milk over him, and some others should drink the cirṇāmṛt." They came and stood in front of Bhagavān in the forest. Bhagavān said: "Why are you doing this to me? I'm a leper—why are you touching me?" [The brothers said:] "It's a leper that we want. We've been waiting for you for so many days. Today we've found you!" Some of the brothers poured milk over his head, and some drank cirṇāmṛt. Savāī Bhoj drank one handful of cirṇāmṛt. He took

a second handful. When he was about to take a third handful, Bhagavān caught hold of his hand: "Daughter's father, one becomes the lord of the triple world by taking three handfuls . . . !"[61] Yes, that's why Savāī Bhoj is known as such a great *bhagat*. Bhagavān reflected to himself: "They are such *surgyānīs*,[62] these Bagaṛāvats, there's no pair of men or women who are like that." He abandoned that form [of a leper] at that place. That was in a forest. Quickly, he took on the form of a jogī wearing ochre robes.

Viṣṇu subsequently visits Savāī Bhoj's wife, Sāḍū Mātā, in order to test her.[63] However, when she also sees through his disguise he decides to give up the idea of destroying the Bagaṛāvats himself. There is, however, an interesting turn to the encounter that directly links Sāḍū Mātā to the destruction of the brothers. When Bhagavān agrees to accept Sāḍū Mātā's offerings, he asks her for the *sakalp* of 23 of the brothers.[64] Thinking that her husband, Savāī Bhoj, will be spared, Sāḍū Mātā willingly "pours" the sakalp of 23 brothers into Viṣṇu's hands. Viṣṇu reveals to her that it will not be her husband who will survive the great battle, but the eldest of the 24, namely Tejājī, the son of Bāgh Siṃh's wife, who belongs to the merchant (Bānyā) caste. By offering Viṣṇu the sakalp of 23 of the 24 Bagaṛāvats, Sāḍū Mātā ritually seals the fate of the brothers.[65]

In keeping with the Sanskritic notion of saṃkalpa, Viṣṇu simply requests Sāḍū Mātā's *determination* or *intention* to act: the rite itself is to take place later. The use of this term further substantiates the idea that the deaths of the Bagaṛāvats are being perceived as a ritual offering (*dāna*) to the deity. Both Sāḍū Mātā and Viṣṇu are engaged in performing and executing the ritual that culminates in the self-sacrifice of the Bagaṛāvats. As soon as Sāḍū Mātā offers Viṣṇu the sakalp of 23 brothers, Viṣṇu reciprocates by granting her a boon. But the only unfulfilled desire she has is to have a son like Viṣṇu himself (or that Viṣṇu be born in her shoulder sash as her son).

It is as though the lives of the 23 Bagaṛāvats are weighed against the incarnation of Bhagavān as Sāḍū Mātā's son, Devnārāyaṇ. Sāḍū Mātā's covert instrumentality in causing the brother's deaths brings her close in terms of feminine power to the figure of the Goddess, who is overtly involved in slaying the brothers. Through her active participation in their killings, however, the Goddess in the narrative parallels the many Sanskritic as well as regional and local tellings in which the Goddess confronts a demon or demons. In these narratives, and in the rituals of many folk cults, the relationship between the Goddess and the demons she destroys is not always straightforward, as between victor and victim or two warring factions. Often there is an underlying erotic current that is employed by the Goddess in order to entice and weaken her demon adversary. Sometimes, in a more explicit expression of eroticism, the Goddess marries the demon, only to kill him later. Thus, during a temple festival dedicated to the goddess Māriyamman̲ in Kan̲n̲apuram in Tamil Nadu, the Goddess is briefly wedded to a demon, who at the end of the ritual proceedings is "killed." After this the Goddess returns to her independent, "virgin" state.[66] In other contexts the erotic feelings of the demon and his violent encounter with the Goddess is transformed into intense and singular devotion. The demon's death at the hands of the Goddess results in his "conversion" from a "demon" to a "devotee," subsequently elevating his status to that of a guardian and bhakta par excellence of the goddess.[67]

In the *Kālikā Purāṇa*, for example, which is dedicated to the exploits and worship of the Goddess, the buffalo-demon Mahiṣāsūra, upon realizing in a dream that he will be beheaded by the Goddess, asks her for two boons: first, a share in the sacrifice; second; that he remain at her feet forever.[68] Since only the gods (devās) are allowed to have a share in the sacrifice, the Goddess grants Mahiṣāsura's second wish only.[69] As is evidenced by splendid temple reliefs and miniature paintings spanning over two thousand years, Mahiṣāsūra does remain at the Goddess's feet for all time.

The broad pattern of the *Kālikā-Purāṇa* myth and other myths, both oral and written, is also reflected in the Devnārāyaṇ narrative. To begin with, the Bagaṛāvats' great power and unending wealth is the product of a boon, or rather gift, given to them by Śiva on account of their act of extreme sacrifice performed in a previous existence in which they were Ṛṣis. Their deeds of heroic abandon, quintessentially symbolized by the incident in which they pour streams of alcohol onto the earth's surface and down into the underworld, angering Rājā Basak, parallel those of rampant, misbehaving *asuras*. As in the case of demons, a complaint reaches Viṣṇu. Since various gods are unwilling to kill the Bagaṛāvats, Viṣṇu calls on Śakti to destroy them. Before sending Śakti on her mission, Viṣṇu "tests" the brothers himself.[70]. Śakti incarnates herself as the daugher of a Rajput king. Later she is the cause for a battle between the Bagaṛāvats and Rāṇā, the Rajput chieftain of Rān City. The means she uses to incite the factions against one another are those of love and revenge, tricking each side into believing that she belongs exclusively to one of them. But in reality, like a "murderous," "virgin" bride, she makes certain that neither marriage is actually consummated. Thus, during the six weeks she spends with the Rāṇā as his newlywed bride, she refuses to play "dice" with him until he builds her a new palace. Once the palace is completed, she elopes with the Bagaṛāvats and thereby instigates the bloody conflict between them and the Rāṇā, once again avoiding intimate contact.[71]

In contrast to the puranic myth, the Bagaṛāvats are not the Goddess's adversaries who after their defeat become her steadfast devotees. There is no conversion here, since, unlike the asuras of various myths, the Bagaṛāvats are, prior to their deaths, already great bhaktas. In an important sense the Bagaṛāvats, as living symbols of ultimate devotion, *choose* to adopt a course leading to their own destruction.[72]

Devī and Devnārāyaṇ

From the preceding passages it is clear that the two parts of the narrative are significantly informed by two avataric strands, one belonging to the Goddess and the other belonging to Viṣṇu. It is also evident that the motivations and causes for the incarnations of the Goddess and Viṣṇu parallel the motivations and causes found in "classical" or epic sources. But it is also apparent that there are differences in the patterns that are existent in Sanskritic and other vernacular sources (written and oral). One of the primary differences, at least, is in the first part of the narrative, with regard to the consistent motif of "conversion" that is found in the puranic (and allied) myths. Although the brothers are slain by the Goddess on a mandate given to her by Viṣṇu that is identical to the one given in the case of asuras, they are not exactly "demon devotees" whose "mythologies are shaped by a theology of bhakti, or devotion, in which the gods repeatedly convert their demon adversaries—sometimes by defeating them, but more often by killing them (implying the principle of reincarnation)—into their devotees" (Hiltebeitel 1990: 1). Certainly the initial conditions for their destruction at the hands of the Goddess resemble those of errant demons, but the outcome of their encounter with the Goddess is not conversion. On the other hand the mythology of the narrative is definitely also "shaped by a theology of bhakti," but this bhakti is not something that needs to be drilled into the brothers' minds by way of submission and death. The imagery and ideology of bhakti plays a predominant role in the characterization and conception of the 24 brothers from the very opening episodes to its final end in the battle between them and the Rāṇā. Their bhakti is the extreme kind of devotion, characteristic of the lifestyle of warrior-ascetics, for whom renunciation and self-sacrifice in the arena of battle are a viable choice. First as Ṛṣis and later as the Bagaṛāvats, the brothers enter into a self-destructive pact with both Śiva and the Goddess.[73] The evidence of a premature death, precipitated by Śiva's hunger in the face of Brahmā's yajña and Bhavāni's awesome demands in the face of the great battle (mahābhārata) are contained by the ideology of renunciation (*tyāga*), bodily self-sacrifice (*balī-dāna*), and devotion (bhakti).[74] This is the renunciatory and devotional framework that transforms the potential tragedy of the circumstance into the positive qualities and powers of the "good" death of heroes.

Ultimately, both the Goddess and Devnārāyaṇ fulfil the well-known function of destroying those whom the gods have ordained for destruction: whereas Bhavānī slays the Bagaṛāvats, Devnārāyaṇ slays the Rāṇā. This secret pact between Bhavānī and Devnārāyaṇ is also paralleled in the connection between Devī and Kṛṣṇa that, for example, is illustrated in Arjuna's recitation of the *Durgā-Stotra* for the sake of conquering his enemies as he and Kṛṣṇa stand before the armies of the Kauravas: "Kṛṣṇa spoke (those) words for the sake of Arjuna's well-being: 'Having become pure, o great-armed one, being about to engage in battle, recite the *Durgā Stotra* for the sake of conquering (your) enemies.'"[75] Coburn (1991: 27) interprets these lines as a confirmation of the mutual redemptive functions of both Kṛṣṇa and Devī:

> The conclusion seems inevitable: The conception of deity as periodically incarnate for the sake of redeeming the world has been employed in the service of both Krishna and the Goddess. . . . That this affinity is not merely casual is suggested by the fact that virtually all the other early hymns to the Goddess as found in the *Mahābhārata* and *Harivaṃśa* contain the same emphasis on salvific activity in the teeth of adversity.

Similarly C. Vaudeville (1975: 104), in her seminal historical study of Kṛṣṇa-Gopāla, points out the connections between his worship and that of Devī by the Abhīras and other "non-Aryan" pastoral tribes inhabiting a large region of the Indian peninsula:

> It was probably the Abhīras and related castes who spread the legend of their hero, Kṛṣṇa-Gopalā, throughout India. But there is nothing to indicate that these tribes were Vaishnavite, or even that particular beliefs and traditions showed any affinities with the Brahmanical cult of Viṣṇu-Nārāyaṇa, and even less with the teaching of the *Bhagavad-Gītā*. Like all the non-Aryan castes from the North to the South of India the pastoral tribes recognized as the supreme deity the great goddess Devī, in her warlike form of Durgā or her fertile and maternal form of Umā, the wife of Rudra-Śiva. Still, today, even after the invasion of Vaishnava bhakti, the worship of the Devī remains the predominant religion among the lower strata of rural populations, particularly in the West and in Bengal.

Thus the intimate association between Devī and Kṛṣṇa, in structural, historical, and social terms, is deeply reflected in the two halves of the narrative of the Bagaṛāvats and Devnārāyaṇ.

Returning to Soifer's outline of basic motifs related to the avatāras of Viṣṇu, we find that in visible terms there are few parallels with Devnārāyaṇ. There is neither a special relationship to Indra borne out in the narrative nor is there a cosmogonic scenario invoked in which cosmic destruction and recreation are played out. Devnārāyaṇ as an avatāra does not assume the role of a mediator between two opposing groups, nor does he employ "deceit, guile, or trickery" to bring on a victory for the gods against the demons. And, finally, there is no famous "loophole in the law" that allows Devnārāyaṇ to circumvent a situation that has arisen because of a boon granted by the gods (usually Brahmā) to their demon adversaries. In fact the last three motifs would appear to suit the role of the Goddess in the narrative. It is she, more than Devnārāyaṇ, who "mediates" between the two groups represented by the Bagaṛāvats, and the Rāṇā; it is she who uses trickery and deceit to destroy the Bagaṛāvats who have been preordained to die. And, in a sense, it is through trickery and deceit that she also finds a solution to destroying the Bagaṛāvats, who, because of their flawless reverence and devotion to the gods, are considered unworthy of their anger. Devnārāyaṇ, on the other hand, does not assume these roles or strategies in (re)establishing his kingdom and defeating his enemy, the Rāṇā. The confrontation with the Rāṇā, though built up over a period of time in a number of episodes, is straightforward and direct. The strategy Devnārāyaṇ uses to "weaken" the Rāṇā's strength involves letting loose his herd of 980,000 cows and buffaloes into the Rāṇā's crops, thereby destroying the latter's "wealth."

But if we consider the narrative as a whole—invoking the Goddess and Devnārāyaṇ in the first and the second parts, with the "great battle" in the center—we may discern certain other overall features of the checklist provided by Soifer. To begin with, the imagery of the first part, especially in its culmination in the "great battle," is strongly reminiscent of the *pralaya.* Although the battle does not involve the destruction of the entire world, the magnitude of the scene and the pivotal role played by the goddess in secretly decapitating the heroes with her discus and later stringing a necklace of their heads while squatting blood-drenched on the battlefield is nevertheless undoubtedly pralayic in nature.[76] It certainly involves the end of one major generational cycle in the epic, in which rebirths (of the heroes) are also terminated. The pralayic imagery[77] is simultaneously accompanied by the imagery of renewal, re-creation, and rejuvenation. The recreative period is marked by the manifestation of Bhagavān in the person of Devnārāyaṇ. His appearance shortly after the great battle is concluded signifies a reversal of the destructive and sorrow-ridden character of the first part. The key term used here is that of parcyos, or miracles, wonders, and "testimony." It would also be accurate to claim that Devnārāyaṇ appears precisely at the "interstitial" moment of the great war between his ancestors and the Rāṇa. The circumstances of his birth, I will discuss in more detail in chapter 7, are surrounded by the symbols of danger and destruction. But his birth, I have pointed out, ushers in a new *sattā*, or reign of sovereignity or power. While Devnārāyaṇ does not play the role of a mediator accumulating "power by positioning himself 'betwixt and between' two opposing groups," he does represent the avatāric functions of protecting the world and defending the dharma, even if the world and the dharma are only defined by the cosmos of his cult and his devotees. Similarly, he is an "unlikely hero, the 'underling made uppermost' "—an outsider arising as it were not only from the underworld but also from a pastoral background.[78]

In this chapter I have shown that the verbal and visual narrative, or *text*, of Devnārāyaṇ can be understood, or rather *imagined*, by placing it within a framework of *interrelating* texts. It is the intertextual field that determines the constellation of verbal and visual imagery, particularly in the religious context. While certain motifs give the impression of being "fragmentary" elements inserted into the text to support a specific purpose, others occupy a much more central position by determining the overall ideology of the text. This is distinctively true for the idea of the avatāra, which, rather than having the peripheral status of a "late" "strata," lies at the core of the text, serving as a medium for providing its intrinsic literary *and* religious constitution, which on the level of meaning can scarcely be separated from one another. The idea of the avatāra is thus the "code" through which the text receives shape and is made meaningful. This is expressed in the various "foreground" incarnations depicted on the paṛ, as well the "background" incarnations in the verbal narrative with regard to figures such as the Rāṇa, Dīyājī Jodhkā, Devnārāyaṇ's father and brothers, and so on. Above all, it is Devnārāyaṇ and Bhavānī who express this idea in its fullest form, replicating and reworking patterns fundamental to some of the deepest and most intricate structures of Hinduism as a whole. Thus on the one hand the notion of the avatāra is instrumental in establishing linkages within a general field of narratives of which that of Devnārāyaṇ forms a part. On the other hand, it provides a linkage between the two halves of the narrative and their seemingly divergent religious ideologies. Finally, the religious structure of the narrative is intimately informed by the notion of the avatāra and that of bhakti. Given the extremely complex nature of the imagery, conceptualizations, and interconnections that arise in this context, saturated as they are with the motifs of the avatāra, bhakti, rebirth and reincarnation, and destruction and renewal, it would seem virtually impossible to conceive of a slow, purposeful development that began without them.

5
Historical Narrative

> The concept of history . . . has been placed under epistemological scrutiny. Left behind is history "in the raw" and Ranke's dictum of *"wie es eigentlich gewesen ist"* (how things really were). . . . Such polarities as history from below versus history from above, event history versus serial history, the native view of history versus the outsider's view of history all point to the complexity and multiplicity of what we call history.
>
> —E. Ohnuki-Tierney, *Culture through Time*

If the idea of the avatāra serves as a link between different texts and different religious ideologies within the narrative of Devnārāyaṇ, it also, quite obviously, serves as a link between different cycles of time. It provides a bridge between different periods of the past, and to the present, furnishing a framework for establishing temporal and material continuity. Within this framework, the condition of the present is perceived of as a replica of the condition of the past: the present repeats and resembles the past. But it is through the mundaneness of repetition rather than the exclusiveness of linearity, that time itself is embellished and adorned. The narrative is, thus, couched within a discourse on time that in turn creates a discourse on the "history" of Devnārāyaṇ, and the community of people who worship him. The notion of the avatāra coupled with the notion of yugas, or time cycles, therefore, provides the devotees of Devnārāyaṇ with a platform for extending their cult deeply into the past. But besides articulating a history of the deity and his devotees, the narrative also expresses a history that competes with and contests local and regional histories within the cultural and political region of Rajasthan. In other words, the narrative supplies us not only with a religiously oriented "history of the god" but also a politically oriented history that, by virtue of its "peripheral" status within the dominant history of Rajasthan, may be regarded as a "counterhistory." Thus the narrative does not merely provide us with an "oral history" that can be used as a source to reconstruct the history of social groups: it need not be seen as an attempt to record "real" or "testifiable" facts in terms of a "Western" historiography. It is, above all, an "imagined" or "constructed" history of the community of worshipers. But this "imagined" history, as pointed out in the introductory chapter, may be considered no more or no less "subjective" or "objective" than the well-researched history of scholars.[1]

This chapter is devoted to an understanding of the interconnected discourses on time and history that the narrative deals with. The materials for this are primarily provided by the oral telling of the narrative, recited by Śrī Hukamārām Bhopā, along with the opening passages of a recently printed version of the narrative, told by another singer, Śrī Aṇandārām. In addition, there is also a reference to a shorter orally told story that, like the printed text, also deals with the "origins" of Devnārāyaṇ's main devotees, the Gujars.

Although the oral and printed tellings constitute distinct streams within the narrative tradition as a whole,[2] they will, on one level, be treated as belonging to a single, seamless narrative, so as to grasp the breadth of the discourse on history the narrative represents. On another level there will be comparison of the two versions, oral and printed, in order to point out certain important differences. While to a large degree these differences relate to an emphasis on *time* versus an emphasis on *place*, they also result in part not only from there being different versions but also from the transformations the oral narrative undergoes through the medium of the printed text. In very immediate terms, for example, with regard to style, the printed text no longer makes use of the dialogic and repetitive structure of the oral narrative. Instead, there are long spoken passages bordering on monologue.[3] In terms of content, the printed text has an extreme concern with lengthy genealogical lists and the creation of lineages that begin with the very inception of time. In fact, in the printed text we find all the markings of a purāṇa. The puranic character of the text is devised, as will become clear later, by heavily drawing on puranic and epic sources. However, quite explicitly, the printed text flourishes not only by a simple borrowing but by a masterful alteration of these sources. Like the oral narrative, the printed text too is thereby sustained by the reflexive possibilities of intertextuality.

While as a genealogical account, the printed text focuses primarily on the endurance of the Gujar community, the oral narrative contains important passages in which the role and identity of Gujars, along with other social groups, as part of the larger *community of devotees* is reflected upon. The religious framework of the narrative provides us here with metaphors and models for imagining social identities that, in contrast to the reality of everyday life, are perceived of as "commingling," ambivalent, and interchangeable. Sociality too, like the narrative text, has blurred boundaries and is defined in terms of mergers and overlappings.[4] Within this framework there are also sections of the oral narrative that build a case for understanding it as constructing a "counterhistory" that undermines the mainstream Rajput history of Rajasthan. This point is particularly exemplified with regard to the longstanding relationship of kinship *and* conflict between Devnārāyaṇ and his devotees. These are constituted by Gujars, Kumhārs, Guāls, and Bhābhis on the one hand and the Rajput Rāṇā together with his Rajput and Paṭhān confederates on the other.

The Printed Text

Although in the preface to the printed text the publishers claim that the book is a record of the spoken words of the singer, the passages do not in any way read as sections of an oral narrative. It appears that the medium of the written or printed word has pressed the compilers of the text to change the nature of the spoken narrative. There are, therefore, no passages consisting of sung verse (gāv), and no syntactical breaks marking the speech of different singers. Even though the text proceeds on the basis of dialogues between characters, the dialogues themselves are lengthy, giving the impression of spoken passages rather than brief sentences. Moreover, the printed text makes direct use of names and characters from the purāṇas. This is evident in the opening paragraphs, which outline a genealogy beginning with Svāyambhuva Manu and his wife Śatarūpā. Judging from the names of persons[5] and places,[6] and the chronology given here, the compilers seem to have drawn considerably from the *Bhāgavata Purāṇa* to establish their own text. The printed text is entitled:

Bagaṛāvat Bhārat
Śrī Devnārāyaṇ Kī Kathā
(Vīr Gurjar Utpatti)
Speaker:
Śrī Aṇandārām
Writer (Copyist):
Rāmnārāyāṇ
Sole distributors:
Phūlcand Book Seller
Purānī Maṇḍī, Ajmer (Raj.)

The inside cover page also mentions the publishers: *Arcanā Prakāśan, Ajmer.* No publication date is given, but it would be safe to assume that the book was printed between the late 1970s and mid-1980s.

On the page where the narrative begins, the title is elaborated further. Here we have:

Śrī Rāmjī
Devnārāyaṇ Kī Kathā
known as
Bagaṛāvat Bhārat
Vīr Gurjar Utpatti: Gurjar Dharmkathā
Śrī Gaṇeśāya Namaḥ

On the page preceding the commencement of the narrative, there is a photograph of the singer, accompanied by biographical details about both the singer and the copyist. This is called *vācak-lipikār-paricay*, or "singer-writer-introduction." The short biographies identify the village, *jātī*, *got*, and immediate family of the singer and copyist. In addition to this, the religious affiliation of the singer is mentioned as belonging to the Rāmāvat *sampradāya* and the Rām Jaygam *akhāḍā*.[7]

The subtitle of the printed text makes it clear that the Bagaṛāvat Bhārat or Śrī Devnārāyaṇ Kathā is also about the origins of *Vīr Gurjars* or of "brave," "mighty," "warrior," or "excellent" Gurjars, as the Gujars call themselves in order to highlight their status as Kṣatriyas. Thus in terms of the compilers' perception the story of Devnārāyaṇ the god is also the story (or rather history) of the community of his main worshipers, namely the Gujars.[8] An extension of the history of the god into past eons, as the passages that follow show, is simultaneously an elaboration of the history of the community. The community of devotees is, therefore, not just a socially defined unit but an irrevocable part of the religious or sacred discourse built around the figure of Devnārāyaṇ, who, as will be shown, is in reality an incarnation of Pārbṛhm Parameśvar.

After paying reverence to Gaṇeśa (*śrī gaṇeśāya namaḥ*), the printed text begins with a *dohā* (couplet) calling on the the "five" gods Śāradā, Gaṇeśa, Brahmā, Viṣṇu, and Maheśa for protection. Thereafter follows a *kavitta*[9] of six lines, in which Gaṇeśa is again remembered, along with Sarasvatī and one's own guru.[10] After this the text says: "The story of the Gurjars begins" (*Gurjar kathā prārambh*).

> I remember mother Śārad and Surasat, you are full of greatness.[11]
> Reveal to us the secret of how the Gurjars, the Bagaṛāvats, arose.
>
> I take Śrī, Śrī, Śrī 108 Guru Govind's permission.
> I will always sing the Bagaṛāvat-story.
> The Gurjar succession is most excellent.
> Śaṅkar will visit their home.
>
> The world created by grace or by offering[12] was as follows: On Śrī Tenth Sun, Tenth Moon on the twelfth with the authority of ṛṣis, Brahmā and Viṣṇu performed a yajña, out of which [they] first extracted the Paṅvār, then the Piḍyār, then [they] extracted the Solaṅkī, after that they extracted Chatrapati Cuhān.[13]
>
> This is creation through cohabitation: Svāyambhuv [*sic*] Manu, from Satrūpā's womb two sons and three daughters were born; the elder was Utānpād, the younger Prīyavrat. There were three daughters. 1. Ākolī, 2. Prasutī, 3. Devahutī. Utanpād had two wives; the elder Sunitī, the younger Surucī. From Surucī's womb was born Dhunjī Mahārāj. Devahutī was married to a ṛṣi called Kardam. To them Kapil Muni Bhagavān took avatār, and nine girls [were born]. To their husband Brahmājī [were] born nine boys—ṛṣis. Utānpād had Dhunjī Mahārāj; Dhunjī had two boys: Matsya and Aṅgdev. After bestowing them with the kingdom [he] departed to Baikuṇṭh. Prīyavrat's wife's name was Viśvakarmā. From his second wife Barhismatī's womb, who was Dakṣa Prajāpatīs daughter-[from] Barhismatī there were 10 sons. 1. Āgnidhra, 2. Idhmajir, 3. Yajñabāhū, 4. Mahāvīr, 5. Hiraṇyaretā, 6. Dhṛtapṛṣṭh, 7. Savan, 8. Medhatithi, 9. Ditīhom, 10. Kavi. Of these 1. Kavi, 2. Mahābīr, 3. Savan remained child ascetics [*bālbrahmacārī*]. There were three boys from Prīyavratjī's other wife Viśvakarmā, 1. Uttam, 2. Tāmaś, 3. Raivat. The three of them became Manus later on. Prīyavratjī worshiped Satlok. Because of this devotion, he received a chariot of Truth from Satlok.
>
> [He] drove that chariot over the earth, by the tracks made by its wheels. Seven oceans were made; in the seven oceans there re-

mained seven mountains from which seven islands were named: 1. Jambū, 2. Plakṣa, 3. Śālamil, 4. Kuśa, 5. Karogdha, 6. Śāka, 7. Puṣkara. The seven oceans were: 1. Kṣārod, 2. Ikṣursod, 3. Surod, 4. Ghṛtod, 5. Kṣīrod, 6. Dadhi Manḍod, 7. Śudhod. Āgnīdhra became the ruler of Jambū Island; from the womb of the *apsarā* Pūrvaciti were born nine sons to him: 1. Nābhī, 2. Kimpuruṣa, 3. Harivarṣa, 4. Ilāvṛta, 5. Rambaka, 6. Hiraṇmaya, 7. Kuru, 8. Bhadrāśva, 9. Ketūmāl. After dividing his kingdom in nine parts to those sons, Āgnīdhra took refuge by Rāma [*rāmasaraṇ*]. It's after their names that the nine divisions [*khaṇḍa*] and nine temples [*devrā*] of Pārbṛhm Parameśvar have been called. After them during the period of Rāma's avatāra, Gopāl was also a devotee [*bhakta*].

The aforementioned 17 bhaktas existed during the Satjug. Āgnīdhra had nine boys, so together in the lineage of those very nine boys are the nine yoked [*nāglī*] Gujars. Ṛṣis Priyabrat [*sic*] was an inhabitant of Avadhpurī. The lineages of the country of Gujarat are listed in the following: Hor, Mevātī, Rabārī, Gāḍarī, Māhī, Dāṣavī, Candelā, Mareṭhā, Kāmalyā.[14] In the Satjug they were called Gurujar [*sic*] and used to take care of all the cows; all the cows were given to them by Pārbṛhm Parameśvar. "You will receive the fruits of serving them now, later." Suvāī Manu, Satarūpā set up samādhī in the name of Pārbṛhm Parameśvar on Mount Meru. Now many eons passed doing *tap*. Because of their *sat* the lion-throne of Brahmā, Viṣṇu, and Mahādev began quivering. So Viṣṇu Bhagavān departed from Baikuṇṭh; Śaṅkar Bhagavān departed from Kailaś; Brahmājī Mahāraj from Brahmalok.[15]

Each of the three gods sat in their celestial chariots and arrived at Mount Meru. They arrived there where Savāī Manu [*sic*] and Satrūpājī were sitting in samādhī [on] Meru, Sumeru, Acalā, Macalā, Mandrāsī, Droṇācala, Govardhana, Bandecala—there are these eight mountains. Akṣarjī Mahārāj is the guru of these 8 mountains. Brahmājī gazed on the samādhī even then they didn't come out of samādhī. Viṣṇu Bhagavān gazed on the samādhī, even then the samādhī didn't "open." All three gods gazed [on them], but still the samādhī didn't open. They spoke through ether voices: "Oh Suvāī Manu, oh Satrūpā, you've done great service, there's no flaw in your penance. While you did penance, termites have crawled over you. The termites have eaten away your blood and flesh. Only bones remain, even then you haven't stopped from muttering Rām's name. So there's no taint in your penance. We three gods are pleased with you. Oh Savāī Manu, oh Satrūpā, ask for whatever you desire, we will grant you whatever you ask for. We three gods, will give you whatever you want. If you want to rule [over a kingdom] we will give you an inviolable kingdom. If you desire grains and wealth we'll give you plenty of that. If you want to go to Baikuṇṭh we'll put Baikuṇṭh in your reach."

Using the ether voice Savāī Manu, Satrūpā spoke: "Oh, Brahmājī Mahārāj you please go and look after Brahmalok; oh Viṣṇu Bhagavān you too go and look after your City of Baikuṇṭh; oh Śrī Śaṅkar Bhagavān, you too go and look after your Kailāś. We don't ask you for anything!" Then Śaṅkar Bhagavān spoke: "Oh Savāī Manu, oh Satrūpā whose [name] are you repeating? Whose name are you extolling?" Then Suvāī Manu said: "I'm repeating Rām's name and extolling Rām." Then Śaṅkar Bhagavān said: "Who is this other Rām? All the three gods are standing in front of you!" Even Śrī Viṣṇu is present [*se hi had che*]! Then whom are you worshiping?" Then Suvāī Manu, Satrūpā said: "Not one of you three are Rām. You are the three guṇas in Rām: Viṣṇu [is] *satoguṇ*, Brahmā [is] *rajoguṇ*, Śaṅkar [is] *tamoguṇ*. I am meditating on that Rām. I worship him who gave birth to the three gods; gave birth to Brahmā, Viṣṇu, Umeśa." Śaṅkar Bhagavān said: "Oh Suvāī Manu, which Rām is that?" Then Suvāī Manu said: "Oh Śaṅkar Bhagavān, that Rām is Pārbṛhm Parameśvar. He gave birth to Brahmā, Viṣṇu, Mahādev—to these three gods." Then Brahmājī said: "What do you want from that Rām?" Then Viṣṇu Bhagavān spoke: "Oh Suvāī Manu, whatever your wish is, I will fulfil it!" Suvāī Manu said: "Oh Rām, I don't ask for anything from you three gods!"

Brahmājī Mahārāj left for Brahmalok; Śaṅkar Bhagavān left for his Kailāś. Viṣṇu left from there to the untainted, formless [place]. [He] went to Pārbṛhm Parameśvar.

Pārbṛhm Parameśvar spoke: "Welcome Viṣṇu! You've shown great kindness in coming to Nirañjan! Due to what reason have you come?" Śrī Viṣṇu Bhagavān said: "Oh Lord, I have come to you." "If you've come, then speak up! What brings you here?" "Oh Lord, a devotee called Suvāī Manu and his wife Satrūpā, both wife and husband, have set up samādhī on Mount Meru. They are repeating your name. Termite mounds are creeping over them. Many eons have passed in their performing penance. There's no blood or flesh left on their bodies, only bones remain, and [yet] they're worshiping and extolling you. On account of the heat [tap] of those ascetics the entire earth is shaking. They are remembering you. Suvāī Manu and Satrūpā told me that only if Pārbṛhm Parameśvar Jyotiṣa Sadrūpī [*sic*] visits us and grants us darśan will we end our samādhī, only then will we leave our places. Otherwise we will not leave our seats. Only when that Jyotiṣa-Svarūpī [*sic*] Bhagavān Pārbṛhm Parameśvar grants us darśan will we leave our samādhī, only then will our mind's desire be fulfilled. Oh Lord, that Suvāī Manu requests you; when will you grant him darśan?" Pārbṛhm Parameśvar said: "Oh Viṣṇu, on account of the sat of Suvāī Manu and Satrūpā even the lion-throne of Satlok has begun to quiver!"

"Oh Viṣṇu, let's sit in the flower chariot [*puṣpa vimān*] and visit Suvāī Manu!" Śrī Pārbṛhm Parameśvar and Viṣṇu Bhagavān both sat in their flower chariots and went to Suvāī Manu and Satrūpā on Mount Meru. After arriving on Mount Meru, Pārbṛhm Parameśvar gazed at the samādhī of Suvāī Manu and Satrūpā, so they broke their samadhī, and both received copper-colored [*tāmbā-barṇī*] bodies, and both stood up and fell at Rām's feet: "Oh Lord you've done us a great favor by granting us *sadrūp darśan*. Pārbṛhm Parameśvar said: "Oh Suvāī Manu, Satrūpā, you've done lots of [*śāk?*] worship and service, there's no taint in your service. Oh Suvāī Manu, oh Satrūpā, I'm satisfied with you. Ask for whatever you desire, and you shall receive whatever you demand." "Oh Lord, I will certainly ask for something, but I will ask [for it] when you give me a promise. Oh Lord, I request you to give me your word. When you give me your word, I will ask from you what I desire. If you don't give me your word, I will not ask you for anything. This is all I request you to do, to give me your word by your hand." "Oh Suvāī Manu, Satrūpā, here take my word. Whatever you ask for I will give you. Whatever your desire is, just ask for it, you will get whatever you ask for." Satrūpā, Savāī Manu stood and bowed their heads to [his] feet. With folded palms together they say: "Oh Lord, we desire this, we don't want grains, we don't want wealth, and we don't want to be without decay or be immortal. The only request we have is that someone like you take incarnation with us, and be called our son. This our desire and longing, fulfil it! . . .

"Oh Rām! We've seen you as an adult, but we desire and long to see your life as a child [*bāl-caritra*], fulfil [this longing]. Oh Rāṃ! Pārbṛhm Parameśvar, I have the desire and longing to feed you in my lap on two occasions: Please fulfil this [desire]." "Oh Suvāī Manu, oh Satrūpā, what you ask for [from me] is good; I will take incarnation twice, and be known as your son. I will satisfy your desire." Suvāī Manu, Satrūpā bowed and said: "Oh Lord! Please listen to another request of ours. About this lineage of ours which began from the lineage of Prīyavrat from the seven islands, what action and duties will be theirs, and who will they serve?" "Oh Suvāī Manu, oh Satrūpā, all the cows will be given to your lineage, and [your lineage] will serve all these cows, and will enjoy [*khātā-pītā*] butter and dried fruits [*mākhan-mevā*], and you will keep offering me food; I too am very pleased about this matter.[16] I will continue to take avatār in this form, and will continue to eat butter and crystallized sugar [*miśrī*]. What happened did so rightly during the avatāra of Kṛṣṇa; your lineage which appeared as the *govcar* lineage will be called Gūrjar in the satjug.

"Oh Suvāī Manu and Satrūpā! Whatever you asked for, your mind's desire will be fulfiled; now I go—if there's anything else you want, tell me." "Oh Lord! Oh Rām! Since you're going I want to talk [to you] about two things. Oh Pārbṛhm Parameśvar! When will you take incarnation with us? When will my desire be fulfilled? I am asking you this with hands joined together, and tell me this news." "Oh Suvāī Manu and Satrūpā, one time I will take incarnation with you when Ṛṣi Kaśyapjī manifests [himself]. Ṛṣi Kaśyapjī will have two wives, Kudrā and Bīntī. From Kudrā's womb will be born the nine Nāga lineages; from Bīntā's [*sic*] womb two boys will be born, Harūṇ, Garuḍ.[17] Harūṇ will drive Sūrya's chariot; Garuḍ will always remain in Rām's service. Garuḍ will take his mother Bīntā's permission and advice: 'Oh mother! What shall I do?' Bīntā will say: 'Oh son, go, whatever food you come across, eat that, and go into Rām's service.' Listening to this Garuḍ will depart from that place. From there he will go into the ocean; he will catch a big crocodile from the ocean; he will take the crocodile and fly off to Mount Sumer and sit down there; Mount Sumer is of gold: so sitting on it he will think of preparing himself a meal, when, because of the weight of the crocodile and Garuḍ and the swiftness of the wind, the mountain will split apart. Beneath that mountain there will be the samādhī of Kapil Munī. Then Garuḍ will reflect, that when the mountain splits apart the Muni Mahātmā will die; thinking of this, when the mount splits apart Garuḍ will fly off with a piece [of mountain] and the crocodile. [He] will keep circling between the earth and the sky. And, he will keep reflecting upon where he can sit down and eat his food; wandering about he will meet his brother Harūṇ, who will be driving the sun's chariot; he will ask Garuḍ: 'Oh Garuḍ, what are you wandering about for?' Garuḍ will say: 'Where should I sit down and eat?' Harūṇ will say: 'Sit in my hand and eat.' Then Garuḍ will sit down on that Harūṇ's empty hand and begin to eat his meal. Sitting down he will begin to eat; after eating his food he will throw down that crocodile's cage and that piece of gold [from the mountain] onto an island in the seven oceans.[18] Wandering about, Śaṅkar Bhagavān will arrive there and will enquire regarding the kind of devatās who are Gandharvas. 'Oh devatās! From where and from whom did this mountain of gold come?' Then the kind of devatās who are Gandharvas will speak to Śaṅkar Bhagavān with palms joined together: 'Oh Śaṅkar Bhagavān, I don't know who brought it, but Garuḍjī brought it, and Garuḍjī threw it down here.' Then Śaṅkar will call the craftsman called Viśvakarmā; after calling him he had some pieces made of that mountain of gold. Having had that done, he had seven substances taken out of it. And, from those seven metals [he will] make houses; on that island he will set up a great and mighty city; that city's name will be Laṅkā. Listen, hey Suvāī Manu, there will be this many houses in Laṅkā: 5 *kroṛ* houses will be made of stones and 9 *lakh* houses of wood, 3 kroṛ of bronze, 4 kroṛ of copper, 100 kroṛ of reed, 6 kroṛ of silver, 2 kroṛ of jewels,[19] and 100 kroṛ pairs of diamonds. Look, hey Suvāī Bhoj at the length of 13 kos there will be 100 houses of diamonds, 15 kroṛ huts of grass will be made. Look, hey, Suvāī Manu all together there will be 2 *arab*, 15 kroṛ, 4,096 gateways where the king of Laṅkā will live. Musical instruments will play continously for him. There will be seven golden forts in his ocean moat.[20] Look, hey, Suvāī Manu, I'm telling you what is going to happen [in the future], and I told you before the description of Laṅkā; in this very Laṅkā—Bisvejī—who will be Ṛṣi Pulast's daughter—a devotee will be born, and that devotee will worship Śivjī; with her worship Śaṅkar will be pleased. After being pleased[21] Śaṅkar will tell her "Ask for whatever you want." Then Śrī Bhakta Bisvejī will stand in front of Śaṅkar with hands joined together and say: "Oh Śaṅkar Bhagavān, I will ask you only then when you promise me." So Śaṅkar Bhagavān will make her a promise. As soon as [he] makes her a promise [she] will ask for Laṅkā. Śaṅkar Bhagavān will give that Laṅkā to Bisvejī as a gift.

"Look, Suvāī Manu, such a mighty one as Rāvaṇ will be born, [that] Indra will fill water for him, Baimātā will feed his horses with grain, Pavan will do the sweeping. He'll tie Kālan to an arrow-pillar [*tīr thambak*]. He will imprison the nine gods of the planets[22] in nine step cages.[23] He will capture the 33 kroṛ gods and goddesses and put them into prison. His son, Meghnāth, will be victorious over Indra. His elder brother, Kuṃbhakaraṇ, will be victorious over enemies; Kuṃbhakaraṇ will defeat Andra [*sic*] 17 times. Such a mighty warrior Kuṃbhakaraṇ will be. He will have one lakh 80,000 lineage and caste brothers [*nyāti goto*]. Rāvaṇ will have one son named Nārāṇatak,[24] whose birth will take place in the *mūl nakṣatra*. Upon seeing his face, Rāvaṇ's own death will come nearer. He will throw that Nārāṇatak into the ocean, and he will float to Bimal country. In Bimal country a great family of Nārāṇatak's will prosper. In that Laṅkā will be a bhakta called Vibhīkṣaṇ. A great tulsī plant in Rām's name will grow in his house.

"Oh, Suvāī Manu, a *rā̃gaṣ* [demon] will be born to the bhakta called Bisvejī, who will have 10 heads and 10 arms. That rā̃gas will be very badly behaved, and that rā̃gas' name will be Rāvaṇ.[25] That same Rāvaṇ will destroy dharam on this earth [and] increase evil.[26]

"Then, look, hey Suvāī Manu, on the banks of the Sarjū River there will be a city called Ayodhya; in that city there will appear a king called Raghu in the lineage of the Sun; you will have to take birth in the family of that Raghu. In that birth you will have to assume two bodies. In one body you'll have to go and perform tapasya in the form of 23 ṛṣis; in the second body you'll go and become King Daṣarath of Ayodhya; this wife of yours, Satrūpā, will take birth as the king of Kauśalpur. You'll have to take birth at King Kauśal's house. Her name will be Kauśalyā. Then your second wife will be Kaikeī, the daughter of King Kaikay. Then your third wife will be Queen Sumitrā, who will be the daughter of King Samudra [*sic*].

"Look, hey, Suvāī Manu, then I will take avatār with you. Śeśjī will also come, Viṣṇu will also come, oh Suvāī Manu, Dharamrājjī will also come. The four of us will satisfy your desires. We will fulfil our promise completely, the satjug will come to an end, and the *tretājug* will begin. Then I will take avatār, and then I will become your son, and play in your lap, and will show my childhood to you. Of the two promises, one I will fulfil then. Oh, Suvāī Manu, during that time in Janakpur, a king Janak will be born; Rājā Janak's younger brother will be Kuśketū. In the home of that king Janak, Lakṣmī will take birth; her name will be Sītā. Kuśketū will have three daughters: Urmilā, Catrā, Māṇḍavī. These three girls will be born to Kuśketū; then all of us four brothers will be married in Janakpur. Look, hey, Suvāī Manu, my name will be the avatār of Pārbṛhm Parameśvar, Rāmcandra; Śeṣa's avatār Lakṣmaṇ; Viṣṇu's avatāra's will be Bharatjī. Dharamrājjī's avatār will be Satrughnajī; Rāmcandrajī's marriage will be with Jānakījī. Lakṣmaṇjī's marriage will be with Urmilā, Bharatjī's marriage will be with Māndavī. Satrughnajī's marriage will be with Catrā.

"Suvāī Manu, I will then launch an attack on Laṅkā with 18 infantry battalions [*padam bal phauj*], I will build a bridge [*saṣya?*] across the ocean; after killing Rāvaṇ I will hand over the rule of Laṅkā to Vibhikṣaṇ. I will perform this *līlā* when I take avatār with you, I will release all the gods and goddesses from their captivity, and destroy the demons [*rākṣasās*]. I won't let the name *rākṣas* exists on this earth. I will destroy evil. I will increase dharam. I will take this incarnation in the thirty-eighth generation of the Sun Lineage." Suvāī Manu and Satrūpā prayed again with their hands joined: "Oh Lord! When will you come as an avatār a second time, describe that also to us." "Oh Suvāī Manu, oh Satrūpā! I will come as an avatār for the second time when the tretājug will come to an end, and the *kaljug* will begin. I will take incarnation in your lineage [*kul*]. Oh Suvāī Manu, oh Satrūpā! There will be a town called Fort Badnor. Go to Fort Badnor! When your lineage is flourishing, in some lineage of the cattle-grazing Gujars I will take incarnation. This Satrūpā will become Satvantī Sāḍū in Devā̃s in the Country Malwā. The 23 ṛṣis will be with you, together with you, you will be 24; so Śrī Bāghrāvat will manifest in Fort Badnor, and the avatār will be called Bagaṛāvat. Suvāī Bhoj your marriage will be with Satvantī Sāḍū in the village of Devā̃s in Malwā. Then I will come as an avatār the second time, oh Suvāī Manu, oh Satrūpā! When I take avatār for the second time, my younger brothers from the earlier time will also take avatār, Lacchmaṇ, Bharat, Śatrughnajī. In Lacchmaṇ's avatār Bhuṇājī will manifest; in Bharat's avatār Bhā̃gījī. Satrughnajī's avatār will manifest [as] Medujī. My name in the first avatār will be Rāmcandrajī and in the second birth I will appear with the name Śrī Devnārāyaṇjī. That king of Laṅkā Rāvaṇ will become Rāṇājī in Fort Rāṇ in the Country Mārvāṛ. Then that evil demon will resort to old ways [*jūṇī-darsābā*] and will dam up the embankment where the cows drink water from.[27] Oh Suvāī Manu, Satrūpā then I will take avatār with you and kill the Rāṇā of 'nine citadeled' [*nau koṭi*] Mārvāṛ, and lessen the earth's burden. I will free the captivity of the cows. I will show my second avatār in the present. I will dig evil's destruction, [and] increase dharam. In the future I will take sides with the dharam. In order to increase dharam and to destroy evil will I take incarnation. . . .[28]

On the lunar date 7 of the light half of the month of Vaiṣākh in the year Samat [*sic*] 361, the Bagaṛāvats died in the Bhārat.[29] On the lunar date 7 of the light half of the month Bhādrā in the year Samant [*sic*] 361 Līlāgar, the foal took birth from the mare Tejan. On the night of the sixth and seventh, Sāḍū Mātā, in a dream, had darṣan of Pārbṛhm Parameśvar. "Oh, Mother Sāḍū, I gave you a promise in an earlier life. I will fulfil that promise on the seventh day of the light half of the month of Māh at night on Saturday; Mother Sāḍū, the suffering of many lives will be destroyed. . . . The rock split apart on the hill of Mālāserī, a stream of water arose, and in a lotus blossom the radiance of Bhagavān Devnārāyaṇ appeared. Out of the [lotus] blossom's bud [*taḍakī*]—out of the flower's bud, a child took birth into Mother Sāḍū's shoulder sash [*jholī*]. His family name was Dev [*kul mẽ Dev kuhāyā*], on the lunar date 7 in the bright half of the month Māh in the year Samvat 361, Devnārāyaṇ took birth in this family; in Sāḍū Satvantī's shoulder sash Pārbṛhm Parameśvar Bhagavān appeared on his own and was called Dev as the family name.[30] When Dev was born, the forests and gardens [*upvan*] turned green and began blooming, rivers, streams and lakes filled up, on blades of grass various birds delighted, and in Goṭhā Town and in each and every town and village there was celebration; Brahmaṇs performed yajñas, in all the 10 directions the guardians of the quarters were joyous [*harṣa ne bādal*]; circling Mālaserī, the gods showered flowers from the sky seated in their celestial chariots; Vidhyadhars, Gandharvas, Cárṇas played drums [*damāke*] and sang praises; and Uravasī together with other *apsarās* were dancing.

Interpretations

It is significant that the printed text begins with an account of creation from two points of view, namely, through the cosmogonic ritual of the yajña and through the act of procreation. Both these two forms of creation are, not surprisingly, thoroughly rooted in the cosmogonic myths and rituals of the *Śrauta Sūtras* and

Brāhmaṇas. These pervade the ideological and social levels through the notions of *nivṛtti* ("renunciation," religious orders at the periphery of "ordered" society) and *pravṛtti* ("being in the world," duties and obligations of the householder, world-order based on dharma).[31] Although short, the description of creation through Brahmā and Viṣṇu's yajña is important because it recollects the creation of the agni-kula Rajputs. Here four clans are mentioned: the Panvār (Pavār), Piḍyār (Paḍīhār), Solankī, and Cuhān (Cauhān). The Cuhāns are called Chatrapatīs, or "kings with the emblem of a parasol."

In the context of this chapter dealing with the construction of a "Gujar history," at least two names are also significant because they also refer to Gujar clan names that are shared with Rajput clan names: Panvār and Cuhān.[32] The myth of the creation of Rajput clans through cosmogonic ritual is, thus, also appropriated as a story about the origin of Gujar clans. However, as is apparent from its length and detail, a major emphasis in the text is placed on "biological" creation to explain both the origin of Devnārāyaṇ and the Gujars. The forefathers of the Gujars and Devnārāyaṇ are none other than the very first human pair, Svāyambhuva Manu and Satarūpā (Śatarūpā). The genealogy of the god and his devotees therefore extends not to a point in historical memory but to the very beginning of human time in the Kṛta or Satya Yuga. Nine lineages are born from the nine sons of Āgnīdhra: Lor, Mavati, Rabārī, Gāḍarī, Māhī, Dāṣavī, Candelā, Mareṭhā, and Kāmalyā, who in the "satjug" were called Gurjars. It is Pārbṛhm Parameśvar himself who gives them protection over cows. Meanwhile Svayambhu Manu, whose name has already been shortened to Suvāī Manu—strongly resembling his future appellation Savāī Bhoj—meditates together with his wife Satarūpā (who will be called Satvantī Sāḍū later) on the highest godhead, Pārbṛhm Parameśvar. Not satisfied with the manifestations of the three gods Brahmā, Viṣṇu, and Śiva, they continue to wish for a darśan of that "Rām" who is the progenitor of the three gods—the supreme, flawless Being. When Pārbṛhm Parameśvar grants them a boon, there is nothing else they wish for but to have him born on two separate occasions as their son. The first occasion, Pārbṛhm Parameśvar reveals, will be in the "tretājug," when Suvāī Manu will be born as King Daṣarath and Satarūpā as his wife, Kauśalyā. Parameṣvar will be their son, Rāmcandra, who incarnates himself to free the earth of the evil demon-king of Lankā, Rāvaṇa. The second manifestation of Parameśvar will be in the "kaljug" in the region of Marwar. Suvāī Manu/Rājā Daśaratha will be born as Savāī Bhoj, and Satrūpā/Kauṣalyā will be born as Satvantī Sāḍū. Their son will be called Devnārāyaṇ, who, as Rāma in a previous birth, will incarnate in order to once again destroy the evil demon Rāvaṇa, who has appeared as the Rajput ruler of Rāṇ City. It is Devnārāyaṇ who will free the cows that have been captured and tormented by the Rāṇā, thereby lessening the earth's burden of evil.

The most outstanding feature here, in terms not only of genealogy but also "intertextuality," is that the incarnation of Devnārāyaṇ is being coupled with the incarnation of Rāmcandra. The written text does not accede to "traditional" knowledge—however "canonical" this may appear—that Viṣṇu's avatāra as Rāma is followed by his avatāra as Kṛṣṇa, Buddha, and then Kalki. Rāma's avatāra is, in the scheme provided by the printed text, followed by that of Devnārāyaṇ. In fact, moving backward, it is the triad of Savāī Bhoj, Satvantī Sāḍū, and Devnārāyaṇ who manifest in earlier ages, culminating in the triad of the very first "parents" and their object of unwavering worship, Parameśvara. Similarly, Devnārāyaṇ's cousins are avatāras of Lakṣmaṇa (Lacchman), Bharata, and Śatrughna. And, the latter in turn are avatāras of Śeṣa, Viṣṇu, and Dharmarāja, respectively. Thus, while acknowledging Parameśvara's incarnation as Rāma, the printed text simultaneously reworks Rāma's past and future. Devnārāyaṇ is Rāma's kali yuga incarnation. The printed text is not only a recollection of events known but also a restructering of these events that constitute history, or rather the history of a pivotal religious figure, Rāma.[33] It implicitly, thus, dismantles a fixed field of meaning that may have become attached to the Rāma avatāra.[34] In fact, it plays with our memory of the "classical" telling of the Rāma story by Vālmīki, and the sequence of avatāras in Vaiṣṇava theology.[35] The printed text thus involves what may be called a *symbolic translation* of two textual sources: puranic and epic. A symbolic translation is one in which

> Text 2 uses the plot and characters and names of Text 1 minimally and uses them to say entirely new things, often in an effort to subvert the predecessor by producing a countertext. . . . The word *translation* itself acquires a somewhat mathematical sense, of mapping a structure of relations onto another plane or another symbolic system. When this happens, the Rāma story has become almost a second language of the whole culture area, a shared core of names, characters, incidents, and motifs, with a narrative language in which Text 1 can say one thing and Text 2 something else, even the exact opposite.[36]

While referring to characters, places, and incidents from the Rāmāyaṇa, it simultaneously creates a new, different story about the incarnation of Devnārāyaṇ. Rather than remain within the boundaries of the former, it refashions the Rāma story for its own purposes. Whereas the puranic sources are used to establish a genealogy of Devnārāyaṇ's parents, and the historical identity of his worshipers, the epic source is used to establish the divine identity of Devnārāyaṇ himself. And in doing so the printed text involves a recollection of time, as does the oral telling, that gives credence to the subtitle of the book: *Vīr Gūjar Utpattī* ("origin of warrior Gūjars").

In the printed text the connection between Gujars and their profession of cowherding is made explicit through the promise made to them by "Pārbṛhm Parameśvar." Moreover, their own genealogy is clearly Vaiṣṇavite, in that it is traced to Svayambhū Manu and his wife Śatarūpā on the one hand and Rāmacandra or Parameśvara, on the other. But in the following shorter oral story about the origins of the Gujars, we find that it is Śiva who is indirectly responsible for their appearance. Furthermore, there is a much deeper, intimate connection established between the community and the cattle they take care of: it is a cow who bears Gaupāl Gujar, the first Gujar.

> The origin of the Gujars is a very long story. In the beginning the Gujars were [born] from the seed of Śaṅkar. [They] were born from

a cow that used to graze. . . . Pārvatī and Śivjī, what did they do? They performed *tapasyā* on a mountain. Good, while they were performing tapasyā on the mountain, a demon [*rākas*] who saw them doing tapasyā upon seeing Pārvatī got evil thoughts about her. "Well, brother, if I get this woman for myself, only then will [I] be satisfied." So what did he do? The demon danced and jumped in front of Śivjī's fire-place [*dhūnī*], to make Śivjī pleased and happy. So he served Śivjī for twelve years. After that Śivjī said: "Ask [for whatever you want]!" [The demon] said: "Give me your word!" [Śivjī] said: "[You have my] word, brother. You've served me for twelve years. Whatever you say will happen!" [The demon] said: "Well, brother, Mahārāj, I don't want anything else but that bracelet of yours that turns [things] into ash." Śivjī realized: "Hey, I've made a great mistake! All [my] power is in this bracelet." Śivjī handed over the bracelet to the demon. Why? Because he'd given his word hadn't he? He handed over the bracelet. The demon was powerful in any case, but now he had all the power of Śivjī too.

Śivjī said: "Now, move off from here, go away!" [The demon] said: ". . . what do you want?" So then the demon and Śivjī began fighting one another. Śivjī ran away. He started sweating. He grew afraid. He arrived at Bhagavān's court [*darīkhānā*]. "Śivjī is in trouble today!" Then what did Bhagavān do? He went and stood between the demon and Śivjī in the form of Mohinī. He spoke to the demon: "Hey, brother why are you running after that old sādhū? I desire you, let that old man go, and I'll stay with you." He had taken the form of a woman. What does *mohinī rūp* mean? It means a nice appearance that would attract the demon. "But there is one thing that Śivjī . . ." Now who's saying this? Bhagavān is speaking. Whose appearance did he take on? Pārvatī's. Bhagavān says: "I'll certainly accompany you, brother." In the form of Pārvatī he said: "I'll go with you when—Śivjī will dance in front of me everyday. Yes, he will dance—when the time comes—he will dance in front of me everyday, always. Now if you do the same dance everyday then I'll accompany you. Then I'll stay together with you." So then he began dancing in front of Pārvatī. So he pranced and danced about, but moved only one hand above his head; he would never move both hands together above his head. He [Bhagavān] was there in Pārvatī's form: "I'm not pleased." "Why not?" "Well, my husband would move both his hands above his head." So what did he do? The demon was wearing that bracelet wasn't he? When he brought that hand above his head, Bhagavān said: "Bracelet [make] ashes, ashes!" Well, that demon was turned into a heap of ashes. Taking the bracelet with him, Bhagavān returned in his chariot and stood in front of Śivjī: "What are you running away for? Old-man why are you running? What's happened?" "Mahārāj, there's a demon who's giving me the chase," [he] said: "Listen to this. That demon has my power because he's wearing the bracelet, where did you get it from?" "Here, Śivjī, take your bracelet, and go back home." . . .

[Śivjī] said: "Mahārāj, I won't take back the bracelet like that. Show me how you got it, then I'll take back the bracelet." So Bhagavān took on the form of Mohinī immediately, the same appearance, like Pārvatī. Śivjī Mahārāj went into raptures. When he went into raptures, Śivjī lost his seed. Now Nārad was standing close to Bhagavān. [Bhagavān] said: "Nārad, if the seed falls down on the earth, the earth will be burnt up." He cupped his hands and took hold of the seed. The sweat from the body—sweat—being pleased at seeing Mohini—Śivjī dispersed all of it. Nārād Muni caught hold of it in his hand. And [Bhagavān] spoke to Śivjī: "Look, you learnt of this form. That demon returned the bracelet to me because of this form alone." Śivjī grew pale. "Old-man, here take the bracelet and go home!"

Now Bhagavān said: "Well, Nārad, what should we do with this seed?" [Nārad] said: "Mahārāj, the matter is this—Hanumān's mother—Agni"—Whose daughter was she? Hanumān's mother was Agni's daughter. But no, she had been cursed by her father: "May you have the mark of an unmarried woman [*kū̃vārī ko kalaṃk*]." What did she do? As soon as he cursed her, she retreated to a mountain and began performing tapasyā. Hanumān's mother wouldn't see the face of a man. So Bhagavān said: "Agni's daughter, she doesn't have a guru yet. So give her the knowledge one receives from a guru. Thereby finishing off the curse that was put on her." So Nārad Muni and Bhagavān went to the place where Hanumānjī's mother was performing tapasya. She arose from the dhūnī and fell at Bhagavān's feet. Bhagavān turned his back on her. [She said:] "Why Mahārāj?" "You don't have a guru [*sugrī konī tū nugrī hai*]. I don't look at the face of someone without a guru." Who said this? Bhagavān said this. [She said:] "Mahārāj, since you've come, what's missing? You give me a guru, if I'm without a guru, then make me into someone with a guru, Mahārāj!" What happened? Now when she stood up to welcome him—when she stood up—they had poured Śaṅkar's seed into the hollow of a bamboo pipe—Bhagavān took that pipe and blew into Agni's [daughter's] ear. Śaṅkar's seed went into Agni's [daughter's] navel. [She said:] "Mahārāj, what should I call you, husband or father? I'm expecting from the seed that was blown into my ear." Then Bhagavān said: "Don't be afraid. We had to finish that old curse of your father's. The world won't understand what's happened, nevertheless, since it went through your ear, after nine months Hanumān will appear out of your ear."

Now Surjī Mahārāj [the sun] was arising when he was born. Now when the sun arose—right when he was born, he put the sun into his mouth and made [the world] dark. Then Bhagavān said: "Nārad Muni, what's happened? There's no sun, why is there darkness? Find out Mahārāj!" [Nārad] said: "Its that ṛṣi who's been born from Śivjī's seed, from Agni—Hanumānjī who was born of that seed." Now the day that seed was held in his hand it was put into a box, after which he then wiped his hands clean on some grass. That grass was eaten by Mother Cow. A cow ate that grass. Now from eating that grass a man was conceived by her—in the cow's womb from Śivjī's seed. So now what was his jāt? [It was] Gaupāl. Gaupāl Gujar. So now Gaupāl Gujar was born from that cow. From the day he was born he began looking after cows. From that day onward cows began to be looked after. Guāl Gujar's origins are from the cow's womb. Hanumān's birth and the origin of Gujars happened together—they grew from one and the same substance.[37] Yes, sir, the story is that old."

The story related here, thus provides an alternative to the narrative in the printed text, which, as already pointed out, is Vaiṣṇavite in its outlook. Even though in this account Bhagavān plays a significant role in helping Śiva, and directly causing Agni's daughter to give birth to Hanumān, it is the indirect link to Śiva that the narrator emphasizes. Śiva is their father, so to speak, and the cow is their mother. This story not only widens the intertextual web of the narrative tradition as a whole by alluding to well-known stories about Viṣṇu as the enchantress Mohinī, Śiva's seed falling to the earth and being caught by Agni, or Hanumān's swallowing of the sun, it extends the scope of possible interpretations from within the community of Gujars about their own origins and status as cowherds. While the printed text with its puranic character may represent an attempt to consolidate a particular viewpoint, the tradition in its entirety itself consists of different and in some cases even contending perspectives regarding the history and identity of Devnārāyaṇ's chief devotees.[38] Thus while the narratives presented in this chapter[39] stand at crosspurposes to the narratives of other communities (in particular local Rajputs) in the same region, they also represent a system of "cotexts" and "countertexts" vis-à-vis one another.

The Oral Telling

In the oral telling there is also a reference to different ages and different births or incarnations. Two epochs are alluded to, the satya yuga and the kali yuga. No indications are given of other yugas. These two epochal cycles suffice to extend the history of the narrative's characters into the "primordial" past while at the same time anchoring them in the present (or immediate past). Similarly the incarnational structure is, with the exception of the avatāra of Viṣṇu as Devnārāyaṇ, bound to the births, deaths, and rebirths of characters specific to the narrative. For example, although the 24 Bagaṛāvats, including Savāī Bhoj, are considered to be the reincarnations of 24 sages from the satya yuga, they are not (re)incarnations of persons or deities extraneous to the narrative. Savāī Bhoj is not an incarnation of Svayambhū Manu, nor is Satvantī Sāḍū an incarnation of his wife Śatarūpā.[40] While both are reborn from earlier or different lives, the incarnational scheme is provided by the narrative itself rather than (inter)textual reworkings of puranic and epic sources, as is the case with the printed tellings. The same is the case with Devnārāyaṇ who is simply an avatāra of Bhagavān Viṣṇu. No explicit connections are established to Viṣṇu's Rāma avatāra, or to Devnārāyaṇ being a manifestation of Pārbṛhm Parameśvar. A similarity does, nevertheless, exist, in the causal chain that induces Pārbṛhm Parameśvar to incarnate himself. In both the printed and the oral tellings it is either tap or bhakti that impresses the god into manifesting as Satārūpā's / Sāḍū Mātā's son.[41] This is the primary motivation. The secondary motivation is persistently mentioned as being the destruction of evil and evildoers, and the protection of dharma. The latter aspect is particularly emphasized in the printed telling, which most closely mirrors the "classical" notion of the avatāra and that of cyclical moral uplift. Again, while the printed version strongly emphasizes "time," in the sense that it situates the incarnation of Devnārāyaṇ in the context of the epochal past, the oral telling stresses the primacy of place and locality when describing the actual birth of Devnārāyaṇ. Here the reworking of the idea of the avatāra is connected to its directional and locative dimension. The prominent concepts in the oral telling are the Mālāsarī Hill, where Sāḍū Mātā performs tap, Devnārāyaṇ's game of dice with Rājā Bāsak in the underworld, and his movement from there to the surface of the earth on a stream of water.[42] The inherent indexicality of the narrative heightens the sense of the immediacy, concreteness, and accessibility of the event.[43] Along with its emphasis on place, the oral telling, furthermore completely inverts the "classical" notion (implicit in the very etymology of the term avatāra) that an avatāra *descends* from Vaikuṇṭha onto the surface of the earth. Devnārāyaṇ does not descend, he *ascends* onto the surface of the earth from the serpent kingdom of the underworld. As an "ascending" avatāra, Devnārāyaṇ reverses an important locative dimension of the classical avatāras of Viṣṇu. Thus, while both tellings (oral and printed) make use of the concept of yugas as abstract units of epochal time, the oral telling, in addition, makes use of local geography to particularize and fill out events.[44]

The Recurrence of Time

The oral telling, furthermore, deals with *discontinuity* in a particular way by referring to temporal concepts that also involve a metaphysical notion of personhood that allows for a movement of "individual" histories through a series of death(s), birth(s), and rebirth(s). This requires some explanation. To begin with, the "plot" of the narrative is strikingly complex; it is so extensively interwoven with "substories" and "subplots" that it is difficult to speak of a single, overarching "main plot." Given this complexity, it is perhaps more appropriate here to speak of recurring themes rather than a plot. One such theme, encountered in various episodes but predominantly in the first half of the narrative, is that of death. The heroes of the first half, the 24 Bagaṛāvats, die in two different ages. The first time is during the satya yuga, in which they are—as disciples of Lord Śaṅkar—consumed by their hungry guru. Subsequently, in the kali yuga, they are reborn as the 24 sons of Bāgh Siṃh. This time as devotees of Bhavānī, they offer their bodies to the Goddess as a final proof of their devotion, dying in a battle against Rāṇā, their Rajput enemy.[45] Besides the heroes' deaths in two yugas, there are other "deaths" in the narrative that are explicitly connected to the heroes' lives. One "death" is closely linked to the birth of the 24 heroes (or rather the birth of their father, Bāgh Siṃh, who is also Devnārāyaṇ's grandfather). The other "death" is concerned with Śaṅkar's reciprocal act of sacrifice, in which he—as their guru, Rūpnāth—now offers his own body to the Bagaṛāvats.[46] Both these points of cleavage, like the deaths of the heroes, have one quality in common, namely that of regeneration and transformation. Furthermore, these episodes—the birth of Bāgh Siṃh, Rūpnāth's offering of his body, the brothers' deaths—suggests a dual notion of time and personhood, a notion that, as it operates here, contains the possibility of repetition and metamorphosis. But this results in a paradox. As such, the narrative follows a sequence of events moving from a finite beginning to a finite end, creating, on one level, the linearity of time and enfolded within it the time limit of human life. In the narrative there is a reference to what happened earlier, what is happening, and what will happen. Each of these temporal states—past, present, and future—are woven together by a causality of human action intertwined with human fate. But the linearity of time that arises from the sequential structure of the "plot" is embedded in a concept of time that offers the potential for recurrence and transfiguration.

This aspect of the narrative can be understood in terms of the application of a "cultural schema," namely that of the yuga. "Cultural schemas" refer to such "key scenarios" or "root paradigms" that structure cultural choices and social action in a persistent manner through time. They are (Ortner 990: 60)

> preorganized schemas of action, symbolic programs for the staging and playing out of standard social interactions in a particular culture . . . every culture contains not just bundles of symbols, and not even just bundles of larger propositions about the universe ('ideologies'), but also organized schemas for enacting (culturally typical) relations and situations.[47]

By utilizing the notion of "cultural schemas" we can begin to view concepts such as that of the yuga, yajña, or avatāra as historically recurring ideational frames for ordering experience that are then rearticulated and reworked in distinct cultural and social contexts.[48] The usage of this "cultural schema" concerning time, in turn, structures the response to discontinuity. It also defines the way human identity is perceived. Thus the closure of linear time is juxtaposed with the open-endedness of cyclical time, in which the temporality of human life receives an extension: the heroes die in one epoch only to be reborn in another. Whereas cyclical time and rebirth are invariably associated with determinism, karma, and fate (or even fatalism), here we encounter a startling reversal. Transformation and rebirth have a specific goal, namely to bring an end to unfinished business. Rather than serve a notion of mechanistic repetition, the narrative emphasizes the *purposefulness* of being reborn. Furthermore, the fluidity of substance allows the slain lion's head to reappear on the body of Bāgh Siṃh and Rūpnāth's mortal body to transmute into a solid golden one. While the narrative places events and characters in time past, time present, and time future, it also simultaneously extricates them from temporality. The past does not exist as memory alone but also as substance in the physical presence of reborn heroes, a recreated guru, and a refigured lion. In the narrative, thus, three levels of temporal order can be discerned. The first two levels pertain to two distinct yet interwoven aspects of time: (1) the linearity of time intrinsic to the experiential structure of the narrative, which like any other narrative, makes use of different *tempora* in situating events, and (2) the instrumentation of a "time concept" that reverses the inherent temporality of linear time: by framing the narrative in cyclical time, death and disjuncture are coupled with creation and continuity.

While the first level pertains to the experiential structure of time resulting from a succession of events, the second level relates to the application of a "cultural schema" concerning time that challenges linearity. The third and final level of temporality that emerges here deals with the force of the narrative in the domain of "public discourse." At this level we find the occurrence of another crucially significant dimension of time, namely *history*. There are two senses in which the narrative has to be understood as history. In the first sense, as I pointed out previously, the narrative encompasses a statement about the history of Devnārāyaṇ's worshipers—the Gujars. This is evident from the fact that the narrative, particularly in the printed text, juxtaposes the existence and duties of the Gujars with the creation of the world through the primeval parents Svayambhū Manu and Śatarūpā, and the lineages of ṛṣis and kings that follow. It is Pārbṛhm Parameśvar who, in the satya yuga, hands over charge of all cows to the Gujars. Again, when Suvāī Manu and Satrūpā are visited by Pārbṛhm Parameśvar, they ask him: What will become of their lineage, which has sprung from the lineage of Prīyavrat? Parameśvar replies that all cows will be in their protection. Moreover, the cows will provide them with butter, they will enjoy dried fruit, and they will offer Parameśvar food in the form of butter and crystallized sugar that he will consume in his forms as avatāra. In the satya yuga the lineage will be called "Gurjar." The Gujars are in fact direct descendants of Svayambhū Manu and Śatarūpā. Conversely, Suvāī Manu and Satrūpā both belong to the Gujar clan. After his first incarnation in the treta yuga as Rāmacandra, Parameśvara promises to take birth among "some lineage of cattle-grazing Gujars." Suvāī Manu is to take birth as Savāī Bhoj, and Satrūpā as Satvantī Sāḍū. Thus, the successive "incarnations" of the Gujar lineage(s) are coupled with the "incarnations" of Parameśvara, thereby providing the former with a "divine" genealogy. The application of a concept of "time-cycles," together with that of the avatāra, therefore, furnishes community identity with temporal and moral depth. Through the discursive framework of the narrative text, crucial "life events" such as birth, death, and marriage, as well as brotherhood and kinship, "sacrifice," and devotion, are all held together within the context of historical continuity and social cohesion.

In the second sense of "history," the narrative provides us with a statement of the history of the region called Rajasthan. But in what way does the narrative speak to us as a "history" of Rajasthan? Are we to understand it as constituting an oral *source*, from which "real" events and processes can be culled? Is it to be perceived of as an—albeit jangled—historical record? Is it possible to talk of history when no "objective" history is involved? In what manner is the narrative a subjective, community-oriented, "local" history that nevertheless competes within an arena of entrenched, dominant histories of Rajasthan? To what extent—if taken seriously—does it alter our picture of the history of Rajasthan, which is primarily a history of ruling families and dynasties that have been placed in the foreground of both regional consciousness from within and Western situated historiographies from without (both in India and Europe)? To concur again with Ohnuki-Tierney (1990: 3),

> Historical records themselves result from the subjective and cultural sifting of perspectives, insights, and "facts." Any attempt at historical representation, then, must take into account the subjectivity of those who made the record, written or oral, and the role of memory. . . . The same subjective and cultural factors inherent in historical texts—verbal and nonverbal—affect their interpretations, and both historians and anthropologists are often unwillingly constrained by their membership in a particular period in history, by their gender, age, and class, and, most important, by the power inequality that often exists between the observed and the interpreters of history. Historiography in any intellectual tradition is not an objective science but is constrained by the same subjective, cultural, and political factors.

The narrative of Devnārāyaṇ as a statement about the deity and his main devotees certainly embodies both a history from "below" as well as the "native" view of history. It forms part of a wider network of stories, commentaries, and counternarratives, engaging us in a "counterhistory" of pastoralists, potters, leatherworkers, and jogis that undermines both the mainstream and local (Rajput) history of Rajasthan. This is particularly evident in the conflict that the narrative traces between the multicaste, pastoral Bagaṛāvats and Devnārāyaṇ, the "cowherd" king, on the one side and the politically powerful Rāṇā and his other "ruling-class" vassals on the other. One of the critical instances provided here is given in the founding story of the historically important Sisodiya Rajput clan of Mewar that is conspicuously different from the Sisodiya's own claims.

Tod offers two etymologies for the name Sisodiya. In the first (1957: vol 1, 176 n. 3) he says that "the origin of this name is from the trivial occurence of the expelled king of Cheetore having erected a town to commemorate the spot, where after an extraordinarily hard chase he killed a hare [*sussoo*]." For the second etymology, he relates the following story:

> In these wilds, an ancient Rana of Cheetore had sat down to a *gote* (feast) consisting of the game slain in the chase; and being very hun-

gry, he hastily swallowed a piece of meat to which a gad-fly adhered. The fly grievously tormented the Rana's stomach, and he sent for a physician. The wiseman (*béd*) secretly ordered an attendant to cut off the tip of a cow's ear, as the only means of saving the monarch's life. On obtaining this forbidden morsel, the *béd* folded it in a piece of thin cloth, and attaching a string to it, made the royal patient swallow it. The gad-fly fastened on the bait, and was dragged to light. . . . the curious Rana . . . when he heard that a piece of sacred kine had passed his lips, he was determined to expiate the enormity . . . and to swallow boiling lead (*seesa*)! . . . half a *seer* soon melted . . . he boldy drank it off; but lo! it passed through him like water. From that day, the name of the tribe was changed from Aharya to *Seesodia*.[49]

Both these etymologies speak for the warrior-like qualities of endurance and strength of the founders of the royal family. The "founding story" given at the tail end of the narrative of Devnārāyaṇ has a radically different, if not "subversive," message. After the five brothers have joined forces, they attack the Rāṇā; Bhāṅgījī singlehandedly destroys Rātā-Koṭ ("Red-Fort"), the Rāṇā's stronghold. He slays the Rāṇā's generals with his "club," a mortar taken from an oil press. The Rāṇā, seeing his fort and generals destroyed, flees in order to save his own life. Four brothers mount on their horses and ride after the Rāṇā. Devnārāyaṇ, who will not attack anyone from behind, rides with his horse into the underworld and covers the distance between him and the Rāṇā swiftly under the surface of the earth. Then he emerges in front of the Rāṇā, turning to face him:

He got in front and Rāvjī got afraid. He stopped immediately. *Yes, he stopped*
Bhuṇājī was ahead. When Rāvjī stopped—*mhe*—
He slung a bow around Rāvjī's neck—right here—from behind.
"Throw the enemy in front." *Throw* . . .
Bhuṇājī slung the bow around his neck.—*mhe*—
And Dev struck him with a lance.—*vāh vāh*—
Both brothers were together. The other brothers stood behind.—*mhe*—
They threw Rāvjī down. Yes, Rāvjī died right there.
By God's grace, when Rāvjī died—*mhe*—
the Bagaṛāvats' Bhāṭ came running along and began tearing open his stomach. *Yes, he jumped on Rāvjī's stomach.*
They said: "Hey Bhāṭ, don't tear open his stomach!"—*vāh vāh*—
The Bhāṭ said: "You don't realize—*mhe*—
The Bagaṛāvat's revenge is inside his stomach.—*vāh vāh*—
After tearing open his stomach I'll fill it up with stones." *I'll fill stones in it.*
So, Bhūṇājī was standing nearby. Tears started flowing from Bhūṇā's eyes. *Yes, tears flowed from his eyes*
Dev Māhārāj, who was standing in front, noticed: "Bhūṇā!—*mhe*—
After killing an enemy, everyone is happy." *And why do you cry?*

Bhūṇājī said: "Śrī Mahāraj, he is the enemy, *he's no friend.*
But he took care of me—he raised me. Yes, he took good care of me!
He was my father!—*mhe*—
That's why I'm sad. There's no other reason. *No other matter*
He's no friend!—*mhe*—
He's an enemy!"—*vāh vāh*—
Dev Mahārāj said: "Bhūṇā, did he take such good care of you?"
Bhūṇā said: "Yes, Mahārāj!" *He kept me well!*
Dev Mahārāj said: "Then, brother, the Bagaṛāvats' and my revenge has been completed." *Yes, we've taken it.*
He said: "It's taken since he's dead.—*mhe*—
I'll join on his head.—*vāh vāh*—
I'll revive him." *I'll revive him*
So Bābā Rāvjī's severed head Bhuṇājī—*mhe*—
Cleaned of dust.—*vāh vāh*—
He stuck it on again.—*mhe*—
He said: "There you are, Mahārāj, I've stuck it on." *Stuck it back on.*
Dev Mahārāj cast a look of mercy.—*mhe*—
Rāvjī came alive again abruptly.
Dev Mahārāj said:
"Brother, the Rāv of Rāṇ City is finished as of today. *Yes, it's gone.*
And that title of Rāv. *Yes, that too is gone.*
Brother, listen, so many days you were called Maṇḍovar.—*mhe*—
And, which Paḍihār—Maṇḍovar. *Maṇḍovar Paḍihār*
From today onward, the title of Maṇḍovar is finished.—*mhe*—
And by God's grace, the town that Rāṇājī will establish will be called Udaipūr after my name. *Yes, he'll establish Udaipūr*
And he'll be called Śīsodiyā Rāṇā, brother.—*vāh vāh*—
I stuck his head on and revived him, didn't I!—*mhe*—So, the day Bhagavan stuck on his head and revived him—*vāh vāh*—
From that day the title of Śīsodiyā Rāṇā came to be.—*mhe*—
And the town Udaipūr that Rāṇājī established was called after the name of Dev. *Yes, establish it in my name. It's your name, and the name of the village is mine*
"It's mine, brother."—*vāh vāh*—
So, Rāṇājī got the title of Śīsodiyā.
By God's grace, Rāṇājī came to Udaipūr *and established it*
The Bagaṛāvats' revenge was taken completely.—*vāh vāh*—
Dev Mahārāj's cows were freed. Speak: Victory to Śrī Dev, victory, victory, victory, brother.

The passage makes it clear that the entire founding of the Sisodiya clan is based on an act of mercy supplied by Devnārāyaṇ. Had not Bhūṇā been sad over his foster father's death, Devnārāyaṇ would not have revived him. However, the

Rāṇā's revival is "conditional": by sticking his severed head back onto his body, Devnārāyaṇ also determines the identity the Rāṇā will receive. The Rāṇā cannot revert back to his prior identity as the Rāv of Rātā Koṭ. He is compelled to take on a new appellation that is "etymologically" connected to the word *śīs*, or "head," and *diyā*, or "having given." Thus, having "offered" his head, or rather having had his head severed, the Rāṇā is then called Śīsodiyā. He is commanded by Devnārāyaṇ, who has both subjugated and revived him, to establish the great city of Udaipur in Mewar. Again, an "etymology" is used here that institutes a link between Devnārāyaṇ and his epithet Ud and the city of Udaipur, which conventionally is associated with the name of Uday Siṃh.[50] Thus Devnārāyaṇ is responsible not only for the Rāṇā's defeat but also for the foundation of the kingdom of Mewar and its palatial capital of Udaipur. Through this act of resurrection, coupled with the establishment of one of the major ruling houses, Devnārāyaṇ's jurisdiction extends not only to his immediate devotees but also to Rajput "ruling classes." In fact, the final victory over the Rāṇā, seen both in his slaying and revival, is something of a "crowning event" in the long-drawn-out friction between the main actors of the narrative and their Rajput opponents.

The Sisodiya Rajputs are not the only Rajputs who "owe" their origins to Devnārāyaṇ. In a prior incident that also carries the symbolism of death and revival, Devnārāyaṇ creates the clan of Sindhan Rajputs. The event occurs after they have passed the Lake of Māṇḍal in Bhilwara District, where Devnārāyaṇ together with Sāḍū Mātā and his newlywed wife Pīpalde are returning to his ancestral lands from Malwa. They reach the pass of Richor, where "Śaṅkar Mahārāj" has placed his disciples and told them to tax travelers crossing over the pass. A quarrel ensues between Devnārāyaṇ's cart-drivers and Śaṅkar's (or Rūpnāth's) Jogīs, whose leader is Nevā's son Bhāṅgī, who has been adopted from birth by Rūpnāth. While Sāḍū Mātā is "proving" Devnārāyaṇ's divinity to Rūpnāth, the cart-drivers and Jogīs fight and kill each other. When Devnārāyaṇ appears on the scene he casts his "nectar gaze" and revives the cart-drivers. Bhāṅgījī, who has by now accepted the fact that Devnārāyaṇ is an avatāra, and that he is his brother, asks him also to revive his people (that is, the Jogīs):

> Bhāṅgījī said: "O Incarnate One—*mhe*—
> You revived those of yours that died.
> And, the people who live with me—mhe—
> they're lying dead.
> *Yes, they're lying here dead*
> I'll perform their last rites, and follow afterward.
> Devnārāyaṇ said: "O Elder Brother Bhāṅgījī," *Yes, what last rites will you perform?*
> Bhāṅgījī said: "I'll perform the last rites—*mhe*—
> I'll dig holes—*mhe*—
> And gather them together. *Yes, I'll give them all a samādhī.*"
> Devnārāyaṇ said: "Then it'll take a lot of days. *Yes, it'll take us many days.*

I don't recognize them. You recognize your people having lived together with them
You join them together!—*mhe*—
I'll revive them, brother."
Bhāṅgījī had at that time consumed a quarter and a half maṇ of intoxicants.
He stuck somebody's arm on somebody else.
And stuck somebody's head on somebody else.
Somebody's foot he fastened on somebody else.
He covered them all with blankets. *Yes, put them all to sleep.*
He said: "Here, brother, Incarnate One, here you are. *Asleep they are ready, now revive them.*"
All the Jogīs woke up saying: "Dev, Dev."
As soon as they woke up they began quareling.
They said: "Why is my arm stuck on you, brother?"
Yes, how come my arm is stuck on you?
They said: "Hey, why is my foot stuck on you?"
Yes, how come my foot is fastened on you? Bhāṅgījī said: "O Incarnate One, you've done a great job. You revived them all right.
But you've created a quarrel. You've caused a fight among them!"
On the day Dev Mahārāj revived those Jogīs—*mhe*—
On that day he made the Sindhan Rajputs out of the Jogīs.
That's where Sindhans come from.
Yes, so Prince Bhāṅgījī joined up—*mhe*—
Dev Mahārāj, the lord of the three worlds, gave testimony.
Speak: Victory, brother, to Śrī Devnārāyaṇ Bhagavān, victory.

Reviving the jogis, as in the instance of the Rāṇā's revival, first involves rejoining severed bodily parts back onto torsos. But here, confusion is created because of Bhāṅgījī's inebriated state, and—somewhat as in the myth of the transposed heads—the Jogīs receive arms, legs, and heads that are not their own. While being reattached they are also mixed together and are cast, thereafter, into new identities as "Sindhan" Rajputs. They "wake up" acknowledging the authority of Devnārāyaṇ, against whose cart-riders they had taken up arms shortly before. His "enemies," once revived, take his name. And their revival as Rajputs again extends the social domain of Devnārāyaṇ's sovereignity.[51]

The "history" provided in the narrative, to return to the questions posed earlier, is both a "history" of the Gujars and of particular Rajput clans seen from the perspective of the Gujars. The history outlined in the narrative is not only a temporal account but, as I will discuss in more depth in the next chapter, also a description of social interrelationships that forge the identity(s) of the Gujars. It is clearly a "local" history that does not enter into the textbooks and compendiums on the history of Rajasthan. Nor does it enter into the historical imagination of the ruling families of Rajasthan, who, I was told, would not listen to its tale of defeat and slaughter.[52] Nevertheless, we need to take it seriously if we are to extend our understanding of history and culture as being composed of different and differing perspectives—not as a "single totalizing discourse but as a universe of discourse and practice in which competing discourses may contend with and play off each other . . . compose ironic commentaries on or subvert one another, or reflexively interrogate a given text or tradition or power relation" (Raheja and Gold 1994: 3). Thus we need not consider it to be a "source" from which an objective, "tangible" history can be winnowed, away from mythological and legendary matter. Even if this were the case—even if it did contain allusions to "historical" characters, real battles, recorded escapades, and verifiable marriages between royal and pastoral communities—we would still be missing the point if we were to only scrutinize these materials and discard the other imaginative fabric. It is precisely the imaginative web of the text that brings forth its purpose and fills it with meaning. And this cocoon of meaning is composed of "fictional" genealogies and fantastic liaisons, of "strange encounters" between brothers and villains, of the impetuous deeds of a clowning bard, a loudly laughing god, and his demonstrations of divinity.[53] Rulers, in this subversive scheme of things, are ridiculed. Intellectual and physical weaklings in the face of unlikely adversaries such as cowherds and minstrels, they sink in esteem as they are pushed with each small disaster toward the final fiasco.

6
Social Narrative

In chapter 5 I have shown that the narrative develops within it ideas about tradition and history that are important for the community that is chiefly associated with the cult of Devnārāyaṇ. By placing events within the framework of different world-ages, and by identifying Devnārāyaṇ and other figures from the narrative with deities and heroes (or villains) from the past, the text extends the identities of the god and his devotees in temporal terms. The interconnections made here also concern ideas about sociality in general, since social interrelationships too are expressed in terms of the past and the present. This chapter focuses on the way social interrelationships are perceived and defined. Broadly speaking, these interrelationships are articulated in more than one way: through ancestry, kinship, conflict, political alliances, marital bonds, and so on. The nature of these interrelationships both declare and explain which groups belong to the community of worshipers and why, as well as which groups tend to be located at the periphery of the "core community." Although at some point different groups are pictured as interrelated and "commingling," differences between groups are also accentuated in terms of mutual enmity. This is particularly evident in the example of the Gujar heroes and local Rajputs, in the garb of the Rāṇa, whereby the former belong to the "core community," and the latter, in some cases, belong to the domain of enemies (and villains).[1] The images of sociality that are articulated here are driven by one of the primary underlying concerns of the narrative, namely a concern with the sources of social, "secular,"[2] and divine power. The passages discussed in this chapter bring to the surface not only the ways power as such is perceived but also the tensions involved in establishing the supremacy of one kind of power over the other. Thus, for example, the encounter between Devnārāyaṇ's bard and the Rāṇā's brother points to a confrontation between divine and secular power; Devnārāyaṇ's mother, Sāḍū Mātā, and the other wives of the 24 brothers embody aspects of social and religious power; and Queen Jaimatī, or the Goddess Bhavānī, is a source of divine but also destructive power.

While the story of Udaipur quoted in the previous chapter speak for a "counterhistory" in terms of the origins of one of the most powerful kingdoms of Rajasthan, it also quite clearly tells us something about the way social and political relationships between the narrative's protagonists and their adversaries are perceived. But even lesser calamities than the ones described in this story add fuel to the contestation the narrative provides in the face of the secular power that the Rāṇā and his generals represent.[3]

One of the chief actors in this arena of contestation is the Bagaṛāvats' genealogist, Chochū Bhāṭ. Eulogizer, coward, clown, trickster, and Devnārāyaṇ's bard and devotee, Chochū Bhāṭ both infiltrates the "enemy lines" and instigates his master to pursue the course of revenge. The episodes in which he appears thus provide not only comedy but also "testimony" to his master's divine nature. One such significant episode occurs at a point when it has been decided that Bhūṇo should be informed of his parentage. Bhūṇo, or Khaṇḍerāv, as he is called by the Rāṇā, has grown up in the latter's court. He is unaware of the fact that he is the son of Bāravat, one of the 24 Bagaṛāvats, and Salūṇ, who is Sāḍū Mātā's sister. He is the last of the five cousins who still is in the "captivity" of the Bagaṛāvats' enemy. The other three cousins, Bhāṅgī, Medu, and Madno, have, under varying circumstances, joined forces with Devnārāyaṇ, who, on the advice of his mother, has postponed a confrontation with the Rāṇā until all the brothers are reunited. The task of locating and convincing Bhūṇo is the most treacherous and difficult of all, because it involves entering the enemy city itself. The episode that deals with the brothers' attempt at locating Bhūṇo is called the *hero* ("search") of Bhūṇo. As in many other sections of the narrative, here too Devnārāyaṇ, who conducts the "search," is not directly involved in the "action." Rather it is his "allies" Kālā and Gorā Bherū̃, and, importantly, Chochū Bhāṭ who function as his active counterparts. Chochū Bhāṭ volunteers to undertake the task of finding Bhūṇo. This is an extremely risky assignment because Chochū has to penetrate Rāṇ Śahar (Rāṇ City), where he is well known from the Bagaṛāvats' frequent visits to the Rāṇā prior to their enemity. In order for the Bhāṭ to be able to proceed with his mission without arousing the suspicion of the enemy, Devnārāyaṇ alters Chochū's physical appearance into that of a young man of 25 with features identical to his own. Before leaving for Rāṇ City, the Bhāṭ visits his old mother, Delū Mātā, to see whether she recognizes him or not. Since she cannot place him, he carries on in the direction of the enemy city:[4]

> After the Bhāṭ had spent a couple of nights in the city, one morning he went to the bazaar [*aṛadū kā bazār*]. He tethered his horse inside an old, broken-down shop, hung his bīṇ[5] and water-bottle on a nail, and went down to the middle of the street. There he collected piles of sand in his shield and started throwing the sand into the wind as one does with chaff.
>
> Now just at that time the king's younger brother, Nīmde, was passing through with his entourage. The leading Sirdār[6] said to the

Bhāṭ: "Hey, Dholīyo,[7] move over! Can't you see that King Nīmde's entourage is passing through?" But the Bhāṭ replied: "Hey, Sirdārs, I don't care whether Nīmā or Pīmā lives here in this city. I've lost something that belongs to me in this bazaar and I'm not moving till I've found it." He continued throwing up the sand. The horsemen shook their clothes free of the sand and said: "Oh, let him be—let's move on!" Just then King Nīmde's entourage arrived. So, what did King Nīmde say to the Bhāṭ? "O brother Dholīyo, you have costly shoes and your clothes are white, why do you fling up sand in my bazaar?" Now who said this? King Nīmde said this upon arriving in the bazaar.

The Bhāṭ thought to himself: "Let me find out whether Nīmde is clever or if he is just a 'broken drum' [*phūṭīyo ḍhol*]." So, what did the Bhāṭ say to King Nīmde: "Yes, the shoes on my feet are expensive and the clothes I wear are white. O Nīmā, I've lost twenty-four rubies and one diamond and I'm looking for them here." Now King Nīmde was not that clever that he could understand what the Bhāṭ had said. The Bhāṭ hadn't even told the smallest lie: he'd made the 24 Bagaṛāvats into rubies and Bhūṇojī into the diamond. But King Nīmde didn't understand anything. The Bhāṭ thought to himself: "The enemy doesn't understand, he's a broken drum. I'll finish him off right now." So what did the Bhāṭ say: "O Nīmājī, it's true that my shoes are studded with diamonds and pearls, but it's time for my opium now. If only I could find some gold coins belonging to the Bagaṛāvats. O King Nīmde, I've heard that in some bygone age the Bagaṛāvats lived here. They used to string necklaces together of gold coins weighing 5 *tolās* each, which they'd tie around their horses' necks. Then they'd gallop down this road and the necklaces would break, scattering the coins everywhere. If only I could find one coin I'd be able to buy enough opium for today's supply."

King Nīmde said: "Hey, Muṅgtā, which country are you from?" "I come from across the seven seas." "What's your profession?" "I'm the bhāṭ of kings." "Name?" "People calle me Jagīśyo." "Listen Jagīśyo, do you know how many years ago that was? There are no such coins here today, idiot!" The Bhāṭ thought to himself: "If I can find some coins here, then I'll be able to put him in his place." So he prayed to Lord Devnārāyaṇ for some coins: "O Lord, put five gold coins into my shield, so I can teach the enemy a lesson." He took Devnārāyaṇ's name and put his shield down on the ground. The Lord of the Three Worlds [*tīn tilokī ko nāth*] was present in Causle Kheḍā. He laughed aloud [*bak bak hāsiyā.*] The pheph blossoms[8] came into bloom. Bhairūnāth asked him: "O Lord, why do you laugh?" [Devnārāyaṇ said:] "Look, the Bhāṭ wants gold coins to appear in the dust!" Bhairūnāth said: "Lord, we should grant the old man his wish." The Bhāṭ took Devnārāyaṇ's name and pulled out a string of gold coins. He showed them to Nīmde: "Look carefully,

Nīmde. Are these the gold coins which the Bagaṛavāts scattered here?" Nīmde stuck his finger into his mouth and said: "Sirdārs, give the poor man whatever he wants and let's move on." King Nīmde did not understand anything.

As Nīmde was about to leave he saw the Bhāṭ's bīṇ. He said: "Dholīyo!" "Yes, Lord?" "Who does the bīṇ belong to? Is it yours?" "Yes, Lord, it belongs to me." King Nīmde said; "It's been so long since I heard someone playing the bīṇ. Long ago the Bagaṛāvats' bhāṭ used to play the bīṇ when he accompanied them. Play me a little [tune]!" "Yes, certainly Lord." King Nīmde said: "You play the bīṇ very beautifully. O Brother, tell me, where do you come from? I haven't followed!" The Bhāṭ thought to himself: "He's a broken drum anyway. Just tell him anything you like—he won't understand." So the Bhāṭ said: "Well, I have places to live in all four corners of the world. I'm King Harcand's Bhāṭ. My residence is in Mathura." Now the Bhāṭ didn't tell even the smallest lie: he made Savāī Bhoj into King Harcand and Ṭhākur Devmahārāj's residence into Mathura."

Now King Nīmde wasn't that clever that he could follow this. He asked his horsemen: "Where does this King Harcand live?" They replied: "O Lord, the country is long and wide—there are so many places—who knows where he lives? Who should keep a watch?" King Nīmde said: "Sirdārs, let's move on." The Bhāṭ thought to himself: "The enemy's moving on without my having put him to shame. Let me sing a song of praise [*āsakā*] to the entourage." What song of praise did he sing for King Nīmde?—"The Rāṇā's army is full of princes and kings from other lands. There are many Mughals and Paṭhāns. Accept the blessings of Jagiśyā Bhāṭ—[they] will bring you fame!" The leading Sirdār listened carefully to the Bhāṭ's song. He said to King Nīmde: "O Lord, the song was really wonderful, but he gestured with his left hand." King Nīmde gave the Bhāṭ a shove: "Hey, Muṅgtā, why did you gesture with your left hand? Am I not a king?" The Bhāṭ said: "Forgive me, Lord, but that right arm, you know, it doesn't belong to me!" "Then who does it belong to?" "I pawned it off to someone." "Hey, Dholīyo, you pawned off your own arm? What do you take?" The Bhāṭ said: "I eat opium don't I?" "How much?—A *pāv*[9] or so?" "More than that!" "A *ser*[10] or two?" "Oh, no, more than that!" "Then what, five or ten ser?" "No, no, more than that!" "Listen Jagiśyā, you had better tell me how much you consume." The Bhāṭ said: "Well, you see, Lord, people don't ask me how much I consume. If they do and I tell them then they have to supply me with all that I need. I don't let the person move ahead till he fulfils my demands! I'll tell you if you can fulfil my wishes, otherwise just move on down the road."

King Nīmde said: "Listen, Dholīyo, I'm King Nīmde. That's no small thing, is it? I'm the Rāṇā's younger brother. I'll get you what you need, just tell me now! You can't be consuming a maṇ[11] or two, could you?" "No Lord, much more than that!" "Tell me, how much?" What did the Bhāṭ tell King Nīmde? "At dawn I swallow one and a half maṇ of opium, after that seven baskets full. I eat that much to begin with. Later on there's no limit to bits and pieces. So, when I wake up it's one and a half maṇ. Then I go to the sons of kings and they throw me bits and pieces. There is no measure of those!" King Nīmde said: "Sirdārs, we've found a great opium-eater [*amaḷdār*]." "Is there anything you eat along with the opium?" he asked. "Yes, I do. I chew up two and a half maṇ of roasted chickpeas [*bhūṅgaṛā*]. Then I consume one and a half maṇ of bhāṅg. And if I'm still not intoxicated then I order a couple of portions of poison." "What sort of poison?" "Oh things like *ākaṛā, nīmaṛā,* and *dhaturā.* I mix them all up." King Nīmde said: "Sirdārs, we've found a great opium-eater!"

King Nīmde gave the command. In no time they brought one and a half maṇ of opium, two and a half maṇ of chickpeas, one and a half maṇ of bhāṅg. They churned the ākaṛā and nīmaṛā together and got two *tablas* full ready. "There you are Dholīyo." The bhāṭ said: "You may be a great king, but you don't have a spot of sense. Yes, you're a broken drum. You brought all these huge chunks of opium and have thrown them in front of me—how am I supposed to eat them? Cut them up into smaller pieces." The Rajpūt's son had a knife, so it didn't take long cutting up the large chunks into smaller pieces. "There you are, Jagiśyā. The opium is ready." The Bhāṭ said: "Nīmde, you don't have a spot of sense." "Now what's the matter?" The Bhāṭ said: "Look how I'm surrounded by your horsemen. If I eat the opium in front of them, I'll explode and die. Yes, I'll explode and die like the pod of a chickpea explodes. Set up a tent. I'll only eat the opium in a tent." It took no time for a tent to be set up. King Nīmde said: "There you are, brother Dholīyo," and pushed him inside the tent. "Call out when you're finished."

Now the Bhāṭ had never even touched opium, not even when he had been offered some. He thought to himself: "If I eat even a pāv of this poison I'll die inside here. But if I go outside without eating it then King Nīmde is sure to kill me straight away. If there's anything like death calling, then this must be it." The Bhāṭ thought: "Let me try some of it at least—is it sweet or bitter?" He put some of it on his tongue. "Damn, was it bitter! Oh, was it bitter, bitter, bitter!" He spat it out! Then he thought to himself: "God has sent you here, hasn't he—think of him, he'll help you." So, the Bhāṭ prayed to Devnārāyaṇ: "Listen to my plea. The Bhāṭ of the Bagaṛāvats is about to die here!" Lord Devnārāyaṇ laughed aloud. Bherū̃nāth asked him: "O Lord, why are you laughing?" Devnārāyaṇ said: "Look, Bherū̃nāth, Bābā Bhāṭ's calling." Bherū̃nāth said: "Lord, we should fulfil the old man's wishes." Devnārāyaṇ said: "Bherū̃nāth, go over there and take whatever offerings are being made. Let the Bhāṭ be victorious!" So the 52 Bherū̃, 64 Jogīṇī, and 78 Khetrapāl quietly entered the tent and asked the Bhāṭ: "O Bhāṭjī, why did you call us?" The Bhāṭ said: "I'm in bad trouble!" "What trouble?" The Bhāṭ took some opium in his hands and offered it to Kālā and Gorā Bherū̃. The 52 Bherū̃ and 64 Jogīṇī swooped down on all the opium, bhāṅg, and chickpeas. Gorā Bherū̃ drank up all the poison. And then he said: "Any other wish?" The Bhāṭ thanked them and said he would now manage on his own.

He waited awhile in the tent and then ripped it open on the side and came out yawning: "Hey Nīmde," he said, "That was useless stuff, where did you get it from! It didn't intoxicate me at all." Nīmde turned around to his horsemen and said: "Sirdārs, the man's consumed the harvest from seven villages and says he's still not intoxicated." The Bhāṭ said: "Oh that doesn't matter, I'll have some more when we go to the fort." Nīmde said: "You hear that, he's eaten away the harvest from seven villages and now he wants to eat the rest of the reserves we have in the fort! If he stays here a day or two he'll finish off everything we have. Give him a lakh [of rupees] and tell him to leave." Just then one of the horsemen said: "Shouldn't we check whether he's really eaten the opium?" The Sirdār went inside the tent and saw that even the sand had been eaten away in the tent—not even a pebble remained. That was what Ṭhākur Devmahārāj did when he heard the bhāṭ calling for him.

In this episode, as in many others, Chochū Bhāṭ plays the role of Devnārāyaṇ's alter ego. Twenty-five years young, with the same physiognomy as Devnārāyaṇ, Chochū is sent out to search for Bhūṇā, while the god continues dwelling at his residence in Causlā Kheḍā. All along the bhāṭ is a great improviser. Both boastful and timid, not quite sure of how far to push his luck, he always takes courage from Devnārāyaṇ's divine abilities. The sole intention here is to ridicule the Rāṇā's younger brother, King Nīmde. He tests the king's cleverness by posing riddles like the one about the lost diamond and 24 rubies. Gradually he grows more and more insolent until he openly calls the king a fool. When he finds the gold coins magically created by Devnārāyaṇ, his cheekiness increases. He sings a eulogy without the proper decorum and begins boasting about the gigantic quantities of opium he consumes every day. Ad-libbing throughout in order to humiliate the powerful king, the claim about his daily consumption of opium and bhāṅg reaches unimaginable dimensions: tens of kilos at a single session, along with a mixture of poisonous herbs and plants (ākaṛā, nīmaṛā, dhaturā). The king, both mistrustful and wonderstruck at the Bhāṭ's tall claim, repeatedly turns to his soldiers with the phrase: "Sirdārs, we've found a great opium-eater." Ultimately there is no escape for the Bhāṭ except to prove that his assertions are true or to die. In all these situations he relies on Devnārāyaṇ's powers to rescue him. In the final scene, where all the Bhāṭ's demands have been met and he has to face up to the mounds of opium, bhāṅg, and poison plants, Devnārāyaṇ dispatches his assistants, the Bherūs, Jogīṇīs, and Khetrapāls to receive all the "offerings"—the mounds of intoxicants—the Bhāṭ deliberately comes out of the tent pretending to be most bored and disappointed, indicating to Nīmde that the produce of his land is quite useless. An astounded Nīmde hastily turns down the Bhāṭ's request to take him into the fort and feed him with the supplies of opium stored there. Instead he tells his horsemen to gift the Bhāṭ with a large sum of money as a reward for his gargantuan feat.

In this episode the Bhāṭ's foolhardiness and boasting is backed up with inner strength because of his steadfast trust in Devnārāyaṇ's powers. While on an explicit level the intention is to deride King Nīmde (and his elder brother, the Rāṇā, symbolizing perhaps the Rajput community as a whole), there is an equally significant aspect to the incident that is related to the larger purpose of the narrative. The dangerous circumstances the Bhāṭ finds himself in and the solutions he seeks to save himself are closely connected to the issue of "testimony" (parcyo). The incident is about "divine proof" that surfaces every time the Bhāṭ is rescued by Devnārāyaṇ. Whereas the Bhāṭ is convinced of his master's divinity, King Nīmde, in contrast, is portrayed as being too dull to realize the divine significance of the unusual events taking place before him. The issue of divine intervention is taken up again in the ensuing encounter the Bhāṭ has with Bhūṇā, who finds it hard to share the Bhāt's faith in Devnārāyaṇ. Soon after Chochū has met Bhūṇā, they both travel to the famous pilgrimage town of Puṣkara, during the period of the annual fair in the month of Kārttika. Bhūṇā has been given jurisdiction over Puṣkara for the duration of the fair. In his habitual manner, Chochū begins to provoke Bhūṇā. He chides Bhūṇā for not taking up arms against the Rāṇā's generals, who also happen to be camping outside Puṣkara. Bhūṇā remains even-tempered, until out of exasperation he confronts the Bhāṭ, demanding "proof" (parcyo) of Devnārāyaṇ's divine powers:

> "When Dharamarāj[12] Devjī left on account of Sītā, O Bhūṇā, how large was the army he took along with him on that day? When he left on account of Sītājī, how large an army did he take along with him on that day?" (Yes, "how many did Bhagavān have with him, tell me!"). Bhūṇājī said: "Hey, Muṅgtā, is the one who left on account of Sītā your master?" (Yes, "is he yours?") [Chochū] said: "He is one and the same. ("Exactly the same one.") [Bhūṇā] said: "Muṅgtā, how long have you been about?" He caught hold of [the bhāṭ's] arm and took him down the ghāṭs[13] in Puṣkara. (Yes, "he took him right down in front.") "Just you wait, Bhāṭ," [he] said. (Yes, "just wait!") "[You say] your master left on account of Sītā ("We'll find out now!")—I'll find out now!" Bhūṇājī placed Dūdā's sword, which had been given to him, on the steps. The bow and arrow(s) [he also placed on the steps.] "Listen, Bhāṭ, he is your master, isn't he!—[If] the sword leaves its sheath on its own, and the arrow strings itself on the bow, [only then] is your master the one who left on account of Sītā! If not, then Muṅgtā, I'll drown you in the water, after I cut off your head. (Yes, "I'll make an offering of you in

Puṣkar.") The Bagaṛāvat's Bhāṭ spat on his hands—without removing his shoes, he jumped into Puṣkar and went under. What did he cry out to Bhagavān, as he came up? Let us see. ("We'll know it by saying it—let's see—by saying it.")

By God's grace, [the Bhāṭ] said the following: ". . . If you listen to my call here, then I'll return alive and bring Bhūṇā with me! If not, watch the Bagaṛāvat's scroll drown!" He took a second dive. ("He took a dive"). "I'll stay in the water now!" (Yes, "I'll die here," [he] said). Devmahārāj was present in Causlā Kheḍā. Kālā and Gorā Bhairavānāth. . . .[14] Devmahārāj laughed out aloud [*bak bak hāsīyā*]. The pheph blossoms [bloomed]. Bhairavānāth asked: "Śrī Mahārāj, what's the reason for your laughter? (Yes, "why is it so today?") [Devjī] said: "Bābā Bhāṭ's asking for a miracle now on the steps. (Yes, "he's going to drown and die.") [Bhairavānāth] said: "Śrī Mahārāj, you should do what the old man wants you to do!" "Bhairavānāth, get the Bhāṭ out quickly, otherwise the Bagaṛāvat's scroll will drown! Go swiftly!" Like speaking to the wind, by God's command, Bhairavānāth went and caught hold of the Bhāṭ's arms. He pulled the Bhāṭ out: "Why are you drowning?" (Yes, "why are you drowning and dying?") [The Bhāṭ] said: "Bad times have befallen me, that's why!" [Bhairavānāth] said: "What bad [times]?—If you say so, I'll turn everything in the Melā[15] upside down." (Yes, "I'll destroy it—turn it all upside down!") [Chochū] said: "No, No, No, No. ("Not that kind of thing.") By God's command, that arrow should string itself onto the bow (Yes, "if it does that on its own") and that sword should leave its sheath on its own. ("If it comes out of its sheath.") Do these two things. (Yes, "just do that much") . . . And then sit on Bhūṇā's right arm for a while." . . .

Gorājī Mahārāj strung the arrow onto the bow. By God's grace, Kālājī Mahārāj, drew out the sword from its sheath. (Yes, "and placed it there.") This came to Bhūṇā's attention. Bhūṇājī said: "Bābā Bhāṭ, come out of Puṣkar—come out of the water. (Yes, "my ancestor's chronicle will drown—come out quickly!") Hey, some *goyalā*[16] animal might devour you! Come out! I consent! Your master is the one who brought Sītā [back]. ("He's the very same one," [he] said.) I agree, brother. Now I'll fight anyone you say in the Melā. (Yes, "I'll do it now!") By God's command, Bhūṇājī said: "Bābā Bhāṭ, don't wait any more!" ("Don't delay things any longer.") (Yes "begin the fight soon!") [This is how] the Lord of the Three Worlds, Bhagavān Dev, created a miracle. [And] Bhairavānāth sat on Bhūṇā's arm.

As in the previous episode with King Nīmde, the Bhāṭ goes to the extreme in taunting Bhūṇā, to the extent that a situation is created that poses a threat to his own life. Undoubtedly the fear and courage he expresses gives the situation a comic touch—even when he is about to drown in the lake of Puṣkar. As always, at this point, the Bhāṭ cries out to Devnārāyaṇ for help, "blackmailing" him with the threat that the Bagaṛāvats' genealogy and genealogist will be wiped out. As always, Devnārāyaṇ is unperturbed, laughing his loud, radiant laugh.[17] Again, he sends Kālā and Gorā Bherū̃ to rescue the Bhāṭ. The pair of Bherū̃'s successfully (and invisibly) perform the test Bhūṇā has set up for the Bhāṭ. Once again the Bhāṭ is retrieved from the dire straits he has involved himself in. Although the immediate purpose is to save the bhāṭ, the lasting aim is to provide "proof" of Devnārāyaṇ's powers. By putting his own life into danger, the Bhāṭ elicits an urgent response on the part of Devnārāyaṇ. The appearance of this miracle convinces Bhūṇā also of his brother's divine qualities and of the reality of the Bhāṭ's claims.

The commonly occurring role of the court jester is altered in the figure of Chochū Bhāṭ. His teasing and taunting is not directed toward his own divine master but toward the enemy king. Chochū Bhāṭ's position as a satirical figure within the narrative is thus different from to that of other famous jesters such as Birbal, at the court of the Mughal emperor Akbar, or Tēnāli Rāma at the court of the Vijayanagar king Kṛṣṇadevarāya.[18] The Bhāṭ's character and role, like that of other major players in the narrative, such as Sāḍū Mātā and the 24 brothers, is informed by an ideology of bhakti, which in turn colors his allegiance to Devnārāyaṇ.[19] In fact the radical role of the jester, clown, and bard is transformed in the figure of Chochū Bhāṭ by the strong element of devotion that characterizes the religious discourse of the narrative as a whole. Nevertheless, Chochū Bhāṭ generously brings to surface the subversive thrust of the narrative. This dimension of the narrative is, not surprisingly, also shared by his master Devnārāyaṇ, who himself is an "underling made uppermost."[20]

Metaphors of Multiplicity

The ambivalent nature of the relationship between Gujars and Rajputs, characterized by the simultaneous kinship and conflict mentioned earlier, is intrinsic to the idea of sociality pervading the narrative in general. In fact, the heroes of the narrative cannot be said to possess a "clear-cut" lineage at all. They are, as I pointed out earlier, the sons of the multicaste wives of Bāgh Siṃh, a man-lion, who in turn is the product of a "mixed" marriage between a Rajput and Brahman, or a Rajput and a Banyā, or a Gujar and a Brahman, depending on different versions of the story. Furthermore, Bāgh Siṃh has—among his 12 wives—a Rajput wife, who bears Savāī Bhoj and his sister Bhojī.[21] Following this socially broadbased genesis, the narrative's heroes and the cult of Devnārāyaṇ as a whole are "appropriated" into a better defined caste or group identity through their marriage exclusively to Gujar women:

> By God's command, to each mother [the wives of Bāgh Siṃh] two [sons] were born together with Bhoj. There was a sister. There were 23 Bagaṛāvats. So they grew up gradually. Now people are telling the king of Ajmer: "You're a king, the country's master! Who is going to [marry them]? The Rajputs won't, because they are of 12 jāts."

So the king of Ajmer said: "Look, you're right, what should we do? Now, there's this Gujar jātī who lives here." So all the big—nowadays they say *netā* [leader]—otherwise they're called *Patel*—[he] got them together. "Come, Patels! Brothers, get together." So the king of Ajmer sat them all down. He took liquor and began offering it to them. The Gujars said: "No Mahārāj, we won't take it." "But, I'll tell you how. Today you must!" [The Gujar said:] "Rājā Sahab is offering it to us, why not accept it?" He [the king] gave it to everyone. [Then] he poured [liquor] in the same cup and drank it himself. Who [did that]? King Bisaldev [did that]. Then the Gujars stood up and put their palms together in respect: "Why Mahārāj, why did you drink liquor from the same cup we had drunk from? What's the matter?" King Bisal says: ". . . Give us women!"[22] All of them [i.e., the Gujar leaders] looked down. Now who would say "I'll give you a girl [in marriage]?" . . .

So there was Dulojī Khaṭāṇo. What about him? He had two wives. But both of them were childless. A mahātmā used to practise tap in front of their home. They looked after the mahātmā and served him for 12 years. After 12 years were over, in the evening [the mahātmā called out:] "Dūlā Bābā, come over here!" "Yes, Mahārāj!" "I'm leaving the dhūnī today." "What for, Mahārāj?" "[I'm leaving] because my tapasyā is complete after 12 years. That's the reason!" "Why, Mahārāj, aren't you happy?" Well, anyway Dulojī went back to tending his cows and buffaloes. And, Bābājī prepared to leave. Before he left, he said: "Look, [Dulā] Bābā, take care of my dhūnī [when I'm gone]." It was some time before Dulojī [went home]. He went home and ate his food. He asked his wives: "Did either of you say something to the mahātmā yesterday? Did you not give him his food or milk at the proper time?" "No we didn't do anything [wrong]!" "Well, Bābājī's left today! He's left the dhūnī." [The wives said:] ". . . we served Bābājī. And, because of him we're childless. [Should] we ask for something? Is there nothing we could ask for? So what did Bābājī say?" "All he told me was to take care of his dhūnī in the morning." [Dulojī's wives decided:] "Let's do the following. Let's go [down the road]. If we find Bābājī, then we'll stop him, we won't let him go any further. If we don't catch up with him, we'll tend his dhūnī." So Dulojī's wives got ready, they washed their hands, and went towards the dhūnī. [But] they didn't find Bābājī. So they tended the dhūnī. From the dhūnī there came out a ball. And, out of it a baby girl appeared. (I'm telling you about Devnārāyaṇ's mother's birth.) So Dulojī said: "Bābā didn't give us a baby boy. He gave us a baby girl. And, that's fine." Dulojī's eldest wife pressed Sāḍū to her chest. She gave her her breast. Milk began flowing out of Dulojī's wife's breast. [Later] two boys were born—Āmo [and] Nīmo. And, one girl by the name of Salūṇ was born. She was Bhūṇājī's mother, and was married to Bāravat.

> Dulojī reflected to himself: "She's been given to us by the mahātmā . . . I'll get her married to Savāī Bhoj." So immediately he got up like a leader and said: "I'll give my daughter to Savāī Bhoj in marriage!" When that Patel stood up, all the Gujars saw that Pateljī has stood up. "What's it to us? Nothing at all." [So] all of them stood up [too] and started saying: "I'll give one, I'll give one." This way the 24 Bagaṛāvats got married into the Gujar jātī. So the Gūjars—how do you say *deyajā* . . . *dahej* [dowry] . . . they gave 20 cows and one bull. All together 21 cattle. So that added up to 20 times 24 [cows] and 24 bulls. So what did the Bagaṛāvats do? They tended cattle. Now among [these cattle] there were cattle from the city—from Ajmer.[23] What did they do? They began grazing the city's cattle, and their own in the [on the slopes] of Nāg Pahāḍ. All right . . .

In this passage it is evident that the Bagaṛāvats, because of their "mixed" background, have difficulties in being socially acceptable to the extent that they can lead "normal" married lives. On the verge of remaining "bachelors," or "recluses," permanently, the Bagaṛāvats' fates are taken care of by the king of Ajmer, Bisaldev, who in a previous instance also allowed their grandparents, Harī Rām and Līlā Sevrī (also of different castes), to marry. Bisaldev proposes an alliance with the Gujars, who inhabit the countryside of Ajmer.[24] His manner of convincing the Gujar leaders to offer their daughters in marriage once again, if only in a potently symbolic gesture, blurs the distinction between their respective caste identities. By drinking out of the same cup from which they have drunk, he initiates an act of commensality that implies brotherhood between the king and the Gujar patels. This act of commensality, or "commingling," is one in a series of social "transgressions" that are characteristic of the opening episodes of the narrative.[25] It is also reminiscent of the "turban exchange" that the Bagaṛāvats perform with Rāvjī, the Rāṇā of Rātā Koṭ (their later enemy). It also speaks for the magnanimity of the Gujar leaders and community in offering their daughters in marriage to men of socially dubious origins. At the same time, Śrī Hukamārām Bhopā's comment that it is from this juncture onward that the Gujars enter into the narrative is significant: not only do they enter into the narrative at this point but also from now on the narrative also becomes *the story of* the Gujars. Prior to this moment the narrative is, as Śrī Hukamārām Bhopā points out, a narrative of the Rajputs. But, as mentioned earlier, all throughout the narrative there are points of merger and separation between the main protagonists, namely the Gujars and the Rajputs.[26]

❁ Images of Women ❁

Within the discourse on sociality there is a "subdiscourse" concerning relationships between men and women. Crucial to this "subdiscourse," as also to the larger discourses on sacrality and intergroup relationships, as I pointed out earlier, is a notion of power. However, given our understanding of the "martial" nature of the narrative, we may tend to assume that the narrative is dominated by a set of values and ideas that is sustained by men only, who define and wield power, being chiefly interested in war, politics, and the retrieval of lost property. Seen from this perspective, women are often automatically relegated to subordinate or "passive" roles that solely support the agendas of men. Although this observation is partially true, it is still worthwhile to examine the question of what "power" is and how it can be defined; and whether there are different sources and forms of power, each with a capacity to influence and dictate events. Perhaps it is precisely because of their normally understood marginal status that women, or rather images of women, provide a window into the many ramifications of power structures in the narrative.[27]

Some of the questions that may further be asked are: What are the different contexts in which women are represented? How are they represented? Are they represented as passive objects? Or are they represented as active but sometimes covert players? What are the different contexts in which power issues from women? How is power defined in these different contexts? To what extent do certain overall themes such as devotion, social diversity, or subversion in the face of secular power also inform the roles of women? What do these different contexts tell us about the representation of women in the narrative as a whole? Is the perennial vision of the Indian woman "as a silent shadow, given in marriage by one patrilineal group to another, veiled and mute before affinal kinsmen, and unquestioningly accepting a single discourse that ratifies her own subordination and a negative view of femaleness and sexuality" (Raheja and Gold 1994: 3)[28] corroborated through the narrative?

Women feature in a variety of different contexts in the narrative. In some they appear anonymous and passive. In others they emerge as immensely powerful, deciding matters of life and death. In still other cases they seem to work as catalyzers and "hidden" integrators in situations that have a potential for conflict. Moreover, women are represented in terms of a number of social and religious identities: as mothers, daughters, wives, sisters, widows, devotees, and goddesses. Some women feature more prominently in the narrative than do others. For example, Devnārāyaṇ's mother, Sāḍū Mātā, plays a central role throughout the narrative, not only as the wife of Savāī Bhoj and the mother of Devnārāyaṇ but also as a paramount devotee of Bhagavān. Conversely, one does hear of the other 23 brothers' wives, but not all of them recur in the narrative. And while we are told that Devnārāyaṇ marries on three different occasions, it is only his third wife, Queen Pīpalde, whom we encounter in a number of episodes in the narrative. And, as I discussed in chapter 3, it is she who occupies a central position in the cult as well. Queen Jaimatī—perhaps the most powerful person in the narrative next to Devnārāyaṇ—draws her power from being the incarnation of the goddess Bhavānī, who is ultimately responsible for the slayings of the 24 Bagaṛāvats. Images of women and the power accorded to them express themselves in three main contexts. The first is that of marriage and social liaisons; the second is that of religious devotion; and, the third, which overlaps the second, is that of divine power.

Sons and Wives

Although there are a number of marriages throughout the narrative, marriage as a theme is predominant in the first part of the narrative. The very first series of marriages occur in the so-called preamble to the narrative. There are three successive incidents in which marriages take place.[29] In each case the context in which the marriages are to take place is problematic, and marriage itself shows up as a thorny issue that requires ingenuity and initiative in order to be brought to a satisfactory conclusion. And in all three cases it is the social identities of the persons involved that create a problem. The marriages narrated in the "preaṃble" all relate to Devnārāyaṇ's ancestors, namely Hari Rām and Līlā Sevrī, Bāgh Siṃh and his 12 wives, and the 24 Bagaṛāvats.

In all of the three cases that occur here, marriages are between unequal or mismatched partners—unequal and mismatched either in social or in purely "physical" terms. Whereas in the first case Hari Rām and Līlā Sevrī belong to different castes, in the second case Bāgh Siṃh himself is half human and half animal, and his wives are human. The Bagaṛāvats, who are born of Bāgh Siṃh and his multicaste wives, do not have a perceptibly clear social or caste identity. They in turn are married to women who belong to a single well-defined social group.

In the case of Hari Rām and Līlā Sevrī, it appears that Līlā Sevrī is the more powerful of the two, since it is she who has taken a vow not look at a man's face, and it is she who insists that Hari Rām now marry her, although from a conventional point of view this would seem impossible. It is the king who then overrides social conventions and allows the two to marry. However, Līlā Sevrī's curse that Hari Rām's son will have the face of a lion and the body of a man comes to fruition when their son, Bāgh Siṃh, who is half man and half lion, is born. Regardless of his potential divinity, Bāgh Siṃh is "exiled" to a garden far away from the main settlement, where he lives alone except for his Brahman care taker. Whereas the marriage between Hari Rām and Līlā Sevrī could be seen as resulting from an "accident," the bond between Bāgh Siṃh and his wives is clearly the result of deceit and trickery. The innocent young girls are manipulated into circumambulating Bāgh Siṃh on the promise of being able to use his silken swing. Here too there is a relationship of social unequals or, at any rate, of socially distinct individuals. Bāgh Siṃh, a child born of an unconventional marriage, marries women from different jatīs. The women enter into a bond with Bāgh Siṃh unknowingly and therefore also passively. Once the marriages are consummated, the strengths of the children born thereof are determined by the character and strengths of the caste identity of Bāgh Siṃh's wives. For example, the son born from his Banyā wife has the personality of a "typical" Banyā, the son born of a Rajput wife has the "typical" qualities of a Rajput, and so on. Thus the character and qualities of the 24 Bagaṛāvats is not so much fixed by their father as by their respective mothers. This in turn results in the multiformity of the Bagaṛāvats. The point in this example is that although Bāgh Siṃh's wives are represented in an anonymous, passive, and nonvolitional manner, they do play a central role in an underlying causality that determines who the Bagaṛāvats will be as heroes. Thus to return to the notion of sociality, it appears that social diversity and nonuniformity are, at least in the discourse of the narrative, valued higher than clear-cut, unchanging social boundaries. This nonuniformity also provides a model for the shifting, "uncertain" and socially speaking "negotiable" nature of Devnārāyaṇ's cult in terms of who may or may not become his devotee.

The "passive" role of Bāgh Siṃh's wives is then reversed: it is the Gujar women who under the advice of their fathers take on an "active" role in marrying the Bagaṛāvats. Whereas Bāgh Siṃh is successful in assimilating many different groups through his marriages, the Gujar women are successful in assimilating the heroes and, as a consequence, also the cult into the fold of a single group. This, then, becomes a point of reference for the cult in general, and for social relationships within the community of worshipers. If Bāgh Siṃh's wives are about social diversity and ambiguity, the Gujar women are about social appropriation and self-definition. For the first time here there is no trickery or deceit involved in the process of marriage: the Gujar women volunteer to marry the Bagaṛāvats. By doing so they also lay the foundations for Devnārāyaṇ's birth in their community. And, in terms of a chronicle of births, the Gujar women, especially Sāḍū Mātā, tie up with Līlā Sevrī, and Bāgh Siṃh's wives, who in each case determine the nature of their offspring. It is Līlā Sevrī who curses Hari Rām so that their son will have the body of a man and the head of a lion; the social background of Bāgh Siṃh's wives determines the personal qualities of each Bagaṛāvat; and it is Sāḍū Mātā's devotion that draws Bhagavān into incarnating himself as Devnārāyaṇ.

In terms of the representations of women in the context of marriage, we can perceive both an underlying consensus as well as an underlying shift in the narrative. The underlying consensus relates to the notion that women prevail over the domain of birth, not only in an obviously physical sense but also in the sense of providing their children with essential qualities that will mark their journey as heroes in the narrative. The underlying shift relates to the movement from women representing different groups to women representing a single group. Both aspects are important for the cult as a whole, which simultaneously has a relatively well-defined social reference point and a relatively open access for other social groups. The metaphor of marriage, therefore, reveals that images of women relate to both social control and social assimilation. The narrative via the metaphors of marriage and commingling thereby inscribes within itself a discourse about the openings and occlusions of the cult of Devnārāyaṇ, which even though not generally attended to by Rajputs is patronized by a broad variety of other "peasant" castes such as cowherds, potters, weavers, gardeners, and farmers.[30]

Sāḍū Mātā: Devotee, Ascetic, Mother

I will now turn to the second context mentioned earlier, namely devotion: How does devotion, or bhakti, figure as a source of power? What kind of power issues from devotion? To what extent is the role of Devnārāyaṇ's mother, Sāḍū Mātā, determined and defined by bhakti? To what degree is Bhagavān's incarnation as Devnārāyaṇ explainable in terms of his mother's devotion?

If we examine various episodes featuring Sāḍū Mātā, we find that they are characterized by both devotion and asceticism. The first episode, which has been related earlier in the story about Dulojī Khaṭāṇo, narrates the circumstances of her birth and the meaning of her name. Sāḍū Mātā is, thus, born out of an ascetic's fire-place. Her name is said to derive from *sādhu* (ascetic/mendicant). While the ascetic component visible in the story of her birth is strengthened in the scene in which she practises tap on the Mālāsarī Hill while awaiting the manifestation of Bhagavān, the devotional component is well displayed in a prior encounter between her and Bhagavān, who approaches her disguised as a wandering mendicant.[31]

> [Bhagavān] went there and sat down in front of the door. At that time Sāḍū Mātā had prepared to bathe. [She] had taken off her clothes and all, and was bathing. At that time [the Jogi] said: "Alakh!" [Sāḍū Mātā] said: "Maidservant go—Jogeśvar is calling . . ." The maidservant went and said: "Mahārāj, what do you want?" "No, no, I won't take anything from you!" "Well, then?" "I want it from—the mistress of this house—the mistress—I'll take it from her hand. You're a maidservant." "Well, Mahārāj, should I fetch my mistress?" "Yes!" "On your guru's name promise you won't leave these steps!" Then Bhagavān said: "Go to your mistress. If she dresses up and all, I won't accept anything [from her]. She should appear in front of me in the way she's sitting outside. Then I'll accept [her offering]." The maidservant went to Sāḍū Mātā: "Well, maidservant, what have you come for?" "What for, Mahārāj? Today the sādhu won't receive anything from me. He's calling you. And, he's summoning you—the way you're sitting here—he's says to come that way." Sāḍū Mātā said: "Go, don't worry!" She quickly—like one does when one bathes—tied her hair together into a knot, and took a plate [of offerings].
>
> So, when Sāḍū Mātā showed up, Bhagavān turned his back to her. "Why, Mahārāj, why did you turn away?" [Bhagavān said:] "Mother, put on some clothes!" "Now, you sent for me, did you send for clothes? [No,] you sent for me to come like this!" There's no shame for sons and daughters in front of parents. What's there to be afraid of in front of one's parents. I've come to you in exactly the way you'd sent for me." So, he said: "Mother, open the knot in your hair." Mājī Sā [Sāḍū Mātā] opened the knot of hair. Now when her hair hung down long, Bhagavān cast a look of mercy, and created a dress of long hair. When the dress [covered her] Bhagavān turned around. Sāḍū Mātā said: "Well, here Mahārāj." "Give me your word!" "I promise!" Bhagavān said: "Look, the matter is this, give me the sakalp of 23 Bagaṛāvats with your hand." She poured the sakalp of 23 Bagaṛāvats with her hand. Then Sāḍū Mātā thought:

> "Now, why did this happen?" She grew a bit unresolved. Bhagavān said: "Why are you afraid? Have you let down your promise?" "I won't forsake my word!" "Well then? Give me the sakalp!" "I'll give it to you, Mahārāj!" "Don't be afraid! Look, of the 24 brothers, one will be let off! One of them won't die." Then Sāḍū Mātā reflected to herself: "If one of them is going to be let off, it'll be my husband who'll be let off." Then Bhagavān said: "Mātā, it won't be the way you thought!" "Then [how]?" "You thought of your husband. [But] your husband will die. The eldest of [the brothers], Tej Siṃh, the Banyā's child, will be let off! Your husband will surely die! And, you—you'll be immortal—your husband will die [in battle]! Give me the sakalp, or break your word!" "Mahārāj, I won't break my word." Sāḍū Mātā gave it to Bhagavān: "Here you are Śrī Mahārāj, it's yours. Do whatever you like [with it]!"
>
> Then he said: "Mother, what do you want?" "What should I ask for? I've no dearth of money, wealth—there's no dearth of anything. Now, what should I ask for?" "Anything you desire." "Well, Mahārāj, you give me your word too!" He was Bhagavān: "I give you my word." "Well, then Mahārāj, I want a son like you in my shoulder sash. I want you in my shoulder sash." Then Bhagavān said: "Mother, someone like me is myself. Who else is like me?" "I want you—to feed you. I have no other desire [but] to feed you." "Mother, someone like me is myself, and you did a good thing in opening the shoulder sash. Otherwise I'd falter in my word. If you had said come into my womb, then I'd have to come and suffer in the womb. That was a good thing you did [asking me] to come into the shoulder sash. I won't have to wallow in dirt and fat. When Bhoj's thirteenth day arrives, after he dies, when his *satīvāḍā*[32] takes place, on that day I'll take avatār with you on the Hill of Mālāsarī." This was Bhagavān's word: "The others will die, be burnt. Don't you leave that place. Do bhajan,[33] then your promise will be fulfilled." So there was a pact between Sāḍū Mātā and Bhagavān Dev for the thirteenth day. Bhagavān gave his word. Speak: Victory to Śrī Dev Mahārāj, victory!

By obeying Bhagavān's command to present herself "as she is," Sāḍū Mātā is able to impress Bhagavān of her "knowledge" (*gyān*). Sāḍū Mātā realizes that the mendicant is Bhagavān, which is why she addresses him with the collective "parents." Her ability to recognize the mendicant's true nature arises also from her own asceticism-induced, miraculous birth.[34] But the alms the mendicant desires are truly awesome and foreboding: the lives of 23 of the 24 Bagaṛāvats. Sāḍū Mātā, thinking that the life of her husband Savāī Bhoj will be spared, complies with the mendicant's wish. But he soon dissolves her illusions by telling her that her husband will die in battle and that it is the eldest brother, Tej Siṃh, or Tejājī, the son of a Banyā woman, who will survive the "mahābhārat."

However, after demanding the deaths of 23 Bagaṛāvats, Bhagavān reciprocates by granting Sāḍū Mātā a boon. Sāḍū Mātā wishes nothing more than to have Bhagavān to be born as her son. Bhagavān agrees to her wish, promising to manifest himself on the thirteenth day after Savāī Bhoj has been slain in battle. Whereas the Bagaṛāvats are actively slain by Bhavānī in the battle, it is Sāḍū Mātā who initiates their deaths through her promise to Bhagavān. The word used here is *sakalp*, which can mean "an offering," "the intention to offer," or "a promise."[35] Sāḍū Mātā thus utters the intention to offer, and Bhavānī receives the offering in the sacred field of battle. Sāḍū Mātā and Bhavānī both play a decisive role in the slayings of the Bagaṛāvats. Both are joined to the Bagaṛāvats in a singular fashion: Sāḍū Mātā as Savāī Bhoj's wife, and Bhavānī, or Queen Jaimatī, as his lover. However, while Bhavānī is overtly involved in their killings, Sāḍū Mātā is covertly involved in the process that results in the Bagaṛāvats' deaths. Bhavānī and Sāḍū Mātā represent two sides of the same feminine power. Both preside over life and death, although Bhavānī is the more pronouncedly divine of the two. In Sāḍū Mātā's case it is her bhakti that characterizes her role as the mother of Devnārāyaṇ. Her wish for a son echoes the fulfilment of a bhakta's desire found elsewhere in religious narratives.[36] She relinquishes her status as a married woman for the sake of a son "like" Bhagavān. And in doing so she violates the powerful norm of a widow's fate as a satī. Even so she is called "Sāḍū Satvantī," or "Satī Mātā," in the narrative, that is, she is considered to embody the qualities of a satī even though she has not committed the act of satī.[37]

The third context in which images of women are embedded is that of divine power. Of all the women in the narrative, it is Queen Jaimatī who is central to this context. She is considered to be an incarnation of the goddess Bhavānī, who has manifested herself in order to destroy the 24 Bagaṛāvats. The episode describing her intention to destroy the brothers is paralleled by puranic myths in which the gods, after declaring their inability or unwillingness to destroy a demon, summon the goddess to slay him. In the narrative, Bhavānī explains that she will have to destroy the Bagaṛāvats through deceit, since they cannot be defeated otherwise.

In the episode that has already been outlined in chapter 4, Bhavānī succeeds in slaying the Bagaṛāvats by deceiving them. The means she uses to incite the Rāṇā and the Bagaṛāvats against each other are those of love and marriage, allowing each group to believe that she solely desires each one of them. In reality she makes sure that neither marriage is actually carried to the full. Thus, in the six months spent with the Rāṇā she refuses to play "dice," which is a euphemism for sexual activity, with him, until he has built a new palace for her. Later when she joins up with the Bagaṛāvats, she incites a quarrel between them and the Rāṇā, leading to the deaths of the former, once again avoiding sexually intimate relations.

The Ambivalence of Power

In the previous sections I have examined images of women in the narrative of Devnārāyaṇ from the point of view of different women in different contexts:

those of marriage, devotion, and divine power. The social and religious identities of the women involved were formed by each of these contexts. Thus, they were successively wives, mothers, devotees, and goddesses. In their status as wives the women appeared predominantly in anonymous and passive characterizations. Notwithstanding this image, the women were shown to exercise an important influence in the domain of birth with regard to the qualities of their respective offspring. Moreover, they also acted as integrators and assimilators of different social groups within the frame of the narrative and the cult. In the second example of Sāḍū Mātā, we find that her identity is only partially determined through her status as the wife of Savāī Bhoj. More prominent is the position and authority she derives from being a devotee of Bhagavān. As a devotee she is closer to her divine "parent" than she is to her human husband. She is represented in a more independent and volitional manner than are the women in the first examples. Her power is derived from her status as a devotee, and finally as mother of Devnārāyaṇ. In the third and last example we find the most extreme and overt expression of power issuing from the fact that Queen Jaimatī is an incarnation of the goddess Bhavānī. Although Queen Jaimatī enters into marital relations with both the Rāṇā and Savāī Bhoj, her identity is least of all determined by marriage. In fact, as I have shown, she skilfully avoids the consummation of these marriages. Whereas in the first examples, women are "tricked" into marriage, in this case it is the Rāṇā and the Bagaṛāvats who are tricked into getting married by the goddess. Queen Jaimatī represents the most independent, volitional woman in the narrative, standing alone in her destructive power.[38]

Taken together, these examples point to a continuum rather than an opposition of images.[39] On one end of the continuum, women's identities and the power they wield is derived from their status as wives. On the other end of the continuum a woman's identity is derived from her divine origin. Midway between these two extremes is the figure of Sāḍū Mātā, who represents a break from a complete identification with a human husband to an identification with Bhagavān.[40] This identification characterizes her both as a devotee and as the mother of Devnārāyaṇ.[41] Whereas in the first cases women wield influence in the domain of birth, in the second and third cases women wield power over both birth and death. In both the latter cases, devotion is of central importance. In Sāḍū Mātā's case, it is devotion that brings forth creative powers that then result in the birth of Devnārāyaṇ. In the case of Bhavānī, the situation is reversed, in that she is the focus of devotion. The Bagaṛāvats' devotion to her, however, leads to the war between them and the Rāṇā and to their destruction. But it is their voluntary death that in turn elevates their status as heroes in the narrative and cult. The images of women discussed here mirror crucial concerns of the community of devotees articulated in the narrative: social interrelationships, religious power, and religiopolitical solidarity and disparity. Women thus traverse different domains—domains accredited both to women and to men. They move skilfully between interior domestic realms of marriage and childbearing and exterior political realms of battle and bloodshed, thereby showing that the borders between these realms are interpenetrating and fluid.[42] Thus the discourse on sociality, and on the sources of social, secular, and divine power, is itself represented in terms of a wide range of shifting contexts. At times there is commingling, and at other times confrontation. At times there is submission and compliance and at other times fear-inspiring power and the strength derived from devotion.

7
Divine Testimony

Parcyo

In addition to the sections in the narrative called gāv and arthāv, consisting of song and declamatory speech,[1] there are also larger subdivisions brought under the heading of "parcyo," which is the Mārvāṛī equivalent of "proof" or "divine testimony."[2] These subdivisions relate to incidents in which Devnārāyaṇ provides testimony of his divinity. The submission of "proof" through various divine acts dictates the overall characterization of the second part of the narrative. This is in contrast to the first part, which is said to be marked by *dukh* (suffering, pain, disharmony). The notion of parcyo approaches the idea of an episodic structure of the narrative, which is comparable to the idea of *parvāṛos* in the epic of Pābūjī. Parvāṛos are considered to be "story-episodes" into which the epic of Pābūjī is divided. According to Smith (1991: 17) the singers of the epic do not have a unitary term for the epic (such as "the epic of Pābūjī") but call it a "collection of individual episodes" (*Pābūjī rā parvāṛā*). In the case of Devnārāyaṇ, Śrī Hukamārām Bhopā refers to various parcyos that, as deeds of the god, also single out individual episodes. Śrī Hukamārām Bhopā also adds that the parcyos are not named individually but numerically (first, second, third, fourth, and so on). The first parcyo occurs at the very birth of Devnārāyaṇ, when he brings back to life the Kacchāvā Sirdars of Amerav, together with their five hundred horses and five hundred soldiers. The second parcyo occurs when swords in Rāvjī's court start rattling on their own and the balconies of his fort topple down. The third parcyo is when Devnārāyaṇ confronts the Jogīṇīs in Sindhbāḍā and revives Chochū Bhāṭ, who has been devoured by them. The fourth parcyo happens when Devnārāyaṇ, while camping on the outskirts of "Ujjini Dhār," assaults the demons of Fort Gājanā and gains the hand of the demon's daughter, Princess Cā̃vaṭi. The fifth parcyo involves the attack on Dīyājī's Fort Sāvar, in which Devnārāyaṇ frees the mare Bāvlī from captivity and breaks Dīyājī's teeth. Another parcyo describes Devnārāyaṇ and Bhūṇājī's assault on the Dhārāpati's Fort Pilodā. Devnārāyaṇ casts his "poison gaze" on the fort and burns it to the ground. After this he provides testimony to Jetū Birāṇī, a woman belonging to the Banyā caste, who is childless and whose husband has died. On her way to the funeral ceremony, she salutes

Devnārāyaṇ, who happens to say: "Live well, child!" [The Birāṇī replied:] "My husband has expired, and I'm going to burn myself." Devnārāyaṇ keeps his word, and brings back Jetū Birāṇī's husband to life so that she can continue to live, and their marriage remains intact.[3] The next parcyo is when Devnārāyaṇ, after he has set up court in Causlā Kheḍā, attacks Rāṇ City for the first time, after Rāvjī has demanded a tax from him. After this parcyo Devnārāyaṇ finally proceeds to free his cows from captivity, before returning to Indrāsan in Baikuṇṭh.

Almost all of the passages pointed out by Śrī Hukamārām Bhopā relate to "martial" events and deeds of Devnārāyaṇ. Even though in some incidents he revives individuals from death, the circumstances are nevertheless, up to a point, confrontational. Other parcyos deal explicitly with assaults on enemies or enemy forts. The overall sense emerging from this list of parcyos is one of a strong deity reversing the defeats of his ancestors, the Bagaṛāvats. But the "martial" incidents of the second part are different from those of the first, in the sense that they are the result of Devnārāyaṇ's divine powers. The "battles" he wins are not won forcefully but "miraculously." And it is these miracles that in turn provide "testimony" of his divinity. The episodic division of the narrative into different parcyos establishes a link between the narrative structure and the religious discourse of the narrative. One could perhaps even describe the narrative as displaying an "epiphany" of divine testimony, through which Devnārāyaṇ "enrolls" his devotees and establishes his cult. Finally, Devnārāyaṇ's parcyos are comparable to the *līlās* of Kṛṣṇa, in that they also mark the itinerary of the god in a region that is actively infused with his divine power and play.

❁ A Journey through Realms ❁

In the sections to follow, the focus is on the different chapters in Devnārāyaṇ's biography, which is largely qualified by the various instances of the testimony he provides. The aim is not to furnish an exhaustive description of each and every event but to supply the reader with a selection of moments from the journey of the god's life. The biography of the god is not just about Devnārāyaṇ; in reality it constitutes him. The narrative *is* Devnārāyaṇ, and, vice versa, Devnārāyaṇ is manifest in the spoken narrative. The presence of the god is spread over the entire narrative, in each of its utterances and episodes. Devnārāyaṇ moves through each instance of the narrative while at the same time being created through it.

The sequence followed here is supplied by the narrative's own progression, beginning with Devnārāyaṇ's birth. This path of description makes possible, along with an acquaintance with the narrative's religious and symbolic meanings, an appreciation of the details of the story itself.

Birth

The account of the birth of Devnārāyaṇ is the first parcyo in a long line of miracles through which he supplies testimony of his divine provenance and consolidates his sovereignty over different realms. The imagery of the event is suffused with striking religious and bodily symbols. Danger and calamity are juxtaposed with hope and protection. The great war between the Bagaṛāvats and the Rānā has only recently come to an end. The wives of 23 brothers, except for Savāī Bhoj's wife, Sāḍū, all burn themselves on their husbands' funeral pyres. In the aftermath of that annihilating war, Sāḍū, disheveled and wild in appearance, prays to Bhagavān in the stark wilderness of a hilltop. Eleven days have gone by. Bhagavān has promised to appear in her shoulder sash on the thirteenth day after Savāī Bhoj's death—at the end of the time after which death generates pollution. It is in the aftermath of the war also that the Rāṇā realizes that his chieftains have not captured three things of great value: first, the golden image gifted to Savāī Bhoj by his guru, Rūpnāth (alias Śaṅkar); second, the cow of plenty, which the Bagaṛāvats likewise received from Rūpnāth; and third, Savāī Bhoj's wife, Sāḍū, who unlike the other wives has survived the decimation of the battle. Since the golden image, which is under Tejājī's protection on the mountain of Richor, cannot be retrieved,[4] the Rāṇā decides to concentrate on capturing the Bagaṛāvat's cow(s) and Savāī Bhoj's wife, Sāḍū Mātā.[5] When Nāpā, one of the Bagaṛāvats' cowherd chieftains, hears of the Rāṇā's intentions, he sets out on a search for Sāḍū Mātā. He finds her on the Hill of Mālāsarī "singing praises of Bhagavān." He mistakes her hideous, awesome, and dreadful appearance (bikharālrūp) for the result of grief and insanity on account of the Bagaṛāvats' deaths. He does not realize the hidden affinity between her and Queen Jaimatī, who on the battlefield had also resumed her terrifying blood-drenched aspect as the goddess Bhavānī. He does not realize that her appearance is the result of both the danger and the uncertainty set free after the cataclysmic battle, and the ascetic heat she draws from her single-minded penance. Nāpā treats her as an almost "hysterical," grieved, and nearly deranged woman in need of being coaxed into sheltering herself from the impending threat of the Rāṇā. His stubborn disbelief in Sāḍū's claim that Bhagavān will soon be born as her son is contrasted with her steadfast trust. Sāḍū Mātā knows of her bond with Bhagavān. Her penance on the hilltop and her earlier recognition of Bhagavān in the guise of a wandering mendicant speak for her qualities as a bhakta.[6] But, underlying Nāpā's attempt to "save" Sāḍu Mātā by removing her from the scene of her penance is also the age-old attempt to both scatter and contain the powers of an ascetic. It is only on account of her devotion that Bhagavān grants her the wish to become the mother of God. The intimate relationship between Sāḍū Mātā and Devnārāyaṇ is thus not only between mother and child but also between devotee and god.

When Sāḍū Mātā refuses to leave the hilltop, Nāpā's scepticism leads to rage, and he draws out his sword to slay her and thus save the Bagaṛāvats' honor. At the point of this rash and disastrous event, Bhagavān is far below the surface of the earth, in the "thirteenth" underworld, the deepest depths of the subterranean realms. Down there in the kingdom of the Nāgas, he is immersed in a game of dice with Rājā Bāsak, the king of the underworld. There are no reasons given for this game of dice. It almost seems as if they are playing the game out of pure leisure. Unlike in other, sometimes famous, dice games of the *Mahābhārata* or between Śiva and Pāravatī, nothing seems to be overtly at stake. They appear to play because they have the time to play. After all it is still another two days before Devnārāyaṇ has promised to manifest himself as Sāḍū's son. But it is precisely this uneventful scene of dice-playing in the thirteenth level of the underworld that fits into the cataclysmic imagery surrounding Devnārāyaṇ's birth. A generation ago it was the same dice partner of Bhagavān, Rājā Bāsak, who was the first to initiate the Bagaṛāvats' deaths. It is his complaint of falling drops of dārū (locally made liquor), seeping through the earth into his kingdom far below, after the Bagaṛāvats have steeped an entire hillside with the substance, that is sent to Bhagavān. It is his demand that a means be found to destroy the violating brothers. And now, after that demand has been fulfilled, he sits playing a game of dice with Devnārāyaṇ. The first round—so to speak—has been won by Bāsak: the Bagaṛāvats are dead. What is at stake this round? Is it perhaps Bhagavān's promise of birth, renewal, and healing? Rājā Bāsak is Devnārāyaṇ's dark, venomous, underworld counterpart, who, as the verbal narrative and paṛ both tell us, spits his poison breath onto the exquisite symbol of life and transcendence, the lotus-blossom that Devnārāyaṇ holds in his hand. But before the flower can shrivel away, Devnārāyaṇ restores it to perfection with his nectar gaze. The blossom is in a perpetual state of balance. Poison-breath and nectar-gaze; night and day; chaos and order.[7]

Thus, beneath the fragile situation on the hilltop, a game of balance is being played out, and a decision is being made. Will the god disengage himself from his dark companion, from the glittering, bedazzling, jewel-bedecked underworld kingdom, to rise—unlike other avatāras, who descend—to the earth's surface, to take part in another kind of game? Two days before the promised date, Bhagavān cuts short the game of dice, with the claim that someone is "troubling my satī." His departure reverses the imagery of the first instance, in which the Bagaṛāvats' presence was felt in the underworld. He rises on a jet of water that is strong enough to bore a path through the solid rock of the hilltop and split it apart. The descent of alcohol is replaced by the ascent of water, keeping the symbols and domains of father and son—Savāī Bhoj and Devnārāyaṇ—apart. The jet of water bears a lotus blossom that bears the infant Devnārāyaṇ. The lotus blossom falls into Sāḍū Mātā's lap, and in the blossom "Dev Mahārāj, the lord of the three worlds, was manifest on his own." But Nāpā, the cowherd chief, continues to be doubtful even of this very tangible manifestation of Bhagavān. He accuses Sāḍū Mātā of being a sorceress who has conjured up a human infant through magic powers she has acquired in Malwa.[8] Nāpā demands "proof" of the infant's divinity. When Sāḍū Mātā tries to defend Devnārāyaṇ by pointing out that he is only a child, Nāpā comes up with an intriguing metaphor: snakes' "children" are not "small," they are just as "big" as full-grown snakes. In other words, neither the potency of a snake nor that of god is diminished through physical size. If Devnārāyaṇ is really God, then he should be able to revive two Rajput confederates of the Bagaṛāvats, and their armies. The allies of the Bagaṛāvats are Khaḍak Siṃh and Nirvān Siṃh, two Sirdārs of the Kachāvā (Kacchavāhā) Rajput clan[9] who have been killed by the Rāṇā's forces while protecting the Bagaṛāvats' cattle. Devnārāyaṇ revives the two Rajput chieftains, who also meet up with the cowherds assembled at the hill of Goram. The Sirdārs claim that another *sattā* ("power," "sovereignty," or "force") has established itself, heralding a new period in which the powers that have been will be overruled. This first parcyo of Devnārāyaṇ that is connected to the symbols of the martial realm provides a sign, so to speak, for the founding of a new "rule." This new "rule" is not linked to any particular royal dynasty but to the sovereignty of God himself.[10] The revival of the two Kachāvā brothers, who claim Devnārāyaṇ's supremacy, is comparable to later incidents in which Devnārāyaṇ revives individuals who thereafter also swear allegiance to him. The most important of these incidents is the one in which the Rāṇā is killed and revived and given a new Rajput identity as the Sisodiya king who establishes the city of Udaipur in Marwar.[11]

Childhood

Devnārāyaṇ's childhood is a variation on two interconnected themes. On the one hand it resembles the Indo-European myth of the hero's birth being followed by an attempt to kill him (and other innocent children) and the hero being raised by foster parents, ignorant of his true divine or royal identity.[12] On the other hand, it follows a pattern set by a myth much closer to the region of its provenance, namely the myth of Kṛṣṇa. The parallels that become apparent between the childhood of Devnārāyaṇ and that of Kṛṣṇa point both to deeper patterns operating in the structure of these myths, as well to aspects of intertextuality that continuously surface throughout the narrative of Devnārāyaṇ. Again, these larger patterns are bound to the more specific context and intention of the narrative as a story that successively deals with the establishment of Devnārāyaṇ's divinity. From this perspective, the overcoming of threats to his life and other related incidents, it is the question of "divine testimony" that is at stake. When Devnārāyaṇ manifests himself on the Hill of Mālāsarī, the Rāṇā sees a number of signs and omens in his palace: swords begin rattling on their own, elephants and horses stop eating *talavā cūrmā* and *rātab ghās*,[13] and three balconies collapse on their own. He summons his paṇḍits and tells them to read the horoscope and explain these strange happenings. The paṇḍits, who are from Kāśī, tell the Rāṇā that the avenger of the Bagaṛāvats, Bhagavān, has taken incarnation. Fearful of the paṇḍit's prophecy, the Rāṇā asks them whether there is any one powerful enough to kill Devnārāyaṇ immediately. The paṇḍits reply that they can do so on the condition that the Rāṇā hand over half his kingdom to them, which he then agrees to do. Four paṇḍits, thereafter, depart on their murderous mission to Sāḍū Mātā's house in Daṛāvat (or Goṭhā).

This incident is one of the extremely rare occasions in which paṇḍits or Brahmans feature in the narrative. Except for two other brief instances, the occurence of Brahmans is practically nonexistent. In a prior episode involving Devnārāyaṇ's grandfather, Bāgh Siṃh, it is a Brahman who looks after the man-lion in the garden that is his home. In a passage following Devnārāyaṇ's birth, it is, intriguingly, Devnārāyaṇ himself who takes on the guise of a Brahman in order to confuse his uncles[14] into abandoning the cradle in which he is being carried by them on the way to Malwa. Apart from these three occurrences, there is no mention of members of this—at least in the construction of sociologists and anthropologists—excessively important community of ritual specialists, and priests. True, there is a pattern to be found in all three incidents in terms of the representation of Brahmans: they preside over the realm of rituals, omens, horoscopes, and mantras, and they are—at least in the first two cases—shown to be affiliated with persons wielding temporal power (Bāgh Siṃh and the Rāṇā). But the representation of Brahmans does not stop here. They are pictured as wanting almost greedily to partake of the material benefits of the realm of their masters. The Brahman caretaker of Bāgh Siṃh desires to marry one of the 13 women Bāgh Siṃh has embraced, and the Rāṇā's paṇḍits ask him to hand over half his kingdom to them. But the Brahman's avaricious attempts at gaining more "possessions" have negative or even paradoxical results: Bāgh Siṃh's caretaker chooses a woman from the lowest caste, whom he cannot ordinarily marry, but he is forced into doing so because of the promise he has given Bāgh Siṃh not to consider the woman's social position while choosing her as his bride. The four paṇḍits who set out to kill Devnārāyaṇ, as I will now show, only return confused and quarreling among each other, having utterly failed in their mission. As in the case of many other folk narratives and cults that emphasize martiality and a warrior ethic, the narrative of Devnārāyaṇ also deemphasizes the values and hierarchies of the *varṇa* system, and its inherent separation as well as interlinking of social groups on the basis of ritual purity and impurity. It is true that Brahmans need to be consulted regarding questions concerning esoteric and ritual matters. But their authority does not extend beyond this domain. They are not major players in the narrative. The major players are cowherds, potters, weavers, washerwomen, Rajputs, Paṭhāns, and so on. The narrative does not, therefore, constitute an example of what M. N. Srinivas (1952) has called "Sanskritization" or what Shulman (1989: 7) more recently calls "the process of Brahmanical restructuring." The paradigm that is being reflected and emulated, if any, is not a Brahmanical one. Matters of social and ritual prestige are not negotiated by incorporating the terms, metaphors, paraphernalia, or even narrative framework of "Brahmanical culture." Such elements are almost consciously ignored and underplayed. The narrative in its representations itself reflects and represents a cultural milieu that occupies a large space that is adjacent and concurrent to the Brahmanical creation of social order and ritual.

When the paṇḍits visit Sāḍū Mātā in Daṛāvat, they send her off to fetch water in a pot of "unburnt clay."[15] Meanwhile, they approach the cradle in which Devnārāyaṇ is lying, one by one, with the intention to kill the infant. But instead of finding Devnārāyaṇ each of them is confronted with a different form that Devnārāyaṇ has assumed. Devnārāyaṇ is a great "artist," "magician," and "wizard," and the four different forms he shows the Brahmans speak loudly for these abilities. However, the four forms he appears in are also symbols of different aspects of the god and of his powers in the material, transient world. In the first manifestation he appears as a serpent, as "Śes Nāg," sleeping under a costly shawl, but fanning its hood when the Brahman looks beneath the shawl. The serpent, as I have pointed out earlier in reference to Bāsak Nāg, is Devnārāyaṇ's dark, underworld counterpart, also suggesting doom and death. In the second manifestation, Devnārāyaṇ appears as an extremely old man who is about to breathe his last. This form complements the fourth manifestation, in which he appears as a child suckling its own big toe. The second and fourth manifestations thus symbolize the major junctures of mortality, namely birth/childhood and death/old age. The third manifestation, which in reality is a "nonmanifestation" because Devnārāyaṇ "appears" as "emptiness," signifies his formless, transcendent aspect as *nirākar* (formless) and *nirañjan* (unblemished). The emptiness of the cradle conveys the potentiality of different possibilities that Devnārāyaṇ combines within himself.

Confused by these different appearances, the paṇḍits begin quarreling among themselves, and they return to Rān City as soon as possible. Over there a *dūtī* ("female messenger," "evil woman") volunteers to set out and slay Devnārāyaṇ. This "female messenger" and the means she uses—she smears her breasts with venom—falls closest to the image of Pūtanā, the demoness who tries to kill the infant Kṛṣṇa. Although the passage in the oral narrative is less elaborate and less dramatic than the one in the *Bhāgavata Purāṇa*, the resemblances are powerfully striking. Like the demoness Pūtanā, the dūtī too assumes another shape, that of Sāḍū Mātā's elder sister from their uncle's elder brother's side. The disguise is perhaps less seductively dazzling than that of Pūtanā, who had "jasmine bound to her hair . . . cast sidelong glances and smiled sweetly . . . being mistaken for Śrī herself," but it is certainly effective in convincing Sāḍū Mātā that the dūtī should be allowed to suckle her nephew. Here, like Pūtanā, the dūtī too smears her breasts with poison. But Devnārāyaṇ, like Kṛṣṇa, suckles the woman so intensely that all her inner organs are sucked out in the process, and the dūtī is killed. In the oral narrative the dūtī does not, like Pūtanā, undergo a transformation after having being killed by Devnārāyaṇ.[16] Instead, Sāḍū Mātā takes this thwarted threat as an opportunity for her to leave Daṛāvat and return to her natal home in Malwa.

The Flight to Malwa

Once Sāḍū Mātā realizes that her life, and that of Devnārāyaṇ, is in danger, she decides to return to her natal home in Malwa. She is accompanied by her brothers Āmo and Nīmo and by the two Bhīls Salā and Malā. At this point in the narrative we are informed that Devnārāyaṇ's horse, Līlā (Līlāgar), was born at the same time as Devnārāyaṇ. Līlāgar is the foal of Sāḍū Mātā's mare Kāḷavī. There is a pact between Devnārāyaṇ and Līlāgar that they will suckle their respective mothers always concurrently. Horse and rider are inseparable, seamlessly connected. This bond also informs the central incident of their journey to Malwa, in which Devnārāyaṇ is abandoned by his uncles. In the third occurrence of a Brahman in the narrative, Āmo and Nīmo are stopped by a solitary Brahman. The Brahman is none other than Devnārāyaṇ himself, who has assumed this form in order to test his uncles' "power." The Brahman prepares a horoscope for the infant, claiming that according to his calculations the boy will bring great harm to his family: he will destroy both his paternal and maternal homes. Āmo and Nīmo believe the Brahman rather than their sister's claim that the boy is an avatāra. They tip over the cradle into one of the many streams flowing through the forest they are journeying through. Once abandoned, Devnārāyaṇ is sheltered by a lioness, who suckles him. As soon as Devnārāyaṇ suckles the lioness, his horse, Līlāgar, also begins to suckle his mother, Kāḷavi. Sāḍū Mātā admonishes the foal for breaking his promise to Devnārāyaṇ, but Līlāgar insists that Devnārāyaṇ is also doing the same thing at that very moment. Sāḍū rides back to her brothers and discovers that they have turned over the cradle into one of the streams flowing through "that country." Sāḍū Mātā finds the lioness suckling Devnārāyaṇ. Thinking that she can easily frighten the lioness away, she commences shooting a barrage of arrows at it, but with no effect. The lioness responds by claiming that she will not give away her child. Then Sāḍū Mātā changes her tone and addresses the lioness as her "dharam-sister." She requests that the lioness hand back the child to her. The lioness's response is interesting, in that she once again lays more claims to motherhood over Devnārāyaṇ than Sāḍū Mātā has: she has suckled him with seven teats, whereas Sāḍū Mātā has offered him only one! Her response also has a didactic element to it: she tells Sāḍū Mātā not to trust anyone and not to entrust anyone else with anything of her own. This instructive content of her speech to Sāḍū Mātā parallels other instances in the narrative in which animals either consistently voice didactic and moral themes or are the subjects in short tales that are used to press a particular point home to one or more of the characters in the narrative.[17]

In this short passage, situated in a forest on the way to Malwa, three things are important. The first, of course, is the temporary abandonment of Devnārāyaṇ, a feature that is common to the lives of other Indian (and Indo-European) "epic" heroes. The second is the instrumentality through which Devnārāyaṇ is abandoned: he is abandoned because of a stratagem of his own creation. In a rare change of identity, he becomes a member of a social group that has so far in the narrative generally received a negative representation. To be sure, the Brahman's authority over the realm of astrology is not doubted. But his appearance, like that of the four paṇḍits earlier in the story, is detrimental to Devnārāyaṇ's well-being. However, his abondenment leads to the third important aspect of the passage, which is his being sheltered by a lioness. Symbol of strength, martial prowess, and, not insignificantly, also the Goddess, the lioness plays the role of surrogate mother in the forest of abandonment. Sāḍū Mātā competes with the lioness in laying claim to the child and can regain possession only after becoming the lioness's "sister," a symbolic bond that signifies equality and perhaps even subordination on part of Sāḍū Mātā. But the appearance of the lioness as surrogate mother has another deeper significance in terms of Sāḍū Mātā's decision to flee to Malwa. As will become apparent later, especially in Sāḍū Mātā's attempt to dispose of Chochū Bhāṭ, the Bagaṛāvats' genealogist and bard, the journey to Malwa and Devnārāyaṇ's time spent there are linked to his location in the maternal realm. In the maternal realm it is, of course, Sāḍū Mātā who has authority and control. Here she can guarantee a sheltered, conflict-free, idyllic environment in which her son Devnārāyaṇ is kept away from the gory and tragic past, ignorant of his destiny as king and god. The passage through the forest with the appearance of the lioness-mother strengthens the movement that is propelling Sāḍū Mātā and Devnārāyaṇ towards his carefree, pastoral childhood in Malwa. This continues until the visit of Chochū Bhāṭ and his mother Deḷū Mātā to Malwa. Although Sāḍū Mātā never completely relinquishes control over decisions that are made by Devnārāyaṇ and his four cousins, it becomes clear that Devnārāyaṇ's resolution to later leave Malwa and return to Causlā Kheḍā, near Bhilwara, marks the commencement of a shift toward the "paternal realm" and its concerns.

Chochū Bhāṭ in Malwa

The Bagaṛāvats' kuldevī, Bijorī Kājrī, informs Chochū Bhāṭ that Devnārāyaṇ has taken incarnation after his masters have passed away. Chochū reaches Malwa, together with his old mother, Deḷū Mātā (and not with his wife, as one might expect of a grown man). This fact again characterizes Malwa as the "maternal" realm (not necessarily the feminine one). We encounter sets of mother-and-child relationships: Sāḍū Mātā and Devnārāyaṇ; Kāḷavī Ghoṛī and Līlāgar;[18] Deḷū Mātā and Chochū Bhāṭ. Fathers and wives are absent. But Chochū Bhāṭ is both symbol and messenger of the world of fathers, and this is what Sāḍū Mātā immediately realizes. She plans to eliminate the Bhāṭ. The three attempts she makes at having him slain are important because they mark the beginning of a series of events in which the Bhāṭ's life is first threatened and then protected by Devnārāyaṇ. The vulnerability and courage that is simultaneously expressed by the Bhāṭ make him one of Devnārāyaṇ's closest associates.[19] In each of the three attempts by Sāḍū Mātā, Devnārāyaṇ saves the Bhāṭ's life. In one case it is his attendants Kālā and Gora Bherū who pull the Bhāṭ out of a pond into which he has been drowned by Sāḍū Mātā's cowherds. In the second case she prepares a poisoned meal for the Bhāṭ and a meal with *amṛt* (nectar) for her son. To her horror, Devnārāyaṇ exchanges plates with the Bhāṭ, eating the poisoned food himself and letting the Bhāṭ eat the food with amṛt. Here again, we encounter the two complementary substances of nectar and poison and Devnārāyaṇ's ability to deal with both in a creative manner. After eating the poisoned food, he coughs up "black scorpions," that is, he creates the venomous creatures from the poison he has consumed. The scorpions "begin serving Bhagavān" from then on. In fact, Devnārāyaṇ is also lord of scorpions and snakes, both of whom feature as part of his "entourage" in iconographic representation, for example, on the paṛ.[20]

The last instance is revealing in many senses. Here Sāḍū Mātā sends Chochū Bhāṭ to Sindhbāḍā, a sacred banyan tree occupied by Jogīṇīs. The Bhāṭ is supposed to carry an offering of one and a half rupees' worth of prasād for the Jogīṇīs. But as it turns out, the prasād is only a ploy to get him there; the real "offering" is the Bhāṭ himself. Sāḍū Mātā informs them that she is sending such an offering to them, the offering of a human being. When the Bhāṭ reaches the Jogīṇīs' banyan-tree residence, they swoop down on him and devour him, bones and all. After discovering that Sindhbāḍā is no village but a fatally dangerous place where Jogīṇīs reside, Deḷū Mātā pours out her lamentation to Devnārāyaṇ. Together with his attendants Kālā and Gorā Bherū̃, Devnārāyaṇ then proceeds of Sindhbāḍā. On the way Bherū̃ spots a fox, which, in order to get at some yellow berries growing on bushes and trees, swipes them with his tail, causing the berries to fall down. The insertion of this brief section in the narrative, like the previous one featuring the lioness, has an instructive purpose. Upon reaching Sindhbāḍā, Bherū̃nāth repeats what the fox has done: he catches hold of the tree trunk and shakes it vigorously, causing the Jogīṇīs, who are sitting on the tree's leaves to rapidly fall to the ground and into a nearby well. Devnārāyaṇ makes the Jogīṇīs vomit out the Bhāṭ's remains, even though three days have passed since they have devoured him. Devnārāyaṇ puts the remains together; but one rib and its flesh are missing. Recovering those pieces leads Devnārāyaṇ to Rājā Bāsak, a mango tree, and a deer.

Supposedly a thief has stolen the pieces and has hidden them in the underworld. Rājā Bāsak challenges Devnārāyaṇ to a game of dice, bringing up this motif for a second time in the narrative. What is at stake is much more explicit now: it is a game of win or die, as Rājā Bāsak says: "If I lose, cut my head off. If you lose, then I'll cut your head off." Devnārāyaṇ wins all three rounds of the game. Bāsak offers Devnārāyaṇ one of his hundred hoods to cut off. But Devnārāyaṇ, as with Bherū̃ and the banyan tree earlier, is not interested in the "branches" but in the trunk, that is, in the source of the hundred hoods. Rājā Bāsak capitulates quickly, agreeing instead to offer Devnārāyaṇ first his own and then his brother-in-law's daughter in marriage.

Devnārāyaṇ returns from the underworld having married for the first time. His Nāgkanyā wife is the first of three wives, all of whom he marries during the course of the return journey. But his marriage to the Nāgkanyā does not resolve the issue of the Bhāṭ's missing rib and its flesh. Devnārāyaṇ procures the rib by cutting a branch off a mango tree and the flesh by cutting it off a deer. When the tree and the deer complain that he will be setting a bad example by doing this, Devnārāyaṇ assures them that they will always be protected from harm. Anyone worshiping Devnārāyaṇ who will either cut wood from a mango tree or harm a deer will be violating the god's word. Such a devotee's offerings will not be accepted by the god. By making this claim Devnārāyaṇ, is, in fact, connecting his worship and the cult to the issue of "environmental protection." The protection of mango trees and deer is in this case religiously legitimized by this statement of the god's.

The passage discussed here thus has both a didactic and "environmental" aspect featuring animals and trees. The other tree occurring here, namely, the banyan (*baḍ*), moreover, has a religious and ritual significance transcending that, for example, of the mango. It is the residence of the flesh-eating, hungry helpers of Sāḍū Mātā, the Jogīṇīs.

The motifs of the banyan tree, the flesh-eating Jogīṇīs, Bherū̃'s shaking of the tree trunk, Devnārāyaṇ's competition with the hundred-headed serpent king, and Sāḍū Mātā's association with the Jogīṇīs each have a deeper symbolic significance that becomes apparent when the story is compared to other regional narrative traditions, especially those related to the *Mahābhārata*. Thus, for example, in Rajasthani and Garhwali oral tellings of the epic, there are passages that connect Kuntī, the banyan tree, the Kauravas, and Bhīma together. Sharma[21] summarizes the passage in the Rajasthani telling as follows.

> Kuntī wanted to plant a tree. But since such a thing could cause enmity on the part of the Kauravas, Bhīma forbid (her from) planting a tree. Kuntī did not agree, and she planted the tree anyway. A little while later the tree grew large and dense, and its shade began to spread over a wide (area). When they saw its nice, deep shade, the Kauravas went there to play. Nakula went there with the Eternal Food (nitya bhojan). He hung the food on a branch and played together with the Kauravas. He always gave away the strike off and never got the opportunity to play the lead. Because of this distress, he began to wither away by day and night. When Bhīma noticed his condition, he asked: "Are you getting too little to eat? Are you being troubled by the Forest Witch or is Mother Kuntī disturbing you?" Nakula explained to him that his weakness had nothing to do with these (causes), on the contrary he always gave the lead to the Kauravas, and never had the opportunity himself for the strike off. It was because of this distress that he was so weak. Bhīma commanded Nakula to stay at home, and decided to go instead of him. Bhīma wrapped rags round his feet, poured thickened sweet milk (into them), he took a well rope in his hand, and when he arrived there he fell asleep under the tree. The Kauravas arrived there at the usual time. When they didn't find Nakula, they woke up Bhīma, asked him the reason for Nakula's absence, and explained to him their method of striking off. Bhīma said that they should begin when Nakula came. The Kauravas said that due to Nakula's absence they would play against Bhīma. Bhīma explained that he was sick and shook his foot. The thickened sweet milk trickled out of the rags. The Kauravas took this to be pus. But Bhīma said that he would—on the condition that the Kauravas took down the food that was hung up and gave it to him to eat—give away the strike off in Nakula's place. The game began after Bhīma had finished eating. The Kauravas threw the ball far away and climbed up the tree. Bhīma encouraged them to climb even higher. As soon as they had climbed up, Bhīma took hold of the tree and shook it vigorously. The Kauravas fell down and died.

In the Garhwali telling, the ball game does not take place under a banyan tree but under a pīpal tree. There is no mention of "Eternal Food," and the Kauravas do not die in the process of falling down from the tree:

> Arjuna withers away because he is bullied by the Kauravas. He plays ball with them during the day. In the evening Duryodhana throws the ball away and tells him to look for it. But because he can't find it, he becomes completely emaciated. Bhīma promises to teach the Kauravas a lesson. He goes to Kurukṣetra with a ball made of wood and places it on the tip of a Pīpal tree standing there. The Pāṇḍavas and Kauravas play against each other the whole day long. In the evening Bhīma tells Duryodhana that they should now play Kud-

> budūṛi, and since Duryodhana has till now always thrown the ball away, Bhīma himself would like to throw the ball away once. He throws it high into the sky, and as the Kauravas grow tired of watching it, it falls down into the Pīpal tree. Bhīma then tells the Kauravas they have till next morning to find the ball. They look all over but cannot find it. The next morning Bhīma shows them the ball in the Pīpal tree and challenges them to retrieve it from the tree. The entire tree is full of Kauravas. But when they climb up, the ball descends, and when they climb down, the ball goes up. Finally Bhīma gives the tree a huge blow and the Kauravas tumble down like "Apricots in August."[22]

As Zoller points out, both the Rajasthani and Garhwali tellings make it clear that the "ball-game" under the banyan or pīpal tree is in reality a deadly earnest matter in which life and death are being wagered. This wager has in the narrative of Devnārāyan been transposed to the game of dice played between Devnārāyaṇ and Rājā Bāsak, who shelters the thief who has stolen the Bhāṭ's rib and its flesh, which "fell into the underworld and . . . flew into the sky." The dice game is being played in the bowels of the earth, where the roots of the Banyan tree—the world-tree—have their hold. Also transposed is the metaphor of the tree to the body of the serpent king, as is the image of a hundred opponents falling dead to the ground when the trunk is shaken or even severed outright. While Bhērū is a multiform of Bhīma shaking the banyan tree above the surface of the earth, Devnārāyaṇ[23] is the latter's multiform beneath the surface of the earth challenging the hundred-hooded Rājā Bāsak, who has hidden parts of the Bhāṭ's mortal remains, without which Devnārāyaṇ cannot rejuvenate him.[24]

In the course of the narrative it becomes clear that Sāḍū Mātā personifies the same qualities and role as does Kuntī in the *Mahābhārata*. Sāḍū Mātā, like Kuntī, represents the virtuous, motherly, dutiful, sheltering aspects of feminine power in the narrative. She stands in contrast to the violent, bloodthirsty, bewitching qualities of Queen Jaimati, alias Bhavānī. Like Kuntī, she is the "mother" not only of Devnārāyaṇ but also of his other four orphaned cousins, Bhūṇā, Bhāṅgī, Medu, and Madno. Although she is not, as in the case of the Pāṇḍavas, the "biological" mother of all five brothers, being the foster mother of four, she nevertheless has the status of their "real" mother. After they have been united, it is she who advises and guides them, resolving potential conflicts between them.

The motherly and sheltering qualities of Sāḍū Mātā do not, however, explain her treatment of Chochū Bhāṭ, whom she sends as a human offering to the Jogīṇīs in the banyan tree. How does one reconcile her maternal and protective attributes with her links with wayward, flesh-eating witches? A partial answer to this ambivalence is available in the underlying association that exists between her and Bhavānī. This connection surfaces at the point when Sāḍū Mātā offers Viṣṇu the "sakalp" of 23 of the 24 Bagaṛāvats. By expressing the intention to offer the brothers an offering she seals their fate. Later it is Bhavānī who actively receives the "offering" of the Bagaṛāvats. Similarly, in the case of Chochū Bhāṭ, Sāḍū

Mātā, while not being the recipient of the offering, is instrumental in making it available to the Joginīs. In both cases, while staying clear of the gory outcome of the "offerings," it is obvious that Sāḍū Mātā is not an unambivalently, protective, motherly figure. While it is true that she primarily fulfils the latter role, it is also worthwhile noting that she presides over the fate of individuals closely connected to her: her husband, Savāī Bhoj, the other Bagaṛāvats, and Chochū Bhāṭ, their genealogist. In order to fully understand the "wild" undercurrent in Sāḍū Mātā's otherwise benevolent personality, it may be helpful to once again turn to another regional tradition in Garhwal connected to the performance of the *Mahābhārata.* In the Pāṇḍavlīlā, the *Mahābhārata* is enacted in a ritual setting that is sponsored by dominant-caste Rajputs (Sax 1996: 356):

> Prominent among female characters in the drama are Kuntī, mother of the five Paṇḍavas brothers, and Draupadi, their common wife . . . the elderly Kuntī is associated with motherhood, sexual modesty, nurturance, and especially virtue, while the dangerous and sexually active Draupadī is explicitly identified as Kālī, and is sometimes the recipient of dramatic blood sacrifices.

Moreover, Kuntī is so closely "identified with truth and virtue that the normal epithet for her is "Truthful Mother Kuntī" (Satī mātā Kuntī) . . . Kuntī is also associated with service (sevā)—in particular, she serves the gods in order to obtain her five sons" (Sax 1996: 368). But as Sax points out the distinction between the dangerous Draupadī and the benevolent Kuntī gets blurred when other narratives are included, such as one in which Arjuna is told by Kuntī to travel to a "huge tree" that is hollow inside and is inhabited by Yoginis. It is these 64 Yoginis who will decide whether the Kauravas or the Pāṇḍavas will win or lose the war. Kuntī tells Arjuna to hide in the tree's hollow and listen to what the Yoginis have to say:

> The sixty-four yoginis began to arrive and Arjun would hear the flapping of their wings. One after another they came, in the shape of vultures. . . . Some were like Chandi, some had skulls, some were bloody, some were like mothers or sisters, some ate the living, some ate the dead. The eldest was an old mother, and she sat in the largest chair. She was of high caste, religious and learned and well-spoken. She said "The war (bhārat) is about to happen. You are all gathered together here; now tell me who should lose and who should win." One hag, who was also known as Kālī, stood up and said "Let the Pāṇḍavas lose, and the Kauravas win!" A second hag fought with the first one: "How can you say such things?" . . . The second returned and said: "Hey, elder sisters! What nonsense this is! How can we be satisfied by the blood of only four brothers? If the sixty Kauravas die, then all our stomachs will be filled. So my mothers, arrange the Pāṇḍavas' victory, and the Kauravas' defeat . . . The old yogini certified that the Pāṇḍavas would win and that the Kauravas would lose . . . Arjun emerged along with his horse . . . [and] went straight to

> his mother. . . . He fell at her feet, and said: "I've seen the whole world, but nothing is greater than your dharma. There was an old mother sitting there amongst the yoginis who was like you. She was just like you!" Mother Kuntī said: "Tell me quickly, what did the yoginis say?" and Arjun replied: "Listen, my mother, I think that this whole affair is your doing! You are the taker, you are the eater, you are the one who has done this Kurukṣetra. I already told you, there was an old woman there just like you. Why are you asking me? You already know!"

Arjuna, who has hidden in the hollow of the "huge tree" (presumably a banyan tree), comes to the unexpected realization that the old mother hag and his own mother are no different from one another. "Differences between Draupadī and Kuntī are effaced. They have kept their true identities secret from the Pāṇḍavas, who innocently regard them as wife and mother. But in reality, both of them are dangerous, blood-thirsty hags, jointly responsible for the carnage of the Mahābhārata war" (Sax (1996: 378). Judging from the parallels that exist between Kuntī and Sāḍū Mātā, one may also infer from the above passage the latter's affinity to Sindhbāḍā's Jogīṇīs, who, even though not explicitly presiding over the fates of the Bagaṛāvats, do dispose of the last traces of their physical memory embodied in the person of Chochū Bhāṭ. However, as I have mentioned earlier, Devnārāyaṇ sees to it that this repository of memory is resurrected after the Jogīṇīs have disgorged the Bhāṭ's remains.

Devnārāyaṇ's Marriage to Pīpalde

Pīpalde is undoubtedly the most important of Devnārāyaṇ's three wives. In fact, there is practically no mention of his other two wives (the Nāgkanyā and Cāvtī Rāṇī) in subsequent sections of the narrative. It is Pīpalde who figures as his queen, giving birth to his two children, Bīlā and Bīlī. At this point I will not enter into the role played by Pīpalde in the narrative but will focus on the significance of Devnārāyaṇ's marriage to her, which also supplies a further example of the god's sovereignty over different realms. Devnārāyaṇ leaves Malwa together with the Bhāṭ, Sāḍū Mātā, oxen carriages, and a herd of cattle. After exactly 45 days of traveling they reach the fabled city of Ujjain ("Ujjini Dhār"), the capital of the legendary King Vikramāditya, after whom the Vikram Era is named.[25]

The king's daughter, Pīpalde, is a cripple: she is lame, blind, and afflicted by leprosy and has horns on her head. On the outskirts of the city, where Devnārāyaṇ and his companions have stopped to rest, there is a temple dedicated to the Goddess. Every day the princess is brought on a palanquin carried by four men to this temple, which they circumambulate in the steadfast hope that the Goddess will cure the princess's diseases and deformations. Devnārāyaṇ's tent and the entrance to the Goddess's temple face each other. On its daily visitation of the temple, Pīpalde's palanquin passes by Devnārāyaṇ, who "awakens" the princess casting his nectar-gaze on her, thereby causing her body to turn pure or immaculate ("golden"). Pīpalde's afflictions are healed by Devnārāyaṇ: she begins to see and to walk again, and the horns and other protrusions disappear. At first people believe that it is the Goddess who has finally cured the princess. But Pīpalde makes it clear to her father that it is not "his" goddess but "the man with the tent who's staying in front of the temple" who has given her "the gift of life." With this statement Pīpalde clearly suggests that the powers of Devnārāyaṇ are superior to those of the king of Ujjain's "own" goddess. Not only that, she also insists on being married to the man. But the king, taking Devnārāyaṇ to be one of the many cowherds from Marwar who pass on the road going to Malwa, does not want Pīpalde to marry him. The princess is quick to point out that Devnārāyaṇ is not a cowherd but an avatāra. Although she, like Sāḍū Mātā and later Bīlī (Devnārāyaṇ's daughter), does not need any elaborate convincing that he is divine, her father is sceptical of her claims. He sets up the condition that a Devnārāyaṇ, as proof of his divinity, recover doorway made of many (or seven) metals that has been stolen by the Daitya. Devnārāyaṇ, unaware of the fact that this is a test in fulfilment of a marriage condition, agrees to retrieve the doorway in return for having rested so long in the territory of the king. Devnārāyaṇ goes to the Daitya's fort together with Bherū̃nāth. Rather than return the doorway, the Daitya sets up another condition for Devnārāyaṇ, which is to marry his own 13-year-old daughter! The Daitya promises to make a dowry gift of the doorway. Bherū̃nāth and Devnārāyaṇ both decide that it is more convenient to accept the marriage offer rather than fight the demons. So while retrieving the doorway for the king of Dhār, which will ultimately lead to his third marriage, Devnārāyaṇ marries the Daitya's daughter, Cā̃vṭī. Having returned the doorway Devnārāyaṇ, lies down to sleep. The king of Dhār tells Chochū Bhāṭ that Pīpalde wishes to marry Devnārāyaṇ. Chochū Bhāṭ advises them to perform the marriage ceremony while Devnārāyaṇ is asleep,[26] because having being married twice already, he will not marry a third time. Brahmans are summoned, a fire-pit is dug, and all the other paraphernalia for the wedding are brought. Chochū Bhāṭ warns the participants to run away or hide as soon as Devnārāyaṇ awakens lest his poison-gaze fall on them. He tells Pīpalde to stand in front of Devnārāyaṇ with a jug of water that will cool his gaze. When the ceremony has been completed and Devnārāyaṇ is about to awaken, all the participants scatter, except for the officiating Brahmans, who greedily try to pick up this and that. The god's poison-gaze falls on them, turning them to stone. But Pīpalde is able to cool him by presenting herself, along with the jug of water. Whereas the Brahmans remain as stone, the four poles (of the awning of the palanquin) are turned into trees by Devnārāyaṇ.

Pīpalde's marriage to Devnārāyaṇ is in fact an inversion of what happens in the marriages known to us from the first part of the narrative. The marriages in the first part are characterized by accident, deceit, and trickery. Invariably women are tricked or persuaded into marrying (excepting in the case of Queen Jaimatī, who tricks the Rāṇā of Savāī Bhoj into marrying her) their husbands. In this case, Devnārāyaṇ is tricked into marrying Pīpalde, who has quite independently chosen to wed him. In fact Devnārāyaṇ is a reluctant suitor throughout. In each of his two earlier marriages, his wives are almost forced on him as part of a bargain in which the retrieval of an object that has been stolen is at stake. Also conspicuous is the absence of socially important themes such as the caste identities of the marriage partners, unlike the instances of marriage in the first part. His marriages to the Nāgkanyā and Cāvṭī are somewhat "liminal": they both belong not to the domain of humans but to other worlds inhabited by serpents and demons. Pīpalde is his only "human" wife. However, here too the marriage is not foregrounded in the social themes that predominate in the marriages of the first part of the narrative[27] but in the fact that Pīpalde is a recipient of the god's grace and powers of healing. It is her experience of Devnārāyaṇ's divinity that awakens in her the desire to marry him. Pīpalde is not only a wife but also a devotee. As she says: "Śrī Mahārāj, I want to stay at your feet. I don't need a home. I've found refuge with you. That's all I desire. There's nothing else I want."

What is the meaning of the marriage between Pīpalde and Devnārāyaṇ, and of Pīpalde's and Devnārāyaṇ's connection to the goddess of Ujjini Dhār? Myths about deities and their multiple wives are widespread in India, both in puranic and folk contexts. Well-known examples are to be found in Śiva's marriage to Pārvatī and Gaṅgā, Khaṇḍobā's marriage to Mhālsā and Bāṇāī, Brahmā's marriage to Sāvitrī and Gāyatrī in Puṣkar, and in the myths of Murukaṉ. According to G. D. Sontheimer (1989: 7), the pattern expressed in all such myths is

> mostly the same: The first wife comes from an upper stratum (or heaven) and the second wife from a lower stratum of society (or the underworld). The second wife usually belongs to a forest tribe or migrant community and, in any case, comes from a spatially separated area, such as a forest or a pastoral region.

While the first wife tends to be more "orthodox" and "distanced," the second wife is earthy, erotic, and devoted. Usually the god's second wife is his "favorite" spouse, with whom he shares a much more intimate and sexually accented relationship. Furthermore, the god's wives also symbolize linkages between different social communities and their participation in a particular cult. Thus, for example, in the Khaṇḍobā cult, his second wife Bāṇāī belongs to the Haṭkar Dhangars, a pastoral community that plays an extremely central role in the worship of the god. Similarly, in Puṣkar, Brahmā marries a local woman belonging to the Ābhīra or Gujar community. After a peculiar purificatory rite she is named Gāyatrī. Today it is she and not Sāvitrī who is seated next to Brahmā in the temple in Puṣkar.[28]

The spatial distinction that Sontheimer mentions regarding the origins of the wives also refers to the complementary domains of settled area (*kṣetra*) and wilderness (*vana, araṇyaka*).[29] Clearly, Devnārāyaṇ's three wives also occupy spatially distinct locations. His first wife, the daughter of the serpent king, lives in the underworld, which Devnārāyaṇ enters from the desolate and dangerous regions of Sindhbāḍā, where the Jogīṇī-inhabited banyan tree grows. His second wife, Cāvṭī, the daughter of a Daitya chief, on account of her demonic origins also resides in a both spatially and socially peripheral "wild" region that stands in contrast to the ordered region of the territory of Jaisalrāj Pūvār's kingdom of Ujjini Dhār. It is only Pīpalde who dwells in a "settled," orderly, and presumably morally unambiguous region of the city. As the daughter of a king, she also symbolizes the organized space of sedentary civilization created by human beings. Nevertheless, there are some unexplained, strange dimensions to the way she is presented to us: her disabilities, her illness, and perhaps most of all the protrusions growing out of her head. These features, as well as the fact that she regularly visits a goddess, situated on the outskirts of Ujjini Dhār, point to irregularities within the system of order. Perhaps Pīpalde is not the perfect representation of the kṣetra we may have initially made her out to be. A clue to Pīpalde's "real" identity and the cause of her deformities is given toward the end of the first part of the narrative. After the Bagaṛāvats have been killed on the battlefield, Nevājī's wife, Netū, the mother of Bhāṅgījī, prepares herself to become a satī. Before committing satī, she removes the nine-month-old fetus she is pregnant with and hands over the baby to the care of the Bagaṛāvats' guru, Rūpnāth. But, then while she is sitting on the funeral fire, she begins to curse Queen Jaimatī:

1. This Netū Nekāḍaṇ began giving curses to Queen Jēmatī:
2. Yes, she was sitting in the funeral pyre.
3. And Netū Nekāḍaṇ said (her) tidings,
4. Look, look, Queen Jēmatī, you come into our homes.
5. But look, at that time,
6. I shall go after giving you only this curse.
7. You became happy. You demanded the heads of the twenty-four.
8. Yes, first of all you demanded (them) just as vegetables before bread.
9. Cataracts will appear in your eyes.
10. And buck horns will grow upon (your) head.
11. Yes, look, (your) legs will become crippled.
12. And oozing from each and every hair, leprosy will appear.
13. I give you only this curse.[30]

In the next section Queen Jaimatī asks Netū how she shall be freed of her curse. Netū replies (Miller 1994: 721):

1. Yes, look, Queen Jēmatī.
2. Yes, the incarnation of Naraṅjan Nirākār will come to my sister-in-law Sāḍū.
3. The simple Sālagrām will come.
4. Yes, the child Lord Kṛṣṇa will wed you.
5. Yes, you will be called Queen Pīpalde Paṅvār.
6. Yes, so only that Devnārāyaṇ will perform the liberation of your body.
7. Only he will reform your life.
8. Yes, the child Lord Kṛṣṇa will wed you.

9. In these homes you will return and after coming you will touch the feet of my sister-in-law.

These lines make it clear that Pīpalde is in reality a reincarnation of Queen Jaimatī, or Bhavānī, who is suffering on account of the devious and violent acts she has performed in the first part of the narrative. But the awesome power of her earlier manifestation is transformed here. As wife and daughter-in-law she is now represented as a considerably humbler, devoted figure. Freed from Netū's curse, she does not revert to her old powerful self; rather she accepts Devnārāyaṇ's powers as supreme. This act of "submission" on the part of the most dominant and strong figure in the first part of the narrative once again is an indication that Devnārāyaṇ's biography involves a "conquest" of different domains and sources of power. In this case, by healing Pīpalde more efficiently than the king's goddess and by acquiring a (reincarnated) goddess as his spouse, Devnārāyaṇ shows his sovereignty over the Goddess and her realm.[31]

Furthermore, in the telling just presented, we also see that Devnārāyaṇ's spouse is the goddess Bhavānī, who in the first part of the narrative is chosen by Viṣṇu to destroy the Bagaṛāvats. While Viṣṇu's classical spouse Śrī or Lakṣmī represents the epitome of auspiciousness, being a deity who bestows fortune and prosperity, Bhavānī or Durgā represent more ambiguous, violent, warring, and at times inauspicious aspects of feminine divine power. On the surface the marriage of Devnārāyaṇ (or Nārāyaṇ or Viṣṇu or Kṛṣṇa) to a reincarnation of the bloodthirsty Queen Jaimatī does not match Viṣṇu's connection to the benevolent goddess Śrī. However, Queen Jaimatī has undergone a double transformation: one time through the crippling curse that Netū gives her, and a second time through her "conversion" upon being healed by Devnārāyaṇ. Pīpalde is, thus, much closer to the image of Viṣṇu's benevolent consort than is Queen Jaimatī. Regardless of these connections, and more important, the reincarnation of Queen Jaimatī as Pīpalde needs to be placed within the framework of kin relationships and the hierarchies attached to them. Thus Savāī Bhoj's erstwhile lover, Queen Jaimatī, returns as his wife Sāḍū Mātā's daughter-in-law. Her status as daughter-in-law requires her to touch the latter's feet, an act of reverence and a hierarchical positioning within the authoritative domain of the mother-in-law.

On all accounts the pattern that Sontheimer outlines concerning "the myth of the god and his two wives" is not repeated here. Certainly Devnārāyaṇ does have more than one wife, but his three wives do not represent the polarities of settled space and wilderness in the distinct manner suggested in Sontheimer's observation, and in the examples provided here. Devnārāyaṇ's first wives undoubtedly do belong to spatial and symbolic regions that fall within the domain of the *vana*, or forest (underworld/demon fort). And his third wife undoubtedly does belong to the quintessential symbol of the kṣetra, or civilized field, namely the city and the kingdom. But surprisingly it is his third wife, belonging to the kṣetra, who is Devnārāyaṇ's most important spouse and not the two whose origins lie in the vana. It is Pīpalde who is Devnārāyaṇ's "favorite" wife, embodying the devotional qualities of a bhakta. Moreover, given the minimal reference to his two other wives, it is almost as if we are dealing with a monogamous god here.

What is the meaning, and explanation, if any, for this nonconformity to a constantly recurring pattern in other myths and religious cults of similar deities in other regions? Why is it that the devotional quality otherwise present in the personality of the god's wife who belongs to the forest or pastoral region occurs here in the wife who belongs to the "higher" social strata of the settled region? In order to arrive at a satisfactory understanding of these inversions, it is perhaps worthwhile to begin with Devnārāyaṇ himself and examine the way he too differs from the deities (Khaṇḍobā, Murukaṉ, Brahmā, Śiva) mentioned in this context.

To begin with, it is worth pointing out that the other deities enumerated here are "well-established" gods with spouses from the "upper stratum" by the time they enter either physically or metaphorically into the forest or pastoral region to marry a second time. This is particularly evident in the cases of Khaṇḍobā and Murukaṉ who woo Bāṇāī and Vaḷḷī respectively, by entering the shepherd's camp or the hunter's jungle preserve. Khaṇḍobā, for example, disguises himself as an old man who tends sheep in order to be near Baṇāī, the *mirdhin* of the shepherd's camp (Sontheimer 1989: 40):

> Like Vaḷḷi, the beloved of Murukaṉ in the Cankam literature, she is not related to any celestial being. She is just there, is tremendously rich. Owns nine lakh of sheep and goats, not counting the barren ones, and is the leader of twelve cattle camps (bārāhaṭṭi) each inhabited by a different clan. Her divinity is rooted in tellurian fertility and prosperity based on cattle wealth. She is the source of the life-giving gift of water to Khaṇḍobā, the god on earth.

Khaṇḍobā's encounter with Bāṇāī and his subsequent marriage to her reveals the story of her "conversion." Gradually she accepts the "old man's" divinity and sees through his disguise. In the myth of Brahmā in Puṣkar, the god does not physically enter the territory of his second spouse; rather she is "abducted" and brought to the site of his *agniṣṭoma-yajña*. The young Ābhīra girl is purified and Brahmanized to the extent that she is called Gāyatrī. Her pastoral connections are, however, kept alive in a folk etymology that associates Gāyatrī with the Hindi *gāy*, or cow. Nevertheless, she too fulfils the pattern of the myth by providing a contrast to Brahmā's first wife, Sāvitrī, who abandons him to settle as a solitary goddess on a hilltop on the outskirts of the town of Puṣkar. In each case the god oversteps the established boundaries of his ritual and social sphere to make connection with "other" symbolic, spatial, social, and ritual fields through the binding act of marriage.

Thus there is a movement from "center" to "periphery," whereby both center and periphery are then symbolically merged through the dialectics of the myth. In the case of Devnārāyaṇ, many of these points are reversed. Although he is an avatāra of Bhagavān, his position, in terms of an understanding of the narrative, is not one of a self-evident deity who moves from center to periphery and back. In fact, the itinerary of the narrative and the conceptual thrust of the notion of parcyo are about moving from periphery to center. In other words, the sequence of the god's deeds in the narrative serve to construct and institute his importance and singularity as a deity, which even though he is an avatāra are not a given. Moreover, Devnārāyaṇ is first and foremost a "pastoral" deity, that is, his wealth and prosperity rest, like those of Bāṇāī, in the possession of cattle. The social milieu in which he is first raised, and then worshiped, is primarily one consisting of cattle herders and grazers. Furthermore, returning to his birth story, we find that his "origins" too are not in the settled region but in the peripheral zone of the underworld. Even on the surface of the earth, the circumstance of his birth is suffused with descriptions of wilderness: the awesome, disheveled appearance of his mother; the solitary hill near the battlefield; the dangerous, polluting, and calamitous period subsequent to the annihilating war. Into this forbidding landscape, Devnārāyaṇ transports the symbols of fertility, well-being, and regeneration: water, and the lotus blossom in which he manifests himself. These sources of nourishment also have a direct association with wilderness, albeit with its less foreboding and more revitalizing life-giving aspects.[32] Devnārāyaṇ is thus not an "established" god of the settled, organized region, but a god of the "peripheral" (from the perspective of "settled" communities) region of cattle keepers and grazers.[33]

Thus we encounter yet another reversal: the wife belonging to the settled space becomes the favorite spouse of the god from the wilderness. Perhaps we could say, following Sontheimer's hypothesis, that Devnārāyaṇ through his marriage to Pīpalde is able to establish a link to communities belonging to the settled region, in this case represented by Rajput royalty. But the evidence is not as strong as in the case of Khaṇḍobā, Murukaṉ, or Brahmā, who are worshiped by the communities personified by their respective spouses. While shepherd, hunter, and cattle-herder communities are actively involved in the cults of the three gods, the Rajputs as a whole do not feature prominently in the list of communities who worship Devnārāyaṇ. In fact, Pīpalde gives up her comfortable existence as a princess to join Devnārāyaṇ, even though he warns her beforehand that she will suffer being with him:

> "O Queen, my hut is in the heavens—*mhe*—In my clan I am the one who is completely poor. Hey, queen, you'll regret very much being at my home. O Queen, you'll suffer a great deal."
> Pīpalde said: "Śrī Mahārāj!—*mhe*—
> I want to stay at your feet—*vāh vāh*—
> I don't need a home
> *Yes, that's all I want*
> I've found refuge with you—*mhe*—
> That's all I desire
> *Yes, I desire nothing else*
> There's nothing else I want."

While the image of Pīpalde expressed in these lines closely parallels the ideal of a devoted wife, or *pativratā*, it also resonates with the ideal of devotion to God. It is by way of being healed through Devnārāyaṇ that Pīpalde "converts" to being his devotee *and* wife.

To return to the questions posed at the beginning of this section, we may conclude that the reason for Devnārāyaṇ's marriages not following the pattern found elsewhere lies in the kind of deity Devnārāyaṇ himself is. Unlike the other gods, Devnārāyaṇ is a god from the "outside." He is, in a sense, an "outlandish" deity, who, after arising from subtarrenean realms, must continously prove his divinity before his cult and kingdom are established.

The Return to Causlā

Devnārāyaṇ's return from Malwa also involves passing through localities that invoke the memory of his ancestors. In fact, the closer he and his companions approach the Bagaṛāvats' capital, the more the landscape is suffused with the signs of their tragic tale. However, since Devnārāyaṇ is working at not only establishing his cult but reestablishing the kingdom and territories of his ancestors, he is also concerned about smoothing out the scars of the past. At the Lake of Māṇḍal he performs purificatory rites because an ancestor of his, King Māṇḍal, committed suicide by drowning himself in the lake. Later, when Sāḍū Mātā refuses to come down from the monument built at the Lake of Māṇḍal[34] because she is grieving after seeing the "evil" River Khārī's banks where the Bagaṛāvats lost their lives, Devnārāyaṇ coaxes her into descending. He reassures her that he will now proceed to reestablish the Bagaṛāvats' capital city of Causlā. But his mother, burdened by the memory of the tragic events of the past, urges him not to reestablish the city. Interestingly, she addresses him as her son Bhīm here:

O my Bhīm, elder brother of Arjan
O my Bhīmjī Mahārāj, avoid Causle."—*vāh vāh*—
Devnārāyaṇ said: "Listen, O Mother—*mhe*—
Bhoj's royal residence was first in Causle."
Yes, he established the territory of this place
Sāḍū Mātā said: "Hey, Son—*mhe*—
You know Causle Kheḍā is the root of strife
Yes, it's been the root of strife right from the beginning
It can't exist at all without strife.
So Son you're alone now—*mhe*—
On the day the five brothers meet, and the hand becomes strong—
    vāh vāh—
Then there's no problem."

But Devnārāyaṇ does not heed her words; rather he consults the omens that manifest before he establishes Causlā again:

"Look, Bhāṭ, the snake enters his hole backward—*vāh vāh*—
Backward does the cat climb up and sit on the Khejaṛā tree
Hey, according to the omens we will destroy the enemy Rāv—*mhe*—
We'll put the enemy's head into the ground and his feet above
Hey, Bābā Bhāṭ—*mhe*—
Look, what omen is it?"
Yes, what kind of augury is it, tell us

The Bhāṭ said: "Oh Śrī Mahārāj, a mortal would never have this
kind of augury
You're an incarnate person, aren't you—*mhe*—
You've received this kind of omen."
Hey, with this omen no one will be able to defeat you
Śrī Mahārāj—*mhe*—
The augury is such that whoever is defeated, you will defeat
There is no one who will defeat you
O King, the time is auspicious now.—*mhe*—
The time is right.—Establish the territory of Causle!"

It would appear that the retrograde actions of the snake and the cat characterize the upside-down fate that awaits Devnārāyaṇ's enemy! But the important point here is that the god disregards his mother's counsel to establish Causlā. It is Chochū Bhāṭ who supports his intentions. His decision thus also implies a further relinquishment of control and authority on the part of Sāḍū Mātā. Devnārāyaṇ's establishment of Causlā, the capital of his father, Savāī Bhoj, thereby entails an almost final disassociation from the maternal realm, in which his mother has tried to keep him sheltered. We find Sāḍū Mātā merging increasingly with the "patriarchal" quest to restore ancestral honor and territories. With the establishment of Causlā, we also find that there is a shift in the representation of Devnārāyaṇ as a deity. This is also evident in the majority of parcyos that are to follow.

Whereas the kind of testimony Devnārāyaṇ has provided up to this point has been predominantly composed of miracles of healing, resurrection, and transmutation, the testimony he provides after his establishment of Causlā is of a decidedly confrontational and martial nature. These are the deeds of a strong warrior-king whose intention is to regain the losses of the past and to lay the foundation of a kingdom. Subsequent episodes, therefore, forcefully bring out the idea that Devnārāyaṇ is both a deity and a sovereign. The idea of a religious territory of the cult is, in the narrative at least, congruent with the idea of a physical and geographical territory. This does not, however, imply that Devnārāyaṇ becomes the ruler over the territories of those chieftains and kings he defeats, but that the reinstatement of ancestral territories involves acts of physical assault and resistance.

Before turning to the parcyo that involves a confrontation between Devnārāyaṇ and Dīyājī Jodhkā, one of the Rāṇā's generals, it will be worthwhile to briefly look at one incident preceding the establishment of the capital of Causlā Kheḍā. The incident involves the recovery of one of the brothers, Bhāṅgī, from a group of Nāth Yogis in whose company he has grown up. His foster-father, Bābā Rūpnāth, who is also the Bagaṛāvats' guru, is not so readily willing to part with Bhāṅgī. His ward, who is the son of Nevā and Netū, knows of no other parents but bhāṅg and Bābā Rūpnāth. From Rūpnāth's perspective, Devnārāyaṇ's abilities need to be tested and proven before he can acknowledge a power greater than that residing with the Nāths. At stake is also the claim to the vacant throne of the Bagaṛāvats, which Rūpnāth feels should be occupied by Bhāṅgījī, and not Devnārāyaṇ—a "boy" from Sāḍū Mātā's natal home in Malwa. Like Nāpā, the cowherd in the opening episode of the narrative, and Bhūṇā at the banks of Pushkar, Rūpnāth demands a very specific act that he considers to be "proof":

"The Nāths demand this kind of proof:—*mhe*—
See, this fire is ablaze[35]
Yes, it's strongly and abundantly ablaze
There are logs of wood lying there dry at one end
Yes, dry at one end
They burn in front and are dry at the back—*vāh vāh*—
If on the dry parts fresh green leaves one and a half cubits long
spring out, *if they grow green*
Then I'll believe in your "incarnation"
Otherwise, get back just the way you came."

Confronted with Bābā Rūpnāth's paradoxical demand to have green leaves sprout out of burning logs of wood, Sāḍū Mātā prays to Devnārāyaṇ. As in the earlier incident with Nāpā, Sāḍū Mātā does not address Devnārāyaṇ as her mortal son; rather she addresses the mystery of his godly identity: imperceptible, faultless, and formless. Implicit in her prayer to Devnārāyaṇ is also a threat to take her own life, burning in the Jogis' fire-place. She thus parallels Chochū Bhāṭ's threat to take his own life by drowning in the waters of Lake Puṣkara. This somewhat childish but serious threat is swiftly reciprocated by Devnārāyaṇ supplying the miracle of having green leaves grow from burning firewood. At this point Rūpnāth accepts Devnārāyaṇ, and dispatches a letter to Bhāṅgījī explaining to him that he should "return" the saffron robe to the Nāths and become Goṭhā's Rajput. In other words, Bhāṅgījī should abandon his ascetic role and take on his identity as a warrior of another kind. Devnārāyaṇ's miracle at this point and Bābā Rūpnāth's recognition of it is a strong statement about the god's appropriation of the powers issuing from the domain of the ascetic Nāths.

The miracle Bābā Rūpnāth expects from Devnārāyaṇ is similar in content to the miracles of transmutation that have occurred earlier in the narrative in connection with Rūpnāth and that are part of the larger magical lore associated with Nāth Yogis.[36] In the first instance, grains of cereal sticking to the seams of a sack gifted to Savāī Bhoj from Rūpnāth, in exchange of the milk consumed from the latter's cow, turn into precious gems the morning after the brothers have fed the cereal to pigeons and other birds. This wonderous event teaches them of the supernatural powers of Bābā Rūpnāth, whom they adopt as their guru. In the second incident, which soon follows, Rūpnāth's body, after falling into a cauldron of boiling oil, turns golden. His golden body (porso) has the capacity to provide unlimited wealth for a limited period of 12 years, after which the Bagaṛāvats too will have to part with their bodies in equally bizarre acts of sacrifice. These acts propound an alchemical transformation from relatively inert substance (practically from death) into the substances of prosperity, well-being, and wealth (if not life itself). This transmutation is also inherent in the growth of green leaves from logs of dry, burning wood. This easily mastered transition from dead to living substance by Devnārāyaṇ convinces the Nāth guru of the former's control over the phenomenal world, which bespeaks of his access to the supernatural and godlike. Even though his acceptance of Devnārāyaṇ is rather swift, the incident is significant in extending the deity's jurisdiction over a further realm, that of ascetic power.

Once Devnārāyaṇ establishes Causlā Kheḍā, other incidents with an overtly violent, sacrificial quality follow, once again redefining his character as a deity. The first incident occurs when Chochū Bhāṭ and Devnārāyaṇ are on their way to the court of the king of Ajmer in response to a summons from the latter to pay tax. Devnārāyaṇ reacts to the king's summons by telling Chochū Bhāṭ: "So Bhāṭ, the village[37] has hardly been set up, and the oppression has already begun!" Then in an ironic tone he says: "Bābā Bhāṭ, let's go and deliver the tax first." Of course, he has no intention of paying tax; on the contrary, he plans to square off a "debt" the king owes him. After three tiles from his fort, Tārā Gaḍ, fall down on their own, the king grows apprehensive of Devnārāyaṇ's visit. Paṇḍits advise him to let loose black buffaloes smeared with vermilion and oil in front of Devnārāyaṇ. They presume the god will return to his village after seeing these bad omens. Rather than return, Devnārāyaṇ decides to "knock their omen [back] onto them." But before doing this he creates a pond full of water for the buffaloes to wallow in and green grass for them to eat:

> Bhagavān took Ind's name—*mhe*—
> In a flash, rain fell—*vāh vāh*—
> And in a moment green grass
> *Yes, it appeared*
> And that pond which was created in a moment—*mhe*—
> The pond is named Ūsrī—*vāh vāh*—

Seeing the green grass and the pond full of water, the buffaloes leave the road. After they have eaten the fresh grass and wallowed in the pond, Devnārāyaṇ draws his sword and beheads them:[38] "The cut-off heads of both buffaloes flew back to the court of Ajmer and *Yes, they went and fell in the court.*"

Later, when he is in the court of the king of Ajmer, the king asks him to ride on a horse of his that is extremely difficult to train. The god sits on the speckled horse, and it begins to walk to and fro in a gait that is even better than that of Devnārāyaṇ's own horse, Līlāgar. But then

> Suddenly Bhagavān gave the horse a kick with his heels
> He sent the horse down into the thirteenth underworld
> Bhagavān said: "Bhāṭ of the lineage—*mhe*—
> Tell Grandfather,[39] hey, brother, that this Mother Earth
> *Yes, it demanded an offering of a horse*
> I gave the Earth the offering of a horse."

In this encounter with the king of Ajmer, Devnārāyaṇ does not hesitate to slaughter buffaloes and dispatch a horse. His treatment of animals here is markedly different, for example, from the incident in Sindhbāḍā, where he promises protection to the mango tree and deer in exchange for a piece of wood and a portion of flesh. The buffaloes and horse are mute and anonymous, they do not speak to us, and they are not sheltered by the god. His killing of the animals has, as mentioned earlier, a sacrificial and ritualistic quality. Thus the buffaloes are allowed to bathe and feed before he beheads them. Similarly, the horse disappears into the underworld as an offering to Mother Earth.

Subsequently while passing through a dense forest on the way to Fort Sāvar (which belongs to Diyājī Jodhkā), Devnārāyaṇ is confronted by Pārvatī's mount, the lion. Devnārāyaṇ and Chochū Bhāṭ make their way through the forest infested with "lions, panthers, and robbers." They are spotted by Pārvatī, who together with Śaṅkar, is residing in the "Baraḍ of Soner" (the Banyan Tree of Soner). Pārvatī is curious to know who this rider is:

"Look, traveling above the ground!—*mhe*—
Bholānāth, a strange rider is coming
On his way to the Soner. Open your eyes,—*mhe*—
And look at what kind of vehicle of Dev's is going by
Hey, it's moving above the ground!"
Yes, what kind of vehicle is that of Dev's?
Mahādev said: "Caṇḍī, that is Dev—Dev!"—*vāh vāh*—
She said: "What Dev?" *What Dev is he?*
"There are four Devs." She thought to herself: "There are only
four Devs.—*mhe*—
"I don't know of a fifth one, brother."—*vāh vāh*—
By God's grace, which were the four Devs? She said: "Anndev—
mhe—
Jaldev—*vāh vāh*—
Pavandev—*vāh vāh*—
And, by God's grace, did I mention Agaṇ . . . Pavan, Jaḷ, Ann,
these are the four Devs on earth that I believe in.
Yes, I only see four
You've created that fifth Dev yourself today!"
Yes, where did you get him from?
Śaṅkar said: "Listen, Caṇḍī—*mhe*—
The lord of the three worlds, Bhagavān, has arrived." *On his own
he has arrived*
She said: "What is he doing?"—*mhe*—
He said: "He's going to Sāvar." *He's going to Sāvar*
He said: "Just like the one before went to Sāvar."[40]
Yes, he's going just like that
She said: "Don't rely on him this time!"—*mhe*—
He said: "What are you going to do?"—*vāh vāh*—
She said: "The same thing—I'll release the lion!—*vāh vāh*—
And it'll roar twice and frighten him off."—*mhe*—
He said: "You'll be on foot then, Caṇḍī!"
Yes, that doesn't matter

By God's grace, Pārvatī got up and gave the lion a slap: "Hey, brave one, go on in front and roar!"—*vāh vāh*—

When Dev's and the lion's eyes meet, the lion crouches down, whereupon Pārvatī prods him a second time urging him to go and scare Devnārāyaṇ. In order to observe the fight that will ensue between the two, Pārvatī assumes the form of a kite and perches on the branch of a nearby tree. Upon seeing the lion, Devnārāyaṇ advises it to go and take a "ceremonial bath" in the Kāliyā Pond before being slain. The lion does exactly what Devnrāyāṇ tells him and jumps into the pond.[41] After the "bath," the lion comes bounding back to Devnārāyaṇ, who immediately beheads it. Chochū Bhāṭ, who has upto this point hidden in a tree, jumps down and begins stabbing the dead lion's torso with his dagger, claiming that Devnārāyaṇ doesn't really know how to kill a lion:

You don't know how to kill a lion!
Yes, what do you know!
You severed one vein.—*mhe*—
Look at the substance of nine veins and seventy-two billion! *I'm extracting them with my dagger*
I've killed the lion!"—*vāh vāh*—

In order to counter Chochū Bhāṭ's boastful claim, Devnārāyaṇ revives the dead lion. He creates two lions, one from the head and another from the torso, but Chochū Bhāṭ, instead of killing them, runs away. Devnārāyaṇ sends one of the lions back to Pārvatī and the other into the forest.

In this encounter between Devnārāyaṇ and the lion, it once again becomes apparent that Devnārāyaṇ is establishing his sovereignity. It is Pārvatī who, by releasing her own mount, tries to test him. She is confused about who this "fifth" Dev or god could be, in addition to the "classical" four gods whom she enumerates. The gods she speaks of actually embody the three elements: wind, water, and fire, as well as "nourishment" or "food" (*ann*).[42] Devnārāyaṇ is the fifth god, who in comparison to the other four is unknown and therefore also new to Pārvatī. Moreover, by calling him the fifth god, Pārvatī unconsciously places him in league with the five fundamental elements of the universe. Furthermore, Pārvatī's lion, who in other mythologies vanquishes world-conquering demons,[43] is not able to intimidate this "fifth" god. The way his great-grandfather Hari Rām did once, Devnārāyaṇ swiftly slays the lion, after having it ritually cleanse itself in the Kāliyā Pond. This motif of cleansing the victim before it is killed is similar to the incident in which the vermilion-colored buffaloes, sent from the ruler of Ajmer to frighten Devnārāyaṇ, are allowed to first wallow in ponds before being beheaded by the god. Taking the incident with Pārvatī's lion together with the earlier two involving animals from the court of Ajmer, we may observe that Devnārāyaṇ slays creatures who have associations with strength, virility, valor, and martiality in general: the buffalo, horse, and lion. His victory over these animals symbolizes a victory both over their possessors as well as the realms they preside over. In the case of Pārvatī's lion, the connections do not stop between her and

Devnārāyaṇ. Pārvatī or rather Devī, is Dīyājī Jodhkā's ally. This also makes it clear why she lets her mount loose on Devnārāyaṇ, who is on his way to Dīyājī's fort in order to reclaim his father's mare, Bāvlī Ghoḍī, which can "catch a live boar in its teeth." The clash between Devnārāyaṇ and Dīyājī Jodhkā provides the context for another important parcyo.

Dīyājī Jodhkā

It is Chochū Bhāṭ who enters the Fort of Sāvar to set Savāī Bhoj's mare free. He slips into the fortification unnoticed during the celebrations for Dīyājī's son's wedding and challenges Dīyājī in a manner similar to that of his subsequent meeting with the Rāṇā's younger brother, Nīmde. He claims that his "prince" was able to catch a boar with his horse even though the boar was running much further away. Then he says:

> "Cowherds happened to be in the forest—*mhe*—
> My prince spoke to Dīyā's water-bearers when they arrived
> Hey, they say that Savāī Bhoj's mare is with you.—*mhe*—
> It can catch a live boar in its teeth
> By God's grace, I was told that Bhoj's mare is with you."
> My prince said, brother, if Bhoj's mare, Bāvlī, would only be here,—
> *mhe*—
> And catch the boar alive, see, then I would be pleased.
> *Yes, then I'd be pleased*
> I've promised five villages already.—*mhe*—
> And afterward I'll give you five more—I'll give you ten.
> *Yes, I'll do my best and give you five more villages*
> What will you do? Go and ride the mare, I'll catch the boar."—
> *vāh vāh*—

Chochū Bhāṭ convinces Dīyājī that he can get the mare ready for Dīyajī to ride so that he can catch the boar. In this way Chochū Bhāṭ can approach Savāī Bhoj's mare, "Mother Cā̃vaṇḍā,"[44] which has been kept in captivity for 11 years now.[45] Once Chochū Bhāṭ is in the mare's stable, a long conversation unfolds between him and her. She has grown timid from being held in captivity and fed only on water and scraps of food. Chochū Bhāṭ pours liquor into the her drinking bowl so as to revive her spirits. The mare, too, has heard of Devnārāyaṇ's incarnation. She expects to be freed by him and shown the land of Badnor again.[46] But Chochū Bhāṭ coaxes her to carry the enemy Dīyājī for once on her back to the Pond of Ṭīm, where Devnārāyaṇ is waiting.

Even though his wife's dream and other omens warn against riding the mare to the place where Chochū Bhāṭ's "prince" is resting, Dīyājī climbs onto the horse. His wife prophesies:

> He's being sucked away by time, O Hīḍāgar maidservants!—*mhe*—
> Fort Sāvar's chief is passing away!
> Look and see!

Yes, he's going today pulled away by time
He'll be struck by Dev Mahārāj's spear—*mhe*—
And four of my husband's teeth will break."

On the way to the pond Dīyājī's helmet falls off because of the mare's unsteady movements. This again is a bad omen. But Chochū Bhāṭ cajoles him to ride on. He meets women water-bearers returning from the pond and asks them whether "the ill-fated prince has alighted at the Pond of Ṭīm."[47] The water-bearers respond by saying they know nothing of an "ill-fated" prince, but that two suns are blazing at the pond![48] Dīyājī grows suspicious again. Once more Chochū Bhāṭ persuades him to continue, explaining that the water-bearers are talking about the sun in the sky and its reflection in the water. But then, having arrived on the opposite bank of the pond, Dīyājī sees Devnārāyaṇ and realizes that he has been tricked. He turns the mare around and gallops away as fast as he can. At first Devnārāyaṇ does not follow him since he has taken a vow not to chase someone who is trying to flee. Again, it is Chochū Bhāṭ who compels him to take up pursuit of the Rajput chieftain. When Devnārāyaṇ catches up with him, Dīyājī changes his shape into that of a pigeon pecking at grains of millet. As a response to this, Devnārāyaṇ changes into a hawk, warning Dīyājī that he will spare him this time but that during the great battle of Rātākoṭ he will take away the Rajput's "life-force." Then, as Dīyājī returns to his human shape, Devnārāyaṇ strikes his front teeth with the rear end of his spear.[49] As prophesied by his wife, Dīyājī looses four teeth in this encounter with Devnārāyaṇ. But this is only a trifling loss compared to the complete defeat and destruction that will happen later in the "great battle of Rātākoṭ." In the "assault of Sāvar" thus Dīyājī loses four teeth, and Savāī Bhoj's mare is released from captivity.[50]

As I pointed out in chapter 4, there is a deep thread of enmity between Devnārāyaṇ and Dīyājī that is provided by the incarnational scheme of the narrative. Thus while Devnārāyaṇ is an avatāra of Bhagavān/Kṛṣna, Dīyājī is an avatāra of Kaṃsa. The enmity between them is stronger and more violently carried out than, for example, the enmity between Devnārāyaṇ and his four cousins and the Rāṇā, who is no less than an avatāra of Rāvaṇa. But, as I mentioned earlier, the interrelationships between the Rāṇā and the Bagaṛāvats and their sons are ambigious. The Rāṇā is not clearly identified as the enemy who exists as the completely "other." As in the *Mahābhārata*, here too there are interconnections between rival groups that arise from both real and imagined kinship ties. The Rāṇā is therefore addressed by the five cousins as "Grandfather." Three of the cousins have been raised either by the Rāṇā or by allied Rajput chieftains. The case of Bhūṇā is particularly important in this context, because the Rāṇā is his foster father.[51]

After Bhūṇā departs from the city of Rāṇ in the direction of Daṛāvaṭ, he passes by the Khārī River. This is the location of the great battle between the Bagaṛāvats and the Rāṇā. The river bank is studded with *devlīs*, or memorial stones, commemorating the deceased heroes and their wives who have performed satī. Bhūṇā enquires from the Bhāṭ[52] about the memorial stones:

"Banū Bābā what's this arrangement here?"
Yes, why have so many stones been erected?
The Bārahaṭh said: "Śrī Mahārāj, the battlefield of your ancestors
has arrived
Bhūṇā said: "Here?"
Yes, they are devlīs
"Devlīs, Śrī Mahārāj."—*vāh vāh*—
Bhūṇājī said: "Well then, brother, if it's the battlefield, then surely
there is the devlī of my father and my mother."
Yes, are they here?
The Bārahaṭh said: "They are, sir. *They are*
Your mother's name was Salūṇ—*mhe*—
The devlī with the name Salūṇ belongs to your mother."—*vāh vāh*—[53]

Bhūṇā wanders about the battlefield until he finds the devlī with his mother's name on it. What follows is a moving conversation between Bhūṇā and the memorial stone of his mother, whom he has never known:

The Bagaṛāvat's son cuts grass away on the threshold.—*vāh vāh*—
With a shoulder wrap he sweeps away Mother Satī's dust
"Eleven years we were separated.—*vāh vāh*—
Speak to me with your mouth
Well, brother, you're my mother's—Salūṇ's—devlī aren't you?
Speak to me from your mouth.
Yes, show me your presence
Then I'll believe—*mhe*—
That it's my mother's devlī."[54]
Bhūṇājī came to the battlefield.—*mhe*—
The Raj-bearing Rajpūt came
Wearing bangles[113] she took her arm out of the devlī—*mhe*—
And placed it on Bhūṇā's head.—*vāh vāh*—
On that day milk spurted out of the devlī
By God's grace, a stream of milk flowed from the stone—*vāh vāh*—
Falling onto Bhūṇā's moustache.
Bhūṇājī said: "Hey, Banū Bābā—*mhe*—
After eleven years today I again tasted Salūṇ's milk."

In the subsequent dialogue between mother and son, Salūṇ enquires whether her son has been looked after properly in the custody of the Rāṇa; Bhūṇā for his part asks why his mother had to become an object of stone. She answers his incredulous question by saying:

"Son, I hung up the ivory bangles on a nail in the wall.—*vāh vāh*—
I wore only the fire-goddess's bangles
By God's grace, hey, Bhūṇā, I burnt up and became ash after your
family
I burnt up after your family, brother."

Thereafter, when Bhūṇā turns his attention to the sounds of the early morning service for Devnārāyaṇ in Daṛāvaṭ, the presence of the devlī disappears. He then, with the help of Sujā Paṭel from the village called Cāmpānehrī, finds Savāī Bhoj's memorial, The conversation between uncle and nephew is much shorter than the first. Again, Bhūṇā's attention is drawn toward the early morning service for Devnārāyaṇ, and "the light that was in the devlī, / it disappeared." Finally Bhūṇā proceeds to Daṛāvaṭ, the village where his four cousins and his aunt, Sāḍū Mātā, are assembled.

The way the four cousins, who are already in Daṛāvaṭ, meet with Bhūṇā is unusual. Each individual meeting carries a different degree of mutual respect with it. The way the brothers unite with one another also tells us something about the quality of their interrelationships and the underlying hierarchy that exists among them. Similarly, the order in which they meet is also expressive of the rank and importance the brothers bear. First Bhūṇa is met by Medū and then by Madno; they both embrace him. Medū does so after "touching the earth" in front of Bhūṇā. Then it is Bhāṅgī's turn. Bhūṇā notices him and asks the bhāṭ who this "Jam"[55] is with eyes like a lion? Impressed by Bhāṇgī's mighty presence, Bhūṇā moves forward to embrace him. But Bhāṅgī catches hold of his arm, and even though Bhūṇā has the "strength of 11 elephants," he cannot cause his brother to stir "the space of a sesame seed." Bhāṅgī, however, knocks Bhūṇā about, vanquishing the might of 11 elephants with the utmost of ease, till the latter tells him to let go of his arm, which has "turned red," presumably from being squeezed. Bhāṅgī speaks to him in his rough habit: "I am Nevā's Prince Bhāṅgaḍo, you remain Bārāvat's Bhūṇ. / Don't look at me today—*vāh vāh*— When we go for revenge, shortly . . . / I'll show my strength there.—*vāh vāh*— / Why should I show you today!"[56]

The meeting with the last of the brothers, Devnārāyaṇ, is even more enigmatic. Bhūṇā asks his bhāṭ how he should approach the brother "who is called an incarnation." The bhāṭ tells him to "stop the horse, and get down.—*mhe*— / And remove your weapons.—*vāh vāh*— / Join your hands together. / Go to Bhagavān's assembly and stand there. / You'll get him naturally." Būṇā considers this to be a solution for beggars rather than for equal brothers. He enters Devnārāyaṇ's assembly riding his horse. Then Devnārāyaṇ shouts three times. Each time Bhūṇā, together with his entourage, is turned about-face. After the third time, Bhūṇā, in a temper, decides to leave Daṛāvaṭ, not wanting to have anything to do with "such a harsh brother." Chochū Bhāṭ coaxes him into waiting a little while he goes and advises Devnārāyaṇ on the value of the family: "A brother resides in the shelter of another brother.—*mhe*— / When the swords resound in the Rāṭhors' heroic field,—*mhe*— / if there is a brother there, he'll act in your favor." A major portion of Chochū Bhāṭ's subsequent dialogue with Devnārāyaṇ consists of a long didactic section in which Chochū Bhāṭ narrates the story of a family of sandpipers (*ṭīṭoḍī*), who, out of virtue of being united, are even able to confront the mighty ocean. As in the examples of the lioness and fox mentioned previously, we find that a didactic message is expressed with the assistance of nonhuman, animal, or bird characters. Owing to the length of the story and the importance of its theme, I present it here below in a summarized form:

The Bhāṭ said: "Śrī Mahārāj, the Ṭī̃ṭoḍī creature laid eggs on the side of the ocean.—*vāh vāh*—
For three days she sat on the eggs
Yes, she sat on top off them
The Ṭī̃ṭoḍā came and said: "Ṭī̃ṭoḍī, why are you famishing yourself! Go, eat and drink!"
Yes, go, eat and drink
The Ṭī̃ṭoḍī said: "Brother, who'll keep an eye on the eggs?"
Yes, who'll protect the eggs?
"I'll protect them."—*vāh vāh*—
So, the Ṭī̃ṭoḍī flew into the forest to eat and drink
The Ṭī̃ṭoḍā creature, what did it do? It lay with its back down on the eggs.—*vāh vāh*—
The ocean brought its wave near and said: "Creature, why are you suffering, brother? Lie down properly."
Yes, "Sit straight!" it said.
The bird said: "Don't you say anything."
Yes, don't talk to me
"Why not?"—*mhe*—
The bird said: "I'm looking after the eggs."
Yes, I'm protecting my eggs
"Protection against what?"
Yes, what kind of protection is this?
The bird said: "Should the sky fall down from above—*mhe*—
I'll catch it in my two feet.
Yes, I'll keep it on my feet, raised above
And, if you come with a wave—*mhe*—
I'll catch you in my wings."
Yes, I'll capture you in my wings
The ocean thought: "Know your mother—it's a small creature . . ."
Yes, he's controlling you
Right then, with a roar, the ocean let loose a wave.
Crying out "Ṭau, ṭau," the Ṭī̃ṭoḍā flew up into the sky
And the ocean grabbed the eggs and took them within.
The Ṭī̃ṭoḍī came back. She said: "Ṭī̃ṭoḍā, where are the eggs?"
Yes, why are you flying around above?
He said: "Your father! The ocean took them away yesterday!"
Yes, it took them away yesterday
She said: "You've done great wrong, brother!—*mhe*—
Hey, I was here for three days, the ocean didn't take notice of me.
Yes, the ocean didn't take my name
You offended the ocean."
Yes, you've done something or the other wrong!
Here, brother, Ṭī̃ṭoḍī; the Ṭī̃ṭoḍī spoke in such a way.—*mhe*—

"What shall we do now?"
Yes, what shall we do?
She said: "Let's go to our clan and family.—*mhe*—
Let's summon them together."—*vāh vāh*—
So, all the creatures born of eggs,—*vāh vāh*—
They went to them, brother.—*vāh vāh*—
They said: "The ocean has taken away our eggs, therefore come, brother, Have them returned to us."
Yes, we'll fight
All the feathered creatures that existed—*mhe*—
They all gathered together on one side of the ocean.—*vāh vāh*—
They said: "We've gathered together, but how shall we fight the ocean?"
What's the solution for that!
There was a creature called Puṭīyā, in the meantime it said:
"Brother, set me up as lord, king amongst all—*mhe*—
Then I'll tell you a plan.
Yes, I'll tell you a plan all right
But you'll have to make me king."—*vāh vāh*—
The birds said: "O King, we'll believe in you only."
Yes, we'll believe you are the king, what's it to us?
They made a small heap with sand—*mhe*—
And gave the throne to the Puṭīyā creature.
Yes, have him sit on the throne
"Here you are, King, sir, speak!" *Now tell us*
Puṭīyā said: "What should I say, brother—all you creatures dive into the water.—*mhe*—
Take some water in your stomachs, some on your wings, and some *take in your beaks*
These white dunes of sand—*mhe*—
Go to them and pour out the water.
While coming back, take some sand on the curve of your wings
And take some in your beaks
Make two or three runs; on its own . . .
Yes, the ocean will leave it's place."
It took no time at all—*mhe*—
By God's grace, in the time they made two or three runs, the ocean left the place.
Yes, at different places they erected mounds of sand in the water
The ocean said: "Hey, creatures, why are you making me leave my place?"
Yes, what's the matter?
The birds said: "We are fighting you, because you took away the eggs.
Yes, return this Ṭīṭoḍī's eggs!

Otherwise we won't let this place of yours exist!"—*vāh vāh*—
The ocean said: "Then, brother, don't fill up my shore with sand.—
mhe—
I'll give you your eggs." *I'll return them*
The ocean let loose a wave—*mhe*—
And brought the eggs back and placed them on the shore.
Yes, here you are, take them
"The family stood behind.—*mhe*—
Then the family won the fight," the Bhāṭ said.—*vāh vāh*—

The Bhāṭ concludes this parable by urging Devnārāyaṇ to reconcile with his brother Bhūṇā, who is already heading back to his foster home. When Sāḍū Mātā finds out that Bhūṇā is leaving Daṛāvaṭ, she angrily enquires about the person who has insulted him. Devnārāyaṇ tries to hush things up, but Bhāṅgī tells her that it was Devnārāyaṇ who has grieved Bhūṇā:

"O mother, he sat with his back turned against Elder Brother
Bhūṇā.
No one else has any fault—*mhe*—.
All the fault is with your Devjī. *Yes, it's with him!*
Today he's angered and sent back this brother.
Tomorrow he'll anger and send me back.
The place where Bhūṇājī's going—*mhe*—
I'm going there to meet him!" *There you are, take care of your throne!*
Bhāṅgījī picked up his mortar and pestle and departed behind
Bhūṇājī.—*vāh vāh*—
Dev Mahārāj thought to himself:
"Brothers have split up!"

Realizing that he has created an undesirable situation, Devnārāyaṇ requests Sāḍū Mātā to ride after Bhūṇā and bring him to a halt within the boundary of Daṛāvaṭ. Then Sāḍū Mātā tries to convince Bhūṇā that he has not encountered Devnārāyaṇ in the assembly because the latter always goes out grazing cattle in the early morning, returning in the afternoon together with the herd. In the meantime Devnārāyaṇ enters the earth on his horse and emerges on the road ahead of where Bhūṇā and Sāḍū Mātā are standing. Bhūṇā is, of course, amazed to see him coming from the direction in front: "He thought to himself: 'Hey, the very same horse and the very same boy! *Yes, he's the same as that one, yes /* But how did he come this way?' " Feigning ignorance of the entire situation, Devnārāyaṇ asks Sāḍū Mātā:

"Hey, Mājī Sāī—*vāh vāh*—
why did you come to the jungle? *Yes, why did you come to the jungle
today?*
Whose cavalry is it, and why did you come . . . ?"
Sāḍū Mātā said: "Son, that's your brother Bhūṇājī—*vāh vāh*—
Someone in your court played a joke on him—*mhe*—

So, in anger this Bhūṇā is going away. *Yes, he's turning back*
In order to appease him I've *yes, come into the jungle*. . . .

Bhūṇāji is quite confused, but the brothers embrace each other in the jungle anyway.[57] As a sign of grace, Devnārāyaṇ makes Bhūṇā's little finger grow back that had been cut off by the Rāṇā's brother-in-law when Bhūṇā was a child.[58] This act convinces Bhūṇā of Devnārāyaṇ's divine abilities: "Bhūṇājī thought to himself: 'Hey, he's God!' *Yes, 'what matters are hidden from him?'* He said: 'Truly you only create, and you only destroy.' "

Tangibly in this entire episode there is a strong tension between Bhūṇā and Devnārāyaṇ. Bhūṇā's scepticism regarding Devnārāyaṇ's divinity goes back to earlier incidents featuring his conversations with Chochū Bhāṭ.[59] Devnārāyaṇ is equally unrelenting toward Bhūṇā, until the very last moment when the union of the brothers is on the verge of breaking apart. Only a crafty ploy can come to the rescue of the precarious situation. While Medū and Madno are represented as being mild and accommodating,[60] Bhūṇā, Bhāṅgī, and Devnārāyaṇ are portrayed as definitely more independent and demanding. But in the final count, there is no overruling the authority and sovereignity of Devnārāyaṇ, who, being the youngest of the brothers, reverses the conventional ranking according to age, replacing it with a hierarchy based on magical and elusive, godly power.

The Conquest of Realms

The aim of this study has been to show how an oral tradition and folk cult are conceived and constructed on the basis of different kinds of interactions on many different levels. The purpose of this exercise has been to both illuminate the particular example of Devnārāyaṇ and also to provide material for a broader understanding, within the framework of Indian culture, of a set of questions: how is orality conceptualized and practiced? To what extent do concepts and practices from the tradition itself demand a revision of our own academic frameworks? For example, what is the relationship between the spoken and the visual sign? What kind of an approach is required for understanding the nature of, in this case, "folk" textual traditions? What kinds of discourses are articulated in such narratives? How are the discourses on religiosity, sociality, and historicity envisioned within the discursive frame of the narrative? How are these discourses interrelated to one another? Finally, how is Devnārāyaṇ, the god, represented and constituted through these discourses?

To draw a metaphor from the linkages between texts discussed in the study, it could be said that the answer to each of these questions can be conceived in terms of an "intertextual" field that, to paraphrase Ramanujan (1989), elicits the self's own language in terms of the other. Thus it is the other's voice that is continuously present in each of the interactions described. The "other's" voice is literally present in the exchange that takes place between the two singers in the oral delivery of the narrative, and within the narrative itself in terms of the dialogues spoken by individual characters. It is present in the interrelationship between the verbal narrative and the visual narrative. Each "encroaches" on the other's terrain, creating an "oral-visual" narrative, in which the oral and the visual sign comment on and reflect on each other. The narrative *text* is composed of a deep play between itself and other narrative texts, some belonging to the puranic and epic streams of texts and others to "folk" streams. The intertextual dimension of the narrative text reworks and repeats patterns found in other texts, which themselves draw from a "common pool" of ideas, motifs, and values. Then again, the dimension of intertexuality is used to establish a temporal (and spatial) framework for identifying the god and his worshipers in the past and present. Like the construction of the narrative text, historicity too is carved out of the possibilities that present themselves to devotees within a field of historical narratives, again predominantly puranic but also "local" in nature. While historicity is about defining the self in terms of time, sociality is about defining the self in terms of other social communities. Thus the narrative presents an array of concerns regarding the identities of the community of devotees. But social identities, like the other elements, are also not sharply defined. They are ambiguous and fluctuating. More often than not they "transgress" well-known norms of social interrelationships found in India. They emphasize the fluidity and negotiability of individual and social identities, at least in the context of the religious community of devotees. Finally, the "dialogic overtone" that Bakhtin speaks of is lucidly expressed in the discourse on religious power expressed in the biography of Devnārāyaṇ himself.

Devnārāyaṇ's biography portrays a god moving through different realms. The movement from his birthplace to his natal home, and back, is a metaphorical journey, a cadence of events that describes his entry into different domains, physical, metaphysical, and divine. Like a traditional king engaged in a *digvijaya* (conquest of realms), he moves from region to region equipped with an "army" of cows and cowherds, proving his power to those whom he encounters. Like the singers of the narrative who engage in a conversation with one another, and the characters in the story who speak to one another, Devnārāyaṇ too "converses" with the representatives of different realms in his journey. But even while being God, he is not recognized as such. In order to induce a recognition of this kind, he must "prove" who he is. He must rally and participate with different individuals and situations before being able to create a discourse about himself in the perception of others. The biography of Devnārāyaṇ is thus a story of the construction of a discourse on religious power that attempts to establish itself within other discourses that already exist. It is a "conquest" of realms that is achieved by the god's engagement in those realms rather than his turning away from them. In these terms, his biography again mirrors the nature of this narrative and religious tradition as a whole as being forged out of series of interactions.

As the "grand" yet "strangely incompatible visions" (Shulman 1989: 7) of South Asianists such as Dumont, Biardeau, Heesterman, and others, who attempt to describe South Asian culture, religion, and society through holistic frameworks, through the workings of single, deeply rooted structures that are oblivious to disjuncture and agency—are called into question, it becomes increasingly clear that South Asia is characterized by things "multiple": multiple identities, multilayeredness, multidirectionality, and so on. Within things "multiple" there are ambivalences, inversions, subversions, and an understanding of identity that is flexible and fluid.[61] But flexibility and fluidity are not "irrational" or "accidental"; they are situational and contextually determined. Underlying the epistemic noncontradiction of ambiguity and fluidity there lies an appreciation of uncertainty in many life situations. In fact, to return to the attempt at positing overarching principles, one might claim that South Asian culture is deeply rooted in a philosophical and experiential notion of uncertainty. Specific cultural systems, traditions, and religious configurations are, among other things, expressive of attempts to "manage" uncertainty and its manifold forms in everyday life. But this also means that solutions and answers are not predetermined or given: they are continuously being "worked out."

The narrative of Devnārāyaṇ also calls the aforementioned theories into question precisely because it inscribes within itself an interaction, perhaps even a "struggle," out of which discourses and practices emerge. This is quintessentially represented in the identity of Devnārāyaṇ, whose divinity is never something simply "there"; it has to be demonstrated. But his identity, as are also the character of his narrative and cult, is "holistic" in another sense of the term: in having the capacity to establish *linkages*—linkages between religious ideologies, narrative texts, social communities, the past and the present, the spoken word and the visual image. And out of these linkages emerge overlappings, in-between spaces, and multiple meanings but also boundaries, fixity, and directedness.

❁ TRANSLATION ❁

In this translation of *Śrī Devnārāyaṇ Kathā*, the oral structure of the narrative has been retained to the maximum extent possible. Thus instead of the flowing sentences of a prose work the translation contains the sometimes fragmented utterances of an oral delivery. This is particularly reflected in the fact that the narrative is built of a series of exchanges between two singers, in this case Śrī Hukamārām Bhopā and his companion, Śrī Moṭārām Gūjar. While Śrī Hukamārām is the main speaker, it is the job of his companion, Śrī Moṭārām, to repeat, reformulate, complement, or even punctuate the former's lines with expressions such as *mhe* or *vāh vāh*.[1] These elements have not been edited so as to expunge from the text the idiosyncrasies of the oral delivery. Every item belonging to the oral style as a whole, and the individual styles of the singers, has been reproduced as far as possible, so as to provide an impression not only of the contents of the narrative but also its form as a spoken text. Thus, for example, "formulaic" and repetitive phrases and expressions have been retained: "God willing," which is used frequently by Śrī Hukamārām; "know it by saying it, by saying it," which is mentioned in this or variant forms before each sung passage; or "yes" at the beginning of Śrī Moṭārām's response. Similarly, Śrī Hukamārām also says "hey," "and," and "brother" as part of his verbal style even at places that do not require these words.

In the majority of cases, the voice of the second singer is shown in italics to mark it off from that of the main singer. In some cases, determined by syntax, the two singers' lines have been combined to produce a coherent sentence. In such cases as well the second singer's voice is distinguished through the use of italics.[2] The expressions *mhe* and *vāh vāh* (which are explained in chapter 2) have been left in their original form in the translation. Often details such as characters' names are not mentioned explicitly by the singers. For example, Śrī Moṭārām regularly ends his response with the word "said" without referring to the person who has spoken. The speaker can usually be located in the previous lines spoken by Śrī Hukmārām. In the translation "said" has frequently been deleted, since the identity of the character whose speech it is remains easily recognizable. In a number of cases Śrī Moṭārām uses "said" even though no one in particular is being referred to. The nonspecific "said" at the end of such utterances has also been edited because of the stilted effect it has in translation. In addition Śrī Moṭārām also uses the phrase *jī kīyo*, which has been translated as "said sir."

The succession of chapters and subchapters presented here is not derived from an episodic division internal to the narrative. In fact, no such episodic succession is given to the narrative by the singers. The chapters and their individual names are based on an understanding of the importance of various events in the narrative. Ultimately, however, they are solely my creation, having been introduced in the hope of facilitating the appreciation of the narrative by users of the written and printed word. Besides this substantial alteration to the original, certain other frequent, though minor, changes and additions have been made in order to enhance the flow of the reading. Finally, the sung sections of the narrative, called *gāv*,[3] have not been translated here, since they are repeated almost word for word in the declamatory sections, called *arthāv*. On the whole, then, the following pages are an attempt at producing a translation of the narrative that evokes the dialogic, spoken nature of the original oral rendering.[4]

Contents

Devnārāyaṇ's Birth 177

Sāḍū Mātā's Flight to Malwa 187

Sāḍū Mātā and Devnārāyaṇ in Malwa 191

The Return to Causle Kheḍā 205

Devnārāyaṇ Establishes Causle Kheḍā 226

The Search for Bhūṇājī 271

Bhūṇājī Returns to Rāvjī's Court 346

Devnārāyaṇ Releases 980,000 Cows into the Fields 383

Kālū Mīr and Dīyājī Try to Capture the 980,000 Cows 407

Devnārāyaṇ Prepares to Attack Rātākoṭ 468

Devnārāyaṇ Departs to Baikuṇṭh 492

Devnārāyaṇ's Birth

Sitting in the turret called "Bhairū̃," Rāv Maṇḍovar—*vāh vāh*—
Brother, summoned Kālū Mīr and Dīyā Jodhkā—*mhe*—
"O, brother, Dīyā, where is Bhoj's inexhaustible golden image?[5]—*mhe*—
Where Bhoj's wish-fulfilling cow?
Listen, Kālū Mīr and Dīyājī—*mhe*—
There were only three things in the Bagaṛāvats' possession.
Yes, none of the three things came as part of our loot
They did not come in our booty—the Mahābhārat is over—yes, everything was under our close attention during the Mahābhārat, but we did not notice those three things, brother—*vāh vāh*—
So tell me what did we really get?—*mhe*—
The golden image gifted by Śaṅkar, that too remained behind; and the cow presented by Śaṅkar that would have come in use—even that one
Yes, she too we did not get
Then, there was this Sāḍū Satvantī—there's no knowledge about her either. All the Gūjar women went to the satīvāḍā,[6] but there's no knowing of her whereabouts."—*vāh vāh*—
God willing, Dīyā Jodhkā said:
"Śrī Mahārāj!—*mhe*—
I know about the golden image—Tejājī took it and ran up the Mountain of Rīchor"
Yes, he climbed up the mountain
God willing, Rāvjī's younger brother, Nīmde, said—*mhe*—:
"Śrī Mahārāj,
I seized the golden image. But, he caught up with me within seven kos, cut my shoulder, and seized it.
Yes, he seized it back
Under no circumstances will Tejājī let it go."—*vāh vāh*—
Rāv said: "Sāḍū's whereabouts are still not known.
Yes, there's no knowing where she is—vāh vāh—
We don't know where she is
And the cows that the cowherd took grazing—we don't know where they are."
Yes, there's no knowing about where they are or where they're not
Then Rāv said: "Sirdārs, pay heed to the following, brothers—*mhe*—
We didn't get any loot belonging to the Bagaṛāvats—*vāh vāh*—
Yes, if these three things didn't come in the loot, then nothing came as loot.

Yes, since nothing at all accrued—prepare to attack again
Prepare a second assault. Wherever the cows may be, capture them!"—*vāh vāh*—
So, Rāvjī Sā had his fifty-two forts launch a second assault there and then—*vāh vāh*—
So, in that assault there were two Kacchāvā brothers, Sirdārs from Āmerāv, whose names were Khaḍak Siṅg and Nirvāṇ Siṅg—*vāh vāh*—
They had five hundred horses
They had five hundred cavalry—*mhe*—
Rāvjī Sā gave them a salary.
Yes, they were in Rāvjī's service
Long ago, they visited Savāī Bhoj—*mhe*—
And affection grew between them. They became dharam-brothers—*vāh vāh*—
They considered the following: "Hey, brother, it's not our dharam to go with them.
Yes, it is not our dharam to capture the cows
Why?—Because we drank the milk of those cows—*mhe*—
Now, if we go to capture them, then where is dharam?—*vāh vāh*—
So, for the sake of those cows, we and our forces are to offer our bodies' breath. When we die protecting the cows, then at least our dharam will be saved."
Yes, at least our dharam will be saved. We won't let the cows go to Rāvjī
God willing, both these brothers turned their soldiers around, and faced Rāvjī's army outside the village entrance—*vāh vāh*—
They said: "Look, brother, whoever goes to capture the Bagaṛāvats' cows should first fight with us."
Yes, first fight us!
Rāvjī's general said: "Brother, if a small bird takes away an ocean's water in its beak, this ocean's water hardly becomes less.
Yes, it doesn't come to an end
And this army of Rāvjī's is the ocean—*mhe*—
You are the bird." *What power do you at all have?*
The brothers said: "Whatever it is—we are going to die."—*vāh vāh*—
When they said this, Rāvjī's forces launched the attack. God willing, the armies of those two brothers were slain.
Yes, they were slain protecting the cows. Said sir.[7] And the Sirdārs, they certainly died—*vāh vāh*—
So, Rāvjī's generals went to the Goram Hill, and surrounded the cows.—*vāh vāh*—

The Search for Sāḍū Mātā

Now, the cowherds did not know that the Bagaṛavāts' mahābhārat had already taken place.
Yes, they did not at all know
They had gone out grazing, grazing cattle—*mhe*—

So, what did the cowherd do? The cowherds had not been taken captive by Rāvjī's generals, God willing—*mhe*—

Now, there was another general of Rāvjī, who somehow was acquainted, and related, to the Bagaṛāvats—*mhe*—

He said: "Who are you fighting for?

Yes, your masters have been slain

And, God willing, a second assault will be made—*vāh vāh*—

Your cows won't remain here either—*mhe*—

You do this—Bhoj's wife Sāḍū Mātā didn't go to the sativāḍā.

Yes, find out where she is and take her to some refuge!—vāh vāh—

Hide her!

Otherwise, Rāvji's generals will capture her—and the world will say that Rāvji's queen was taken away by the Bagaṛāvāts—*mhe*—

And Rāvjī's queen was taken away by the Bagaṛāvats, and the Bagaṛāvats' queens

They were taken away by Rāvjī. *He captured them*

It would be an equal matter."

God willing, Nāpājī was Dev Mahārāj's chief cowherd—*mhe*—

They told him: "Here, Nāpā, brother, go you now!"

Yes, go and find out, while I protect the cows

God willing, Rāvjī's general said: "You can keep the cows surrounded if you want, but I won't let you take them.

Yes, not even one

Why?—Because five hundred horses and five hundred cavalry of the Kacchāvā Sirdārs have died for them.—What do you propose to do?"

Yes, what power do you have?

God willing, what did Nāpā Guāl, who was the chief, do? He rode his horse that stood near the cows—*vāh vāh*—

God willing, when he went to the land of Goṭhā.—*vāh vāh*—

At that time, there were satī memorials by the banks of the Khārī river.—*mhe*—

He noticed that what the fellow had told him, had really happened. He went near Savāī Bhoj's memorial stone and looked over there—*vāh vāh*—

Now at the time when Sāḍū Mātā was atop the Mālāsar Hill, the elephant—Gajmaṅgal—wandered all around it.

Yes, wandered about it

The Guāl saw the elephant as it wandered about the hill. He reflected to himself: "There is sure to be someone where the elephant is."

Yes, surely Bhuvājī[8] *is over there!*

He raced his horse—*mhe*—

God willing, what did he do? From the Goram Hill he reached the Mālāsar Hill

So, Sāḍū Mātā was singing praises of Bhagavān—*vāh vāh*—

She was sitting there in a fearsome form[9]—*mhe*—

The Guāl thought to himself: "Bhuvājī's gone mad!

Yes, she's deranged

That's because the Bagaṛāvats died—they were such great people—that's why she's beside herself.

Yes, now there's no sense left in her

What did the Guāl do? He went quietly up to her and said: "Bhuvā Sāī,[10] get up from here—Rāvjī's general has come to capture you."

Yes, let's go!

Bhuvājī speaks.—*vāh vāh*—

Let's see what news she tells her nephew. *Now, by saying it, know it, let's see, how it's said*

I'll say it now, Lord Dev Bhagavān willing, let's see.—*vāh vāh*—

—*gāv*—

"Let Rāṇā attack—let Rāv attack—*vāh vāh*—

Let the earth's greatest kings attack

Hey, in the month of Mā̃h,[11] I'll certainly perform austerities[12] on Mālāsarī, in the manner of a demoness[13]—*mhe*—

O Nephew, I'm remembering Bhagavān now![14]—*vāh vāh*—

Don't interrupt me, brother!"

Yes, don't disturb me

The Guāl thought to himself: "Hey, look at Bhūvājī!

Yes, her mind is deranged

Her mind's gone. She's saying senseless things. She's longing for Bhagavān!"—*vāh vāh*—

He said: "O Mother, what is Bhagavān telling you now?"—*mhe*—

Sāḍū Mātā said: "Hey, look, nephew, there's an agreement between Bhagavān and me.

Yes, there's a promise,"

As soon as Bhoj's thirteenth day[15] arrives *on that day Bhagavān will enter my door."* Nāpā said: "All right, agreed—he'll come—*vāh vāh*—

Why? The Bagaṛāvats were such great people—such great devotees of Śaṅkar and even they've departed

Of course, Bhagavān will come to your home!"

Yes, to your door!

Sāḍū Mātā said: "Hey, Guāl, he will definitely come!"—*vāh vāh*—

Nāpā said: "I don't believe it!

Yes, I don't believe this Bhuvājī!

God willing, leave this place—*vāh vāh*—

Look, otherwise I'll not let Rāvjī's generals capture you.

Yes, I won't let them capture you!

I'll sever your head, and throw you onto Phūphājī's[16] funeral pyre. You'll be cremated together."

Yes, I'll perform your satī like this right away!

—*gāv*—

"Let Rāṇā attack—let Rāv attack—*mhe*—
Let the earth's greatest lords attack
Hey, brother, in the month of Māh I'll perform austerities on Mālāsarī—*mhe*—
I'll burn camphor incense for Bāḷā Dev."[17] Nāpā said: "All right, agreed, Dev Bhagavān will come to your door."—*mhe*—
Sāḍū Mātā said: "Guāl, he is sure to come!"—*vāh vāh*—
God willing, Nāpā became enraged.—*mhe*—
He had a sword with him. He drew the sword.
Yes, take this
"Take this, Bhagavān, brother, Bhuvājī, Bhagavān is . . . God willing now, take this!" he said, "I'll throw you onto Savāī Bhoj's pyre!"—*vāh vāh*—
He drew out the sword
Sāḍū Mātā prayed to Bhagavān—*mhe*—:
"Look, brother, Bhagavān, there's a promise between you and me—that you'd play in my jolī.[18]
Yes, there is a promise of the thirteenth day
The Guāl won't let the thirteenth day arrive.
Yes, he won't let it pass. What will happen to your promise?
Today is only the eleventh day. Come into my joli today, come now!"

Devnārāyaṇ's Birth on Mālāsarī Hill

The lord of the three worlds, Bhagavān, was playing caupaḍ[19] with Bāsak down in the thirteenth underworld.[20]
He said: "Hey, Rājā Bāsak, someone's troubling my satī—*mhe*—
I have to go, brother!
Yes, I can't wait!
Bhagavān departed from the place, didn't he?—*mhe*—
What emerged from the earth? From the thirteenth underworld, a jet of water arose. Splitting the hill apart, the stream of water fell into Sāḍū Mātā's lap—*vāh vāh*—
In that stream a lotus blossom *manifested, which fell into her lap*
In the lotus blossom Dev Mahārāj, the lord of the three worlds, was manifest on his own.[21] *Said sir.*
Sāḍū Mātā said: "Here you are nephew! What did you say?—*mhe*—
When will Bhagavān come and where? *Here he's come!*"
Nāpā said: "Brother, O Mother, you've lived in the country of Mālāgar[22]—there are crafts in Malwa. You've created some child through magic!"[23]
Sāḍū Mātā said: "Guāl, he's not born of magic, brother."
Yes, he's manifest on his own. He's Bhagavān
Nāpā said: "If he's manifest on his own, then, brother, tell your Bhagavān to give me some proof!"
Sāḍū Mātā said: "Guāl, brother, what proof can that child give now?"
Yes, tell me!—He's an infant—just a child!

Devnārāyaṇ's birth on Mālāsarī Hill.

Nāpā said: "Listen, hey, Bhuvājī, a snake's offspring are neither small nor big.
Yes, neither small nor large—they are all the same—always big
If he's Bhagavān, then he's not small—*mhe*—
And, if he's not Bhagavān, then he's smaller than all."
Yes, he's small because you've created him through magic!
The lord of the three worlds shouted. He said: "Don't fear, Mother!
Yes, ask—what proof does the Gūal want from you?"
She said: "Hey, Gūal tell me, brother." *Tell me, what do you want?*
Nāpā said: "I want only this proof"—*mhe*—

Devnārāyaṇ Revives the Kacchāvā Rajputs

"The Bagaṛāvats were killed because they fetched the queen.[24]
Yes, they were killed
Why should I ask for them now?
Yes, no point asking for them—they've departed!
But the two generals, the Kacchāvā brothers from Āmerāv, Khaḍak Siṅg and Nirvāṇ Siṅg—*mhe*—
died for the sake of the Bagaṛāvats today.
Yes, they died protecting the cows. If their armies come alive again *and the two brothers come alive*
And meet together with the cows and cowherds, *come together and the blockade around the cows is ended*

Then I'll certainly believe in his incarnation . . ." *Only then is your Bhagavān an avatār, otherwise he's nothing at all*
So, the Lord[25] was in Sāḍū Mātā's lap—*mhe*—
He shouted
On account of his shout, the armies of the two Sirdārs came alive again on the outskirts of Rāṇ Śahar—*vāh vāh*—
After coming back to life, God willing,
They met at the Goram Hill with the cowherds.
Yes, and stood there
They said: "Guāls, be strong, brother.
Yes, now, nothing will go wrong, the cows won't go away. All these days there was one power—*mhe*—
Now there is a another power and it is ours."

So, at the time when the lord of the three worlds, Bhagavān, took incarnation, he first provided testimony.—*mhe*—
The armies of the Sirdārs of Āmerāv came to life again, the blockade of the cows was lifted.—Speak victory to Śrī Devanārāyaṇ, brother, speak victory, everyone, both great and small!

What did the Guāl do?—*mhe*—
He collected wood from that spot on the hill.—*vāh vāh*—
And at the time when Bhagavān gave testimony, he made a cradle, placed it on his head, and brought it to Goṭhā.—*vāh vāh*—
By God's grace, at the time when Dev Mahārāj took incarnation—*mhe*—the news reached Rāvjī Sāī.—*vāh vāh*—
By God's grace, swords started rattling on their own in the court.—*mhe*—
And the elephants gave up eating talavā cūrmā.[26] And the horses gave up rātab ghās.[27] Rāvjī Sāī asked: "Sirdārs—*mhe*—
How has this happened today?"
Rāvjī Sāī's bed began to shake
They said: "Mahārāj, call the paṇḍits"—*vāh vāh*—
So then the paṇḍits were summoned, by God's grace, and shown the horoscope.
Yes, an enquiry was made
He said: "O Paṇḍits, brothers, why have the swords begun moving on their own in my court?
Yes, the swords started moving on their own
Three balconies of the fort broke on their own and *fell down! What's the matter?*
They said: "Śrī Mahārāj—*mhe*—
Since you went to capture the cows—*vāh vāh*—
And caused the great battle you had with the Bagaṛāvats—Bhagavān, their avenger, has taken incarnation.
Yes, Bhagavān has taken incarnation in their home today
The one who'll take the Bagaṛāvats' revenge on you.—*vāh vāh*—
He said: "So, brother, by God's grace, is there any one who can kill him?"

Yes, is there anyone?
So the Paṇḍits who were from Kāśī said: "Mahārāj, the expenses will be very great
Yes, but we'll kill him
We'll offer him to the fire rites.—*mhe*—
But first give us half of the kingdom of Rāṇ City *then we'll . . .*
Then we'll finish him off." Rāvjī Sāī said: "Here, O Brahmans, I'll give you half the kingdom.
Yes, take half the kingdom!

Brahmans Try Killing Devnārāyaṇ

Four Paṇḍits departed from there
Now Sāḍū Mātā had taken the cradle to Daṛāvat and hung it up there.—*mhe*—
So those Brahmans came to Sāḍū Mātā
They went and asked: "O Mother, you have a child—*mhe*—What about the child's name, brother?"
Yes, have it named by us—we'll name it!
She said: "Hey, Brahmans, I'm barren from birth, can't you tell?"
Yes, what naming do you want done?
They said: "O Mother, we've heard that you had a child."
Yes, that's why we've come

Devnārāyaṇ's cradle protected by snakes and scorpions.

She said: "No brother, I've had no child and neither is there need for any naming and all.
Yes, why should there be a naming?
If you want to eat and drink—*mhe*—
Then I'll prepare a meal for you."
Yes, that can be done
They said: "O Mother, we won't take our meals with this water.—*mhe*—We'll take our meals with water from an unburnt clay pot.
Yes, we'll take our meals with that water, not with yours
We're Paṇḍits from Kāśi aren't we?" *We want pure water*
Now Sāḍū Mātā was Bhagavān's devotee.—*mhe*—
She said: "O divine beings, sit for a while, brother."
Yes, I'll go and fetch water
Sāḍū Mātā came to the water well.—*vāh vāh*—
She went to the Kumahārs and got a pot of unburnt clay.—*mhe*—
And with Bhagavān's help she returned to the water
What did the Brahmans do in the meantime?—There you are—now take care of the house
Yes, now let's find out where the child is
So the first Brahman went to the cradle
The cradle was covered with a costly shawl and was swinging to and fro.—*mhe*—
By God's grace, the lord of the three worlds took the shape of a snake at that time.—*vāh vāh*—
What did the Brahman do? In no time he put the shawl aside—Ses Nāg was sleeping in the cradle
Yes, the snake fanned its hood
As it fanned its hood he put back the shawl on it and ran away.
Yes, he came and said "It's not a child"
He came and told the Brahmans: "Hey, brother, there's no child here—he would have eaten me—it's a snake."
Yes, there's a snake in there
They said: "There is, there is! You sit down." The second Brahman went to the cradle.
Yes, he went there
What did Bhagavān do this time—*mhe*—
He became a hundred years old.
Yes, he became an old man clearly
And, in the flash of an eyelid he took on the form of someone who was about to breathe his last.—*vāh vāh*—
The Brahman "god" thought to himself: "Brother, why should we kill him and sink in sin?"
Yes, where's the snake here—he's an old man of a hundred years
"He'll die on his own"
Yes, he's about to die
He went and said: "Brother, there isn't a snake there"

Yes, there's no snake in the cradle—you're a liar
"There's a man who's a hundred and twenty years old!—*mhe*—
He's an old man—about to die, brother.
Yes, his neck is about to break!
He said: "You're a liar—absolutely—I just saw a snake.—*mhe*—
He said: "Both of you sit down at one place!" The third Brahman went to the cradle. *Said sir.*
This time Bhagavān showed an empty cradle to the Brahman
Yes, it was swinging to and fro empty
He said: "Brother, there's neither a snake—*mhe*—
Nor an aged man—*vāh vāh*—
The cradle's empty this time!" *It's swinging absolutely empty!*
They said: "You're a liar too, brother!"—*vāh vāh*—
The fourth Brahman went to the cradle
At that time Bhagavān assumed the form of a child.—*mhe*—
And he was sucking his big toe in the place of a breast
Yes, he was sucking on his big toe
The Brahman put the shawl aside and saw a child sleeping in the cradle.—*vāh vāh*—
What did the Brahman "god" do when he returned?—*mhe*—
He took off his sandals.—*vāh vāh*—
And started beating the other Brahmans with the sandals.
Yes, he started beating them
That one's pigtail fell into this one's hands, and this one's pigtail into that one's hands
Sāḍū Mātā came back with the water
She said: "O Brahman gods, why are doing this, brother?"
Yes, why are you fighting like this, brother?
"Eat and drink. I'll give you dakhiṇā.[28] Receive my offering!" They said:
"Mājī Sā, we've taken the full offering!—*mhe*—
And we've had enough to eat, brother.
Yes, we're very satisfied, Mājī Sā!
You just show us the way to Rāṇ City." *Tell us that, so that we may be able to return—we appeal to you with hands joined!* She said: "Hey, brother, why?"
Yes, what has happened?
They said: "Your child is extremely artful, Mājī!
Yes, he's a wizard
By God's grace, you said there was no child—*mhe*—
We came to name him. Yes, but you named us"
Yes, you got our names pronounced first!
By God's grace, the Paṇḍits went back as they had come
And they went to Rāvjī and said: "Śrī Mahārāj, we can't do this work"—*mhe*—

Then Rāvjī Sā made a proclamation again
"Is there some strong person capable of killing the child? *If there is one, then tell me*"
By God's grace, the Dutī said: "Śrī Mahārāj, I'll go and kill him!"
Yes, I'll go and kill him right away
Taking the shape of a demoness, this Dutī—*mhe*—
Took shape of Sāḍū Mātā sister—*vāh vāh*—
And reached Daṛāvat
She asked Sāḍū Mātā: "Sister, how many days old is Nephew and how many days not?
Yes, tell me about that, Sister
We're sisters from our uncle's elder brother's side
Yes, we're both sisters from the uncle's elder brother's
You haven't known that all these days—*mhe*—
But Sister I know that, I'm elder to you."—*vāh vāh*—
Sāḍū Mātā said: "I don't know, Sister!" The Dutī said: "I heard that a nephew was born to you
Yes, that's why I came
I came to feed him—*vāh vāh*—
to feed him, Sister!" So, Sāḍū Mātā took Bhagavān from her lap and gave him to the Dūtī—*mhe*—
What did the Dūtī do? She had smeared poison on her breasts—*vāh vāh*—
So, she gave Dev Mahārāj her breast smeared with poison
In no time Dev Mahārāj suckled her and pulled out all her inner organs
he sucked them all out and removed them
The Dūtī was killed completely.
Sāḍū Mātā said: "Brother, it won't be possible for us to live here any more
Yes, it's not possible here
First we threw out the Brahmans—*mhe*—
And again this Dūtī came—*vāh vāh*—
And more so than that Rāvjī generals will be coming."
Yes, they'll be coming. It's not possible for Dev Mahārāj to live here.

❁ Sāḍū Mātā's Flight to Malwa ❁

So, Sāḍū Mātā sent a letter to her maternal home—*vāh vāh*—
She sent a letter to Salā and Malā, the Bhīls.—*mhe*—
And she sent a letter to her brothers Āmo and Nīmo
By God's grace, Bhagavān departed at night—*mhe*—
And Sāḍū Mātā departed at night
So, now at the time Dev Māhārāj took incarnation—*mhe*—

At that time Līlā, the horse, also took incarnation with him.
As soon as they took incarnation, a promise was made between Līlā and Dev Mahārāj
He said: "Listen, brother, Horse!—*mhe*—
You take to the teat of this Kāḷavī Mare—*mhe*—
And I'll take to the breast of this Gūjar Mother."
Kāḷavī was the horse that Sāḍū rode—*mhe*—
The Līlāgar horse started suckling her teats
By God's grace, they went five kos—ten kos; at that time the brothers, they appeared in front of Sāḍū Mātā—*vāh vāh*—
They said: "O, Aunt!—*mhe*—
Give us Bhagavān's cradle, brother
Yes, lift up the cradle to us; it's our custom."
She said: "You take it, brother"
Yes, you take it, brothers
Sāḍū Mātā goes ahead; the cowherd goes in front of Sāḍū
Bhagavān's maternal uncles took the cradle on their heads and departed.

Devnārāyaṇ Disguises Himself as a Brahman

Dev Mahārāj thought in his mind
He said: "Let's see how resolute the uncles are, let's see"
Yes, let's see what kind of strength they have
He took the shape of a Brahman—*mhe*—
And stood alone
As they saw the figure of the Brahman, Dev Mahārāj's uncles thought in their minds: "Hey, Sister has had a nephew now—*mhe*—
So there are no Brahmans there.
Yes, where are the Brahmans there . . . Let's ask about his horoscope."
Which constellation was he born under?
They said: "Brother Brahman, make a horoscope." The Brahman said: "That's my business, brother
Yes, what other work shall I do?"
They said: "A nephew has taken incarnation with our sister; take a look at him
Yes, what kind of constellation was he born under
He was born on this time and this hour"—*mhe*—
The Brahman said: "I won't tell lies"
Yes, I'll tell the truth
By God's grace, Dev Mahārāj said:—*mhe*—
"Listen brother, my books show such and such a conjunction"—*vāh vāh*—
He said: "He'll eat his paternal home as soon as he's born
And now that child's on his way to eat his maternal home
That's the kind of conjunction given in the books."

Dev Mahārāj's uncles thought to themselves: "Brother Brahman, didn't go there[29] to see what happened—*mhe*—
What he's saying must be true
Yes, he's said it after consulting the books
And what he is saying exactly that'll happen to us in the future *exactly that will happen—he'll devour us as soon as we reach*
We don't want such a nephew"—*mhe*—
A number of rivers and streams—*vāh vāh*—
Flow through the forest—*mhe*—
The uncles, you know, overturned Dev Mahārāj's cradle into a stream
Yes, yes, they threw it down—there you are!—We don't need a nephew like that!

Sāḍū Mātā and the Lioness

After they went away, by God's grace, there was a lioness in that forest.—*mhe*—
She placed her chest against Dev's cradle and put her teat to Dev's mouth
Yes, she started suckling him
Now there was a promise with Līlā that they would suckle at the same time
Yes, they would suckle together
So the Līlāgar horse turned in front of the mare—*mhe*—
And started suckling the Kāḷavī horse's teat
Mājī Sā whipped it
She said: "What promise is there between you and Dev, brother?"
Yes, you were supposed to suckle together! Why are you suckling first?
The horse said: "Mājī Sāī—*mhe*—don't disturb me
Yes, you're disturbing my habit
Your Dev is suckling at this moment
Yes, that's why I began suckling
Let me complete my regular habit at least."—*vāh vāh*—
She said: "Hey, brother, I, his mother, am over here—*mhe*—
Who can suckle him other than me?"
Yes, who is the other?
The horse said: "Listen, O Mother *he has a lot of mothers*
There are a lot of mothers like you for him
Take a look!"—*vāh vāh*—
Mājī Sāī turned around and raced her horse. The brothers were empty-handed.
Yes, where was the cradle?—The brothers were walking empty-handed
She said: "Brothers, where is Bhagavān's cradle?"—*mhe*—
They said: "What Bhagavān? We dropped the cradle in a river of this country *we threw it away over there*
Where's Bhagavān over here?" *He's not Bhagavān—his horoscope is not good, Sister*
She said "You've done great wrong!"—*vāh vāh*—
Sāḍū Mātā raced the horse, by God's grace, she reached that river's banks—*vāh vāh*—

Now the cradle was lying in the river bed—*mhe*—
The lioness was there with her chest toward the cradle and Dev Mahārāj was suckling her teat
Sāḍū Mātā thought: "I'll frighten the lioness away with arrows"
Yes, she'll go away
She used up as many arrows as she had—*mhe*—
The lioness didn't budge
Yes, the lioness didn't move at all from that place
By God's grace, the lioness said: "Gūjrī,[30] you can shoot any number of arrows"
Yes, don't shoot arrows like that—I won't give you that child of mine anyway
By God's grace, Sāḍū Mātā said: "Brother, I'm your dharam-sister—*mhe*—
So give the child back to me in my bodice."
The lioness said: "I'll give him back, if from today onward you don't trust anyone—*mhe*—
And not entrust someone else with something of yours
You gained motherhood by giving him just one breast—*mhe*—
I'm giving your Dev the seventh teat today"
Since Sāḍū had taken the name of a sister, the lioness left Dev—*mhe*—and returned into the forest. Sāḍū Mātā took Dev Mahārāj's cradle back onto the basket on her head—*mhe*—and started off again.
As the lord of the three worlds approached Malwa—*mhe*—
By God's grace, Sāḍū Mātā appealed to the lioness
She appealed to the lioness.
Speak: Victory to Śrī Devnārāyaṇ Bhagavān *victory*

Sāḍu Mātā confronts the lioness.

Dūdī Nīm

Now three kos before Dūdīyā Kheḍā there was one Dūdī Nīm—*mhe*—
They say that Bhagavān's cradle alighted there on its own *It alighted under the nīm tree*
As long as Dev was on the road to Malwa—*mhe*—
For that many days he suckled the Gūjrī's breast
But after the cradle alighted at that nīm tree they say, and tell, that he suckled that many days
Yes, he didn't suckle beyond that
He used to suckle till they reached that nīm tree—*vāh vāh*—

❁ Sāḍū Mātā and Devnārāyaṇ in Malwa ❁

Now the Bagaṛāvats' Goddess[31] was Kā̃jrī; she came to test the Bagaṛāvats—*mhe*—
Now what did the Bagaṛāvats do on that day? They presented her a double-stringed necklace and told her: "Go, brother, and test the country's wealthy people *Test them!*
If there's anyone who offers a greater gift[32] than us then forget our name and start taking the name of the other one"
She went away to test the wealthy people of this country—*mhe*—
In the meantime the Bagaṛāvats' great war took place
Yes, it took place—they were killed
By God's grace, they she returned after they died—*vāh vāh*—
She had made Śaṅkar promise that: "Brother, when I return I want to meet the Bagaṛāvats unharmed."
Śaṅkar was very intoxicated at that time—*mhe*—
Inadvertantly he said: "Go, Caṇḍī, you'll meet them unharmed
Return and you'll find the Bagaṛavāts unharmed
Nothing will be harmed"—*vāh vāh*—
So she came to Śaṅkar and began asking for her Bagaṛāvats—*mhe*—
And Śaṅkar said: "Look, they had an old vow—the time for that vow has come, brother
Yes, the vow has been fulfilled
Now they've gone to Indra's residence"—*mhe*—

Six months' time passed—*vāh vāh*—
So Bijorī Kā̃jarī went to Tejājī at the Richor Hill—*mhe*—
Tejājī went to look for the Bagaṛāvats—*vāh vāh*—
In the direction of Nagaur
When the Bagaṛāvats died the Bhāṭ went to his maternal home in Nagaur—*mhe*—

Speechless, he wandered about the land
Yes, he wandered about mute—where was the sovereign?
The masters had died. By God's grace, Bijorī asked: "Hey, Bhāṭ, why are you wandering about in this country?"
Yes, why are you wandering about in this land?
He said: "The masters have died and I'm wandering about aimlessly."
Yes, I've fallen naturally into decay
Tejājī said: "The masters haven't gone away—*mhe*—
Bhagavān, the lord of the three worlds, has taken incarnation after the masters died—*vāh vāh*—
As soon as he took incarnation, Dev Mahārāj went to Malwa. Go Bhāṭ,
Bring Bhagavān back from Malwa!
Get him back from Malwa—bring him back!
Establish Goṭh Kheḍā after that!"—*vāh vāh*—
The Bhāṭ said: "Bijorī, you know about the matter—you know for sure."
Bijorī said: "Yes, brother!"
Yes, don't make problems for me!

—*gāv*—

Chochū Bhāṭ's Journey to Malwa

The Bagaṛāvats' Bhāṭ departed from Nagaur—*mhe*—
The Bhāṭ reached the rivers, the waters
O Deḷū Mātā, we'll go to the land of Mālāgar—*vāh vāh*—
To Ṭhākur Dev's court
On that day the Bhāṭ's mother was together with him—*mhe*—
So now many days passed. When they reached the Sapra river—*vāh vāh*—
Deḷū Mātā asked: "Hey, Bhāṭ—*mhe*—
How far have we come and how far is Malwa now?"
Yes, how far is Malwa?
The Bhāṭ said: "Mother, hardly a pāv has been ground from a maṇ
Yes, we've traveled only a short distance
Malwa's three hundred kos from here
Yes, it's not close by"
Deḷū Mātā said: "Hey, Bhāṭ, the ceremony of the twelfth day will be done for me here on the way[33]
Yes, it'll be done on the road—let alone my going to Malwa
And if you reach Malwa—*mhe*—there's no returning."
There's no question of returning.
So after crying, Deḷū Mātā—*mhe*—
And the Bagaṛāvats Bhāṭ—by God's grace—both mother and son went to sleep on a rock that was on the banks of the Saprā river
Yes, both mother and son went to sleep

And the horse *was tethered to that rock.*
By God's grace, the lord of the three worlds was present at Dūdīyā Kheḍā. He spoke to Bhairūnāth:
"Bhairūnāth! The bhāṭ of my lineage is in difficulty, brother
Yes, go and fetch him!
He's sleeping on the banks of the Saprā river."—*vāh vāh*—
He was like a flash of lightning.—*mhe*—
Yes, by God's grace, in the movement of an eyelid Bhairūnāth reached there—*vāh vāh*—
He picked up the rock from the Saprā river into the air—*mhe*—
There was the Kāḷyode pond in Malwa's territory
Yes, he brought it and left it there as it was
Deḷū Bhāṭaṇī awoke at dawn—*vāh vāh*—
Now that water was flowing—*mhe*—
And this water was stationary *The pond there was filled with water*
Deḷū Mātā said: "Hey, Chochū—*mhe*—
Get up, brother, it's not the same place that we slept at night!"
The Bhāṭ awoke and said: "Mother—*mhe*—Malwa's territory is right here, brother."
Yes, we've gone and reached Malwa
Deḷū Mātā said: "At night you said it would take six months—*mhe*—
And was three hundred kos away. How did we reach Malwa as we slept?"
Yes, how did that come about, brother?
The Bhāṭ said: "Our Dev Mahārāj—Bhagavān—brought us here—*vāh vāh*—
Now I went to Savāī Bhoj's marriage—*mhe*—
On that day Savāī Bhoj's in-laws gifted me a horse
Yes, they gave me a horse
I didn't take to that horse—*vāh vāh*—
I cut its tail off—*mhe*—
And threw it into this Kāḷyode pond *I left it here*
It's that Kāḷyode."
Yes, it's that pond
What did Sāḍū Mātā do? The Bagaṛāvats' cows—*mhe*—were tended by the Bagaṛāvats' cowherd. She put him to work at home *Some other work at home*
And, by God's grace, she sent her maternal home's brothers' children to look after the cows.

Sāḍū Mātā Tries to Kill Chochū Bhāṭ Three Times

She told them: "Hey, brother, an enemy of mine is following me
Keep a look out for in case he comes *Don't let him come ahead of here—kill him on the way*
They asked: "O Aunt, what signs and marking are there to know him?"

Yes, tell us about that

Sāḍū Mātā said: "The horse he rides is called Phūlrīyo—*mhe*—his old mother accompanies him, and he keeps large gourds around his neck.[34]

At the time when he comes—*mhe*—at that time these cows—*mhe*—and that person will talk like

People talk to one another." At dawn, Bhagavān's cows reached Kāḷyode.

As the Bhāṭ saw the cows—*mhe*—he strung the surbīṇ around his neck *and began playing*

The lineage's Bhāṭ speaks—what does he say to Mother Cow? Let us see

Know it by saying it, Bhopājī Mahārāj, see it by saying it

I'll say it now, by Dev's grace, let's see—*vāh vāh sā*—[35]

—*gāv*—

O Mother, there's plenty of water and grass in this region—*vāh vāh*—

Bumblebees hum loudly

The lineage's Bhāṭ asks you: "Nāglī Mātā, why are you so thin?

Why are you thin, brother?

Yes, why are you so thin?

So much water—*mhe*—! So much grass to eat! The bumblebees hum, don't they, daughter's father!"—*vāh vāh*—

Now Suremātā spoke—*mhe*—

Let's see what she says to the Bhāṭ *Let's see what she replies. Know it by saying it, by saying it*

I'll tell it now, by Dev's grace

—*vāh vāh sā*—

—*gāv*—

"There's plenty of water and grass in this region—*mhe*—

By God's grace, the bumblebees hum loud

By God's grace, Jāsā's Nirpāl didn't feed me!—*mhe*—

Once upon a time you used to enjoy even the royal *produce*

Listen, O Bhāṭ—*mhe*—

This is what my trouble is, brother.

Yes, I used live off the monsoon harvest of wheat and chickpeas—I didn't get any of that

If I want to go to the west—*mhe*—then, look, the bare-headed cowherd strikes my horns and moves me ahead."

Yes, he moves me ahead by hitting me

Sure Mātā went to the Bhaṭ's home—*vāh vāh*—

Dev's cowherd was behind the cows. He climbed up on a high edge of the pond.

He said: "Hey, cowherds—*mhe*—the man Bhūvājī told us about has come today."

Yes, our enemy has come today. By God's grace, they took sticks and surrounded the Bhāṭ. *They encircled him*

So Suremātā freed the Bhāṭ from the cowherds' encirclement—*vāh vāh*—

Nāglī went to the Dūdī Nīm tree and prayed to Darbār—*mhe*—:
"Śrī Mahārāj, the lineage's bhāṭ has arrived and the cowherds are beating him"
Yes, your cowherds—the ones that Bhūvājī brought are beating him
By God's grace, Devnarāyāṇ spoke to Bhairūnāth: "Bhairūnāth—*mhe*—it's a cowherds' race, brother—*vāh vāh*—
The Bhāṭ and his mother will be finished off.
Yes, bring them here
Go, bring them here."—*vāh vāh*—
So Kālā and Gorā Bhairūnāth reached them
What did the cowherds do in the meantime? The cowherd caught hold of the Bhāṭ and tied—*mhe*—
A stick between his elbows and knees,[36] and dropped him into the Kāḷyode pond.—*vāh vāh*—
Bhairūnāth freed him from the log of wood,—*mhe*—
And said: "Here you are, Bhāṭjī, I'll take you to your master"
Yes, come along now
After the Bhāṭ had left the Dūdīyā Nīm tree, at that time the Bagaṛāvats' Bhāṭ sang a song of praise to Bhagavān, as soon as he arrived
By God's grace, it's the Bagaṛavāts' lineage Bhāṭ, isn't it—*mhe*—?
He gave a song of praise—*vāh vāh*—
He said: "From King Ād came King Jugād. From Jugād came Kācchap; from Kācchap Raṇdhol—*mhe*—
From Raṇdhoḷ came Kajaḷī; from Kajaḷī came Maṇḍalī—*mhe*—And from Maṇḍalī came Harīrāmjī—*vāh vāh*—To Harirāmjī Bāgh was born; from Bāgh came Bhoj and from Bhoj came Dev
Arisen from the fire-pit, the great family of the Cauhāns.
The soles of his feet have the mark of lotuses[37]
His shoulders are the shape of betel leaves
Through the strike of Līlā's hooves a surge of cold water arose from the underworld—*vāh vāh*—
And split open the hill
On the day that Dev took incarnation, the space between the sky and the earth was lit up
Hey, Bhoj's Udal—*mhe*—he held up the falling sky"
Devnārāyaṇ said: "Welcome, Bhāṭjī, welcome
I haven't met anyone yet who sang such a song of praise
And it doesn't seem like I'll meet another one."
What does the Bhāṭ say?—*mhe*—
And, let's see what he tells Bhagavān
Know it by saying it; let's see now, by saying it.

—*gāv*—

"Summer dust is blowing today—*mhe*—
O King of Goṭhā̃, the winds of north and east are blowing
Come to Goṭhā, come Dharamarājā Devjī—*mhe*—
Hey, the season of rain will come now

O giver of nourishment, come to Goṭhā."
Yes, don't stay here any more
Devnārāyaṇ said: "Come, Bhāṭ, come now"—*vāh vāh*—
The cowherds went and spoke to Māt Khaṭāṇī,[38] "Here, brother, Bhūvāji"
Yes, he went just as he came
By God's grace, Sāḍū Mātā thought in her mind: "This stupid Bhāṭ's come, hasn't he—*mhe*—! He won't leave Dev alone—he'll take him away."
Yes, he'll take him away from here—won't leave him here
By God's grace, Sāḍū Mātā made a plate of food with poison for the Bhāṭ
For Dev Mahārāj she made a plate of food with amṛt
"Go, O maidservants—*mhe*—give the lord the plate with amṛt—*vāh vāh*—
And slide that Bhāṭ the plate with poison
By God's grace, if the stupid fellow dies, I'll be rid of the bad fortune.—*vāh vāh*—
The enemy Rāvjī destroyed the twenty-four brothers—*mhe*—
What power does he[39] have?"
Dev Mahārāj saw the plate with food.—*mhe*—
He reflected in his mind: "Hey, the old woman has played a trick."
Yes, she'll kill the Bhāṭ
The plate of aṃrt that was in front of—given to Bhagavān, he placed in front of the Bhāṭ—*mhe*—And the plate with poison, he slid over to his side
Sāḍū Mātā, standing high in the palace, noticed this
How does she descend from the palace—*mhe*—
Let's see what she tells her sister-in-law.[40]
Know it by saying it, let's see by saying it

—*gāv*—

Mājī Sā climbed up the steps and descended the steps—*vāh vāh*—
She goes step by step to her brothers' front door
"The maidservants gave the stupid Bhāṭ poison—*mhe*—
That's about to be swallowed by Ṭhākur Dev
Go, sisters-in-law, someone get up and run."
Yes, Devjī is eating the poisoned food!
The sisters-in-law said: "Mājī Sāī, it's your business—your Bhagavān's business *We're not concerned with this*"
So the lord of the three worlds ate the poisoned food—*mhe*—and coughed
On that day he created the scorpion from the poison
The black-spotted scorpion began serving Bhagavān
The lineage's bhāṭ went to his lord—*mhe*—
Dev Mahārāj gave the plate of food with amṛt to the Bhāṭ—*vāh vāh*—
Speak: victory to Śrī Devnārāyāṇ, victory!

Now Bhagavān asked—*mhe*—
He said: "Bhāṭjī—*vāh vāh*—
All right I'll travel to your country—*mhe*—the people from the village who have accompanied me and Sāḍū Mātā, brother, go and inform them

Yes, go and tell them the news, so that we start off
Prepare the wheels and oxen for our carts, brother"—*vāh vāh*—
So how does the Bagaṛāvats' Bhāṭ approach the people of the village—*mhe*—
and what news does he tell them, let's see
Know it by saying it, let's see by saying it

—*gāv*—

Bhāṭjī wore sandals; he wore shoes on his feet—*vāh vāh*—
He goes here and there to the people of the village
"Hey, will anyone go to the land of his birth?—*mhe*—
The lord is going to send back the cows from Mālāgar today! O, people of the
village—*mhe*—
Prepare the carts, brother"
Yes, return now
He told Sāḍū Mātā: "Mājī Sāī—*mhe*—take leave of your brothers."
Yes, take leave, and prepare to depart!
Sāḍū Mātā said: "Welcome, Bhāṭjī, welcome—I waited many days—you've
come now—*vāh vāh*—
It's been many days that I've been waiting
Yes, it's been many days I said we'll go when he comes
But do this—I'm ready—*mhe*—
But the day I came here, you know—*vāh vāh*—on that day I promised an
offering of sweets worth one and a half rupees for Bhagavān in
Sindhbāḍā
Yes, I've promised an offering—go and make the offering
Come back" *Come back and we'll go*
So the Bhāṭ was enthusiastic, that's why the matter will be successful, brother.
Yes, Mājī is ready right now
The Bhāṭ said: "Hey, Mājī Sāī, give it to me."—*vāh vāh*—
Māt Khaṭāṇī tied one and a half Rupees to the border of the Bhāṭ's clothes—
vāh vāh—
She said: "Say this
Yes, as soon as you reach there—
The offering that Sāḍū Mātā wants to give you is ready, take it"
Yes, receive it!
She sent the Bhāṭ off after tying the offering to his clothes—*vāh vāh*—
In the meantime Sāḍū Mātā offered seven spoons of water in the Jogīṇīs' name
Yes, there you are now Jogīṇīs! There's a person of mine coming
Devour him as soon as he arrives! Take my offering of a person *vāh vāh*—
By God's grace, the Bagaṛāvats' Bhāṭ reached Sindhbāḍā
He went and sat down under the banyan tree—*mhe*—and said: "Here you are,
brother, Jogīṇīs—*mhe*—the offering that Sāḍū Mātā sent you is ready,
take it."
Yes, it's ready, take it
It took no time saying this
The Jogīṇīs swooped down and devoured each bone and sinew of the bhāṭ.

Yes, not even one bone was left
By Gods' grace, the Jogīṇīs finished off the Bhāṭ
Three days went by—*mhe*—
The Bhāṭ's mother Deḷū had gone along, hadn't she—*vāh vāh*—
She asked the people of the village: "Hey, brother, who is Sindhbāḍā?"
Yes, where is Sindhbāḍā, O cowherd brothers?
They said: "Old woman what do you want there?"
Yes, what work do you have there? She said: "It's been three days since my son's gone there, brother."
Yes, he hasn't returned again
They said: "Listen Mother—*mhe*—! Sindhbāḍā isn't a village.
Yes, there's no village there
That place is the residence of the Jogīṇīs—*vāh vāh*—
Anyone who goes there doesn't come back"
Yes, a person doesn't come back. They said: "He won't come back."
Deḷū Mātā started crying and wailing on the spot. How does she go to Dev's court? What does she pray to Bhagavān, let's see *What prayer does she give as she reaches, let's see*

—*gāv*—

"By God's grace, I came on Chochu Bhāṭ's saying from the land of Nagaur—*mhe*—
I've been to Medū and brought a letter
Hey, you have great power,[41]but still I'm fed up.—*mhe*—
Send me back just as I came. Both mother and son came together, but send them back just as they came."
Yes, get them back exactly as they came
How does Deḷū Mātā wail and cry; what does she tell Bhagavān, let's see
Know it by saying, let's see by saying it

—*gāv*—

"I came here because of him from the land of Suhāvaḷ—*mhe*—
I've been to Medu and brought a letter from Ajmer
You have great power, but still I'm fed up.—*mhe*—I've gone and lost a jewel like my Chochū
I had a jewel like Chochū
Yes, he who is mine has been lost."—vāh vāh—
She spoke in front of the giver of nourishment.—*vāh vāh*—
The lord of the three worlds speaks now—*mhe*—
What does he tell Deḷū Bhāṭaṇī?
By saying it, Bhopājī Mahārāj, by saying it
I'll just say it, by Dev's grace, here you are—*vāh vāh sā*—

—*gāv*—

Crying, crying, don't you cry mother—*mhe*—
Deḷū have courage for a little while

I'll bridle Līlā just now—*mhe*—
I'll create four of your Chochūs with one shout
Have you lost one of yours?
Yes, have you lost only one?
Deḷū Mātā said: "O giver of nourishment, a hungry person trusts when he is satisfied. I don't need four"
Yes, get me just one at least
Devnārāyaṇ said: "Mother, be a little patient"—*vāh vāh*—
How does Bhagavān saddle Līlāgar with a cotton rug and bridle him in the territory of Mālāgar? And let's see what kind of assault he puts up to revive the Bhāṭ, let's see
Know it by saying it, let's see, by saying it
I'll just say it, by Bhagavān's grace—*vāh vāh jī*—*vāh vāh*—

—*gāv*—

Devnārāyaṇ and the Jogīṇīs

By God's grace, now who all took up the assault of Sindhbāḍā?—*mhe*—
Kālā and Gorā Bherū̃nāth—*vāh vāh*—and Dev Mahārāj and Pālosāyaṇī.[42]
Yes, all four took up the assault
Dev Mahārāj, riding on his horse, travels along the road—*mhe*—
Bherū̃nāth travels off the road—*vāh vāh*—
By God's grace, Bhagavān said: "Bherū̃nāth *come onto the road, why are you running amongst the thorns off the road!*
Bherū̃nāth said: "Śrī Mahārāj, I've learnt a trick"—*vāh vāh*—
It was the month of Kārttik then—*mhe*——the time when those yellow berries grow on the bushes and trees—*vāh vāh*—
It was the month of Kārttik—the bushes were full of berries *They were utterly full.*
Now a fox would come by and give them a swipe with its tail
The berries all fell down on the ground
The fox began picking up the berries and eating them—*vāh vāh*—
Bherū̃nāth said: "Śrī Mahārāj, I've learnt one trick!"
Yes, I've learnt one at least! Devnārāyaṇ said: "What trick?"—*mhe*—
Bherū̃nāth said: "That fox that is standing by the bush. I'll go to Sindhbāḍā and do exactly the same to the Jogīṇīs." So when they arrived in Sindhbāḍā—*mhe*—both Bherū̃nāths caught hold of the tree trunk—*vāh vāh*—
After catching hold of the tree trunk they shook it. There were Jogīṇīs sitting on each leaf. Crack, crack, crack, crack they all came and fell down, sir said.
By God's grace there was a well close by—*mhe*—
They went and fell into the well
Bherū̃nāth said: "Śrī Mahārāj we threw them down with difficulty—the whores have gone and fallen into the well."

Bherū̃nāth shaking the Jogīṇīs' tree at Sindhbāḍā.

Yes, you didn't stand in their way!

Devnārāyaṇ said: "They've collected at one place, brother."

Yes, they won't go anywhere! Bherū̃nāth took a whip and entered into the water.

Yes, he entered the inside of the well

He made them run—*vāh vāh*—

The Jogīṇīs ran up—*mhe*—

As they ran up, the lord of the three worlds was standing on the steps of the well

Yes, he was standing in front of them

They said: "Hey, daughter's father, O Bhagavān *why are you harming us?"*

Devnārāyaṇ said: "The lineage's Bhāṭ came here—where is he?" *If you return him, I'll have you freed immediately*

The Jogīṇīs said: "Hey, Śrī Mahārāj, three days have passed since we swallowed him"

Yes, we ate him up

Devnārāyaṇ said: "The Bhāṭ of my lineage is ending—*mhe*—Bring him up again[43]

Yes, throw up and mix him together

The Jogīṇīs said: "My lord, he has been swallowed!"—*mhe*—

Devnārāyaṇ said: "Throw up whatever's been swallowed"

Yes, throw it up at least! So the Jogīṇīs put their fingers in their throats—*mhe*—and started vomiting in pretense—*mhe*—What did Dev Mahārāj do? He put those pieces in their proper places—*vāh vāh*—

Two things were not found amongst them—*mhe*—

One rib was not found—*vāh vāh*—and the flesh of that rib was not found

Devnārāyaṇ said: "Jogīṇīs—*mhe*—two things were not found"

Yes, two things were not found—say where they are
The Jogīṇīs said: "We don't have those two things."—*vāh vāh*—
Devnārāyaṇ said: "Where have they gone?"
The Jogīṇīs said: "The dumb person fell into the underworld and the crazy one flew into the sky."

Devnārāyaṇ's Marriage to Nāgkanyā

Stepping aside from the well, the lord of the three worlds—*vāh vāh*—departed
He spoke to Bāsak Rājā: "Hey, Bāsak Rājā a thief of mine has come here."
Return the thief that has come to you
Bāsak Rājā said: "Mahārāj, he's come—*mhe*—but this is a place of refuge—*vāh vāh*—Now that he's taken refuge here, I won't return the thief, brother
Yes, I won't give him back to you just like that! If you want to play win or lose with me
Yes, if I lose, then take him"
Devnārāyaṇ said: "What will I win?"
Yes, tell me about that!
Bāsak Rājā said: "If I lose then cut my head off—*mhe*—and if you lose—*vāh vāh*—then I'll cut off your head!"
The lord of the three worlds began playing dice against Bāsak in the thirteenth underworld.—*vāh vāh*—Every time Bāsak throws the dice, by God's grace, it's a bad throw, and when Dev Mahārāj throws the dice—*mhe*—it's an absolute winner. Dev Mahārāj won three times.
He asked Bāsak: "Bāsak, what do you say?"—*mhe*—Bāsak said: "Mahārāj, you've won
I have a hundred hoods—cut off any one you like best *Cut off one hood.*"

Devnārāyaṇ said: "No
Yes, I want the other
These are just branches on top—*mhe*—but there's one trunk
Yes, give me the trunk"
Bāsak said: "Brother, Mahārāj, don't do this, brother—*vāh vāh*—"
Devnārāyaṇ said: "Marry your daughter to me instead, then the enmity will be resolved"
Yes, the enmity will be over
Bāsak said: "I have a daughter, a thirteen-year-old Nāgkanyā—*mhe*—
I'll get her married to you." Devnārāyaṇ said: "Tell me, which clan of Nāgs do you belong to?"
Bāsak replied: "I belong to the Gog Cauhān clan."—*mhe*—Devnārāyaṇ said: "What! I took incarnation amongst the Cauhāns, tell me."
Yes, how can there be a union between me and your daughter! Bāsak said:
"Śrī Mahārāj—*mhe*—there are nine clans of Nāgs—*vāh vāh*—
I'm a Nāg of nine clans!—*mhe*—
My wife's brother's daughter is with me." *I'll marry her to you*

So Devnārāyaṇ got married for the first time to Bāsak Rājā's brother-in-law's daughter in the thirteenth underworld
Dev's marriage took place—*vāh vāh*—in the underworld—*mhe*—

After getting married Bhagavān returned—*vāh vāh*—
Bhairūnāth said: "Śrī Mahārāj, you went to catch a thief didn't you?"
Yes, you're going about getting married instead! Devnārāyaṇ said: "Bhairūnāth, it happened on its own—naturally, brother!—*vāh vāh*—But, brother,
Tell me what shall we do about the Bhāṭ?"
Bhairūnāth said: "The thief won't be caught anymore."
There was a mango tree growing there, Devnārāyaṇ told him: "Go and cut one cluster"
Yes, cut a piece of its wood
The mango tree said: "Śrī Mahārāj, if you cut a piece, then how will the world let me be?"
Yes, the world won't let me be at all! Devnārāyaṇ said: "Whoever worships me—*mhe*—will avoid you. He won't cut a branch of yours—*vāh vāh*—if he cuts one—*mhe*—and burns it in the stove, by God's grace, I vow, that on the day he makes an offering to me—even if a single thorn of yours is burnt—I won't accept the offering.
Yes, his savāmaṇī[44] *will be annulled—I won't recognize it*
Give me assistance today.
Yes, you'll have to help me
Then after that you'll have freedom."—*vāh vāh*—
By God's grace, he went to the deer and said: "Cut the deer's flesh, brother."—*vāh vāh*—The deer said: "Śrī Mahārāj, if you cut my flesh, how can the world let me be?"
Yes, the world won't let me be at all! Devnārāyaṇ said: "To slaughter is a serious business—whoever worships me—*mhe*—
He won't even point at you with his finger." *He won't point with his finger any time*
How does Bhagavān revive the lineage's Bhāṭ—*mhe*—and what story is made, let's see
Know it by saying it, let's see now, by saying it
I'll say it now, by God's grace—*vāh vāh*—*vāh vāh*—

—*gāv*—

Bhagavān made the Bhāṭ's rib from the mango tree—*vāh vāh*—and flesh from the deer
Hey, he revived the lineage's Bhāṭ—*mhe*—
On that day Bhagavān blew on the flute. He blew into it.—*mhe*—
Bhagavān blew into it.
The Bhāṭ sat up with a shout
He said: "Hey, Śrī Mahārāj, you've woken me up in the midst of deep sleep."
Yes, I've been having such a sweet sleep

Devnārāyaṇ said: "Bhāṭ, you've had as much sleep as you can have, brother"—*vāh vāh*—, *now get up and let's go!* Bhagavān's first marriage took place with the Nāgkanyā in the underworld—*vāh vāh*—On the day he went to revive the lineage's Bhāṭ—*mhe*—

So Bhagavān revived the Bhāṭ and Bhagavān's first marriage took place

Brother, victory to Śrī Devnārāyaṇ

Say it both big and small

Devnārāyaṇ's Departure from Malwa

By God's grace, after Bhagavān had revived the Bagaṛāvats' Bhāṭ—*mhe*—he returned home. Devnārāyaṇ said: "Deḷū Mātā, here you are, brother, take him

Yes, here take your Bhāṭ

He's the same one, isn't he!"

Deḷū Mātā said: "Hey, Śrī Mahārāj, lord, you are great, brother, to have revived my dead one—*vāh vāh*—

But still, Śrī Mahārāj, I'm doubly fed up[45]—*mhe*—Give me leave to go"—*vāh vāh*—Devnārāyan said: "Delū Mātā, we'll go together.—*vāh vāh*—

Bhāṭjī, go to Mājī[46] take leave of her.

Yes, let's go

Since I've come to Malwa, I haven't been to visit my aunts.—*vāh vāh*—So brother, let me go and exchange a couple of words with them."

Yes, let's meet them, and depart after that

So how does the lord of the three worlds go to his aunts' home, and what does he say to his aunts upon reaching, let's see. *Know it by saying it now, Bhopājī Mahārāj, by saying it*

I'll just say it, by Bhagavān Dev's grace, let's see—*vāh vāh*—*jī vāh*

—*gāv*—

I stayed well and gained happiness—*mhe*—My cows grazed well. There'll be no drought in your country—*mhe*—Great amounts of white millet will grow! Here you are, brother, I stayed well—*vāh vāh*—

There'll never be famine.

Yes, famine in your country, aunt

That's my promise.—*vāh vāh*—*no famine!* What do the aunts say to Dev, let's see

Know it by saying it, lets see, by saying it

—*gāv*—

"O aunt's nephew, you stayed well and gained happiness—*mhe*—your cows grazed well. May famine not fall in your country—*mhe*—A guest like you will always be welcome." Devnārāyaṇ said: "O aunt, you caused me harm this time—*vāh vāh*—

I won't go about saying it."—*mhe*—
The aunts said: "There are nine citadels in Marwar—*mhe*—In one citadel there will definitely be drought. That's my promise in my divine land." Dev Mahārāj said: "Listen, brother, O Aunt, there'll be a lot of harvest, but always wear shoes on your feet—*mhe*—
And don't wander about barefoot
In my country you'll find a ser of gold in each household."
Yes, wander about wearing shoes

—*gāv*—

By God's grace, this news was told to the carriage drivers by Bhagavān—*mhe*—: "Put the spokes back on to the carriage wheels—*vāh vāh*—
Get the cows moving on toward our country
Is anyone coming along to the country of their birth?—*mhe*—Hey, Bhagavān's going to get the cows moving back from Mālāgar today!
We are to go together—*mhe*—Depart now!"—*vāh vāh*—
Devnārāyaṇ spoke to Māt Khaṭāṇī: "Mājī Sāī—*mhe*—You too take leave from your brothers."
Sāḍū Mātā said: "Son, where to?
Yes, I won't go
By God's grace, you do what the Bhāṭ says—*mhe*—Hey, the twenty-four Bagaṛāvats—he destroyed them by creating quarrel upon quarrel. You're five youths—what strength do you have?"
Devnārāyaṇ said: "Mājī Sāī—*mhe*—the work won't be complete unless Goṭh Kheḍā is established—*vāh vāh*—So, by God's grace, Mājī Sāī I have to go, brother!"—*vāh vāh*—
Sāḍū Mātā said: "Son, it was difficult taking care of you—difficult raising you—I won't let you go.
Yes, I won't let you go
If you go like this—*mhe*—then at least return the milk I fed you with all these days. Leave after that—get on the road"
Yes, get on the road—leave!
The lord of the three worlds, Bhagavān, vomited—*mhe*—
And filled up the pond in front with all the milk that he had suckled from Sāḍū Mātā
Yes, he filled back the pond
"There you are Mother, take back your milk—I've brought it up, now you Put it back into your breast."
Sāḍū Mātā couldn't handle the milk—*mhe*—She said: "Son, I've understood
Yes, I understand, now I've understood
I didn't know about your powers all these days.
Yes, I didn't know
I can't put back the milk into my breasts."
Yes, I can't put it back
Devnārāyaṇ said: "If it won't go back, then Mājī Sāī, start off *Come on*"

So on the day the lord vomited and created a pond of milk—*mhe*—That pond is called Dūdī Pond today—*vāh vāh*—

—*gāv*—

The Return to Causle Kheḍā

Devnārāyaṇ Camps at Dhār City

Nārāyaṇ Dev's carriages were ready—*mhe*—The dust from those carriages rose now to the sky
Bhagavān drove them on day and night—*vāh vāh*—On the forty-fifth day camp was set, upon reaching Dhār's outskirts.[47]
It took forty-five days—*vāh vāh*—
Ujjini Dhār was reached in forty-five days—*vāh vāh*—
Dev Mahārāj spoke.
He said: "Hey, brother, the carriage-bullocks' fodder is finished today—*mhe* and the cows are thin.
Yes, they are tired
So at this place the water looks good—*mhe*—and the fodder looks good too." He said: Set up the tents on the outskirts of Dhār—*mhe*—
Leave the cows to graze in the grass—*vāh vāh*—Dev Mahārāj's tent has been set up—*vāh vāh*—
The cowherd has begun grazing the cows
Now the Pūvār king of Ujjini Dhār had a daughter—*mhe*—who was lame in her feet and blind in her eyes. Her body was diseased with leprosy. On her head there were horns—*vāh vāh*—
There was a temple to the goddess on the outskirts of the village—*mhe*—
Four men would lift up the palanquin—*vāh vāh*—
High and circumambulate the temple.
Yes, they'd circumambulate it and take her back
The door to that temple was directly in front of Dev Mahārāj
Dev's tent and the door to the goddess's temple faced each other—*vāh vāh*—
On that day Queen Pīpalde's palanquin came by—*mhe*—Dev Mahārāj awoke
Bhagavān, the lord of the three worlds, cast a look of mercy—*mhe*—
Queen Pīpalde's body became golden—*vāh vāh*—
And the horns and protrusions disappeared and her body became golden—*vāh vāh*—and she began seeing with her eyes, and Dev Mahārāj gave her feet.
Yes, she began walking with her feet
So he healed Queen Pīpalde's body—*mhe*—gave her eyes—*vāh vāh*—and, by God's grace, he healed her life. Victory to Śrī Devnārāyaṇ Bhagavān, *victory*!

By God's grace, when Bhagavān gave the queen feet to walk—*mhe*—trumpets and drums were played. There was pomp and fanfare

They said: "Pīpalde's palanquin has being going there for so many days—*mhe*—After so many days the goddess is pleased today."

Today the goddess is pleased

So now Queen Pīpalde's body turned into gold—*vāh vāh*—

Pīpalde went to her father and said: "Śrī Mahārāj, Father, my body wasn't healed by the goddess.

Yes, the goddess didn't heal it

The man with the tent who's come—*mhe*—that man has given me the gift of life. So what I say is cut green bamboo[48] and tie me to the border of his costume, marry me, marry me." *Get me married to him!*

The king said: "Look, Pīpalde, that's the road to Malwa—*vāh vāh*—So the people of Marwar—*mhe*—they travel along this road every day.

Yes, they travel daily along this road

Lots of cowherds travel along here—*vāh vāh*—So I'll hardly get my daughter married to a cowherd."

Yes, never will she be married

She said: "Father, he's not a cowherd!

Yes, he's Bhagavān,

He's considered to be a divine person."—*mhe*—

The king said: "If he's considered to be a divine person—then once upon a time there used to be a doorway in Dhār made of all the metals—*mhe*—

The demons of Fort Gājanā in Dā̃tā̃, they came and carried away the door.

Yes, they took it away

If my door is put back here, then I'll certainly believe he is an avatār." The king of Dhār wrote a letter—*mhe*—and sent it to Dev's tent.

Yes, here you are

Dev Mahārāj read the letter and said to the Bhāṭ:

"Hey, Bābā Bhāṭ, I've got a job to finish, brother!"

Yes, I've got work

The Bhāṭ asked: "O Śrī Mahārāj, what kind of work have you got?"

Dev Mahārāj said: "Listen Bhāṭ, we've lived in his country—*mhe*—and were content.—*vāh vāh*—

So we too can do the little that he's requested, brother."

Yes, we'll pull down the door!

So now who participated in the assault on the demons' Fort Gājanā in Dā̃tā̃?

Only the two of them, Bhairū̃nāth and Dev Mahārāj went there.—*vāh vāh*—They arrived at the demon's Fort Gājanā. All the demons came and fell at Bhagavān's feet. *Said sir.*

Devnārāyaṇ's Marriage to Cā̃vṭī

Dev Mahārāj said: "Hey, brother, now you've come to me, but listen first to the reason for which I've come to you!"

The demons said: "What's the reason?"
Yes, tell us why you've come, Mahārāj
Devnārāyaṇ said: "There's used to be a door in Ujjini Dhār made of many metals—give that back!"
Yes, return it
The demon said: "Śrī Mahārāj, I won't return even a tiny bit of something I've taken today. I'll never give it back!—*vāh vāh*—
I fell at your feet because my daughter Cā̃vṭī—a girl of thirteen—is unmarried—*mhe*—I don't encounter any living persons—
Yes and if I do encounter someone—*mhe*—I finish him off right away.—*mhe*—Because you've come her unmarried state can be resolved.
Yes, I have to do away with my daughter's unmarried state
I'll gift you the door in marriage
I'll offer it to you.—*vāh vāh*—There's no other way I'll give you the door."
Yes, I won't give it away just like that
Dev Mahārāj said: "Bhairū̃nāth, what do you say, brother, what should we do?"
Yes, what shall we do?
Bhairū̃nāth said: "Who wants to fight with these demons!"
Yes, who wants to fight—I prefer marriage
Let's get our work done with humor." *Why not get married?*
The day he went to the demons' Fort Gājanā, Dev Mahārāj had his second marriage with Cā̃vṭī. *Said sir.*

Now by God's grace, when he got married to Queen Cā̃vṭī—*mhe*—when the marriage took place—the demon offered the door made of many metals to Dev Mahārāj
The demon said: "Here you are, Śrī Mahārāj." *Here take the door*
Dev Mahārāj said: "Go and return it, brother!" *Go and bring it back!* The demons placed it on their heads—*mhe*—and delivered it to the outskirts of Dhār town
Then Dev Mahārāj came back and went to sleep
Day arrived. People saw the door and ran off.—*mhe*—"Śrī Mahārāj, that door of yours is back." *Your door is back*
The king of Dhār saw the door and—*mhe*—
Said: "Brother, I made a mistake in formulating the matter."
Yes, I've made a mistake
If I had said that the door should be put back onto the doorway, then it would have been fixed on.
Yes, it would have been fixed on
But now I'll have to marry my daughter." *The door won't be fixed onto the doorway and it's become necessary to marry my daughter to him.*

He went to the Bhāṭ—*vāh vāh*—
And said: "Bhāṭ, I want to arrange your master's marriage!"—*mhe*—
The Bhāṭ said: "My master's already been married twice!"
Yes, now why should he get married—he's already married twice! The king said: "My daughter's being stubborn, brother!"—*mhe*—
The Bhāṭ said: "Well if she's decided then—Dev Mahārāj is lying down now—get him married while he's sleeping
There's no other way my master will get married.
Yes, he won't get married any more
Bring whatever materials are necessary for the marriage over here."—*vāh vāh*—
So all the people from the village collected together.—*mhe*—The king of Ujjini Dhār brought his daughter along. The materials for the marriage were taken along
The Bhāṭ said: "See, brother, listen—*mhe*—
The moment Bhagavān begins to wake up—*vāh vāh*—I'll make a sign. *Each and everyone should run away.* He told Queen Pīpalde: "Look, you hide beneath the litter."
Yes, hide underneath the litter
Take this jug of water—*mhe*—When he awakes put it front of Bhagavān. Bhagavān's gaze will fall on the jug, and will get cooled."—*vāh vāh*—
The Paṇḍits made the fire-pit and prepared the materials—*vāh vāh*—and the marriage ceremony began.—*mhe*—The Bhāṭ took out lots of gold coins in Dev's name from his pockets—*vāh vāh*—and filled up the pits completely with coins. After saying three marriage mantras Pīpalde's circumambulation ceremony took place—*vāh vāh*—
During the third round Bhagavān twisted his body
Yes, he changed his side
The Bhāṭ made a sign, and said: "Hey, brother, he's going to wake up—run."
Yes, everybody run
The people of the village ran away immediately
The Brahmans reflected in their minds—*mhe*—: "Hey, brother, pick up this and take that."
Yes, the coins will be left behind here!
As soon as the lord of the three worlds, Dev Mahārāj, awoke, he cast a gaze of poison, and the four Brahmans were turned to stone on the spot
Queen Pīpalde hid under the litter
As Dev Mahārāj sat up and looked about, Pīpaljī quickly stood in front of him
Yes, she stood there with the jug of water
Devnārāyaṇ said: "Hey, Bhāṭ—*mhe*—! Who's responsible for this now?"
Yes, I've done two, who's done the third?
The Bhāṭ said: "Śrī Mahārāj, you've done two, and I've got one done!"
Yes, I got one marriage done.

—*gāv*—

"O Queen, my hut is in the heavens—*mhe*—In my clan I am the one who is completely poor. Hey, queen, you'll regret very much being at my home. O Queen, you'll suffer a great deal." Pīpalde said: "Śrī Mahārāj!—*mhe*—

I want to stay at your feet—*vāh vāh*—

I don't need a home

Yes, that's all I want

I've found refuge with you—*mhe*—

That's all I desire

Yes, I desire nothing else

There's nothing else I want." By God's grace, they say, whether true or false, that the four poles that were driven in—*mhe*—

Bhagavān turned those four into trees, brother—*vāh vāh*—

And the Brahmans are still present as stones.

Yes, all four are still there as they were

Today in front of the fire-pits over there, they say. Dev Mahārāj spoke: "Hey, Bhāṭ—*mhe*—I've married in this country—*vāh vāh*—

It's not correct for me to drink water here

Yes, I won't drink water here

By God's grace, tell the cows, tell the cowherds, that I'm departing, brother."—*vāh vāh*—Sāḍū Mātā's bullocks that she had brought from her brothers were also there

The maidservant, Padmāvatī, was with Sāḍū Mātā—*mhe*—

Devnārāyaṇ at Lake Māṇḍal

One maidservant was given to Queen Pīpalde by her father—*vāh vāh*—

So Queen Pīpalde's and Sāḍū Mātā's carriages were aligned together

The cows and cowherds and Dev Mahārāj reached the lake of King Māṇḍal—*vāh vāh*—

Dev Mahārāj said: "Hey, brother, tell me which country does this lake belong to?"

Yes, which country is it in?

They said: "This lake belongs to your ancestors—*vāh vāh*—

Once upon a time there was King Māṇḍal—*mhe*—

The lake has been dug by him." Devnārāyaṇ said: "The lake is very nice."—*vāh vāh*—

The Bhāṭ said: "O giver of nourishment, Śrī Mahārāj, the lake is very nice—*mhe*—but there is a small blemish to it."

Something is wrong

Devnārāyaṇ said: "What's wrong?" *What Bābā Bhāṭ?*

The Bhāṭ said: "King Māṇḍal spent a lot of money on making it—*mhe*—

He had it dug well—*vāh vāh*—And he looked after it well

But there came such a time—*mhe*—when King Māṇḍal abandoned his life and drowned with his horse in this lake."

The Bhāṭ continued: "The lake's become impure."
Yes, it's not pure
"I won't go any further without making it pure."—*mhe*—
The lord of the three worlds began performing ceremonies—he summoned Paṇḍits and Brahmans—*vāh vāh*—
And the ceremonies were begun—*vāh vāh*—
"Only if that lake is purified, will we move ahead, brother!" The cows and cowherds went ahead
The pass of Pichor was reached—*mhe*—
Śaṅkar Mahārāj had stationed his disciples at that place—*vāh vāh*—
Śaṅkar told them: "Tax whoever comes and goes, brother!"
Yes, demand tax, drink bhāṅg, and enjoy yourselves! By God's grace, the Jogīs spoke—*vāh vāh*—
What conversation takes place between the Jogīs and carriage drivers, let's see!

—*gāv*—

The Cowherds and Jogīs Clash

Dev's carriages reached the pass of Pichor, brother—*mhe*—
A tension arose on the carriages
"Hey, the driver has arrived without paying tax
Park the carriage according to Śaṅkarnāth's demands.
It's Śaṅkar's vow, if you move the carriage any further—*vāh vāh*—
Because, brother, I have Bābājī's command.
Yes, it's a command!
I take tax from those who come and go, brother—*vāh vāh*—
Pay the tax, and then continue ahead."
Dev's driver speaks now—*mhe*—
What does he tell the Jogīs, let's see!
Know it by saying it, let's see, know it by saying it
I'll just say it, lets see, by God's grace, here you are—*vāh vāh*—*jī*—*vāh vāh*—

—*gāv*—

"Your matted hair is brown—*vāh vāh*—
By God's grace, I respect the saffron-colored robe
I'll knock off your earrings with a stick—*mhe*—
Your ears will appear bad without earrings
O wise one, you'll look bad. *It'll seem bad*
What tax are you levying now?"—*vāh vāh*—

—*gāv*—

"Your matted hair is brown—*mhe*—
Raw cotton clothes to wear

Let go of the carriage's harness and move over to one side—*mhe*—
Or you'll be killed, Jogeśar Avadhūt
You'll be killed straight away." *You'll get killed*

—*gāv*—

There is brown matted hair on your head—*vāh vāh*—
By God's grace, you've smeared ash on your body
Let go of the carriage's harness, and move over to one side—*mhe*—
O Nāth, I'll hit you with a stick and have your siddhis go flying off!
These powers of yours
Yes, I'll have them fly off
Move over to one side!"—*vāh vāh*—
The Jogī said: "You can leave after paying tax."
"O Jogī, there is brown matted hair on your head—*vāh vāh*—
I see raw cotton clothes that you wear
Let go of the carriage's harness, and move over to one side—*mhe*—
You'll be killed, O Jogeśar Avadhūt!
Hey, you'll be killed straight away."—*vāh vāh*—
Now what does the Jogī say—*mhe*—
This is a tale about Babajı's story—*vah vah*—
Let's see what he tells the cowherd, let's see
Know it by saying it, know it by saying it, know it by saying it
I'll just say it, by Lord Dev's grace!

—*gāv*—

Who said this news?—the Jogī said it *The Jogī said it*
He said: "Pay up the carriage driver's tax—*mhe*—
Now doom and destruction comes upon your carriage
Hey, I'll fling a tong full of ash onto your carriage—*mhe*—
Hey, I'll turn both your cart and oxen into stone!
I'm a disciple of Śaṅkar
Yes, I'll turn them into stone!
Look, I have that much power—*vāh vāh*—
You'll become stone."—*vāh vāh*—
By God's grace, in the meantime Māt Khaṭāṇī's carriage drew by
She enquired: "Hey, brother, why have you stopped the carriage?
Yes, why have you halted the carriages
The cowherd said: "Mother, look at the naked ascetic,[49] look at the Jogī standing in the way
Yes, he demands tax
Sāḍū Mātā speaks—*mhe*—
What does she say to the Jogīs, let's see
Know it by saying it, let's see by saying it
I'll just say it by Lord Dev's grace, let's see—*vāh vāh—jī—vāh vāh*—

—gāv—

"I've journeyed across the entire earth—*mhe*—
Where King Kācchap's orb rises[50]
Hey, I've come from my maternal home and am on way to my father-in-law's place, O Bholānāth!—*mhe*—
So far I haven't heard of a tax
O Nāthjī—*mhe*—
Tell me where did you get this new tax from?"
Yes, where did you create that tax from!
The Jogī said: "Listen, O Mother—*mhe*—
I have Śaṅkar's command—*vāh vāh*—
I'll demand tax from those who come and go
And then drink bhāṅg
It's Bhagavān's order!"—*mhe*—
By God's grace, Māt Khaṭāṇī said: "Hey, brother—*vāh vāh*—
A morsel[51] given by the Nāths has got stuck inside our vital organs."
Yes, it's got stuck inside
By God's grace, the lord of the three worlds has stayed back at King Māṇḍal's lake—*mhe*—
He'll come and pay the tax
So let's move ahead!"

Bhāṅgījī amongst the Jogīs

She said: "Release the carriages, brother."—*vāh vāh*—
The lord of three worlds' carriages were released on the other side of the pass of Pichor—*vāh vāh*—
The maidservants were given the order
Queen Pīpalde's carriage was released—*mhe*—
Sāḍū Māta's carriage was also released
Sāḍū Mātā says: "Maidservant Padmāvatī!—*mhe*—
There's a well here, fetch water from it
Yes, fill up the water jug, and bring it
So I can have a bath and perform worship."
One maidservant of Queen Pīpalde's went to fetch water
And one of Sāḍū Mātā's went
Yes, Maidservant Padmāvatī went to fetch water
There was a banyan tree above the well—*mhe*—
Half of the Jogīs were sitting beneath the banyan tree playing caupaḍ—*vāh vāh*—
The other half of the Jogīs were sitting on the well's steps
Yes, they were on the steps
Nevājī's son Bhāṅgījī was sitting in the midst of those Jogīs like a lord
Yes, he was sitting in their midst like a master

Upon seeing the Jogī's face—*mhe*—the maidservant swooned on that spot—*vāh vāh*—
Not even did she fill up the jug
What happens when the maidservant returns?—*mhe*—
What does Padmāvatī tell Sāḍū Mātā now?
Yes, what does she say upon her return, let's see, know it by saying it, Bhopājī
I'll just say it, by Dev's grace, I'll say it—*vāh vāh*—

—*gāv*—

"In the middle of the well there's a twisted banyan tree—*mhe*—
O Mother, as I went down there, I saw a group of Jogīs
I saw one Jogī—*vāh vāh*—
With the face of our brother-in-law, Nevā
Nevājī features—*mhe*—
And the Jogīs features were identical, O Mother!"
Yes, they are exactly the same
The maidservant told this to Sāḍū
Dev Mahārāj's carriages arrived at the pass of Pichor
Speak: Victory, brother, to Śrī Devnārāyaṇ!

—*gāv*—

"I'll cut your tongue out—*mhe*—
I'll smear your tongue with black salt
Can the Bagaṛavāts who died of the sword on the Khārī river leave behind such a sign?—*vāh vāh*—
Padmāvatī, who became a Jogī from amongst them?
The Bagaṛāvats were hardly such a feeble family that one of them would join the Jogīs."
Yes, go and mix with the Jogīs
Maidservant Padmāvatī speaks—*mhe*—
Māt Khaṭāṇī stands listening.
Know it by saying it, let's see by saying it
I'll just say it, by Lord Dev's grace, let's see—*vāh vāh sā*—

—*gāv*—

"Why do you cut my tongue out?—*mhe*—
O Mother, why do you apply black salt on my tongue?
Neither has Tejā Rāvat's Madan Siṅg joined the Jogīs—*mhe*—
Nor has Bāravat's Bhūṇ become a Jogī
I didn't spot those two at all."
Yes, I didn't see them at all
Sāḍū Mātā said: "Padmāvatī—*mhe*—
Which place, come on and show me."
Yes, come and show me!
So Sāḍū Mātā and Maidservant Padmāvatī—*mhe*—

Went back to that well
Yes, they returned
By God's grace, Nevājī's son and prince, was sitting in the midst like a lord
When Sāḍū Mātā saw the Jogī's face—*mhe*—
Even Sāḍū Mātā fell unconscious
"O Maidservant, that face belongs to this family!"
Yes, it belongs to this family
Māt Khaṭāṇī speaks—*vāh vāh*—
What does she say, let's see! *Know it by saying it, let's see.*

—*gāv*—

"The Jogī's feet are like lotuses—*vāh vāh*—
Diamonds shine on his forehead
I'm false and you're true, O Maidservant—*mhe*—
you've brought my sweet ones'[52] fire back, Padmāvatī—*mhe*—
That face belongs to this family,
Yes, it does belong to this family
But brothers, who knows of which king
Yes, this is not known
Let's ask the Jogī
Yes, if we ask him then we'll know
We'll know the matter right away."—*vāh vāh*—
Māt Khaṭāṇī speaks. What does she say to Prince Bhāṅgījī, let's see!
Know it by saying, let's see by saying it
I'll just say it, by Lord Dev's command, here you are *vāh vāh*—

—*gāv*—

Brown matted hair upon your head—*mhe*—
Brown is your hair
Mother Gūjrī asks: "Nāthjī which country may you belong to?
Which country are you a Jogī from, brother?"
Yes, where did you come from and become Bābājī's disciple?
By God's grace, Bhāṅgījī speaks—*mhe*—
Let's see what he says to Māt Khaṭāṇī. *Know it by saying it, let's see Bhopājī Mahārāj, by saying it*
I'll say it now, by God's grace, here you are—*vāh vāh—jī—vāh vāh*—

—*gāv*—

"Brown matted hair upon my head—*mhe*—
brown is my hair
Mother Gūjrī, I've seen no country—*mhe*—
What country shall I tell you of now
I don't know what country means."
Yes, I don't know what a country is
Sāḍū Mātā reflected to herself: "He doesn't know about his country—*mhe*—
He'll certainly know about his parents."[53]

Yes, he'll know about that
Māt Khaṭāṇi speaks. What else does she say to Bhāṅgījī
Yes, let's see what she asks about his family

—gāv—

"The matted hair is brown—*mhe*—
Raw cotton clothes to wear
This Gūjrī Mother asks you now—*mhe*—
O Nāth, which family might you belong to?
Which family are you a Jogī of—tell me this."
Yes, tell me which is your family
Bhāṅgījī speaks. What does he tell Mother, let's see!
Know it by saying, let's see by saying it
I'll just say it, by Lord Dev's grace, here you are—*vāh vāh—jī vāh vāh*—

—gāv—

"Brown matted hair on my head—*mhe*—
raw cotton clothes for me to wear
O Mother Gūjrī, brother, I haven't tasted milk—*vāh vāh*—
What family shall I tell you about now
What should I tell you?"
Yes, which family am I related too?
By God's grace, Māt Khaṭāṇī spoke to the maidservant: "Maidservant—*mhe*—
he's doesn't know about his country nor does he know about his family—
O Nāth, do you perhaps know the names of your mother and father?"
Yes, do you know the names of your mother and father
The Jogī said: "Yes, certainly I know."
Sāḍū Mātā said: "Tell me then!"—*vāh vāh*—

—gāv—

"See, bhāṅg is my mother—*mhe*—
And austerity my father
Yes, austerity is my father
And our measure of our enjoyment is bhāṅg—*mhe*—
O Mother Gūjrī, I have no knowledge about my mother and father—*vāh vāh*—
You see the Jogī Rūpnāth on that hill performing austerities,
He's my mother *and he's my father as well.*
There you are, brother."
Māt Khaṭāṇī said: "Padmāvatī, brother, we haven't found out
Yes, we haven't found out again
The face belongs to this house."—*mhe*—
She said: "O Nāth, you were not born of Jogīs."
Yes, you weren't born of Jogīs
The Jogī said: "Mother—*mhe*—I was born of Bābājī, brother!
Yes, I'm born of Jogīs
I don't know of anyone else." *I don't know*

Sāḍū Mātā said: "O Nāth, it's been so long that you've been working for Bābājī—*mhe*—
Some days work turns out well *and some days work gets delayed*
If work gets delayed, then one is sure to remember bygone things
And if work is done well *then also one is certain to remember things of the past*
If there's something you recall, tell me about that."
Yes, something that Bābājī when you were with him, told you about
The Jogī said: "Here, brother, Mother, a conversation that took place one day has come to my mind
Yes, it's come in my recollection
I'll tell you about that."
Yes, I know about that, I'll tell you
Sāḍū Mātā said: "In that case, relate it to me."—*vāh vāh—let's see how it is told*
I'll just say it, by God's—Dev's grace, let's see, here you are—*vāh vāh sā—*

—*gāv*—

"Disciples upon disciples, brother, O Mother, laid the garden—*mhe*—
I planted the saplings of bhāṅg well
Once pleased and satisfied, Bholānāthjī said—*vāh vāh*—:
'Well done, my son[54] of Nevā'
Who knows who Nevājī is, O Mother, brother *I don't know about this matter* Bābājī only took this name."
Yes, that's all he spoke of and related
Sāḍū Mātā said: "Maidservant Padmāvatī we've found him
Yes, now we've got him
On the day brother-in-law Nevājī died on the heroes' field[55]—*mhe*—
on that day Netūjī[56] had a six-month-old fetus in her womb
Yes, she had this six-month-old fetus in her womb
After tearing open her womb—*mhe*—
She went and threw the fetus down at Śaṅkar's seat[57]
This is that fetus
Yes, it's the six-month-old fetus, he doesn't know about his family
He's truthful *What does he know about country*
Neither has he seen country—*mhe*—
Nor has he tasted milk."—*vāh vāh*—
Māt Khaṭāṇī speaks—*mhe*—
What does she tell Bhāṅgījī?
Yes, let's see what she says; know it by saying it Bhopājī Mahārāj
I'll just say it, by God's grace—*vāh vāh—jī.*

—*gāv*—

"Son, your maternal grandfather's home is in Nāgar—*mhe*—
You are Nekaḍīyā's son and your home is in Daṛāvat City
Give back the saffron robes to the Nāths—*mhe*—
And you too take up the sweet ones' revenge."
Who said that? *Sāḍū Mātā said it*

Bhāṅgījī said: "Mājī Sāī—*mhe*—I've been a Jogī since birth—*vāh vāh*—
I even put ash on my buttocks
What enemies do I have?"
Yes, what enmity do I have?
Sāḍū Mātā said: "Son, a bygone one—not even one of the other Jogīs have it.
Yes, not even one has an enmity But you certainly do have one."

—*gāv*—

"Neither Nāgar nor my maternal grandfather's place have I seen—*mhe*—
I haven't seen your capital of Daṛāvat city
Brother, I've become a Jogī from birth, O Mother Gūjrī—*mhe*—
What enmity is there for us Jogīs?
I put ash on my buttocks
I'm a Jogī since birth, I hardly have an enmity!"
Yes, what enmity do I have?
Sāḍū Mātā said: "Listen son—*mhe*—not one of the other Jogīs have an enmity, but you certainly have one.
Yes, you certainly have one!
Where's your Bābājī?" *Tell me*
Bhāṅgījī said: "He's performing austerities on the hill in front."
Sāḍū Mātā said: "Come, lets go over to Bābājī."
Yes, come on!
Bhāṅgījī said: "You have the need—you go! *I'm not going anywhere!* I have Bābājī's command to take in one and a quarter maṇ of bhāṅg straight away—*vāh vāh*—
See, the effect is full; at the same time I demand tax, brothers
Yes, I take taxes
Bābājī makes thick bread in the kitchen
I get it right here, brother—*mhe*—
If you have the need, then you go over to Bābājī; I'm not going." *I'm not going.*

Sāḍū Mātā Talks to Rūpnāth

So, the lord of the three worlds, Bhagavān, was having rites performed at the lake of King Māṇḍal
And Māt Khaṭāṇī left for the mendicant's fire-place.
In the meantime the Jogī and carriage driver were left alone—
Many Jogīs were killed—*mhe*—
And many carriage drivers were killed over there
On the way Māt Khaṭāṇī saw them—*mhe*—
Bābājī saw her and thought: "Meṇāde Gūjrī has come—she's sure to bring on a complaint."
There was a cave nearby. He went right inside the cave and placed a boulder in front of the cave's opening.

Māt Khaṭāṇī went there, by God's grace, the fire-place was still alight—*mhe*—
Mātā says. Let's see what she says to Nāthjī, let's see!
Know it by saying it, let's see by saying it
I'll just say it, by lord Dev's grace, let's see—*vāh vāh sā*—*vāh vāh*—

—*gāv*—

"You ran inside a deep cave—*mhe*—
O innocent Nāth, and sat with your eyes closed
Hey, you made the Bagaṛāvats' offspring black—*mhe*—
O Nāth, hey, you smear ash on the entire world!
See, the Bagaṛāvats served the likes of you
Yes, in a true manner
But, no, you did the right thing to make their offspring into a Jogī." Bābājī reflected to himself: "Mājī can see well."
Yes, she sees where I am
By God's grace, Māt Khaṭāṇī speaks—*vāh vāh*—
What does she tell Bābājī, let's see!
Know it by saying it, now, let's see by saying it now.

—*gāv*—

Sāḍū Mātā said this
She said: "I put my foot on the first step, hey, Bholānāth—*vāh vāh*—
And I took the second step
Leave the cave and come out—*mhe*—
Otherwise I'll use the dagger lying at your fire-place and die
O Nāth, I'll scatter splashes of blood!" *vāh vāh*—
Bābājī reflected to himself: "Hey, this Meṇāde Gūjrī!—*mhe*—
What is she saying!"
Yes, what if, in distress, she really goes and does that?
So after knocking the boulder aside, Nāthjī came and stood on the outside
Māt Khaṭāṇī fell at his feet—*vāh vāh*—
Nāthjī said: "Welcome, Meṇāde, welcome." *Welcome*
Sāḍū Mātā said: "I've come Nāthjī, but you did a great thing—*mhe*—
Nobody does such a great thing!"—*vāh vāh*—

—*gāv*—

"By God's grace, the sons of Bāgh died valorously in wars—*mhe*—
They died valorously on the banks of the river Khārī
You didn't perform the rites of the twelve days[58]for Bhoj—*mhe*—
You preferred going to your maternal home
I know about what you say—*vāh vāh*—
You tell me I've run into a deep cave.
Yes ! But I know of your faithfulness!"
Yes, you didn't perform Bhoj's rites of the twelve days—you ran off before that!
Sāḍū Mātā said: "O Nāth, I didn't perform the rites."—*mhe*—
Bābājī speaks. What does he say to Sāḍū Mātā, to the Gūjrī—let's see!

Know it by saying it, let's see by saying it
I'll just say it, by Dev's grace, here you are—*vāh vāh sā*—

—*gāv*—

"You abandoned Causle Kheḍā to your left—*vāh vāh*—
And Rāṇ City to your right
Hey, you ran away to the country of Mālāgar *vāh vāh*—
Leaving Savāī Bhoj's pyre ablaze
Bhoj's pyre was still aglow *and you got up and ran away!*
You think I don't know!"
Yes, I know everything about you on that day!

—*gāv*—

"Don't you know you used to wear gold and silver—*mhe*—
Mājī you would suffer under the weight of pearls
One calamity came and fortune changed—*mhe*—
In the time of distress you ran fifty kos on foot
You left Causle Kheḍā at night."
Yes, not until fifty kos did your feet halt.
Sāḍū Mātā said: "Bhagavān incarnated himself with me."
Yes, that's why I left.
Bābājī said: "I agree with that—*vāh vāh*—
Your destiny must be great!
Yes, that Bhagavān came to take incarnation with you!
You've brought a boy from your natal home! From where? From Malwa!
Wherefore? Because of the throne!
Yes, to sit him on the throne!
Listen, I brought up Nevājī's son, Bhāṅgījī—*mhe*—
He was an unripe fetus of six months
Yes, I brought him up!
If you want to put him on the throne then take Bhāṅgījī with you
Yes, take him from here and leave!
Otherwise go back just like you came." *Get back!*
Sāḍū Mātā said: "Look, Nāthjī, he's not a boy of my brothers'
Yes, I haven't brought a boy belonging to my brothers, he is in fact Bhagavān."
Bābājī said: "Sāḍū, he's Bhagavān is he?"
"Yes, sir, he is"
"By God's grace, then show me some proof!"
Yes, then show me some proof of your Bhagavān!
Sāḍū Mātā said: "Nāthjī, what proof do you accept?"
Yes, what do you demand, Nāthjī?
Bābājī said: "The Nāths demand this kind of proof:—*mhe*—
See, this fire is ablaze
Yes, it's strongly and abundantly ablaze
There are logs of wood lying there dry at one end
Yes, dry at one end

They burn in front and are dry at the back—*vāh vāh*—
If on the dry parts fresh green leaves one and a half cubits long spring out, *if they grow green*
Then I'll believe in your "incarnation"
Otherwise, get back just the way you came."
Yes, go back to Malwa
So what proof does Māt Khaṭāṇī provide through Bhagavān, let's see!
Know it by saying it, let's see by saying it now Bhopājī Mahārāj
I'll say it just now, by lord Dev's grace, I'll say it—*vāh vāh sā*—

—*gāv*—

Devnārāyaṇ Provides Proof to Rūpnāth

"You alighted in a lotus blossom—*mhe*—
Even superior individuals have not understood your mystery
O chief of Goṭhā, provide testimony at the fire-place
Hey, pay heed to Mājī's cry, O imperceptible, faultless Ūd![59]
O formless Bhagavān—*mhe*—
If you respond to my prayer
Then I'll ask for Bhāṅgījī and bring him.
If not then, see, I'll burn in this fire." *I'll burn and die right here.*
Sāḍū Mātā stepped toward the fire
The lord of the three worlds, Bhagavān, was performing ceremonies—*mhe*—
He laughed radiantly, the phep-blossoms[60] went into bloom
Bhairūnāth, drinking bhāṅg, also enquired.
The Bhāṭ said: "Śrī Mahārāj, why, why are you laughing?" *What great thing has happened?*
Devnārāyaṇ said: "Bābā Bhāṭ—*mhe*—
Hey, look, Māt Khaṭāṇī's asking proof for Nāthjī"
Yes, she's asking for it at the fire-place
The Bhāṭ said: "Śrī Mahārāj, one should do what an old person says."
The lord of three worlds cast a look of mercy.

—*gāv*—

So over there the logs burn—*mhe*—
Bhagavān made one-and-a-half-cubit-long green leaves grow from the burning logs—*vāh vāh*—
This came to Bābājī's notice
Bābājī reflected in his mind: "Hey, there has certainly been an incarnation
Yes, it can hardly remain hidden from me
Why cause Meṇāde Gūjrī sorrow!"—*vāh vāh*—
He said: "O Mother, today I have accepted him"
Yes, I've accepted him
Bābājī speaks—*mhe*—

Let's see what he says to Māt Khaṭāṇī.
Know it by saying it, let's see by saying it

—*gāv*—

Bābājī wrote a letter and dispatched it. In it he wrote: "O son of those who hold the peacock-feathered rod, return the saffron robe to my Nāths—*mhe*—
And become, O son, Goṭhā's Rajpūt
Bhāṅgī, Goṭhā is yours
Yes, go there and
By God's grace, become the throne's lord—*vāh vāh*—
And this one who comes to you, accept her as your mother."—*mhe*—
"Here you are, Meṇāde Gūjrī—*mhe*—
Take this letter to my Bhaṅgījī and give it to him!
It'll take time to give it to him, but it won't take time for him to join you."
Yes, it won't take time
So Bāḷā Ṭhākar, the lord of the three worlds, gave testimony at the fire-place—*mhe*—
Bābājī gave Bhāṅgījī the command
Speak: Victory to Śrī Devnārāyaṇ, victory
Say it both great and small!

Devnārāyaṇ Revives the Jogīs

By God's grace, what happened? Māt Khaṭāṇī got up from the fire-place—*mhe*—
The lord of the three worlds who was at King Māṇḍal's lake
Yes, he stayed there and left
In the meantime the matter between the Jogīs and carriage drivers had gotten bad, hey—*vāh vāh*—
Mother and son both reached there at the same time
The King asked: "Mājī Sāī—*mhe*—why did you let this matter happen like this? *Why did you let it happen like this?*
We would have established Causlā Kheḍā eternally.—*mhe*—
But before that the ochre-robed ones were struck *and were killed*"
Sāḍū Mātā said: "Son, where was I here?" *I wasn't here*
Devnārāyaṇ said: "Where did you go to?" *Whom did you go to?*
Sāḍū Mātā said: "I went to your uncle's son, among the Jogīs, whose name is Bhāṅgī.
Yes, I went to Bābājī in order to get him
I went to ask for him—*mhe*—
Hey, in the meantime, son, the carriage drivers and Jogīs were all killed."
The lord of the three worlds cast a look of mercy
The carriage drivers sat up saying "Dev, Dev!" *All of them came back to life*
Sāḍū Mātā went and gave the letter to Bhāṅgījī
Bhāṅgījī said: "Mother—*mhe*—I accept,

Yes, I accept
You are my mother—*vāh vāh*—
Bābājī's written a letter."
Yes, you are my mother
Dev Mahārāj asked: "So now, O Elder Brother Bhāṅgījī, what will you ride on?"
Yes, take your transportation, and move on
Bhāṅgījī said: "O Incarnate One—*mhe*—you revived those of yours that died.
And the people who live with me,—*mhe*—
They're lying dead.
Yes, they're lying here dead
I'll perform their last rites, and follow afterward."
Yes, I'll come afterward
Devnārāyaṇ said: "O Elder Brother Bhāṅgījī"
Yes, what last rites will you perform?
Bhāṅgījī said: "I'll perform the last rites—*mhe*—I'll dig holes—*mhe*—
And gather them together
Yes, I'll give them all a samādhī"
Devnārāyaṇ said: "Then it'll take a lot of days
Yes, it'll take us many days
I don't recognize them—*mhe*—
You recognize your people—having lived together with them
You join them together!—*mhe*—
I'll revive them, brother."
Yes, I'll be able to revive them
Bhāṅgījī had at that time consumed a quarter and a half maṇ of intoxicants
He stuck somebody's arm on somebody else
And stuck somebody's head on somebody else
Somebody's foot he fastened on somebody else
He covered them all with blankets
Yes, put them all to sleep
He said: "Here, brother, Incarnate One, here you are.
Asleep they are ready, now revive them."
The lord of the three worlds cast a look of mercy
All the Jogīs woke up saying "Dev, Dev"
As soon as they awoke they began quarreling—*vāh vāh*—
They said: "Why is my arm stuck on you, brother?"
Yes, how come my arm is stuck on you?
They said: "Hey, why is my foot stuck on you?"
Yes, how come my foot is fastened on you?
Bhāṅgījī said: "O Incarnate One, you've done a great job.
Yes, you revived them all right
But you've created a quarrel."
Yes, you've caused a fight amongst them!
On the day Dev Mahārāj revived those Jogīs—*mhe*—
On that day he made the Sindhan Rajpūts out of the Jogīs—*vāh vāh*—

That's where Sindhans come from
Yes, so Prince Bhāṅgījī joined up—*mhe*—
Dev Mahārāj, the lord of the three worlds, gave testimony
Speak: Victory, brother, to Śrī Devnārāyaṇ Bhagavān, victory.

Sāḍū Mātā at Māṇḍal's Monument

What did Māt Khaṭāṇī do? She went and sat on top of Māṇḍaljī's monument
Yes, she climbed up the monument
Dev Mahārāj said: "Hey, brother, where's the old woman gone to?
Yes, where's Mājī Sāī gone off to?
I'm going to stake the territory of Causle."—*vāh vāh*—
Then the Sirdārs said: "Śrī Mahārāj, your mother can be seen sitting high up on that monument"
Yes, she's sitting high up there
The king went and asked:
"Hey, Mājī Sāī—*mhe*—
Climb down
Yes, we'll go and stake the territory of Causle"
Sāḍū Mātā said: "Son, don't get me down!"—*mhe*—
Sāḍū speaks. What does Bhagavān listen to, let's see *know it by saying it, let's see by saying it*
I'll just say it, by Dev's grace, here you are—*vāh vāh sā*—

—*gāv*—

"O son, I climbed up Māṇḍal's tall monument—*vāh vāh*—
Look, in front I saw the evil Khārī river's banks
Hey, a necklace of pearls did the Khārī swallow—*mhe*—
She swallowed up my sister-in-law's brave ones; O Bhagavān, my heart is full of sadness."
Yes, my heart can't take it anymore
Devnārāyaṇ said: "Don't reproach yourself—come down"—*vāh vāh*—
Sāḍū Mātā speaks. Let's see what she says
Know it by saying it, let's see by saying it

—*gāv*—

"Son, I climbed up Māṇḍal's monument—*vāh vāh*—
Look, I saw the Bagaṛāvats' cattle trough
Hey, I used to feed the cattle with arms full of fodder, O Son—*mhe*—
Hey, the cattle trough lies empty."
Dev Mahārāj said: "Mājī Sāī, what good is reproach?"
Yes, come down!
Māt Khaṭāṇī speaks. Lets see what she says! *Know it by saying it, let's see,*
Bhopājī Mahārāj now by saying it
I'll just say it, by God's grace—*vāh vāh*—*jī*.

—*gāv*—

"I climbed up high on Māṇḍal's monument—*vāh vāh*—
I saw the thorny ker bush
Son, the heaps of green fodder that never used to dwindle—*mhe*—
The Bagaṛāvats were finished, on every step I have a foe
O Son, an enmity has arisen for me in this country
Yes, I have great foes
So Son, Rāṇ City is near this place."—*mhe*—
Devnārāyaṇ said: "Mājī Sāī, climb down—*vāh vāh*—
We'll certainly establish the territory of Causle Kheḍā!"

—*gāv*—

"Sīvlī's stable-boy never alights—*mhe*—
Nor does Līlā's saddle come off
My heart's grief doesn't disappear—*mhe*—
Hey, the evil child-eating Rāṇ City resides nearby
O Son, Rāṇ City is very close by here."
Yes, it resides nearby
Sāḍū Mātā speaks—*mhe*—
Who said this?—Sāḍū Mātā said this *to Dev Mahārāj,—vāh vāh*—
Dev Mahārāj speaks—*vāh vāh*—
Let's see what he says to Gūjrī Mātā.
Know it by saying it, let's see now by saying it.

—*gāv*—

"Sīvlī's stable-boy never alights—*mhe*—
Nor does Līlā's saddle come off
My heart's grief won't go away—*mhe*—
Hey, the evil, child-eating Rāṇ City resides nearby
I'll have donkeys plough in child-eating Rāṇ."

—*gāv*—

By God's grace, Sāḍū Mātā said
She said: "O son, was it a nice thing that Yam's wretched one's cut down the Bagaṛāvats' youth?
I'll give you a reward with my own wealth, O brave one—*mhe*—
Bring the Bagaṛāvats back just one time into the world of mortals."
By God's grace, Sāḍū Mātā said this
Dev Mahārāj speaks—*mhe*—
What does he say *Let's see, know it by saying it, Bhopājī Mahārāj, now by saying it*
I'll just say it by Lord Dev's grace, let's see—*vāh vāh sā*—

—*gāv*—

"Was it a nice thing, mother, that Yam's wretched one's cut down the Bagaṛāvats' youth?

If rewards would be accepted, then not even one person would be able to die in the world of mortals!
The whole world would pay fare according to their power and ability!
If you start taking fare, then people won't die!"—*vāh vāh*—
The lord of the three worlds, Bhagavān speaks—*mhe*—
Let's see what he says to his mother.
Know it by saying it, let's see by saying it
I'll just say it, by God's grace, let's see—*vāh vāh sā*—

—*gāv*—

"Don't cry—*mhe*—
O Mother, crying causes harm
The Bagaṛāvats won't come back because of crying—*mhe*—
O Mother, you fill up rivers with your crying
Even if you start a river with your tears—*mhe*—there will be no coming back for the Bagaṛāvats
Mājī Sāī—*mhe*—crying now is only spoiling your eyes—*vāh vāh*—
Come down!—*mhe*—
We'll stake the territory of Causle."
Sāḍū speaks. What does she say to Dev, let's see *Know it by saying it, let's see by saying it*
I'll say it by God's grace—*vāh vāh sā*—

—*gāv*—

"Don't establish Causle—*mhe*—
Causle is said to be a kingdom of four villages
Hey, establish Tejā's Maṇḍārīyā Kheḍā—*vāh vāh*—
Get together the kingdom's five brothers
When the five brothers meet
Yes, establish the territory of Causle on that day
O Son, you are alone at the moment—*mhe*—
One person alone never has the authority."—*vāh vāh*—
Devnārāyaṇ said: "Mājī Sāī,—*mhe*—
Causle's territory will be established!"
Yes, Causle village will be established

—*gāv*—

"You know Causle Kheḍā—*mhe*—
Don't establish it.—*vāh vāh*—
Causle is said to have a border of four villages
Hey, establish Tejā's Maṇḍārīyā Kheḍā—*vāh vāh*—
O my Bhīm, elder brother of Arjan
O my Bhīmjī Mahārāj, avoid Causle."—*vāh vāh*—
Devnārāyaṇ said: "Listen, O Mother—*mhe*—
Bhoj's royal residence was first in Causle."
Yes, he established the territory of this place

Sāḍū Mātā said: "Hey, Son—*mhe*—
You know Causle Kheḍe is the root of strife
Yes, it's been the root of strife right from the beginning
It can't exist at all without strife.
So Son you're alone now—*mhe*—
On the day the five brothers meet, and the hand becomes strong—*vāh vāh*—
Then there's no problem."
Yes, if you establish the territory on that day, then there's no problem.
By God's grace, what prophecy does the lord of three worlds make—*mhe*—
What omens does he read while establishing the territory of Causle, let's see.
Know it by saying it, let's see by saying it
I'll just say it, by Dev Bhagavān's grace, let's see—*vāh vāh sā*—

—*gāv*—

❁ Devnārāyaṇ Establishes Causle Kheḍā ❁

"Look, Bhāṭ, the snake enters his hole backward—*vāh vāh*—
Backward does the cat climb up and sit on the Khejaṛā tree
Hey, according to the omens we will destroy the enemy Rāv—*mhe*—
We'll put the enemy's head into the ground and his feet above
Hey, Bābā Bhāṭ—*mhe*—
Look, what omen is it?"
Yes, what kind of augury is it, tell us
The Bhāṭ said: "O Śrī Mahārāj, a mortal would never have this kind of augury
You're an incarnate person, aren't you—*mhe*—
You've received this kind of omen."

—*gāv*—

"While Dev established Causle, deer sported with one another.
O Giver of Nourishment, on account of this omen, a thief won't be able to steal your cows—*vāh vāh*—
Hey, with this omen no one will be able to defeat you
Śrī Mahārāj—*mhe*—
The augury is such that whoever is defeated, you will defeat
There is no one who will defeat you
O King, the time is auspicious now.—*mhe*—
The time is right.—Establish the territory of Causle!"

—*gāv*—

The seventh day in the bright half of Māh—*mhe*—
The sixth of Bhādvā; Ākhā Tīj; on these kinds of auspicious dates

Feed Nārāyaṇ Dev in such a manner, O Khaṭāṇī—*mhe*—
Dev will put us across the ocean of life
By God's grace, the Bagaṛāvats' land lay desolate for seven years—*vāh vāh*—
On Ākhā Tīj day Bhagavān came and established the territory of Causle
Yes, he established the territory again
So, by God's grace, Bhagavān related three equal days of worship—*vāh vāh*—
Great are the seventh day in Māh—*vāh vāh*—
And the sixth of Bhādvā—*mhe*—
And Ākhā Tīj. There are three days of worship of Bhagavān the fruits of which are the same
Yes, the fruit of the three is equal
Some believe in burning incense on Ākhā Tīj, even then it has the same fruit; some worship Bhagavān by burning incense and meditation on the seventh of Māh, even then it has the same fruit; on the sixth of Bhādvā it's the same result. The seventh of Māh is the worship of the coming because at the time Bhagavān took incarnation it was the night of the sixth; on Saturday the sixth, at four in the morning Dev was born—*vāh vāh*—
Following that it was dawn of the seventh, that is why worship is done on the seventh only
Yes, it's done on the seventh—there's no question about doing it on the sixth
Yes!

—*gāv*—

Brother, Nārāyaṇ Devjī resided at Causle—*vāh vāh*—
He resided on the high place of the bearer of honor
Hey, on the throne of Maṇdvā Rāvat Bhoj—*vāh vāh*—
Bhagavān, even the sun bows in front of his emblem on the doorway

—*gāv*—

Nārāyaṇ Devjī resided at Causle—*vāh vāh*—
He resided on the bed with bells
In front Meghnāth plays a musical instrument
Chochū Bhāṭ, who came from far away, now gave him great praise

—*gāv*—

If you take Dev's name, then, brother, it's always a blessing
Then it was said: "Brother, Nārāyaṇ Devjī resided in Causle Kheḍā—*mhe*—
He resided there on his own
Nārāyaṇ Devjī heals the sores of lepers. O Lord, remove my past and future sins!
The lord of the three worlds began healing the sores of lepers—*mhe*—
He began giving sight to the blind
By God's grace, Rāvjī Sāī's Gā̃go Bhāṭ—*mhe*—
He heard, brother, that Bhagavān has appeared, who heals the sores of lepers—I'll also go to him."

Yes, my body too is diseased
Rāvjī's Gā̃go Bhāṭ, who had "snake" leprosy—*vāh vāh*—
Came to Dev's feet—*mhe*—
By God's grace, Bhagavān cast a look of mercy, and turned his body into gold
Now Gā̃go Bhāṭ speaks—*mhe*—
He said: "The Gaṅgā is here, and the Gomatī is here—*vāh vāh*—
Hey, eighty-six pilgrimages are at this place here" *Here!*
Rāv's Gā̃go Bhāṭ says: "I'll never leave Bhagavān's feet and go anywhere else
I'll stay here at Bhagavān's feet."
So the Bagaṛāvats' land had lain desolate for seven years—*mhe*—
Bhagavān established the territory of Causle Kheḍa, and healed the body of Gā̃go Bhāṭ.
Speak: Victory, brother, to Śrī Devnārāyaṇ Bhagavān. *Speak: Victory both great and small.*

Rāvjī, Dīyājī, and the King of Ajmer Demand a Tax

By God's grace, after he established the territory of Causle—*mhe*—
At all other places some people began to know a little about this—*vāh vāh*—
Because Devji's cows would go into the pasture lands and not return till they had eaten the fodder of fifteen or even twenty villages
Now what letter does the king of Ajmer send first—*mhe*—
And what, by God's grace, what do Rāvjī Sā and the king of Ajmer agree upon?—*vāh vāh*—
And what letter do they send to Bhagavān Dev, let's see
Know it by saying it, let's see by saying it

—*gāv*—

"Brother, you grazed the cattle at the Hill of Goram—*mhe*—
While coming and going they appear to leave their hoofprints on Rāvjī's lands
Hey, those hoofprints, by God's grace, caused Bābā Rāv pain—*mhe*—
I was pained by the sweet one Bhoj
Bhoj is such an enemy
Yes, that I didn't even think of him
By God's grace, not even our cows' marks are liked by the people."—*vāh vāh*—
In the meantime his letter of complaint
Yes, it arrived afterward
What happens when Bhagavān reads the letter?—*mhe*—
Let's see what he says. *Know it by saying it, now by saying it*

—*gāv*—

"The cows stood on the lands—*mhe*—
While coming and going they ate stacks of Dīyā's wheat and chickpeas
Dīyājī missed these stacks—*mhe*—

Hey, I missed Bhoj's clever and pure Bãvlī[61]
Dīyā has a treasure like Bãvlī
Yes, I didn't even think of that horse!
Hey, somebody scattered even our cow's fodder, but look Dīyā didn't like that."
Yes, he didn't like that and sent a letter of complaint
By God's grace, Rāvjī wrote a letter—*mhe*—
And sent it to Ajmer—*vāh vāh*—
He said: "The Bagaṛāvats used to always pay tax—*mhe*—
Dev Mahārāj has come from Malwa and established Goṭh Kheḍā. He didn't even think of you!
Yes, he didn't remember you
Either go and collect the tax—*mhe*—
Or Dev Mahārāj's horse that he rides, Līlāgar
Yes, go and demand it in lieu of tax
And if he doesn't give it—*mhe*—
There's the cow Suremātā gifted by Śaṅkar *Go and collect it*
And if he doesn't even give it—*mhe*—
Bhagavān has a bath with a stone pot—you go and collect that
Yes, there's a stone water vessel, go and collect that
Devjī's in possession of only these three marvelous things."
Yes, there's no fourth marvel
The king of Ajmer wrote a letter—*mhe*—
He sent it to Dev—*vāh vāh*—
Dev speaks—*vāh vāh*—
What does he say, let's see
Know it by saying it, let's see by saying it

—*gāv*—

"The cows went onto the pasture lands—*vāh vāh*—
Hey, while coming and going it appears they ate some saplings of wheat and chickpeas
Grandfather took a liking to the saplings—*mhe*—
I took a liking to camels packed with gold coins
It's written here in these papers, brother—*mhe*—that when the Bagaṛāvats' Mahābhārat began—*vāh vāh*—
It is said, that at that time seventy camels filled with gold coins were brought by Uncle Nevājī to the court of Ajmer
Yes, he brought them there
But I didn't think about them till now
Yes, I didn't even think about that many gold coins
So why did Grandfather take an interest in taxes so soon?"—*vāh vāh*—
Right after that, another letter demanding tax arrived—*vāh vāh*—
It said: "Either deliver the tax quickly—*mhe*—
Otherwise, brother, go back the way you came

Yes, get back to your place, back to the country of Mālāgar
Hey, you went and became king without informing us or asking for permission."—*vāh vāh*—
The lord of three worlds, Bhagavān, speaks—*mhe*—
What does he say to the Bhāṭ, let's see—*mhe*—
Know it by saying it, by saying it
I'll just say it, by Bhagavān Dev's grace, I'll say it—*vāh vāh sā*—

—*gāv*—

"Hey, Bhāṭ, I read the letter written by Grandfather's hand—*vāh vāh*—
Now in my mind there arose pain
Grandfather is interested in tax, O lineage's Bhāṭ, what hunger does Grandfather still have?
Is he hungry because he doesn't have my tax?"
Yes, he can't be feeling like that
The Bhāṭ said: "Śrī Mahārāj, don't take it badly—*mhe*—
The Bagaṛāvats used to pay tax."
Yes, it's been taken right from the beginning
Devnārāyaṇ said: "Bābā Bhāṭ, then we'll also have to pay the tax!"
Yes, Śrī Mahārāj!
"They take one and a half measurements, O Mahārāj."—*vāh vāh*—
Devnārāyaṇ said: "So Bhāṭ, the village has hardly been put up, and the oppression has already begun!—*vāh vāh*—
We won't be able to live here
Yes, settling here will be hard
Why?—because Dīyā's letter has arrived, here Rāvjī's letter has arrived, there the king of Ajmer's letter *has arrived*
Bābā Bhāṭ then let's go to deliver the tax first."
Yes, we'll do that work first
The Bhāṭ said: "Yes, Śrī Mahārāj, let's go and deliver it."—*vāh vāh*—
What command does the lord of the three worlds give to Pālāsāṇī?—*mhe*—
How does he saddle the horse Līlāgar?—*vāh vāh*—
How does the assault of the tax take place? *Know it by saying, let's see now Bhopājī Mahārāj, by saying it*
I'll just say it, by God's grace, let's see—*vāh vāh sā*—

—*gāv*—

"O Bhairavnāth!
Yes, where did the battles take place
My "begging" bowl[62] is full
Yes, it won't fill
Why not? You know which place it is the battle of? *Dev Mahārāj is going to Ajmer to pay tax*
The lord of the three worlds saddled the horse Līlā—*vāh vāh*—
And put his feet into the stirrups.

The Incident with the Buffaloes

Three tiles from the ramparts of Tārā Gaḍ broke off by themselves and fell down
The king of Ajmer asked:
"Hey Sirdārs—*mhe*—how come these stones have broken off by themselves, brother?"
Yes, there's no wind or storm, nor are there any drops of rain
The Sirdārs said: "Śrī Mahārāj, what do we know? *We don't know about this matter*
Call the Paṇḍits."
Yes, ask them
The Paṇḍits were summoned and asked: "Hey, brother, Brahmans—*mhe*—how come these stones broke off on their own?"
Yes, look in the almanac and tell me—they looked in the almanac
The Paṇḍits said: "Śrī Mahārāj, yesterday you sent a letter, didn't you—*mhe*—
About the tax—*vāh vāh*—
That lord is about to leave his home *to pay the tax—he's put his feet in the stirrups.*"
The king said: "O Brahmans—*mhe*—
If the stones break off when he puts his feet in the stirrups—*vāh vāh*—
Then when he comes here *what will happen?*"
The Brahmans said: "Everything will be destroyed, brother"—*vāh vāh*—
That's the way things are going to be
The king said: "In that case I don't want the tax!"
Yes, make a plan for me with which he will return
Make one Brahmans!—*mhe*—
That individual is not to enter our village."
Yes, think of such a plan
The Brahmans said: "Śrī Mahārāj, it's Bhagavān's battle—*mhe*—
Now, he won't return in a hurry
Yes, Bhagavān's come to pay tax, how can he return?
But there's one thing, Śrī Mahārāj—*mhe*—
Send for black buffaloes—*vāh vāh*—
Smear their bodies with vermilion and oil
Now, let them loose on the road at the outskirts of Goṭhā
Yes, let them loose in front of Goṭhā
He's a divine person—if he sees it's a bad omen *then he'll return*
Otherwise, he won't go back at all." *vāh vāh*—

So much was said—*mhe*—
Black buffaloes were sent for—*vāh vāh*—
They were smeared with vermilion and oil and let loose on the outskirts of Goṭhā
Yes, they were let loose in front of Goṭhā

Bhagavān noticed them coming
He asked the Bhāṭ: "Bābā Bhāṭ—*mhe*—These animals ahead, brother."
Yes, what are these black animals, hey, brother
The Bhāṭ said: "Śrī Mahārāj, after the Bagaṛāvats died, I've no longer any eyesight
Yes, he said, I can see only faintly
Tell me all the details." *Then I'll tell you what animal it is*
Bhagavān said: "O Bhāṭ of the Lineage, it appears to me to be a black animal—*mhe*—
Smeared with vermilion and oil, brother." *They were thoroughly smeared*
The Bhāṭ said: "Hey, Śrī Mahārāj, Pāliyo's and my doom has come
Yes, it's death all right
No harm will come to you
Yes, you're a divine person, nothing of yours will be spoiled
You wanted to destroy the Bagaṛāvats' ancestral record, *that's why you took me along.*"
Bhagavān said: "Hey, Bhāṭ, what's happened?"
Yes, what happened? What's the matter
The Bhāṭ said: "Śrī Mahārāj, it's a bad omen"
Yes, it's a bad sign
Bhagavān said: "So now *what should we do?"*
The Bhāṭ said: "What shall we do, brother, Mahārāj, do whatever you think is right!"
Yes, you know what's best in this matter
"Turn back, Śrī Mahārāj!"—*vāh vāh*—
The lord of the three worlds, Bhagavān, speaks—*mhe*—
Let's see what he says to the Bhāṭ.
Know it by saying it, let's see, by saying it
I'll tell it now, by Dev's grace, let's see—*vāh vāh sā*

—*gāv*—

"Hey, Bhāṭ, only if the turban eats the head—*vāh vāh*—
And the cow eats the lion
If Dvārkā is built in place of Mathurā *vāh vāh*—
Shall my cavalcade turn back
You know that don't you
Yes, only if that much work is done will my cavalcade return
Returning their fame will increase—*mhe*—
Their fame is already great enough."—*vāh vāh*—
The Bhāṭ said: "By God's grace, Śrī Mahārāj, then I won't survive!"
Yes, it'll be my death
Bhagavān said: "By God's grace, hey, Bābā Bhāṭ, don't fear!
Yes, tell me a plan that will save us
By God's grace, then I'll knock their omen back onto them." The Bhāṭ said: "Then my lord
What more do you need?—*vāh vāh*—

But, Śrī Mahārāj, the animal that's coming belongs to the water and forest
If its wish is fulfilled—*vāh vāh*—
Then things will be all right." *Then they'll work*
Bhagavān said: "Bābā Bhāṭ, how can its wish be fulfilled?"
Yes, tell me about that
The Bhāṭ said: "Śrī Mahārāj, there should be good rains—*mhe*—And knee-high green grass
Yes, if it stood there
This animal is hungry, if it eats grass now—*mhe*—
And later if there's a pond full up with water
If after it drinks water from it—*mhe*—
It wallows in the pond,—*vāh vāh*—
Only then will the old creature be satisfied."
The lord of the three worlds left Līlāgar's stirrup right away—*vāh vāh*—
He took Ind's[63] name—*mhe*—
Wrapped the best blanket around himself and lay down
Yes, he went to sleep

—*gāv*—

By creating clouds he created heat—*mhe*—
By God's grace, in a moment Bhagavān created green grass
He cut off the buffaloes' heads—*mhe*—
The Great Lord kept captive the clouds
Bhagavān took Ind's name—*mhe*—
In a flash, rain fell—*vāh vāh*—
And in a moment green grass
Yes, it appeared
And that pond which was created in a moment—*mhe*—
The pond is named Ūsrī—*vāh vāh*—
Bhagavān filled that Ūsrī pond with a great amount of water—*vāh vāh*—
Now the animals were going down the road
And as they saw the grass—*mhe*—
They quickly left the road and began eating the grass
They ate the grass—*vāh vāh*—
They looked around and saw the water in the pond
Yes, they noticed the full pond
They went there and began wallowing[64] in the water
In the meantime, by God's grace, the king[65] got up and drew his sword—*mhe*—
The heads of both buffaloes went back to the court of Ajmer and
Yes, they went and fell in the court
The king of Ajmer enquired of the Brahmans
The king said: "O Brahmans—*mhe*—
What has happened here?"
Yes, what has happened here?
The Brahmans said: "Śrī Mahārāj, your portent has been swept back to you."
The king said: "Now what . . . ?" *Now what will happen?*

The Brahmans said: "Brother, he'll come and start things off."
Yes, now he'll come, he won't stop
The king said: "By God's grace, have the doors sealed!
Yes, lock the doors!
Leave the windows open, he won't enter through the windows
He's a divine person, who knows, he might turn back from this place—even then it'll be good."
Yes, it's a good thing!
At bright midday the king of Ajmer had the doors sealed—*vāh vāh*—
And had the windows opened
The lord of the three worlds and the Bhāṭ reached the gate
Dev Mahārāj said: "Hey, Bhāṭ of the lineage,—*mhe*—
Why has the door been closed at bright midday?"
The Bhāṭ said: "They closed it out of fear of you
Śrī Mahārāj, you see this window—*mhe*—a horse together with rider—a man-ridden horse—can fit into it
Yes, a man-ridden horse fits into it—enter the window and go in!
So then Dev Mahārāj speaks—*mhe*—
What does he tell the Bhāṭ, let's see! *Let's see by saying it, now by saying it*
I'll just say it, by Bhagavān Dev's grace, I'll say it—*vāh vāh sā*—

—*gāv*—

"O Bhāṭ, if the turban eats the head—*vāh vāh*—
And the border of the field comes and eats the field
Hey, if river waters flow back to the mountains—*mhe*—
Then my horse and I will enter through the window
If water from the mountain climbs back up again, then my horse and I will turn back
Yes, otherwise we won't turn back
Pālo his fame is great—*mhe*—
Hey, we're hungry—come on—let's go to the court of Ajmer—we're friends and acquaintances of theirs
Yes, we'll receive praise right on entering—two plates now—if you come then they'll give you the bowls."
Pālosānī and the Bagaṛāvat's Bhāṭ of the lineage—*mhe*—
Entered the windows dragging their horses
This is something that happened in Ajmer. *This very Ajmer*
The lord of the three worlds pulled the horse's reins back at that spot—*vāh vāh*—
The horse stepped back, stepped back, stepped back till it stopped at a distance of three kos—*vāh vāh*—
At that place, Dev, lord of three worlds, tightened the horse's saddle
So on the day he came to pay tax—*mhe*—
They say that on that day Dev Mahārāj tightened Līlā's saddle on that spot—*vāh vāh*—
So now I haven't seen it myself till today, but people say there's a Temple of the Saddle there even now—*vāh vāh—three kos to the south*

By God's grace, after creating the Temple of the Saddle at that place—*mhe*—
Bhagavān lifted up the horse's reins
Yes, he lifted them up
The Bhāṭ and Pālosānī hadn't even reached yet—*mhe*—
The lord of three worlds sprang over the door
Yes, and arrived in the court
The Līlāgar horse gallops one and a half arm-lengths above Mother Earth—*vāh vāh*—
The saddle stays one and a half arm-lengths above the horse—*vāh vāh*—one and a half arm-lengths above the saddle sits Bhagavān.
Yes, he's sitting above it
On his head a parasol weighing one and a half maṇ
Yes, even the one-and-a-half-maṇ parasol is one and a half arms-lengths in the air
And above the parasol—above Bhagavān—the banner is flying—*vāh vāh*—
In this manner Bhagavān rides the horse Līlāgar back and forth in the court
Yes, he was riding it back and forth in front of the court
Just then the Bagaṛāvats' Bhāṭ arrived in the court—*vāh vāh*—
He said: "Hey, Pāliyā—*mhe*—
Look we left Dev behind us, in spite of that he's gone in front
Yes, he's come ahead of us!
We have not fathomed his greatness."
Yes, there's no limit to his greatness
After that the Bagaṛāvats' Bhāṭ sang a song of praise for the king of Ajmer—*vāh vāh*—:
"King Ād—from Ād came Jugād—from Jugād Kācchap—from Kācchap Raṇdhol—*mhe*—
From Raṇdhol came Kajaḷī—from Kajaḷī Maṇḍalī—from Maṇḍalī came Harīrāṃjī—*mhe*—
From Harīrāṃjī came Bāgh, and from Bāgh came Bhoj
From Bhoj has come Dev
Arisen from the fire-pit the great lineage of Cauhāns
The soles of his feet have the mark of lotuses
His shoulders are the shape of betel leaves
Through the strike of Līlā's hooves a surge of cold water arose from the underworld—*vāh vāh*—
And split open the hill
On the day that Dev took incarnation, the space between the sky and the earth was lit up
Hey, Bhoj's Udal.—*mhe*—
He held up the falling sky.

Devnārāyaṇ Trains the King of Ajmer's horse

The king of Ajmer said: "Look, brother, the song of praise
Yes, was very good

Hey, Bābā Bhāṭ!" "Yes, Śrī Mahārāj?"—*mhe*—
"Is that your lord?"
Yes, is he yours?
The Bhāṭ said: "He's the very one that's mine."
Yes, Dev is mine
The king said: "The horse has been ridden back and forth superbly."
Yes, he rides a horse back and forth very well
Hey, Bābā Bhāṭ, ask your lord to ride in my pony."
Yes, there's a horse in my kingdom, that he could ride in, and look, have trained
The Bhāṭ said: "Śrī Mahārāj, Grandfather wishes to have a horse trained."
Yes, would you train it?
Bhagavān said: "Hey, Bhāṭ of the lineage, tell Grandfather—*mhe*—
To let the horse roam outside, brother. *Have it sent out, I'll train it*
I'll do what's been commanded."—*vāh vāh*—
By God's grace, the Bhāṭ said: "Śrī Mahārāj, call for it."
Yes, send for it
The king said: "If I let it roam free, then Bhāṭ
Yes, I might as well train it
I can train it. *I can train it*
I won't free the horse!"—*vāh vāh*—
The Lord said: "Bābā Bhāṭ, just ask which stable the horse is in."
Yes, which place is it tied to
The king of Ajmer said: "It's tied in the stable there in front. It's a speckled horse."—*vāh vāh*—
What did Dev do? He removed Līlāgar's bridle
And arrived *at the speckled horse's stable*
As soon as he went there he gave the horse a slap
The horse was immediately prepared to be ridden
By God's grace, as the speckled horse stood there, the lord climbed onto it and stood there—*vāh vāh*—
Now, you know how Līlā's gait is—*mhe*—! It began moving even better than that!
The king of Ajmer said: "Great, brother!"
Yes, your lord certainly knows how to train horses
For a while, the lord of the three worlds, Bhagavān, rode the horse
Yes, back and forth
Suddenly Bhagavān gave the horse a kick with his heels
He sent the horse down into the thirteenth underworld
Bhagavān said: "Bhāṭ of the lineage—*mhe*—
Tell Grandfather, hey, brother, that this Mother Earth
Yes, it demanded an offering of a horse
I gave the Earth the offering of a horse."
By God's grace, the king of Ajmer speaks.—*mhe*—
What does he say to Dev. *Let's see by saying it, now by saying it*
I'll just say it, by God's grace, I'll say it!—*vāh vāh sā*—

—*gāv*—

"He killed my black buffaloes—*vāh vāh*—
Hey, he reduced my horse to ashes
By God's grace, I'm satisfied with your service and tax—*mhe*—
Take your lord back the way you came—I'm completely content with your service and tax
Hey, Bhāṭ, I yield, brother!"
Yes, here take this note
The king of Ajmer went and wrote a note—*mhe*—
Stamped it with his seal—*vāh vāh*—
And gave it to the Bhāṭ
The king said: "O Bhāṭ, I won't ever demand tax or service
Yes, I'll never ask—you go away
I didn't realize this earlier—*vāh vāh*—
Buffaloes worth lakhs of rupees were devastated—*mhe*—
And the horse worth one and a half lakhs *was finished off*
The Bhāṭ took the note to Dev—he showed it to Bhagavān—*mhe*—
Bhagavān said: "Bābā Bhāṭ, tell Grandfather, if he needs anything else, then,
Yes, I'll satisfy him some more."
The king said: "No, Śrī Mahārāj, you please leave—I'm content! *I've had enough!*
Dīyājī Jodhkā was the king of Ajmer's nephew[66]—*mhe*—
He thought: "Stupid, Dev shouldn't return just the way he came![67]
Yes, he hasn't got to know me!
Dīyājī Jodhkā's such a great archer—let's find out at least!" *Let's test this Dev*
So he filled a cauldron with oil—*mhe*—
Looking at the reflection in it—*vāh vāh*—

Devnārāyaṇ's First Encounter with Dīyājī Jodhkā

In its home in the sky—a kite—Dīyājī shot down with an arrow
Yes, immediately the kite fell down
Bhagavān noticed the kite as it fell near him
He said: "Hey, Bābā Bhāṭ!—*mhe*—
What's that creature that's fallen down—bring it to me over here!"
Yes, "Bring it here, let's see!"
The lord of the three worlds lifted up the kite, and took all of its feathers
He cast a look of mercy. As many feathers there were—*mhe*—
That many kites arose
Yes, he made them fly off
He said: "Dīyā, kill! What's the big deal in killing one?"
Yes, kill now! He said, "Let's see your skill now—how much of an archer you are!"
Dīyā speaks—*mhe*—

What does he tell Dev, let's see.
Know it by saying it, let's see by saying it
I'll just say it by God's grace—*vāh vāh sā*—

—*gāv*—

By God's grace, who said this? *Dīyājī said this*
"O Gūjrī's son, I'll come running to Daṛāvaṭ—*mhe*—
Otherwise you come running to my Sāvar
Hey, I won't slay you this time—*mhe*—
In the Mahābhārat of Rātākoṭ—vāh vāh—
By God's grace, I'll kill you like a cat swallows a chicken
The way a cat kills a chicken—*mhe*—
I won't take even that much time!"
Yes, no time at all—great Dīyājī!
By God's grace, the lord of the three worlds, Bhagavān, speaks this time—*mhe*—
What does he tell Dīyā? *Know it by saying it, let's see, now saying it*
I'll just say it, by Bhagavān God's grace—*vāh vāh sā*—

—*gāv*—

"O Dīyā, you made me into a chicken—*mhe*—
You turned into a true feline
Hey, I'll single you out from the armies on the battlefield of Rātākoṭ and kill you—*mhe*—
On that day you'll see the true lord of the three realms
Why should I kill you now?—*vāh vāh*—
If I kill you here, O Dīyā—*mhe*—
Then without you who will face me in the Mahābhārat of Rātākoṭ?
Yes, who will endure a fight with me?
Hey, at least you'll put up a little resistance!—*vāh vāh*—
On that day I'll single you out from the army and extract your life." He said—*vāh vāh*—
Who said this to Dīyājī?
Dev Mahārāj said this *Dev Mahārāj said this to Dīyājī*
The king of Ajmer speaks—*mhe*—
What does he say, let's see. *Know it by saying it, let's see*
I'll just say it by God's grace, let's see

—*gāv*—

"O Bhāṭ, take your lord back to the pond of Ūsrī—*mhe*—
Hey, I'll send Dīyā off to the mountain of King Ajaypāl
Look, both these heroes entered the court—*mhe*—
As though water and fire met
Both of them are warriors aren't they?—*mhe*—
They can't tolerate each other
Yes, they can't endure each other here." He said, "Take them away."
"Hey Bhāṭ, take your lord away quickly now!"—*vāh vāh*—

The Bhāṭ went and spoke to Dev Mahārāj: "Śrī Mahārāj, it's Grandfather's wish—*mhe*—
That—Grandfather can't bear you any more here—"
Yes, please leave
"It seems to me, Bābā Bhāṭ, that you're easily satisfied."
The king of Ajmer . . . Prince Medūjī was taken away by the ṭhākur of Bhairūdā, who was the dharam-brother of the Bagaṛāvats—*mhe*—
Now when the king of Ajmer realized that Medū, brother, belonged to him—*vāh vāh*—
He looked after Prince Medū, gave him an education—*mhe*—
And married Prince Medū to the house of the Salāv Rajpūts—the lord of Ajmer did—*vāh vāh*—

Medū's Wife Departs with Devnārāyaṇ

He gave Medū the jurisdiction over the region of Baṭṭūṭ
He started living in Baṭṭūṭ, brother.—*vāh vāh*—
The lord of the three worlds, Bhagavān, paid the tax—*mhe*—
. . . and was pardoned the tax. Taking the note—*vāh vāh*—
He took leave and journeyed back
Sitting in the palace, Medū's princess speaks. What does she say to her brother-in-law,[68] let's see.
Yes, know it by saying it, let's see by saying it
I'll just say it, by Dev's grace, here you are—*vāh vāh sā*—

—*gāv*—

This was what said by Medū's princess—*mhe*—
She said: "By God's grace, wait, my dear brother-in-law!—*mhe*—
I'll come having harnessed these oxen!
Hey, my dear brother-in-law!—*mhe*—
He's begun today to go around and assemble the sweet one's clan
Sirdārs!—*mhe*—
He's not come to pay tax!
Yes, he's come to take me along!
He's bringing his own clan together now!"—*vāh vāh*—
So Medū's princess prepared the chariot—*vāh vāh*—
The day Dev Mahārāj came to pay tax, she departed together with Dev
Yes, she came to Daṛāvaṭ
He paid taxes—*mhe*—
He showed the lord of Ajmer
Yes, his miraculous powers
Medū's princess came together with him
Proclaim victory to Śrī Devnārāyaṇ Bhagavān—victory—say this both great and small!

Sāḍū Mātā Meets Medū

The lord of Ajmer reflected to himself: "Hey, now that Medū's princess has left—*mhe*—how will Medū stay with you any more?"
Yes, he won't stay
He wrote a letter.—*mhe*—
And, by God's grace, sent it off to Baṭṭūṭ.—*vāh vāh*—
"Medū, Dev Mahārāj came here, brother, and has taken your Padmaṇī along with him.
And in the meantime he's also established Goṭh Kheḍā." He said
"As Bhoj's son, you are the heir apparent.—*mhe*—
What claim does Dev have to the throne?"
Yes, you're the lord of the throne
What happens when Medūjī, by God's grace reads the letter written by Grandfather?
What does he say to the Sirdārs, let's see. *Know it by saying it, let's see, now by saying it.*

—*gāv*—

"I read the letter written by Grandfather.—*mhe*—
Today I understood Grandfather's intention
After I lost my land-deed, Sirdārs, I'll never drink water
My authority has been taken away—*vāh vāh*—
O Sirdārs, I won't drink water on this earth, brother."—*vāh vāh*—
Prince Medū got his horse ready.—*vāh vāh*—
And then he raced his horse—*mhe*—
By God's grace, he went to the king of Ajmer and said:
"Grandfather, why did you do this?"
Yes, what is this?
The king said: "Prince Medū, brother, I've said this in your favor.—*vāh vāh*—
Hey, you're the lord of the throne!—*mhe*—
Dev didn't ask or enquire of you—he just became the lord of the throne on his own!—*vāh vāh*—
Go Medū, I'm on your side, brother!—*mhe*—
One day I'll send him back to Malwa just the way he came." *I'll send him back—he*[69] *can become the lord of the throne.*
Prince Medū got into a great rage—*vāh vāh*—: "The smart fellow, took away my wife from here—Dev's become the lord of the throne all on his own!—*vāh vāh*—
It's an audacious thing that he's done!"
Yes, there's no mention of me at all!
Without saying farewell, Prince Medū departed—*vāh vāh*—
As he'd reached some distance, what did he do?—Dev Mahārāj's cows were grazing in the forest—*vāh vāh*—
The Guāl was singing praises of Dev and Chhapanjī Bhairūjī—*mhe*—and playing the flute.—*vāh vāh*—

By God's grace, Prince Medū speaks—*mhe*—
What does he tell the Guāl, let's see. *Know it by saying it, let's see by saying it*
I'll just say it by Dev's grace, here you are!—*vāh vāh sā*—

—*gāv*—

"Brother, Sirdārs, by whose name do these cows go?—*mhe*—
Whose name do you go by, O Guāl?
The son of a Rajpūt king asks you—*mhe*—
On whose strength have you destroyed the king's produce, O Guāls!—*mhe*—
Why have you gathered together the harvest of wheat and chickpeas here?"
Yes, tell me why have you collected the summer harvest?
Now Sāḍū Mātā had told the Guāl.—*mhe*—
She said: "Hey, brother, listen, when you go into the forest—*vāh vāh*—if someone asks you who the cows belong to—
Yes, whose will you say they are?"
Don't say they belong to Devjī, brother!—*vāh vāh*—
My dear Medū lives in Ajmer—*vāh vāh*—
Say that the cows belong to him!
Yes, say that the cows belong to him, to Medū
Don't take the name of the lord of the three worlds there!"—*vāh vāh*—
Dev's Guāl speaks—*mhe*—
What does he say to Prince Medū, let's see *Know it by saying it, let's see*
I'll just say it by Dev Bhagavān's grace, let's see—*vāh vāh sā*—

—*gāv*—

By God's grace, the following was said.—*mhe*—
The Guāl said: "O brother, these cows belong to Medū.—*vāh vāh*—
I'm a Guāl from Sāḍūjī's mother's home
Hey, son of a Rajpūt king, whose protection do I have?—*mhe*—
I came to the royal harvest on my own strength
When do I ever need someone else's protection, brother?
If there's fight or quarrel here, then I rely on my own strength!—*vāh vāh*—
And the cows—there's Prince Medū who resides over Baṭṭūṭ—
Yes, they belong to him
Hey, brother, I'm a Guāl from Malwa—Sāḍū's natal home."—*vāh vāh*—
Like sprinkling water onto boiling milk—*mhe*—
Soothing drops fell onto Prince Medū's body
Yes, he calmed down immediately
"Hey, the cows belong to you.
Yes, then the throne is yours! It's yours!
The world—people—are all false
Yes, they do things to create strife
Brothers are being made to fight brothers!—*vāh vāh*—
Hey, brother, graze the cows!"
Yes, graze them—take them around and around

After Medū's princess had come to Daṛāvat, Sāḍū Mātā paced up and down high up in the palace
She heard the sound of Medū's horse's footsteps—*mhe*—
Sāḍū Mātā speaks—*vāh vāh*—
What does she say, let's see. *Know it by saying it, Bhopājī Mahārāj, by saying it*
I'll say it now, by Bhagavān Dev's grace, let's see—*vāh vāh sā*—

—*gāv*—

"I recognized Medū's feather plume and steed!—*mhe*—
I recognized the pace of my dear young one!
Hey, maidservants, I've forgotten his face long ago.—*mhe*—
Today, my one and only rider has come!
Medū's coming, brother!"—*vāh vāh*—
Sāḍū Mātā speaks. What does she say, let's see.
Know it by saying it, by saying it, let's see
I'll say it now, by God's grace, let's see—*vāh vāh*—*sā*

—*gāv*—

"Prepare a cup of saffron!—*vāh vāh*—
O maidservants, fill up a plate with pearls!
O maidservants, prepare an āratī for Medū, who is coming!—*mhe*—
Today my dear master of the kingdom has come!
O maidservants—*mhe*—
The master of the kingdom has arrived!"
Yes, today he's come
Sāḍū Mātā speaks—the Bhāṭ of the lineage had come near—what does she tell him, let's see *Know it by saying it, by saying it, let's see*
I'll just say it, by Dev's grace, here you are—*vāh vāh*—

—*gāv*—

"O Bhāṭ of the lineage, prepare a cup of saffron!—*mhe*—
Bring my dear prince who has come to me!
Hey, the ṭīkā[70] and coconut meant for the person occupying the throne—*mhe*—
Now give that to my dear Prince Medū!
Bābā Bhāṭ!—*mhe*—
Medūjī has come today!
Yes, put the king's mark on Medū's forehead
By God's grace, all these days everything was all right—Dev Mahārāj was residing, brother.—*mhe*—
My dear Medū has come, he's the lord of the kingdom!
Yes, he's the eldest
Bhoj's heir, you know—*mhe*—
He's come now!"
Yes, it's Medūjī!
The Bhāṭ speaks.—*vāh vāh*—
What does he say, let's see.

Know it by saying it, let's see
Prince Medū came near—*vāh vāh*—

—*gāv*—

"Don't be pleased by seeing brightness!—*mhe*—
By God's grace, the flower-shaped lamps shine in the garden
O Mother, he who sees the radiance of Nārāyaṇ Dev—*mhe*—
by God's grace, his body and mind grows powerful[71]
Today Medūjī has come—*mhe*—
And you're giving the throne to Medūjī
If, tomorrow morning, Tejājī's son Madan Siṅgjī arrives
Yes, tomorrow morning you'll say give him the throne!—
Because he's the leader's son too.—*mhe*—
Mājī Sāī, who all will you give it to?—*vāh vāh*—
Now only Bhagavān will remain the lord of the throne."
Yes, only Dev Mahārāj will be so.
Prince Medū thought to himself: "Hey, what Mājī Sāī said was right.
Yes, she spoke in your favor
But that old Bhāṭ has spoiled the deal.
Yes, he's spoiled the matter!
By God's grace, speak a little sternly now." *So that they give me the throne—otherwise I won't see the coconut ceremony*
Prince Medūjī speaks. Let's see what he says. *Know it by saying it, let's see by saying it*
I'll just say it, by Dev's grace, brother—*vāh vāh*—

—*gāv*—

"You didn't take permission from your uncles,[72] brother!
You didn't respect the honor of your uncles
In pouring rains I'll throw your mattresses back to Mālāgar.—*vāh vāh*—
Know then that my name is Medū!
You didn't ask anyone and didn't request anyone!
You became the lord on your own!—*vāh vāh*—
What do you demand for this land?"—*mhe*—
By God's grace, Prince Medū said that—*vāh vāh*—
Sāḍū Mātā speaks.—*mhe*—
Let's see what she says to Medū *Know it by saying it, let's see, by saying it*
I'll just say it, by Dev's grace, here you are—*vāh vāh*—*jī*—*vāh vāh*—

—*gāv*—

By God's grace, this was said by Sāḍū Mātā—*mhe*—
"O son, I'll have the spokes fixed onto the carriages' wheels—*vāh vāh*—
And move the cows that are mine back to Mālāgar
O son, this land belongs to you and your father.—*mhe*—
Sow plenty of mustard and fenugreek in it
You didn't like me."

Yes, I'll return to the country of Mālāgar
That is what was said. *Sāḍū Mātā said it*
Now Queen Pīpalde, who was Dev Mahārāj's wife—*mhe*—
She heard what had been said.—*vāh vāh*—*what had been said*
Yes, sir!—*vāh vāh*—
Queen Pīpalde speaks—*mhe*—
What does she say in return, let's see.
Know it by saying it, let's see, by saying it
I'll say it now, by Bhagavān's grace—*vāh vāh*—

—*gāv*—

Pīpalde's Altercation with Medū

"O mother-in-law, why did you have the spokes fixed onto the carriages' wheels?—*vāh vāh*—
Why did you drive back the cows to Malwa?
This land, which belongs to father-in-law Savāī Bhoj—*mhe*—I will divide and take half of it from brother-in-law Medū in the morning
Not even more than a point of a spear will I let Medu have half of."
Medūjī reflected to himself:
"Who is this arbiter of half of the territory?"
Yes, who is this,
"Sāḍū Mātā!—*mhe*—
Where did you get this one from?"—*vāh vāh*—
By God's grace, Sādū Mātā said: "Hey, son—*mhe*—
That's Dev Mahārāj's wife!"
Yes, Pīpalde.

—*gāv*—

"O Sister-in-law Pīpalde, you talked a great deal of nonsense—*vāh vāh*—
Your eyes painted with collyrium.
O mother, send Pīpalde back to her maternal home.—*vāh vāh*—
By God's grace, Medū says he'll take her life now!
I can't bear it anymore!"
Yes, I can't bear it anymore
Prince Medū said that
Dev Mahārāj's wife speaks.—*vāh vāh*—
What does she say to Prince Medū, let's see.
Know it by saying it, let's see, by saying it
I'll just say it sir, by Dev's grace, let's see—*vāh vāh sā*—

—*gāv*—

"O Brother-in-law, tell me, when did you learn to strike and destroy?—*mhe*
Didn't you feel any shame saying this?

In the heroic field of the Rāṭhors—*mhe*—the enemy Rāvjī killed Bhoj.—*vāh vāh*—
Why didn't you fight that enemy on that day?
You're prepared to kill me——*mhe*—
But you didn't kill Rāvjī!
Yes, did you send your valor off wandering[73] *on that day?*
Where were you then?"—*vāh vāh*—
By God's grace, Prince Medū didn't quite know how to answer.—*mhe*—
Medū speaks now—*vāh vāh*—
What does he say, let's see—
Know it by saying it
I'll say that now, by Dev's grace! *vāh vāh sā*

—*gāv*—

"O Sister-in-law Pīpalde, you talked a great deal of nonsense,—*mhe*—
Sitting in your palace with your face turned away!
Your father married you off to a traveling palanquin—*mhe*—
Having seen, O Queen, my brother's match
Because there are brothers like me—
Yes, that's why your father married you off to a traveling palanquin
He turned the opposite way and married you off."—*vāh vāh*—
Medū said that.
Queen Pīpalde speaks.—*mhe*—
What answer does she give to her brother-in-law, let's see

—*gāv*—

"I talked a great deal of nonsense to you—*mhe*—sitting in the palace with my face turned away
Your infant brother went in times of trouble to the land of Mālāgar.—*mhe*—
On that day, O Brother-in-law, there was no match of brothers!
Where were you?
Yes, tell me where you were!
Bhagavān went there alone and returned alone!—*vāh vāh*—
Brother-in-law had told a lie!"—*mhe*—
By God's grace, he thought to himself: "Women are in control in this place!—*mhe*—
By talking to these women your own interests
Yes, will be disregarded
Just by saying so they seem to sing the old Bhāṭ's tune—*mhe*—
Which is why right on my arrival they turned down the throne on me!
Yes, they turned it down
That's why Queen Pīpalde over there is answering this way!
Yes, turning away!
Hey, there's the Bagaṛāvat's Guru—let me inform him at least!"
Yes, whatever the Guru says, that will be done

—gāv—

By God's grace, Prince Medū wrote a letter and sent it off—*mhe*—
"O Bābā Nāth, upon receiving it, read it straight away
Dev and I have had a falling out because of the throne.—*vāh vāh*—
O Guru, you come and confer rule
Whoever you give it to he's the right one—I'll accept!—*vāh vāh*—
Messenger!—*mhe*—
Take this letter and deliver it to Śaṅkar's fire-place, brother!"
Yes, bring it to Rupāyalī
The messenger took the letter and raced his horse right away.—*vāh vāh*—
By God's grace, he reached Rupāyalī
He took the letter and gave it to Bābājī
Bābājī said: "Wait, brother!—*mhe*—
Take a letter written by me."
Yes, back with you—this way I won't trouble some Jogī
Bābājī speaks—what letter does he write, let's see!
Know it by saying it, now by saying it

—gāv—

"You're both sons of Bhoj.—*mhe*—
O Medū, I can't tell a lie!
Hey, only the son of Bhoj will receive the coronation—*mhe*—
Who goes to Sāvar to rescue Dīyā's mare
Dīyā has your father's mare.—*mhe*—
It's in captivity—in pain now!
Yes, you want the throne?
Go and free the mare from its captivity and I'll confer the throne on you."
Yes, I'll give it to whoever is worthy of having it
"Messenger!—*mhe*—
Here take this, brother." *Take this letter and give it to Medū*
The messenger took the letter and turned his horse back from that place
By God's grace, he brought the letter and gave it to Medū
Medujī said: "Bābājī's gone and turned the matter upside down.—*mhe*—
By God's grace, hey, Bhāṭ of the lineage!—*mhe*—
I'm going to go to Sāvar—are you going to come along or not, brother?"
Yes, are you going to accompany me or not?
The Bhāṭ said: "Śrī Mahārāj, with others I would go on foot . . .
Yes, with you I would go on my head!"
They didn't ask Dev and didn't ask Sāḍū.—*mhe*—
So, brother, they departed. *Let's go*
Without informing anyone, the Bhāṭ of the lineage and Prince Medū departed.—*vāh vāh*—

By God's grace, they arrived at the banyan tree at Soner—*vāh vāh*—
Pārvatī and Mahādev were meditating in it

After Pārvatī saw him she spoke to Śaṅkar: "Hey, by God's grace, Bābājī, look!"
Yes, who is this traveling on horseback?
Śaṅkar said: "Caṇḍī, that's Bhoj's son.—*mhe*—
And he's going on the assault of Sāvar."—*vāh vāh*—
Pārvatī said: "For whose sake?" *For whose sake are they going?*
Śaṅkar said: "Dīya's got his father's mare."
Yes, which he's going to rescue.

By God's grace, when Prince Uttam Rāī went to get married—*mhe*—
She said: "I'll release this lion of mine now
I'll make two strokes of my sword
Dīyājī is my closest disciple.—*vāh vāh*—
I'll support Dīyā fully."—*mhe*—
By God's grace, Pārvatī gave the lion a slap
"Get up, let's see your play"
Yes, go and roar
It didn't take much time after the slap that the lion began leaping nine lengths of three and a half yards.
Prince Medū saw it approaching
He said: "Hey, Bābā Bhāṭ!—*mhe*—
Hey, there's an animal coming that's taking leaps of three and a half yards."
Yes, it's taking leaps
The Bhāṭ said: "Śrī Mahārāj, after the Bagaṛāvats died I can't see anymore!
Yes, I don't see—I see only very faintly
Tell me all the details, *then I'll be able to guess*
Prince Medū speaks.—*mhe*—
What details does he tell of . . .
Know it by saying it, let's see by saying it
I'll just say, by God's grace, here you are—*vāh vāh sā*

—*gāv*—

"O Bhāṭ, like a cat it has stripes—*mhe*—
And a head big and round like the wheel of a well
Bhāṭ of the lineage, it lives in the banyan of Soner.—*mhe*—
What animal is that?
Take a look and see *what animal it is."*
The Bhāṭ said: "O my master, that's a lion that's come!"
Yes, a lion!
Medū said: "My grandfather has come!"
Yes, it's Bāgh!
The Bhāṭ said: "It's not your grandfather!
Yes, that animal belongs to the jungle
Your grandfather was a man.—*mhe*—
Only his head was that of a lion.—*vāh vāh*—

That's a lion of the jungle!"—*mhe*—
Medu said: "What does it do?"

—*gāv*—

"I went away at night and returned in the morning.—*mhe*—
I took a very brief span of time
Savāī Bhoj's mare, Mātā Cā̃vaṇḍā—*mhe*—
O Giver of Nourishment, can only be brought back by someone brave."[74]
Dev said: "Bābā Bhāṭ—*mhe*—don't you and Elder Brother Medū have moustaches?"
Yes, no moustaches at all?
The Bhāṭ said: "No, Śrī Mahārāj, they stand thick and strong!"
Yes, they stand thick and strong
Dev Mahārāj said: "What's the point in their standing?—*mhe*—
The mare hasn't come back!"—*vāh vāh*—
Dev said: "Hey, Bābā Bhāṭ, you've put the matter onto the wrong track!—*mhe*—
Tell Medū—*mhe*—
if he wants to rule, then rescue the mare from its captivity quickly!
Yes, rescue and bring it back!
And if the mare does not return—*mhe*—
Then, brother, see that witness platform—*vāh vāh*—
Which belongs to the throne of justice—*mhe*—
Occupy that!" *Occupy that!*
Prince Medū said: "Hey, Bhāṭ, tell Dev, brother—*mhe*—
That this throne is very difficult to occupy *I don't desire it!*
I'll take this platform of justice.
Yes, I'll do that work
I'll decide henceforth on the justice of those who come and go."—*vāh vāh*—
He spoke to Sāḍū Mātā. "Mājī Sāī—*mhe*—
Do the coronation ceremony for me for the throne of justice."
Yes, do it soon!
The day when Prince Medū arrived from Baṭṭūṭ, on that day Māt Khaṭāṇī did the coronation ceremony of the platform of justice for him.—*vāh vāh*—
She said: "Justice belongs to you—*mhe*—
And the village belongs to Bhagavān Dev!" *to Dev*
When Medū was crowned for the platform, and joined together with the king
Say victory to Śrī Devnārāyaṇ Bhagavān! *Victory!*

Devnārāyaṇ Encounters Pārvatī's Lion

Dev Mahārāj said: "Hey, Bhāṭ of the lineage—*mhe*—
I won't sit on the throne.
Yes, I won't sit on the throne now!
If the mare is released from captivity, then I'll certainly sit on the throne,
Bābā Bhāṭ, let's go!"

Yes, come on
The Bhāṭ said: "Śrī Mahārāj, where else should I go? I'll stay with you!"—*vāh vāh*—
Pālāsānī placed the saddle on the horses, brother.—*vāh vāh*—
The lord of the three worlds, the Bhāṭ of the lineage—*mhe*—
And Pālāsānī
Yes, the three of them set out
They set out to release the mare Bāvlī from captivity.—*vāh vāh*—
By God's grace, they went to that place in the forest—*mhe*—
where the path split into two
Dev Mahārāj *spoke:* "Bābā Bhāṭ—*mhe*—
Tell me why the road ahead has two paths?"
Yes, which road goes to Sāvar, tell me
The Bhāṭ said: "Śrī Mahārāj, both go to Sāvar."
Dev Mahārāj said: "Bābā Bhāṭ, hey, tell me why does one village have two paths?"
Yes, why is it like this?
The Bhāṭ said: "Śrī Mahārāj, one path takes six months.
Yes, it takes six months"
One path is such—*mhe*—
That we'll reach there in three days! *Amazing!*
Dev Mahārāj said: "Bābā Bhāṭ, what's the advantage of the path with six months.—*mhe*—
What's the disadvantage of the one of three months?"[75] The Bhāṭ said: "Śrī Mahārāj, the three-day path is full of lions, panthers, and robbers
It can never be traversed!—*vāh vāh*—
The six-month path—*mhe*—
If anything of ours gets lost in it,
Yes, only we ourselves will come and retrieve it, no one else will pick it up."
Dev Mahārāj said: "Hey, listen, Bhāṭ of the lineage—*vāh vāh*—
I haven't made that much of a promise[76]
Yes, I don't have such a promise!
We'll take the three-day path." *We'll quickly rescue the mare and return!*
So Bhagavān, the lord of the three worlds, put his horse, Līlā, onto the three-day path.—*vāh vāh*—

Pārvatī saw the Lord's horse
What does she get up and tell Śaṅkar?
Know it by saying it, let's see, by saying it
I'll say it now, by Dev's grace, here you are!—*vāh vāh*—

—*gāv*—

"Look, traveling above the ground!—*mhe*—
Bholānāth, a strange rider is coming
On his way to the Soner. Open your eyes,—*mhe*—
And look at what kind of vehicle of Dev's is going by

Hey, it's moving above the ground!"
Yes, what kind of vehicle is that of Dev's?
Mahādev said: "Caṇḍī, that is Dev—Dev!"—*vāh vāh*—
She said: "What Dev?" *What Dev is he?*
"There are four Devs." She thought to herself: "There are only four Devs.—*mhe*—
"I don't know of a fifth one, brother."—*vāh vāh*—
By God's grace, which were the four Devs? She said: "Anndev—*he*—
Jaldev—*vāh vāh*—
Pavandev—*vāh vāh*—
And, by God's grace, did I mention Agaṇ . . . Pavan, Jaḷ, Ann, these are the four Devs on earth that I believe in.
Yes, I only see four
You've created that fifth Dev yourself today!"
Yes, where did you get him from?
Śaṅkar said: "Listen, Caṇḍī—*mhe*—
The lord of the three worlds, Bhagavān, has arrived." *On his own he has arrived*
She said: "What is he doing?"—*mhe*—
He said: "He's going to Sāvar." *He's going to Sāvar*
He said: "Just like the one before went to Sāvar."
Yes, he's going just like that
She said: "Don't rely on him this time!"—*mhe*—
He said: "What are you going to do?"—*vāh vāh*—
She said: "The same thing—I'll release the lion!—*vāh vāh*—
And it'll roar twice and frighten him off."—*mhe*—
He said: "You'll be on foot then, Caṇḍī!"
Yes, that doesn't matter
By God's grace, Pārvatī got up and gave the lion a slap: "Hey, brave one, go on in front and roar!"—*vāh vāh*—
It took no time for the lion to rise. Dev's and the lion's eyes
Yes, they met
Then the lion sat back onto the ground!
Yes, it crouched back right at the same place
Pārvatī gave it another slap
The lion looked down and did not raise its eyes.—*vāh vāh*—
Pārvatī thought in her mind: "This is an outrage."—*mhe*—
She spoke to Śaṅkar: "O Bholā Mahādev—*mhe*—
What should I do with him?"
Yes, I want to create a quarrel
He said: "Who are you, by your saying now—*vāh vāh*—
The lion will make him run away?"
Yes, release him at least!
She said: "Then your and my ways are different, there you are."
Yes, I don't like it!
Taking the shape of a golden bird—*mhe*—she went and sat on a branch nearby.—*vāh vāh*—

Śaṅkar said: "Come back, don't make trouble."
Yes, come back
She said: "No, I'll come back only after I create a quarrel between the lion and Nārāyaṇ
He said: "Don't reproach me later—I don't care—you'll have to go on foot!"
Yes, I'm not concerned about this, you'll have to go on foot
She said: "Even if I have to go on foot—*vāh vāh*—
I'll create a quarrel."
Create one quarrel
By God's grace, Śaṅkar got up and gave the lion a slap:
"Go brave one and roar once!" *Come on*
So how does the lion move?—*mhe*—
What does Bhagavān say to the lion when it comes, let's see.
Know it by saying it, let's see, by saying it
I'll just say it, by Dev's grace, here you are!—*vāh vāh—jī—vāh vāh*—

—*gāv*—

"I am Nārāyaṇ.—*mhe*—
You are the forest's lion. You'll be defeated
Hey, I'll kill you, forest's lion. *mhe*
Dip your head into the Kāliyā Pond
Go and take a ceremonial bath."
Yes, I'll release you today
It didn't take long after hearing this for the lion—*vāh vāh*—
To run back on the same way he came
The Kālīyā Pond was full.—*mhe*—
The lion jumped into it.
Jumped and fell into it
Water flew up nine yards high
The Bhāṭ reflected to himself: "I know your mother! It'll do the same with us that it's done with the water."
Yes, it'll do the same to us now when it comes—mhe—
The Bhāṭ began walking around the tree—*vāh vāh*—
He thought to himself: "If I climb up on top"
Yes, I'll be able to save myself like this
The Bagaṛāvats' Bhāṭ would catch hold of a clump of grass—*vāh vāh*—
The dead grass would break off, and the Bhāṭ would come falling down right away
He started blabbering—*vāh vāh*—
Dev Mahārāj said: "Hey, Bābā Bhāṭ, why are you blabbering?"
Yes, why are you climbing up and falling down?
The Bhāṭ said: "Śrī Mahārāj, the horse has been hungry since yesterday.
I'm looking for some fresh fodder
I can't find any."
There's only rotten fodder
Dev Mahārāj said: "I know where there is grass."

Yes, come here near me
Come let's fight the lion!"—*vāh vāh*—
The Bhāṭ said: "Hey, Śrī Mahārāj when did I ever quarrel?"
Yes, I'm frightened of fighting a lion
Dev Mahārāj said: "Then come close Bhāṭ!—*āh vāh*—
I'll protect you!"—*vāh vāh*—
The Bhāṭ said: "How are you going to do that, Śrī Mahārāj?"
Yes, tell me that!
Dev Mahārāj said: "Bābā Bhāṭ, I'll tie you down on top of this rock."
Yes, keep sitting up there
The Bhāṭ said: "Great, great, hey, my lord, you thought good!"—*vāh vāh*—
Dev Mahārāj said: "Pāliyā—*mhe*—
Protect the Bhāṭ up there!"
Yes, tie his arms firmly to the rock and come back!
"By God's grace, tie the Bhāṭ up on the branch"—*mhe*—
He took the sash, wrapped it around the branch—*vāh vāh*—
And gave it a knot
He said: "Dev Mahārāj told me to do this, what's your idea, brother, Bābā Bhāṭ?" *What's your idea*
The Bhāṭ said: "Great, Śrī Mahārāj, if the rock falls, then *I'll fall tied to it*
Now I won't leave it.—*vāh vāh*—
Before being tied, I would have fallen down in between when you and the lion fought, because my hands would have left their hold.
Yes, they would tremble
Dev Mahārāj said: "Pālā Sānī,—*mhe*—
Tie up Līlāgar." He said.—*vāh vāh*—
"There's going to be a fight now."—*vāh vāh*—
Pālā Sānī took the horse and tied it to that rock.
The Bhāṭ said: "Hey Pālyā—*mhe*—where there is a rock, there is Līlā.
There is Līlā
Did you bring your father to tie up here—isn't there another one?
Yes, tie it at another rock—you'll harm me this way
The horse given by the Dūdās could kick out now and uproot the rock—
Your father."—*vāh vāh*—
He said, who said it now—Pālā Sānī.—*mhe*—
What does he say to the Bhāṭ, let's see.
Know it by saying it, let's see, by saying it, how does he say it

—*gāv*—

By God's grace, who said this, Pālā Sānī said this.—*vāh vāh*—
He said: "You were fifty, and became sixty.—*mhe*—
Hey, you've become an old man of seventy
You've left this eleven-year-old child in front of the lion.—*mhe*—
O Bhāṭjī, now how much time do you have left?
Hey, daughter's father, aren't you ashamed—how many days?
Yes, how many days do you have to live?

You've sent this child in front of the lion, and you're talking about living on!"—
vāh vāh—
Now Pālā Sānī said that.
Yes, he said that to the Bhāṭ
The Bhāṭ speaks—what does he say to Pālā.
Know it by saying it, by saying it

—*gāv*—

"By God's grace, you're the two sons of Raṇsī.—*mhe*—
I'm my mother Deḷū's only one
Hey, don't say bray like a donkey, you who belong to the clan of Kumahārs!—
mhe—
See the work of Dev now!
Look at the deed Dev will perform.
Yes, see what Dev Mahārāj is going to do, let's see
What he's going to do, let's see!"—*vāh vāh*—
Pālā Sānī said: "We'll see, daughter's father—don't you have any shame?"—*mhe*—
The Bhāṭ said: "I had shame, but, look you are two—if one dies then one will remain.—*mhe*—
I'm the only one of my mother!—*vāh vāh*—
Hey, when the Jogīṇīs ate me up in Malwa, Bhagavān revived me on account of my being one!"—*vāh vāh*—
By God's grace, in the meantime, the lion bathed—*mhe*—and returned
What kind of fight takes place between the lion and Dev? Let's see!
Know it by saying it, by saying it, let's see
I'll say it now, by Dev's grace, here you are.—*vāh vāh sā*—

—*gāv*—

The ill-fated lion returned.—*mhe*—
The lion came bounding on its front feet
The king cut down the forest's lion.—*mhe*—
The king cut it into pieces.
The lion fell on one side.—*mhe*—
The head *went and fell on another side*
The lineage's Bhāṭ was high up on the branch.—*mhe*—
Some of the sash he tore with his teeth
Some of the knot, by God's grace, he opened with his hands.
Immediately he fell down. *He jumped and fell down*
He pulled out the dagger from his waist
He pulled out the dagger and caught the tail.—*mhe*—
And started stabbing the lion
Dev Mahārāj said: "Hey, Bhāṭ, why are you stabbing a dead body.
Yes, why are you destroying it?
It'll come in handy for some ascetic.
Yes, "The skin will come in use," he said, "it can be spread out and sat upon."
The Bhāṭ said: "Listen, O Dev.—*mhe*—

Devnārāyaṇ beheads Pārvatī's lion.

Pālā Sānī praised you, and you got flattered instantly!
You don't know how to kill a lion!
Yes, what do you know!
You severed one vein.—*mhe*—
Look at the substance of nine veins and seventy-two billion! *I'm extracting them with my dagger*
I've killed the lion!"—*vāh vāh*—
Dev Mahārāj said: "Bhāṭ of the lineage can you kill a lion?"
Yes, I can kill one
The Bhāṭ said: "Sit and watch! *I won't take any time*
By God's grace, when I used to bring the Bagaṛāvats' shepherds' meals to the Mountain of Goram,
A couple of lions would come in front
I would catch the back of their necks.—*mhe*—
One I would scare them off in that direction
Yes, I would throw off their heads in that direction and go on my way."
The lord of the three worlds cast a look of mercy
One lion revived from the torso
One revived from the head.
"There you are Bhāṭ, both are prepared," he said.
Yes, here are two lions, now kill them
The Bhāṭ was in front and the lions were behind.
Yes, both lions got behind
The Bhāṭ turned back
And went around and the lions followed behind.—*vāh vāh*—

Dev Mahārāj said: "Bābā Bhāṭ, why are you doing this?"
Yes, why are you running away
The Bhāṭ said: "Hey, Śrī Mahārāj, my tongue is very fickle!
Yes, it's very fickle
What lion have I seen, and when did I kill one!
You manage your road on your own."
Yes, I can't traverse it
"Bābā Bhāṭ, can't you kill the lion?" *Can't be killed by you?*
"Hey, my lord, I haven't even seen one, and you're talking about killing one!"
The lord of the three worlds beckoned to the lions with a gesture.—*mhe*—
He said: "Go, brother, one of you return to the company of Pārvatī
One of you go into the forest."
Now in the forest where the lion had been released a caravan had passed through some six months earlier
Taking on a scent, the lion—*mhe*—
Departed and went in search of the caravan.
Dev said: "Hey, brother, call that creature back!"
Yes, "Call it back," he said, "it's taken up a scent of something
It won't spare the humans in the caravan."—*vāh vāh*—
After calling it back and taking hold of the back of its neck—*mhe*—
Dev Mahārāj hit it on the nose with his fist
"From now on you won't scent anything!"
Yes, you won't take up a scent at all!
"If a clever cowherd whistles, then jump away into the hills and mountains
If a king's drummer comes,
Then climb up and roar in front of him!"
Yes, come in front
He told Pārvatī's lion: "You return to the company of Pārvatī."—*vāh vāh*—

Chochū Bhāṭ Speaks to Mare Bāvlī

What did the king, the lord of the three worlds do—he departed.—*vāh vāh*—
So the Bhāṭ walked off the road.—*mhe*—
And Dev Mahārāj walked along the road
Dev Mahārāj said: "Bābā Bhāṭ,—*mhe*—
Why are you walking off the road?"
Yes, "Come onto the road," he said, "why are you running through the bushes?"
The Bhāṭ said: "Śrī Mahārāj, Dīyā's court is ahead.—*mhe*—
I'm saving myself."
Yes, I'm protecting my life!
The Bhāṭ had a sash.—*mhe*—
By God's grace, partridges were flying about in the forest.—*mhe*—
The Bhāṭ would throw his sash onto the ones that he saw.—*vāh vāh*—
He'd catch them alive.
Yes, he'd catch the partridges alive

He'd throw his sash onto partridges he saw walking in the grass.—*vāh vāh*—
He'd catch them alive
Catching hold of live partridges—*mhe*—
He tied them to his waist.—*vāh vāh*—
Dev Mahārāj said: "What are you doing?"
The Bhāṭ said: "Śrī Mahārāj, in Dīyā's court one has to provide testimony for truth and falsehood.
Yes, there's a divine discus
"If you lie—*mhe*—
Then your head falls off straight away.
It's a boon granted to him by Devī.—*vāh vāh*—
Without telling a lie, Dīyā will not release the mare."
By God's grace, he caught five or ten partridges—*mhe*—
And tucked them alive into his waist.—*vāh vāh*—
They arrived at the pond of Ṭīm.
Dev Mahārāj said: "Hey, Bābā Bhāṭ—*mhe*—
The outskirts of Sāvar have come, and Sāvar itself can be seen.—*vāh vāh*—
I'll send all of Sāvar to Baikuṇṭh *All of Sāvar will go to Baikuṇṭh*
I've come so far.—*mhe*—
Draw out the enemy on the mare this far.
The rest is between me and Dīyā!"
The Bhāṭ said: "Śrī Mahārāj—*vāh vāh*—
Dīyā won't release the mare without our telling a lie.—*mhe*—
If I lie, then right there and then my head
Yes, it'll fall down
Who'll bring the mare?"
Yes, the mare won't come here
Dev Mahārāj said: "Bhāṭ, the amount of salt we mix into flour—*mhe*—
For that much falsehood there's pardon. *"If you lie that much it's all right," he said, "I won't let any harm come to you."*
The Bhāṭ said: "Hey, Śrī Mahārāj, with that much falsehood, who knows how much I can achieve!"
Yes, I'll plant that town over here, and this town over there!
"Settle it there!"—*vāh vāh*—
By God's grace, the Bagaṛāvats' Bhāṭ departed for Sāvar.—*mhe*—
The lord of the three worlds stayed back at the pond. *He resided there*
By God's grace, Dīyā's water-bearers came to the water.—*mhe*—
They saw Bhagavān's face—*mhe*—
And fell in swoon.—*vāh vāh*—
They said: "Hey, water-bearers, two sun gods have arisen today at the pond!"
Yes, two sun gods have arisen!
On the day the Bhāṭ went to Sāvar—*mhe*—
At that time Dīyā's Prince Uttam Rāī's marriage was taking place
Dīyājī's Prince Uttam Rāī's marriage was on that day—trumpets and drums were played.
Amidst the fanfare the Sirdārs did not recognize anyone.—*vāh vāh*—

The Bhāṭ speaks—*mhe*—What does he tell Dīyā upon going there, let's see.
Know it by saying it, let's see, by saying it
I'll say it now, by the lord Dev's grace, here you are!—*vāh vāh sā*—

—*gāv*—

By God's grace, the Bhāṭ said this right upon going there
He said: "Dīyā Jodhkā, the day has set over your head.—*vāh vāh*—
Hey, the shadow of your great fort has subsided
How did such carelessness creep into Dīyā's kingdom—*mhe*—
That a guest receives no meal?
Hey, daughter's father, I'm dying of hunger!—*vāh vāh*—
By God's grace, who's paying attention here?"
Yes, who's keeping a watch?
So what does the Bhāṭ say? What conciliatory news does he tell Dīyā, let's see.
Know it by saying it, by saying it, let's see
I'll say it now, by Lord Dev's grace, I'll say it!—*vāh vāh*—*jī*—*vāh vāh*—

—*gāv*—

"O Dīyā, on others you showered money like rain in the month of Sāvan Bhādvo—*mhe*—
Hey, but in my case you took the rain away!
I ate with my own expenses, Mājhī Jodhkā.—*mhe*—
I've spent five months in your Sāvār
Hey, daughter's father, all my expenses have come to an end!"
Yes, five months have gone by!
Hey, I spent five months here, but tell me who is spending all the money?—*vāh vāh*—
You call musicians, but have lost your mind in the prince's wedding!"—*vāh vāh*—
Dīyā speaks.—*mhe*—
What does he tell Kālū Mīr, let's see.
Know it by saying it, now by saying it
I'll just say it, by Bhagavān's grace.—*vāh vāh*—*jī*

—*gāv*—

"By God's grace, don't play that kettle drum!—*vāh vāh*—
Don't play that trumpet
Hey, some seller of beads in the court has stayed hungry.—*vāh vāh*—
Now he's showering me with complaints
Hey, fathers of daughters," he said—*mhe*—
"You've kept the seller of beads hungry!—*vāh vāh*—
Stop the music!"—*mhe*—
So, by God's grace, what did the Bagaṛāvats' Bhāṭ do?—*vāh vāh*—
He wrote a false letter.—*mhe*—
And made up a plan of his own.—*vāh vāh*—
He took that letter and gave it to Dīyā:
"Here Dīyā, read this letter, brother."

Yes, take this letter
Dīyā said: "Hey, brother, where are you from?"
Where did you come from?
The Bhāṭ said: "I belong to Ajmer."—*vāh vāh*—
"Tell me, what's your name?"
"People call me Jagīśyā."—*vāh vāh*—
"Jagīśyā—*mhe*—
Ajmer is no new place for me—I've been coming and going there for a long time." *I've been coming and going there for a long time, but I never saw you*
"Yes, Śrī Mahārāj, you're right—you didn't see me.
Yes, you didn't see me
How would you see me? You know the ill-fated boy that was born to the Bhāṭ of Ajmer.—*mhe*—
He was born under an inauspicious sign
As soon as he was born, he was sent off to his natal home, and I accompanied him.
Yes, I was sent along
Śrī Mahārāj, tell me, how should I see you?"—*vāh vāh*—
The Bhāṭ speaks. What does he tell Dīyā, let's see. *Know it by saying it,*
Let's see, by saying it

—*gāv*—

"A boar has run from the boundaries of Ajmer
It came and hid at the Ṭīm Pond
First the prince gave me a small village with the proper authority—*mhe*—
Afterward the prince gave me five villages.
Yes, he said it on your name
Here, take these. *Take these, look after five villages*
By God's grace, my prince chased a boar with his horse.—*mhe*—
The boar ran at a distance of an arm's length, at a distance of an arm's length."—*vāh vāh*—
By God's grace, Dīyā said: "Hey, Bhāṭ, who told you, hey, brother, that the boar running at such a distance can't be caught."
Yes, tell me about that

—*gāv*—

"Cowherds happened to be in the forest—*mhe*—
My prince spoke to Dīyā's water-bearers when they arrived
Hey, they say that Savāī Bhoj's mare is with you.—*mhe*—
It can catch a live boar in its teeth
By God's grace, I was told that Bhoj's mare is with you."
Yes, it can lift up a living boar between its teeth
"My prince stopped at that place."
Yes, he left the horse's stirrups, alighted, and sat down
The water-bearers said: "Look, what kind of rider he is!"—*mhe*—

Hey, the water-bearers didn't get hold of the boar, which was an arm's length away.
Yes, didn't catch it,
"If, at this time, our lord, Dīyā, was riding
Yes, if he was riding the mare Bā̃vlī,
He would catch this boar alive now."—*vāh vāh*—
"My prince said, brother, if Bhoj's mare, Bā̃vlī, would only be here,—*mhe*—
And catch the boar alive, see, then I would be pleased.
Yes, then I'd be pleased
I've promised five villages already.—*mhe*—
And afterward I'll give you five more—I'll give you ten.
Yes, I'll do my best and give you five more villages
What will you do? Go and ride the mare, I'll catch the boar."—*vāh vāh*—
Dīyā said: "Hey, Bhāṭ—*mhe*—
It's been eleven years since the mare was taken away.—*vāh vāh*—
The mare hasn't been let free for eleven years, brother.
Yes, it hasn't been freed from the stake
You free it and bring it.—*mhe*—
I'll be able to get on it and ride, brother."
Mīr said: "Friend, Dīyā, something's amiss.
Yes, something seems wrong in the matter
Haven't you realized?"
Yes, this is the Bagaṛāvats' Bhāṭ!
Dīyā said: "You're not the Bagaṛāvats' Bhāṭ of the lineage are you—I've been cheated!"
Yes, I've been cheated in this matter!
The Bhāṭ said: "If I'm the Bagaṛā̃vāts' Bhāṭ, then I vow on this creature's life:—*vāh vāh*—
The partridge will die, *the Bhāṭ will survive.*"
Dīyā said: "Hey, Mīr,—*mhe*—
He's given an oath, brother!—*vāh vāh*—*he's truthful, he's not a liar!*
By God's grace, if he'd spoken a lie, then Devī's discus would have flown on its own.
Yes, Devī's divine discus would have flown, and the Bhāṭ's head would have fallen over there
Hey, Bhāṭ, go on, free the mare!"
The Bagaṛāvats' Bhāṭ had bottles of wine filled up.—*vāh vāh*—
He put them inside his shirt and went away.
The Bhāṭ speaks—*mhe*—
What does he say, let's see.
Know it by saying it, by saying it, let's see

—*gāv*—

The Bhāṭ said this—*mhe*—
"By God's grace, I searched Ḍhākā and Bengal, O mare, Mother Cā̃vaṇḍā!—*mhe*—

O Savāī Bhoj's mare Mother Cā̃vaṇḍā,—*mhe*—
if you're in the hills, then speak up

—*gāv*—

"By God's grace, I searched Ḍhākā and Bengal.—*mhe*—
I searched the four corners of Sāvar
Did the enemy Dīyā sell you to merchants?—*vāh vāh*—
Did Bhoj take you up to Bhagavān's Indra-Throne in heaven?
You went with Bhoj to heaven.—*mhe*—
The enemy Dīyā sold you off to merchants."
The Bhāṭ of the lineage said this
The mare speaks.—*mhe*—
What does she say, let's see.
Know it by saying it, by saying it

—*gāv*—

"O Bhāṭ, first you spoke at the market square.—*mhe*—
The second time you spoke at the enemy Dīyā's court
I recognized the Bhāṭ's language of home.—*mhe*—
That's why I neighed, Bhaṭ
I recognized you the very first time you spoke!"—*vāh vāh*—
Mother Mare spoke to the Bhāṭ.—*mhe*—
The Bhāṭ went to the black horse. Victory to Bhagavān Śrī Devnārāyaṇ, victory!
Say it both small and great, brother!

—*gāv*—

By God's grace, so when the Bagaṛāvats' Bhāṭ went to the mare, the black horse—*mhe*—
The mare spoke.—*vāh vāh*—
The Bagaṛāvats' lineage's Bhāṭ stands, how does he listen, let's see.
Know it by saying, now by saying it
I'll say it now, by Dev's grace, I'll say it.—*vāh vāh*—
"O Bhāṭ, in winter I suffered the cold wind.—*vāh vāh*—
In summer I was burnt by the hot wind
Look, Savāī Bhoj went up to Indra's throne.—*mhe*
That pain, O Bhāṭ, I'll only forget at death
Listen, hey, Bhāṭ—*mhe*—
I'll forget when I'm dead."
Yes, I won't forget before that
The Bagaṛāvats' Bhāṭ, by God's grace, thought in his mind: "It's been so many years since the mare was intoxicated, that's why she speaks so timidly. Here!"—*mhe*—
He poured liquor into the stone bowl.—*vāh vāh*—
He poured it into a bowl.—*vāh vāh*—

By God's grace, Mother Mare had the wine that was in place of the milk in the bowl.—*mhe*—
And became drunk.—*vāh vāh*—
What does she say to the Bhāṭ, let's see.

—*gāv*—

"My hooves, O Bhāṭ, look, brother, have become bad.—*vāh vāh*—
On my neck long hair has grown
Hey, Bhāṭ, they say that in Goṭhā̃ God has manifested, who'll show me the land of Badnor
By God's grace, is there anyone who'll show me the land of Badnor, O Bhāṭ?"
Yes, has anyone been born
The Bhāṭ said: "Be a little patient!"—*vāh vāh*—

—*gāv*—

"Look, O Bhāṭ, I drink water from the roof's drain.—*mhe*—
And the enemy Dīyā throws me trays of food
I've heard of Bāḷā Dev's incarnation.—*mhe*—
It looks as though the resident of Mathura has come to take me away
Bhāṭ is it him?"
Yes, is it him that's come or someone else?
The Bhāṭ said: "It's him
But Mother be a little patient."—*vāh vāh*—

—*gāv*—

"By God's grace, look, I drink water from the roof's drain.—*mhe*—
The enemy Dīyā throws me trays of food
Hey, I've heard of Dharamrājā Dev's incarnation.—*mhe*—
By God's grace, they say that Mathura's resident has arrived," said the mare.—*mhe*
The Bhāṭ said: "Brother, be a little patient!—*mhe*—
It's the resident of Mathura they speak of who's come along.—*mhe*—
It's that very one who's come to take you away."—*mhe—sā*

—*gāv*—

"I'll destroy your chains and wooden stake.—*mhe*—
O Mother Mare, I'll sever the rope around your neck
The Bhāṭ of the lineage is talking to you.—*mhe*—
O Mother, endure Dīyā's riding you a little
Listen, O Mother—*vāh vāh*—
You'll have to endure Dīyā's ride."—*vāh vāh*—
The mare said: "Hey, Bhāṭ—*mhe*—
I don't like very much what you're saying, brother.
Yes, I don't like this business of enduring Dīyā's ride
Only Bhoj sat on my back.—*mhe*—

With the exception of Bhoj, no one has climbed on my back, hey, brother, Bhāṭ."
Yes, I won't let anyone climb on
The Bhāṭ said: "Mother—*mhe*—
Of course Dīyā is an enemy, but he won't take you away."—*vāh vāh*—

Dīyā's Wife Reads the Bad Omens

"Bhagavān's shied away, brother.
Yes, you'll have to go to the Pond of Ṭīm
Bhagavān won't come this far."—*vāh vāh*—
The mare said: "Listen, hey, brother, Bhāṭ, I don't have the desire—on seeing the enemy, by God's grace, my eyes burn!—*mhe*—
But all right."
Yes, let's go!

—*gāv*—

He severed the chains around the mare's legs.—*mhe*—
And the Bagaṛāvats' Bhāṭ severed the rope around her neck
He let the mare loose on the outskirts of Fort Sāvar.—*mhe*—
Kiśan Murārī Dev's come to take her
"The one who's called Bhagavān you know—*mhe*—
That very one has arrived, but you'll have to go to the outskirts of Sāvar and carry the enemy on your back, brother."—*vāh vāh*—
What did Dīyā do to the mare? Mīr said: "Hey, brother, Dīyā, I'm not convinced.—*mhe*—
That's the Bagaṛāvats' Bhāṭ. *He's come along*
Do the following.—*mhe*—
It's the Bagaṛāvats' Bhāṭ—the Bhāṭ and the mare talk to one another.
Put a spy onto them!"
Yes, put spies onto them who can catch the conversation
Dīyā sent off four spies after them
The spies listened well to the conversation between the mare and the Bhāṭ
Then they went and said: "Śrī Mahārāj—*mhe*—
The mare and that man talk just like people talk to one another."
Yes, they do it very well
Thereupon Mīr called Dīyā: "Friend Dīyā, Dīyā Jodhkā, the Bagaṛāvats'
Bhāṭ has come."
Yes, it's him all right
Dīyā said—*mhe*—: "By God's grace, you're the Bagaṛāvats' Bhāṭ, brother."—*vāh vāh*—
The Bhāṭ said: "Śrī Mahārāj—*mhe*—
If I'm the Bagaṛāvats' Bhāṭ, then I swear on this creature's life.
Yes, I swear on this creature
The partridge will die, *the Bhāṭ will remain alive.*"

Dīyā said: "Mīr, what do you say, brother?"
Yes, he's not the Bhāṭ
Mīr said: "No, I see deceit, brother, I don't like it!"—*vāh vāh*—
Dīyā said: "Listen, hey, Bhāṭ!—*mhe*—
I sent my spies after you.—*vāh vāh*—
You and the mare talked like people talk to one another, hey, brother," he said.
Yes, you spoke very easily
The Bhāṭ said: "Śrī Mahārāj, it's a fact
If they lie then . . .
Yes, they're no liars
When the mare turned on me, I scolded it . . .
Yes, the well brought forth an echo!
They thought that we were talking!"

—*gāv*—

"Now the horse is a *kāgaḍā*.—*vāh vāh*—
While scraping its feet on Mother Earth it eats grass.
Hey, Mājhī Jodhkā, horses don't speak from their mouths.—*mhe*—
God made its tongue dumb
By God's grace, there are horses in your kingdom. *Vāh vāh, show me one at least!*
Hey, there are thousands of horses, bring one at least!—*vāh vāh*—
Daughter's father, he's lying!"—*mhe*—
Mīr said: "Dīyā, there's something wrong all right, brother.—*vāh vāh*—
By God's grace, he claims he's not the Bagaṛāvats' Bhāṭ.—*mhe*—
Bring the horse's bridle to the lord."
Mīr said: "Brother, Bhāṭ, I won't ride without a saddle.—*vāh vāh*—
Go to the stable, get the mare's saddle and bring it over."
The Bhāṭ thought: "The right thing's happened!"—*vāh vāh*—
By God's grace, the Bhāṭ reached the stable.
There were plenty of harnesses of ponies and horses.—*mhe*—
He pulled them down and threw them aside
At the same time he came upon the mare's saddle.—*mh*—
Bhoj's ruby helmet was tied onto of the mare's saddle.—*vāh vāh*—
The chain of armor,
Yes, that too was tied on it
The earrings also lay there
Now the sevenfold ornamented weapons—*vāh vāh*—
Of Bhoj, all of them were tied onto the top of that saddle.
Yes, yes, said sir.
The Bhāṭ thought: "The right thing has happened!"—*vāh vāh*—
Quickly Dīyā took it and, by God's grace, placed the bridle on the horse.—*vāh vāh*—
Mīr said: "What do you think!" *Isn't it the same Bhāṭ?*
"How should he otherwise know which bridle belongs to this mare," he said.

Yes, it's this bridle
Dīyā said: "Hey, Bhāṭ, I'm not coming with you!"—*vāh vāh*—-
"Why not? *Why aren't you going now?*"
"Because you're the Bagaṛāvats' Bhāṭ."
Yes, belonging to the Bagaṛāvats!
"O Śrī Mahārāj—*mhe*—
What did you recognize?" *How did you recognize me?*
Dīyā said: "Bring the bridle along—*mhe*—
Untie the mare and bring it over."
The Bhāṭ said: "Śrī Mahārāj, is this mare's bridle a secret for me?
Yes, it's not secret
The Bagaṛāvats would come and go through Ajmer all the time
I've put the saddle on this horse three times a day."
Yes, I've put it on
He told the complete truth there, brother.—*vāh vāh*—
"If you have a doubt, then I swear on this creature's life.—*vāh vāh*—
The partridge will die, and the Bhāṭ will remain alive."
By God's grace, Dīyā was cajoled and fooled into getting onto the horse

Dīyā's queen—*mhe*—
Said: "Maidservants—*vāh vāh*—
Today's a very bad day.
Go and stop my husband!"
Yes, go and stop him—I had a very bad dream at night
She commanded the maidservants: "Go, maidservants, by God's grace, tell him that his wife's calling him
Yes, don't go out now,
On this day!"—*vāh vāh*—
The maidservants arrived and said: "Śrī Mahārāj, it's our mistress's command that you don't go out today!"
Yes, don't step out!
The Bhāṭ thought: "I'll collect small stones and make a wall."
—*vāh vāh*—
Dīyā said: "Hey, Bhāṭ, I won't go now, hey, brother.
Yes, now I won't go along
You know my wife who is inside."
Yes, my wife's forbidden me
The Bhāṭ thought: "A darn thing indeed."—*vāh vāh*—

—*gāv*—

"In my house there are two wives
Two quarreling women
Hey, I smash one's omen into the other's!—*mhe*—
It shouldn't happen to me later, brother, Dīyā.
If I expect a hundred thousand—*mhe*—
What do both my wives come and do—they hold me back."

Yes, "Don't go out, don't fight," they say
Then I beat them two, four times with my shoes
If I go out expecting a thousand, a hundred thousand—*mhe*—
Then I get four hundred thousand.—*vāh vāh*—
You too go and break the omen a bit!"
Yes, my master, break the omen
Dīyā got into a rage—*mhe*—
And climbed up the palace of pleasure
By God's grace, he went up and struck the queen with a whip. *Said sir.*
The queen fell onto a pillar.—*vāh vāh*—
She received great pain from the pillar.—*mhe*—
Only once she was struck—the whip cracked, and the maidservants who
Were there took flight.
Yes, they ran away
The Bhāṭ turned around standing on the staircase.—*vāh vāh*—
He slapped each maidservant that came down and caught them all
He'd give them a slap and send them all down.
Yes, go!
Dīyā struck the queen thrice with the whip—*mhe*—
And returned down
In front of him the staircase was full with the maidservants.
Yes, they were crowded in the staircase
Dīyā said: "Hey, Bhāṭ, what did you do?" *What's this that you've done?*
The Bhāṭ said: "Śrī Mahārāj, you took the grain. *I've gathered the husks*
I was agitated in my mind.—*mhe*—
The queen gave the order, *but these maidservants came and forbade you themselves.*
That's why I broke the omen a little."
Yes, I'll smash this one's omen into the other one's
Dīyā thought: "*Beggar* sure is clever!"—*vāh vāh*—
By God's grace, Dīyā got onto the mare again. *Yes*—*vāh vāh*—
Now the queen speaks.—*mhe*—
Let's see what she says.
Know it by saying, let's see by saying it

—*gāv*—

"Look, to the left of my husband a kocarī[77] has spoken
O maidservants, the mountain has spoken its council
Lord Dev's spear—*mhe*—
Will strike. My husband's armpit will be full of blood
Brother, there's been such an omen.—*vāh vāh*—
Bhagavān's spear—*mhe*—
Will surely strike my husband!"
Yes, he won't escape being struck today!
By God's grace, the queen speaks.—*mhe*—
What kind of omen does she talk about? *Know it by saying it—by saying it*
I'll tell you now by Lord Dev's grace!—*vāh vāh*—*jī*—*vāh vāh*—

—*gāv*—

"Look, my husband met a cart pulled by black oxen.—*vāh vāh*—
O maidservants, he met water-carriers
He's being sucked away by time, O Hīḍāgar maidservants!—*mhe*—
Fort Sāvar's chief is passing away!
Look and see!
Yes, he's going today pulled away by time
He'll be struck by Dev Mahārāj's spear—*mhe*—
And four of my husband's teeth will break."
Yes, he'll have his teeth broken and return!
By God's grace, Dīyā encountered those very omens.—*vāh vāh*—
He came across a cart with black oxen.—*mhe*—
And met with water-carriers
Now, by God's grace, the mare was already prancing and dancing around with Dīyā on her.—*mhe*—
The Bhāṭ had a lemon with magic spells.—*vāh vāh*—
He hit the mare between the ears with it
By God's grace, the mare, hit by the lemon, became quiet immediately.—*mhe*—
Dīyā climbed on to the mare, donning the helmet and coat of armor.—*vāh vāh*—

The Bhāṭ said: "Great, great, brother, when Bhoj rode the mare he would shine.—*mhe*—
Dīyā, today you shine on the mare!"
Yes, you've shone
The horse sprang up—*vāh vāh*—
On to the gate and jumped down.—*vāh vāh*—
There was a crash on her jumping down.—*mhe*—
Dīya's helmet fell down with the impact.

Yes, it flew off in the other direction
Dīyā got off the mare
The Bhāṭ said from behind—*vāh vāh*—: "What's happened Śrī Mahārāj, why did you get down?"
Yes, why did you get off again?
Dīyā said: "Hey, Bhāṭ, a bad omen has happened, brother."—*vāh vāh*—
"What? *What bad omen has happened?" asked the Bhāṭ*
"The helmet from my head has fallen down, brother.
Yes, it's fallen down!
If something I take pride in falls down, then I'm sure to be defeated."
Yes, I'll lose—I won't ride now
The Bhāṭ said: "My lord, did it fall behind you or in front of you?"
Yes, tell me about that
Dīyā said: "To the front." *It fell toward the front*
The Bhāṭ said: "So you weren't in front?"
Yes, you won't go?

He jerked the helmet and placed it back on Dīyā's head
He placed it on his head and tightened it properly.
Yes, he fixed the button
"If the mare jumps up the enemy shouldn't stop again."
Yes, you shouldn't fall
The Bhāṭ said: "Śrī Mahārāj, be on your way now!"
Yes, go now
On the way, Dīyā came across the water-carriers
Dīyā speaks, let's see what he says to the water-carriers. *Know it by saying it, by saying it.*

He said: "Maidservants, water-bearers!"—*mhe*—
"Yes, Śrī Mahārāj, what is it?"
Dīyā said: "Is the ill-fated prince at the Pond of Ṭīm?"
Yes, has the ill-fated prince alighted there?
The water-bearers said: "Śrī Mahārāj, we don't know of any ill-fated prince.—*mhe*—
There were two suns blazing at the pond."
Yes, we saw two suns rise
Dīyā said: "Hey, Bhāṭ, I've been cheated again.—*vāh vāh*—
What are the water-bearers talking about?"
Yes, why are they talking of two suns?
The Bhāṭ said: "It's true what they are saying *they are truthful*
The mother-in-law told the daughter-in-law that she didn't have breakfast.
Yes, she hasn't eaten a meal
They came to the water—*mhe*—
And of course saw one sun outside, *and one they saw in the water*
You take a look too—I'll show you.
Yes, they are truthful
Not untruthful."—*vāh vāh*—
He convinced Dīyā completely.—*mhe*—
By God's grace, he cajoled and convinced Dīyā into arriving at the pond of Ṭīm.—*vāh vāh*—

Devnārāyaṇ Breaks Dīyā's Front Teeth

Dev Mahārāj, lord of the three worlds, was standing there astride on Līlā.—*mhe*—
Dīyā's and Dev's eyes met.
Yes, they met as soon as Dīyā reached the high bank.
Dīyā said: "Hey, Muṅgtā,—*mhe*—
You've deceived me greatly haven't you!"—*vāh vāh*—
Saying this he turned the mare about.
Yes, turned it about again
The mare's hooves rang out.—*mhe*—

The Bhāṭ said: "Śrī Mahārāj, I brought him here with great difficulty."
Yes, he shouldn't return now that he's come.
Dev Mahārāj said: "Bābā Bhāṭ—*mhe*—
I've a vow.
Yes, I won't chase someone who is running away
He's run away."—*mhe*—
The Bhāṭ reflected to himself: "Dev's denied the matter. Let's see, I'll speak to his horse, let's see."
Yes, let me tell the horse
The Bhāṭ speaks to the horse Līlā. Let's see what he says.
Know it by saying it, let's see, by saying it

—*gāv*—

"I'll break your shins—*mhe*—
By God's grace, Horse Līlā, I'll cut your mouth piece
Hey, at the distance of an arm's length—*mhe*—
Look, the enemy Dīyā is taking away the mare Bā̃vlī
Daughter's father, you're just standing there!" he said
Yes, what are you standing and looking at? Run and stop her
The horse said: "Bhāṭ, why have you gone crazy?—*mhe*—
Whose mare is it? *"Who is it, tell me!" Līlā said*
It's my maternal aunt—I won't run after my maternal aunt."
Yes, I won't chase my maternal aunt—won't look at her back
The Bhāṭ thought to himself: "Dev's turned down going after the mare—*mhe*—
Seeing the mare, Līlā also turned down the matter after him
So what is Dev to blame for?"—*vāh vāh*—
The Bhāṭ speaks. What does he tell Dev, let's see.
Know it by saying it, let's see, by saying it

—*gāv*—

"A horse encountered a horse.—*mhe*—
A chieftain met a chieftain; we met a horse's offspring
At least send these partridges flying off into the forest, O Giver of Grain!—*mhe*—
Which ones—the dead ones!—*vāh vāh*—
Revive these!" he said.—*vāh vāh*—
"Fly off these partridges into the forest, O king of Goṭhā̃, Chochū Bhāṭ is now free of his responsibility
It's up to you and your Dīyā and that mare.—*vāh vāh*—
I just had to do the introductions, which I did
I did the introductions," he said.
The lord of the three worlds cast a look of mercy—*mhe*—the partridges flew up and off into the forest
He pressed down Līlā's reins.—*vāh vāh*—
The horse went and passed in front of the outskirts of Fort Sāvar
Dīyā noticed it
—*vāh vāh*—

The lord of the three worlds stood in front of him.—*vāh vāh*—
Dīyā thought to himself: "Hey, look, I left the enemy way behind."
Yes, he's come up in front
By God's grace, what trick did Dīyā perform?—*mhe*—
Pigeons were pecking at grains of millet. He left the mare's reins
And changed his body.—*vāh vāh*—
He turned into a pigeon and began pecking at the grains inside the carts
The king thought, he's done some magic all right.—*vāh vāh*—
The lord of the three worlds left the horse's reins
And became a hawk, *said sir.*
By God's grace, what does he say; and let's see, what he says.
Yes, know it by saying it, now by saying it

—*gāv*—

Dīyā became a pigeon—*mhe*—
The lord of the three worlds became a hawk.
"I won't kill you this time, Dīyā!" Dev said.—*vāh vāh*—
"In the great battle of Rātākoṭ, I'll steal away your life-force
Get back onto the horse—don't fear, I won't kill you!" Dev said.
Yes, I won't kill you now!
Now, by God's grace, Dīyā thought: "He changed his body—*mhe*—
When you changed yours.—*vāh vāh*—
He'll strike you three or four times."
He thought to himself: "He won't leave you alive here!"
Yes, he won't leave you!
He caught hold of the pigeon's feet.—*vāh vāh*—
The lord of the three worlds said: "Dīyā, take on your own body again and get onto the horse!"—*vāh vāh*—
So Dīyā took on his body again—*mhe*—
And got up on the horse again
The lord of the three worlds got up onto Līlā, *said sir.*
As soon as he faced him, Bhagavān struck Dīyā with the back of his spear
Yes, onto his front teeth
His four front teeth broke off and fell down
Dīyā went into a daze and fell down off the Mare Bāvlī.—*vāh vāh*—
The Bhāṭ saw this
Yes, standing nearby
By God's grace, he picked up the teeth that fell to the ground—*mhe*—
And gave them to Dīyā: "Here, keep them, brother!"
Yes, I told you about the four villages!
"Look I told you I possessed them, didn't I!"
Yes, take these four villages!

Then the Bhāṭ started breaking up the chain of armor and tearing up the earrings.—*vāh vāh*—
Dev Mahārāj said: "Hey, Bābā Bhāṭ, why are you doing this?"

Yes, what are you doing?
The Bhāṭ said: "Śrī Mahārāj, who knows what you'll do—your father's mare is in hand.—*vāh vāh*—
I've only got the remainder
Yes, I have only this in hand"
By God's grace, Dev Mahārāj said: "Hey, Bhāṭ—*mhe*—
Let Mother Mare go, brother!
Yes, leave her!"
We've come to release the mare that God has given us from captivity.—*vāh vāh*—
We've freed the mare.
Yes, we've released it
Now if you were happy in Bhoj's home, then go onto Daṛāvaṭ!
Yes, go there!
If Dīyā kept the mare well, then it's all right for her to return to Dīyā's court!"
Yes, go to Sāvar
It took no time letting go of the mare
The mare leaped onto the path to Sāvar.—*vāh vāh*—
Now, the lookout with his friends and my friends in Dīyā's court
"Keep a watch," they said, "on the mare that throws off its rider. It's coming now."
Yes, it's coming after throwing off Dīyājī
The mare took three or four rounds of the fort.—*vāh vāh*—
They said: "Sirdārs, it won't enter like this.
Yes, it can't be caught this way,
Release the fillies that came along with it
Release them and catch them again
The mare will enter together with them." By God's grace, fillies had been captured along with the mare.—*mhe*—
All their chains were broken.—*vāh vāh*—
They joined the mare.—*mhe*—
When all the fillies were released the mare gave a leap.—*mhe*—
It didn't stay in the hold of any Sirdār.—*vāh vāh*—
It took the path to Daṛāvat
Dīyā's four teeth were broken; Bāvlī Mare's chains were cut after eleven years
Brother, victory to Śrī Devnārāyaṇ, victory!

Devnārāyaṇ Kills Uttam Rāī with his Stirrups

After Bhagavān released the Mare Bāvlī from its captivity—*mhe*—
He arrived at the Sā̃khlī Pass.—*vāh vāh*—
In the meantime, Prince Uttam Rāī arrived at Sāvar.—*mhe*—
He saw his father like this.
Yes, with broken teeth
The Prince got into a rage.—*vāh vāh*—
By God's grace, he came and stood in the way at Dev's Pass.—*mhe*—

"Let's see where you'll go now, brother," he said.
Yes, now I won't let you pass
Dev Mahārāj said: "Hey, brother, Prince Uttam Rāī—*mhe*—
you didn't take off the bracelets from your wrists, or worship the gods of the village
By God's grace, go back the way you came,
Yes, go on back
If you want an auspicious omen."—*vāh vāh*—
But Uttam Rāī was in a rage, why should he go back. He stood in the way.
Yes, he stood in the way
Then the king came in front of the horse.—*mhe*—
He struck out with the stirrups. The prince's head went and fell in the other direction.
Yes, "It fell in the other place," said sir.
With the impact of the stirrups.—*vāh vāh*—
It's written in the paṛ
By God's grace, he struck out with Līlā's stirrups so much that the prince's head broke with the stirrups!—*vāh vāh*—
By God's grace, the Bhāṭ spoke to the princess: "Śrī Mahārāj, widow, he stood in the way, the god struck him down first.—*mhe*—

The Search for Bhūṇājī

The lord of the three worlds, Bhagavān, came back—*vāh vāh*—
And sat down on the throne: "There you are, Bhāṭ, now I'll sit down, brother!"
Yes, now I'll sit on the throne
He resided on the throne.—*mhe*—
As soon as he sat down what happened, let's see—he summoned the Bhāṭ of the lineage, let's see.
Know it by saying it, let's see, by saying it

—*gāv*—

Devnārāyaṇ and Chochū Bhāṭ Plan Revenge

Now Dev resided on the royal carpet.—*mhe*—
Hey, brother, he summoned the Bhāṭ of the lineage
By God's grace, the lord of the three worlds, says: "Bābā Bhāṭ, Nirjan[78] is asking you about the truth
Bhāṭ of the lineage, be just—don't be unjust, brother.—*vāh vāh*—*Tell the truth!*
The way things happened,—*mhe*—

Tell me exactly what happened."
The Bhāṭ did not speak.—*vāh vāh*—. *He stayed silent*
The lord of the three worlds, Bhagavān, speaks.—*mhe*—
What does he tell the Bhāṭ, let's see. *Know it by saying it, let's see, by saying it*
I'll say it now, by Dev's grace!—*vāh vāh sā*—

—*gāv*—

"You're a man of previous times.—*mhe*—
Bābā Bhāṭ, you know about old matters
Look, in the battle the chief of Rāṇ was in the wrong—*mhe*—
My father Savāī Bhoj was in the right
Savāī Bhoj, you know, he was completely in the right
Rāvjī Sā was in the wrong." *Said sir.*
Who said this? *Dev Mahārāj said it*
Now the Bhāṭ of the lineage speaks.—*vāh vāh*—
What answer does he give to Bhagavān, let's see.
Know it by saying it, let's see, now by saying it

—*gav*—

"I'm a man of previous times.—*mhe*—
I know about all matters.
In the battle, the chief of Rāṇ was in the right.—*vāh vāh*—
Your father Savāī Bhoj was in the wrong
Savāī Bhoj fought wrongly.—*mhe*—
Rāvjī Sā absolutely fought rightly."
Dev Mahārāj said: "Hey, Bābā Bhāṭ—*mhe*—
Those whose salt and water you've taken."
Yes, you're slandering them
The Bhāṭ said: "Śrī Mahārāj, what do you suggest now?"
Yes, I spoke the truth
Dev Mahārāj said: "This is Dev's royal carpet—Bhagavān's court!—*mhe*—
Don't tell a lie here!"—*vāh vāh*—
The Bhāṭ said: "Śrī Mahārāj, I tell you only the truth!"
"Bābā Bhāṭ—*mhe*—how were the Bagaṛāvats in the wrong and how did
Rāvjī Sā get to being in the right—tell me about that in detail."
Yes, tell me in proper detail
By God's grace, the Bhāṭ speaks.—*vāh vāh*—
What does he say to Dev, let's see.
Know it by saying it, let's see, by saying it
I'll say it now, by Lord Dev's grace, let's see.—*vāh vāh—jī*

—*gāv*—

"The Paḍihār sons of Bāghjī exchanged turbans, brother.—*vāh vāh*—
They exchanged turbans sitting under the shade of the four-windowed balcony
Rāvjī Sā extended them his small finger.—*mhe*—

The Bagaṛāvats swallowed the whole arm together with the hand!
They swallowed it all."—*vāh vāh*—
Dev Mahārāj said: "Bhaṭ, you say you're not lying.
Yes, you've gone and told a lie
Hey, certainly a finger can fit into a human mouth.—*mhe*—
How do these hands and arms go in?
Yes, tell me how do they fit inside?
By God's grace, tell me this properly—I haven't understood at all!"—*vāh vāh*—
By God's grace, the Bhāṭ of the lineage speaks.—*mhe*—
What does he tell Bhagavān Dev, let's see.
Know it by saying it, let's see, by saying it now.

—*gāv*—

"By God's grace, the sons of Bāgh would drink cups of wine.—*mhe*—
The Bagaṛāvats brought unhappiness to the merriment
Hey, they eloped with Hindvā Rāv's queen.—*mhe*—
The Bagaṛāvats laid explosives in Rāvjī's palace
Rāvjī thought of his duty in such a manner—*mhe*—: The Bagaṛāvats were nephews seven times removed.
Yes, said sir.
He gave them to eat and drink
He considered them to be equal brothers.
And the Bagaṛāvats thought of their duty in such a manner:—*mhe*—
We'll lay our hands on Rāvjī's queen.
Yes, they laid explosives in his palace
Śrī Mahārāj, the Bagaṛāvats were killed because they took away the queen."—*vāh vāh*—
Dev Mahārāj said: "Bābā Bhāṭ, tell me whether the queen belonged to Rāvjī or to the Bagaṛāvats."
The Bhāṭ said: "Śrī Mahārāj, of course the queen belonged to Rāvjī!"—*mhe*—
Dev Mahārāj said: "Hey, Bhāṭ, then who received the mark on the forehead and the coconut from the great Śakti of Bū̃vāl first?"
Yes, who received it, tell me
The Bhāṭ said: "I'll tell you, hey, Śrī Mahārāj,—the mark on the forehead and coconut was received by the Bagaṛāvats."
Dev Mahārāj said: "By God's grace, who did Hīrādāsī first worship in Bū̃vāl?"
Yes, whom did she worship?
"Śrī Mahārāj, she worshipped Bhoj first."
"Who struck down the toran first?"—*mhe*—
The Bhāṭ said: "Śrī Mahārāj, the Bagaṛāvats struck it down."
"And did the queen circumambulate the sword before or after Rāvjī?" *Tell me was it before?*
The Bhāṭ said: "Śrī Mahārāj, Bhavānī Rāṇī said her stomach was paining.—*mhe*—
She asked for the sword first.

Yes, she took a round of the sword before she married Rāvjī
In pretence she sat together with Rāvjī and did the ceremonial rounds," *said sir.*
"In that case, Bābā Bhāṭ, what does Rāvjī want of the queen?
Yes, the queen belongs to Savāī Bhoj
He became the queen's husband just like that!"—*vāh vāh*—
The Bhāṭ said: "Śrī Mahārāj, only in pretense did the queen belong to Rāvjī.
Yes, she belonged to Rāvjī."
Dev Mahārāj said: "It's because of the queen that so much happened.—*vāh vāh*—
Bhāṭ, all this happened because of the queen."
Yes, because of the queen!
The Bhāṭ said: "Yes, Śrī Mahārāj!"—*vāh vāh*—
The lord of the three worlds speaks.—*mhe*—
What does he say in return, let's see.
Know it by saying it, let's see, by saying it
I'll say it now by Lord Dev's grace, let's see.—*vāh vāh*—*jī vāh vāh*—

—*gāv*—

"I'll return two queens for one.—*mhe*—
Bābā Bhāṭ, with one shout I'll make one thousand queens
Hey, we demand the sons of Bāgh back from Rāvjī.—*mhe*—
Bābā Bhāṭ we demand those very horses and those very riders!
The Bagaṛāvats took away one queen didn't they.—*mhe*—
I'll return two for one.—*mhe*—
If you want two hundred from two, I'll give them!
We want our Bagaṛāvats back."
Yes, give us them back!
By God's grace, the Bhāṭ said:
"Śrī Mahārāj, you're a divine person.—*mhe*—
You can turn one hundred thousand into two hundred thousand, and two hundred thousand into four hundred thousand.
Yes, who knows?
But Rāvjī Sā is born of humans.—*mhe*—
Not even one horse and one rider belonging to the Bagaṛāvats can he revive!"
Dev Mahārāj said: "Hey, Bābā Bhāṭ—*mhe*—
Rāvjī can't revive the Bagaṛāvats."
Yes, no they won't revive, Śrī Mahārāj
"No they won't revive, Śrī Mahārāj."—*vāh vāh*—
Dev Mahārāj said: "Then think of some quarrel through which I can extract the Bagaṛāvats' revenge," he said.
Yes, we can take revenge
The Bhāṭ said: "Śrī Mahārāj, whatever kind of quarrel you want, I'll create
In three hours or in three days—*mhe*—
I'll carry this mountain there, and that mountain there. I'll settle this town over there!"

The Bhāṭ said: "Śrī Mahārāj, do the following—*mhe*—have a well dug at the border of our forest and that of Rāvji's
Plate it over with gold
Rāvjī's water-carriers will come from that direction—*mhe*—
Ours will go from this direction
Like the species that women are, they won't be able to be without quarreling on the steps of the well
Some will exchange pads for carrying water pots, some shoes
Some will exchange bucket ropes. Rāvjī's water-carriers will go and call out to Rāvjī
And our water-carriers will call out to us
Rāvjī will come riding for battle from over there.—*mhe*—
We'll come riding for battle from over here
And strike again and again with our swords.—*mhe*—
We'll extract the Bagaṛāvats' revenge in a good way by the well."
Dev Mahārāj said: "Bābā Bhāṭ—*mhe*—
I don't like this quarrel."
"Why?"
"*Because it's a quarrel involving women*
It was in quarrel over women that the twenty-four Bagaṛāvats got killed. *vāh vāh*—
We're just five boys.
Yes, I don't like this idea
Look, brother, we're not all together yet."—*vāh vāh*—
The king's eyes opened wide when he talked about getting together: "Hey,
Bhūṇājī isn't with us!—*vāh vāh*—
By God's grace, hey, Bābā Bhāṭ, I don't like this quarrel at all."—*mhe*—
The Bhāṭ said: "Śrī Mahārāj, should I create another one?"
Yes, I'll create another one
"When it rains in the month of Jeṭh, Bhagavān—*mhe*—
What do our farmers and Rāvjī's farmers do? They sow the fields from east to west
Tell our farmers to sow the fields from north to south.
Rāvjī's farmers will go and give their petition to him
Our farmers will come and give their petition to us
From that side Rāvjī Sā will get ready for battle and arrive
From this side we'll get ready for battle and go.—*mhe*—
In the forest we'll extract the Bagaṛāvats' revenge in a good manner."
Dev Mahārāj said: "Hey, Bhāṭ—*mhe*—
Twelve months in a year, the farmers plough the fields for a living there.—*vāh vāh*—
We give people bread, brother, not take away people's work.
Yes, I can't bring myself to snatch away something, Bābā Bhāṭ
We're Givers.—*Vah vāh*—
This is bad—I don't like it."

The Bhāṭ said: "Śrī Mahārāj, I'll create a third quarrel now."
Yes, I'll put a third one to use
Dev Mahārāj said: "Yes, do it!" *Do it, Bābā Bhāṭ*
"You've been in the country of Mālāgar.—*mhe*—
You were looked after well by every household
You have nine lakh and eighty thousand cows.—*mhe*—
Tell the Nirpāl of Jāsā—*vāh vāh*—
When he sees Rāvjī Sai's full-grown summer harvest of wheat and chickpeas.
Yes, destroy the harvest
So let dharam be dharam and karam be karam
By God's grace, Rāvjī Sā will say: You destroyed my harvest
And we'll say: You captured our cows
We'll extract the Bagaṛāvats' revenge in proper manner!"
At this point, Dev Mahārāj praised the Bhāṭ:—*vāh vāh*—
"Great, great, hey, Bhāṭ you're a master quarrel-maker
All three ideas have come together
Yes, my home has all three things now
If the cows eat wheat then wealth increases there.—*mhe*—
Cow's milk increases with that
We'll extract the Bagaṛāvats' revenge there."
By God's grace, Dev Mahārāj said: "Bābā Bhāṭ—*mhe*—
Now where is Elder Brother Bhuṇā?
Yes, tell me that
How can we release those cows into the fields?—*vāh vāh*—
When our brothers are still scattered about?"—*mhe*—
The lord of the three worlds speaks.—*vāh vāh*—
What does he tell the Bhāṭ, let's see.
Know it by saying it, by saying it

Devnārāyaṇ Alters Chochū Bhāṭ's Appearance

By God's grace, Dev Mahārāj said: "Hey, Bābā Bhāṭ—*mhe*—
the search for Bhūṇo can't take place without you!"
Yes, go and find him
The lord of the three worlds said this.—*mhe*—
So what does the Bhāṭ say, what does he say to Dev, let's see. *Know it by saying it, let's see, by saying it.*

—*gāv*—

"O Giver of Grain, searches are done by Mīṇās and Bāvrīs.—*mhe*—
The kingdom's clever Mīṇā will do it
I'm the Bhāṭ of the lineage.—*mhe*—
Make me a twofold gift of money
Śrī Mahārāj, I'm a receiver of gifts!

I'll accept a double gift of money, if I will. How should I go about this business of searching for someone?"—*vāh vāh*—

Dev speaks:—*mhe*—

What does he say to the Bhāṭ, let's see. *Know it by saying it, now, by saying it, let's see.*

—*gāv*—

"You've let me down, Bhāṭjī," he said.—*mhe*—
"Gone away from work and duty
Hey, live in some pilgrim town.—*mhe*—
Then beg for grain and eat, go!
What worth are you for me?—*vāh vāh*—
You don't do my work, that's why you've let me down."—*vāh vāh*—
The Bhāṭ said: "Hey, Śrī Mahārāj, why are you doing this?
Yes, why do you say such things
Even if a dog belonging to the Bagaṛavāts' home enters Rāṇ City—*mhe*— enemy Rāvjī will have it killed.
If I go as a person, every boy knows me!
Yes, everyone in Rāṇ City knows me
Śrī Mahārāj—*mhe*—
If you want to destroy the ancestral record, then I'll go there.
If not, then, by God's grace, I can't manage the matter."—*vāh vāh*—
The lord of the three worlds cast a look of grace.—*mhe*—
He changed the Bhāṭ's body.—*vāh vāh*—
Dev speaks.—*mhe*—
What does he say to the Bhāṭ.
Know it by saying it, by saying it

—*gāv*—

He was sixty years old—*mhe*—
Fifty arrived—*vāh vāh*—
"You've become a strong youth, brother
You've become like a young man—take a mirror in your hands brother Bhāṭ.—*mhe*—
Look at your princely visage
Bhāṭ, take a look!"
Yes, what kind of face do you have[79]
Yes, the lord of the three worlds showed the Bhāṭ his face in the mirror.—*vāh vāh*—
He gave the Bhāṭ his own form—*mhe*—*he turned him into a youth of twenty-five years*
Bhagavān changed the Bhāṭ's body on account of the search for Bhūṇā.—*vāh vāh*—
The Bhāṭ's body was changed.—*mhe*—
They talked about the search for Bhūṇojī
Victory to Śrī Devnārāyaṇ Bhagavān, brother, victory!

The king said: "Hey, Bhāṭ—*mhe*—
Go to your mother, go to Deḷū.—*vāh vāh*—
If your life-giver recognizes you
Yes, then they'll recognize you in Rāṇ City
Otherwise you'll have to take up the search for Bhuṇā."—*vāh vāh*—
The lord of the three worlds, Bhagavān, gave the command for the Bhāṭ to go and meet his mother Deḷū.—*vāh vāh*—
Bhagavān gave the Bhāṭ his own features.—*mhe*—
By God's grace, the Bagaṛāvats' Bhāṭ arrived at his home.
So the Bhāṭ's mother speaks.—*mhe*—
Let's see what she says to the Bhāṭ, let's see.
Know it by saying it, let's see, by saying it
I'll say it now, by God's grace, here you are.—*vāh vāh—sā*

—*gāv*—

Chochū Bhāṭ Meets His Mother and Wife

Deḷū Mātā said—*mhe*—: "O King, the shining robes give you splendor—*mhe*—
With their golden seams
Deḷū Bhāṭṇī is talking to you, Śrī Mahārāj—*mhe*—
What made you come today to the lane in which Bhāṭs live?
Hey, Giver of Grain, why did you come to my street?"
Yes, why have you come?
The Bhāṭ said to himself: "She hasn't recognized me!"—*mhe*—
The Bagaṛāvats' Bhāṭ speaks.—*mhe*—
What does he tell his mother. *Know it by saying it, let's see, by saying it*

—*gāv*—

"The shining robes give splendor," he said—*mhe*—
"Inside they have golden seams
I came out to play ball.—*mhe*—
I didn't pay attention and came into the lane where Bhāṭs live
Brother, I didn't pay attention."
Yes, I turned up here playing ball
Then as the Bhāṭ laughed, the Bhāṭ's wife saw his thirty-two teeth.—*vāh vāh*—
So the Bhāṭṇī—the Bhāṭ's wife, speaks.—*mhe*—
What does she say, let's see.
Know it by saying it, let's see, by saying it.

—*gāv*—

"O Mother-in-law, his features look like my husband's.—*mhe*—
His face is like the flame of a lamp
The Bhāṭ's wife says to you—*mhe*—
O Mother, how did you forget the features of your offspring?

Isn't that your son?"
Yes, have you forgotten your son's features?
Deḷū Mātā was grinding rice and lentils together at the time.—*mhe*—
You know that thing, a pestle—some call it *kevaṭṇo.*
Yes, some call it kevaṭṇo, and some
Call it mūsal. *Some call it mūsal*
She took the pestle in her hands and went after the Bhāṭ
"By God's grace, my son's an old man—have you come to deceive my son's wife!
Yes, have you come to cheat her?
By God's grace, you're falsely making Dev, the Lord, into my son."—*Vāh vāh*—
She took the pestle and went after him. Over there she scolded her daughter-in-law.—*vāh vāh*—
The Bhāṭ laughed.—*mhe*—
He said: "Mother, why are you doing this—aren't I your son, Chochū?"
Yes, I'm really him
He had laughed a little when he spoke to Deḷū Mātā.—*mhe*—
She noticed his teeth, and said: "Why is there no difference in these damn teeth?"
Yes, they look exactly the same
Deḷū Mātā speaks, what does she tell the Bhāṭ?
Know it by saying it, let's see, by saying it

—*gāv*—

"Brother, Chochū, which ascetic's fire did you tend?—*vāh vāh*—
Which place did you meditate? Your mother says to you:—*mhe*—
Hey, Son, which man changed your body?
Who transformed your body, brother?"
Yes, who gave you this form
The Bhāṭ speaks. What does he tell his mother, let's see. *Know it by saying it, let's see, by saying it*

—*gāv*—

"Bhoj's ascetic fire in Daṛāvaṭ—*mhe*—
I tended because of his moral strength, the ascetic fire—*vāh vāh*—
Hey, I meditated in Goṭhā̃
Dharamrājā Devjī has ordered the search for Bhūṇo. *My body was transformed by Ūdojī*
You know that Devjī of ours.
Yes, he changed my body
But Mother we're conducting a search for Bhūṇojī—what do you say to that?"
Yes, tell me that!
Deḷū Mātā said: "Hey, son, I suckled you and did not recognize you—how will the chief of Rāṇ City recognize you?
Yes, how will they recognize you

Go without fear," she said.—*vāh vāh*—
As the Bhāṭ got ready to go—*mhe*—
Dev Mahārāj said: "How can this be!
Yes, how can this be!
Bābā Bhāṭ take a letter along," he said.—*vāh vāh*—

—*gāv*—

Bhagavān wrote a letter and sent it off.—*mhe*—
In it he wrote many lines.
"Read the letter and return soon, Bhūṇojī—*vāh vāh*—
Hey, your father's Bāgor lies barren
I've established the Bagaṛavāts' village.—*mhe*—
But your father's village of Bāgor
Yes, it lies barren."
Sāḍū Mātā said: "Wait a moment, Bhāṭjī!"
Yes, take one letter written by me!
Pā̃cyā Paṭel said: "It shouldn't happen that I don't send my greetings to Bhūṇā!"—*mhe*—

—*gāv*—

Sāḍū Mātā wrote a letter and sent it off.—*mhe*—
She wrote it on a letter leaf
"Read the letter and return soon,—*vāh vāh*—
Because your mother has become very old
Son, I'm about to fall now, brother!
Yes, I'm about to go!
You have to meet me!"
Yes, come soon!
Queen Pīpalde thought to herself: "You'll be left behind!"
Yes, you too write a letter to Elder Brother-in-law with the others

—*gāv*—

Now Queen Pīpalde wrote a letter and sent it off.—*mhe*—
She wrote it behind her veil
"Read the letter and return soon, my dear brother-in-law.—*mhe*—
While coming strike down upon the enemy's roof
Don't let it happen that you come without making a mark!"
Yes, definitely make a mark and return
By God's grace, as the Bhāṭ was about to depart, Dev Mahārāj's wife, Pīpalde's—*mhe*—
senses all became enthralled.—*vāh vāh*—
A good deed had been done.

—*gāv*—

She wrote a second letter and sent it.—*mhe*—
She wrote it on a letter leaf

"Read this letter and return soon!—*mhe*—
Hey, who will keep the dignity of this young wife?
I'm the child amongst you."
Yes, if you come then my honor will be raised
By God's grace, Bhāṅgījī said: "Hey, Bābā Bhāṭ—*mhe*—
Take a small letter from me too!"
Yes, take one from me too

—*gāv*—

Bhāṅgījī wrote a letter and sent it off.—*mhe*—
He gave his moustache a twirl
"Read the letter and come soon.—*mhe*—
Otherwise I'll ground you together with the enemies like chilis
You'll be ground together with the enemies.—*vāh vāh*—
I don't care!—*mhe*—
I take one and a quarter maṇ of bhaṅg at dawn.—*vāh vāh*—
After that I can't discern between my own and others
Here Bhāṭ, take this small letter of mine and give it,
Yes, to Bhūṇājī."
By God's grace, what other letter does Bhāṅgījī give, let's see.
Yes, know it by saying it
I'll say it now by Dev's grace

—*gāv*—

Bhāṅgījī wrote the letter and sent it off.—*vāh vāh*—
By God's grace, he wrote heaps and heaps.
"Read this letter and come soon.—*mhe*—
With one hit of my club I'll destroy your Bābājī's nine-yard-high Red Fort
I keep a whip in one hand.—*mhe*—
I'll give one lash with my whip and destroy the Red Fort.—*vāh vāh*—
So much strength!" he said.
Yes, your Bābājī has only so much strength
Pā̃cyā Paṭel told the Bhāṭ: "Hey, Bhāṭ,—*mhe*—
Brother, take a letter written by me too!"
Pā̃cyā Paṭel wrote a letter and had it sent. In it he wrote a lot of lines.
"Read this letter and come soon, brother Prince Mahābalī.—*mhe*—
Your father's Bāgor lies barren
Look, Bhūṇo, the village of Bāgor lies barren," he said—*vāh vāh*—
By God's grace, "There you are, go now, sir."
Yes, go
"Put the letters into the bag—*mhe*—
We've written very special letters—Bagaṛāvats' Bhāṭ fill up the bag with the letters."—*mhe*—
And, by God's grace, the horse Phūlrīyā's body hadn't been changed.—*vāh vāh*—
The Bhāṭ said: "Hey, Śrī Mahārāj, you've done my body—*mhe*—
But should this horse get through?"

Yes, he's the same old horse
Dev Mahārāj said: "Bhāṭ, think of me—*mhe*—
I'll handle it, if bad times befall you, then remember me.
Yes, whenever you want, remember me
Wherever you are, I'll be present at that place."—*vāh vāh*—
The Bhāṭ said: "Great, great, Lord, then I have no fear!"
Yes, then I'll bring Bhūṇojī back for sure
By God's grace, Bhūṇojī climbed onto the horse Phūlrīyo.—*mhe*—
He rode off with the horse
By God's grace, in the forest—*mhe*—
There was a śīras tree. What did the Bagaṛāvats do—when they came to that spot they would rest under the śīras tree.—*vāh vāh*—
They would spread out a carpet, strew flowers, and play a game of caupaḍ pāsā on it
On the branches they would hang leather bags full of liquor, by God's grace, they would hang leather bags.—*vāh vāh*—
What did the śīras tree do after the Bagaṛāvats died?—*mhe*—
It dried up and became withered
After Dev incarnated—*mhe*—
What did it do? Its roots turned green again.
Yes, they turned green again, said sir.
By God's grace, the Bhāṭ speaks—how does he reprimand the śīras tree, let's see.
Know it by saying it

—*gāv*—

"O Śiras, why didn't a porcupine dig up your roots?—*mhe*—
Hey, by God's grace, why didn't some summer wind shake you from side to side?
Hey, how did you forget those men, O enemy śīras?—*mhe*—
How did your branches turn green today?—*mhe*—
By God's grace, you've forgotten those men!—*mhe*—
And have turned so green!"—*vāh vāh*—
The tree said: "Bhāṭ, why have you gone crazy?
Yes, why are you crazy?
Do you have any idea why the dry branches turned green again?
Yes, do you have no idea at all?
Why should a porcupine dig out my roots?—*mhe*—
Why should a summer stream catch hold of me?
Bāḷā Ṭhākur Dev has taken incarnation in Goṭhā̃—*mhe*—
That's why my roots have grown down into the underworld
They returned to the underworld—*vāh vāh*—
At the time when Bhagavān took incarnation."
Yes, that's the time they turned green again
The Bhāṭ thought. "I know your mother—even a tree of the forest recognizes Bhagavān.—*vāh vāh*—

Now what?"—*mhe*—
So the Bhāṭ departed from the śīras, he reprimanded it.—*mhe*—
And Bhūṇā's search took place, the Bhāṭ departed. Victory to Śrī Devnārāyaṇ.

By God's grace, afterward Bhagavān told the Bhāṭ: "Look, Bhāṭ—*mhe*—
I don't have much time—don't delay things!"
Yes, don't take too much time!
By God's grace, the Bagaṛāvats' Bhāṭ reached the well of Ambesar, *said sir.*
The Bhāṭ thought to himself: "It'll take a lot of time talking to the well's water-bearers.—*mhe*—
And the water-bearers seeing me, won't recognize me."
Yes, let's see if they recognize me or not
Nārdī Bhāṭ sat down on the steps and began washing his face and rinsing his mouth
Now the water—*mhe*—
When the Bhāṭ sat down there—after the Bagaṛāvats died, the well's water sank back into the underworld.—*vāh vāh*—
So Bhāṭ said: "Hey, Well—*mhe*—
Why have you become so deep, tell me about that!"
Yes, speak

The well said: "Bhāṭ, what sort of thing are you asking!—*mhe*—
The Bagaṛāvats collected rocks together," it said.—*vāh vāh*—
By God's grace, they made the well out of expensive stone—say one praise of the Bagaṛāvats, and the water will leap up nine steps high.
By God's grace, I was dug by them.—*mhe*—
Sing one praise, brother
Yes, say one praise and I'll leap up the steps
The Bhāṭ said: "I'm Bhagavān's messenger, can't you see?—*vāh vāh*—
Look at these letters."—*mhe*—
By God's grace, taking the Bagaṛāvats' name, taking Dev's name, the water surged up from the underworld
It came up nine steps to the Bhāṭ
The Bhāṭ washed and rinsed his mouth—*mhe*—and departed from that place.

Chochū Bhāṭ Stays Overnight with Leṇūdī Kumahārī

He arrived at Leṇūdī Kumahārī's house, *said sir.*
The sun had set—*vāh vāh*—*time to eat and drink*
The Bhāṭ thought to himself: "Kaḷālī's big house is far off
I'll stay here the night at Leṇūdī's home. *Then things will be all right*
The Bagaṛāvats' Bhāṭ goes to Leṇudī Kumahārī's home
What does he say to the Kumahārī, let's see.
Know it by saying it, let's see, now, by saying it
I'll say it now, by Bhagavān Dev's grace, let's see.—*vāh vāh*—*jī*—*vāh vāh*—

—*gāv*—

"The sun has set over my head.—*mhe*—
Everywhere there is darkness
I want to stay for the night, O Kumahār's daughter, I'll leave at dawn whether
It rains or storms
When it's dawn—*mhe*—
I'll be on my way soon."
Who said this? *The Bhāṭ of the lineage said this, said sir.*
Leṇūdī Kumahārī speaks.—*mhe*—
Let's see what she tells the Bhāṭ.
Know it by saying it, let's see, by saying it
I'll say it now, by Bhagavān Dev's grace, here you are.—*vāh vāh jī*

—*gāv*—

"Only a widower stays inside the gate.—*mhe*—
Hey, in the lanes there are Chālar, and Bhī̃ḍal cows
Stranger, set up tent in the Aḍadū Bazār.—*vāh vāh*—
If you're hungry, come in and eat some rābaḍī
There's no question of staying here at home, brother.
Yes, there no question—no place at all here
If you're hungry or thirsty—*mhe*—
Then drink some rābaḍī in my house, and move on."
The Bhāṭ speaks
What does he say to Leṇūdī Kumahārī, let's see.
Know it by saying it, let's see, by saying it

—*gāv*—

"I'll lay out the blanket belonging to my horse.
I'll go and sleep behind your kitchen where pots are cleaned[80]
I'll get up early and get on the road, Kumahār's daughter.—*mhe*—
I'll wash the blanket in the pond ahead
The blanket could get a little dirty, nothing else will happen.—*vāh vāh*—
I'll go ahead and wash it myself.—*mhe*—
And I'll use soap, Surf,[81] what else could I do?—*vāh vāh*—
Give me refuge for the night!"
Yes, let me stay here
She said: "Hey, no, Bhāṭ—*mhe*—
There's no question of staying here."
Yes, no question about it here
By God's grace, what did he do—he thought to himself: "Dev Mahārāj told
me to."—*mhe*—
Taking Dev's name, the Bagaṛāvats' Bhāṭ put his hand in his pocket
Five golden coins appeared, *said sir.*
He said: "Leṇūdī Kumahārī,—*mhe*—
Here, brother, give me a place to stay if you wish to.

Yes, if you like to, then do so
These five coins were given to you by Sāḍū Mātā for a bodice."
Leṇūdī Kumahārī said: "Hey, Bhāṭ—*mhe*—
Don't you belong to the Bagaṛāvats?
Yes, you're not the same one are you?
The Bhāṭ said: "I'm the very same one!"
Yes, I am
She said: "Hey, Bhāṭ, after the Bagaṛāvats died I don't see too well, brother.—*mhe*—
I didn't recognize you!"
Yes, I didn't recognize you!
He said: "And now?" *Now I recognize you*
By God's grace, what does Leṇūdī Kumahārī tell the Kumahār to do.—*mhe*—
How does she give the Bhāṭ a place to stay, let's see. *Let's see, know it by saying it, know it by saying it*

—*gāv*—

"Get the donkeys together from the gate.—*mhe*—
Get together, brother, the Chālar, and Bhī̃ḍal cows from the lanes
Hey, brother, this stranger has come after many days.—*mhe*—
I want to talk about those past matters
We'll talk about good and bad times, brother.
Yes, we'll talk about the good and bad times in the house of the Bagaṛāvats
Kumahār, bring two cots for the Bhāṭ."—*vāh vāh*—
The Kumahār ran and got two cots for the Bhāṭ and set them up
On one cot the Bhāṭ untied the bags tied around his waist.—*mhe*—
On one cot he sat down.
The Kumahārī made hot water and pressed his feet
She gave the horses a bag with about five kilos or so of chickpeas and oats
She made good bread from wheat and gave King Bhāṭ to eat, *said sir*
Both of them talked the night through about good and bad times of the house of the Bagaṛāvats
Then dawn came
The Bhāṭ put back the saddle on the horse Phūlrīyo
After he put back the saddle, he thought to himself:
"At night Bhagavān gave you the gold coins.—*mhe*—
That's why she gave me shelter
I've come on account of Bhūṇājī.—*mhe*—
Who knows whether it'll take six months or twelve months
This evening I may or may not be given gold coins.
How many days can I stay on here handing out gold coins?
Things will work only if I get these gold coins back."
While departing he said: "Leṇudī Kumahārī!"—*mhe*—
"Yes, brother Bhāṭ, what is it?"
Yes, at night I made a great mistake
"What mistake?" *Tell me*

The Bhāṭ said: "I stayed in Nagaur.—*mhe*—
Look in Nagaur, times were bad, I had used ample coins
The coins Sāḍū Mātā gave me, they're in this pocket
Lady, I gave you false coins at night.—*mhe*—
That was wrong."
Yes, that went the wrong way, mother!
She said: "O Bhāṭ, one shouldn't give a sister or daughter a bodice.—*mhe*—If one does, then a very good one
That can be washed and worn twelve months long
When it tears, it can be put into a blanket, and be wrapped around and worn twelve months long like that."
He said: "Gold coins exactly like those, *return them to me!"—vāh vāh*—
So Leṇūdī Kumahārī standing close by said: "Here take last night's gold coins back!"—*mhe*—
The Bhāṭ put his hand in his pocket
By God's grace, he took out a bag of coins
"Here, brother, Leṇūdī Kumahārī—*mhe*—
This coin's for the night spent here. *Take it*
And this coin's for the fodder given to the horse.
Yes, take it for that
This coin's for the two round loaves of bread you gave me.
Yes, take this
Woman, it's amounted to only three coins—you've pocketed the fruits of hard labor—not your husband's earnings—the golden coins don't belong to your father!"
Yes, taking five gold coins weighing fifty grams each!
Having said this he rode his horse off.—*vāh vāh—let's go!*
The Kumahārī thought to herself: "Damn, it's good thing he did!—*mhe*—
He stayed here the night.—*mhe*—
And took back the gold coins.
But you do this.—*mhe*—
Go and tell the Rāṇā's generals before he reaches."
Yes, they'll put him into the grain grinder and squash him as soon as reaches
So Leṇūdī Kumahāri climbed high up onto the palace.—*mhe*—
Let's see what she shouts out to Rāvjī's generals. *Know it by saying it,*
Bhopājī Mahārāj, know it by saying it, now
I'll say it now by Dev's grace, here you are.—*vāh vāh—jī—vāh vāh*—

—*gāv*—

"Listen to my summons, King Nīmde!—*mhe*—
Hey, listen Dīyājī, strong warrior
That Bhāṭ of the Bagaṛāvats has come to Rāṇ City today.—*vāh vāh*—
At dawn he'll take away Bhūṇojī, the great warrior
Bhūṇojī, who is with you—*mhe*—
His claimant has come, brother."
Yes, his claimant has arrived

The Bhāṭ said: "The widow is getting me killed!"
Yes, she's tattling on me
She said: "What should I do? You went and did a good thing!"—*vāh vāh*—
He said: "Just you wait!" *Wait right here*
The Bagaṛāvats' Bhāṭ halted his horse.—*vāh vāh*—
He halted his horse and spoke to it. What did the Bhāṭ say, let's see.
Know it by saying, Bhopājī Mahārāj, by saying it now, let's see
I'll just say it, by the Lord's grace, brother.—*vāh vāh sā*—

—*gāv*—

"Listen to this summons now, brother, Dīyājī Jodhkā.—*vāh vāh*—
Listen to the summons Prince Nīmājī
Hey, the Bagaṛāvats' indestructible golden image—*mhe*—
Is with this Leṇūdī
All the Bagaṛāvats' wealth and money,
Yes, it's with this Leṇūdī Kumahārī."
The Kumahārī said: "Goddammit, you'll finish me off"
Yes, you've done me great good
The Bhāṭ said: "I haven't done anything yet! *Now I'll do it, just wait!*
I've just entered Rāṇ City!"—*vāh vāh*—
She said: "I won't take your name!
Yes, go on!
You go on ahead!"—*vāh vāh*—
The Bagaṛāvats' Bhāṭ is riding through the bazaar.—*mhe*—
He met the Rāv's Bhāṭ, Gā̃go.—*mhe*—
They clasped each other and met well—*vāh vāh*—
The Bagaṛāvats' Bhāṭ was from Nagaur.—*mhe*—
And Gā̃go Bhāṭ's mother too was from Nagaur. *Said sir*
They were maternal cousins.—*vāh vāh*—
Gā̃go Bhāṭ said: "Hey, Bhāṭ, where were you at night, brother?"
Yes, where were you at night?
The Bhāṭ said: "I was at Leṇūdī Kumahārī's home."
Gā̃go Bhāṭ said: "And today?" "*Today I'll go to your house*
There you are!"—*vāh vāh*—

—*gāv*—

"The horse ran off, brother—*mhe*—
Neighing. Look, at home the children have been affected by Mātā[82]
Stranger, pitch your tent in the marketplace.—*vāh vāh*—
If you're hungry, then come drink rābaḍī at my home
There's no question about staying here.
Yes, there's no question about staying here—the children have been affected by Mātā
You have a horse with you.
Yes, if some fodder falls down, Mātā could get enraged."
Who said this? *Gā̃gā Bhāṭ said it, said sir.*
The Bagaṛāvats' Bhāṭ speaks. What does he say to Gā̃gā Bhāṭ again, let's see.

Know it by saying it, Bhopājī Mahārāj, now, by saying it
I'll say it now, by Lord Dev's grace, I'll say it, brother.—*vāh vāh jī—vāh vāh*—

—*gāv*—

Take the name of Demālī Nāth—*mhe*—
Always. *Very good, said sir.*
By God's grace, Chochū Bhāṭ said this.—*mhe*—
He said: "In other people's homes, you and your father used to untie the pouches on their waists on two cots each.—*vāh vāh*—
You've always been a great talker
Hey, you never gave any Bhāṭs who came a place to stay.—*mhe*—
Gā̃glā Bhāṭ, you've always been avoiding people because of expenses
This house has always been an avoider of expenses.
Yes, you've always avoided
No one will remember giving a son of the community rābaṛī to drink, brother.—*vāh vāh*—
You know when you go home."
Yes, how people really are. Gā̃gā Bhāṭ said: "Hey, Bhāṭ, if Rāvjī's generals find out—*mhe*—
That the Bagaṛāvats' Bhāṭ is at Gā̃gā Bhāṭ's home . . .
Hey, they'll kill you anyway. *But, they'll kill me together with you too*
Why are you asking to die, hey, brother!"—*vāh vāh*—
The Bhāṭ said: "Don't worry—don't be afraid!—*vāh vāh*—
I'm going to big people's homes.—*mhe*—
The path doesn't cross homes of people like you!"
Yes, "I'm not staying here"

Chochū Bhāṭ Visits Pātū Kaḷālī

He came to Parmā Modī's store at the entrance of the marketplace.—*vāh vāh*—
When the Bagaṛāvats used to come to Rāṇ City—*mhe*—
Goods were ordered from Parmā Modī's store.
Everything would go from there, said sir
By God's grace, the Bagaṛāvats' Bhāṭ speaks.—*mhe*—
What does he say to Parmā Modī upon arriving. *Know it by saying it, let's see now, by saying it*
I'll say it now, sir, by Dev's grace, let's see.—*vāh vāh—jī—vāh vāh*—

—*gāv*—

"Throw open the store—*mhe*—
Parmā Modī's son, I'm getting late by the minute!
Hey, the sons of Bāgh Siṅg have returned from Indra's throne.—*vāh vāh*—
Their camp is at the very wonderful Nolke Garden
The Bagaṛāvats have returned from Indra's throne.—*vāh vāh*—
All the things that used to go before from your store, for cooking and so on."

Yes, get all those things ready and deliver them
By God's grace, Parmā Modī speaks.—*mhe*—
What does he say to the Bhāṭ, let's see.
Know it by saying it, now, let's see, by saying it

—*gāv*—

Take Demālī Nāth's name—*mhe*—
Always! *said sir*
Parmā Modī said: "It looks like the stupid Bhāṭ has gone crazy!—*vāh vāh*—
He's become like a peacock in the middle of the forest!—*mhe*—
Hey, where have you brought the sons of Bāgh from?—*mhe*—
Bhāṭ, you must have seen some others on the road
It's the month of Kārttik now.—*vāh vāh*—
On all the roads pilgrims are journeying to the Puṣkar Fair.
Many drum-playing Sirdārs got here.—*mhe*—
It used to be a kings' fair earlier.—*vāh vāh*—
Which one? *The Puṣkar Fair*
Horses and others would certainly come.—*vāh vāh*—
By God's grace, why did you come—tell me that."
Yes, tell me exactly
The Bhāṭ diverted Parmā Modī's attention.—*mhe*—
Taking Dev's name, he put his hand in his pocket and out came five gold coins, which he hid inside the store.
Yes, he hid them secretly, said sir.
The Bhāṭ said: "Parmā Modī, so you won't give the things!"
Yes, I won't deliver the things
"Have you gone crazy—what things? Do you know when the Bagaṛāvats died?—*vāh vāh*—
You've made such a racket!"—*mhe*—
The Bhāṭ picked up a basket of sweets and ran off.
Parmā Modī said: "Just you wait—you've been stealing things for many days."
Yes, there's a thief!
After taking off his shoes—*mhe*—
Parmā Modī caught up with the Bhāṭ—*vāh vāh*—
The city's Mahājans[83] collected together.—*mhe*—
They said: "He's a prosperous, grand man. He has the finest clothes to wear
The finest pair of sandals are his
By God's grace, why are you dishonoring him, brother, hey!"
Yes, Parmā Modī, why are you doing this?
The Bhāṭ said: "Traders, bankers—*mhe*—
Take stock of his store, brother—how many goods does he have?"
Yes, how much goods and money is he the proprietor of?
They said: "A hundred or two would be a lot for him to have."—*vāh vāh*—
The Bhāṭ said: "What about gold coins?" They said: "Not even his father or his grandfather ever saw gold coins!"
Yes, where should he have them from?

The Bhāṭ said: "If you find gold coins in the store, then Parmā's the thief.
Yes
If not, then, brother, I'm the thief."
The person who went to check found gold coins blazing like burning coals in the interior of the store, *said sir.*
He said: "Parmā Modī, you took the gold coins, but haven't done the accounts yet.
Yes, haven't done them
And the man's ruining the Bhāṭ's honor!"—*vāh vāh*—
The Bhāṭ removed his shoe, and beat Parmā Modī three or four times with his shoe, *said sir.*
Parmā Modī said: "Hey, Bhāṭ, why are you doing this!
Yes, why are you doing this?
Speak up truthfully about the reason why you've come!"
The Bhāṭ said: "I've come on other work.—*mhe*—
But you're not giving me a place to stay—you won't let me stay here.—*vāh vāh*—
I've forgotten the road to the Kaḷālī's mansion."
Yes, tell me where the road to Kaḷālī's mansion is
So Parmā Modī speaks.—*vāh vāh*—
How does he tell the Bhāṭ about the road to the Kaḷālī's mansion, let's see.
Know it by saying it, Bhopājī Mahāraj, know it by saying it, let's see
I'll say it now, by Bhagavān's grace, here you are.—*vāh vāh*—*sā*

—*gāv*—

"Go on ahead, Bhāṭ," he said.—*mhe*—
"Don't take time waiting,
In front one can see the quarters of dancers and prostitutes.—*vāh vāh*—
Over there doves peck at lentil seeds
You know the creature called Parevo—*mhe*—
It's found only in the Kaḷālī's mansion and nowhere else."
Yes, it's not found anywhere else
By God's grace, Parmā Modī speaks.—*mhe*—
What complete verse does he tell the Bhāṭ.
Know it by saying it, let's see, by saying it
I'll say it now, by Dev's grace, let's see

—*gāv*—

Always take Dev's name. *Very good, said sir.*
"By God's grace, you go on away," he said.—*vāh vāh*—
"Nāradī Bhāṭ don't go down any other lanes
Hey, the sons of Bāgh had made costly blossoms of gold
Blossoms of gold.
Yes, it belongs to that lane
No other house either in a village or city has it."—*vāh vāh*—

—gāv—

"Now go ahead," he said.*—mhe—*
"Nāradī Bhāṭ, don't dally!
Up front one can see the quarters of dancers and prostitutes.*—vāh vāh—*
A banana tree sways outside, Bhāṭ*—mhe—*
Look a banana tree grows only at that one place."
Yes, there's no other place
The Bagaṛāvats' Bhāṭ rode the horse Phūlrīyo toward that place
So, by God's grace, the Bhāṭ arrived at the Kaḷālī's residence
Now the door at the gate was locked.*—mhe—*
The window lay open.
Aṇandrāmjī of the gate who had gone blind, lay asleep in front of the gate—*vāh vāh—*
The Bhāṭ speaks. What does he say to Aṇandrāmjī upon arriving, let's see.
Know it by saying it, let's see, by saying it
I'll say it now sir, by Dev's grace, here you are.*—vāh vāh—jī vāh vāh—*

—gāv—

"Open up the gate, brother!*—mhe—*
Aṇandrāmjī of the gate, I'm getting delayed by the minute!
The sons of Bāgh Siṅg have come from Indra's throne to drink wine again.—*mhe—*
Their camp has been put in the Nolke Garden
Aṇandrāmjī of the gate, open up the gate!"
Aṇandrāmjī of the gate speaks.*—mhe—*
He said: "Hey, Bhāṭ—vāh vāh—
It's been eleven years since the gate was locked.
The window's open, isn't it . . .
Yes, come inside

—gāv—

"It's been eleven years since the door has been locked.*—mhe—*
O Bhāṭ, the lock has rust clinging to it
Hey, taking the bunch of keys, the woman of pleasure climbed up high onto the palace's balcony.
Since the Bagaṛāvats died, she hasn't come down. The keys aren't with me.
Yes, the keys are no longer in my hands
To open the gate*—mhe—*
Go down beneath the Kaḷālī's mansion.
Yes, go outside
The window's lying open. *When you come in, just come through the window*
A rider together with his horse can pass through."*—vāh vāh—*
The Bhāṭ said: "Aṇandrām of the gate*—mhe—*
Why should I go through the window, hey?"
Yes, why go through the window?

The Bhāṭ goes outside Kaḷālī's mansion.—*vāh vāh*—
And the Bhāṭ began to play on his surbīṇ.
He started playing out the Goḍī Malāgirī rāg
Kaḷālī heard it high up in the pleasure palace
She said: "O Hīṛāgar Maidservants—*mhe*—
A sound like that of the Bagaṛāvats' Bhāṭ's bīṇ has come into the palace."
Yes, hey, go and find out where the bīṇ is being played
So her friends stuck their heads out of the balcony
And took a look around.—*vāh vāh*—
The Bhāṭ looked up and saw the maidservants.—*vāh vāh*—
The Bhāṭ speaks.—*mhe*—
What does he say to the maidservants, let's see.
Know it by saying it, now, let's see, by saying it
I'll say it now, by Dev's grace, here you are.—*vāh vāh jī*

—*gāv*—

"I see seven friends like cranes.—*vāh vāh*—
You have delicate blankets to wrap around
A stranger asks you—*mhe*—: Who, brothers, amongst you is Pātū?
Who is the one who is called Pātū amongst you?" *Please tell me that!*
So the friends speak.—*mhe*—
What do they say to the Bagaṛāvats' Bhāṭ in return.
Know it by saying it, let's see, by saying it
I'll say it now, by Bhagavān's grace, here you are.—*vāh vāh*—*jī vāh vāh*—

—*gāv*—

"By God's grace, we are seven merry sisters.—*mhe*—
We have fine shawls to wrap around
Hey, stranger, we are Pātū's girls.—*vāh vāh*—
Pātū herself you'll see in the pleasure palace
We are Kaḷālī's maidservants!"
Yes, O brother, she's not here
The Bhāṭ said: "Well, then, ladies, why should I talk to you!"—*vāh vāh*—
The maidservants go back into the palace
Let's see what they say to Kaḷālī.
Know it by saying it, let's see, Bhopājī Mahārāj, now, by saying it
I'll say it now, by Dev's grace, here you are.—*vāh vāh*—*jī*

—*gāv*—

"O Lady, the stranger wears fine shoes.—*vāh vāh*—
In his hand a cane of the Kailū tree
O Lady, the stranger's name and village we've forgotten.—*mhe*—
But once upon a time, there would come together with the dear . . .
Together with the Bagaṛāvats there used to come . . . *he looks like that Bhāṭ to us*
But no, there is some difference.
Yes, there is some small difference

Those days together with the Bagaṛāvats he was an old man of sixty.
O Lady, today he's a youth of twenty-five.
All the signs are the very same.—*mhe*—
He has the same water gourd about his neck.—*mhe*—
And the same horse Phūlrīyo with him."
Kaḷālī said:
"Maidservants—*mhe*—
Don't you know about it?" she said—*vāh vāh*—
"It's the search for Prince Bhūṇā.—*mhe*—
The Bagaṛāvats' Bhāṭ has come—the Bhāṭ's body has been altered by Bhagavān.
Yes, Dev Mahārāj has changed his body and sent him
Here take the bunch of keys—there!
Yes, go and give it to Aṇandrāmjī of the gate,
Open the gate on one side—*mhe*—
So that the Bhāṭ can come inside.
He whose master is proud, *his 'beggar' too is proud*
How can the Bhāṭ enter through the window?"—*vāh vāh*—

By God's grace, the maidservants went and gave the bunch of keys to Aṇandrāmjī of the gate
Aṇandrāmjī of the gate tried using those keys—but how should the lock that hadn't been opened for eleven years open?
Yes, it was completely coated with rust, said sir.
The Bhāṭ said:"Hey, Aṇandrāmjī of the gate—*mhe*—
What are you up to? *It's taken such a lot of time—hasn't the lock opened yet or what!*"
Aṇandrāmjī said: "Hey, Bhāṭ, the keys don't fit, brother," he said.—*vāh vāh*—
The Bhāṭ said: "Throw them off to the side!
Yes, cast them off to one side
Take Dev's name and put your hand on the lock!"
Yes, keep saying Dev, Dev, and place your hand on the lock
He went on taking Dev's name, and placing his hand on the lock—*vāh vāh*—
The latch fell off to one side, *said sir.*
The gate opened and the Bhāṭ rode inside
By God's grace, Aṇandrāmjī of the gate said:
"Bhāṭ!—*mhe*—
When the Bagaṛāvats had the gate opened by me at sunrise,
They used to give a gold coin. *Said sir.*
Hey, daughter's father, give me a copper coin at least.—*vāh vāh*—
You've had me open the door for nothing!"—*mhe*—
Taking Dev's name, the Bhāṭ put his hand in his pocket
The same gold coins blazing like burning coals appeared. *Said sir.*
"Here, hey, brother, Aṇandrāmjī of the gate—take the gold coins, or rupee coins, money, if you want to call it that."
Yes, here take them

Dev's family's Bhāṭ gave gold coins to Aṇandrāmjī of the gate.—*mhe*—
He had been blind for twelve years.—*vāh vāh*—
His eyes opened in a flash
So the Bhāṭ entered the gate, and put his hands in his pocket
Dev Mahārāj's name was taken; Āṇandrāmjī of the gate's eyes opened, *said sir.*
Victory to Śrī Devnārāyaṇ, victory!
Say it, brother, hey, small and great, everyone!

The Bagaṛāvats' Bhāṭ arrived at the palace of Kaḷālī, *said sir.*
Kaḷālī was praying in silence.—*vāh vāh*—
She was repeating God's name.
The Bhāṭ speaks.—*mhe*—
What does he say to Kaḷālī upon arriving, let's see.
Know it by saying it, let's see, now, by saying it
I'll say it now, by God's grace, here you are.—*vāh vāh jī*—*vāh vāh*—

—*gāv*—

"Kaḷālī, your quarters are halfway up the hill.—*mhe*—
The balcony at your wonderful window looks splendid
Kaḷālī, the Kaḷāl sits there, still alive.—*mhe*—
How come you've renounced the sixteen hundred–fold dresses?
You've given up the sixteen hundred–fold dresses and thirty two hundred–fold ornaments.
Yes, why have you given them up already?

Chochu Bhāṭ visits Pātu Kalālī in her mansion.

Why have you taken to a widow's white dress?"—*vāh vāh*—
The Kaḷālī speaks. What does she say to the Bhāṭ, let's see.
Know it by saying it, let's see, by saying it

—*gāv*—

"By God's grace, I've taken a vow of four things, Bhāṭ, after the Bagaṛāvats died.—*mhe*—
And without grain you can't live
I'll put on sixteen hundred-fold dresses and thirty-two hundred-fold ornaments,—*mhe*—
Hey, if the Bagaṛāvats came to the golden cup now
If the twenty-four brothers sat and drank wine from the golden cup—*vāh vāh*—
Then I'll put on sixteen hundred-fold dresses and thirty-two hundred-fold ornaments."
She said: "Bhāṭ—*mhe*—
Hey, after the Bagaṛāvats died, you've gone mad.
Yes, you wander about crazy
You've gone crazy, Bhātjī, you've—*vāh vāh*—become stupid. You look like a peacock in the midst of the forest
Where did you get the sons of Bāgh?—*vāh vāh*
You saw someone else on the road
You saw someone else going on the road, brother."—*vāh vāh*—
So, the Bhāṭ of the lineage speaks.—*mhe*—
Kaḷālī speaks and the Bhāṭ listens.
Know it by saying it, Bhopājī Mahārāj, now, let's see, by saying it
I'll say it now, by the Lord's grace.—*vāh vāh*—*jī*—*vāh vāh*—

—*gāv*—

"On the Bagaṛāvats' cremation grounds, a khejaṛā tree has grown
By God's grace, knotted grass has grown
Where did you get sons of Bāgh from?—*mhe*—
Bhāt, cows graze on their cremation grounds
Cows graze there during the day.—*vāh vāh*—
Where did you get the Bagaṛāvats from?"
Yes, where did you bring them back from!

—*gāv*—

"Khejaṛā trees have grown on the Bagaṛāvats' fields.—*mhe*—
By God's grace, age has circled over.
Where did you get the sons of Bāgh?—The murderous evil woman sacrificed them with her own hands, *said sir.*
With her own hands she destroyed them.—*vāh vāh*—
Bhāṭ, where've you revived and brought them?"
Yes, where did you get them back from
The Bhāṭ said: "Kaḷālī!—*mhe*—
The Bagaṛāvats have come to drink wine!

Yes, they've come—get the place prepared
The 'drunken' times you used to have with the Bagaṛāvats.—*mhe*—
Today after twelve years there will an outright 'session' today."
Yes, it'll be celebrated

—*gāv*—

"If they'd gone to the village, Bhāṭ, they could return.—*mhe*—
And if they'd gone to other lands and countries, they could return, brother.
Where did you get the sons of Bāgh from?—*mhe*—
Bhāṭ, by which lane did the Bagaṛāvats go?
You know whether the Bagaṛāvats took the road of return or of no return!
Yes, don't you know which road they took?
Bhāṭ, the Bagaṛāvats didn't take the road of return.—*vāh vāh*—
They went down the road of no return.—*vāh vāh*—
They won't come back!—*mhe*—
You tell me the reason why you've come."
Yes, tell all the details!

The Bhāṭ said: "Kaḷālī, I've come, brother, by God's grace, to see the place where the Bagaṛāvats lived."
Kaḷālī said: "So then why are you sitting here?
Yes, come with me, I'll show you!
The Bagaṛāvats' place and the golden cup"
Yes, I'll show you
Catching hold of his arm, she took the Bhāṭ up to the golden cup and left him there.—*vāh vāh*—
So the Bagaṛāvats had a large kettle drum—when they drank wine, they would strike it—strike it with a drumstick.—*mhe*—
The drum was in Kaḷālī's mansion.—*vāh vāh*—
The Bhāṭ noticed it
He said: "Kaḷālī, Kaḷālī,
Yes, what's this, woman?"
She said: "It's a kettle drum . . ."
Yes, it's a kettle drum
The Bhāṭ said: "What are you doing with a kettle drum?"
Yes, what use do you have for it?
Kaḷālī said: "When the Bagaṛāvats used to drink wine worth one hundred thousand in my mansion,
They struck the drum once
When they drank two hundred thousand, they would give two strikes.
When they drank down three lakhs of wine—*mhe*—
They would give three strikes
Rāṇ City would all tremble, *said sir.*
They would know in Rāvjī's camp that today wine worth three hundred thousand have been drunk down.
Yes, they've been consumed at the Bagaṛāvats' camp, said sir

The Bagaṛāvats' Bhāṭ alighted from his horse, got down on his knees and with great strength he turned the drum right side up.
Yes, he turned it right side up
By God's grace, let the drumstick strike again at least.—*mhe*—
He didn't keep a count.
Yes, he went on striking four or five times with the drumstick
So, by God's grace, Kaḷālī said: "Hey, Bhāṭ—*mhe*—
You've blessed my house.
Yes, you've blessed my home!
Come over here—I'll show you more of the Bagaṛāvats' place."
Yes, I haven't shown you this—let me show you the next thing. Come along
She fastened locks on seven doors behind the Bhāṭ. *Fastened locks*
"Damn it, your destiny is such—let the bats eat you."
Yes, stay here, hey, the bats will eat you

In Rāvjī's court it became known.—*mhe*—
Rāvjī said: "Dīyā, Mīr, the kettle drum has sounded in Kaḷālī's mansion after eleven years today. *Why did it sound today?*
Either there's some Sirdār who drinks wine worth three hundred thousand
Yes, he has come today. Bring him in front of me
Or Kaḷālī has hidden an inscription belonging to the Bagaṛāvats, that *she's disclosed today*
Bring it also to me.—*vāh vāh*—
Go!" *Attack immediately!*
Kālū Mīr and Dīyājī took five hundred horses and five hundred riders.
Yes, they went on attack
They started their horses off.—*vāh vāh*—
By God's grace, they reached Kaḷālī's mansion, *said sir.*
What did Kaḷālī do?—*mhe*—
Talking hold of big iron hammer—*vāh vāh*—
She climbed up high onto the pleasure palace
She broke off parts of the roof *and put them onto the kettle drum. Said sir.*
She started praying in silence and repeating God's name
Dīyā spoke to Mīr: "Hey, Mīr, take a look, brother. Speak to Kaḷālī."
Yes, tell her
Mīr came up and said: "O Kaḷālī, Kaḷālī!"
Yes, speak, brother, speak
Mīr said: "Either you bring the Sirdār who drinks wine worth three lakhs in front of me
Yes, bring him out!
Or you've hidden an inscription of the Bagaṛāvats *that's you've disclosed today. Bring that out in front.*"
Kaḷālī said: "O Śrī Mahārāj!—*mhe*—
Where on earth are there any Sirdārs left who drink wine worth three lakhs?
Yes, there are none left
And where do I have *an inscription from the Bagaṛāvats to hide*

When the Bagaṛāvats were alive—*mhe*—
They spent a lot of money at my place
I had houses set up far away, *said sir.*
After the Bagaṛāvats died no one spends even a little money at my place
The town's urchins have become so frivolous
The walls still don't have lime on them.
Yes, the lime is not even on when they jump around on the roof at night
The ledge of the roof breaks off and the kettle drum beats on its own."
Mīr was standing there. Dīyājī said: "Hey, Mīr . . ."
Yes, take a look, let's see
By God's grace, when Mīr went there, there were three or four stones lying
Yes, on top of the drum, said sir.
Mīr said: "Friend, Dīyā—*mhe*—
There's no fault of the poor thing.
Yes, no fault of Kaḷālī
The roof breaks off on its own, *the drum beats on its own*
Let the cavalry return."
The cavalry departed.
Yes, Dīyā and Mīr's cavalry started back, said sir.
After the cavalry went away Kaḷālī opened the lock and got the Bagaṛāvats' Bhāṭ out
"Bhāt, right in broad daylight, you blessed my house, daughter's father."
Yes, why did you come out here—tell me exactly.
The Bhāṭ said: "Listen, O Kaḷālī—*mhe*—
I've come on the search for master Bhūṇājī.
Yes, I've come on a search for Bhūṇājī
Take to me to Bhūṇā."—*vāh vāh*—
Kaḷālī said: "By God's grace, Bhāṭ." Kaḷālī speaks now.—*mhe*—
What does she say to the Bhāṭ, let's see.
Know it by saying, let's see, by saying it
I'll say it now, by Dev's grace, let's see.—*vāh vāh*—*jī*—*vāh vāh*—

—*gāv*—

"Bhāṭ, one hundred oxen are laden with Bhūṇā's goods.—*mhe*—
All hundred carry weight
Brother Bhāṭ, Bhūṇājī is not in Rāṇ City.—*mhe*—
Rāvjī has sent him to buy horses from the mighty fort of Lahore
There are good horses in Lahore.
Yes, he's gone there to buy—to get horses
Bhūṇājī is not here—*vāh vāh*—
The Bhāṭ said: "Kaḷālī—*mhe*—
Is my master Bhūṇājī not in Rāṇ City today?—*mhe*—
Lady, there's no virtue in my staying here.
Yes, there's no virtue in my drinking water here
Tell me the road to Lahore." *I'll go right away*

Kaḷālī speaks. What road does she describe, let's see.
Know it by saying it, let's see, by saying it

—*gāv*—

"There are lots of hindrances in the hilly area without a road.—*mhe*—
On the way rivers run each with nine streams
Your horse looks old to me.—*mhe*—
Bhāṭ, it won't be able to cross over to the river's other bank
Bhagavān Dev Mahārāj changed your body.—*mhe*—
By God's grace, your horse *is the same old aged horse*
How will the rivers be crossed?" *You'll drown in the river*
By God's grace, the Bhāṭ speaks.—*mhe*—
What does he say to Kaḷālī.
Know it by saying it, let's see, by saying it
I'll say it by Dev's grace, here . . . —*vāh vāh*—*jī*—*vāh vāh*—

—*gāv*—

"Let there be hindrances in the hilly area without a road.—*mhe*—
Let rivers flow with nine streams each
Look, Dharmarājā Devjī has taken incarnation in Goṭhā.—*vāh vāh*—
Kaḷālī, he'll take me over to the rivers' far banks
My Lord will take me across rivers. *He's backing me*
Listen Kaḷālī—*mhe*—
Show me the road to Lahore as quickly as possible."—*vāh vāh*—
Kaḷālī said: "Hey, Bhāṭ—*mhe*—
I've the nature of a whore—Bhūṇājī is here!"
Yes, "Bhūṇājī is here," she said, "he hasn't gone to Lahore."
The Bhāṭ said: "Where is he here?"
Yes, tell me about that!
Sometimes you say Lahore and sometimes you say here."—*vāh vāh*—
Kaḷālī said: "Bhūnājī has gone to hunt wild boars in the hills of Goram.
He's about to come back in a short while.
By God's grace, rest a little.—*vāh vāh*—
We'll leave together soon."—*mhe*—
So the Bhāṭ tied his horse, and began resting.—*vāh vāh*—
What did Kaḷālī do? She put grains of green lentil and pearls onto a platter—*mhe*—
Climbed up onto the pleasure palace's balcony and sat down
She said: "Bābā Bhāṭ,—*mhe*—
When the drums of Bhūṇājī's returning army sound,
The green lentils and pearls will collect in one place on their own.
Then we'll know that Bhūṇājī's drums
Yes, beat and the cavalry is returning."
By God's grace, Kaḷālī put the green lentils and pearls on the platter and climbed up the pleasure palace.—*vāh vāh*—

Bhūṇājī's army returned from the hills of Goram
So the army's drums sounded
By God's grace, the green lentils and pearls collected together on their own, *said sir.*
What happens when Kaḷālī comes down from the pleasure palace
What does she say to the Bhāṭ. *Let's see, know it by saying it*
I'll say it now, by Dev's grace, here you are . . .*vāh—vāh vāh—vāh—*

—gāv—

"The day here has gone by in sleep.*—mhe—*
By God's grace, Rājā Kacchapajī's orb has set.
Seek out your master, now,*—mhe—*
Bhāṭ in the midst of both armies
I don't know who the groups belong to
One army belonged to Bhūṇājī.*—mhe—*
One army, they say accompanies King Nīmde."
She told the Bhāṭ about these two factions.*—vāh vāh—*
The Nāradī Bhāṭ got up.*—mhe—*
He saddled the horse Phūlrīyo.
The Bhāṭ was about to leave, when Kaḷālī said: "Bhāṭ, how can you leave?"
Yes, you hardly know Bhūṇājī
You don't recognize him.*—vāh vāh—*
The Bhāṭ said: "When did I eat rice pudding made by Bhūṇājī himself?"*—mhe—*
Kaḷālī said: "Just wait a little."
Yes, I'll describe Bhūṇājī to you
Kaḷālī speaks.*—mhe—*
What details about Prince Bhūṇā does she tell the Bhāṭ, let's see.
Know it by saying it, Bhopājī Mahārāj, by saying it
I'll say it now, by God's grace, here you are.*—vāh vāh jī—vāh vāh—*

—gāv—

"Bhūṇājī ties his turban tilted to the left side.*—vāh vāh—*
On the right side he keeps his scabbard and dagger
You'll recognize him straight away because Bhūṇā has the same gait like Bābā Bāvājī
Bhūṇājī walks exactly the same way Bāvājī Bagaṛāvat walked.
You won't find that gait in someone else's army."*—vāh vāh—*
The Bhāṭ began to leave.*—mhe—*
Kaḷālī said: "Wait don't leave."
Yes, don't depart, wait—I'll tell you the complete description

—gāv—

"By God's grace, Bhāṭ, in Bhūṇā's army there is a horse with the mark of a hare; a palanquin
The palanquin glitters with diamonds
You'll recognize him straight away—Bhūṇā rides a black horse

What does one call 'susro'? It's the mark that is found on stallions and mares
on their chests."—*mhe*—
So she said, "The 'susro' is only on the black horse and no other."—*vāh vāh*—

—*gāv*—

"In Bhūṇā's army—*mhe*—
There is the horse with the mark of a hare; a palanquin.—*vāh vāh*—
By God's grace, the palanquin is studded with a thousand diamonds
You'll recognize him straight away—Bhūṇā walks the sweet ones' gait
The way the Bagaṛāvats walked, *Bhūnājī walks exactly the same way*
Wait a little." *I'll tell you more about Bhūṇājī—where he usually sits—I'll tell you.*

—*gāv*—

"His trousers are made from the cloth called Sohraṭo
A drawstring of red color
You'll recognize him straight away—Bhūṇā walks his uncle Nevājī's gait
Nevājī's gait and Bhūṇājī's gait are one and the same."
Who said that? *Kaḷālī said it*
Now the Bagaṛāvats' Bhāṭ speaks.—*mhe*—
What does he say to Kaḷālī, let's see

—*gāv*—

"I'll recognize him with eyes closed.—*mhe*—
Kaḷālī why are you telling me in such a longwinded way?—*vāh vāh*—
Is the recognition of my master something hidden from me?
My master isn't hidden from me."
Yes, he's not some secret that you need to tell me so many details
Woman, since when do you speak such nonsense?"—*vāh vāh*—
Kaḷālī said:
"Here you are, hey, Bhāṭ—*mhe*—
I'll tell you the complete details, hey."

—*gāv*—

"You'll find Bhūṇā at the wide crossings—*vāh vāh*—
Or in the diamond-seller's store
Sometimes Bhūṇājī will be found at the wine-sellers' drinking wine—*vāh vāh*—
Or he'll be at Durjan Sāl's court
There you are, brother, at these places he'll be found for sure
Yes, Bhūṇājī sits at these places
Hirā Gānī is Bhūṇā's close friend.—*mhe*—
It's certain he'll always do two things.
Yes, he won't continue without meeting them
If he's at the crossing, then you'll meet Bhūṇājī right upon going there
He's certain to come to the wine-sellers' mansion.—*vāh vāh*—
He stays at this many places.—*mhe*—
Seated on the left of Rāvjī,

Yes, you'll also find Bhūṇājī."
Kaḷālī speaks—*mhe*—
What does she say to Bhūṇā.
Know it by saying it, let's see, by saying it

—*gāv*—

Always take Dev's name. *Very good, said sir.*
"Hey, Bhāṭ, I'm sad when I see the mansion's spires
Then I'm sad when I see the mares Bor and Bāvlī
These three reasons for sadness the Bagaṛāvats left behind. *I see them when I awake*
The fourth they left in Rāṇ is the mighty Bhūṇā
How can I forget him.—*mhe*—
Bhūṇājī is the Bagaṛāvats' child who is living in Rāṇ City."
Yes, he lives in Rāṇ City. I can't bear it, if I see him wandering about
"Hey, Bhāṭ it's pain,
The Bagaṛāvats left me with pain."—*vāh vāh*—

—*gāv*—

"Now go," she said.—*mhe*—
"O Bhāṭ, you will have a good omen
Hey, in the Aḍadū Bazaar—*vāh vāh*—
Ahead you'll meet Bārāvat's Bhūṇā
It's Dev's grace.—*mhe*—
Hey, Bhāṭ, you'll meet Bhūṇājī ahead.—*vāh vāh*—
Go!"—*mhe*—
By God's grace, Kaḷālī bade the Bhāṭ farewell.—*mhe*—
Kaḷālī and the Bhāṭ talked to one another.—*mhe*—
The Bagaṛāvats' Bhāṭ departed.
Victory to Śrī Devnārāyaṇ Bhagavān, victory
Say it, brother, everyone—big and small

Chochū Bhāṭ Taunts King Nīmde with Riddles

By God's grace, the Bagaṛāvats' Bhāṭ arrived in the bazaar
So he saw a broken-down shop, *said sir.*
He drove the Phūlrīyo Horse into the inside of the shop
He hung the sūrbīṇ on a nail
He had a water bottle with him.—*vāh vāh*—
He hung it up on the nail, *said sir.*
Some distance away in the bazaar he collected together dust.—*vāh vāh*—
The Bagaṛāvats' Bhāṭ began flinging the dust up into the wind.
Yes, he put it into his shield and began flinging the sand up
By God's grace, Nīmde's cavalry was up ahead.—*mhe*—
The Sirdār who was leading said:

"Hey, brother, Sandy!—*mhe*—
Move over to one side, Prince Khāṇḍerāv's[84] cavalry . . .
Yes, King Nīmde's cavalry is coming."
The Bhāṭ said: "Hey, Sirdārs!—*mhe*—
Brother, maybe Nīmā lives here or maybe Pīmā.
Yes, lives in Rāṇ City
If Nīmā or Pīmā say so I won't leave—I've lost something of mine in the bazaar."
Yes, I won't leave it here and ride off
Filling up his shield with sand—*mhe*—
All around the cavalry he'd fling it up.
Yes, give it a fling, and coat the clothes with dust
The men would ride ahead and shake off the dust: "There you are, let him burn away."
Yes, let him go!
King Nīmde, yes, King Nīmde's canopied horse came
So Nīmde speaks. What does he say to the Bhāṭ now, let's see.
Know it by saying it, let's see, by saying it

—gāv—

"Brother, Dandy, on your feet costly shoes.—*mhe*—
Your clothes are *bright and* white
King Nīmde is asking you:—*mhe*—
"Hey, why are you flinging up shields full of sand in my bazaar?
You look like a wealthy man, brother.—*mhe*—
You have costly clothes to wear
Hey, why are you grappling with dust?" *Tell me that!*
Who said this? *King Nīmde said this upon arriving*
By God's grace, the Bhāṭ thought to himself—*mhe*—
"Let's see, I'll put Nīmā to test—let's see whether he's all-knowing or unknowing."
Yes, is he a broken drum, an ignoramus, let's see
The Bhāṭ speaks. Let's see what he says to Nīmde.
Know it by saying it, Bhopājī Mahārāj, by saying it, let's see

—gāv—

"On my feet there are costly shoes.—*mhe*—
My clothes are *bright and* white
Twenty-four rubies were dropped in your bazaar—*mhe*—
Nīmā, and one diamond was lost
Twenty-four rubies were dropped—*mhe*—
And one diamond
Yes, got lost
I'm looking for those, brother."
Yes, I'm looking for them!
King Nīmde was hardly all-knowing.

Yes, that he'd understand the matter
The Bagaṛāvats' Bhāṭ didn't tell even a speck of a lie.—*vāh vāh*—
The Bagaṛāvats he made into rubies.—*mhe*—
And the Bhūṇājī he made into the diamond
King Nīmde didn't follow.—*vāh vāh*—
Nīmde speaks.—*mhe*—
What does he say to the Bhāṭ, let's see. *Know it by saying it, let's see, now, by saying it*

—*gāv*—

"I can see the diamonds on your shoes.—*mhe*—
Hey, son, and the pearls on your shoes
By God's grace, King Nīmde asks you.—*mhe*—
What wealth did you lose in my Bazaar?
What great wealth was lost, hey, brother—*vāh vāh*—
That you're grappling with dust?"—*mhe*—
By God's grace, the Bhāṭ thought to himself: "The enemy hasn't understood.
Yes, he certainly is a broken drum—an ignoramus. Hey, I'll throw him
Down right in this place.—*mhe*—
He's just roaming around like that."

—*gāv*—

"I have shoes studded with diamonds.—*mhe*—
O Nīmā, my shoes are lined with pearls
It's time for opium and water.—*mhe*—
If only I would find a gold coin from the time of the Bagaṛāvats, today, lying here
Hey, I'm an opium-eater."[85]—*mhe*—

So Nīmde spoke about a hundred thousand rupees.—*mhe*—
The Bagaṛāvats' Bhāṭ speaks.—*vāh vāh*—
What does he tell Nīmde.
Know it by saying it, let's see, now, by saying it
I'll say it now, by Dev's grace, let's see.—*vāh vāh*—*jī*—*vāh vāh*—

—*gāv*—

"Nīmā, all these days one would get pure gold in Rāṇ City—*mhe*—
Today you fill my lap with copper coins
Hey, King Nīmā, someone was accompanied by lions, a jackal played with a lion."
Nīmde said: "Hey, beggar—*mhe*—
Forget about past matters.
Yes, tell me, who is a jackal
And who a lion? Speak about that!"
The Bhāṭ said: "I'll tell you Mahārāj."—*vāh vāh*—

—gāv—

"By God's grace, both the brothers Bāvājī and Nevā would roar like lions, brother.*—mhe—*
Those lions were caught and kept in a cage
Hey, you accompanied those lions*—mhe—*
Nīmā, you standing here, played the jackal
The Bagaṛāvats were the lions. *They used to be lions*
You were the jackal." *You are the jackal*
By God's grace, King Nīmde's Sirdārs said:
"Śrī Mahārāj, look*—mhe—*he's made the master into a jackal," they said.*—vāh vāh—*
Nīmde said: "The beggar's blood has begun flowing the wrong way
Move our cavalry ahead.
Yes, he's going to die in a little while
By God's grace, he's a beggar of a noble house.*—mhe—*
Some Sirdār will hand us a serious complaint."
King Nīmde's cavalry departed.*—vāh vāh—*
The Bhāṭ thought to himself: "Hey, the enemy is going away like he came!"
Yes, put him to some shame
The Bagaṛāvats' Bhāṭ speaks.*—vāh vāh—*
What more does he say to Nīmde.
Know it by saying it, let's see, by saying it
I'll say it now, by Lord Dev's grace, I'll say it.*—vāh vāh jī—vāh vāh—*

—gāv—

"An unmarried daughter.*—mhe—*
Plenty of debts on my head.*—vāh vāh—*
I need a hundred thousand rupees
Be liberal to the point of hundreds of thousands, then continue ahead.*—mhe—*
Otherwise tell me where the mighty Bhūṇā's camp is pitched.
Listen, hey, Nīmā,*—mhe—*
I have four girls at home, brother*—vāh vāh—*
I don't even have one paisa to spend on them
And, I don't want to burden anyone else.
Yes, I don't want to have a competitor Bhāṭ pay for expenses
I thought*—mhe—*
If I meet a Sirdār, who'll make an offering of a hundred thousand,
Then the daughters would get a marriage mark on their forehead.
Yes, with hennaed hands, I'd send them off
By God's grace, son, Nīmā, I've come because of you, brother."
Yes, I've come because of this matter!
Nīmde speaks*—vāh vāh—*What does he say to the Bhāṭ, let's see.
Know it by saying it, let's see, by saying it
I'll say it now, by Dev's grace, here you are.*—vāh vāh—jī vāh vāh—*

—gāv—

"Bhūṇājī rode my horse.—*mhe*—
He consumed my wealth
Entering into this Rāṇ City, O brother Bhāṭ—*mhe*—
Who told you the name Bhūṇā?
Yes, tell me about that
Tell me, who said Bhūṇājī?—*vāh vāh*—
Whoever said Bhūṇājī, I'll put him in the press and have oil extracted from him!—*vāh vāh*—
Isn't he called Prince Khāṇḍerāv?"
Yes, don't you know about that name?
The Bhāṭ thought to himself: "I've caught the old man in a sore spot."
Yes, this time I've got caught in the matter
The Bhāṭ speaks. Let's see what he says to Nīmde, let's see.
Yes, let's see how he confuses him.

—*gāv*—

"By God's grace, brother, in the forest cowherds told of a rumor—*vāh vāh*—
They put water on my fire. *The water-bearers lit a fire*
Hey, I stayed so long in Pilodā's quarters.—*vāh vāh*—
The Kumahār from Pilodā told me about Bhūṇā's name
I went to Pilodā because I wanted an offering of a hundred thousand.—*mhe*—
I thought, why this Sirdār is mighty too.
Yes, he might make an offering of a hundred thousand
He said, brother, I can't come up with an offering of a hundred thousand.
Yes, I'm not capable
There's a son of the Bagaṛāvats' called Bhūṇā, who makes offerings of a hundred thousand.
Yes, every day before he cleans his teeth, he offers a hundred thousand and then cleans his teeth
He doesn't clean his teeth without donating a hundred thousand—*vāh vāh*—
When the sun rises, he gives away a hundred thousand rupees.—*vāh vāh*—
Then what's the trouble, brother?
Yes, there's no problem in that
Śrī Mahārāj, the Dhārāpatī Sirdār told me, here you are.
Yes, he told me the name
Now on the one hand which cowherd from which lane should I go and ask?
Yes, who should take his name, said sir.
Even stags run away from his name."—*vāh vāh*—
Nīmde said: "Let the beggar burn away." *"Let him go," he said, "it's because of the opium*
That he's fantasizing."—*mhe*—

Chochū Bhāṭ Tests Bhūṇājī with Riddles

By God's grace, what did the Bagaṛāvats' Bhāṭ do?—*mhe*—
At that place he went and began collecting dust again, *said sir.*

Nīmde left.—*vāh vāh*—
Prince Khāṇḍerāv's cavalry rode up.
The leading Sirdār said: "Hey, brother, Sandy—*mhe*—
Why are you doing this with the sand? Your white clothes are dusty."—*vāh vāh*—
He said: "Sandy, move over to one side, Prince Khāṇḍerāv's cavalry is approaching now!"
Yes, Prince Khāṇḍerāv is arriving!
The Bhāṭ said: "Sirdārs!—*mhe*—
Rāṇ City is settled over twelve—twenty-four kos.
Something belonging to me I've lost, should I leave it behind?"
Should I get up and go?
By God's grace, he'd put sand in the shield and toss it all around the riders.—*vāh vāh*—
He'd go some distance away and jerk his clothes free of sand.
Yes, he wouldn't stand still
By God's grace, Bhūṇā on his horse came up.—*vāh vāh*—
Immediately, Bhūṇā halted his black horse.—*he*—
After looking and reflecting, Bhūṇājī speaks.—*mhe*—
What does he say to the Bhāṭ now.
Know it by saying it, let's see, by saying it

—*gāv*—

"Brother, costly shoes on your feet.—*mhe*—
Your clothes white and bright
Prince Khāṇḍerāv asks you.—*vāh vāh*—
Sandy, why are you throwing up shields full of sand in the bazaar?
Daughter's father, you look like a prosperous man.—*mhe*—
You have clothes to wear worth hundreds of thousands
Why are you wrestling with sand?"
Yes, tell me about that!
The Bhāṭ reflected to himself—*mhe*—: "Tell your master the same thing.
Yes, the very same thing you told Rājā Nīmde, tell him
If he's all-knowing, *then he'll understand*
If he's a broken drum, then he can go the way Rājā Nīmde went now.
Yes, he'll go that way. What's the point of bringing him together with the brothers!"

—*gāv*—

"On my feet I have costly shoes.—*mhe*—
My clothes are white and bright
Hey, twenty-four rubies were lost in your bazaar.—*vāh vāh*—
O Prince, I've lost one diamond
Listen, O Prince, twenty-four rubies were lost,
One diamond fell."
By God's grace, Bhūṇājī asked: "A man of what country are you?"
Yes, tell me that!

The Bhāṭ said: "Śrī Mahārāj, I come from across seven seas."
Yes, I do
"What community do you belong to?"—*mhe*—
The Bhāṭ said: "I'm the Bhāṭ of kings."
Yes, I am
"Your name?" *What is it?*
"Śrī Mahārāj, people call me Jagīśyo."
"Hey, Jagīśyo—*mhe*—
Those rubies that fell down have been lost."
Yes, they're gone forever
"Śrī Mahārāj, the rubies are lost.
Yes, they've been lost beyond recovery
"Now there's hope of finding the diamond."
By God's grace, Bhūṇājī spoke to the Sirdārs:
"Hey, Sirdārs!—*mhe*—
Some child of his master has got lost.—*vāh vāh*—
He's wandering about looking for him.
He's driving people crazy."—*mhe*—
When Bhūṇājī said this, the Bhāṭ reflected to himself: "Your master is all-knowing.
Yes, he's certainly all-knowing
He's all-knowing, not ignorant."—*vāh vāh*—
Bhūnājī said: "Jagīśyā!—*mhe*—
The administration of fifty-two forts is in my hands.
Yes, everything is settled through my authority
If the name of your 'diamond' appears in the fifty-two forts,
Then I'll settle all accounts—*mhe*—
Strike his name off, and return your 'diamond' to you."
Yes, I'll strike his name off—so you can take him
The Bhāṭ said: "Śrī Mahārāj—*mhe*—
Will you really find my 'diamond'?" *Will you certainly procure my 'diamond'?"*
Bhūṇājī speaks.—*vāh vāh*—
What does he say to the Bhāṭ, let's see.
By saying it, know it, by saying it
I'll just say it, by Dev's grace, here you are

—*gāv*—

"A great deal of rain has fallen on your 'diamond.'
It's looks like your 'diamond' has gone away over the banks of the River Narmadā
You won't find the diamond in the sand.—*mhe*—
Look carefully amongst the royal families
Daughter's father, you're making a fool of everyone.
Yes, there's no diamond in the sand
Sirdārs, he's been wandering about looking for a child.—*vāh vāh*—
All right," he said—*mhe*—

"Come to the cattle enclosure at Bhinay."—*vāh vāh*—
By God's grace, having said so much, Bhūṇājī
Yes, he gave the horse a dig with his heels
The Bhāṭ reflected to himself: "I didn't give the arriving cavalry a song of praise
I'll certainly give the departing cavalry a song of praise."
The Bagaṛāvats' Bhāṭ speaks.—*vāh vāh*—
What song of praise does he compose. *And what song of praise does he offer to Bhūṇājī, let's see*
I'll say it now, by God's grace, let's see.
Know it by saying it, Bhopājī Mahārāj, by saying it

—*gāv*—

"By God's grace—*mhe*—
In the prince's army there are kings from many lands.—*vāh vāh*—
And there are a lot of Mughals and Paṭhāns
Accept Jagīśya's song of praise—*mhe*—
By God's grace, O Sā̃mar Rāy Cauhān."
Taking Sā̃mar and the Cauhān's name, the Bhāṭ sang Bhūṇājī a song of praise
Seven and a half times Cauhān Sirdārs used to be employed by the prince
"They've gone away, brother, my Bhāṭ."
He said: *My Bhāṭ*
The Bhāṭ reflected to himself: "You've offered a song of praise—*mhe*—
But my master *didn't let it finish, he stopped it in the middle."*
He composes another song of praise. *And, what song of praise does he offer to Bhūṇājī. Know it by saying it, Bhopājī Mahārāj, now, by saying it*
I'll say it now, by Lord Dev's grace, here you are—*vāh vāh jī*—*vāh vāh*—

—*gāv*—

"By God's grace, in Rāvjī's gardens there are kevaṛā flowers from Ajmer.—*mhe*—
All the flowers are collected together
Hey, from long before
I'm giving the best flower a song of praise.—*mhe*—
At some time the Cauhāns ruled over Goṭhā̃."
Taking Goṭhā̃'s name, *he offered a song of praise to Bhūṇājī*
All the Sirdārs denied the matter.—*vāh vāh*—
"Not even one of us is from Goṭhā̃. We're Cauhāns from other villages."—*vāh vāh*—
Bhūṇājī said: "Hey, Sirdārs—*mhe*—
Why are you quarreling amongst yourselves?
Yes, what are you fighting amongst yourselves for?
What name did he take when offering this song of praise now?
Yes, he's offered it to the best flower
Today I am your leading flower.
He's addressed the song of praise to me."
Bhūṇājī turned his horse around and rode back:

"Hey, beggar—*mhe*—
Tell me, why did you offer me a song of praise in the name of the Cauhāns?
Yes, why did you offer it today?
Don't you know the name of my father, and grandfather?"
Yes, don't you know or what?
The Bhāṭ said: "When did I come to eat your father's, and grandfather's rice-pudding?"
Yes, when did they feed me rice-pudding and bread?
By God's grace, Bhūṇājī said: "Listen, hey Bhāṭ—*mhe*—
I haven't secretly been a Maṇḍovar Paḍihār."—*vāh vāh*—
When he took the Paḍihār's name, then the Bhāṭ became angry from foot to head.
Yes, became angry
By God's grace, the Bagaṛāvats' Bhāṭ speaks.—*mhe*—
What does he say to Prince Bhūṇā, let's see. *Know it by saying it, let's see, by saying it*
I'll say it now, by Dev's grace, here you are.—*vāh vāh—jī—vāh vāh*—

—*gāv*—

"You've changed your jāt, Prince Mahābalī—*mhe*—
The way, brother, a Ṭhaṭhīyārā changes copper
For so long you were called a Cauhān in Goṭhā.—*mhe*—
Today Dīyā has mixed you together with the Paḍīhārs
A good thing has happened!"
Yes, you've changed your jāt
By God's grace, how did Bhūṇā and they become related?
What is this that has happened?—*mhe*—
So now those Cauhān Sirdārs—*mhe*—
They all denied the matter.—*vāh vāh*—
They said: "There's not even one Sirdār from Goṭhā among us."
By God's grace, Bhūṇājī speaks.—*vāh vāh*—
What does he say, let's see. *Know it by saying it, now, Bhopājī Mahārāj, by saying it*

—*gāv*—

By God's grace, he said: "They say that Bābā Rāvjī went on a tour into the country.—*mhe*—
Brother, they say he went across the seven seas
Hey, captured at the age of six months, I came to Nautherī Rāṇ City.—*mhe*—
After that day till now, Maṇḍovar Paḍihār
Is what people call me, brother."—*mhe*—
"Well, Bhūṇā.—*vāh vāh*—
He captured you from across the seven seas.—*vāh vāh*—
Brother, you ask why I offer you such a song of praise, since you're not born of Rāvjī.—*vāh vāh*—
You say you were captured from across seven seas.

I don't have this sort of song of praise.
Yes, for an adopted heir I don't have a song of praise
For an adopted heir."
Yes, sir
By God's grace, Bhūṇājī reflected deeply—*mhe*—:
"If this Bhāṭ, this beggar is left free in the bazaar—*vāh vāh*—
Then I'll be called an adopted heir.—*vāh vāh*—
Let the cavalry move on."
Yes, let it move on
By God's grace, Bhūṇājī rode off on the Black Mare.
The Bhāṭ thought to himself:—*vāh vāh*—
"The master who arrived is going. *Who will let me meet him elsewhere?*
He doesn't recognize you.—*vāh vāh*—
But this mare should recognize me."
Yes, speak to it
So the Bhāṭ speaks.—*vāh vāh*—
What does he tell Mother Mare, let's see. *Know it by saying it, let's see*
I'll say it now, brother, by Dev's grace, let's see.—*vāh vāh*—*jī.*

—*gāv*—

Bhūṇājī Strikes Chochū Bhāṭ Thrice

"If you move ahead from here, O Mare Cā̃vaṇḍā—*mhe*—
Then you'll be abandoned by the twenty-three brothers!
O Mare!
Yes, don't move ahead
It's the Bagaṛāvats' oath, brothers—*vāh vāh*—
That the way a pillar is grounded—*mhe*—
In the same way the mare will be grounded."
Bhūṇājī would kick the mare with his heels, but the mare would jump back.
It wouldn't take a step forward
Bhūṇājī thought to himself: "The beggar just said he lived seven oceans away, didn't he!
Yes, 'I am,' he said.[86] He's bewitched the mare!"
Yes, he's done some magic
Bhūṇājī said: "Beggar, why have you bewitched the mare, brother?"—*vāh vāh*—
So the Bhāṭ didn't say anything.—*vāh vāh*—
Bhūṇājī said: "Watch out, my lance is coming at you."
Yes, let it come
"Let it come, brother, Dev's iron slab is across my head." *Across*
Bhūṇā's first lance was hurled on the Bhāṭ's head
The way a horse's hooves resound against an empty cauldron—*mhe*—
In the same way *the lance resounded on his head, said sir*
Bhūṇājī said: "What do you say Bhāṭ?"

Yes, I'm still standing at the same place
The Bhāṭ said: "Not a hair has been disturbed so far."—*vāh vāh*—
Bhūṇājī thought to himself: "What's happened? He's protected his head through wizardry.
Yes, he's protected his head through magic
By God's grace, strike him on the side, so that his life will be completely finished off.
Bhūṇājī said: "So now, beggar, it's coming, brother!"
Yes, right ahead!
"Let it come!—*mhe*—
Dev's iron slab is going to protect me."
Bhūṇājī's second lance struck the Bhāṭ on his side
In the same manner, by God's grace, the lance slid by.—*vāh vāh*—
Bhūṇājī thought to himself:—*mhe*—
"The beggar has protected his side firmly with magic.—*vāh vāh*—
Strike him on his back, so that his heart will be removed from inside." *Tear it out*
Taking strength, Bhūṇājī said: "Now it's coming!"
Yes, "Let it come," said the Bhāṭ
Bhūṇājī struck the third lance on the Bhāṭ's back.—*vāh vāh*—
The lance went and resounded like a horse's hooves against a cauldron.
Yes, it resounded and fell down
"Hey, Bhāṭ, so now what do you say?"
Yes, I'm standing at the same place!
Bhūṇājī thought to himself:—*mhe*—
"By striking him, I'll be . . .
Yes, disgraced
By God's grace, if some general of Rāvjī sees me—*mhe*—
He'll say Bhūṇājī is reprimanding himself.
Hey, from which country did you meet a beggar,
Yes, to whom no harm has come even though Bhūṇājī hurled three lances?"—*vāh vāh*—
By God's grace, Kālū Mīr and Dīyājī, were watching this spectacle, *said sir.*
Mīr said: "Dīyā!—*mhe*—
Have you realized or not?
Yes, do you know or don't you
Who is that? *Tell me*
By God's grace, the Bagaṛāvats' Chochū Bhāṭ has met with Bhūṇā."
Yes, it's him all right
Dīyājī said: "Hey, Mīr—*mhe*—
You say that one doesn't speak falsehood in the Muslim caste.
Daughter's father, when the Bagaṛāvats were alive, the Bhāṭ was an old man of sixty.
Hey, he's a twenty-five-year-old youth . . .
Yes, today."
Mīr said: "Hey, you don't know!—*mhe*—

There is a search on for Bhūṇā.—*mhe*—
And, by God's grace, the lord of the three worlds has altered his body."
Yes, he's altered his body and sent him here
He said: "Then tell me."
Yes, "Tell me," he said, "let's see"
He said: "Here you are, what delay can there be, now."—*vāh vāh*—

—*gāv*—

By God's grace, the following was said:—*vāh vāh*—
"O Bhāṭ, who would catch a snake's tail.—*vāh vāh*—
Hey, who would tease a lion on its way
The man who would fight Bhūṇā today,—*mhe*—
Would die without age.
There's no one to fight your master today."—*vāh vāh*—
Mīr speaks.—*vāh vāh*—
What does he say to Prince Bhāṭ, let's see, *what he says to the Bhāṭ, let's see, by saying it, know it, by saying it*
I'll just say it, by Bhagavān's grace, here you are!—*vāh vāh—jī*

—*gāv*—

"Your face is sweet—*mhe*—
Hey, since when do you, O Bhāṭ, speak the truth?
You, from the sheep pen, Bhāṭ Nāradī?—*mhe*—
Hey, now don't open a departing lion's chains
I fought in front of him.—*mhe*—
Brother, let me go and burn in the sheep pen.
Inform your master after that.
Let me move to safety."—*vāh vāh*—
The Bagaṛāvats' Bhāṭ gave a clap with his hands.
Yes, he gave one: "Move on," he said
"Otherwise I'll have you killed now!"—*vāh vāh*—
Mīr said: "Dīyā, what do you say now, brother?" *Isn't it the same Bhāṭ?*
Dīyā said: "It is the very same one, brother."—*vāh vāh*—
So both these generals departed.
Bhūṇājī thought to himself:—*mhe*—
"Hey, all of Rāvjī's generals have gone away.
Standing here alone, you look foolish.—*mhe*—
My going away is also the right thing now."
Yes, let's leave
By God's grace, Bhūṇājī moved his horse off again.—*mhe*—
So the Bhāṭ thought to himself: "He hasn't realized yet.—*vāh vāh*—
And the master is going back the way he came—the enemy won't let me meet him again.
Yes, they won't let us meet
By God's grace, so I told the horse about this—*mhe*—

And it halted."—*vāh vāh*—
So, by God's grace, Pātū Kaḷālī was watching the spectacle from the pleasure palace
She saw the spectacle and went up to the high balcony
Pātū Kaḷālī speaks.—*vāh vāh*—
What does she say, let's see. *Know it by saying it, let's see, by saying it*
I'll just say it, brother, by God's grace, let's see.—*vāh vāh*—

—*gāv*—

Bhūṇājī Reads the Letters Written to Him

"O Bhūṇā, why are you lashing the Black Mare with the whip?—*mhe*—
And why are you kicking it with your heels?
Hey, by God's grace, Bhūṇā, the Bhāṭ belongs to you and your father.
Seeing you, he is uttering strong words
Looking at you, he's speaking sternly."—*vāh vāh*—
Bhūṇājī turned his sight above:
By God's grace, what is Pātū Kaḷālī saying, brother?
Yes, what is she saying?
Bhūṇājī calls Pātū Kaḷālī "Aunt"—*mhe*—
But he doesn't know which branch of relatives
Yes, she is an aunt of
That branch *or this one*
Kaḷālī speaks—*mhe*—
What more does she tell Prince Bhūṇā. *Let's see, right away*

—*gāv*—

"Why are you mixing together ākaṛā and nīmaṛā?" she said.—*mhe*—
"Bhūṇājī, why do you kill your family's Cāraṇ Bhāṭ?
Hey, kill Durjan Sāl Paḍīhār instead—*vāh vāh*—
Hey, he's destroyed your fair father Bhoj
What is the point of killing him, brother?[87] Kill Rāvjī—*mhe*—
So that at least one enmity will be avenged."—*vāh vāh*—
By God's grace, Bhūṇājī thought to himself:
"Hey, if Aunt Pātū is saying such things, then the search is for you!"
Yes, the search is for you and no one else
He said: "Hey, Bhāṭ—*mhe*—
Are you going to someone else, or have you come for me?"
Yes, you've come for me!
The Bhāṭ said: "Śrī Mahārāj, I don't have to bring any invitations ahead
I've come only because of you."
Bhūṇājī said: "Then did you bring letters from my brothers?"
Yes, I've brought them
The Bhāṭ said: "There are plenty of them."—*vāh vāh*—

By God's grace, the bag was full of letters.—*mhe*—
So the Bhāṭ placed them in front of Bhūṇājī
Let's see, what the first letter written by Dev reads.—*vāh vāh*—

—*gāv*—

The first letter he read, brother, was written by Dev.—*vāh vāh*—
Dev Mahārāj wrote lots of lines:
"Come as soon as you read the letter, Prince Mahābalī.—*vāh vāh*—
Your father's village Bāgor lies barren
All the other villages belonging to the Bagaṛāvats are inhabited, brother.—*mhe*—
Your father's village . . .
Yes, is without inhabitants

—*gāv*—

Brother, he read the letter written by brother Bhaṅgerīyā.—*mhe*—
Bhāṅgījī wrote, giving his moustache a twirl:
"Yes, come soon upon reading the letter.—*mhe*—
Otherwise I'll throw you together with the enemies and pound you like chilis
By God's grace, you'll be killed together with the enemies—I don't care!"—*vāh vāh*—
Bhūṇājī said: "Bābā Bhāṭ, is that a brother of mine?"
Yes, he is a brother, sir
"Śrī Mahārāj, he's your brother."—*vāh vāh*—

—*gāv*—

Brother, he read the letter written by Pīpalde.—*vāh vāh*—
Queen Pīpalde wrote it on letter leaf:
"Come soon after reading the letter.—*vāh vāh*—
Without you who will maintain this young bride's honor?
O Brother-in-law, if you come, then my honor too . . .
Yes, will increase

—*gāv*—

By God's grace, he read the letter written by Mother.[88]—*vāh vāh*—
Brother, Mother wrote on a letter leaf:
"Hey, Prince Mahābalī, come soon after reading the letter
Son, your mother has grown very old
I'm about to fall down like a leaf from a tree—I may fall tomorrow, son!"
Yes, if you come, then we can meet
By God's grace, Bhūṇājī said: "Hey, Bābā Bhāṭ—*mhe*—
Is she my mother?" "Yes, Śrī Mahārāj, she is your big mother," the Bhāṭ said.
She's your big mother.

—*gāv*—

He read the second letter written by Queen Pīpalde—*mhe*—
Queen Pīpalde wrote, taking shelter behind her veil:

"Go quickly to attack after reading this letter, my dear brother-in-law—*vāh vāh*—
While coming strike down on the enemy's roof
Leave a mark on the enemy and come."
By God's grace, brother, he read the letter written by Tejājī's son Madnā.—*mhe*—
Madan Siṅg wrote a lot of honorable salutations:
"Read the letter and come soon.—*mhe*—
Brother, there's a marriage procession in Goṭhā without a bridegroom
There are a lot of people in the procession . . .
Yes, but nobody to be the bridegroom
Elder brother, Bhūṇā, come soon, brother!"—*vāh vāh*—

—*gāv*—

The Bhāṭ slid his feet out of the horse Phūlrīyā's stirrups.—*vāh vāh*—
Now the mighty Bhūṇā has returned!
Hey, the master and his disciple embraced each other in the bazaar.—*vāh vāh*—
Who watches this miracle?
The city's traders spoke:
"Sirdārs!—*mhe*—
Look, for so much time they fought . . .*both of them quarreled*
And, now, every few minutes, they are behaving like friends.—*mhe*—
They embrace each other and both meet together in the bazaar
We haven't be able to understand them!"—*vāh vāh*—
So, by God's grace, the Bagaṛāvats' Bhāṭ met with Bhūṇā.—*mhe*—
He read the letter written by Dev
Bhūṇā recognized the Bhāṭ.—*mhe*—
Victory to Śrī Devnārāyaṇ Bhagavān, victory!

Bhūṇājī and Chochū Bhāṭ in Puṣkar

By God's grace, Bhūṇājī met with the Bhāṭ after eleven years.—*vāh vāh*—
Rāvjī's generals, Kālū Mīr and Dīyājī, both these heroes arrived in the court.
Yes, they reached before, said sir.
Upon reaching it they told him their concern
Rāvjī said: "Mīr!—*mhe*—
Whose 'concern' did you bring here?"
Mīr said: "Śrī Mahārāj, you know that Bhāṭ of the Bagaṛāvats.—*mhe*—
He's met with Prince Bhūṇājī today."
So Rāvjī's generals arrived at Rāvjī's court
So Prince Bhūṇājī and the Bhāṭ—*mhe*—
Arrived at the outskirts of Bhināy, *said sir.*
Mīr said: "Do what I say!"—*mhe*—
"What is it Mīr?"
Yes, tell me about that
Mīr said: "It's the month of Kārttik—there is the fair in Puṣkar Rāj.—*mhe*—
Send Prince Bhūṇā for one month to oversee the fair."

Yes, send him there to oversee for one month. We'll survive one more month
Rāvjī Sāī wrote off a letter.—*mhe*—
And, he had it brought to Prince Bhūṇā's camp
Bhūṇājī read the letter.—*mhe*—
What did he tell the Bhāṭ, let's see.
Know it by saying it, let's see, by saying it
I'll say it now, by Lord Dev's grace, here you are.—*vāh vāh—jī—vāh vāh*—

—*gāv*—

"Catch hold of the message, Bābā Bhāṭ—*vāh vāh*—
Ask for the Sirdār's message soon
Hey, the hungry sword is demanding an offering, Bhāṭ of the lineage.—*mhe*—
Pray now to Pokharjī[89]
Bābā Bhāṭ, let's go to Puṣkar."
Yes, come on
The Bhāṭ said: "Great, wonderful, my master, you thought a good thing.—*mhe*—
By God's grace, that's a great idea!
Yes, I could have a ritual bath there
My small bones will loosen up in old age."—*vāh vāh*—
Bhūṇājī departed from the outskirts of Bhināy with an entourage of eighteen thousand, *said sir.*
Mīr spoke to Dīyā:
"Hey, friend Dīyā!—*mhe*—
Do what I say!"
"What?" *What should be done, Mīr?*
Mīr said: "Bhūṇā's army is about to enter the bazaar now
You know our Maṅgānā elephant.—*mhe*—
Give it alcohol *and let it loose in front of Bhuṇājī*
The enemy will be torn into two in one stroke.
Yes, the elephant will do it straight away!"
They didn't ask Rāvjī.—*mhe*—
Without asking him, they released the elephant in front of Bhūṇā.
The Bhāṭ saw that elephant coming
He thought to himself: "An elephant has been released by the enemies.
What fear do you have?—*mhe*—
Your master is standing close by, isn't he!"
Yes, Bhūṇājī is with you, what do you fear?

—*gāv*—

Bhūṇājī Slays Maṅgānā Elephant

"The elephant has two tusks.—*mhe*—
Bhūṇā, in your mouth there are thirty-two teeth!
Hey, slay the battle-winning elephant, Rāyjādā Mahābalī!—*mhe*—

Now sever Airapat's head!
Make two pieces with one stroke!"—*vāh vāh*—
Bhūṇājī thought to himself: "Hey, where did this dull-headed fellow turn up from!—*vāh vāh*—
By God's grace, I heard of the Bhāṭ with my ears—*mhe*—
And saw him with my eyes."
Yes, he is a dull-headed fellow all right
By God's grace, the Bhāṭ speaks; what does he tell Bhūṇā, let's see. *By saying it, know it, by saying it*

—*gāv*—

"Bhūṇā, it's considered evil to kill the enemy's dog.—*mhe*—
And upon you comes swaying an elephant worth a hundred thousand
When it comes, kill the battle-winning elephant, Rāyjādā Mahābālī.—*mhe*—
The enemy treated me badly
Bhūṇā!—*mhe*—
It's good if the enemy's dog is dead!" he said.—*vāh vāh*—
Bhūṇājī thought to himself: "Ruin worth a hundred thousand—how will Bābājī[90] bear the day?"
Bhūṇājī didn't speak at all.—*vāh vāh*—
The Bhāṭ thought to himself: "He has 'white eyes' all through.
Yes, there's no rage in him
What will you do taking him to the other brothers?"
The Bhāṭ speaks.—*vāh vāh*—
By God's grace, what does he tell Prince Bhūṇājī, let's see. *By saying it, know it, by saying it, let's see*
I'll say it now, by Dev's grace, here you are.—*vāh vāh*—*jī*

—*gāv*—

"Bhūṇā, why weren't you born as Bārāvatjī's daughter?—*mhe*—
You would have looked after the home well
Upon departing the lady would have given the Bhāṭ a place to repose.—*mhe*—
Upon departing I would get a long embrace
Why did you, with 'white-eyes,' take birth of the Bagaṛāvats?
Yes, why did you take birth?
If you'd been born as a woman.
Yes, you'd look after the household well
I would have received food then."—*vāh vāh*—
Bhūṇājī thought to himself:—*mhe*—
"Hey, I heard of Bābā Bhāṭ with my ears, *but I saw him with my eyes only today*
"He certainly is the root of trouble, brother!"—*vāh vāh*—

—*gāv*—

"Hey, Bhūṇā, as soon as you were born in the quarters of Daṛāvaṭ,—*vāh vāh*—
On that day the gong sounded

When you were born, the oil that burned in the night hasn't returned to my home yet
Your father gifted four elephants to beggars
He gave away four elephants.—*mhe*—
Leave alone the matter with the elephants.—*vāh vāh*—
The oil that burned when you were born—*mhe*—
Hey, that hasn't been returned to me till today."
Yes, I haven't received the value of that oil till today; leave the elephants be
By God's grace, Bhūṇājī thought to himself:—*mhe*—
"The Bhāṭ certainly is the root of trouble."—*vāh vāh*—
The Bagaṛāvats' Bhāṭ speaks.—*vāh vāh*—
What does he say to Prince Bhūṇā, let's see.
By saying it, know it, by saying it, let's see
I'll say it now by the Lord's grace, here you are.—*vāh vāh jī*—*vāh vāh*—

—*gāv*—

"There would be a lot of fighting at Rāṭhoḍā's Pond.—*mhe*—
Swords crisscrossed there
Hey, at this moment Nevā's Prince Bhāṅgaḍo isn't present.—*mhe*—
That elephant would run back like a jũjalo[91]
You with the 'white-eyes',—*mhe*—
I told you—*vāh vāh*—
If I tell my Bhāṅgījī—*mhe*—
Then the time taken to kill a jũjalo, not even that much time would he take to kill the elephant." *To kill this elephant*
Bhūṇājī thought to himself—*mhe*—he said: "Ever since Bābā Bhāṭ has
come, he only takes the name of some Bhāṅgījī.
Yes, he mentions it him a lot
And in Rāvjī's court I heard the name."
Yes, said Bhūṇājī
He said: "Dev's Daṛāvaṭ belongs to him.—*mhe*—
Over there, Nevā's brave khān, Bhāṅgaṛī Khān, the mighty one.—*mhe*—
Forts, castles, and *strongholds*
A brother ruling over castles, strongholds, forts, is backing you.—*mhe*—
What matter do you have to fear?"
By God's grace, how does Bhūṇājī attack the elephant
How does the fight between the elephant and Bhūṇā take place in the bazaar, let's see.—*vāh vāh*—

—*gāv*—

The prince pulled out his sword from its sheath.—*mhe*—
With might equal to Hanumān he arrived
Prince Mahābalī slew the battle-winning elephant.—*mhe*—
Masters, thunderous strength rose into Bhūṇā in the bazaar
So the elephant's body went and fell to one side

His trunk fell to one side
The elephant-driver fell to one side. *Said sir.*
By God's grace, Mīr spoke to Dīyā
He said: "Dīyā!—*mhe*—
Alas, alas, alas, alas, alas, alas, alas!
Yes, we made a great mistake!
Hey, we didn't ask Rāvjī—*mhe*—
We released this elephant without taking permission
Rāvjī Sāī will give us a big scolding!" *He'll give us a scolding*
Mīr went and placed an entreaty in front of Rāvjī.—*vāh vāh*—
Rāvjī said: "Mīr!" *What's the matter*
Mīr said: "Śrī Mahārāj, you know the Maṅgānā Elephant that used to be in the court."—*mhe*—
Rāvjī said: "It was there."
Yes
"Bhūṇājī killed it today."—*vāh vāh*—
Rāvjī said: "By God's grace, when it was tied to the stake?" *Why did Bhūṇājī kill it when it was tied to the stake?*
Mīr said: "No, no!" *He didn't kill it when it was tied to a stake*
"So then, hey, Mīr, who released the elephant in front of Bhūṇā?"—*mhe*—
"Śrī Mahārāj, I released the elephant.—*vāh vāh*—
I thought—*mhe*—
That the elephant would kill Bhūṇā now in the bazaar
It would be a matter of convenience for you."
Rāvjī said: "Hey, Mīr—*mhe*—
You let loose one elephant on Bhūṇā
Bhūṇā has the strength of eleven elephants.—*vāh vāh*—
If you tie eleven elephants to the toe of Bhūṇā's foot,
He'll drag them to the outskirts of Bhināy.
Why did you get one elephant killed, hey, brother?"
Yes, why did you get it killed off?
By God's grace, Bhūṇā set off for the fair in Puṣkar Rāj.—*vāh vāh*—
The letter written by Rāvjī Sāī said, "Bhūṇā, don't let any rowdiness or trouble happen in the fair.—*vāh vāh*—
Keep a watch over things
The one-month-long fair's supervision is under you, brother," he said.
The Bagaṛāvats' Bhāṭ went and halted in between on the way.
Yes, he dug in his heels deep; he said: "I won't go."
Bhūṇājī said: "Bhāṭ!—*mhe*—
Are you angry or what?"
Yes, are you angry or what, O Bābā Bhāṭ?
The Bhāṭ said: "This always happened—even when the Bagaṛāvats were alive I was angry."—*mhe*—
Bhūṇājī said: "Why have you halted?"
Yes, won't you go to the fair?
"Śrī Mahārāj, I'm going to return."

Yes, I won't go to the fair
"Why?" *Why won't you go, brother?* The Bhāṭ said: "My ritual bath is very difficult.
Yes, it is
And it is easy, Grain-Giver."—*vāh vāh*—
"How can it be of two kinds, Bhāṭ?" The Bhāṭ said: "After the Bagaṛāvats' Mahābhārat had taken place,—*mhe*—
At that time, the Bagaṛāvats' wealth—Rāvjī's fifty-two forts—*mhe*—
Got distributed under the fifty-two forts more or less . . .
Yes, it went as booty
Without coming here, the Sirdār . . .
Yes, won't leave the fair
If he brings wealth from the Bagaṛāvats' home,—*mhe*—
And I see it with my eyes,
Then my ritual bath will become difficult to complete
If there is someone born after the Bagaṛāvats—*mhe*—
Who'll retrieve the wealth from the others *and place it in front of me,*
I'll take it and deposit it in Dev's Daṛāvaṭ—
Then that ritual bath of mine will be good."
Bhūṇājī said:
"Listen, hey, Bhāṭ, I was born in the lineage of the Bagaṛāvats.—*mhe*—
Go! *Go to the fair*
I'll arrange your 'bath'."—*vāh vāh*—
The Bhāṭ said: "Wonderful, hey, my master, there's trust," he said.
Yes, "This trust rests on you," Bhūṇājī said.
The assault of the fair took place.—*mhe*—
Bhūṇājī and the Bhāṭ departed to the fair
Say victory to Śrī Devnārāyaṇ, victory
Say it, brother, everyone—small and great!

So, by God's grace, near the fair in Puṣkar, Bhūṇājī's assault took place.—*vāh vāh*—
Prince Bhūṇā's camp, by God's grace, was set up at Sudhā Bāī.—*vāh vāh*—
The Bagaṛāvats' Bhāṭ hung the gourd around his neck like me[92]
And started wandering about in the fair.—*vāh vāh*—
He didn't encounter any wealth belonging to the Bagaṛāvats
So the Bagaṛāvats' Bhāṭ, who ate two bread rolls, didn't have any satisfaction. *He ate two bread rolls, said sir.*
He couldn't digest them. *There was no quarrel, said sir.*

Chochū Bhāṭ Incites the Dhārapatīs' Bards

So all four Bārahaṭ brothers of the Dhārapatīs', wandering about in the fair, met with the Bhāṭ, *said sir.*
So they were friends and acquaintances of each other.—*mhe*—

Taking each other in arm, they met warmly.—*vāh vāh*—
The Bagaṛāvats' Bhāṭ speaks.—*mhe*—
What does he tell the Dhārāpatīs' Bārahaṭs.
Know it by saying, let's see, now by saying it

—*gāv*—

The Bagaṛāvats' Bhāṭ said this to the Bārahaṭs
"Puṣkar's lake is full to the limits, O brother Bārahaṭs.—*mhe*—
People from far and wide have crowded into the fair
Hey, why didn't your masters come to the fair?—*mhe*—
Before everyone would come, hey, brother, Rāvaḷjī and Raṇsī would come
Both brothers, Rāvaḷjī and Raṇ Siṅg, used to come before everyone
Everyone used to go only after them to the fair.
The supervision of the fair belonged to the Dhārāpatīs."
Yes, "It was always theirs."
Who said this? *Bhāṭjī said it*
The Bārahaṭ thought to himself:—*mhe*—
"He's a friend and acquaintance of your masters.
Yes, he is
Talk about some happiness or sorrow."

—*gāv*—

"Bhāṭ, there was tumult in the quarters of Pīlodā.—*mhe*—
Many flag-bearers wandered about in the camp.
My master will come now to the fair.—*mhe*—
I left him tightening the harness on the elephant.
By God's grace, ladders were being placed against the elephant.—*mhe*—
It was being adorned with ornaments.
He's about to come to the fair in few minutes' time."
Who said this?
The Dhārāpatīs' Bārahaṭjī said it
By God's grace, the Bagaṛāvats' Bhāṭ speaks.—*mhe*—
What does he say to the Bārahaṭs, let's see,
By saying it, know it, by saying it, let's see

—*gāv*—

"Your master drank wine on Bāsak's head
The Rajpūts are always in a drunken state
Your master won't come at all to the fair, brother Bārahaṭ.—*mhe*—
They are afraid of my master Prince Bhūṇā
Don't you know?
Yes, Bhūṇājī's camp here has been set up at Sudhā Bāī today.—*mhe*—
Your masters may want to come as much as they want.—*vāh vāh*—
In the fair, by God's grace, out of fear they won't sleep with legs stretched out."—*vāh vāh*—

That news was told, by God's grace, by the Bagaṛāvats' Bhāṭ.—*vāh vāh*—
The Dhārāpatīs' Bārahaṭ speaks.—*mhe*—
What news does he tell, let's see.
Yes, by saying it, know it, let's see, by saying it

—*gāv*—

"By God's grace, who descends from a home in the sky?—*mhe*—
Who would reside on a lance?
You talk about fear—*mhe*—
Sitting next to my master, what two things could your master Bhūṇājī talk about?
He wouldn't know how to converse with him.—*vāh vāh*—
Fear is a great thing!" *I'm the strong arm of the Bārahaṭs*
By God's grace, the Bagaṛāvats' Bhāṭ speaks.—*mhe*—
What reply does he give to the Bārahaṭs in return. *By saying it, know it, by saying it*
I'll say it now, by Lord Dev's grace, let's see.—*vāh vāh*—*jī*—*vāh vāh*—

—*gāv*—

"It's possible to descend from the sky-house with Inderpag[93]—*mhe*—
Hey, for a living, acrobats reside on the point of a lance.
By God's grace, my master will be strong in the battle of Rātākoṭ.—*vāh vāh*—
Sādū Siṅg will smash his head on his own, and die
Your masters have a remaining life of six months.
Yes, why be troubled?
They'll die on their own.—*vāh vāh*—
You're crazy—how many days more will they live."—*mhe*—
The Bārhaṭ thought to himself—*mhe*—: "The Bagaṛāvats' Bhāṭ is becoming strong
Yes, he's talking very haughtily
I'll inform my masters." *Then things will be settled*
Four Bārahaṭ brothers had come to the fair.
Two stayed back in the fair.—*mhe*—
Two turned their horses back to face Pilodā.—*vāh vāh*—
By God's grace, they went to the outskirts of the town and considered

"Brother, do such a deed
Yes, so that the first strike, great! upon reaching
Is ours; have such a deed done.
Yes, so that he listens to us
What should we do? *How should we do it?*
Put the horses' heads in front and the riders' turned about.
Yes, turn the riders' faces about
Enter the court sitting back-to-front on the horses, they'll speak to you right away on their own."

Yes, they will say Why have you come like this?
The Dhārāpatīs' Bhāṭ entered the court sitting back-to-front on his horse.—*vāh vāh*—
Behind them were Sirdārs.—*mhe*—
They said:
"Hey, why have you come astride back-to-front?" *"Speak!" they said*
They began beating the Bārahaṭs with green bamboo sticks.—*vāh vāh*—
The Dhārāpatī said: "Hey, brother, Sirdārs—*mhe*—
Don't beat the Bārahaṭs! *Ask them what the matter is*
Why have they entered like this?"—*mhe*—
The Sirdārs said: "What's the matter? Tell us the news in detail, why have you entered riding back-to-front!"
The Dhārāpatīs' Bhāṭ speaks.—*mhe*—
What news does he tell. *By saying it, know it, by saying it*

—*gāv*—

"By God's grace, look, the carpet gets cut by the lance's blade.—*mhe*—
Your brothers' court was attended well
Ride up and fight in the fair, master of Citauṛ.—*mhe*—
Hey, in the fair you were called rider of the Mare Mule
The people in the fair speak lightly of you
But I can't bring myself to say it. *Can't say it*
The people in the fair say that—*mhe*—
By God's grace, the Dhārāpatī Kumahār boy—that donkey-rider—hasn't come.
Yes, why didn't he arrive?
The lying world says that.—*vāh vāh*—
But I can't speak at all, Śrī Mahārāj."
Yes, what more should I say?
The Dhārāpatī Sirdār speaks.—*vāh vāh*—
What news does he tell, let's see.
By saying it, know it, by saying it, let's see
I'll say it now, by Lord Dev's grace, here you are.—*vāh vāh*—*jī vāh vāh*—

—*gāv*—

"Brother, in whose camp was there fun made of me?—*mhe*—
Who amongst the Rajpūts betrayed me?
Show me that adversary, O Sudānā Bārahaṭjī—*mhe*—
Look, after severing his head,—*mhe*—
I'll urinate on him
By God's grace, I'll sever his head.—*mhe*—
And have boys piss on it.—*vāh vāh*—
On the one who has taken my name."—*mhe*—
So, by God's grace, the Bārahaṭ speaks; what news does he tell, let's see. *By saying it, know it, by saying it, let's see*
I'll say it now, by Dev's grace, here you are.—*vāh vāh*—*jī*—*vāh vāh*—

—gāv—

"In Bhūṇā's camp fun was made of you.*—mhe—*
And the Bagaṛāvats' Bhāṭ, wandered about the fair betraying you.
Ride and fight in the fair, master of Citauṛ.*—mhe—*
In the fair you're called the rider of Mule and Donkey
Those people of the fair speak lightly, I can't speak at all."
Yes, Śrī Mahārāj, I can't speak
The Dhārāpatī Sirdār said:
"Prince Mokaḷ Siṅg*—mhe—*
You know that Bhūṇājī—who's been fostered by Rāvjī—he's behaving curiously today. *He's behaving very strangely*
So brothers Ratan Siṅg, Mokaḷ Siṅg, do the following:*—mhe—*
Prepare an assault of the fair.*—vāh vāh—*
By God's grace, we have his father's elephant with us.
Take the elephant along.*—mhe—*
Go and show it to Bhūṇā:
"It's your father's elephant, brother!" *Take a look, there it is with us*

—gāv—

The Jaymaṅgalā and Gajmaṅgalā Elephants Meet

The Dhārāpatī Sirdār went to the stall of the Jaymaṅgalā elephant.*—vāh vāh—*
Both brothers stood with hands folded in salutation
"Ask for an offering Lord Guṇeś.*—mhe—*
O my dear elephant-king of the plantain-woods, go to the fair
Lord Guṇeś, proceed to the fair
Proceed to the fair.*—vāh vāh—*
Prince Mokaḷ Siṅg, bring the elephant, brother," he said.*—vāh vāh—*
Prince Mokaḷ Siṅg said:
"Śrī Mahārāj*—mhe—*
There's an augur in your court.
Yes, there's an augur
For prophecies, we employ him
And, for prophecies he receives offerings of grain
We didn't have any work for the augur, for so many days
Today, there's work for our going to the fair
Ask him about an omen."
Yes, let's ask the augur about an omen
By God's grace, how does the Dhārāpatī call the augur.*—mhe—*
How does he ask about an omen for the fair, let's see.
By saying it, know it, by saying it, let's see
I'll say it now, by Dev's grace, let's see.*—vāh vāh—*

—gāv—

"Consider an omen, brother, augur of Fort Pilodā!—*mhe*—
Speak, brother, your news about the omen
Should we release Jaymaṅgalā elephant from the quarters of Pilodā?—*mhe*—
Hey, will it or won't it return to the throne of Pilodā?
Augur!—*mhe*—
Consider this prophecy!"
Yes, look at the omens, and tell us truthfully
The augur said: "Śrī Mahārāj—*mhe*—
I don't falsify my omens!"
Yes, "I will say what I see."
The Dhārāpatī said: "Go ahead, augur, you're pardoned seven times over!—*vāh vāh*—
Tell us the matter the way you see it, brother."—*mhe*—
So, now how does the augur prepare an omen for the Dhārāpatī
Yes, consider an omen—how does he tell the Dhārāpatī the news about the omen, let's see. *By saying it, know it, by saying it, let's see*
I'll say it now, by Bhagavān's grace, let's see.—*vāh vāh—jī*

—*gāv*—

"By God's grace, O King, the Uḍarmerī[94] spoke at the place called Mān hī Samundrā.—*mhe*—
Buvāṇī[95] spoke in the direction of the banyan tree on the left side
I saw you defeated, King of Fort Pilodā—*mhe*—
Brother, the mighty Bhūṇ won in the fair
I saw Bhūṇā victorious
And you I saw defeated,
Whether you launch the assault of the fair, *or whether you don't.*"
The Dhārāpatī said: "Augur—*mhe*—
you've told the matter wrong!"
Yes, look carefully at the omen, and speak!

—*gāv*—

By God's grace, the Dhārāpatī said: "Augur!—*mhe*—
You said Dev and Medū have met.—*vāh vāh*—
And you corrupted matters
I cut down Savāī Bhoj in the battlefield with my hands.—*mhe*—
Then what matter now, is Bhūṇā, the son, for me?
Bhūṇājī is, after all, born of him.—*vāh vāh*—
The 'big' father of Bhūṇājī,—*mhe*—
I cut him down."
Yes, I killed him with my hands in the battlefield.
Who said that news—the Dhārāpatī Sirdār said it.
The augur thought to himself: "Hey, it's not possible for you to survive here.
Yes, there's no staying here at all
The way you've seen things, *tell it exactly that way. Say it exactly the way it's been seen by you.*"

—*gāv*—

"By God's grace, Kākālī Devī took the son of Bāgh Siṅg—*mhe*—
That man went the way of Ād Sagat
Hey, in the battlefield of the Raṭhors—*mhe*—
Brother, who among you struck Bhoj with a pointed lance?
I was present there.
Yes, who among you killed him, tell about that!
He was taken away by the Great Sagat.—*mhe*—
Hey, her discus flew—he died on his own."—*vāh vāh*—
The Dhārāpatī Sirdār said:
"Hey, augur—*mhe*—
For one you're asking us for a secret, and for another *you're speaking about matters concerning omens.*"
The augur said: "Śrī Mahārāj, I say the things that I see."
Yes, I say them the way I see them
The Dhārāpatī said: "Augur! Listen, brother,—*mhe*—
That moment was different, this moment is different
Things change moment to moment.—*mhe*—
Consider a second omen."
Yes, give us a second opinion now, let's see
The augur said: "Śrī Mahārāj, I don't falsify the omens.—*vāh vāh*—
I will read the omen exactly the way I see it."
The Dhārāpatī said: "You're pardoned seven times over," he said. *Speak*
"Tell us whatever you see."—*vāh vāh*—
What prophecy does the augur prepare
By God's grace, what news about the omen does he tell.
By saying it, know it, Bhopājī Mahārāj, by saying it

—*gāv*—

"O King, this time both lion and goat spoke together at the foot of the banyan tree.—*mhe*—
I considered the same omen
I saw you defeated.—*mhe*—
Right upon entering the fair, Jaymaṅgalā elephant, was captured in the Kāśmirī tent by Bārāvat's Bhūṇ
There you are sir, whether you launch an assault *or whether you don't*
I saw Bhūṇājī victorious,
You I saw defeated."

—*gāv*—

"By God's grace, hey, the ruler's augur is false, false!—*mhe*—
By God's grace, since when did you speak matters of untruth?
Let me go to the fair and come back, O ruler's augur;—*mhe*—
Returning I'll cut off both your hands, and nose
I'll leave you a cripple without hands or legs."—*vāh vāh*—

The augur thought to himself:—*mhe*—
"After going to the fair, there is no way that the enemy will return
And, over here, if he lets out a command, to cut hands and nose—*mhe*—
Ruin will come down on me.
Yes, there will be ruin waiting at home
After going to the fair, there is no way he'll return."
By God's grace, the king said: "Hey, augur—*mhe*—
Leave aside past matters!—*vāh vāh*—
How did the lion and goat meet together at one place?" *Speak about that*
The augur said: "Śrī Mahārāj, the shepherd took the goats and sheep, and went into the hills
A tired nanny goat stayed back in a cave.
Night fell.—*mhe*—
By God's grace, at night a lion lived in the cave.—*vāh vāh*—
Roaring—*mhe*—
It came out of the den.
Frightened, the goat cried out aloud.—*mhe*—
The lion thought to itself—*vāh vāh*—: 'For so many days there was no animal that could face you in this land or in these hills.
Today the animal that faces you,
Yes, that animal is capable of facing you
That is great today.'—*vāh vāh*—
Roaring, it came out of the den,
Putting its tail between its haunches—*mhe*—
The lion retreated into its den, *said sir.*
Goṭhā is this goat—*mhe*—
Fort Pilodā the lion
The lion I saw defeated, the goat *I saw victorious*
You are the lion.—*mhe*—
In front of you, Bhūṇājī,
Yes, is the goat
Śrī Mahārāj, I saw the goat victorious.—*vāh vāh*—
Whether you launch an assault or don't."
The Dhārāpatī said: "Augur, you've mixed all matters together.—*vāh vāh*—
By God's grace, what will happen now, if I don't cut off your hands and nose."—*vāh vāh*—
The augur thought to himself: "There will be ruin waiting at home!"
Yes, now it won't take any time for his command to be discharged
So the Dhārāpatīs' augur spat in his hands and ran away.—*vāh vāh*—
A Sirdār said:
"Śrī Mahārāj, the augur has run away." *"Let him run away," the Dhārāpatī said*
"Let him go!—*vāh vāh*—
Prince Mokaḷ Siṅg, now go and raise the assault of the fair."

—*gāv*—

"Prince Mokaḷā, put on the elephants' ornaments and silken garments—*mhe*—
Let the gong resound
Hey, Lord Guṇeś asked for an offering—*mhe*—
My elephant-king of the plantain-woods is going to the fair
Lord Guṇeś, proceed to the fair.—*vāh vāh*—
Mokaḷ Siṅg, brother, it's going to be the battle of the fair."—*vāh vāh*—

—*gāv*—

"Ṭhākurs, wrap the cloth around your turbans.—*mhe*—
Drink great quantities of opium!
Tighten the belt of Sāmbhar leather, courageous men.—*vāh vāh*—
Fasten, brother, the shield of real rhinoceros hide
Hey, from our court get out old turbans used in battle
Saddle up fresh Arabian horses.—*mhe*—
Black horses, Dhātī horses
Ṭhākurs, red-faced ones, others white, very white."
With moustaches of iron the Kumahār got astride his horse—*mhe*—
His lance rained death
Astride his horse the Dhārāpatī Sirdār rode out of the gate.—*mhe*—
Five and a half thousand horses
Taking five and a half thousand horses—*mhe*—
He launched the assault of the fair.—*vāh vāh*—
By God's grace, they crossed the village's outer limits. *Said sir.*
Both the brothers received a jolt.
Yes, they remained standing
The Dhārāpatī Sirdār said: "Prince Mokaḷ Siṅg—*mhe*—
Hey, brother, the assault of the fair, both you brothers take it on."
Yes, only you go
"Why?"—*mhe*—
The Dhārāpatī brothers said "If both of us brothers go to the fair, we have a fierce sort of reputation.—*vāh vāh*—
By God's grace, these days Bhūṇājī has a powerful streak.
If the Goddess's sway holds—*mhe*—
If he's struck by iron and Bhūṇājī gets killed,
Rāvjī Sāī will give us a big scolding.
And, who knows, Bhūṇājī might get in a rage and our legs will be broken—*mhe*—
Even then Rāvjī Sāī will give us a scolding:
'I didn't go the fair, but my son went.'—*mhe*—
The Dhārāpatī Sirdārs were beaten, so they ran away.—*vāh vāh*—
Then too I would get a bad name.
Both you brothers go.—*mhe*—
If he makes you run, then I'll take care of the matter later on:
'I didn't go, Śrī Mahārāj—*mhe*—
My boys went.—*vāh vāh*—

Your Bhūṇājī made my boys run off.'—*vāh vāh*—
And if you go and kill Bhūṇājī, then too I'll take care of the matter:
'Why did your Bhūṇājī trouble my boys.
Yes, why did he trouble them,
He was killed being struck by iron.—*vāh vāh*—
Now what will happen?'—*mhe*—
I'll straighten out the whole thing later on."—*vāh vāh*—
So, by God's grace, with five horses, the Dhārāpatī Sirdār prepared to return to the Fort Pilodā:—*vāh vāh*—
"Prince Mokaḷ Siṅg, both you brothers, go to the fair, brother."
Yes, only you go!
Both Sirdārs departed to the fair.—*vāh vāh*—
By God's grace, they arrived in Puṣkar Rāj, *said sir.*
At Sudhā Bāī, indeed there was Prince Bhūṇājī's camp.—*mhe*—
And at Old Puṣkar, the Dhārāpatīs' camp
The Dhārāpatī Sirdār set up camp.—*vāh vāh*—
The Rajpūt's son spread out the tent.—*mhe*—
And began sharpening the blades of lances—sharpening the tips of lances, sharpening the blades of swords.
Preparations for food and water
Yes, were made, said sir.
The Bagaṛāvats' Bhāṭ wandered to and fro in the fair.
Yes, he roamed about the fair
By God's grace, he saw the elephant standing there.—*vāh vāh*—
So, afterward he arrived at the Dhārāpatīs' camp, *said sir.*
A carpet was laid out.—*mhe*—
He went onto the carpet and
Yes, Bhāṭjī, sat down
The Bhāṭ speaks.—*mhe*—
What news does he tell the Dhārāpatīs' princes, let's see. *By saying it, know it, let's see, by saying it*
I'll say it now, by the Lord's grace, here you are.—*vāh vāh—jī—vāh vāh*—

—*gāv*—

"You did wrong bringing the elephant.—*mhe*—
O Prince, you did very wrong!
Deliver this elephant to Bhūṇā's camp.—*mhe*—
Bhūṇā's ears are being filled by the terrific Chochū Bhāṭ
There's that Bhāṭ of the Bagaṛāvats.—*mhe*—
There's talk of your elephants over and over."[96]
Yes, talk about elephants and elephants is going on there
By God's grace, the prince said:
"Hey, which country do you belong to!" *Tell me about that*
The Bhāṭ said: "I'm from across seven seas."—*mhe*—
"Name?" "People call me Jagīśyo."—*vāh vāh*—
"Jagīśyā, bring the elephant's claimant over here *and you come with him*

"Hey, Śrī Mahārāj, I spoke in your favor.
Yes, I spoke in your favor
You considered it bad of me."—*mhe*—

—*gāv*—

"By God's grace, I didn't get the elephant by begging for it.—*mhe*—
Nor did I get it for the price of a sale
I brought the elephant from the Rāṭhors' battlefield—*mhe*—
After breaking Bhoj's sharp swords
I rent apart Bhoj's liver.[97]—*vāh vāh*—
Only then did the elephant come into my hands.—*vāh vāh*—
It's not been begged for and gotten that I'll hand it over to you."
The Bhāṭ said: "Śrī Mahārāj, I spoke then in your favor.—*mhe*—
These things are not meant to be kept standing in the fair.
Yes, they're meant to be taken about
If it's taken about in the fair, then at least people can see it.—*vāh vāh*—
It's a thing for people to see.—*mhe*—
It's in the form of Guṇeś, isn't it."—*vāh vāh*—
Every cell of the Dhārāpatī Siradār's body was thrilled: "The matter is right."
"Śrī Mahārāj, your splendor will increase.—*vāh vāh*—
People will ask: 'Whose elephant is it?'—*mhe*—
And say: 'it's the Dhārāpatī's.' "
Yes, it's the Dhārāpatī's.

By God's grace, in the Dhārāpatī's camp, the Bhāṭ got the elephant from the Bagaṛāvats' house released.—*vāh vāh*—
He began walking it about in the fair.—*mhe*—
The Bagaṛāvats' Bhāṭ went to Bhūṇājī's camp and said:
"Hey, Sirdārs, where's Bhūṇājī, speak up!"
Yes, where is he?
The Sirdārs said: "He's gone to Puṣkar.—*vāh vāh*—
He's taking a 'bath' on the steps.—*mhe*—
The Bhāṭ said: "It's good that he's taking a 'bath' on the steps.—*vāh vāh*—
Hey, the Dhārāpatis' elephant is roaming about the fair.—*mhe*—
Release this elephant of ours, and walk our elephant about the fair.
The Jaymaṅgalā elephant belonged to the Bagaṛāvats' house.
Yes, it did
In Bhūṇā's army there was the Gajmaṅgalā elephant—it too belonged to the Bagaṛāvats' house, *said sir.*
Release the elephant from Bhūṇājī's camp."—*vāh vāh*—
By God's grace, he told the elephant-driver: "Hey, take the elephant for a walk in the fair, brother.—*vāh vāh*—
Elephant will recognize elephant."—*mhe*—
The elephants met with their trunks. *Said sir.*
They made a knot with their trunks.—*mhe*—
The elephants met again.—*vāh vāh*—

By God's grace, Bhūṇā had the Gajmaṅgalā elephant from the Bagaṛāvats' house.—*mhe*—
It was with its master, so what unhappiness could there be?—*vāh vāh*—
Rāvjī Sāī brought it as a trophy.—*mhe*—
By God's grace, the Jaymaṅgalā elephant, it was in captivity, brother.—*vāh vāh*—
The Jaymaṅgalā elephant, by God's grace, when both elephants met—*mhe*—
At that time, tears came into its eyes. *vāh vāh*—
The Bagaṛāvats' Bhāṭ speaks; what news does he tell the elephant.
By saying it, know it, by saying it
I'll say it now, by Dev's grace, here you are.—*vāh vāh*—*jī*—*vāh vāh*—

—*gāv*—

"Patience, patience, Lord Guṇeś.—*mhe*—
The tears from your eyes show sorrow
Hey, today you're tied to the enemy's doorway.—*mhe*—
Tomorrow I'll tie you to Daṛāvaṭ's foremost gate
Tomorrow I'll tie you there!"—*vāh vāh*—
Who said this news? The Bagaṛāvats' Bhāṭ said it.—*vāh vāh*—
The elephant speaks.—*mhe*—
What news does he tell the Bhāṭ, let's see.
By saying it, know it, by saying it, let's see

—*gāv*—

By God's grace, that news the elephant did tell—*mhe*—: "Brother, in Pilodā, many servants roam about," it said.—*vāh vāh*—
"Strong are the bow and arrows of those Sirdārs.
Hey, brother, how are you going to tie me to the quarters of Daṛāvaṭ so easily?—*mhe*—
Pilodā is known as the second Rāṇ of eight-four forts.
You think it's such an easy business!
Yes, it's no light matter
Rāvjī Sā fears Pilodā.—*vāh vāh*—
He doesn't accept it as the eighty-four-fort second Rāṇ City.—*mhe*—
O Beggar, will you turn everything upside down?—*vāh vāh*—
Am I not at the right place?—*vāh vāh*—
I'm in a big household."—*mhe*—
By God's grace, after eleven years the Bhāṭ made the elephants meet.—*vāh vāh*—
He said: "Hey, brother, I was to arrange your meeting today, which I did for you."
By God's grace, the Bhāṭ told the Dhārāpatīs' elephant-driver: "You take yours away, brother."—*mhe*—
And told the elephant from Bhūṇājī's camp: "You go to your camp."
The Bagaṛāvats' Bhāṭ arrived at the steps of Puṣkar Rāj, *said sir.*
At that time, Bhūṇājī was sitting on the steps taking a ritual bath.
At that time, the Bhāṭ arrived.

The Bhāṭ speaks. What does he tell his master, let's see.
By saying it, know it, by saying it, let's see

—*gāv*—

Devnārāyaṇ Saves Chochū Bhāṭ from Drowning

"By God's grace, why are you bathing at the canal with good water?—*mhe*—
Bhūṇā water and oil flow together
Hey, look, Jaymaṅgalā stands at the enemy's doorway.—*mhe*—
Hey, Bhūṇā, you bear the enemy's spears on your body
Daughter's father, the elephant is tied up with the enemy.—*mhe*—
Hey, you're taking a 'bath.'—*vāh vāh*—
Did you think a 'bath' would be appropriate at this time?"—*mhe*—
Bhūṇājī said: "Come, Bābā Bhāṭ, come. *Come*
I heard of you with my ears, *but I saw you with my eyes only now*

—*gāv*—

"By God's grace, brother, Dev has many a brother.—*mhe*—
Bhūṇā how often should I now remember you?
Hey, the elephant can't be captured by you.—*vāh vāh*—
Put on a gourd stringed instrument in the fair, and become Rām's mendicant
Merchants and traders are feeding lāḍūs today.
Yes, don't miss the lāḍūs
You eat as well!—*vāh vāh*—
You won't be able to capture the elephant."—*mhe*—
By God's grace, Bhūṇājī said: "Bābā Bhāṭ, you're the root of trouble.—*vāh vāh*—
It seems to me that you had the Bagaṛāvats killed by causing trouble like this over and over again."—*mhe*—

—*gāv*—

"The grey elephant is standing in the fair.—*mhe*—
A thousand diamonds give it splendor
Brother, the Bagaṛāvats used to have Sālagrām worshipped.—*mhe*—
Bhūṇā, riding on that elephant the Pilodā's son-prince is wandering about
'White-eyed-one,' where else should he go, but ride and wander about—
after the Bagaṛāvats, the likes of you were born!"—*vāh vāh*—
Bhūṇājī saw: "This Bhāṭ is the root of trouble."—*vāh vāh*—
So, talk went on between Bhūṇā and the Bhāṭ on the steps.—*mhe*—
Speak: Victory to Śrī Devnārāyaṇ Bhagavān, victory.
By God's grace, Bhūṇājī said: "Hey, Bhāṭ,—*mhe*—
Take a look, I weigh out the tolas.—*vāh vāh*—
And I distribute gold to the Brāhmans
You too pick up some gold too.
Yes, "You take some small bits and pieces too," he said, "great, brother!"

By God's grace, the Nārad-like Bhāṭ speaks.—*mhe*—
What news does he tell Prince Bhūṇā in return, let's see.
By saying it, know it, let's see, by saying it, how does he take the gold

—*gāv*—

"Whether you give me one lakh or two lakhs—*mhe*—
Hey, I consider your lakh worth dust!
I won't take even a gift from a self-willed Sirdār.—*mhe*—
And if I do, then I don't even take small change from a self-willed Sirdār."
Yes, I won't accept your small coins today
Bhūṇājī said: "Bābā Bhāṭ,—*mhe*—
Who is self-willed?" *Who is?*
The Bhāṭ said: "You are! *You are, my master, who else?*
You're not born of Rāvjī," he said.—*mhe*—
"On the day you get together with the brothers—together with Dev,
Yes, on that day, give me a towel one and a half hands long
I'll consider it the same as a lakh.—*vāh vāh*—
So, by God's grace, Bhūṇājī, what good was it being born of the Bagaṛāvats,
Hey, brother?" he said.—*mhe*—
Bhūṇājī said: "Hey, Bābā Bhāṭ—*mhe*—
Why does this world of merchants and administrators collect together in the fair?"
Yes, for what reason?
"Śrī Mahārāj, to take a bath they collect together.
Yes, for what else have they got together
To do acts of merit and virtue
Yes, they've collected together."
Bhūṇājī said: "Bābā Bhāṭ—*mhe*—
The world of people do acts of virtue.—*vāh vāh*—
And should we destroy duty?"
Yes, where is our duty?
The Bhāṭ said: "Śrī Mahārāj, whatever virtue happens, it will happen to you.—*mhe*—
And the sin that happens, *that will happen to me,*" *he said:* "*Free the elephant!*
Puṣkar Rāj has always been hungry for an offering.[98] You give Puṣkar an offering.—*vāh vāh*—
Puṣkar Rāj will be very happy with you."
Yes, Puṣkar Rāj will be happy then!
Bhūṇājī said: "By God's grace, Bābā Bhāṭ—*mhe*—
These five days belonging to the pilgrimage of five places.[99]
Yes, let these pass at least
And on the day of the 'first,' we'll do whatever business you say afterward.
Yes, we'll do it afterward
Today, by God's grace, is the day of the 'eleventh,'[100] brother.—*mhe*—
On the day of the 'eleventh,' we won't do business." *vāh vāh*—
The day of the "eleventh" went by, and the day of the "twelfth" went by.

The Bagaṛāvats' Bhāṭ said: "Hey, my master,—*mhe*—
You said five days, exactly five years are going to pass!"
Yes, the days seem very long to me
He went out into the fair, taking his gourd stringed instrument like me.[101]—
vāh vāh—
He wandered about on the day of the "eleventh" in the fair, and wandered about the day of the "twelfth" in the fair, and wandered about the day of the "thirteenth" in the fair
On the day of the "fourteenth" too he wandered about in the fair, *said sir.*
On the day of the full moon, after taking a ritual bath,—*mhe*—
As soon as the sun-king rose, he arrived at Bhūṇā's camp.
At that time, by God's grace, Bhūṇājī was sporting with his Sirdārs.—*vāh vāh*—
Food and drink were being prepared.
Yes, he was serving food
Onto some Sirdārs' platters he served sāg,[102]—*mhe*—
Onto some Sirdārs' platters he served flat bread.
The Bhāṭ remained standing at some distance.—*vāh vāh*—
The Bhāṭ speaks.—*mhe*—
What does he tell Bhūṇā let's see. *By saying it, know it, let's see, by saying it*
I'll say it now, by the Lord's grace, here you are.—*vāh vāh*—*jī*—*vāh vāh*—

—*gāv*—

"By God's grace, there were thirty-six varieties of foods at Manvā Bhoj's.—*mhe*—
There used to be an authority over these thirty-six kinds of foods
Today I've seen such a spectacle in the fair.—*mhe*—
Instead of the barber, food was well served by a Sirdār
Is there no barber left in the control of the Bagaṛāvats, brother?
Yes, you became the barber.
You did a good thing, Bhūṇājī."
Who said that news? The Bagaṛāvats' Bhāṭ of the lineage told Bhūṇā right upon arriving.
Bhūṇājī speaks.—*mhe*—
What news does he tell the Bhāṭ, let's see.
By saying it, know it, let's see, by saying it
I'll say it now, by Dev's grace, let's see.—*vāh vāh*—

—*gāv*—

"Bhāṭ, I'll worship the Goddess Sā̃mrā, now
I'll give the Goddess Mother-Nausar offerings
Hey, let's go to the land of birth.—*mhe*—
Listen, hey, Bhāṭ, we'll give out this warning."
Yes, it's a warning
The Bhāṭ said: "Śrī Mahārāj—*mhe*—
This is no warning of yours. *This isn't it*
This is a warning of the barbers!—*mhe*—
If you have any weapons, then give them to some Sirdār

And a good pony.
Yes, give it away to the Sirdār
So that's your warning.
Yes, prince, sir, that is your warning
This warning is of barbers.
Yes, it's a warning of barbers
They'll say, we went to Bhūṇājī's camp, he fed us food well, brother, the barber was good.
Yes, he used to feed us well
Śrī Mahārāj, that's hardly your work!" he said.
Bhūṇājī speaks. What does he tell the Bhāṭ, let's see. *By saying it, know it, let's see, by saying it.*
I'll say it now, by Lord Dev's grace, here you are.—*vāh vāh—jī—vāh vāh—*

—*gāv*—

"To ride you have the horse Phūlrīyā.—*mhe*—
To wrap around a blanket with five colored threads
You've been getting me to fight the Dhārāpatīs today.—*mhe*—
Hey, how much of an army does your master Dev have on his side?
How much might does your master Dev have?
Yes, how much of an army does he have, tell about that
Beggar!—*mhe*—
Since you've come you've been saying 'fight, fight.' "—*vāh vāh*—
The Bhāṭ speaks. What news does he tell Bhūṇā in return.[103]
By saying it, know it, by saying it
I'll say it now, by Dev's grace, here you are.[104]—*vāh vāh*—

—*gāv*—

—*gāv*—

Bhūṇājī Confronts Dīyājī Jodhkā and Kālū Mīr

"Now be prepared Bābā Bhāṭ.—*mhe*—
Climb onto the horse Phūlrīyā
Stop at the Nausar Pass.—*mhe*—
Stop at Sudhā Bāī
Hey, Rāyjādā Mahābāli became enraged in the fair.—*mhe*—
Bhāṭ, the Kumāhār's son, won't go anywhere alive." *They won't return alive*
Having said this, Bābā Bhāṭjī got ready.—*mhe*—
He climbed up onto the horse Phūlrīyo, brother.
"Hey, Baṇīyās pick up your shops.—*mhe*—
Brother, pick up the shops and the stands in the bazaar's lane
People, climb up onto the hills, brother.—*mhe*—*Climb up high*
The sweet ones will fight now in the bazaar
Like the Bagaṛāvats' Bhārat.

Yes, that kind of battle is going to happen here. All of you climb up high
You'll be killed without cause."—*vāh vāh*—
Brother, Kālū Mīr and Dīyā met on their own in the fair
Let the elephant go.—*mhe*—
Take the Mare Bāvalī, Savāī Bhoj's revenge, from Dīyā
He has the Mare Bāvalī.
Yes, take it first, why? Because it's in front of us
Why, we'll free the elephant afterward."—*vāh vāh*—
By God's grace, Mīr and Dīyājī Jodhkā met and—*mhe*—
Came to take a "bath" in the fair
Mīr said: "Alas, alas, alas, alas, Dīyā!—*mhe*—
O brother, the fast has been spoiled now! *Now the fast is spoiled*
Hey, we gave Prince Bhūṇā the command ourselves.
Yes, we didn't remember that matter!
Look, here he's come!"—*vāh vāh*—
Bhūṇājī speaks.—*mhe*—
What does he tell Dīyā first.
By saying it, know it, let's see, by saying it
I'll say it now, by Dev's grace, here you are.—*vāh vāh*—*jī vāh vāh*—

—*gāv*—

By God's grace, Prince Bhūṇājī told that news to Dīyā.—*vāh vāh*—
"Brother, you are called Sakrām Siṅgjī from Fort Sāvar.—*mhe*—
Your 'caste' is Dīyā. *Dīyā, Dīyājī's name was Sakrām Siṅgjī.*
On the battlefield of the Rāṭhors, who among you took credit for having killed Bhoj?"
Yes, who took credit, tell about that!
What is jas? That is, who went and told Rāvjī Sāī, "I killed Bhoj?"
Yes, I killed such-and-such, that is jas.
Mīr said: "Alas, alas, alas, alas, alas," Mir spoke.—*mhe*—
With great tact he spoke.—*vāh vāh*—
Mir said: "Friend, Dīyā—*mhe*—
Speak with great tact."
Yes, speak carefully—death has come!
Dīyājī speaks.—*mhe*—
What news does he tell Prince Bhūṇājī in return.
By saying it, know it, let's see, by saying it
I'll say it now, by Dev's grace, here you are.—*vāh vāh jī*—*vāh vāh*—

—*gāv*—

"I'm Sakrām Siṅgjī of Fort Sāvar.—*mhe*—
Of 'caste' I'm a Dīyā
I don't know about the glory of slaying Savāī Bhoj, brother, Prince.—*mhe*—
A Bhaṅgī[105] took away the clothes."
Who takes away a Sirdār fallen in battle? *A Bhaṅgī does*
"Śrī Mahārāj, a Bhaṅgī takes away a dead man's clothes.—*mhe*—

I was a commander of the army on that day. Overseeing Rāvjī's forces, I went to the bank of the Khārī River at that time.—*mhe*—
Savāī Bhoj's corpse lay on the ground.
Yes, the torso was lying below
And the mare was standing close by.—*vāh vāh*—
The sparkling pearls from his ears were lying there too.—*mhe*—
The mail of chain was on Bhoj's body.
Yes, it was worn
I went near and unfastened it.—*vāh vāh*—
The helmet I took with me.
Yes, I took it
And the sparkling pearls, I took them.
The mare's reins were in Bhoj's hand.—*mhe*—
Giving it a jerk, I freed the reins, and brought the mare.—*vāh vāh*—
So I certainly brought the mare belonging to the Rajpūt who had fallen in battle.
Yes, but I don't know who killed Bhoj
I don't know about his slaying.—*vāh vāh*—
The mare is with me. If you say so, I'll have her brought to you.—*vāh vāh*—
And, if you say so,
Yes, then I'll have it brought to Dev Mahārāj in Daṛāvaṭ."
Bhūṇājī said: "Great, brother, Dīyā, it's all right, it has already come," he said. *It'll come*
Mīr said: "Alas, alas, you spoke very nicely."
Yes, you spoke nicely—saved our lives.
Bhūṇājī speaks. What does he tell Mīr.
Yes, by saying it, know it, let's see, by saying it

—*gāv*—

"Manvā Bhoj used to have buffaloes.—*mhe*—
They would sit body against body
The buffaloes were taken away by Kālū Mīr together with Birjā and Birmā Goḍ who were with him
Where did you leave those buffaloes?" *Tell me that!*
Mīr said: "Prince, sir—*mhe*—
I took away five hundred, brother.—*vāh vāh*—
Today there are a thousand.
Yes, they went away and are with me
O Prince, hey, if you say so, then I'll have them brought to you.—*mhe*—
If you say so, I'll have them brought to your Dev."
I didn't eat a single one, if at all, I consumed their milk.
Bhūṇā said: "It's all right, brother!—*mhe*—
Mīr, they'll come, no worry at all."—*vāh vāh*—
Mīr said: "Hey, O Prince, I sent you to oversee the fair—*mhe*—
What's this business you've done? *Why did you start a fight?*
The fair, the people, all are in tumult."—*mhe*—

Bhūṇā said: "Mīr, that's the Bhāṭ of my lineage.—*mhe*—
He says, brother, that the Dhārāpatī Sirdārs have an elephant belonging to my father."
Yes, I'm going to free it
Mīr said: "O Śrī Mahārāj, why free the elephant through such noise and fight.
Yes, I and Dīyājī will go now
We'll mediate a settlement.—*vāh vāh*—
And we'll go and collect the elephant."—*vāh vāh*—
Bhūṇājī said: "Mīr, actually I don't want to stage a fight.
Yes, I only want the elephant
I need the elephant, brother."—*vāh vāh*—
Mīr said: "So then, Śrī Mahārāj, you just stay standing here."
Yes, wait here—I'll go
Kālū Mīr and Dīyājī—*mhe*—
Reached the Dhārāpatī's camp.—*vāh vāh*—
By God's grace, what talk about a settlement happens?—*mhe*—
Now talk between the prince and Mīr and Dīyājī takes place.
By saying it, know it, let's see, by saying it
I'll say it now, by God's grace.—*vāh vāh*—

—*gāv*—

"By bringing the elephant, you did a very foolish thing!—*mhe*—
Mokaḷ Siṅg, you decided a foolish thing
Now turn over the elephant to us.—*mhe*—
Wily Chochū Bhāṭ has started to fill Bhūṇā's ears in the fair
You shouldn't have brought the elephant to the fair.
Yes, not good to bring it
By God's grace, in the fair today, everybody is pushing talk about the elephant.—*vāh vāh*—
Give me the elephant.
Yes, so that I can have it sent to Bhūṇājī's camp
There will be no trouble for the people in the fair, there will be no trouble . . ."
Yes, for you; you'll reach your home alive and well
Mokaḷ Siṅg said: "By God's grace, Dīyā—*mhe*—
Why didn't you bring the elephant's claimant along, brother?"
Yes, didn't you bring him along?
Prince Mokaḷ Siṅg speaks.—*vāh vāh*—
What news does he tell Dīyā.
By saying it, know it, let's see, Bhopājī Mahārāj, now by saying it
I'll say it now, by Dev's grace, here you are.—*vāh vāh jī*—*vāh vāh*—

—*gāv*—

"I hardly begged for the elephant and got it!—*mhe*—
I didn't get it by buying it.
Hey, I got the elephant from the Rāṭhors' battlefield.—*vāh vāh*—
After breaking Savāī Bhoj's sharp swords

I burst apart Savāī Bhoj's lungs.
Yes, only then did the elephant come to into my hands
The strength from my hands and arms hasn't faded out yet, daughter's father!—*mhe*—
I won't give the elephant just like that!"—*vāh vāh*—
Dīyājī said: "Hey, Prince Mokaḷā—*mhe*—
You're a Kumahār of the losing kind; you will lose.
Yes, you will lose
I know you!—*vāh vāh*—
Your father! Today Bhūṇājī stands enraged in the fair.—*mhe*—
Do you know him?"—*vāh vāh*—
Talk took place between Dīyā and the prince.—*mhe*—
Bhūṇājī grew mighty in the fair
Speak victory to Śrī Devnārāyaṇ Bhagavān, victory!

By God's grace, Dīyājī said: "Hey, Prince Mokaḷ Siṅg, brother,—*mhe*—
You are the kind of Kumahār that loses; you'll lose now."—*vāh vāh*—
Prince Mokaḷ Siṅg speaks. What news does he tell Dīyā, let's see.
By saying it, know it, by saying it, let's see
I'll say it now, by Dev's grace, here you are.—*vāh vāh*—

—*gāv*—

"My shoes have worn down, Dīyājī, brother.—*mhe*—
And my sword has worn down through damage
Hey, by God's grace, when did you learn to keep an elephant?—*mhe*—
In the end you ride the Mare Mule
What's your jāt after all?"
Yes, don't you know about that?

—*gāv*—

By God's grace, Dīyājī spoke this news: "Hey, Ratan Siṅg, you keep dung and rubbish.—*mhe*—
You concern yourself with dirt.
Hey, when did you learn to keep an elephant?—*mhe*—
In the end you ride Mare Mule
Those are your ancestors."—*vāh vāh*—
The prince speaks. What news does he tell Dīyā, let's see.
By saying it, know it, by saying it, let's see
I'll say it now, by Dev's grace, let's see.—*vāh vāh*—

—*gāv*—

"Listen, brother, Dīyā.—*mhe*—
My sandals have been worn down by the stirrups.—*vāh vāh*—
My sword worn down by damage
I'm the grandson of the king of kings.—*mhe*—
My grandfather liked the title Kumahār

My grandfather liked Kumahār
That's why you take the name Kumahār and speak.
Otherwise I'll smash the head of the person who takes the name Kumahār."—
vāh vāh—
Dīyā said: "Listen, brother, Prince Mokaḷ Siṅg," he said—*mhe*—
"Brother, hey, I came to tell you a correct thing, listen to me at least.—*mhe*—
The ancestors of the losing kind of Kumahārs are rotten.
You'll loose right now in front of Bhūṇā."—*vāh vāh*—
Mokaḷ Siṅg said: "Go! By God's grace, bring Bhūṇa along and you come too."
Yes, come together again, I'll deliver you the elephant!

—*gāv*—

By God's grace, who delivered that news? Prince Mokaḷ Siṅg did.
He said: "You came to mediate, hey, Leader of the Jodhkās.—*mhe*—
Since when do you speak against me?
You want me to give away the elephant.—*mhe*—
Now, you give away Bhoj's pure and clever Bāvlī
Daughter's father, by my name, you're sitting with twice as many goods."
Yes, you have twice as many goods!
Dīyā said: "I measured it all. I made a promise to your father and came!"
Yes, I measured the goods and came
Mokaḷ Siṅg said: "You might have measured it, brother, I won't measure it!—
vāh vāh—
I burst open his lungs and got the elephant.—*mhe*—
And, if there is any who'll take it under the clash of lances, I'll give it away."

—*gāv*—

"Both of us generals came to mediate, brother.—*mhe*—
Hey, you two brothers, discuss things on your own
We two generals will go home now.—*mhe*—
You and your Bhūṇājī figure out what's to be done in the fair
Both of you find out, brother." *vāh vāh*—
Mokaḷ Siṅg said: "Go! Send the elephant's claimant—*vāh vāh*—
And why do you go home—why don't you come with him?"—*mhe*—
By God's grace, the brothers didn't accept the mediation.—*vāh vāh*—
Dīyājī and Mīr returned to Bhūṇā, *said sir*.
They said: "Hey, Prince, Prince!—*mhe*—
They didn't accept the mediation."
Yes, didn't accept it
Bhūṇājī said: "When did I say so, brother, hey.—*vāh vāh*—
They'll accept on their own, now."—*vāh vāh*—
They said: "O Prince, we have a fierce sort of reputation.
Yes, we have a big name
If it's your command, then we'll get going toward our home
If we join you—*mhe*—
Then we'll get a scolding

And if we join them—*mhe*—
Then Rāvjī will give us a scolding in any case, you too will be unhappy."
Yes, you'll become unhappy
Bhūṇā said: "It's all right, go, brother!" *Go!*
In front the Dhārāpatī Sirdār had the drums of war beaten.—*vāh vāh*—
He said: "Come on, brother, fight if you want to take away the elephant."—*vāh vāh*—
In Bhūṇā's camp, the drums of war sounded.
"I'm coming," he said. So, by God's grace, what talk takes place between the Dhārāpatī Sirdār and Bhūṇā, let's see.—*vāh vāh*—
The Dhārāpatī Sirdār gives Bhūṇā a message.—*mhe*—

—*gāv*—

"Look, with my hands I slew Savāī Bhoj in the battlefield.—*mhe*—
But who among us has begun to want him back?
Is there someone who'll take Savāī Bhoj's revenge?"
Yes, tell me!

—*gāv*—

To take the king's name is always good, *said sir.*
"By God's grace, Bhagavān has descended onto Bhoj's throne, brother.—*mhe*—
Sometime he'll take back the leaves, flowers, nectar, *said sir.*
Listen, brother.—*mhe*—
The one who's going to take the Bagaṛāvats' revenge has come," he said.
The Dhārāpatī Sirdār said: "No worry at all," he said,
"Mokaḷ Siṅg, get ready, brother."—*vāh vāh*—
By God's grace, Bhūṇājī sent back a message to the Dhārāpatī's camp
What does Bhūṇājī tell the Bhāṭ.—*mhe*—
By God's grace, let's see, how he stages a fight against the Dhārāpatīs first, let's see.
By saying it, know it, let's see, by saying it

—*gāv*—

"Make pots *and enjoy yourselves."*
By God's grace, Bhūṇājī freed his father's elephant that was captured by the Kumahārs, and said: "Here you are, O Prince, this is not your work.—*mhe*—
Your work is making pots."
So the Dhārāpatīs were defeated.—*mhe*—
Prince Bhūṇājī was victorious in the fair; he took the elephant.—*vāh vāh*—
Speak victory to Śrī Devnārāyaṇ Bhagavān, victory!

Devnārāyaṇ and Bhāṅgījī Destroy Fort Pilodā

Bhūṇajī said: "Now what, Bābā Bhāṭ?"—*mhe*—
The Bhāṭ said: "Superb, great, hey, my master!"—*vāh vāh*—

He said: "Give me that elephant, Śrī Mahārāj.—*mhe*—
I'll take it to Dev's carpet[106] and tie it there
The news about when you will be coming . . ."
Yes, tell me about that
Bhūṇajī said: "Hey, Bābā Bhāṭ, tell your master Dev—*mhe*—
That I won't come like this.
Yes, I won't come like this
If your master Dev destroys Fort Pilodā—*mhe*—
only then will I return.
Yes, otherwise I won't come at all
Without providing proof, I won't come," he said.—*vāh vāh*—
By God's grace, after taking a "bath" and praying, on the day of the full moon, Bhūṇājī—*mhe*—
Gave away the elephant, and sent Bābā Bhāṭ off.—*vāh vāh*—
And he himself departed for Rāṇ City.
How does the Bagaṛāvats' Bhāṭ arrive in Daṛāvaṭ.—*mhe*—
How is the elephant worshipped, Lord Guṇeś, let's see. *By saying it, know it, by saying it*
I'll say it now, by Dev's grace, here you are.—*vāh vāh—jī—vāh vāh*—

—*gāv*—

"Brother, Hiṛāgar maids, the elephant has arrived, swaying its trunk—*mhe*—
There won't be a search for it again.
Why did you come alone, brother, hey, Lord Guṇeś?—*mhe*—
Why didn't you bring along the "sweet one" Bhoj?
You didn't bring along your master, brother!"
Yes, you didn't come together with him!
The Bhāṭ said: "Listen, Mājī Sā, don't reproach us in this way.—*vāh vāh*—
Is it possible to see one who has gone there again?"
Yes, there's no coming back now
Bhagavān has come alone, worship him!"—*vāh vāh*—

—*gāv*—

"Fill up the copper cup," she said.—*mhe*—
Maids, fill up the platter with pearls.
Prepare to worship the elephant that has arrived and the Bhāṭ.—*mhe*—
Today my solitary rider has come
The elephant has come alone, brother, no rider on top.—*mhe*—
But, no, worship Lord Guṇeś—*vāh vāh*—
Filling a platter with seeds and pearls."—*mhe*—
And Lord Guṇeś's worship was done.—*vāh vāh*—
So after eleven years, the elephant returned to the Bagaṛāvats' home
The Bhāṭ's victory took place.—*mhe*—
Sāḍū Mātā prepared worship. Speak: Victory to Śrī Dev Bhagavān, victory!

Dev said: "Bābā Bhāṭ—*mhe*—
Elder Brother Bhūṇā didn't come.—*vāh vāh*—
The Bhāṭ said: "He's told you to destroy Fort Pilodā.—*vāh vāh*—
If you destroy Pilodā, then Bhūṇājī will join the brothers."
The mention of Pilodā; it didn't take long for the king:—*mhe*—
"Pālā Sānī, saddle up the horse, brother, quickly.—*vāh vāh*—
Saddle up the horse." Who attacked Pilodā? The five brothers, by God's grace, weren't together.—*mhe*—
Medūjī, Dev Mahārāj, and, by God's grace, Prince Bhāṅgījī—*vāh vāh*— attacked Fort Pilodā.—*vāh vāh*—
They went to the outskirts, Dev Mahārāj said:
"Hey, by God's grace, Elder Brother Bhāṅgī—*mhe*—
I won't enter the town, brother.
Yes, riding on the horse, I won't enter
If I enter the town at this moment—*mhe*—
Fort Pilodā will completely go to Baikuṇṭh."
Yes, everyone, the whole thing will go to Baikuṇṭh
Prince Bhāṅgījī said: "Elder Brother, you stay over here, I alone will take care of Pilodā." *I'm sufficient enough alone*
By God's grace, Dev Mahārāj set up tent at the outskirts of Fort Pilodā.—*mhe*—
Food and drink began to be prepared
Bhāṅgījī took the mare Kāḷvī—*mhe*—
Reached Fort Pilodā alone
At that time, the Dhārāpatī Sirdār was residing on his carpet
He went along, by God's grace, he'd just consumed one and a quarter maṇ of bhāṅg.—*mhe*—
He took his club and threw it down in the middle of the carpet.—*vāh vāh*—
He said: "Here, brother, Sirdārs.—*mhe*—
Rotate my club with one hand."—*vāh vāh*—
The Sirdārs all tried their hand, but Bhāṅgījī's club didn't move at all.—*mhe*—
Bhaṅgījī said: "Listen, Sirdārs.—*mhe*—
I'll rotate it now.—*mhe*—
If your heads shatter, if you die, I don't care, brother."
Yes, now I don't know about that, be alert, be ready
Prince Bhāṅgījī rotated the club.—*vāh vāh*—
The Kumahār's court was full, they all ran out.—*vāh vāh*—
Prince Bhāṅgījī rotated his club, the lord of the three worlds, Bhagavān, cast a look of poison, cast his poison gaze, Pilodā burnt down right away.
All of it burnt down, said sir.
So, Rāvjī Sā was sitting up high in his palace.—*mhe*—
He said to Bhūṇājī:
"Hey, Bhūṇā,—*mhe*—
Why is there smoke rising from Fort Pilodā today, hey?"
Yes, why is smoke pouring out of it?
Bhūṇājī said.—*vāh vāh*—
What news does he tell Rāvjī, now, let's see.

By saying it, know it, let's see, by saying it
I'll say it now, brother, by Bhagavān's grace, let's see.—*vāh vāh—jī—vāh vāh—*

—*gāv*—

"The Dhārāpatī's plough remained worn down.—*mhe*—
The seed remained in the sack
It looks like the king's ridden the attack, at the first day of the third in the month of Sāvan
Hey, Rāvjī,—*mhe*—
God has ridden the attack!"—*vāh vāh*—
"Hey, Bhūṇā, then why is there so much smoke?"
Yes, why is smoke pouring out?
Bhūṇā speaks. What news does he tell Rāvjī, let's see. *By saying it, know it, let's see, by saying it*

—*gāv*—

If you take Demālī Nāth's name—*mhe*—
It's always good, *said sir.*
"There are many unmarried daughters of the Dhārāpatīs.—*mhe*—
It seems that today marriages are being celebrated in all the homes
No time to make pots
There are lots of girls.
Yes, marriages are being celebrated simultaneously
The Kumahār didn't give away any pots.—*mhe*—
Rāvjī Sā, hey, the Dhārāpatī Sirdār baked with his own hands."—*vāh vāh*—
Rāvjī Sā thought to himself: "Hey, why did Bhūṇā talk like this today?"—*mhe*—
He said: "Bhūṇā, tell me things like they are, brother!" Bhūṇā said: "Śrī Mahārāj, the lord of the three worlds, Bhagavān, has ridden to attack.—*vāh vāh*—
I brought back the elephant.—*mhe*—
And Bhagavān destroyed Pilodā today," he said.—*vāh vāh*—
Rāvjī said: "Hey, Sirdārs, Bhūṇā has now grown mighty, brother."—*vāh vāh*—
"Bhūṇājī doesn't belong to you any more."
Yes, now he isn't ours anymore
Bhūṇājī arrived in Bhināy—*vāh vāh*—
By God's grace, when he went to Bhināy.—*mhe*—
Then what did he do, Bhūṇājī started to depart for his country.—*vāh vāh*—
Then he thought to himself: "Hey, brother, I'll go and meet Rāvjī, Bāījī, and everyone well, brother."
Yes, I'll meet them, and then leave.

Bhūṇājī Returns to Rāvjī's Court

Rāvjī Plots to Kill Bhūṇājī

Rāvjī thought to himself: "Who knows whether Bhūṇā will meet you or not—*mhe*—
But before he goes to his country, he'll certainly meet with Bāījī."
He said: "Sirdārs, do this—Bhūṇājī will certainly come to the court, brother."—*mhe*—
Mīr said: "Do what I say! I have a clever idea!"
Yes, do what I say
"What, hey, Mīr?"—*mhe*—
"Spread out chickpeas on the floor in the court
When Bhūṇājī enters the court—*mhe*—
Then we'll crush him like this when he slips over here.—*vāh vāh*—
We'll slay him, right here."
Rāvjī said: "Superb, great, hey, Mīr you're the wazir of wisdom!"
Yes, there's a lot of wisdom in you
Chickpeas were spread out.—*mhe*—
And the door was fastened shut.—*vāh vāh*—
By God's grace, both the generals sat down behind the door with daggers and swords.

Rāvjī (extreme right) in his court with Kālū Mīr (extreme left) and other courtiers.

Yes, both Kālū Mīr, Dīyā sat down firmly
"When Bhūṇājī puts his head into the doorway—*mhe*—
At that time strike him on the neck, keep him down." *Keep him right here*
By God's grace, Bāī thought to herself: "The enemy sure has fixed together a trick."—*vāh vāh*—
By God's grace, Bhūṇājī arrived at the door's latch.—*mhe*—
Bāī thought to herself: "Hey, Bhūṇājī's coming, and now Elder brother Bhūṇā's death has arrived."
So Bhūṇājī comes to the door's latch.—*mhe*—
What news does Bāī say, let's see.
By saying it, know it, by saying it

—*gāv*—

Bhūṇājī Foils the Plot to Kill Him

Bhūnā's dagger is curved—*mhe*—
In a golden sheath
The door clapped when he flung it open.—*mhe*—
Kālū Mīr, Dīyā, both generals jumped over the *wall*
By God's grace, they were sitting behind the door to kill him—*mhe*—
When the knock on the door sounded.—*vāh vāh*—
Mīr said: "Friend Dīyā, your father's come, run away."
Yes, run
Dīyā jumped away and Mīr stumbled and fell, by God's grace, went and fell to Bhūṇā's feet
As he fell, Bhūṇājī placed his foot on his chest.—*vāh vāh*—
"O Prince, sir, what are you doing, aren't I your black cow?"
Yes, I'm your black cow
Bāījī was sitting high up on the balcony
By God's grace, Bāī speaks.—*mhe*—
What news does she tell Bhūṇā?
By saying it, know it, now, by saying it

—*gāv*—

"Don't take your foot off his chest.—*mhe*—
Hey, Bhūṇā this enemy will depart in the direction of the sky
Hang up the milking pail of the black cow on a nail.—*mhe*—
We will profit without the cow now
Bhūṇā there's no gain in this cow!—*vāh vāh*—
Kill the enemy, when the opportunity comes later."—*mhe*—
He said: "Brother, it's not a Hindu's faith.—*vāh vāh*—
He's become a cow.—*mhe*—
It's not a Hindu's faith to kill a cow!"
Yes, I won't kill a cow

In a flash, Bhūṇājī pulled his foot back.—*vāh vāh*—
Bāī said: "Bhūṇā, you have great qualities, brother.—*mhe*—
This enemy won't let you live now."
Yes, there are a lot of enemies of yours
Bāījī speaks. What news does she tell Bhūṇājī, let's see. *By saying it, know it, by saying it, let's see*
I'll say it now, by Bhagavān's grace, brother, let's see.—*vāh vāh*—

—*gāv*—

"Bhūṇā, Rāvjī is cunning, cunning!—*mhe*—
Look, Bhūṇā, cunning Rāvjī spread out the chickpeas because of you
Now stop going in and out of the court through the door.—*vāh vāh*—
Elder Brother Bhūṇā, there are a lot of ill-wishers against you.
Those generals of Rāvjī—*mhe*—
They all have ill-will toward you.
Yes, all of them are your ill-wishers
If you come like this, then, brother, there's my window for coming and going, come this way through it."

—*gāv*—

By God's grace, Bhūṇājī said the news
"If the turban eats up the head;—*mhe*—
The embankment eats up the field
If Dvārkā takes the place of Matharā.—*mhe*—
Then my horse will come in through the window
Why, have you gone crazy?"
Yes, I'm not going to come in through a window!
She said: "Bhūṇā, you have great powers.—*mhe*—
In the court there are many ill-wishing people."

—*gāv*—

"Bābā Rāvjī is very cunning.—*mhe*—
Bhūṇā, cunning people are sitting now in our palace
Hey, stop coming and going into the court-room, Bhūṇā.—*vāh vāh*—
If you have to go, then pass through my window
You only have to meet me.—*vāh vāh*—
What are you taking to the court?"
Yes, what business do you have?
Bhūṇājī said: "Bāī Sāī—*mhe*—
I'll come straight through the doorway."—*vāh vāh*—
"I won't ever come in stealthily."
By God's grace, when Bhūṇājī entered the court—*mhe*—
the chickpeas were spread all about.—*mhe*—
By God's grace, when Bhūṇājī departed, then the chickpeas—like when it enters Mother Earth——*mhe*—
Like that all the chickpeas burst apart.—*vāh vāh*—

Bhūṇājī didn't get afraid.—*mhe*—
By God's grace, all the Sirdārs ran off scared of Bhūṇājī.—*mhe*—
Only Rāvjī Sā remained sitting on the throne.
What does Rāvjī do? He stands up and falls down
Again he gets up and falls down at the same place.
Bhūṇājī said.
"Bābā Rāvjī, why are you doing this?"
Yes, why are you doing this?
Rāvjī said: "Hey, Son Bhūṇā, what am I doing?"—*mhe*—
Before you freed me from captivity—*vāh vāh*—
You used to greet me saying 'Rām Rām' to me
And after you freed me from captivity in Khanār—*mhe*—
Brother, hey, I say 'Rām Rām' to you first.
Yes, I do
I thought I'll meet Bhūṇā.—*mhe*—
I can't get up, son!"—*vāh vāh*—
Bhūṇā said: "Bābā Rāvjī, I've found out about you!"—*mhe*—
What did Bhūṇājī do?
He got up in the court-room.—*vāh vāh*—
Rāvjī Sā said:
"Bhūṇā you'd fixed the law yourself, why did you break it, brother?
Yes, you broke the law
The law was laid down by you—*mhe*—
That no weapons are to be carried into the court-room."—*vāh vāh*—
Bhūṇājī speaks. What news does he tell, let's see. *By saying, know it, let's see, by saying it*

—*gāv*—

"I wandered all over the earth—*mhe*—
Bringing my sword back after exchanging blows with other swords
This dagger on my waist, Rāvjī, remained hungry on my waist.—*mhe*—
Today it demands, hey, Bābā Rāv's offering
You know your paunch—my dagger is pushing to enter it."—*vāh vāh*—
By God's grace, Rāvjī began trembling with fear.—*mhe*—
He thought to himself: "Hey, there's a change come about in Bhūṇā.—*vāh vāh*—
He's ready now! He'll take revenge right here."—*vāh vāh*—
Bāī speaks. What news does she tell Prince Bhūṇā, let's see.
By saying it, know it, by saying it, let's see
I'll just say it, by Dev's grace, let's see.—*vāh vāh*—

—*gāv*—

Queen Sā̃klī Tries to Poison Bhūṇājī

"Bhūṇā, don't commit regicide!—*mhe*—
By God's grace, don't kill Bābā Rāv

Hey, by God's grace, by committing regicide, you'd kill Rāvjī who is your adopted father[107]
O brother, he's yours and my adopted father," she said.—*vāh vāh*—
"Bhūṇā, don't kill off the old man."—*mhe*—
When Bāī says something, then at that time, by God's grace, Bhūṇā must listen to what she says.—*vāh vāh*—
By God's grace, Queen Sā̃klī prepared two platters of food.—*mhe*—
For Rāvjī, she made one with amṛt
And for Bhūṇā she made one of poison
In her mind she thought: "The enemy has come.—*mhe*—
I'll poison him so that the bother will be finished off[108] right here."
Yes, he'll die
At the time when Queen Sā̃klī sent the poisoned food—*mhe*—
Bhūṇājī took a jar of water—*vāh vāh*—
And began cleaning his teeth and rinsing his mouth
Sitting in the palace, Bāī spoke.—*mhe*—
What does she explain to Bhūṇā, let's see.
By saying it, know it, by saying it, let's see
I'll say it now, by God's grace, here you are.—*vāh vāh*—*jī vāh vāh*—

—*gāv*—

It's always good to take Dev's name, hey, brother, *said sir.*
By God's grace, the news was said by Bāī.—*mhe*—
"Bhūṇājī, rivers flow speedily.—*mhe*—
Cranes vault up and down
Hey, understand what I say.—*mhe*—
Your last moment has arrived."
So, by God's grace, the queen had prepared a meal of poison for Prince Bhūṇājī.—*mhe*—
So, by God's grace, tearing off a piece of bread, Bhūṇājī threw it to a bitch standing near
It took no time throwing it
Why, because Bāijī had said that news.—*mhe*—
Bhūṇājī thought to himself: "The news that Bāījī told you."
Yes, she's only told you
It's good to understand."—*vāh vāh*—
By God's grace, he threw the piece to the bitch; the bitch went into a swoon, it went around in a circle and fell down.—*vāh vāh*—
Bhūṇājī pulled out his dagger from his waist—*mhe*—
And pierced it in the middle of the platter
Rāvjī Sā said:
"Bhūṇā!—*mhe*—
Why did you do this?
Yes, why did you do this today?
Hey, in a platter of gold,—*mhe*—
Why did you put a silver nail?"

—*gāv*—

"I've wandered all the earth.—*mhe*—
By God's grace, I brought my sword after exchanging blows with other swords
This dagger hanging on my waist has remained hungry.—*mhe*—
Rāvjī, it wants an offering of your paunch
It's not going to be satisfied without entering your paunch."—*vāh vāh*—
Rāvjī Sāī began trembling with fear.—*mhe*—
Bāījī came and said: "Elder brother Bhūṇā, don't do this, brother," she said.—*vāh vāh*—
"The old man's life will be snuffed out from fright."—*mhe*—
When Bāī spoke, then Bhūṇā, by God's grace—at home we give boiling milk a sprinkle of water—*mhe*—
Like that his body received a sprinkle.[109]
Bhūṇājī said: "Bāī Sāī—*mhe*—
I've come to meet you.—*vāh vāh*—
I'm going to my land now."—*mhe*—
So, by God's grace, what talk happens between Bhūṇājī and Bāī Tārāde.
By saying it, know it, let's see
I'll say it now, by Dev's grace, here you are

—*gāv*—

Bhūṇājī Leaves Rich Gifts for Sā̃j's Wedding

"Dear Bhūṇā you're going to your country.—*mhe*—
Brother, there's no one protecting me who I can call Brother
When you go to your country, who'll wrap silk cloth from the Deccan around me at Sā̃j's wedding?
There is your niece, Sā̃jā̃ Bāī.—*mhe*—
Who'll come in her wedding, brother?" *Tell me that*
Bhūṇājī speaks. What news does he tell Bāī, let's see.
By saying it, know it, by saying it, let's see
I'll say it now, by Dev's grace, let's see

—*gāv*—

"Bāījī, I'm going to my land," he said.—*mhe*—
"This time when I come I'll bring brothers Medū and Madnā
I'll come to Sā̃j's bhāt.[110]—*mhe*—
Medū will wrap around you silk cloth from the Deccan."
This news was said by Prince Bhūṇā.
Bāī said: "Hey, now Elder Brother Bhūṇā—*mhe*—
Do you have a lot of business or what?—*vāh vāh*—
Think of matters to come.—*mhe*—
When you get together with your brothers in Daṛāvaṭ—vāh vāh—
Then this issue will be over for you.

Yes, this matter will be forgotten
Later on plans will be made to kill Rāvjī, the enemy.—*vāh vāh*—
Revenge is your destiny, isn't it Bhūṇā?" she said. "By God's grace, if you want to do my māyrā[111]—*mhe*—
Do it now."
Yes, do it now and go!
After getting together with the brothers, Elder Brother Bhūṇā you won't return."—*vāh vāh*—

—*gāv*—

"Bāījī, I'm going to my land.—*mhe*—
I'll gather together a herd of cows and buffaloes
Give away only the most excellent cows in Bāī's dowry.—*mhe*—
The rest, my sister, return to me
The ones that you find excellent, give just those ones in Bāī's dowry."
Tārāde Bāī speaks; in what manner does she tell Prince Bhūṇā news, let's see.
By saying it, know it, by saying it, let's see
I'll say it now, by Dev's grace, here you are

—*gāv*—

"If Jāṭs and Gūjars give cows and buffaloes in dowry, then the Mers will be happy
Bhāṭī of Jaisalmer is coming to marry Bāī. He demands a mighty elephant in marriage
Only Jāṭs and Gūjars would be happy
So Bhūṇājī speaks and what does Bāī Sā listen to.
By saying it, know it, Sir, by saying it

—*gāv*—

"By God's grace, I'll make one trip to the plantain wood.—*mhe*
Sister, I'll gather together a herd of elephants
Give an excellent elephant in Bāī's dowry.—*mhe*—
They won't all fit into the Bhāṭī's Jaisalmer
I won't fill Jaisalmer with all of them," he said.—*vāh vāh*—
"You thought well, Crazy, great!"—*vāh vāh*—
By God's grace, she said: "Elder Brother Bhūṇā!—*mhe*—
Hey, after meeting together with the brothers, the māyrā won't be filled."—*vāh vāh*—
Bhūṇājī thought to himself: "Hey, there's no friendship with Rāvjī Sāī, brother.—*mhe*—
Just enmity."—*vāh vāh*—

—*gāv*—

Prince Mahābalī went to the bazaar, brother.—*mhe*—
He bought a silk cloth from the Deccan

He wraps Tārāde: "Sister, now brother Bhūṇā wraps the silken cloth about you
Bāī Sā, wrap it around—what else, brother?—*vāh vāh*—
Take this in advance.—*vāh vāh*—
Afterward, who knows Bāī Sā, after meeting together with the brothers, who knows, I may not be able to come."
Yes, to come

—*gāv*—

Rāyjādā Mahābalī went to the bazaar.—*mhe*—
He took only a small moment
Hey, seventy thousand coins Bhūṇājī put in Bāī's platter.—*mhe*—
Rājā Kāchab stopped his chariot
They say that sun-king stopped and looked for a moment at Bhūṇājī's māyrā
So he filled Bāī Tārāde's daughter, Sā̃j's bhāt.—*mhe*—
And Bhūṇājī filled the māyrā in Rāṇ City
Speak victory, brother, to Śrī Devnārāyaṇ Bhagavān, victory

—*ārati*—

—*ṭhumrī bhairū̃jī*—

Bhūṇājī Departs for Causle Kheḍā

So, by God's grace, after filling Bāī's daughter, Sā̃j's māyrā, Bhūṇājī—*mhe*—
Began to depart. *Said sir.*
Rāvjī's generals spoke.—*mhe*—
Mīr said: "Do what I say. Be sensible."
Yes, be sensible
Mīr said: "Should I tell you?"
Yes, "Tell me," Rāvjī said
Mīr said: "Śrī Mahārāj, there's his father's well, dug by Bhūṇājī's father.—*mhe*—

Bhūṇājī will certainly go there
Dīyājī and I will go there.—*mhe*—
On the well, when he enters the well, then—the enemy—at that place we'll kill the enemy!"
Yes, we'll keep him in the well
Rāvjī Sāī said: "Great, Mīr, you're certainly the wazir of wisdom."
Five hundred horses, five hundred riders—*mhe*—
The Sirdārs took and were setting up tents at the well.—*vāh vāh*—
"Keep a watch, brother, when Bhūṇājī, the enemy, comes he is to be killed on the spot," he said.
Yes, to be killed here
So, who arrived? Dīyājī Jodhkā arrived, and Kālū Mīr's army arrived.

Ṭoḍā's Solaṅkī was Rāvjī Sāī's son-in-law
Yes, his army came too
Bāī noticed this, Tārāde did.—*mhe*—
Tārāde and Bhūṇā.—*mhe*—
The day Rāvjī Sāī captured Bhūṇā and took him away in the Mahābhārat—*mhe*—
Then Bhūṇājī was six months old.
Yes, he was
So, Bāī Tārāde was Rāvjī Sāī's daughter.—*vāh vāh*—
So, when she suckled, together with her, by God's grace, Bhūṇā also suckled. The queen was told: "Suckle him too.
Yes, suckle him too!
Give one breast to Bāī.—*mhe*—
Give one to Bhūṇājī."
So, because both sister and brother had suckled together, they used to have "respect of milk"—*vāh vāh*—
Bāī thought to herself: "Hey, the enemy, look he's married to you, is about to deceive your brother."
Bāī Tārāde speaks. What news does she tell Prince Bhūṇā, let's see.
By saying it, know it, let's see, now by saying it
I'll say it now, by Bhagavān's grace, brother

—*gāv*—

"Bhūṇā, I'll place a spinning-wheel in front.—*mhe*—
And I'll put a shelf behind
Hey, while slaying your enemy, Bhūṇā,—*mhe*—
Don't worry about your Bāī Tārāde
You think that Bāī will wear a lā̃bī-kā̃clī?[112]—*mhe*—
Don't worry about that.—*vāh vāh*—
I'll spin cotton cloth and fill my stomach.—*vāh vāh*
But the enemy, look, your brother-in-law has turned traitor on you."
Yes, he's keeping a watch
Bhūṇājī started to depart.—*mhe*—
Bāījī speaks.—*vāh vāh*—
What news does she tell her brother.
By saying it, know it, let's see, by saying it
I'll say it now, by Bhagavān's grace, let's see

—*gāv*—

"Once we used to swing in the cradle.—*mhe*—
Dear Bhūṇā, we suckled together
Hey, we didn't know about jāt-pā̃t for so many days.—*mhe*—
Today we found out.—*vāh vāh*—
You're a Gūjar, I'm a Rajpūt
Bhūṇā you're a Gūjar.—*mhe*—
I'm a Rajpūt, brother.—*vāh vāh*—

But so many days we suckled together and swung together.—*mhe*—
It didn't come to our attention."
Yes, we took no notice
By God's grace, Bhūṇājī began to depart.—*vāh vāh*—
What news does Bāījī say, let's see.
By saying it, know it, let's see, by saying it
I'll say it now, by Bhagavān's grace, here you are.—*vāh vāh*—*jī*

—*gāv*—

"Brother Bhūṇājī is going to his country, brother.—*mhe*—
Hey, he's turned the mare's back on the region of Rāṇ
So bend down a little, O hills of Rān Bhināy.—*mhe*—
Let me see the back of Elder Brother when he goes.
She told the news to the hills. They say that—*vāh vāh*—
The hills of Rāṇ Bhināy bent down a little because of her saying so.—*vāh vāh*—
Prince Bhūṇā, by God's grace, arrived at the well, *said sir.*
Upon arriving he saw those Sirdārs.—*mhe*—
He thought to himself: "Yes, the enemy has come all right."
Yes, they have certainly come
By God's grace, Banū Bārahaṭh was together with him.—*mhe*—
He said: "Hey, Banū Bābā—*mhe*—
Whose well is this?"
Yes, who has it been dug by?
The Bārahaṭh said: "It belongs to the Bagaṛāvats, Śrī Mahārāj."
Yes, it's been dug by the Bagaṛāvats
Bhūṇā said: "Then do the following.—*mhe*—
Cut off the water supply of all of Rāv's generals."
Yes, cut off the water for all of them

Bhūṇājī Speaks with His Mother's Memorial Stone

By God's grace, Bhūṇājī departed from there
By God's grace, he arrived at the Bagaṛāvats' battlefield.—*mhe*—
The Khārī river was flowing as it always did.—*vāh vāh*—
And on the bank of the river devlī upon devlī had been erected.
Yes, devlīs were over there
He said: "Banū Bābā what's this arrangement here?"
Yes, why have so many stones been erected?
The Bārahaṭh said: "Śrī Mahārāj, the battlefield of your ancestors *has arrived*
Bhūṇā said: "Here?"
Yes, they are devlīs
"Devlīs, Śrī Mahārāj."—*vāh vāh*—
Bhūṇājī said: "Well then, brother, if it's the battlefield, then surely there is the devlī of my father and my mother."
Yes, are they here?

The Bāraha̤th said: "They are, sir. *They are*
Your mother's name was Salūṇ.—*mhe*—
The devlī with the name Salūṇ belongs to your mother."—*vāh vāh*—
Bhūṇājī wandered about the entire battlefield.—*mhe*—
When he came upon a devlī with the name of Salūṇ, Bhūṇājī left hold of the mare's reins.—*vāh vāh*—
Bhūṇājī gets down. How does he pay his respects to the devlī. What news is exchanged between the devlī and Bhūṇā on the battlefield.
By saying it, know it, let's see, by saying it
I'll say it now, by Bhagavān's grace, I'll say it.—*vāh vāh—jī*

—*gāv*—

He cuts away the grass on the threshold.—*mhe*—
What's called khaḍ? The grass and stuff growing at the devlī.
Yes, he was cutting that away
And, by God's grace, on the threshold, Prince Mahābalī sweeps Mother Satī's bricks with a shoulder wrap
"We were separated for eleven years, Mother Devlī.—*mhe*—
Dev brought us together now with difficulty
Dev has taken incarnation, Bhagavān has.
Yes, that's why this meeting of mother and son is taking place
Otherwise, Mother Devlī how could our meeting take place?"—*vāh vāh*—
Bhūṇājī speaks. What does he tell the memorial stone. *By saying, know it, by saying it*
I'll say it now, by Dev's grace, brother.—*vāh vāh sā*—

—*gāv*—

The Bagaṛāvat's son cuts grass away on the threshold.—*vāh vāh*—
With a shoulder wrap he sweeps away Mother Satī's dust
"Eleven years we were separated.—*vāh vāh*—
Speak to me with your mouth
Well, brother, you're my mother's—Salūṇ's—devlī aren't you? Speak to me from your mouth.
Yes, show me your presence
Then I'll believe—*mhe*—
That it's my mother's devlī."—*vāh vāh*—
By God's grace, how does light come into the stone.—*mhe*—
What talk goes on after eleven years between mother and son.
By saying it, know it, let's see, by saying it

—*gāv*—

Bhūṇājī came to the battlefield.—*mhe*—
The Raj-bearing Rajpūt came
Wearing bangles[113] she took her arm out of the devlī—*mhe*—
And placed it on Bhūṇā's head.—*vāh vāh*—
On that day milk spurted out of the devlī

Bhuṇājī speaks with his mother's memorial stone.

By God's grace, a stream of milk flowed from the stone—*vāh vāh*—
Falling onto Bhūṇā's moustache.
Bhūṇājī said: "Hey, Banū Bābā—*mhe*—
After eleven years today I again tasted Salūṇ's milk."
Yes, tasted it
The devlī speaks. What does she tell Bhūṇā, let's see. *By saying it, know it, by saying it, let's see*
I'll say it now, brother, by Dev's grace, let's see.—*vāh vāh*—*jī*

—*gāv*—

"Bhūṇā, you departed from Rāṇ City, brother.—*mhe*—
Hey, you turned Bor's[114] back to the region of Rāṇ
Then I got news, hey, Bhūṇā, from Bhagavān's Indra-throne in Baikuṇṭh
In Baikuṇṭh Bhagavāṇ and all the gods got together.—*vāh vāh*—
So at that place they started to talk.—*mhe*—
They said: "Brother, today after eleven years the Bagaṛāvats' son is going to join up with his brothers.—*vāh vāh*—
I thought:—*mhe*—
'Bhūṇājī won't leave without coming to the battlefield
And, just now he'll speak to the stones.'
So, son, hey, you are a person staying in the world of mortals
I'm a person staying in the world of heaven.
Do you know that Mājī Sā is not found normally in the battlefield.
Yes, I'm not in this stone

Hey, son, I filled the stone with light because of you."—*vāh vāh*—
By God's grace, Mother Devlī speaks.—*vāh vāh*—
What does she say to her child, let's see.
By saying it, know it, by saying it

—*gāv*—

"Son, who sang songs to you in the cradle, brother?—*vāh vāh*—
And who suckled you?
Hey, Devlī asks you now:—*mhe*—
Bhūṇā, who kept your honor in Rāṇ?
Son, did you keep badly, brother, *or did you keep well?*
That news . . .
Yes, tell me in detail."
So, after eleven years, Bhūṇā speaks again with his mother.—*mhe*—
What talk happens between mother and son, let's see.
By saying it, know it, by saying it, let's see
I'll say it now, by Lord Dev's grace, here you are.—*vāh vāh sā*—

—*gāv*—

"O Devlī Mother, Uncle Nīmā sang songs to me in the cradle.—*vāh vāh*—
Rāv's queen Sā̃klī Kā̃vlāvatī suckled me
Bābā Rāvjī would sit in the gateway.—*mhe*—
O Devlī Mother, he raised my honor plenty-fold
He kept me very well."
Yes, he kept me very well all right
Bhūṇā mentioned well-being
Devlī Mother speaks.—*mhe*—
What news, by God's grace, does she tell Bhūṇā, let's see. *By saying it, know it, by saying it, let's see*
I'll say it now, by Bhagavān's grace, here you are.—*vāh vāh sā*—*vāh vāh*—

—*gāv*—

"Your mare is making circles like the moon—*mhe*—
It prances around like a witch"
Devlī Mother says:—*mhe*—
"Hey, Bhūṇā, why did you leave the boundary of Rāṇ?
If they kept you so well, then,
Yes, why did you leave Rāṇ and come here?"
Mother and son spoke to one another, from Indra's throne radiance came into the devlī.—*mhe*—
Speak victory to Śrī Devnārāyaṇ Bhagavān, brother, victory!

By God's grace, Devlī said: "Hey, Bhūṇā—*mhe*—
If you gained so much happiness, then, brother, why did you leave Rāṇ City?"

Yes, why did you leave it and come?
Tell me about that, brother!"—*vāh vāh*—
By God's grace, Bhūṇājī speaks.—*mhe*—
What news does he tell Devlī Mother, let's see.
By saying it, know it, by saying it, let's see
I'll say it now, by God's grace, here you are.—*vāh vāh sā*—

—*gāv*—

"By God's grace—*mhe*—
My mare makes circles like the moon—*vāh vāh*—
It prances around like a witch
Devlī Mother I remembered the Bagaṛāvats' revenge.—*mhe*—
I left 'child-eating' Rāṇ quite naturally
Nobody released me from it.
Yes, there was no one to release me
When I remembered the Bagaṛāvats' enmity—*mhe*—
Then Rāṇ City turned sour."—*vāh vāh*—
"By God's grace, son, then no one deceived you did they?"
Yes, no one deceived you, did they?
Bhūṇājī said: "Here you are, brother, Devlī Mother, let me tell you about Dīyājī's deceit."
Yes, tell you that at least
Bhūṇājī speaks. What more does Devlī Mother listen to.
By saying it, know it, let's see, by saying it
I'll say it now, by Dev's grace, here you are!

—*gāv*—

"Dīyājī released a drunken elephant upon me.—*mhe*—
The elephant went and crushed the elephant-driver
Devlī Mother, God Gaṇeś had a good thought.—*mhe*—
It lifted me high up and put me down on its howdah
Dīyājī thought to himself:—*mhe*—
'The elephant will kill the enemy.'—*vāh vāh*—
Drunken,
Yes, he released it
Look, by God's grace, he struck the elephant with a spear, with an elephant-goad—*mhe*—
And let it loose on me.—*vāh vāh*—
What did the elephant do?—*mhe*—
It twisted its trunk *and took me high up in the air and put me down on its howdah," said sir.*
"O Devlī Mother, I was not harmed"—*vāh vāh*—
Bhūṇājī speaks. What does he tell Devlī?
By saying it, know it, by saying it
I'll say it now, by Lord Dev's grace, here you are.—*vāh vāh*—*jī*

—*gāv*—

"Mother, did you slaughter Dīnānāth's cow?—*mhe*—
Did you rob Rāṇ City during broad daylight?
Prince Bhūṇājī speaks to you.—*mhe*—
Devlī Mother why did you become a stone from being a person?
In some age you were a person.—*mhe*—
Why did you turn into stone?" *vāh vāh*—
Devlī Mother speaks. Let's see, what news she tells. *By saying it, know it, by saying it*
I'll say it now, by Dev's grace, here you are.—*vāh vāh*—

—*gāv*—

By God's grace, devlī spoke the news.—*vāh vāh*—
She said: "Son, I didn't slaughter Dinānāth's cow.—*mhe*—
I didn't rob Rāṇ City in broad daylight
Son, I burnt up and became a heap of ash.—*mhe*—
Hey, Bhūṇā, I burnt up after your family
Bhūṇājī!—*mhe*—
Hey, brother, after your family."
Yes, I burnt up
Devlī Mother speaks.—*mhe*—
What news does she tell Prince Bhūṇā, let's see

—*gāv*—

"Bhūṇā, I hung up the ivory bangles on a nail in the wall.—*vāh vāh*—
Hey, brother, I wore only the fire-goddess's bangles on my arms
Bhūṇā, gossip goes around in the world.—*mhe*—
Hey, I would go with you now to meet Sāḍū Mātā, but son, the world would start gossip."—*vāh vāh*—

—*gāv*—

"Son, I hung up the ivory bangles on a nail in the wall.—*vāh vāh*—
I wore only the fire-goddess's bangles
By God's grace, hey, Bhūṇā, I burnt up and became ash after your family
I burnt up after your family, brother."—*vāh vāh*—
In the meantime, Ṭhākur Dev's four o'clock afternoon service started to begin in Daṛāvaṭ.—*vāh vāh*—
The service's drums
Yes, they beat
Bhūṇājī said: "Banū Bābā,
Yes, why did those drums beat?
Banū Bābā said: "Śrī Mahārāj, the service for Dev is taking place in Daṛāvaṭ."
Yes, Bhagavān's four o'clock service is taking place in Daṛāvaṭ
Bhūṇājī gave his complete attention to the service.—*vāh vāh*—
So mother and son talked to one another.—*mhe*—

Bhūṇājī sat in concentration to the service.—*mhe*—
Speak victory to Śrī Devnārāyaṇ Bhagavān, victory!

—*ṭhumrī*—

Bhūṇājī Speaks with Savāī Bhoj's Memorial Stone

So Bhagavān's service of one and a quarter hour took place.—*mhe*—
Bhūṇājī gave his complete attention during that time to the service.—*vāh vāh*—
So Devlī Mother was there.
Yes, she disappeared, said sir.
Later Bhūṇājī looked at her: "Banū Bābā, an outrageous thing has happened, brother.—*vāh vāh*—
I didn't finish talking to this Devlī Mother.—*mhe*—
After having gone to Indra's throne she won't come back now, Bābā Bhāṭ.—*vāh vāh*—
Show me Savāī Bhoj's devlī now."
Yes, I'll meet Bābājī
Banū Bābā said: "Śrī Mahārāj, not even I know about that deval.
Yes, not even I know
They say there is a village called Cāmpānehrī here.—*mhe*—
So in Cāmpānehrī there's one Sūjā Paṭel.—*mhe*—
Call him over and you have him take a look."
Yes, he'll be able to tell us where Savāī Bhoj is
Bhūṇājī sent a messenger on a camel.—*vāh vāh*—
In Cāmpānehrī he called Sūjā Paṭel and brought him.
Bhūṇājī speaks.—*mhe*—
What news does he tell Sūjā Paṭel, let's see.
By saying it, know it, by saying it, let's see
I'll say it now, by Dev's grace, here . . .

—*gāv*—

"I'll give you an elephant in reward.—*mhe*—
I'll give you a land-deed from my own kingdom
Sujā Bābā, if you tell me where the devlī of Savāī Bhoj's stands
Sūjā Bābā!—*mhe*—
Where is Big Father's devlī?" *Tell me that!*
Sūjā Bābā speaks.—*mhe*—
What news does he tell Bhūṇā?
By saying it, know it, let's see, by saying it
I'll say it now, by Dev's grace, here you are.—*vāh vāh*—*sā*

—*gāv*—

"Son, on the high square platform with four divisions.—*mhe*—
Hey, the boundaries of that sinful river Khārī can be seen

See Savāī Bhoj's deval at the place—*mhe*—
Where Medū's Mother Posvāl Gūjrī offered up her body
Medu's mother Posvāl—*mhe*—
She went after Bhoj's death to the satīvāḍā.[115]—*vāh vāh*—
Sāḍū Mātā, afterward, because Bhagavān had made a promise, she went to the Mālāsar Hill and began serving Bhagavān.—*vāh vāh*—
And, Medū's mother—*mhe*—
She became a satī after Bhoj's death."—*vāh vāh*—
By God's grace, Bhūṇājī reached the shore of the Khārī River
He saw Savāī Bhoj's deval.—*mhe*—
Bhūṇājī speaks. What does he say to the deval, let's see.
By saying it, know it, by saying it, let's see
I'll say it now, by Dev's grace, here you are.—*vāh vāh—sā*

—*gāv*—

Bhūṇājī sang at night, at night he played instruments—*mhe*—
He beat brass instruments
"Hey, Bābājī, my watch-time is over.—*mhe*—
Hey, will you twenty-three brothers rise up and show yourselves or not?
You are twenty-three Bagaṛāvats.—*mhe*—
I'll believe in you only if twenty-three brothers meet with me, by God's grace."—*vāh vāh*—
What light comes into Savāī Bhoj's devlī.—*mhe*—
What talk happens between the two of them, let's see.
By saying it, know it, by saying it, let's see
I'll say it now, sir, by Dev's grace, here you are.—*vāh vāh sā*—

—*gāv*—

"Bhūṇā, a person like Sāḍū, became a satī.—*mhe*—
Son, the younger sister Salūṇ became a satī."
Savāī Bhoj's devlī spoke aloud—*vāh vāh*—: "Come nearer, hey, my Bhūṇā, Bārāvat's son
Son, come closer."—*vāh vāh*—
This conversation is happening eleven years after going to Indra's throne.—*vāh vāh*—

—*gāv*—

"Send for lots of freshly distilled alcohol.—*mhe*—
Bhūṇā, send for your goats, do it
Brother, Bhūṇīmal, make all the arrangements now—*vāh vāh*—
Hey, Sirdārs, we'll forget 'child-eating' Rāṇ City
Celebrate well, brother."—*vāh vāh*—
By God's grace, there was talk between father and son.—*mhe*—
Bhagavān's morning service started to take place again.—*vāh vāh*—
That service was the four o'clock one at night.—*mhe*—
And this service was the one of dawn

Yes, that started taking place
Bhūṇājī said: "Banū Bābā—*mhe*—
Why do the drums sound again now?"
Banū Bābā said: "Śrī Mahārāj, it's the dawn service for Bhagavān."
Yes, the dawn service is taking place
So Bhūṇājī once again gave his complete attention to the service
The light that was in the devlī—*mhe*—
It disappeared.—*vāh vāh*—
Bhūṇājī looked again afterward, and said: "Hey, brother, I didn't even finish my talk with him."—*vāh vāh*—
Horse stood in front of horse in the heroic field.—*mhe*—
Rider stood in front of rider
By God's grace, Bhūṇā's cavalry set up tent in the heroic field.—*mhe*—
Dev's dharam-mother, Māt Khaṭāṇī, was walking distraught up and down high up in the pleasure palace
She saw Bhūṇā's armies—*mhe*—
Coming.—*mhe*—
What does she tell the Bhāṭ, let's see. *By saying it, know it, by saying it*
I'll say it now, brother, by Dev Bhagavān's grace, let's see.—*vāh vāh sā*—

—*gāv*—

Sāḍū Mātā Spots Bhūṇājī Approaching

"Hey, Bhāṭ, he's coming after wiping clean the devlī—*mhe*—
He's coming with a good omen
Bābā Bhāṭ, in the heroic field of the Rāṭhoṛs—*mhe*—
Who is the captain of eighty-four villages?
Hey, Bābā Bhāṭ, who is that now?"—*vāh vāh*—
The Bhāṭ didn't speak at all.—*vāh vāh*—
Sāḍū Mātā speaks.—*mhe*—
What news does she tell the Bhāṭ, let's see.
By saying it, know it, let's see, by saying it
I'll say it now, brother, by Bhagavān's grace, let's see

—*gāv*—

"O Bhāṭ, one can see the dazzling mace of the Sirdār.—*mhe*—
One can see the arrow-bearer wearing silken clothes
Hey, which captain of eighty-four villages has entered the heroic field—*mhe*—
Bhāṭ, that all of Daṛāvaṭ shakes?—*vāh vāh*—
My Daṛāvaṭ, isn't it.
Yes, it's all trembling
Who so mighty has arrived?"—*vāh vāh*—
Now the Bhāṭ speaks.—*vāh vāh*—
What news does he tell Sāḍū, let's see.

By saying it, know it, by saying it, let's see
I'll say it now, brother, by Dev's grace, let's see

—*gāv*—

"Brother, I saw the dazzling mace of the Sirdār.—*vāh vāh*—
I saw the arrow-bearer wearing silken clothes
Bāgoṭh's Ṭhākur Bhūṇājī has come as your guest.—*mhe*—
O Mother, in Daṛāvaṭ flower beds of saffron have bloomed
Daṛāvaṭ isn't trembling!
Yes, it's blossoming
Because the city blossomed, it's shaking."—*vāh vāh*—
Sāḍū Mātā said: "Bhāṭ!—*mhe*—
Who has come? Hey, has Bhūṇājī come?"
Yes, Bhūṇājī has come
The Bhāṭ said: "Śrī Mahārāj, he's come."—*vāh vāh*—
"Listen, O Bhāṭjī!—*mhe*—
Lay a carpet under the Pāras Pīplī now.—*vāh vāh*—
And arrange the brothers' meeting."—*vāh vāh*—
So, how does the Bagaṛāvats' Bhāṭ go to the brothers.—*mhe*—
And how does Sāḍū Mātā give the maidservants a command to perform āratī, let's see.
By saying it, know it, let's see, by saying it
I'll say it now, by Dev's grace

—*gāv*—

Bhūṇājī Meets Three of His Brothers

"Place the cup full of saffron.—*mhe*—
Hīṛāgar maidservant fill up the platter with pearls
Hīṛāgar, with lighted lamps adorn Bhūṇīmal who has come.—*vāh vāh*—
Today the master of the people has arrived
The people's master.
Yes, he's come today
Worship him with lighted lamps!"—*vāh vāh*—
The Bhāṭ arrived at Dev's royal assembly
After arriving he said: "Śrī Mahārāj—*mhe*—
Your brother, Bhūṇājī, has come from Raṇ City today after eleven years.—*mhe*—
Go now in order to meet him, go beneath the Pāras Pīplī.
Yes, go on, meet him
Brother meet brother!"—*vāh vāh*—
It took no time saying it, Savāī Bhoj's Medūjī got up first.—*vāh vāh*—
Tejājī's Madan Siṅg got up from that place
Nevājī's prince Bhāṅgījī was there, he too
Yes, got up, said sir.

He got up, took his mortar and pestle, and ground one and a quarter maṇ of bhāṅg.—*mhe*—
So after consuming one and a quarter maṇ of bhāṅg, Bhāṅgījī went together with them—*vāh vāh*—
To meet Bhūṇājī.
Yes, he came beneath the Pāras Pīplī
He spoke to Dev: "Śrī Mahārāj, *you come too.*"
Devjī said: "Bābā Bhāṭ—*mhe*—
Till today I haven't met with any brother.—*vāh vāh*—
Yes, there'll be no meeting.
Yes, there'll be no meeting, why should I meet?
If they want to meet me.—*mhe*—
Then they will come here and meet me."
Yes, they'll come to the assembly
Let's see what happens when Savāī Bhoj's Medūjī meets Prince Bhūṇā first.—*vāh vāh*—

—*gāv*—

Savāī Bhoj's Medūjī embraced Bhūṇā first.—*mhe*—
He met him after touching the earth: "You did a great thing coming away from the enemy today.—*mhe*—
I'll place my horse behind your mare Bor
I'll keep your mare in front now."—*vāh vāh*—

—*gāv*—

Tejājī's Madno too embraced him.—*mhe*—
He kept Prince Bhūṇājī's honor: "You did a great thing coming away from the enemy today.—*vāh vāh*—
Hey, brother, Goṭhā's marriage party is without a groom
We are a lot of people in the marriage party.—*vāh vāh*—
But there's no one amongst us who will become the groom
You've come.—*mhe*—
We'll keep you the chief groom."—*vāh vāh*—
Nevājī's son prince, was standing nearby with mortar and pestle.
Bhūṇājī speaks to Banū Bhāṭ.—*mhe*—
What news does he tell, let's see.
By saying it, know it, let's see, by saying it

—*gāv*—

"Eyes like that of a lion.—*mhe*—
One sees him equipped with an abundance of arms and swords
Brother Bhāṭ, who is this chief of eighty-four villages in Dev's assembly?
What work does Jam[116] have in Dev's assembly?—*vāh vāh*—
Where did you get that Jam from?"—*mhe*—
The Bhāṭ speaks.—*vāh vāh*—

By God's grace, what news is there between the brothers, let's see.
By saying it, know it, by saying it, let's see

—*gāv*—

"Eyes that look like a lion's.—*mhe*—
That is Nevājī's Prince Bhāṅgījī, you, son, are called Bārāvat's Bhūṇ
You belong to Bārāvatjī.—*mhe*—
He belongs to Nevājī."
Yes, he is
Bhūṇājī reflected to himself:—*mhe*—
"This kind of brother is like a lion.—*vāh vāh*—
For so many days, I wrongly ate food at the enemy's.—*vāh vāh*—
I'll meet with the brother."—*mhe*—
By God's grace, so as to meet his brother, Bhūṇājī moved forward.—*vāh vāh*—
Bhūṇājī put his arms around, in the meantime Bhāṅgījī caught hold of his arm.—*mhe*—
He thought to himself: "Hey, I hope I won't get caught in a trap by this great brother, this Jam.
Yes, why did he catch hold of my arm
Not that he'll pull me and throw me to his feet."—*vāh vāh*—
Bhūṇājī had the strength of eleven elephants.—*vāh vāh*—
Eleven elephants would be tied to the toe of Bhūṇā's foot.—*mhe*—
He would drag them seven kos to the outskirts of Bhināy.—*vāh vāh*—
Bhūṇājī thought to himself: "I'll pull this Jam toward myself now."—*mhe*—
Bhūṇājī made as much effort as he could
Bhāṅgījī didn't budge even the space of a sesame seed from there.

Bhāṅgījī gave Bhūṇā a very small knock.—*mhe*—
He was standing at this spot, and was thrown to that spot over there.
Yes, Bhāṅgījī took him there and stood him up, said sir.
The strength of eleven elephants that Bhūṇā had was all vanquished in one go.—*vāh vāh*—
Bhūṇājī said: "Hey, O Jam!—*mhe*—
Let my arm go! It's turned red!"
Yes, my arm has turned red
By God's grace, when he took Jam's name—*mhe*—
Prince Bhāṅgījī said.—*vāh vāh*—
He said: "When smoke rises, when cannon balls are heated in Rātākoṭ, if you see me on that day . . . —*vāh vāh*—
Bhūṇā look, I am Nevā's Prince Bhāṅgaḍo, you remain Bārāvat's Bhūṇ
Don't look at me today.—*vāh vāh*—
When we go to fight revenge, shortly . . .
Yes, see me there in the battle of Rātākoṭ
I'll show my strength there.—*vāh vāh*—
Why should I show you today!"—*mhe*—

Bhūṇājī said: "Accepted, brother!"—*mhe*—
Bhāṅgījī said: "As your uncle's son, I'm your brother."—*mhe*—
Bhūṇājī said: "I believe you now!—*vāh vāh*—
Let go of my arm!"—*mhe*—
So the Bārahaṭh was standing nearby.—*mhe*—
He asked him:
"Bārāhaṭ Bābā, how many brothers were the Bagaṛāvats?"
Yes, how many brothers were they?
The Bārahaṭh said: "Śrī Mahārāj, there were twenty-three brothers amongst the Bagaṛāvats.—*mhe*—
There was one sister too. *She was counted among the twenty-four*
Bhojī was the sister."—*vāh vāh*—
Bhūṇājī said: "Bārahaṭ Bābā, when the twenty-three Bagaṛāvats went to Indra's throne,—*mhe*—
At that time the power of the twenty-three *they gave to this brother Bhaṅgerīyā, and then departed*
I didn't receive even a sesame seed worth of it."—*vāh vāh*—
The Bārāhaṭ said: "Śrī Mahārāj, don't compare yourself with the Bagaṛāvats.
Yes, don't compare their left foot with the big toe
The Bagaṛāvats were so powerful."
Yes, they were so powerful, sir
Bhūṇāji said: "Then tell me about some past incident, some praise about the Bagaṛāvats."—*vāh vāh*—
By God's grace, the Bārahaṭ speaks.—*mhe*—
What past incidents does he relate, let's see. *By saying it, know it, let's see, by saying it*

—*gāv*—

"Bāvā and Nevā, both brothers roared like lions.—*mhe*—
By God's grace, great kings were fearful of them, brother
By God's grace, on that day, Bāsak was frightened in the underworld
Nevājī, Bāgh Siṅg's great warrior son—*mhe*—
After offering his head, without his head he carried on with his sword for eighty three-hour periods of the day
Bhāṅgījī's father's sword carried on for eighty three-hour periods of the day.—*vāh vāh*—
Why should he worry about us?—*vāh vāh*—
He gave his head to Bhavānī.—*mhe*—
Eighty three-hour periods, lord, he did battle.—*vāh vāh*—*eighty three-hour periods make a lot of days*

—*gāv*—

"Bāvā and Nevā both roared like lions, brother.—*mhe*—
By God's grace, great kings were fearful."

—*gāv*—

"Bāvā and Nevā, both brothers—*mhe*—
Roared like lions in Daṛāvaṭ.—*vāh vāh*—
Great kings grew fearful
Hey, because Nevājī, Indra's throne trembled.—*mhe*—
Because of Bāvājī, Śrī Kirtār[117] himself shook.
Bhagavān Mahārāj accepted defeat from him.—*mhe*—
Do you know that!"

—*gāv*—

"The sons of Bāgh served Jogīs—*mhe*—
Which is why Bābājī gave them wonderous wealth and prosperity
Once it was called Bhoj's Daṛāvaṭ.—*mhe*—
Why did it become Sojīālā Saupurī today?
Why have the village's names been turned around?"
Yes, tell me about that!

—*gāv*—

"The Bagaṛāvats were indeed great devotees of Dīnānāth.—*mhe*—
How did unease arise in their minds?
Hey, what great stain fell into their devotion?—*mhe*—
Why did their descendants become homeless?
By God's grace, if the Bagaṛāvats had so much devotion—*mhe*—
Then why were their descendants ruined, brother?"—*vāh vāh*—
By God's grace, the Bārahaṭ said:
"The Bagaṛāvats were great devotees of Dīnānāth. How did unease arise in their minds?
A stain of alcohol fell on the Bagaṛāvats' palms—*mhe*—
Because of that, son you too stray from house to house
The Bagaṛāvats were disciples of Śaṅkar, of Bhagavān, in an earlier birth they were sages.—*mhe*—
So they went to Kaḷālī's mansion.—*vāh vāh*—
They filled a jar of alcohol and brought it.
Yes, that's why!
By God's grace, the Bagaṛāvats didn't drink the alcohol.—*mhe*—
They only went and filled the jar.—*mhe*—
It's because of that, Bhūṇā, that there is a stain, because of that you stray from house to house."—*vāh vāh*—

—*gāv*—

"The Bagaṛāvats sowed wheat in the field of their clan.—*mhe*—
Young Bhūṇājī you too grew up and became green
Nothing died of the Bagaṛāvats.—*mhe*—
A warrior like you appeared on the earth

Because a warrior like you lives, did the Bagaṛāvats become immortal."—*vāh vāh*—
At this news, Bhūṇā's strength that had vanished—*mhe*—
It returned.
Yes, it came back
By God's grace, his strength returned.—*mhe*—
So, how does Bhūṇā's strength return, what news does he tell, let's see.
By saying it, know it, let's see, by saying it
I'll say it now, by Bhagavān's grace, here you are

—*gāv*—

Bhūṇājī's Encounter with Devnārāyaṇ

As soon as this was said, the strap of Bhūṇā's saffron robe broke apart with one stroke.—*vāh vāh*—
Strength like that of Hanumān returned to Bhūṇā
"Blessed, blessed, Kuldevī Āsāvari!—*mhe*—
You kept the great powerful Bagaṛāvats well on earth
Wonderful, great, O Kuldevī," he said.—*vāh vāh*—
You protected my forefathers well.—*mhe*—
Only five brothers remain, now only the essence.—*vāh vāh*—
Banū Bābā, how many brothers have met now?"
Yes, tell me about that
He said: "Śrī Mahārāj, four brothers have met so far."—*mhe*—
"So, the one who is called an incarnation, what about him?" *"I didn't meet him."*
"Śrī Mahārāj, you didn't meet him."—*vāh vāh*—
"So, how should I meet that brother?"
Yes, tell me a means of doing that
Banū Bābā said: "Śrī Mahārāj, stop the horse, and get down.—*mhe*—
And remove your weapons.—*vāh vāh*—
Join your hands together.—*mhe*—
Go to Bhagavān's assembly and stand there.
Yes, stand in front there
You'll meet him naturally."
Yes, you'll meet him on your own
Bhūṇājī said: "Beggar!—*mhe*—
You meet like beggars meet, saying: 'Sir, sir!'
Yes, that's the kind of solution you've told me
He's an equal brother, I'll meet him by way of embracing him."
Yes, I'll meet him well
Banū Bābā said: "Śrī Mahārāj, whatever your wish is, meet him like that."
Yes, meet him like that

So, Bhūṇājī entered the assembly riding his horse.—*vāh vāh*—
The lord of the three worlds gave a shout.—*mhe*—
With the sound of the shout, the front of Bhūṇā's forces turned about face.
Yes, they all turned about face
Bhūṇāji reflected to himself: "What's happened here?"
Yes, why did this happen?
Then again in order to meet Dev, Bhūṇājī turned facing Dev.—*mhe*—
Dev Mahārāj shouted: again the Sirdārs' faces turned about. *They turned about face, said sir.*
Three times in order to meet Dev, Bhūṇā turned to face Dev.—*mhe*—
Three times Bhagavān turned him about face.—*vāh vāh*—
Bhūṇājī thought to himself: "Brother is very harsh.
Yes, that brother is very harsh
Hey, three times we placed our hands together, even then he won't meet."
Yes, he won't meet, he turns around and sits
In a temper—*mhe*—
Bhūṇājī departed again:—*vāh vāh*—
"We don't want to stay with such a brother!"
Yes, I don't want to live near such a harsh brother
At the time when he rode back, he met the Bagaṛāvats' Bhāṭ.
Yes, he met him in front
The Bhāṭ said: "Śrī Mahārāj, why are you leaving astride your horse?"
Yes, why are you leaving?
So, by God's grace, Bhūṇājī speaks.—*mhe*—
Let's see how he chides the Bhāṭ. *By saying it, know it, let's see, by saying it*
I'll say it now, by Lord Dev's grace, here you are.—*vāh vāh sā*—

—*gāv*—

"Over there, Bābā Bhāṭ, I had the blessings of the Paḍihārs.—*mhe*—
Rāvjī would give me Rāṇ City together with trees
Look, here Bandrāban's[118] king was displeased.—*mhe*—
Your Dev's throne moves around without legs
This throne doesn't have any legs.
Yes, just like that, it moves about on its own
Hey, this kind of brother is very harsh but I don't want to give up my status.—*vāh vāh*—
The entire fault is with you.—*mhe*—
You went out to find me, that's why I came, brother!"—*vāh vāh*—
Bhūṇājī got angry.—*mhe*—
Bhūṇājī speaks. What news does he say, let's see.
By saying it, know it, let's see, by saying it
I'll say it now, by Bhagavān's grace, here you are.—*vāh vāh—jī—vāh vāh*—

—*gāv*—

"Over there I had the blessings of Hindvā Rāv.—*mhe*—
Hey, Bhāṭ, I came away after breaking with the ocean

I broke off with the ocean.—*mhe*—
Here Bandrāban's king was displeased.—*vāh vāh*—
Your Sovereign Devjī sat with his back turned about
By God's grace, I came in order to meet him.—*mhe*—
Your Devjī went and turned his back about, brother."—*vāh vāh*—
He said: "Śrī Mahārāj."—*mhe*—
The Bhāṭ says—*vāh vāh*—
"You please wait a little here.—*mhe*—
I'll go to Dev's assembly.—*mhe*—
I'll arrange the brothers meeting for you right now."
Yes, I'll do it
"All right, Bhāṭ, you go, brother, there's nothing to worry about." *Go!*
So, Bhūṇājī astride his horse stands there.—*mhe*—
And the Bagaṛāvats' Bhāṭ goes to Dev's assembly.—*vāh vāh*—
What news does he tell Bhagavān right upon reaching.
By saying it, know it, let's see, by saying it

—*gāv*—

The Tale of the Ṭīṭoḍīs

"It's good to be together with brothers—*mhe*—
A brother resides in the shelter of another brother
When the swords resound in the Rāṭhors' heroic field—*mhe*—
If there is a brother there, he'll act in your favor
Śrī Mahārāj, there are a lot of brothers,—*vāh vāh*—
By God's grace, who are displeased.—*mhe*—
When they kill the enemy, at that time will you jump up and embrace them?
Yes, you'll embrace them?
A brother like Bhūṇājī, whom you've annoyed and sent away."
Yes, you annoyed him
Dev Mahārāj did not say anything.—*vāh vāh*—
The Bhāṭ of the lineage speaks. What complaint does he give Bhagavān,
Dev, let's see.
By saying it, know it, by saying it, let's see
I'll say it now, by Dev's grace, here you are

—*gāv*—

"It's good to be together with brothers.—*mhe*—
Enemies and ill-wishers will honor you
Śrī Mahārāj, the Ṭīṭoḍī[119] raised the ocean—*mhe*—
It raised the ocean on the strength of the family
The Ṭīṭoḍī creature, isn't it—*mhe*—
It won over the ocean because there was the family."—*vāh vāh*—
Dev Mahārāj said: "Hey, Bhāṭ!—*mhe*—

Forget about bygone events!—*vāh vāh*—
How did this Ṭīṭoḍī creature raise the ocean, brother?" *Tell that!*
The Bhāṭ said: "Śrī Mahārāj, the Ṭīṭoḍī creature laid eggs on the side of the ocean.—*vāh vāh*—
For three days she sat on the eggs
Yes, she sat on top off them
The Ṭīṭoḍā came and said: "Ṭīṭoḍī, why are you famishing yourself! Go, eat and drink!"
Yes, go, eat and drink
The Ṭīṭoḍī said: "Brother, who'll keep an eye on the eggs?"
Yes, who'll protect the eggs?
"I'll protect them."—*vāh vāh*—
So, the Ṭīṭoḍī flew into the forest to eat and drink
The Ṭīṭoḍā creature, what did it do? It lay with its back down on the eggs.—*vāh vāh*—
The ocean brought its wave near and said: "Creature, why are you suffering, brother? Lie down properly."
Yes, "Sit straight!" it said.
The bird said: "Don't you say anything."
Yes, don't talk to me
"Why not?"—*mhe*—
The bird said: "I'm looking after the eggs."
Yes, I'm protecting my eggs
"Protection against what?"
Yes, what kind of protection is this?
The bird said: "Should the sky fall down from above—*mhe*—
I'll catch it in my two feet.
Yes, I'll keep it on my feet, raised above
And, if you come with a wave—*mhe*—
I'll catch you in my wings."
Yes, I'll capture you in my wings
The ocean thought: "Know your mother—it's a small creature . . ."
Yes, he's controlling you
Right then, with a roar, the ocean let loose a wave.
Crying out "Ṭau, ṭau," the Ṭīṭoḍā flew up into the sky
And the ocean grabbed the eggs and took them within.
The Ṭīṭoḍī came back. She said: "Ṭīṭoḍā, where are the eggs?"
Yes, why are you flying around above?
He said: "Your father! The ocean took them away yesterday!"
Yes, it took them away yesterday
She said: "You've done great wrong, brother!—*mhe*—
Hey, I was here for three days, the ocean didn't take notice of me.
Yes, the ocean didn't take my name
You offended the ocean."
Yes, you've done something or the other wrong!
Here, brother, Ṭīṭoḍī; the Ṭīṭoḍī spoke in such a way.—*mhe*—

"What shall we do now?"
Yes, what shall we do?
She said: "Let's go to our clan and family.—*mhe*—
Let's summon them together."—*vāh vāh*—
So, all the creatures born of eggs,—*vāh vāh*—
They went to them, brother.—*vāh vāh*—
They said: "The ocean has taken away our eggs, therefore come, brother, have them returned to us."
Yes, we'll fight
All the feathered creatures that existed—*mhe*—
They all gathered together on one side of the ocean.—*vāh vāh*—
They said: "We've gathered together, but how shall we fight the ocean?"
What's the solution for that!
There was a creature called Puṭīyā, in the meantime it said: "Brother, set me up as lord, king amongst all—*mhe*—
Then I'll tell you a plan.
Yes, I'll tell you a plan all right
But you'll have to make me king."—*vāh vāh*—
The birds said: "O King, we'll believe in you only."
Yes, we'll believe you are the king, what's it to us?
They made a small heap with sand—*mhe*—
And gave the throne to the Puṭīyā creature.
Yes, have him sit on the throne
"Here you are, King, sir, speak!" *Now tell us*
Puṭīyā said: "What should I say, brother—all you creatures dive into the water.—*mhe*—
Take some water in your stomachs, some on your wings, and some *take in your beaks*
These white dunes of sand—*mhe*—
Go to them and pour out the water.
While coming back, take some sand on the curve of your wings
And take some in your beaks
Make two or three runs; on its own . . .
Yes, the ocean will leave it's place."
It took no time at all—*mhe*—
By God's grace, in the time they made two or three runs, the ocean left the place.
Yes, at different places they erected mounds of sand in the water
The ocean said: "Hey, creatures, why are you making me leave my place?"
Yes, what's the matter?
The birds said: "We are fighting you, because you took away the eggs.
Yes, return this Ṭīṭoḍī's eggs!
Otherwise we won't let this place of yours exist!"—*vāh vāh*—
The ocean said: "Then, brother, don't fill up my shore with sand.—*mhe*—
I'll give you your eggs." *I'll return them*
The ocean let loose a wave—*mhe*—

And brought the eggs back and placed them on the shore.
Yes, here you are, take them
"The family stood behind.—*mhe*—
Then the family won the fight," the Bhāṭ said.—*vāh vāh*—
"Śrī Mahārāj, a brother like Bhūṇā came to you. *Why do you annoy him and send him away*
So, the Bhāṭ related the Ṭīṭoḍī's plan; Bhūṇājī came to the assembly.
Speak: Victory to Śrī Devnārāyaṇ Bhagavān—victory!

Devnārāyaṇ Persuades Bhūṇājī to Stay

By God's grace, so the news was said to Dev Mahārāj.—*mhe*—
The Bhāṭ said: "Śrī Mahārāj, a mighty brother like Bhūṇā won't be coming—*vāh vāh*—
Whom you've angered and
Yes, turned back
Dev Mahārāj speaks. What news does he tell, let's see.
By saying it, know it, by saying it, let's see
I'll say it now, brother, by Dev's grace, here you are.—*vāh vāh sā*—

—*gāv*—

"I sent a letter for Bhūṇā to Rāṇ City.—*mhe*—
I wrote on paper with black ink
Send Elder Brother Bhūṇā back to Nautherī Rāṇ.—*vāh vāh*—
Tether Bārāvat's Mare Bor
Listen, hey, Bhāṭ!—*mhe*—
Tether Bor together with Līlā.—*vāh vāh*—
Tell Elder Brother—*mhe*—
That Rāṇ City lies there—go back!"
Bhūṇā heard that news.—*mhe*—
Bhūṇājī thought: "Brother didn't call me so that we could meet.
Yes, he called me because of this mare
But I won't give brother this mare!"—*mhe*—
Bhūṇājī speaks. What news does he tell Dev, let's see.
By saying it, know it, by saying it
I'll say it now, by Dev's grace . . .

—*gāv*—

"I didn't get the mare by begging for it—*mhe*—
Nor did I get it by paying a price at the markets
I stood in the way of the enemy from Bhilmāl.—*vāh vāh*—
O Giver of Grain, I brought the mare after breaking the Bhīl's teeth
I broke the Bhīl's teeth—*mhe*—
Then I got possession of the mare.—*vāh vāh*—
Why should I give you the mare just like that?

Yes, I didn't get it by begging for it
My seat is on the Mare Borḍī and your seat is on the Horse Līlā
I stood in the way of the enemy from Bhilmāl, I killed Dānī Bhīl
I killed Dānī Bhīl,—*mhe*—
Only then did the mare come into my possession."
By God's grace, Bhūṇājī said this news.—*mhe*—
Dev Mahārāj, told the Bhāṭ—*vāh vāh*—: "Bābā Bhāṭ!—*mhe*—
Brother seems very brave to me!"
Yes, he's very brave!
Dev speaks.—*vāh vāh*—
What news does he tell Prince Bhūṇā, let's see.
By saying it, know it, let's see, by saying it
I'll say it now, brother, by Dev's grace, here you are.—*vāh vāh sā*—

—*gāv*—

"You grew up among the enemy.—*mhe*—
Bhūṇā you ate pigeons' lentil
How did you claim the Bagaṛāvats' Goṭh village?—*mhe*—
You drew abuse on the clan of the Bagaṛāvats
While thinking of the Bagaṛāvats you attracted abuse."—*vāh vāh*—
Dev Mahārāj said that news to Bhūṇājī
Bhūṇājī speaks.—*mhe*—
What answer does he give back, let's see.
By saying it, know it, Bhopājī Mahārāj, by saying it
I'll say it now, brother, by Bhagavān's grace, here you are.—*vāh vāh sā*—

—*gāv*—

"I grew up among the enemy.—*mhe*—
I ate pigeons' lentil
But like you I wasn't called 'someone who is sent offerings'
You grew up eating food offered by your maternal uncle
You went to your maternal grandparents' home where they offered bread to Brāhmans.—*vāh vāh*—
Earlier your uncles would offer Brahmans one piece of bread:
'Stop giving it to the Brahmans—give it to this nephew.'
Yes, keep giving it to this nephew
I never took away Brahmans' food!—*vāh vāh*—
I flaunted the enemy's authority."—*mhe*—
Dev Mahārāj, my master, laughed aloud:—*vāh vāh*—
"Wonderful, hey, Bhāṭ, great!" he said. "You certainly brought a very brave brother."—*vāh vāh*—
Bhūṇājī thought to himself: "Why meet with my brother?
Yes, let's go
By God's grace, who knows whether the mare is on your side or on Dev's side.
Let me speak to this mare."—*mhe*—

Bhūṇājī speaks.—*vāh vāh*—
What does he tell the mare, let's see.
By saying it, know it, let's see, by saying it
I'll say it now, by Dev's grace, here you are

—*gāv*—

"In the Mahābhārat, Mare, you didn't move well—*mhe*—
You threw my father into the enemy gatherings
If you're going to do to me what you did to my father—*mhe*—
Then tell me right now!"
Yes, tell me in the first place
The mare speaks.—*mhe*—
What news does she tell Bhūnā, let's see.
By saying it, know it, let's see, by saying it
I'll say it now, hey, brother, by God's grace, let's see.—*vāh vāh sā*—

—*gāv*—

"After throwing my reins down
By God's grace, if you say so, I'll take you to Indra's throne!—*mhe*—
Don't give me that bygone complaint.—*vāh vāh*—
Your father didn't do battle sitting on my back!
Yes, my reins were held back
The fight took place face to face.—*mhe*—
Devī's discus flew.—*vāh vāh*—
The Bagaṛāvats offered their heads to Bhavānī.—*mhe*—
I had no hand in the matter."—*vāh vāh*—
The mare speaks.—*vāh vāh*—
What news does she tell Bhūṇā?
By saying it, know it, let's see, by saying it
I'll say it now by Bhagavān's grace, here you are.—*vāh vāh sā*—

—*gāv*—

"Get on, Bhūṇā, great warrior!" she said.—*mhe*—
"Hey, stick to my back
There's no permission of Nārāyaṇ Dev—*mhe*—
Otherwise I'd take you to Indra's throne
I'll show you Vaikuṇṭh.—*vāh vāh*—
But, there's no permission from Bhagavān!"
Yes, there's no permission from Dev!
Bhūṇājī thought to himself: "The mare is on your side all right.—*vāh vāh*—
Now I won't meet brother.—*mhe*—
Let us go now!"—*vāh vāh*—
By God's grace, Bhūṇājī turned the mare Bor back onto the road to Rāṇ City.—*mhe*—
When the mare's footsteps made a sound—*vāh vāh*—
Queen Pīpalde came up into the balcony.—*mhe*—

By God's grace, how does she go to Sāḍū Mātā's mansion
What news does Queen Pīpalde tell Sāḍū upon arriving, let's see. *By saying it, know it, let's see, by saying it*
I'll say it now, hey, brother, by Dev's grace, here you are.—*vāh vāh sā*—

—*gāv*—

By God's grace, Queen Pīpalde said that news.—*mhe*—
She said: "O Mother-in-law, look, Brother-in-law has ridden to the border.—*vāh vāh*—
The headgear on Brother-in-law's horse looks so beautiful
You go and appease Brother-in-law straight away.—*mhe*—
The match of Rām and Lakṣman is going to be separated
Rām and Lakṣman got together at one place,—*mhe*—
Which is what the enemies did not like."
Yes, who has separated them?
Queen Pīpalde speaks.—*mhe*—
What news does she tell Mother-in-law, let's see.
By saying it, know it, let's see, by saying it
I'll say it now, by Dev's grace, here you are

—*gāv*—

"Brother-in-law's mare whinnied when it reached the crossing, O Mother-in-law.—*vāh vāh*—
Dev's Līlāgar whinnied and broke apart the elephants' trough
Appease Brother-in-law right upon arriving.—*mhe*—
Otherwise the honor between brother-in-law and sister-in-law will diminish
Either you appease Brother-in-law and bring him,
Otherwise, Mother-in-law *I'll go to appease Brother-in-law*
Otherwise our honor will be broken."—*vāh vāh*—
By God's grace, how does Māt Khāṭāṇī come to Dev's assembly.—*vāh vāh*—
What news does she tell Dev, right upon arriving, let's see. *By saying it, know it, let's see, by saying it*
I'll say it now, by Dev's grace, here you are.—*vāh vāh sā*—

—*gāv*—

"O chiefs of Dev, I'll cut your tongues.—*mhe*—
I'll smear black salt on your tongues
Hey, who amongst you angered my mighty Bhūṇā?
Who among you angered Bhūṇājī and sent him back, brother?"
Yes, tell me that
Dev Mahārāj said: "Don't anyone speak, brother!—*vāh vāh*—
Mājī Sāī is coming.—*mhe*—
I'll answer her on my own."—*vāh vāh*—
By God's grace, there was Prince Bhāṅgījī.—*mhe*—
He took his mortar and pestle and stood
Yes, up straight

Prince Bhāṅgījī speaks. What news does he tell Mājī Sāī, let's see. *By saying it, know it, let's see, by saying it*

—*gāv*—

By God's grace, Prince Bhāṅgījī said this news.
He said: "O Mother, Bāgoṭ's master met Dev properly.—*mhe*—
And he met him placing both hands together
Because of this the children acquired bad habits—*mhe*—
O Mother, he sat with his back turned against Elder Brother Bhūṇā
No one else has any fault.—*mhe*—
All the fault is with your Devjī.
Yes, it's with him!
Today he's angered and sent back this brother
Tomorrow he'll anger and send me back.
The place where Bhūṇājī's going—*mhe*—
I'm going there to meet him!" *There you are, take care of your throne!*
Bhāṅgījī picked up his mortar and pestle and departed behind Bhūṇājī.—*vāh vāh*—
Dev Mahārāj thought to himself:
"Brothers have split up!"—*mhe*—
By God's grace, Dev Mahārāj speaks. What news does he say, let's see.
By saying it, know it, by saying it, let's see
I'll say it now, here you are, by God's grace, let's see

—*gāv*—

"Why do you cut out my tongue!—*mhe*—
Why do you smear black salt on my tongue?
Mother, I won't let your mighty Bhūṇā disappear beyond the boundary
Mājī Sāī!—*mhe*—
Stop Bhūṇā a little.
Yes, halt a little
Don't let him ride beyond the boundary."—*vāh vāh*—
Kālvī Mare stood in the court, Mājī Sāī—*mhe*—
She got onto the mare as it stood there.—*vāh vāh*—
She rode the mare behind Bhūṇājī.—*vāh vāh*—
By God's grace, she came close to Bhūṇājī.—*mhe*—
Sāḍū Mātā speaks.—*vāh vāh*—
What does she tell Bhūṇājī afterward, let's see *By saying it, know it, by saying it*
I'll say it now, by God's grace, here you are brother!

—*gāv*—

"You reached your destination.—*mhe*—
The fine-spear looked good
Pull up Bor's reins a little.—*mhe*—
Your mother's coming after you calling you

Bhūṇā, stop Bor a little, brother"—*vāh vāh*—
Bhūṇājī said: "Hey, Sirdārs—*mhe*—
Who is this, brother?"
Yes, who is that?
"Śrī Mahārāj, this is your big mother."—*vāh vāh*—
"Hey, I didn't meet the old woman, brother—wait a little!" *Wait!*
So Bhūṇājī halted the cavalry.—*vāh vāh*—
Māt Khaṭāṇī said:
"Bhūṇājī, tell me how come the cavalry is riding back?
Yes, why did you turn it around?
Neither did you meet me nor did you meet Dev.—*mhe*—
Without meeting us why did you ride back, tell me?"
Yes, tell me!
Bhūṇājī said: "Mājī Sāī, I didn't meet you.
Yes, I didn't meet you
And, your Dev, isn't he,—*mhe*—
I met well with him. *I met him well and am coming.*"
Sāḍū Mātā said: "No son, Devjī isn't here."
Yes, he wasn't there in the assembly
"Where did he go?" *Tell me that!*
Sāḍū Mātā said: "Dev is very fond of Suremātā.[120]
Yes, great fondness
As soon as day breaks, he goes with the cows to graze them.
Yes, in the morning he gets up to graze the cows
And during the later hours, at four o'clock,
Yes, he returns leading the cows
Devjī's gone to graze the cows.—*vāh vāh*—
He's not here at all!" *Not here at all*
Bhūṇājī speaks.—*mhe*—
What news does he tell his mother, let's see.
By saying it, know it, let's see, by saying it
I'll say it now, by Dev's grace, here you are.—*vāh vāh—sā*

—*gāv*—

"Horse Līlāgar is tethered in the court.—*mhe*—
An assembly of scorpions and snakes
Bhūṇājī speaks to you.—*mhe*—
If Devjī is two or three times fold, then he doesn't belong to the brothers.—*mhe*—
If there is only one Devjī—*vāh vāh*—then I've seen that Devjī and left."
I've seen him properly!
Māt Khaṭāṇī said: "Hey, listen, hey, son!—*mhe*—
You talk about the snakes and lizards.—*vāh vāh*—
Have you become friends with the village's Jāṭs, goddammit!
Yes, he is friends with all of them
Devjī goes to graze the cows.—*mhe*—

Then they begin to play with them in their lap.
Yes, they play with all of them in their laps, the snakes and those scorpions
Dev's face and people's—Jāṭs' faces look alike, brother.—*vāh vāh*—
That's all there is to it."—*mhe*—
Bhūṇājī reflected to himself: "The old woman is evading me all right!"
Yes, the old woman's lying!
Bhūṇājī speaks. What news does he tell mother, let's see.
By saying it, know it, by saying it, let's see
I'll say it now, by Dev's grace, here you are.—*vāh vāh*—*jī vāh vāh*—

—*gāv*—

"I'll go to Delhi and to Agra.—*mhe*—
I'll go to the Bhāṭṭī's Jaisalmer
The Bagaṛāvats' son is riding to the Bagaṛāvats' revenge.—*vāh vāh*—
Sāḍū distribute the letter on that day
Brother, O Mother, give me then this letter—*mhe*—
When I take my father's revenge.—*vāh vāh*—
I won't go back again.
Yes, now I won't go back to your Devjī!
And, if I don't go near Devjī, then there's nothing like Rāṇ City left to go back to.—*vāh vāh*—
I broke with them."—*mhe*—
The lord of the three worlds, Bhagavān, decorated Līlā—*mhe*—
And what did he do with Līlā' reins—he put them down from the assembly into the earth.—*vāh vāh*—
The horse Līlāgar entered into Mother Earth.—*mhe*—
He went three kos ahead and came out
Dev put the horse back onto the road to Daṛāvaṭ.—*vāh vāh*—
The horse runs one and a quarter hands above Mother Earth.—*mhe*—
And the saddle is one and a quarter hands above the horse
One and a quarter hands above the saddle Bhagavān was present—*vāh vāh*—
A one-and-a-quarter-maṇ heavy parasol is flying above Bhagavān's head
And one flag is flying even above it.
Sāḍū Mātā's attention went to Dev first.—*mhe*—
She told Bhūṇājī:—*vāh vāh*—
"Hey, son Bhūṇā,—*mhe*—
You say that you saw Devjī and came—*vāh vāh*—
Look over there, my Devjī, look he's coming, take a look now!"
Yes, he's coming from the jungle
Bhūṇājī took a look toward the road
So, he saw Līlāgar coming.—*mhe*—
He thought to himself: "Hey, the very same horse and the very same boy!
Yes, he's the same as that one, yes
But how did he come this way?"
Yes, he's coming from ahead
Dev Mahārāj spoke to Sāḍū straight upon arriving:—*mhe*—

"Hey, Mājī Sāī"—*vāh vāh*—
Why did you come to the jungle?
Yes, why did you come to the jungle today?
Whose cavalry is it, and why did you come, tell me news about that!"
Yes, tell me!
Sāḍū Mātā said: "Son, that's your brother Bhūṇājī.—*vāh vāh*—
Someone in your court played a joke on him.—*mhe*—
So, in anger this Bhūṇā is going away.
Yes, he's turning back
In order to appease him I've
Yes, come into the jungle"
Devnārāyaṇ said: "Mājī Sā, is this Elder Brother Bhūṇā?"
Yes, the same one?
Sāḍū Mātā said: "He's the very same one."—*vāh vāh*—
"So, Elder Brother Bhūṇā came, why do you return without meeting me, without talking to me, or what?"
Yes, why are you going back without meeting me?
Bhūṇājī thought to himself: "Damn, was that boy another, or what?
Yes, he was another all right—some nonsensical thought—he's someone else
He spoke sensibly!"—*vāh vāh*—
In front of Bhūṇā, the lord of the three worlds left the horse's stirrups.—*vāh vāh*—
How do the brothers meet in the jungle
What kind of story is it, let's see.
By saying it, know it, by saying it, let's see
I'll say it now, sir, by Dev's grace, here you are.—*vāh vāh*—

—*gāv*—

Bhūṇājī and Dev Mahārāj met each other at half the distance to the border—*mhe*—
Hey, brother, the maidservants sang songs of blessing
In the morning hours marriage cannons fired away.—*mhe*—
Bhūṇā, take a look at the royal custom
At the time when Dev Mahārāj met with Bhūṇājī—*mhe*—
At that time he cast his nectar gaze
All over groups of maidservants began singing songs of joy and blessing.—*vāh vāh*—
Rich and poor started singing songs.
All over there was music and royal receptions
Bhūṇājī took a look all around:
"Hey, know your mother! He's such a divine brother!
Yes, we would have gone away without meeting him
There's no obtaining such a brother again."
Dev Mahārāj said: "Elder Brother Bhūṇā,—*mhe*—
When you lived in Rāṇ City, why were you called Prince Khāṇḍerāvjī?"
Yes, why were you called that?

Bhūṇājī said: "Śrī Mahārāj, the Sāṅkhlā Sirdār of Cāṇdārūṇ cut off my small finger.
He was Rāvjī's wife's brother.—*vāh vāh*—
He said, he'll be my nephew—*mhe*—
What sign should I give him?
Yes, I'll give him a sign and give him another name
On that day my name Bhūṇā was removed.—*mhe*—
They gave me the name Prince Khāṇḍerāv."

Devnārāyaṇ said: "Elder Brother Bhūṇā, it doesn't seem to me that the sword cut off your finger, brother."
Yes, where did the sword cut you—I can't see it.
In what manner does Dev, the lord of the three worlds, show Bhūṇā his finger, let's see.
By saying it, know it, by saying it, let's see

—*gāv*—

"You did very well today coming away from the enemy.—*mhe*—
Child, you looked after the populace in need of protection."
The infant king looked at Bhūṇā with beṇevolence.—*mhe*—
Instantly Bhūṇā's finger grew back
It became uniform.—*vāh vāh*—
Bhūṇā looked toward his right hand.—*mhe*—
The finger looked uniform.—*vāh vāh*—
Bhūṇājī thought to himself: "I've made a mistake."
Yes, it's on the left hand
He looked toward the left hand
The finger looked uniform
Bhūṇājī thought to himself: "Hey, he's God!"
Yes, what matters are hidden from him?
By God's grace, Bhūṇājī said the news.—*mhe*—
He said: "Truly only you create[121] and only you destroy.—*mhe*—
Truly you are the person above the three worlds
Hey, with hands placed together servants serve him—*mhe*—
Salute the perfect, indestructible person, salute, salute!"
The salutation that others make to bhopās—*mhe*—
Bhūṇājī made it to Dev Mahārāj.—*vāh vāh*—
From that day this salutation has begun.—*mhe*—
That's why when someone comes to Dev's priest and to the bhopā, they say: "Bhopājī, salute!—*mhe*—
Salute Dev, brother!"
Yes, a salutation for Dev
Nowadays no one says it to bhopās." So Bhūṇājī came together with the brothers. Bhūṇā and Dev Mahārāj met properly in the jungle.
Speak: victory to Śrī Devnārāyaṇ Bhagavān, victory
Speak, brother, both small and big, everyone!

❁ Devnārāyaṇ Releases 980,000 Cows into the Fields ❁

So, Dev Bhagavān and Bhūṇā met.—*mhe*—
The brothers got together, then they thought
They said: "The brothers have got together." Dev Mahārāj said: "Brother,
I don't have much time now.—*vāh vāh*—
I have a limit of eleven years.—*mhe*—
Seven years passed away in Mālāgar.—*vāh vāh*—
And after coming here more time has passed.
Yes, it's been many days
Think up a plan of how to extract the Bagaṛāvats' revenge."—*vāh vāh*—
They said: "Śrī Mahārāj, hey, each household is good for his.—*mhe*—
Give Jāsā's Nirpāl the command.—*vāh vāh*—
Release the cows now onto the summer harvest of wheat and chickpeas!"
Yes, let them attack

—*gāv*—

The king said: "Place the spear at the proper place, O uncle's son!—*vāh vāh*—
Hey, today Nārāyaṇ Devjī has given the command.—*mhe*—
In the morning he'll demolish the emperor's lands."
By God's grace, the Guāl was enthusiastic since many days, it took no time.—*vāh vāh*—
It took no time releasing the cows into the fields.
Yes, he released them speedily, said sir.
The fields of fifteen, twenty villages
Yes, they surrounded and returned in the evening
Dev had great affection for cows.—*mhe*—
In the mornings he would go out together with them and at the latter time he would *return leading them, said sir.*
Bhagavān went in front of the cows.—*mhe*—
So Suremātā put her face into the fence of branches and leaves surrounding the field, into the fence
Yes, she came to Dev Mahārāj's notice, said sir.
Dev speaks. What reproof does he give to the Guāl, let's see.
By saying it, know it, let's see, by saying it
I'll say it now, by Dev's grace, let's see.—*vāh vāh*—*jī*

—*gāv*—

By God's grace, Dev Mahārāj spoke the news, *said sir.*
"O Brother Guāl, why does Suremātā seem forlorn?—*mhe*—
Why is my Kāmdhen afraid?
Why do you have a fear of dying?—*mhe*—
I'll graze these cows tomorrow morning again, Guāl.
You treasured your own life.—*vāh vāh*—

You didn't treasure the cows."—*mhe*—
The Guāl said: "Śrī Mahārāj, this business of herding is hard.
Yes, I can't do this business of herding
I'll do your work sitting at home!"—*vāh vāh*—
He threw down the grazing stick in front of Dev, *said sir.*
Dev said: "Guāl, why did you do this, brother?"—*mhe*—
The Guāl said: "Śrī Mahārāj, this business of herding is hard, it can't be done by me.
Yes, I can't do it
Another Guāl will go with these cows, now."—*vāh vāh*—
Dev said: "Listen, hey, Guāl, no one else has the authority like you, brother.
Yes, no Guāl has the authority to graze the cows
By God's grace, you have always had the authority for this matter.—*mhe*—
You will have to go with the cows!"—*vāh vāh*—
The Guāl speaks.—*mhe*—
What news does he tell Dev, let's see.
By saying it, know it, by saying it, let's see
I'll say it now, by God's grace, here you are.—*vāh vāh*—*jī*—*vāh vāh*—

—*gāv*—

Devnārāyaṇ Decorates the Cows with Ornaments

"O Giver of Grain, I keep sticks of dhāman.[122]—*vāh vāh*—
I graze Pārbrim's[123] cows
The previous Guāl used to keep Bījaḷsār's lance
Śrī Mahārāj—*mhe*—
With his stick I will be able to get the harvest now.
Yes, some I will get today, some tomorrow
Give the Guāls the ornamentation and armor belonging to a Guāl—*mhe*—
And, the ornaments for a cow, dress the cows with them.—*vāh vāh*—
So, by God's grace, I'll do what you say, I'll go out with the cows again."
Yes, I'll destroy the fields
Dev Mahārāj said: "Guāl!—*mhe*—
I don't know about this, brother.—*vāh vāh*—
What the ornamentation and armor of Guāls are and what the ornaments of cows are.
Yes, what are they?
By telling it I will know!
Yes, what can I know like this?"
The Guāl said: "These are the cows' ornaments
Give me that much, O Bāḷā Devjī, in the morning I'll destroy the emperor's fields."
Dev Mahārāj said: "Guāl!—*mhe*—
You're not talking about destroying the fields.

Yes, this isn't my idea of destroying the fields
You say I should make ornaments for the cows.—*mhe*—
We have nine lakh and eighty thousand cows!—*vāh vāh*—
And when should I decorate and arm them Guāl?
I don't have a lease for so much time, brother!"
Yes, I don't have a promise for that much time
The Guāl said: "Śrī Mahārāj, why make them?"—*mhe*—
The Guāl was there with the Bagaṛāvats from the very beginning.
Yes, the ornaments are all made and ready
"Go to Sāḍū, *and ask for them.*"
The lord of the three worlds, Bhagavān, became a child again after seven years, and went to his mother's lap and began to lie down in it.—*vāh vāh*—
Sāḍū Mātā thought to herself: "What's this?
Yes, why did this happen today?
Hey, why did Bhagavān turn into a seven-year-old child again?"—*vāh vāh*—
Dev speaks. What news does he say to his mother, let's see.
By saying it, know it, by saying it, let's see
I'll say it now, by Dev's grace, here you are.—*vāh vāh sā*—

—*gāv*—

"O Mother, Bāī, open up the safe.—*vāh vāh*—
Take the key in your hand
O Mother, distribute the ornaments to the Guāls in the morning
Distribute the cows' ornaments to the cows—dress them.—*mhe*—
Give the Guāls' armor and ornaments to the Guāls."
Sāḍū Mātā thought to herself: "Damn nuisance! Who sowed this trouble?—*mhe*—
There are three persons from the Bagaṛāvats' time.—*vāh vāh*—
This work is definitely theirs.
Yes, it's their work. There is no fourth person
Either Suremātā has sowed this trouble—*mhe*—
Or the Bagaṛāvats' Bhāṭ.
Yes, Chochū's sown it
There's that cow's Guāl.—*mhe*—
He too is the root of strife." *He is the root, said sir.*
She said: "Śrī Mahārāj, the Bagaṛāvats had ornaments.—*mhe*—
When the Mahābhārat began—*vāh vāh*—
On that day, they opened up the ornaments and stowed them away in this wall over here.
Yes, they are buried somewhere over here, I don't know where.
Who knows, if Rāvjī Sāī took the ornaments away in loot
Even this I don't know.—*vāh vāh*—
And, who knows, son, if they have been left here, even then,
Yes, I have no knowledge about the matter
I have no recollection."—*vāh vāh*—
Dev Mahārāj said: "Mājī Sāī, the ornaments are hardly hidden!"

Yes, they are not hidden from me
The lord of the three worlds speaks.—*mhe*—
What news does he tell his mother, let's see. *Know it, by saying it, let's see, now Bhopājī Mahārāj, by saying it*
I'll say it now, by God's grace.—*vāh vāh sā*—

—*gāv*—

"O Mother, the ornaments are not hidden from me!—*mhe*—
The ornaments lie underneath
You are King Raṇdhīr's granddaughter.—*mhe*—
I won't accept them but from your hands
Listen, O Mother.—*mhe*—
I want to take it from your hands.
Yes, I don't want to take myself
By God's grace, the ornaments aren't hidden from me."—*vāh vāh*—
Māt Khaṭāṇī thought to herself:—*mhe*—
"You have no idea about his powers!"
Yes, what limits are there?
In Mālāgar you demanded milk—*mhe*—
He returned the milk exactly the same way he had drunk it
The ornaments are hardly hidden from him."
Yes, they are hardly hidden from him
Sāḍū Mātā gave Dev the bunch of keys
She opened them and said: "Here, son, take them and go!"
Yes, go and see which one they are in!

The lord of the three worlds reached the underworld.—*vāh vāh*—
In the underworld there was molten lead over the ornaments.—*vāh vāh*—
He kicked it, the glass went and landed far away
Putting it on the workers' heads,
He had the ornaments taken to the cows. *Said sir.*
How does Bhagavān light up lamps
How does he decorate his mother's cows, let's see.
By saying it, know it, let's see, now by saying it
I'll tell you now, by Dev's grace, here you are.—*vāh vāh*—*jī*

—*gāv*—

In the light of lamps, Bhagavān decorated Pārbrihm's cows
There are golden earrings studded with jewels.—*mhe*—
"Hey, put them on the ears of my speckled bull
These large earrings.—*mhe*—
By God's grace, put these on your bull.—*vāh vāh*—
In Nagaur Tehsil they are called Sā̃ḍ.—*vāh vāh*—
And, by God's grace, in the Ajmer Tehsil Sā̃ḍs are called Keraḍo.—*vāh vāh*—

—*gāv*—

Guāl, on some put on ankle bracelets.—*mhe*—
On some put on bracelets with bells
Guāl, that cows' chain worth nine lakhs—*vāh vāh*—
Put that on Nevājī's Nāglī cow
There is Uncle Nevājī's Nāglī cow.
Yes, it's to put on her
The big chain worth nine lakhs!"—*vāh vāh*—

—*gāv*—

Brother, Bhagavān gave Nāpā the chief's helmet
"Hey, Guāl, the strong residence of Badnor.—*mhe*—
Strike the first blow upon attacking."

—*gāv*—

Bhagavān gave Nāpā a palanquin
"Hey, Guāl, plant the flag on Sikarānī now.—*mhe*—
Plant the spear on the enemy Rāv's chest
Put the spear onto the enemy's chest afterwards.—*vāh vāh*—
Guāl!—*mhe*—
Graze the cows, brother!"—*vāh vāh*—

—*gāv*—

Devnārāyaṇ Releases His Cows into Rāvjī's Fields

By God's grace, brother, the Guāl grazed Suremātā in the morning.—*vāh vāh*—
"Destroy Rāvjī's Ṭoḍā chief.
The Ṭoḍā's Sirdār is there.—*mhe*—
Let the cows pass by his mansions."
Yes, let them go
The lord of the three worlds, Bhagavān, gave the command to the cows.—*vāh vāh*—
Dev speaks.—*vāh vāh*—
He tells the Guāl another news, let's see.
By saying it, know it, Bhopājī Mahārāj, by saying it
I'll say it now, by Bhagavān's grace, here you are.—*vāh vāh*—*jī*—*vāh vāh*—

—*gāv*—

The Guāl grazed Suremātā in the morning.—*mhe*—
And he gave her water to drink at Gudale Pond.
"Hey, if you find Gudale's water—*vāh vāh*—
Then while going to Rājā Nīma's Bāndarvāḍe
Yes, give them water, said sir.
Listen, hey, Guāl—*vāh vāh*—
If there's some lack in the cows' decoration, then complain to me

Now if the cows remain hungry or thirsty, *the complaint is on you*
Take good care this time."—*vāh vāh*—
The Guāl reflected to himself:
"Hey, Dev has given you leave.—*mhe*—
Our aunt is Dev's dharam-mother.
Yes!
She is the mistress of the house. *I didn't ask her!*
Let's ask her at least, whether I should graze the cows or not, let's see."
Yes, does she allow me to go into the fields or not
How does Dev's Guāl go to Aunt's residence.—*mhe*—
Right upon reaching he says the news, let's see. Here, I'll tell you now, by God's grace, here you are

—*gāv*—

"O Aunt, that Gudaliyā Pond is near Rāṇ City.—*vāh vāh*—
Rāvjī's generals tie raw cotton
Dharamrājā Devjī gives the cows water to drink.—*mhe*—
In the morning, O Aunt, you will find Kāmdhen's milk sweet
In the morning milk tastes sweet.
Yes, the cows are going into Rāvjī's fields
You find milk sweet, don't you?
Stand in front of the cows and stop them
Stand in front now!—*vāh vāh*—
Afterward you'll scold me!"—*mhe*—*give me a scolding afterward*

—*gāv*—

This news, Sāḍū Mātā,
Yes, told her nephew, said sir
"When the Bagaṛāvats were alive, Nephew, Sikarāṇī would be firm.—*vāh vāh*—
Hey, you would cut branches of the Nolake garden
Nephew, the cows halt in Rātākoṭ.—*mhe*—
Who should I put at Kāmdhen's door, afterward?
Nephew!
Yes, who should I leave at the door?
By God's grace, what did you think of in your mind?"
Yes, how did you think this?
He said: "I didn't think of anything!—*mhe*—
The lord of the three worlds, Bhagavān, has thought of it."
Yes, he has thought of it
Sāḍū Mātā speaks, tells the Guāl news, let's see.
By saying it, know it, let's see, now by saying it

—*gāv*—

"Nephew, Sikarāṇī would often sit strong," she said. *vāh vāh*—
"They would cut bunches of fruit in the Nolke garden
Hey, Nephew, the cows have halted in Rātākoṭ."—*vāh vāh*—

Aunt and nephew wander about in Goṭhā giving out cries.
Yes, you won't get any other share
Guāl!—*mhe*—
By God's grace, what did you think of in your mind?"
Yes, how did you think of this?
The Guāl said: "When did I think up anything?
Yes
Dev, the lord of the three worlds thought this up!"—*vāh vāh*—

—*gāv*—

"When the Bagaṛāvats were alive, they would often sit strong.—*mhe*—
They would cut branches in Nolke Garden
Hey, it's the same Rāvjī—*mhe*—
Who smashed our children against rock
Why do you forget things that have happened?
Yes, Rāv Sāī killed seventy children of ours by smashing them again and again on rock
You've forgotten what happened then!" *You've forgotten completely, daughter's father!*
By God's grace, hey, there are three boys—*mhe*—
So far.—*vāh vāh*—
Of the five brothers two are complete simpletons!
Yes, two are simpletons—amongst the simpletons is Dev Mahārāj too
How did you show so much courage?"—*mhe*—
The Guāl said: "When did I show courage? *This Dev Mahārāj, the lord of the three worlds, has shown courage, said sir.*
The cows are going to go into the fields, whether you say anything or not, Aunt!"—*vāh vāh*—

—*gāv*—

"Nephew, we have enough land.—*mhe*—
Don't do what Dev has proclaimed!—*vāh vāh*—
Graze our cows in our own lands.
Hey, shall we become the lord of beggars?
Yes, we are the lord of beggars
And the people will become the lord of the prosperous, Nephew."
The Guāl said: "Aunt, won't you stand in front the cows and stop them.
Yes, stand in front of them now!
I have Bhagavān's command.—*mhe*—
I will destroy the summer harvest of wheat and chickpeas, brother."
Yes, I can't stay here now without grazing the cows!

—*gāv*—

By God's grace, this news was spoken by Sāḍūjī:—*mhe*—
"Dev and you have become drunk.—*vāh vāh*—
The way clothes are colored red
Hey, don't do what Dev has told you to do!—*mhe*—

Come let's go and see the past
Let's go and look at the days past, brother!"
Yes, why have you forgotten now?
The Guāl said: "Aunt, I have Bhagavān's command.—*mhe*—
The cows will certainly go into the fields!"—*vāh vāh*—

—*gāv*—

"Hey, three people in my court didn't die.—*mhe*—
Chochū Bhāṭ, Jāsā's Nirpāl, and Suremātā, the hasty one.
Three persons from the time of the Bagaṛāvats
Yes, remain
If these three had died together with the Bagaṛāvats,
Yes, then there would have been peace and happiness in my home."
The Guāl said: "How many cows should go into the fields?—*vāh vāh*—
It's Bhagavān's, Dev's command now."—*mhe*—
So, by God's grace, Dev Mahārāj had given the command hadn't he.—*mhe*—
So, Sāḍūjī said: "Brother, whatever pleases Dev and yourself,
Yes, that will happen."
So how does Dev Mahārāj's Guāl graze the cows.—*mhe*—
What kind of story is made up, let's see.
By saying it, know it, Bhopājī Mahārāj, by saying it, let's see
I'll say it now, by Bhagavān's grace, here you are.—*vāh vāh*—

—*gāv*—

A sign was made on the Sikarāṇi.—*mhe*—
A "Naṅgārband"[124] Sirdār was stationed at that spot. They said: "Brother,
If the Guāls get into trouble, then
Yes, beat the drums from here
They'll be heard seven kos away at Daṛāvaṭ.—*vāh vāh*—
So Bhāṅgījī and Dev Mahārāj will get astride their horses and join the Guāls.—*vāh vāh*—
And, over there Rāṇ Śahar's Sirdārs will hear it."
Yes, the attack on the cows has been made now
By God's grace, the cows certainly destroyed the crops of five, ten, fifteen villages.—*vāh vāh*—
The 'five' Patels of the villages got together.—*mhe*—

The Five Patels Complain to Rāvjī

They considered the matter:
"Devjī's cows are feeding on the crop of wheat and gram, brother.
Yes, thrash them and show them Rātā Koṭ—vāh vāh—
The villages' Patels gathered together.—*mhe*—
They came to capture the cows. *vāh vāh*—
Berībāj Guāl used to keep a nine-yard-long bamboo stick.

Yes, that long
He struck it on a hollow stone.—*vāh vāh*—
The Patels reflected to themselves: "Neither can the cows be captured by us.—*mhe*—
Nor can the Guāl be captured by us.
Hey, one is our master!
Let us go to Rāvjī's court.—*mhe*—
Let us tell him about the cowherds' and cows' agitation.—*vāh vāh*—
By God's grace, if he pays attention to the complaint, then we'll settle down in Rāvjī's country
If not, then in the sweet country of Marwar, near Dev."
Yes, we'll settle down over there, near Devmāhārāj
The five Patels got together.—*vāh vāh*—
From the Hill of Goram they took the road to Rāṇ Śahar.—*mhe*—
They said: "We're traveling all right, but how will we be heard by the Rāṇā?
Yes, think of that first," they said
They said: "Wrap turbans with blankets. Pour oil into pails and light fires.
Yes, light fires during the day
And place them on your heads.—*vāh vāh*—
Rāvjī will enquire on his own what the matter is.
Yes, he'll ask when we reach there
So do what you have been told to!"—*mhe*—
What happens when the five Patels reach Rāvjī's court. *By saying it, know it, let's see*
I'll say it now, by Bhagavān's grace, here you are are.—*vāh vāh sā*—

—*gāv*—

"By God's grace, we lit fires during the day.—*vāh vāh*—
We came and cried out at the Paḍihār's gate
Even that one Nāpā wasn't stopped, O Master of Rāṇ.—*vāh vāh*—
Hey, Nāpā created a commotion in the fifty-two districts!
You have fifty-two forts!
Yes, they are grazing cows in all of them!
Not even one Nāpā comes under control!"—*vāh vāh*—
Who said this news?
Yes, the Patel of the villages said it, said sir.
Kālū Mīr and Dīyājī thought it over. Mīr said: "Heaven forbid, heaven forbid, heaven forbid, heaven forbid, heaven forbid, heaven forbid, listen to that brother! Yes, death has arrived!"
Yes, it's our own death!
He said: "Do what I say!"—*mhe*—"What's that?" Mīr said: "When the Patel speaks out his complaint to Rāvjī
Yes, we should make a noise!
In the midst of the noise Rāvjī won't hear, and the Patel will leave right away!"
Yes, he'll get up

When the Patel said that news, at that time Kālū Mīr and Dīyājī made a big noise, the fellows!—*vāh vāh*—
Not even a word fell on Rāvjī's ears.
The Patel thought to himself: "I've said one news, so I'll say another!"
Yes, "Say another one right behind the other, let's see, here listen!"

—*gāv*—

"Devjī has established ninety-six auspicious villages of the Bagaṛāvats.—*vāh vāh*—
Āḷā Rāvat's Āsīn has been established!
That black snake is swaying at the head of your bed.—*mhe*—
Rāvjī asleep in slumber, why are you sleeping?
Yes, how come you're sleeping like this?
Death has surrounded you, hasn't it!"—*vāh vāh*—
The Patel said that news. At that moment Dīyājī and Kālū Mīr made a big noise! *Both of them made a big noise together*
So not even a word reached Rāvjī's ears
The Patel reflected to himself: "Brother, I've said the news twice, why not say it once more!"
Yes, I'll tell it once more right after the last time so the old man will hear it
The Patel speaks. What news does he speak, let's see.
By saying it, know it, by saying it, let's see

—*gāv*—

"Dharamrājā Devjī has come from Mālāgar!"—*mhe*—
He's brought an enormous herd of cows!
Not even that one Nāpā could be controlled by you!—*mhe*—
Hey, Rāvjī, Nāpā's poured down the rains of destruction
It rained a great deal.—*mhe*—
But, that Nāpā threw in destruction!" By God's grace, the Patel said this news
At the moment, by God's grace, Kālū Mīr and Dīyājī made a big noise!—*vāh vāh*—
In the noise the Patel's news couldn't be heard.
Yes, it fell flat in exactly the same way
By God's grace, the Patel speaks again.—*mhe*—
What news does he tell Rāvjī again, let's see.
Yes, let's see some more, how does he say it, by saying it, know it, by saying it
I'll say it now, by Dev's grace, here you are.—*vāh vāh jī*—*vāh vāh*—

—*gāv*—

"The village headmen's cows graze on the hillside—*mhe*—
And the carpenters' cows eat grass
Nothing of yours and Dev's was spoiled!—*mhe*—
What object belonging to both of you was ruined, brother?"—*vāh vāh*—
At that moment Mīr and Dīyā made a big noise again!
In the midst of the noise, Rāvjī didn't hear the news at all!

By God's grace, the Patel speaks again. Let's see what news he says.
Yes, he says it again right after the previous one, let's see

—gāv—

"What object of yours and Dev's, of both of yours, was spoiled?—*mhe*—
Its difficult for someone like me, brother!" *I have it hard, don't I!*
The Patel speaks. What news does he say again, let's see.
By saying it, know it, by saying it, let's see

—gāv—

"The village headmen's and the Jāṭs' cows graze on the hillside.—*mhe*—
The carpenters' cows eat grass
Hey, the Bagaṛāvats' cows graze on wheat and chickpeas.—*vāh vāh*—
Rāvjī, they are moving toward your Maṇḍovar."
He said: "There is the village Maṇḍovar, isn't there!"—*mhe*—
When he spoke of Maṇḍovar, then a little sound fell on Rāvjī's ears
Rāvjī Sā said: "Hey, brother, Nīmā—*mhe*—
Why have these five Patels got together and come here?
Yes, why are they saying Maṇḍovar, Maṇḍovar?
Why did you speak of Maṇḍovar, tell me!"—*vāh vāh*—
By God's grace, the Patel said: "Brother, explain it to him,"
By God's grace, King Nīmde went close to his ear and told the matter.—*vāh vāh*—
He said: "Śrī Mahārāj, these are the five Patels who've come with a complaint about Devji's cows.
By God's grace, they say the cows have been let loose from Mālāgar."—*mhe*—
Rāvjī said: "Nīmā!—*vāh vāh*—
Tell the Patels that
Yes, be a little lenient
Hey, even during the Bagaṛāvats' days, they used to consume all the fields near the forest
Yes, they would destroy the produce of five, ten villages
And, after seven years, the Bagaṛāvats' son founded the village of Goṭhā, and from Malwa
Yes, he's returned
I won't talk to him about this matter yet.
Yes, "I won't do it," he said, "whose child is he?"
Why, because he's a child still.—*vāh vāh*—
Tell the Patels to be lenient—*mhe*—
And pardon the destruction of produce! *There you are!*
There you are, brother!"
The Patels said: "Pardon for what? What will he take?
Yes, what will he take?
As far as your reign spreads.
Yes, the cows have been grazed that far!"

Rāvjī said: "In that case, brother—*mhe*—
The Bagaṛāvats' son has grown mighty.
Yes, battle . . .
He'll avenge the Bagaṛāvats now!"
Yes, now protect yourself!
The officer of goods always
Yes, stayed there
"Take heed of the goods, brother!"
Yes, see what goods there are in our court, and what there might be a scarcity of
Now there were watchmen, they took care of their goods on their own.—*vāh vāh*—
The Patels said: "They are making a noise in front of Rātā Koṭ
Yes, they are making a noise, O King
The grass didn't arrive for the horses.
Yes, this is a little scarce
Order some of this!"—*vāh vāh*—
"From whom should it be ordered?" "Give Bījā Mehtā the command!"
Yes, he'll certainly go and get it

Bhāṅgījī Sets Fire to the Fodder Carts

What does Bījā Mehtā mean? It means he was a Jāṭ, a Caudharī, a Mehtā Jāṭ.
Belonging to the Mehtā Jāt
He said: "Bījā Mehtā!"—*mhe*—
Hey, brother, get the horses' fodder!"
Yes, get the fodder
Bījā Mehtā said: "Śrī Mahārāj, over here in your area there's no fodder available!"
Yes, there's none over here
He said: "Go some distance, brother.—*mhe*—
In that village go and lay a fine of fifteen hundred rupees!
Yes, lay on a fine as it suits you
Have the fine brought to your children *at home so your children can eat and drink from it.*"
The Patel thought: "Brother, our house will be built, brother!"—*vāh vāh*—
By God's grace, he took the document with seal and scepter—*mhe*—
And left from there.—*vāh vāh*—
By God's grace, he had the fine money brought home to his children.—*vāh vāh*—
In this manner he arrived in the Parganā of Pālī Sojat
There was a scarcity of water.—*mhe*—
At that place he obtained fodder.
Yes, the cows hadn't reached that place at all
Devjī's cows hadn't reached there without the water.
Yes, you said there was a scarcity of water

There were seven and a half times twenty carts. Some say: "kiḷaḍakā."—*mhe*—
In our language we say: "Moṭhā kī koraḍ."
Haven't you understood? Each region has a different language. The horses' fodder is the same all over. By God's grace, after filling carts with fodder—*mhe*—
He took leave.—*vāh vāh*—
On the way there were many hills and mountains.—*mhe*—
By God's grace, the road went alongside Nevājī's fort.—*vāh vāh*—
Dev Mahārāj's cows were grazing on the foot of the Hill of Goram.—*vāh vāh*—
So, now the dust from the carts—*vāh vāh*—
Rose up into the sky.
Yes, it rose up high, said sir.
By God's grace, the Guāls were singing praises of Chapannjī Bhairūjī.—*mhe*—
And Caupaḍ Pāsā,
Yes, they were playing.
They saw this dust, and said: "Hey, brother, why this dust?"
Yes, why has so much dust risen?
Dust rises because of three reasons. *Which reasons?*
Now if the Sāhūkār's or Mahājan's procession is on the move,—*mhe*—
Then Surjī Mahārāj[125] becomes hazy.
Yes, when the dust rises
And if Lakhkhi Biṇjārā's bullocks are on the move, then dust
Yes, rises up
Now, if Rāvjī's fifty-two forts prepare for battle—*mhe*—
Then Surjī certainly looks hazy.
Those are the three reasons. It's certainly because of one reason.
Yes, hurry up
They said: "Take a look, brother whether Rāvjī's twenty-two[126] are coming to capture and take away the cows."—*vāh vāh*—
By God's grace, give Padmā the command: "Go, Padmā!"
Yes, you go and find out why dust has risen into the sky
Padmā said: "I'll certainly take a look, but supposing I get into trouble over there, then you'll hardly come to my assistance!" *Will you come to my assistance or no?*
He said: "Make that sign of yours—*mhe*—then as though I'm standing next to you . . . *I'll be on your side as soon as you give the sign*"
Padmā said: "What sign do I have?" *What do I know, Bhopājī?*
He said: "There was a feather—*mhe*—
Which bound to an arrow was released into the sky. *Shot high*
As much strength the feather had, that much it would fly into the sky.
Yes, with as much strength it had, the arrow would rise into the sky
After that it would come down circling.—*vāh vāh*—
So, if I see that, then I'll know that Brother Padmā is in trouble.
Yes, there is certainly trouble
As if I were standing
Yes, near you
There you are, brother, make that sign!"—*vāh vāh*—

Alone, Padmā Posvāl rode his horse from the Hill of Goram.—*vāh vāh*—
By God's grace, he arrived near the carts.—*mhe*—
In front he saw: "Hey, it's Rāvjī's Bījā Mehtā, Patel who has come!
Yes, it's the Patel!
The horse has been troubled for nothing!—*vāh vāh*—
I've come close to Pateljī, so I'll certainly greet him and leave."
Yes, how can I leave without greeting him?
Hey, by God's grace, he's Rāvjī's man!—*mhe*—
If I greet him, then with great respect!"
Yes, I won't greet him empty-handed!
He took Dev's name and put his hand in his pocket
So, five gold coins appeared
Placing the gold coins in his palm—*mhe*—
Going up alongside the bullock-cart, he quietly said: "Pateljī, Rām Rām!"
Yes, Rām Rām, sir!
To himself he thought: "He's an old man, hard of hearing."
Yes, "he didn't say anything." "Pateljī, Rām Rām!"
Yes, Rām Rām!
He didn't hear.—*vāh vāh*—
To himself he thought: "He's hard of hearing."
Yes, he probably hears only louder!
He went up to his ear, and shouted loudly:
"Pateljī, Rām Rām, sir!" *Oh, ho, now he'll hear at least!*
The Patel recognized him.
"Hey, it's the Gūjar's boy!—*mhe*—
What are you greeting me for today?
Yes, I won't greet you today
In the morning I'll summon you to Rātākoṭ with leather water bags on your back.
Yes, greet me over there on that day!
Do it thrice a day!—*vāh vāh*—
Are you crazy today? What is this 'Rām Rām'?"
Yes, "What are you saying 'Rām Rām' for?" he said, "Go away!" he said.
There you are!
The Guāl thought to himself: "It's not what you think, he's spoken to you out of anger."
Yes, he was completely inebriated
By God's grace, he did that very "falling back" thing—*mhe*—
He sat on the ground—*vāh vāh*—
With great strength he released the arrow.
Yes, he released it into the sky, said sir.
As long as the arrow flew it took the feather into the sky—*mhe*—
When the arrow stopped flying, then the feather began,
Yes, it circled
The other Guāls were keeping a watch:—*vāh vāh*—
"Look at Padmā; he's in trouble; the feather is circling"

Yes, "The feather is circling," they said, "get ready for battle."
Fourteen hundred and forty-four Guāls moved forward together from the Hill of Goram.—*vāh vāh*—
The drummer on the village's outskirts began drumming.—*vāh vāh*—
The drumming from the village's outskirts was heard by Devnārāyaṇ.
Yes, then
Bhāṅgījī said: "Hey, Guāls, there's trouble!"—*mhe*—
By God's grace, Bhāṅgījī climbed onto his horse—*vāh vāh*—
And departed.
Yes, he joined the Guāls
So the Guāls and Bhāṅgījī arrived there together.—*vāh vāh*—
Upon seeing Bhāṅgījī coming, the Guāl said: "Hey, Elder Brother Bhāṅgījī has come!"—*vāh vāh*—
He exclaimed: "Bhāṅgījī, Bhāṅgījī"—*mhe*—
By God's grace, Pateljī said: "Hey, which Bhāṅgījī?"
Yes, which one is he?
"Isn't Bhāṅgījī Devjī's brother?"
Yes, it's not him is it?
The Guāl said: "Its quite exactly him!" *It's him*
The Patel said: "Then, brother, you've nothing to fear, I've something to fear!
Yes, I have something to fear!
Open up the cart—*mhe*—
And the bullocks yoked to the cart,
Yes, release them too!
Put me beneath the board and put a heap of grass on top!
Yes, throw a whole heap of grass on top of me; he shouldn't see me
Protect me!"—*vāh vāh*—
By God's grace, Pateljī was protected.—*vāh vāh*—

So Bhāṅgījī enquired, straight away, "Hey, Padmā brother, what's happened?"
Yes, what's up?
The Guāl said: "Nothing's the matter, I have no trouble!—*mhe*—
I just came to meet Pateljī.—*vāh vāh*—
He didn't return my greetings."—*mhe*—
Bhāṅgījī said: "Where is Pateljī?" *Where's he?*
The Guāl said: "Sir, just a moment ago, he was sitting in that cart.
Yes, he was in that cart
Bhāṅgījī said: "He ran away scared!—*vāh vāh*—
You do the following . . . —*mhe*—
These carts are full of fodder, throw that to the cows.
Yes, feed it to the cows
And remove the nose strings from the bullocks." *Put them together with the cows*
He took no time.—*vāh vāh*—
He cut through the bullock's nose strings—*mhe*—
And put them together with the cows.—*vāh vāh; Eat!*
"Graze, brother!" he began emptying the carts of fodder to the cows.

Bhāṅgījī said: "It's taking a lot of time, brother."—*mhe*—
At that time Bhāṅgījī had taken one and a half maṇ of bhāṅg.—*vāh vāh*—
By God's grace, he caught hold of the carts with both hands
Yes, with both hands—mhe—
Two carts of fodder
Yes, are emptied together
By God's grace, after emptying the carts—*mhe*—
He threw the fodder to the cows—*vāh vāh*—
He collected the carts at one place
He put grass all around the carts, and spoke to Guāl: "Listen, brother
Yes, burn this up!
Celebrate Holi!—*mhe*—
There's firewood in these carts."—*vāh vāh*—
By God's grace, Berībāj Guāl celebrated Holi.—*vāh vāh*—
He said: "Holi, Holi!"
Yes, it's Holi, hey it's Holi!
Prince Bhāṅgījī said: "Hey, Guāls!"—*mhe*—
The Paṭel's cart is standing there—put a little bit of fire on to it too!"
Yes, throw it together with the others
The Patel thought: "Your Father! He'll cremate me together with the carts!
Yes, now there's trouble—get away fast!
Now what! Now what shall I do?—*mhe*—
If they put me together with the other carts, then I'll be burnt automatically.
Yes, I'll burn together!
Now, no one else—I don't know anyone else!"—*mhe*—
The Patel said: "Padmājī, brother, 'Rām Rām'; Yes, Padmājī, brother, 'Rām Rām'!"—*vāh vāh*—
The Guāl said: "Now there's no 'Rām Rām' in my hands!
Yes, now it's no longer a matter I can control!
Whatever Elder Brother Bhāṅgījī does, *that's how it'll be, Mr. Caudharī!*
Bhāṅgījī! Here's the Patel—under the board of the cart!"—*vāh vāh*—
Bhāṅgījī moved forward.—*mhe*—
After opening the horse's rope—*vāh vāh*—
He tied the Patel, he tied him to the horse's reins.—*vāh vāh*—
"Come here, Sirdārs," he said. *Come here*
"By God's grace, drag the cart and throw it onto the fire."—*mhe*—

Bhāṅgījī Drags Bījā Mehtā Off to the Stables

By God's grace, Prince Bhāṅgījī returned to Dev's court, *said sir.*
He took the Caudharī to Līlā's stables and tied him. *He took the Bījā Mehtā and tied him to the horse's feet.*
Līlā was a horse content with milk.—*mhe*—
It beats the Patel with its hooves. *It beat him the whole night long*

Pateljī cried aloud
So, the Guāls were victorious.—*mhe*—
Pateljī was tied to the horse, yes, to the stables
Say victory, brother, to Śrī Devnārāyaṇ Bhagavān! *Say victory, small, big, and everyone!*

By God's grace, they went and tied up the Bījā Mehtā, isn't it—*mhe*—in Līlā's stables.—*vāh vāh*—
He cried out during the night.—*mhe*—
When morning came, Dev's court was held.
Yes, it was held
By God's grace, the lineage's Bhāṭ came to Dev Mahārāj.—*mhe*—
And he sang a song of praise—*vāh vāh*—: "Ād Rājā, from Ād Rājā came Jugāj, from Jugāj came Kācchap, from Kācchap came Raṇdhol, from Raṇdhol came Kajaḷī, from Kajaḷī came Harīrāmjī. *Harīrāmjī*
Harīrāmjī had Bāgh, Bāgh had Bhoj.—*mhe*—
Bhoj had Dev, *said sir.*
Arisen from the fire-pit the great lineage of the Cauhāns."
Dev Mahārāj said: "Welcome Bhāṭjī! *Welcome*
But, who was in pain last night in our town?"
Yes, the whole night long he cried!
The Bhāṭ said: "Śrī Mahārāj, probably someone's eyes were hurting."
Yes, that's why he was probably crying!
Dev Mahārāj said: "Hey, Bhāṭ, in my town, somebody's eyes hurt?
Yes, in my town nobody's eyes can hurt
Be careful and speak!"
Yes, tell the truth
The Bhāṭ said: "Śrī Mahārāj, yesterday Bhāṅgījī met up with the Guāls.—*mhe*—
In the shrub he spotted Rāvjī's Bījā Mehtā.—*vāh vāh*—
After catching hold of him, he tied him in the horse's stables.
Yes, he brought him to Līlāgar's stables and tied him up there
Your Līlāgar was content with milk.—*mhe*—
At night he rained his hooves on Paṭeljī.—*vāh vāh*—
The Paṭel cried out aloud!"

Devnārāyaṇ Frees Bījā Mehtā

Dev Mahārāj said:
"Hey, Lineage's Bhāṭ!—*mhe*—
The enmity won't be avenged by *pissing on the boundaries of fields*—*vāh vāh*—
The enmity is between Rāvjī and us.
Yes, its not with the laborers!
Free the Patel, the poor man!"—*vāh vāh*—
The Patel heard what was said. He reflected to himself: "Hey, it's only a small child who is sitting on the throne, but he has a lot of wisdom!

Yes, he's clever all right!
My troubles will be over now!"—*mhe*—
So after freeing the Patel, he was brought to Dev's court and left there.—*vāh vāh*—
Dev Mahārāj called the barber.—*mhe*—
He had him taken care of properly;—*vāh vāh*—
With warm water, he had the Patel bathed.
Yes, he had him bathed
He gave him a new dhoti—*vāh vāh*—
And a fine colored turban.—*mhe*—
He gave him pearl earrings.—*vāh vāh*—
Twenty-five gold coins he handed over to the Patel.
Yes, he gave him another twenty-five gold coins
"Pateljī, if you stay here five days, count this as your home."
Yes, if you stay ten days, then count this as your own home!
The Guāl who treated you so badly yesterday, don't stay with him, stay with me!"
Yes, stay with me!
The Patel thought to himself: "Hey, that boy's really very smart. He took good care of you!"—*vāh vāh*—
Devjī said: "Pateljī, what about a meal?"
Yes, eat something; do you want to eat something?
Pateljī said: "I've been hungry since yesterday; where should I have eaten?"
Yes, I'll certainly take a meal, master

Sāḍū Mātā came to know. She sent the maidservant over: "Go, maidservant, call Pateljī!"
Yes, call him into the kitchen, so that he can eat a meal!
The maidservants came and stood there.—*mhe*—
"Maidservants, why have you come?" *Why have you come?*
The maidservants said: "My mistress has called Pateljī to the Rāvlā."
Yes, she's called him over for a meal
Devjī said: "There you are Pateljī, your invitation for dinner has arrived!"
Yes, please go!
The Patel said: "Yes, sir, I'll go!"—*mhe*—
Sāḍū Mātā thought: "We hardly have the opportunity to have this man visit our home every day."
She prepared excellent rice-pudding from cow's milk—*mhe*—
She mixed sugar in it.
Yes, she poured both sugar and ghī on it
She prepared capatis of wheat flour.—*vāh vāh*—
And, with vegetables and capatis, she nicely prepared Pateljī's plate of food.—*mhe*—
She placed the plate on the bājoṭ.[127]
Yes, she placed it there

So it was a hot summer's day; Sāḍū Mātā took a fan and stood near him.
Yes, so as to fan him with a breeze
By God's grace, she placed twenty-five gold coins beneath the plate.—*vāh vāh*—
What did the Patel do? He looked down at the plate and thought to himself:
"Hey, both mother and son are scared of you! Devjī's got scared,
Yes, Devjī's got scared, and this Sāḍū Mātā has also got scared of me!
Without being scared she wouldn't have done all these things."
Yes, she wouldn't do them!
Now Sāḍū Mātā speaks.—*mhe*—
What news does she tell Pateljī, let's see, *By saying it, know it, let's see*
I'll say it now, brother, by Dev's command, here you are.—*vāh vāh*—

—*gāv*—

"They were Guāls of the jungle.—*mhe*—
Don't take it badly, Pateljī!
Don't take it badly.
Yes, don't misunderstand what the boys have done!
Look toward me and Devjī!"
Pateljī thought to himself: "She's frightened isn't she!
Yes, she's afraid!
Threaten here a little.—*mhe*—
She's already put down twenty-five gold coins, she'll bring another twenty-five."
Yes, she'll place down more now
So the Patel speaks. Let's see what news he tells Sāḍū Mātā.
By saying it, know it, by saying it, let's see
I'll say it now, sir, by God's grace, here you are!—*vāh vāh*—

—*gāv*—

"By God's grace, your Guāls pained me a lot yesterday.—*vāh vāh*—
In the early morning the cows go up on the hill—*mhe*—
In the morning I won't let,
Yes, even one belonging to Syām come down
If you want to drink cow's milk, then do it today! *Tomorrow there won't be any*
In the morning the cows will be waiting."—*vāh vāh*—
By God's grace, Prince Bhāṅgījī also heard this in the court. *He heard this news in the court*
He said: "Hey, Bhāṭ, who's planning to take away my cows in mother's kitchen?"
Yes, who's taking them away from the kitchen?
When Bhāṅgījī's footsteps made a noise, mother thought to herself: "Hey, Bhāṅgeriyā's coming!"
Yes, he'll kill the Caudharī, the Bījā Mehtā!
So when she saw him coming, Sāḍū Mātā reprimanded Bhāṅgījī a lot.—*mhe*—
But how could Bhāṅgījī be subdued?

Yes, how could he be that way?
By God's grace, he struck out.—*mhe*—
It didn't strike the Patel, but the bājoṭ.—*vāh vāh*—
"It's been a long time since you've been herding my cows!"
Yes, it's been many days, just you wait!
Those gold coins scattered all over.—*mhe*—
The plate overturned.—*vāh vāh*—

Catching hold of the Patel's leg as he fell down, Bhāṅgījī set off.
Yes, he dragged him and took him away
Mother thought: "There you are!" *There you are!*
It was Bhairū̃jī's duty at night.—*mhe*—
He would wander about the entire village, the whole night long. *In all four quarters*
By God's grace, Bhāṅgījī took him and handed him over into the custody of Bhairū̃jī.
Yes, here you are
"Here you are, Bhairavānāth, he's in your custody for the night."
Yes, don't let him go!
Bhairū̃jī dragged him all around.—*vāh vāḥ*—
Someplace his dhoti got left behind.—*mhe*—
Someplace, the fire colored turban got left behind.
The earrings from his ears were torn off on thorns.
Yes, they broke and fell down, said sir.
Morning came.—*mhe*—
Dev's court met, and Bhairavānāth went and stood him up in front of Dev.
Yes, stood up the Bījā Mehtā
Dev Mahārāj said: "Bhairavānāth, who put the Patel in your custody?"
Yes, who put him in your custody?
Bhairavānāth said: "Prince Bhāṅgījī!"
Bhāṅgījī said: "Who freed him?"—*mhe*—
Bhairavānāth said: "Dev Mahārāj."
Yes, Dev Mahārāj freed him
Bhairavānāth said: "Brother, after being freed by Dev he can't be tied up again. Hey, you tie up the Patel!"
Yes, now tie him up again
Bhāṅgījī said: "But I won't tie him up, he's been freed by Bhagavān!"
Yes, I won't tie him up; I have respect for Dev.
Dev Mahārāj said: "Bhairavānāth!—*mhe*—
Bhaṅgeriyā won't spare him over here!—*vāh vāh*—
Hand over the Patel to his master, brother!"
Yes, get him to Rāṇ City
Bhairavānāth said: "Pateljī—*mhe*—
Do you want to return?
Yes, or do you want to stay here?"
The Patel said: "No, Śrī Mahārāj, I have to return!—*vāh vāh*—

I have to look after my children."
Yes, I have to look after my children

Devnārāyaṇ Reveals the Triple World to Bījā Mehtā

So by God's grace, Bhairavānāth spoke
He said: "Pateljī won't you take a souvenir from Dev's house?"
Yes, take one before leaving!
The Patel said: "Yes, sir, I'll take one!" *I'll take one*
The lord of the three worlds opened his lotus mouth wide.—*mhe*—
"Take a look Patel! The different things that are inside the mouth, see that marvel." *Tell your master exactly what you see*
So he looked into the master's lotus mouth.—*mhe*—
He saw all the three worlds!—*vāh vāh*—
The Patel thought to himself: "Hey, how can your master defeat him?
Yes, how can he defeat him? He's sitting there with all the three worlds in his mouth.
He can't win!"—*vāh vāh*—
Bhagavān showed the three worlds in his lotus mouth.—*mhe*—
And Pateljī spread out a blanket for a souvenir
Victory to Śrī Devnārāyaṇ Bhagavān, brother. *Say victory, both big and small!*

So by God's grace, the Patel thought to himself:—*mhe*—
"It's the play of the gods—if he gives me a reward, it'll be sufficient for my whole life.—*vāh vāh*—
Gorājī Mahārāj poured on a maund or so of sand, tied it up, and placed it on the Patel's head!
Yes, "Here you are, take this," he said, "Mehtajī, take this away!"
He walked a little and threw down the bundle.
Yes, he threw it down
Gorājī Mahārāj thought to himself: "He's not satisfied!"—*mhe*—
So, by God's grace, there were two maunds there anyway—*vāh vāh*—
He doubled it to four maunds. *He made it four maunds, said sir.*
The Patel thought to himself: "If you throw this damn thing down now!
Yes, it'll become eight maunds straight away!
I'll be squashed underneath this and die!
Good or bad, it's better to carry this load ahead."
Yes, moving ahead some way or the other would be the right thing!
Pateljī walked ahead and got into a sweat, and his shoes filled up with sweat.
Yes, his feet stopped moving
And Bhairavānāth thought: "The mortal will die!"
Yes, he'll die!—mhe—
He took hold of both the bundles.
Yes, move on now Pateljī
So Bhairavānāth brought Pateljī up to the outskirts of Rāṇ City and left him there.—*vāh vāh*—

As Patel was about to enter the gateway—*mhe*—
That time they said: "Let's make a mark on Pateljī!"
Yes, let's make a mark, how will the others know otherwise?
Gorājī Mahārāj cut off the upper lip.
Yes, he cut off the Caudharī's upper lip

Bījā Mehtā Returns to Rāvjī's Kingdom

Kālū Mīr and Dīyājī, sitting up high, were keeping a watch.—*mhe*—
Mīr said: "Hey, Dīyā!—*vāh vāh*—
The Patel's coming from Dev's home.
Yes, he's coming laughing; it looks like Bhagavān has given him some great big reward
He's received a big reward; he's laughing because he's satisfied."—*mhe*—
What should he be satisfied of?—His teeth were showing on their own because his lip had been cut off. Then what did Pateljī do? He went and threw down the sack of sand between the Sirdārs assembled there.
Yes, he threw it down, said sir.
After throwing the sack down, he untied the knot—*mhe*—
And began flinging up the sand. *He began flinging it in all four directions*
In front and behind, he began flinging up the sand saying: "This is Gulāl[128] from Dev's house.
Yes, take plenty of it!
Distribute it.—*mhe*—
If somebody doesn't get any, brother, then I'll have to go again. *I'll go again*
I'll go and get more—*vāh vāh*—
Take it away, brother! This is Gulāl!" What did Mīr do? He gave him a shove: "You're soiling the Sirdārs' attire with dust," he said.
Yes, can't you see
The Patel rolled over thrice.—*vāh vāh*—
He said: "Well then, brother, here you are, I'm leaving Rāvjī's kingdom, now.—*mhe*—
I'll go and settle down in Dev's sweet country of Mevāṛ. We have seven and a half score homes here.—*mhe*—
I'll get the carriage ready right now."
Yes, all of them will leave upon my saying
Rāvjī Sāī said: "Nīmā!—*mhe*—
Why are you sending Pateljī away?"
Yes, call him back!
He commanded Toḍā's Solaṅkī: "Go Son-in-law, you go and call him back!"
Yes, bring the Caudharī back!
Solaṅkī went and called out to him:—*mhe*—
"Sir, Pateljī, Pateljī, Rāvjī Sāī wants to see you!"
Yes, where are you going off to?
The Patel said: "All right, brother, Solaṅkī's son, I wasn't going to go.—*mhe*—
But Rāvjī's son-in-law has come.

Yes, I'll go back with you
He's my son-in-law, because he's Rāvjī's son-in-law.—*vāh vāh*—
I'll have to return, brother!"—*mhe*—
He took the Patel and had him seated.—*mhe*—
Rāvjī Sāī said:
"Pateljī, why are you running away?
Yes, why are you running away like this?
Did Dev Mahārāj keep you well or bad? Speak about those matters!"
Yes, speak the truth!
The Patel said: "What will you do?" *What will you do?*
Rāvjī said: "Whatever you say,
Yes, I'll do that
The Patel speaks. What news does he tell Rāvjī, let's see. *By saying it know it, by saying, let's see*
I'll say it now, by Dev's grace, let's see!—*vāh vāh—jī*

—*gāv*—

"Destroy Mīr's spear!—*vāh vāh*—
Throw the enemy onto a rubbish heap
Give him a tūmbā, and throw him out of the country!—*mhe*—
Rub ash into Mīr's face!
If you'll do what I say, *then do this first to Mīr!"*
By God's grace, Mīr got in a rage, and gave him another kick.—*vāh vāh*—
Pateljī ran away, and departed: "I'm going, sir," he said.
I won't live in your village!
Rāvjī spoke to Dīyā: "Dīyā!—*mhe*—
Why are you annoying Pateljī?" *Bring him back!*
Dīyājī said: "Pateljī, Pateljī, Rāvjī Sāī wants to see you!"
Yes, come back; don't run away like this!
The Patel said: "Dīyā, brother, I wasn't going to go. You've come so I'll return."
Yes, I'll go back!
Dīyājī took him back and seated him on the carpet in the court.—*vāh vāh*—
Rāvjī Sāī said: "Hey, Pateljī, don't run away!
Yes, tell the truth!
Did Devjī keep you well or bad? Speak about those matters!"—*vāh vāh*—
The Patel said: "What will you do?"—*mhe*—
Rāvjī said: "I'll do whatever you say!" *I'll do what you say*
Pateljī speaks. What news does he tell, let's see.
By saying it, know it, by saying it, let's see

—*gāv*—

By God's grace, the Patel spoke the news:
"Make your brother wear bangles of ivory!—*vāh vāh*—
Turn this Nīmde into a woman
Plait him a braid!—*mhe*—

Have him depart and be presented to the brave Nāpā!
Devjī's Gual, Nāpā—*mhe*—
Send Nīmde as his bride!—*vāh vāh*—
If you are going to do what I say, then just do this much to your brother first!"
Nīmde got into a rage again.—*vāh vāh*—
He gave the Patel a kick; the Patel fell over thrice.—*vāh vāh*—
The Patel said: "Hey, I'm going, sir, I'll settle down in Dev's country!" *I won't live here!*
Rāvjī said: "Dīyā, don't chase Pateljī the whole day long!
Yes, don't chase him like this!
Bring Pateljī back and seat him on the carpet."
A Sirdār ran, and said: "Rāvjī wants to see you!"—*vāh vāh*—
The Patel said: "Well, brother, I wouldn't have left, but only if the village's Five Patels say so, then I will leave."[129]
Yes, I'm not going anywhere, I said!
He went and sat back on the carpet.—*vāh vāh*—
Rāvjī said: "Why are you running away?"
Yes, Tell me the truth!
The Patel said: "What will you do?"—*mhe*—
Rāvjī said: "Whatever you say, I'll do that!"
Yes, I'll do exactly that
So, what does the Patel say.—*mhe*—
What more news does he tell Rāvjī, let's see.
Yes, by saying it, know it, let's see, by saying it

—*gāv*—

"By God's grace, you don't tie a turban on your head.—*vāh vāh*—
You hold the chieftain's spear in your hand
Hey, Bāgh's sons took away the former queen.—*mhe*—
In the direction of which clan are you going to send the present queen? *Tell me brother*
Now who are you going to send your queen to?"
Yes, tell me about that!
Rāvjī said: "You talk nonsense!"—*mhe*—
The Patel spat in his hands and ran away.—*vāh vāh*—
By God's grace—*mhe*—
Sirdārs the Bagaṛāvats' sons have great strength!—*vāh vāh*—
Dīyājī was sitting nearby.—*mhe*—
Rāvjī speaks. What news does he tell Dīyā, let's see. *By saying it, know it, by saying it, let's see*

—*gāv*—

"The horn was cut, it became a yogi's earring
It's not the time for anger today.—*mhe*—
Rāv calls you: Come here, brother, *Dīyā. Don't dwell in anger*

And, look, Devjī's Guāls cows have destroyed the fields.—*vāh vāh*—
They've dug up the summer harvest of wheat and chickpeas, daughter's father!"—*mhe*—
He speaks to Mīr, let's see.
By saying it, know it, by saying it, let's see
I'll say it now, by Dev's grace

—*gāv*—

"By God's grace, Mīr you eat the entire harvest.—*vāh vāh*—
You eat up the buffaloes' food
Now deal with the cows and Guāls.—*mhe*—
Or leave my strong fortress Sarvāḍā!
The lease on Sarvāḍ is confiscated from today!"
Mīr said: "Alas, alas, alas, alas, alas, if the lease on Sarvāḍ is confiscated then what will I eat?
Yes, what income will arise for me?
By God's grace, Dīyā be strong!—*vāh vāh*—
And we'll capture the cows and Guāls. Let's go tomorrow!
Yes, let's go in the morning!
I won't survive if the lease is confiscated!"—*mhe*—

—*gāv*—

"By God's grace, both Āvar and Sāvar are enjoyed by you.—*mhe*—
Dīyā, you enjoy the income from Pārā to Guḍgā̃v
Now, deal with the cows and Guāls—*mhe*—
Or leave my forts together with villages
I've given you forts together with villages.
Yes, the leases for those are confiscated from you today, Dīyā!
You may enjoy Āvar or Sāvar—*mhe*—
But the lease is confiscated!"—*vāh vāh*—
Mīr said: "What should we do, Dīyā?"
Yes, now watch the fun!
Mīr speaks.—*vāh vāh*—
Let's see what news he tells. *By saying it, know it, let's see, by saying it*

—*gāv*—

❁ Kālū Mīr and Dīyājī Try to Capture ❁ the 980,000 Cows

"By God's grace, I'll go into the forest.—*mhe*—
I'm known as the Mīr amongst Mīrs

Tomorrow I'll capture the cows and Guāls and bring them to Rātākoṭ.—*vāh vāh*—
Only then will Rāvjī realize that Mīr is the son of the brave!
I'll bring the cows and Guāls in the morning, there you are!" *There you are!*
"Great, wonderful, hey, Mīr, Mīr, Mīr, now there's only hope in you!"
Yes, now the matter rests only with you!
Five hundred horses, and five hundred Amarāvs.—*mhe*—
By God's grace, Mīr took both—*vāh vāh*—
And rode out to capture the cows and the Guāls.—*vāh vāh*—

Kālū Mīr and Dīyājī Confront Nāpā Guāl

Over there, Bhagavān's cows would come to Gudaliyā Pond.—*mhe*—
By God's grace, Mīr went to Gudaliyā Pond.—*vāh vāh*—
He saw the cows come to drink water there. *Capture them right here!*
"The whole herd will fall into our hands."—*vāh vāh*—
The Rajpūt's son went and set up tents
He began having the spears' points sharpened and the swords' edges honed.
Preparation for food and drink,
Yes, began to be made
So, he, by God's grace, set up tents.—*mhe*—
In order to capture the cows and Guāls
Victory, brother, to Śrī Devnārāyaṇ Bhagavān, victory
Everyone speak, both great and small!

So, by God's grace, Dev Mahārāj's cows used to go first to Gudaliyā Pond to drink.—*vāh vāh*—
So, the chief Guāl, by God's grace, he remained up on the hill.—*mhe*—
And the other Guāl reached the front end of the pond together with the cows
By God's grace, Dīyājī speaks.—*mhe*—
Coming to the dam what does he tell the Guāl, let's see.
By saying it, know it, by saying it, let's see

—*gāv*—

"I saw the robes, brother Gual, of fine cloth—*vāh vāh*—
Hey, the Guāls all look the same to me
Dīyājī asks you.—*mhe*—
Where is Baḍ Jāsāvat's Nirpāl?
The one who is called Jāsā's Nirpāl,—*mhe*—
Which one is he amongst you?
Who is the chief Guāl?" *vāh vāh*—
Dev's Guāl speaks—*mhe*—
By God's grace, what does he tell Dīyā, let's see.
By saying it, know it, let's see, by saying it
I'll say it now, by Dev's grace, lets see.—*vāh vāh*—

"Dīyā, the chief Guāl stayed back in the houses of Daṛāvaṭ.—*mhe*—
Hey, he stayed back.
If you go to battle and fight, do it with me!—*mhe*—
You will catch hold of the road while you're running!"
Mīr said:
"Friend, Dīyā Jodhkā, pay attention, what did the Jackal Guāl say?"—*mhe*—
By God's grace, look, the Guāl said.—*mhe*—
Dīyā said: "Mīr, why are you doing such a thing?"—*vāh vāh*—
Dev's Guāl speaks.—*vāh vāh*—
What news, what talk takes place between Dīyā and the Guāl, let's see.
By saying it, know it, let's see, by saying it
I'll say it now, by God's grace, here you are

—*gāv*—

He said: "In the evening you ate sour Rābaḍī.[130]—*mhe*—
In the morning it seems you drank cold buttermilk
Leave the cow's ropes and stand aside!—*mhe*—
Guāl, get away from the cows
These cows of yours—*mhe*—
Wait to be captured by me!"—*vāh vāh*—*Here standing, there taken!*
By God's grace, who said that news? Dīyājī said it.—*vāh vāh*—
Dev's Guāl speaks.—*mhe*—
What news does he tell Dīyājī in reply, let's see.
By saying it, know it, let's see

—*gāv*—

"Dīyā, in the evening I drank Suremātā's milk.—*mhe*—
In the morning I ate as much yoghurt as I wished
I will let go of the cows' ropes only when—*mhe*—
Thousands of Amarāvs like you fall dead in battle
With one hand I'll slay thousands like you, only then know that the Guāl will leave the cows' ropes!—*vāh vāh*—
By God's grace does anyone leave the cows' ropes so simply?"
Yes, has anyone left them like that?
Mīr said: "Look, friend, Dīyā Jodhkā, what has Guāl gone and said!
Dīyājī speaks.—*mhe*—
What news does he tell the Guāl, let's see. *By saying it, know it, let's see, by saying it*

—*gāv*—

By God's grace, Dīyājī said.
He said: "I won't kill Jackal Guāl with my hands.—*mhe*—
By God's grace, I considered Guāl like a Brahman, brother
I'll kill the spear-bearing king with my hands.—*vāh vāh*—
Hey, I won't lay hands on Jackal Guāl now!"
Listen, O Guāl!—*mhe*—

Whether one slays the cows' Guāl or the jackal in the jungle,
One gets the same sin."
By God's grace, a jackal he made—*mhe*—
The Guāl into, didn't he.—*vāh vāh*—
The Guāl speaks—*mhe*—
By God's grace, what other news does he tell, let's see,
By saying it, know, what does he say to Dīyājī

—*gāv*—

"You never killed a Guāl like me on the earth.—*mhe*—
Great kings shiver upon killing those like me!
Hey, even I can frighten Chatarpati Nejādhārī.—*mhe*—
Hey, I won't lay hands on Dīyā or a stag
Whether one kills you—*mhe*—
Or kills a stag.
Hey, whether one kills you or a woman."
By God's grace, this news,
Yes, the Guāl spoke, said sir.
Mīr said: "Tobā, tobā, tobā, tobā, tobā, look, Dīyā, the Guāl has made you into a woman!"
Yes, he's made you into a woman
By God's grace, this news; Dīyājī said: "You keep saying me, mine, but you don't come in front of me!"
Yes, come in front, and get to know!
The Guāl said: "Hey, don't keep saying Guāl, Guāl the whole day long.—*mhe*—
The lord of the temple, God, Dev Mahārāj, isn't he—*mhe*—
He gave me that title!"
Yes, call me by that title!
"What title do you have?"
Yes, how should I know?
The Guāl said: "I'm called Nāpā."—*vāh vāh*—
Mīr said: "Friend, Dīyā Jodhkā, nothing of your father's gets lost, call him Napaliyā."
Yes, say Napaliyā
The Guāl said: "I slay the horses and riders together!
Say it now at least—if you don't say it . . ."
Mīr said: "Dev Mahārāj has given this Guāl the title
Call him Napaliyā!"
By God's grace, the Guāl speaks, what news does he say in return, let's see.
By saying it, know it, let's see, Bhopājī Mahārāj, by saying it
I'll say it now, by Dev's grace.—*vāh vāh*—*sā*

—*gāv*—

"Don't say Guāl!
I don't have the manner of a Guāl
Hey, I'll strike so hard with a spear

I'll knock off the horse together with its rider!"
Mīr said again: "Look, he's giving you a reply."
"Don't call me Guāl," said the Guāl.—*mhe*—
"When you say Guāl, great anger arises in me!
With the horse's reins, I'll throw it away.—*mhe*—
By God's grace, I'll throw you a full twenty-five steps away
You'll fall down at a distance of twenty-five steps."—*vāh vāh*—
That news was spoken by the Guāl.—*vāh vāh*—
The Guāl speaks. What news does he tell, let's see.
By saying it, know it, by saying it, let's see

—*gāv*—

"Don't say Guāl, brother!—*mhe*—
Hey, anger arises in my mind when you say Guāl
I'll throw you away.—*vāh vāh*—
I'll throw you away a full twenty-five steps!
If you say Guāl this time . . .
Yes, don't say it now!
If you say Guāl now, then I'll fling you off."
Yes, in anger, I'll lift you up just as you are!
By God's grace, the Guāl said: "Should I give you the cows, because you've
come here!—*mhe*—
You've forgotten what happened in the past!"—*vāh vāh*—

—*gāv*—

"I grazed my cows on the Hill of Goram.—*mhe*—
On that day, Brother Dīyā, I kept a watch for my master
Hey, when you and I fought on the Hill of Goram—*vāh vāh*—
On that day, Dīyā, I didn't give you a single cow!
Hey, then I was without a master!
Yes, I didn't give you cows even on that day, today a master is backing me!
How can I give you cows! Why should I give you cows?
Do you know, Bhagavān, the lord of the three worlds has taken incarnation!—
vāh vāh—
What should I give you now, fool!"—*mhe*—

—*gāv*—

"A small dagger.—*mhe*—
A long spear. Hey, Mājhī Jodhakā, the supreme captain's helmet adorns you!
You and Elder Brother fought on the Hill of Goram.—*mhe*—
On that day, Dīyā, you stood up with your spear far away!
I didn't give you cows even on that day.—*mhe*—
And, you couldn't capture them
Don't do this to the cows!—*vāh vāh*—
I won't give you the cows!"—*mhe*—
By God's grace, Mīr said:

"Hey, Dīyā Jodhakā, one is told there are fourteen hundred and forty-four Guāls.—*mhe*—
They'll hardly be all exactly like one another.
Give this Padmā a shove
I'll go to the other end.—*mhe*—
I'll gather the cows around and have them reached to Rātākoṭ." *You keep a watch on this Guāl!*
Dīyā said: "Wonderful, great! Hey, Mīr, you're the wazir of wisdom!—*vāh vāh*—
I'll keep an eye on him!"—*mhe*—
By God's grace, Mīr turned his horse around alone toward the other end of the herd.—*vāh vāh*—
Which Guāls kept watch at the other end?—*vāh vāh*—
Lāpaḍo and Jhā̃paḍo, Berībāj Bagūl Siṅgjī.—*mhe*—
By God's grace, Berībāj Guāl speaks.—*mhe*—
What news does he tell Mīr, let's see. *By saying it, know it, Bhopājī Mahārāj, by saying it, now*
I'll say it now, by Dev's grace, here you are.—*vāh vāh*—*jī*

—*gāv*—

"Don't put your horse amongst the cows standing here.—*mhe*—
Believe me, rider of the Mare Maśakī
Mīr gather up the cows that roam free.—*mhe*—
The cows are protected by a Guāl with a man's moustache!
Come here! How can you come!"
Yes, the cows aren't unprotected!
But why should Mīr believe what the Guāl says?—*vāh vāh*—
By God's grace, Dev's Guāl speaks.—*mhe*—
How does he reproach Mīr again, let's see.
By saying it, know it, by saying it

—*gāv*—

"By God's grace, don't bring the horse amongst the standing cows!—*vāh vāh*—
Believe me, rider of the black mare!
I'll bury my spear in your beard—*mhe*—
The way the carpenter's son fixes the point in the plough
The artisan's son fixes the point in the plough, doesn't he!"
Yes, I'll fix the spear in the same way onto your beard
By God's grace, Dev Mahārāj's Guāl, Berībāj, picked up the arrow and bow in his hand
He strung the arrow. Mīr thought: "I'm dead!"
Yes, he's clever
"Well, look," he said: "You said that today in the plough the carpenter fixes the point.—*mhe*—
I'll fix the spear in your beard the same way—*vāh vāh*—
If you come here!"—*mhe*—
By God's grace, Mīr retreated on his feet

He came and spoke to Dīyā:
"Dīyā! Tobā, tobā, tobā, tobā, tobā, I thought," he said, "Hey, why the Guāl at the other end of the herd is not strong.
But, no, he's much braver than Padmā!
He won't break my head, will he?"—*mhe*—
By God's grace, Berībāj Guāl reflected to himself:—*vāh vāh*—
"Rāvjī's great army has come.—*mhe*—
They'll capture the cows.
Yes, they'll capture and take away the cows, and the Gual isn't here!
The chief Guāl, he isn't here.—*vāh vāh*—
So, he'll say, I didn't get to know about it," he said.
Yes, I don't know. What did you do?
"He's stayed back at the Hill of Goram.—*mhe*—
Hey, let me inform Elder Brother."—*vāh vāh*—
He rode alone.
Yes, he turned the horse around
By God's grace, the other Guāl was sitting at the Hill of Goram.—*mhe*—
So, sitting at the Hill of Goram, Berībāj was singing praises of Chappanjī Bhairū̃jī
Dev Māhāraj's Guāl speaks—*mhe*—
Berībāj.—*vāh vāh*—
What news does he tell the chief Guāl right upon arriving, let's see.
By saying it, know it, let's see, by saying it
I'll say it now, by Dev's command, here you are.—*vāh vāh*—*jī*—*vāh vāh*—

—*gāv*—

"O Elder Brother, you're sitting here at the Hill of Goram.—*vāh vāh*—.
Brother Padmā has fallen in battle at the Gudaliyā Pond—*mhe*—
Your cows have been gathered off to Rātākoṭ!
You're sitting here.—*mhe*—
Brother Padmā has fallen in battle at the Gudaliyā Pond—*vāh vāh*—
And the cows Rāvjī's generals,
Yes, have gathered and taken away!"
That news,
Yes, Berībāj Guāl said it right upon arriving, said sir.
The chief Guāl said: "Why did you talk like this?"
Yes, why do you talk like this, brother?
The chief Guāl spoke.—*vāh vāh*—
What news does he tell Berībāj in return, let's see.
By saying it, know it, let's see now, by saying it
I'll say it now, by Bhagavān Dev's grace, here you are.—*vāh vāh*—*jī*

—*gāv*—

"By God's grace, why did you speak so hurriedly?—*mhe*—
By God's grace, you came running away during bright daylight—*mhe*—
By God's grace, you talk without a pause

Hey, how have Nārāyaṇ Dev's cows been gathered together? *Why, brother, did Padmā get attacked?*
Why did you speak so hurriedly?
Yes, tell the truth and speak
Hey, in such a hurry you had the cows in Rātākoṭ, brother, and Padmā fallen in battle."
Yes, I'm not convinced by the matter, Guāl
Berībāj spoke only once.
Yes, he didn't speak again
By God's grace, the chief Guāl speaks again.—*mhe*—
What does he tell Berībāj, let's see.
By saying it, know it, by saying it
I'll say it now, by Lord Dev's grace, here you are.—*vāh vāh sā*—

—*gāv*—

"Guāl, I didn't hear the noise of the battle. I didn't hear the noise of the fight!—*mhe*—
Hey, I didn't hear the blast of cannons!
How have Nārāyaṇ Dev's cows been captured, brother?—*mhe*—
How has the drunken elephant-king been captured?
The entire day, you speak hurriedly.—*vāh vāh*—
Look, the elephant was in the army.—*mhe*—
How did the elephants get captured so easily.
And how did Padmā get slain. Tell me that news carefully!"
Yes, tell the truth!
He spoke only once.—*vāh vāh*—
Berībāj Guāl didn't speak again.—*mhe*—
By God's grace, another Guāl speaks.—*vāh vāh*—
What news does he tell the chief Guāl *let's see, by saying it, know it, by saying it*

—*gāv*—

That news was spoken by the Guāl
He said: "The Guāl has come to the Hill of Goram, brother
Ride to the Gudaliyā Pond.—*mhe*—
Ride to the Gudaliyā Pond.—*mhe*—
Elder Brother, you'll smash the earthen pot into pieces out of confidence
You'll remain seated here out of faith
And the enemy, he'll,
Yes, take the cows away to Rātākoṭ."
Berībāj spoke only once. He turned his horse around.—*vāh vāh*—
By God's grace, the chief Guāl said: "Brother, some treachery could happen!" *Yes!*

—*gāv*—

Riding, the Guāl reached Śivjī's platform.—*mhe*—
Brother, he fell a hundred times at Śaṅkar's feet:

"Hey, Sāvar Fort has attacked me today.—*mhe*—
Śaṅkar, protect me from trouble
Protect me!"—*vāh vāh*—
By God's grace, to Bhairū̃jī's platform,
Yes, the Guāl goes
How does he ask for Bhairū̃jī's powers.—*vāh vāh*—
I'll tell you now, by Dev's grace, here you are

—*gāv*—

Riding, the Guāl reached Bhairū̃'s platform, brother.—*vāh vāh*—
He fell to Bhairū̃nāth's feet:
"Sāvar Fort has attacked me.—*mhe*—
Bhairū̃nāth, protect me from trouble
Protect me, Śrī Mahārāj!—*vāh vāh*—
And you save us."—*mhe*—
By God's grace, riding, the Guāl beat the drums
So, by God's grace, the drums were heard by Rāvjī's generals
By God's grace, Mīr's heart jumped out of its place
The younger brother, Nīmde, the King's brother—*mhe*—
His heart
Yes, jumped out of its place, said sir.
By God's grace, he started to run away.—*mhe*—
Dīyā said: "Hey, what is this, brother?
Yes, hey, why have they done this, Guāl?
By God's grace, I didn't follow your call, *whistle*
You give a call.—*mhe*—
And summon your lord Devjī."
By God's grace, King Nīmde ran away right there.—*vāh vāh*—
Dīyā stands in his way. How does he reprimand him, lets see.
By saying it, know it, by saying it
I'll say it now, by Dev's grace, here you are.—*vāh vāh*—

—*gāv*—

"Nīmā don't run away!—*mhe*—
Running away reduces the Rajpūt's strength
Over there Rāṇ City's Rāv will laugh at you
Hey, Nīmā, Rāṇ City will laugh at you
All of Rāṇ City will laugh at you.
Yes, 'He ran away,' he said, 'he had gone to capture cows'!"
Nīmde said: "Dīyā!—*mhe*—
If they laugh it'll be at me!
I'm going to run away, brother!—*vāh vāh*—
I didn't come to die here!"—*mhe*—
So, by God's grace, Rāvjī's younger brother, you know,
Yes, Nīmdejī
He ran away.—*vāh vāh*—

Mīr said: "Hey, friend, Dīyā!—*mhe*—
Rāvjī's younger brother has run away.
Yes, let us run away too. Blow the bugle for the forces
Blow the bugle for retreat. So let us run!"—*vāh vāh*—
"Why should we run like this!—*mhe*—
Let's try doing that for which we have come, let's see!
Yes, why should we run away like that?
Just like that, daughter's father."
Yes, should we run away
By God's grace, Dīyā said: "Hey, Jackal Guāl!—*mhe*—
Why did you go and do something else!—*vāh vāh*—
You betrayed us, brother!" *Betrayed us!*
By God's grace, Dīyā said: "Guāl!—*mhe*—
I didn't follow your sign, brother.
Yes, I didn't understand it
Guāl, you made a sign,—*vāh vāh*—
And summoned your Dev," he said.—*vāh vāh*—
By God's grace, in the meantime, Mīr spoke.—*mhe*—
What does he say to Dīyā again, let's see.
By saying it, know it, by saying it, let's see

—*gāv*—

"Turn about the elephants' reins, Dīyā!—*mhe*—
Hey, turn us toward the direction of Rāṇ City!
By God's grace, it looks as though Bāḷā Devjī has come on to attack!—*mhe*—
Hey, brother, Dīyā, Bhoj's son has arrived!
He'll take Bhoj's revenge."
Yes, that's why he has come
By God's grace, "Mīr," said Dīyā, "don't run! *Don't run away, wait a little!*
I've spoken to them.—*mhe*—
By God's grace, it's not Devjī."—*mhe*—
"Guāl!" Dīyā said, "Hey, brother, where is Devjī?"
Yes, Devjī has not come along. You asked upon arriving
Dīyā said: "Where is the chief Guāl?" *He's coming now*
"The chief Guāl is on his way."—*vāh vāh*—
Mīr said: "Dīyā, is the chief Guāl really like this?—*vāh vāh*—
A couple of elephants come wandering.—*mhe*—
And spear-points are flashing."
Dīyājī said: "Listen, hey, Mīr!—*mhe*—
If there wasn't a Guāl like this, then
Yes, he would never ever have destroyed Rāvjī's summer harvest!
Guāl, brother, would such a good summer harvest on the outskirts of the village
Yes, be left alone?
The Guāl speaks. What news does he tell Dīyā, let's see.
By saying it, know it, by saying it, let's see

—*gāv*—

"By God's grace, brother, expensive shoes on his feet—*mhe*—
By God's grace, a golden chain around his neck
Hey, look, Dīyā, the point on his turban glitters like fifty gold coins.—*vāh vāh*—
Now, the great Jāsā's Nirpāl has come!
Yes, that Guāl is arriving now
That chief Guāl, he's the master amongst us."—*vāh vāh*—
"Wonderful, brother, Mīr, hey, listen, brother, this is the kind of Guāl Dev has!"—*vāh vāh*—
By God's grace, the Guāl and Dīyā talk to one another.—*vāh vāh*—
In the meantime, the chief Guāl came and said:
"Padmā, what's the matter?" *"What's the matter?" he said, "what's happened?"*
The Guāl said: "What's happened?
Yes, see for yourself!
Look, these enemies, these generals of Rāvjī standing here have surrounded the cows!"—*vāh vāh*—
The chief Guāl said: "It's fine that they surrounded the cows, hey, Padmā—*mhe*—
Did you give the cows to drink or not, tell me that!"
Yes, tell me that news!
The Guāl said: "Elder Brother, you had the thought of giving the cows water to drink, yes?
Yes, I didn't give them water
They spoke respectfully, so I spoke back respectfully
They spoke disrespectfully, so I spoke back disrespectfully.
You remain my support.
I've been awaiting you!"
Yes, I'm just about to feel iron
The chief Guāl said: "No, no, no! *Don't do that!*
Attack the enemy! *Pierce their stomachs!*—*mhe*—
Go, and give our cows water."
Yes, give them water to drink, first
The Guāl said: "O Chief Guāl, brother, I won't fit my dagger into their stomachs there!
Yes, if you can pierce them, then you pierce them
I won't pierce them!"—*vāh vāh*—
The chief Guāl left the horse's saddle and went on foot.—*vāh vāh*—
By God's grace, how does he go to bank of the pond near Dīyā.—*mhe*—
What news does he say upon reaching, let's see.
Yes, by saying it, know it, let's see, Bhopājī Mahārāj, now, by saying it
I'll say it now, by Dev's grace, let's see.—*vāh vāh*—*jī*—*vāh vāh*—

—*gāv*—

By God's grace, the chief Guāl said the news upon arriving
"You say "eleventh," "twelfth,"[131] chief of the Jodhās.—*vāh vāh*—

Hey, you distribute sweets to lepers as a religious observance
Hey, look at the thirsty cows standing on the bank of the pond.—*mhe*—
Dīyājī, you dishonor the Hindu dharam!
Hey, daughter's father, are you a Hindu?
Yes, the cows are standing thirsty
It's not a Hindu's dharam."—*vāh vāh*—
Dīyā didn't say anything.—*mhe*—
The chief Guāl speaks. What does he tell Dīyā, let's see.
By saying it, know it, by saying it, let's see

—*gāv*—

"You say 'eleventh,' 'twelfth.'—*vāh vāh*—
Hey, you distribute food as religious observance amongst lepers
These cows of Nārāyaṇ Dev stand thirsty.—*mhe*—
The reason why a Hindu gets a great fault
Hey, daughter's father!
Yes, why are you accumulating sin?
All the cows are standing thirsty, daughter's father!"—*mhe*—
Mīr spoke: "Friend, Dīyā, that Guāl spoke very sensibly!
Yes, he's very smart!
Hey, there is Padmā Guāl too."—*mhe*—

—*gāv*—

The Guāl said: "Dīyā, the cow takes the Hindu across the Botharnī River when he dies
Dīyā, the cow takes the Hindu across!"
Dīyā said: "Mīr, don't you know!—*mhe*—
The one who is master—*vāh vāh*—
He spoke without strength!"—*mhe*—
By God's grace, Dīyā speaks. What news does he tell the chief Guāl *let's see, what he says, by knowing it, say it*
I'll say it now, by Dev's grace, here you are.—*vāh vāh*—*jī*

—*gāv*—

"Hey, brother, Guāl give these cows water to drink!—*mhe*—
Hey, I'll provide these pale cows shade
While these cows of Nārāyaṇ Dev drink water—*mhe*—
If I strike with my sword, then I swear on Dīyā Jodhkā
Hey, Guāl!—*mhe*—
Give the cows water to drink! *Give them water*
I'm a Hindu, I'm not anything else, brother!"—*vāh vāh*—
By God's grace, the chief Guāl said:
"Padmā!—*mhe*—
The enemy has given the command!"
Yes, give the cows water to drink!
So, by God's grace, Dev Mahārāj's Guāl whistles to the cows.—*mhe*—

How does he give them water, let's see.
By saying it, know it, by saying it, let's see
I'll say it now, by Dev's grace, here you are.—*vāh vāh—jī vāh vāh*—

—*gāv*—

The Guāl took off his shoes.—*mhe*—
On his shoulders he slung sword and shield: "Drink together, O Udājī's cows.—*vāh vāh*—
Berībāj Guāl is giving you water to drink
I'm Berībāj Guāl,—*mhe*—
Who is giving you water today!"
Drink water to your fill
So, it took no time at all
Nine lakh and eighty thousand cows of Dev, gathered together at the pond
By God's grace, Dīyājī and Kālū Mīr—*mhe*—
Stood on the bank.—*vāh vāh*—
Four cows remained standing at a distance.
Yes, they didn't come near the water
Dev's cows drank water—*mhe*—
And climbed back onto the bank
The Guāl climbed back onto his horse
By God's grace, Dīyā said: "Brother Guāl—*mhe*—
Did you give them water?"
Yes, I gave them water
"I gave them water, Dīyā."—*vāh vāh*—
Dīyā said: "Hey, brother, you gave a hundred to drink, but made one thirsty?"
Yes, why did you do this?
"How did I do that?"—*mhe*—
Dīyā said: "I kept a watch, daughter's father, these four cows didn't even come near the water!
Yes, all four animals didn't even come close to the water
The Guāl said: "Dīyā!—*mhe*—
Brother, there's no question about giving them water today."
"Why not?"—*mhe*—
"Well, these cows don't drink water just like that!
Yes, they don't drink like this
Only if I perform daily rites, will these cows
Yes, go and drink water."
Dīyā said: "Hey, Guāl!—*mhe*—
Perform the daily rites today, so that I'll know them.
Yes, when I take them there to Rātā Koṭ, then I too can give them water.
Otherwise the thirsty cows will die!
They'll dry up—I don't care!—*vāh vāh*—
Give them to drink!"—*mhe*—
The Guāl said: "They won't drink like this!"
Yes, I won't give them to drink just like that!

"By God's grace, give them water, hey, Guāl!"—*vāh vāh*—
The Guāl said: "No! You're standing with a spear." "Hey, cart-driver—*vāh vāh*—
Are you afraid of this?" he said.
Yes, I'm afraid of this—like being afraid of a spear
The Guāl speaks.—*vāh vāh*—
What news does he tell Dīyā, let's see. *By saying it, know it, by saying it*
I'll say it, by Bhagavān's grace, here you are

—*gāv*—

"Dīyā, a Hindu's strength never diminishes.—*mhe*—
Nor does Hanūmān's strength
If you want to give these cows water to drink, then, hey, throw down the point of your spear!
He's standing there at the cart with a spear, isn't he.—*mhe*—
As long as he does that I won't give the cows water.
Yes, break the spear!
If you throw it down, then I'll give them water." *Then I'll give them water*
By God's grace, Dīyā said: "Hey, Mīr!—*mhe*—
We'll have to break the spear's point, brother!"—*vāh vāh*—
Mīr said: "Friend, Dīyā, don't break the weapons!—*mhe*—
That Nāplo *will thrash us badly*"
Dīyā said: "It's a Hindu's dharam, brother."
Yes, break it—let's give the cows to drink
By God's grace, he spoke to Mīr: "Hey, Mīr!—*mhe*—
You, too, throw down your spear!"
Yes, break it and throw it down
Mīr said: "Don't break the weapons! Believe me!" he said.
Yes, he'll thrash us badly!
Dīyā said: "By God's grace, Guāl, *give the cows to drink!*
Give them properly to drink, like you do every day!"—*vāh vāh*—
What did Dev Mahārāj's Gual do? First he bathed and prayed.—*vāh vāh*—
He wore a saffron dhotī
By God's grace, he lit a fire.—*vāh vāh*—
He entered the pure water up to his waist, *said sir.*
After going there.—*mhe*—
The useful covering cloth, he laid it out on the water
On the four borders, he laid incense.—*vāh vāh*—
By God's grace, the Guāl took the flute in his hands.—*mhe*—
So, placing the flute to his lips,—*mhe*—
The Guāl played a tune on the flute.—*vāh vāh*—
Hearing the sound of the flute, those four cows moved from the bank.—*vāh vāh*—
They gather at the water.—*mhe*—
What news does the Guāl tell, let's see. *By saying it, know it, by saying it*
I'll say it now, by Dev's grace, here you are

—*gāv*—

"Playing the flute, I instruct the cows.—*mhe*—
Do you follow or not, o my mother of good wishes—*mhe*—
By God's grace, drink water, cows, and go back, now, to Daṛāvaṭ
Don't go into the fields today!"
Yes, today, their master has arrived
By God's grace, because of the Guāl's whistle and the melody of the flute, all four cattle moved from there.—*mhe*—
By God's grace, putting their mouths to the covering cloth—*vāh vāh*—
The cows began drinking water.
Yes, they strained the water and began drinking, said sir.
Dev's Guāl speaks.—*mhe*—
Let's see what news does he tell Suremātā while she's drinking water, let's see.
Yes, he speaks again, said sir.
By saying it, know it

—*gāv*—

"Mother, don't drink in gulps.—*mhe*—
Drink now with ease
Water flows into your body, O cow!—*mhe*—
Look, this horse, because of you, now, this creature suffers
Drink a little water
Look, the enemy's horse stands there."—*vāh vāh*—
Dev's Nāpā speaks. What does he explain to Suremātā, let's see. *By saying it, know it, let's see, by saying it*

—*gāv*—

"O cow, stop drinking water in gulps.—*mhe*—
By God's grace, the water will become a ball in your stomach
Brothers, far away are the chambers of Daṛāvaṭ.—*mhe*—
The enemy's nine-yard-high wall of Rātā Koṭ, too, is far away
If you go to Rātā Koṭ, then too the distance
Yes, is great
Daṛāvaṭ's chambers from here are,
Yes, ahead
That's why, O Mother Cow, drink a little water."

—*gāv*—

"Playing the flute, I instruct the cows.—*mhe*—
Today, I explain to my mother of good wishes
Don't come in the way of Rāv's horse.—*mhe*—
Then drink water, O Mother, and go back, now, to Daṛāvaṭ
It shouldn't happen, that you cross in front of the enemy's horse."
By God's grace, Dev Mahārāj's Guāl began properly to give the cows water to drink.—*mhe*—
Mīr said:
"Hey, Dīyā!—*vāh vāh*—

Look, Nāpalā's giving the cows bad advice!"
Yes, giving them bad advice
Dīyā said: "Mīr, don't talk!
Yes, don't talk, let the cows drink water first
Its our Hindu's dharam."—*mhe*—
Mīr said: "Certainly it's dharam. But you'll find out about your dharam just now."
Yes, you'll know about it soon

—*gāv*—

The Guāl put shoes back on his feet.—*vāh vāh*—
He put on the sword and shield
"Drink water to your satisfaction, Mother, and then—*mhe*—
Return to Daṛāvaṭ
Go to Daṛāvaṭ!"—*vāh vāh*—
Nine lakh and eighty thousand cows belonging to Dev, drank water properly.—*vāh vāh*—
Surematā drank water.—*mhe*—
Dev Mahārāj's Guāl gave the cows to drink
Speak: Victory to Śrī Devnārāyaṇ Bhagvān, victory
Speak, hey, brother, everyone, both great and small!

Kālū Mīr and Dīyājī Consider Capturing Surematā

So, four cows—*mhe*—
Joined the herd of cattle
And, Surematā, that divine incarnation—*mhe*—
She—there was brackish water all over——*vāh vāh*—
Went into the rivulet and suddenly fell down after stepping into mud.
Yes, she fell down. She was an old cow
She changed her form.—*vāh vāh*—
So, what does the cow do? She stands up in the mud and falls down again
She stands up here and falls down there again, *said sir.*
Who noticed this cow? Mīr
Yes, he saw it falling down
Mīr said: "Hey, friend, Dīyā!—*mhe*—
We won't be able to capture the other cows
Give me your horse's rope.—*mhe*—
Hey, I'll tie it around the cow lying in mud.
Yes, let's take this one!
By God's grace, look, Bhagavān gave wealth to this breed—to the Bagaṛāvats.—*vāh vāh*—
Well, look, at this place he put gold onto the cows.—*vāh vāh*—
Hey, where do you get such jewelry and gold, brother?
Yes, where is it available?

By God's grace, this cow's fallen here anyway, *then the ornaments at least will come into our possession*
There are anklets on her feet,
Yes
Those I'll give you. *Those you take*
And, the big chain around her neck—*vāh vāh*—
That I'll place around my wife's neck when I marry again.
Yes, why shouldn't I place it?
There are sheaths of gold on the horns.—*mhe*—
I would have given them to Rājā Nīmde, *but he's left*
Both us generals could take a share each!"
When he spoke of a share,
The Guāl thought to himself: "Hey, what has the enemy made a share of?"
Yes, what will he make a share of?
So, he returned with his horse onto the bank
He returned. Suremātā had assumed another form and was rolling in mud.
Yes, sometimes she falls this way, and sometimes that
The Guāl comes near the cow.—*mhe*—
What else does he tell Suremātā, let's see. *By saying, it, know it, Bhopājī Mahārāj, now, by saying it*
I'll say it now, by Dev's grace, here you are —*vāh vāh jī*—

—*gāv*—

"I would have given you away to the teachers in Puṣkar.—*mhe*—
O, I would have given you away to the thieves of Cāmaḷ
You made us look silly, O cow of Ūdājī.—*mhe*—
Rāvjī's horsemen stand there
Look, Rāvjī's horsemen are standing there.—*mhe*—
O, you made me look silly!" *You made me look silly!*
By God's grace, the Guāl speaks.—*mhe*—
What news does he tell Suremātā, let's see.
Yes, he speaks again, let's see, by saying it, know it, by saying it
I'll say it now, by Dev's grace, here you are.—*vāh vāh*—*sā*

—*gāv*—

"I'd give you away to teachers in Puṣkar.—*mhe*—
And I'd leave you in Brahmājī's temple
O, you made me look very silly, O Ūdājī's cow.—*mhe*—
You made me look silly."
Suremātā speaks. What news does she tell the Guāl, let's see.
By saying it, know it, let's see, now, by saying it
I'll say it now, by Dev's grace, let's see.—*vāh vāh*—
What did the Guāl do? He spoke to the cow over there, didn't he.—*mhe*—
He said: "Brother, look, I came to tie a rākhī. Those Brahmans—*vāh vāh*—
From Puṣkar, *yes, I'd give you away to them*
I would give you away in rākhī.—*vāh vāh*—

O, in Brahmājī's temple
Yes, I would offer you
Let thieves carry you off. All three things I would have done to you."—*vāh vāh*—

—*gāv*—

Juremātā Reveals Her Divine Form to Nāpā Guāl

"My horns are curved like tongs.—*mhe*—
Guāl when did you pray to the creator?
You don't know about these matters yet.—*mhe*—
Hey, I've come to give your Ūdkaraṇ milk
There's a bond between me and Dev.
Yes, there's always been a bond!
I've come to give Bhagavān milk."
By God's grace, the cow speaks.—*mhe*—
What news does she tell the Guāl. *Let's see, by saying it, know it, now, by saying it*

—*gāv*—

"Look, hey, Guāl, now I'm standing in the Gudaliyā Pond.—*mhe*—
Your Dev, yes, was in Mathurā when I was the sixty-four Jogīṇīs—*mhe*—
Then your Devjī was Kṛṣṇa amongst the Gopīs
There's a bond between Dev and myself *right from the beginning*
By God's grace, on that day I was on your Dev's side."—*vāh vāh*—
The Guāl said: "O Mother, leave aside the coquetry *and proceed to Daṛāvaṭ*
By God's grace, the cow speaks.—*mhe*—
What news does she speak, let's see.
By saying it, know it, let's see, by saying it

—*gāv*—

By God's grace, Suremātā told the news.—*mhe*—
She said: "I'll devour all these horses and riders!—*mhe*—
Hey, Guāl, I'll kill all the riders!
Hey, there's no permission of Nārāyaṇ Dev.—*mhe*—
By God's grace, you don't know about these matters—the horse Līlā's rider is standing nearby
By God's grace, standing nearby he's forbidden it.
Yes, Dev Mahārāj has forbidden it, otherwise I would have done the whole thing on my own!
You may find the horse riders too many."—*vāh vāh*—
The Guāl thought: "What's this?"
Yes, I can't see Dev Mahārāj at all. Where is he standing?

The Guāl said: "Suremātā, you told a lie, brother.—*mhe*—
You see Devjī, but I don't see him at all!"
Yes, what's the matter?
Suremātā speaks.—*mhe*—
What news does she tell the Guāl, let's see.
By saying it, know it, let's see, by saying it
I'll say it, now, by Dev's grace . . .

—*gāv*—

"Your birth, isn't it—*mhe*—
I saw in the houses of Daṛāvaṭ.—*vāh vāh*—
Guāl, you tie a turban of raw cotton on your head
You don't know about these matters yet!—*mhe*—
I came to give Ūdkaraṇ milk
By God's grace, I've come to give Bhagavān milk."—*vāh vāh*—
The Guāl said: "O Mother, leave aside the coquetry.—*mhe*—
Proceed to Daṛāvaṭ!"
What did Suremātā do? She took on the five-faces form and gave darśan to the Guāl.—*vāh vāh*—

One face she took on of the mare.—*mhe*—
One of the Uḍanmerī
One of Suremātā—of the cow—was there anyway.—*mhe*—
One she took of Śaktī
"By God's grace, look inside the mouth of Śaktī, Guāl. See, what play there is!"
Yes, look!
So, over there, in Śaktī's mouth the discus was whirling.—*vāh vāh*—
He looked inside the cow's mouth
The way the entire world is created.
Yes, everything was visible
All the three worlds she showed in the cow's mouth
The horses and riders were all there. The cow was standing near Dev Mahārāj.—*vāh vāh*—
The Guāl joined his hands together—*mhe*—
And stood in front of her: "Mother, I didn't know!
Yes, all these days I didn't know that you were like this. I thought you were a cow amongst cows!
That's why Dev Mahārāj comes every day to have your darśan
That's how much power you have!"—*vāh vāh*—
Suremātā said: "Guāl, I'm not a cow amongst cows! I've come to give Bhagavān milk!"—*vāh vāh*—
The Guāl said: "O Mother, leave aside the coquetry. Now, then," he said,
Yes, now proceed, now I know it
Suremātā speaks.—*mhe*—

What news does she tell the Guāl, let's see.
By saying it, know it, by saying it, let's see
I'll say it now, by Dev's grace

—gāv—

"I go waving my tail
Leave the wide plains of Sikarāṇī."—*mhe*—
Suremātā said: "Guāl, it isn't what you think," she said.—*vāh vāh*—
Suddenly, she became a five-year-old calf, and jumped to one side.
Yes, she jumped over and stood on one side
The Guāl came and said: "O Mother, don't turn toward the horses.—*vāh vāh*—
These are going to Darāvāṭ."—*mhe*—
Nāpā and Dev Mahārāj's cow were talking to one another.—*mhe*—
And Mīr was watching the whole spectacle. He went and told Dīyā the news:
"Dīyā, there's no end to the wonder of this cow.
Yes, there's no limit to the wonder!
All this time, she was wallowing in the mud, *and was an old animal*
Look, she's become a five-year-old calf.—*vāh vāh*—
Saddle up the horse.
Yes, the cows are going to run away!
Hey, they'll run away," he said.—*vāh vāh*—
Well, nothing else, by God's grace, the cow went and stood amongst the nine hundred and ninety-nine cows.—*vāh vāh*—
Reaching there the cow turned stiff.—*mhe*—
All the cows turned stiff at the same time, *said sir.*
How do the cows, by God's grace, reach the Hiñvaḍīyā rivulet, let's see. *By saying it, know it, let's see, now, by saying it*
I'll say it now, by Dev's grace, here you are.—*vāh vāh*—*jī*—*vāh vāh*—
Devdātā you protect us, let's see

—gāv—

Going there the cow became a lioness.—*mhe*—
She became Dev's cow
Hey, the cows ran away. And Rāv's generals ran. Pārnimūnī cow ran
Ṭhākurs! The cows reached the Hiñvaḍīyā rivulet
The Hiñvāḍā rivulet flows till Bā̃sā̃.—*mhe*—
The rivulet swelled up when the cows arrived.
Yes, earlier it had dried up
And when Rāvjī's generals went there, isn't it—*mhe*—
At that time *it started flowing back till Bā̃sā̃, sir said*
Mīr said: "Hey, friend Dīyā, the cows' milk isn't sweet."
Yes, let them go! They are about to drown and die!
Now, Dev's Nāpā passed along the bank of the Gudaliyā Pond.—*vāh vāh*—
Wearing a crown
By God's grace, Rāvjī Sā̃ī's generals threatened the Guāl:—*mhe*—
"Dev's Guāl, now you'll be struck

Victory is for Devjī's cows."
Yes, where will you go?
Mīr said: "Friend, Dīyā, what fault is it of his? The Guāl standing there.
Yes, catch hold of him."
The Guāl said: "Brother, what are you fighting for?
Yes, the cows . . .
The cows were released, so they didn't fall into the fields on their own, I drove them there.
Yes, I drove them
I'm standing here, what are you afraid of?"
Yes, what are you afraid of? Come face me!
By God's grace, Dīyā said: "Well, realize!
Yes, now, realize
And, hey, look, Guāl!—*mhe*—
You may not be satisfied—if you want to fight, then do it as much as you want!"
Yes, do it first!
The Guāl said: "What did you say there?
Yes, why have you said an improper thing?
Hey, brother, the master of the fields beats the Guāl, the Guāl beats the master of the fields.
You're the master of the fields
And I'm the cows' Guāl
If you want to fight, hey, Dīyā, then you start first."
Dīyā said: "Hey, Guāl!—*mhe*—
I won't strike a mortal!"
Yes, I won't strike
"What'll you do?"
Yes, I'll just shout. Because of this your life will cease!
"You'll die from my shout!"—*vāh vāh*—
The Guāl said: "Whatever you want to do. The first strike is yours!"
Yes, the first strike is yours. If I have strength after that, then I'll strike
By God's grace, Dīyā left the horse's reins—*mhe*—
and let out a shout.—*vāh vāh*—
He spoke to the Guāl: "Guāl, *well?*"
The Guāl said: "I didn't fall down because of your shout."
Yes, "What sort of shout did you let out?" he said, "I'm still standing here"
By God's grace, Mīr said: "Friend, Dīyā Jodhkā, why are you breaking yourself!—*mhe*—
These aren't things that are going to work through shouts.
Yes, these aren't
He's Guāl of the lord of the three worlds, Dev."—*vāh vāh*—
By God's grace, Dīyā took hold of his bow and arrow:
"Here you are, brother, Guāl, now brace yourself!"
Yes, brace yourself now!
The Guāl said: "Let it come!"—*vāh vāh*—

By God's grace, when Dīyā shot the arrow—*mhe*—
The Guāl turned about on the horse
He hid under the belly of the Koḍalā horse.—*vāh vāh*—
After the arrow passed by, he sat up again.
"Well?"
Yes, I'm still here.
Dīyā threw two spears.—*vāh vāh*—
"Let's see, where he'll go to now!"
Yes, now, where will you go!
"If it's coming, let it come."
Yes, let it come!
It was the magic of Chappanjī Bhairū̃jī.—*mhe*—
Chappanjī Bhairū̃jī repelled the weapons.—*vāh vāh*—
He told Dīyā: "Well?"
Yes, he said, "I'm here!"
Dīyā thought to himself: "Hey, it's an outrage!—*mhe*—
Sister-fucker, not even an elephant stands up to your blow!
Yes, this is a mere mortal. Nothing has happened to him. He's standing there exactly like before!
He didn't even fall down!"—*vāh vāh*—
He threw three spears together
The Guāl speaks.—*mhe*—
What news does he tell Dīyā.
Yes, know it, by saying it, let's see, now, by saying it
I'll say it now, by Dev's grace, here you are

—*gāv*—

"All men strike once.—*mhe*—
After that some strike twice
Hey, a man who strikes three times—*mhe*—
His father is equal to a donkey!
You keep striking the whole day long."
Yes, "Wait," he said, "now take mine!
Take one blow of mine."—*vāh vāh*—
The Guāl took hold of the bow and arrow.—*mhe*—
It gave a loud twang. "Tobā, tobā! By Dev's oath, brother.
Yes, don't release the arrow!
Don't shoot the arrow!"—*vāh vāh*—
So, Rāvjī's generals were frightened of the Guāl's anger
The cows reached the Hĩvaḍīyā rivulet
Dev's nine lakh and eighty thousand cows drank up the water. Speak: victory to Śrī Devnārāyaṇ!

So, by God's grace, "Hey, fight with me, brother, don't run away from the fight! Yes, yes, *now it's my turn."*

So, by God's grace, he said: "Dīyā!" The Guāl said: "What will you do? I know many different ways of fighting!—*mhe*—
What kind of fight should I do with you?"
Yes, tell me what you want to do
Mīr said: "How many kinds are there?" The Guāl said: "There are three ways of fighting that I know."—*vāh vāh*—
Mīr said: "What are their names?" The Guāl said: "One is called Saparloṭ.
And one, by God's grace, is Kā̃kaḍī Buraḍako.—*mhe*—
And there's Guḍabed."
Yes, there are three ways of fighting. Which do you want to do?
Mīr said: "The names of all three are nice, *but what are the good and bad qualities of each? Ask him!"*
Mīr said: "Brother, Guāl, what is Saparloṭ?—*mhe*—
What is Guḍabed?"
The Guāl said: "Listen, brother, Mīr, Saparloṭ is the one in which I spare the horse and kill the rider. *"I kill the rider," he said, "that's Saparloṭ."*
And in Guḍabed I kill only the horse."
Mīr said: "Kā̃kaḍī Buraḍako?" *I slay both the rider and the horse together.*
Mīr said: "Tobā, tobā, tobā, tobā, two names are bad.
Yes, two names are bad
This Guḍabed is right for us. *Let's learn this*
Learn this kind of fight."—*vāh vāh*—

—*gāv*—

Mīr said: "Friend, Dīyā, nothing to worry about, there's no threat to life.—*mhe*—
The horses have died.—*vāh vāh*—
Rāvjī Sā will give us others. *Rāvjī will give us more*
What else happened? Our lives were saved, isn't it?—*vāh vāh*—
I'll feed five fakīrs in Allāh's name when I get back."—*vāh vāh*—
Dīyā said: "You'll feed in Allāh's name, isn't it?—*mhe*—
I'll feed five bhopās of Devī when I get back
God was gracious. We've returned alive, brother."—*vāh vāh*—
There was a rule that Rāvjī had made. He said: "Whoever loses should go to the platform of defeat.—*mhe*—
Whoever wins, should go to the platform of victory.
Yes, go and sit there
The heroes went straight away and sat on the platform of defeat. *They went straight away and sat on the platform of defeat*
By God's grace, Rāvjī said: "It's an outrage!—*mhe*—
Devjī's Guāls won't ever pay tribute!"
So, Rāvjī reflected to himself:—*mhe*—
"Hey, I'll send a message to my son-in-law.—*vāh vāh*—
So, on the day when the cows were surrounded, the day Dev manifested himself—*mhe*—

That day Ṭoḍā Solaṅkī's father was slain fighting for the cows.
Yes, he died there. He died in battle
Then his father's revenge will also be taken.—*mhe*—
And my authority will,
Yes, be made firm."
So, Rāvjī speaks.—*mhe*—
How does he send a message to Ṭoḍāde, let's see.
By saying it, know it, let's see, by saying it

—*gāv*—

Nāpā Defeats the Forces of Ṭoḍā Solaṅkī

Rāvjī wrote a letter and sent it to Ṭoḍā.—*mhe*—
Hey, he wrote to the Solaṅkī's city:
"Solaṅkī's son, after reading the letter come soon!—*mhe*—
It's time to avenge your father Bhisamdās!"
The title "Siṅg" is recent. There was no title "Siṅg" earlier. During the Bagaṛāvats' time Rajpūts bore the title of "Dās." There wasn't this "Siṅg" title.
"By God's grace, Bhisamdās—your father—was killed by the Guāl.—*mhe*—
Take revenge on that, and, by God's grace, capture the cows and cowherds and bring them to Rātākoṭ."
Rāv gave Rāykā the command: "Go, brother Rāykā!—*mhe*—
Take this letter to Ṭoḍā,
Yes, and deliver it there."
Rāykā saddled a young strong camel. He drove the camel along the road to Ṭoḍā.—*vāh vāh*—
By God's grace, Tārāde Bāī, who was sitting high up in the palace—*mhe*—
Thought to herself: "Hey, why has Rāykā brother from my paternal home come today?"
Yes, why has he come?
So, Bāī Sā speaks.—*mhe*—
What does she tell Rāykā, let's see.
By saying it, know it, let's see, by saying it

—*gāv*—

"Brother Rāykā, seat the camel in the Cā̃daṇ Square.—*mhe*—
Place your steps on the stairway in the high palace and come
Hey, Tārāde asks you:—*mhe*—
Brother Rāykā, on what work did you arrive in my fort?
Did you come to take the young camel that father had left behind?—*mhe*—
Did you bring any letter or message?"
Rāykā said: "I didn't even bring one, brother!—*vāh vāh*—
By God's grace, I've come with the cowherds' and cows' petition."

So, by God's grace, how is the letter read out in Ṭoḍā's court, by God's grace.—
mhe—
What story is made, let's see.
By saying it, know it, let's see, by saying it

—*gāv*—

The letter was read out in Ṭoḍā's court—*mhe*—
In the third hour of the day
The Solaṅkī's son set out to attack the cows and cowherds.—*mhe*—
So did Sāvar's Rāv
By God's grace, your fortress is strong, Solaṅkī's son!—*mhe*—
Hey, their fortress is Ujjīnī Dhār!
You'll encounter Dev's cowherds ahead.—*mhe*—
He said: Stop the waters of River Banās.—*vāh vāh*—
Where should the cows of Devjī's cowherds walk?
Solaṅkī's son rode astride and went through the gate.—*mhe*—
Ṭhākurs, he had five and a half thousand horses with him
With five and a half thousand horses—*mhe*—
And, by God's grace, he set up camp at Kalīyāde Pond, *said sir.*
"There, brother, now where will the cowherds give the cows to drink
Gudaliyā Pond is ahead—*mhe*—
And, by God's grace, I won't let them drink in Kālīyāde!"
The Rajpūt's son had the tents set up.—*vāh vāh*—
And preparations began to be made for food and drink
So, by God's grace, at dawn Bhagavān's cows would come to Gudaliyā, isn't it
They would come via Kālīyāde
The Guāl descended from the Goram Hill.—*vāh vāh*—
The Guāl saw Rāvjī's armies.—*vāh vāh*—
Berībāj said: "Hey, Rāvjī's fifty-two forts have come together!"
Yes, they've come to attack today!
So, Berībāj wouldn't say what he intended, he wouldn't listen to others
How does a straight fight happen with the Solaṅkī of Ṭoḍā, let's see.—*vāh vāh*—

—*gāv*—

Ṭhākurs! Dev's Nāpā's arms were heavy with sword and shield
Go back to your country, O army of Ṭoḍā's Solaṅkī. By God's grace, the cows are thirsting
Swords clashed, spears fell
Ṭhākurs! He slew the armies of Toḍā's Solaṅkī with great valor
The waters of the River Banās were released.—*mhe*—
Dev's thirsty cows drank water
Abandoning horse and general, the Solaṅkī's son retreated.—*vāh vāh*—
By God's grace, saving five horses, he came to Rāv's Sāvar Fort
Now Rāvjī Sāī heard his son-in-law's summons
Ṭoḍā's Solaṅkī went and sat on that "platform of defeat," *said sir.*
Mīr said: "There you are, brother!—*mhe*—

The same thing that happened to us through the enemy has happened to Son-in-law."
So, by God's grace, Ṭoḍā's Solaṅkī speaks.—*mhe*—
What news does he tell the warriors, let's see. *By saying it, know it, let's see, by saying it*

—*gāv*—

"O Rāvjī, some horses of mine were worth a lakh—*mhe*—
Some worth a lakh and a quarter
Where did Berībāj retreat after quarrelling?—*mhe*—
He ruined my armor-wielding lineage
You had my horses and generals killed!—*vāh vāh*—
I understood it was only Devjī's cowherd whom I should go and capture!—*mhe*—
Some horses were worth a lakh.—*vāh vāh*—
Some were worth a lakh and a quarter."
Yes, the horse was worth
Mīr said: "Friend, Dīyā Jodhkā, you did a tremendous thing!—*vāh vāh*—
Hey, all his horses died!"—*mhe*—
"It doesn't matter!" Rāvjī Sāī speaks.—*mhe*—
How does he reproach Solaṅkī, let's see.
By saying it, know it, let's see, by saying it

—*gāv*—

"I married my daughter to you," he said.—*mhe*—
"Hey, as dowry I gave away the whole country of Gujarat
You abandoned horse and general and ran away, O Solaṅkī's son.—*mhe*—
How long will you live now?
Hey, daughter's father!
Yes, you returned alive!
By God's grace, how much respect I gave you!—*mhe*—
I married my daughter to you and gave you the country of Gujarat as dowry!"—*vāh vāh*—
That news was spoken by Rāvjī
So Ṭoḍā's Solaṅkī speaks.—*mhe*—
What does he say in reply to Rāvjī, let's see.
By saying it, know it, let's see, by saying it
I'll say it now, by Dev's grace, here you are

—*gāv*—

"Throw your daughter into a well!—*mhe*—
Burn this dowry!
Hey, I'll reach the land of my birth alive.—*vāh vāh*—
I'll go and live in the Mīṇā's settlement
I won't die because I'm married to your daughter!"—*vāh vāh*—

Mīr spoke: "Rāvjī Sāī!—*mhe*—
Your son-in-law, don't say anything
Yes, don't say anything at all!
He'll slay himself. This will cause pain in your daughter Tārāde's bosom!"—*vāh vāh—He'll kill himself and die!*
"What should I do?" said Rāv. "What you should do is respect him again like a Sirdār!"—*vāh vāh*—
"Mīr, what respect should I show him?"—*mhe*—
Mīr said: "Give him horses.—*vāh vāh*—
Give him generals!"—*mhe*—
By God's grace, Rāvjī gave his son-in-law five hundred horses.—*vāh vāh*—
Five hundred generals.
Yes, he gave him soldiers in addition
He did what Mīr had said should be done.—*vāh vāh*—

—*gāv*—

"Mīr, you consume all the harvest.—*mhe*—
And you consume the buffaloes' food
Now, either you manage the trouble with the cows and cowherds—*vāh vāh*—
Or you leave my strong fort Sarvāḍā!"
Rāvjī Sāī told this news
Yes, to Kālū Mīrjī
By God's grace, Mīr said: "Friend, Dīyā Jodhkā!—*vāh vāh*—
If we want to keep the lease over our lands, then be prepared, brother!"—*mhe*—
There's no limit to samcārs. Rāvjī Sāī speaks now to his generals. But I'm telling the main story

—*gāv*—

"Let me go into the jungle.—*mhe*—
Rāvjī, I'm known as the finest Mīr amongst the Mīrs
I'll capture the cows and cowherds and bring them to Rātākoṭ in the morning.—*mhe*—
Rāvjī, know then that Mīr was born of warriors
I'll bring them in the morning!"—*vāh vāh*—
"Great, wonderful, hey, Mīr, wonderful!" Rāvjī said.—*mhe*—
By God's grace, Mīr's forces got prepared.—*vāh vāh*—
Ṭoḍā's Solaṅkī thought to himself: "You've been defeated.—*mhe*—
And tomorrow Mīr will be victorious
You won't be able to stay and show your face.—*vāh vāh*—
How should you stay here, brother?"—*mhe*—
Ṭoḍā's Solaṅkī speaks.—*vāh vāh*—
By God's grace, what news does he tell Mīr.
Yes, by saying it know it, let's see, how it is told
I'll say it now, by Dev's grace.—*vāh vāh—jī*

—gāv—

"Mīr, you sold cotton and bought your mare.—*mhe*—
You sold the threading card and bought the saddle
Up ahead you'll meet Dev's cowherds.—*mhe*—
In the palace your queen Kū̃kaṇde digs a grave
In the palace, Mīr, by God's grace, your wife's already measured it out.
Yes, she's measuring out the grave—three and a half feet, or is it more?
She's keeping the grave dug and ready!"

Kapūrī Dhoban Washes Clothes at Gudaliyā Pond

Mīr said: "Rāvjī Sāī̃!—*mhe*—
This son-in-law of yours is a great stupid beggar!—*vāh vāh*—
He's said don't say anything
My forces won't go now!—*vāh vāh*—
It'll be a bad destiny for the Sirdārs to die in dirty clothes. They will go with a good destiny."
Yes, they'll go with a good destiny
Rāvjī Sāī̃ said: "Hey, Mīr, what are you going for? You've been defeated already!"—*mhe*—
Mīr said: "Śrī Mahārāj, if you have my clothes washed,
Yes, then I'll go"
So, how does Mīr's Rāvjī order the washermen.—*mhe*—
What tales of washing clothes are made. *By saying it, know it, let's see, by saying it*
I'll say it now, by Bhagavān Dev's grace, here you are

—gāv—

Hindvā Rāvjī sent out a summons—*mhe*—
Ṭhākurs! He didn't take any time at all!
Hey, how many washermen are you in the city, brother?—*mhe*—
Rāvjī summoned them to come quickly to the royal court
"Come quickly, brother!—*vāh vāh*—
Because Mīr's clothes have to be washed."—*vāh vāh*—
So, the washermen were waiting.
Yes, they were sitting prepared
So, Rāvjī Sāī̃ sent out a summons. And, by God's grace, he kept Ṭoḍā's Solaṅkī's honor. Speak victory to Śrī Devnārāyaṇ Bhagavān, victory!

By God's grace, it took time to tell the city's washermen, but it took no time for them to come
Rāvjī Sāī̃ had a washerwoman called Kapūrī.—*mhe*—
She got to know
Yes, later

"Why, Rāvjī didn't think of me today
By God's grace, I've always been the royal washerwoman!"—*mhe*—
By God's grace, she left her house—*vāh vāh*—
And arrived in the court
Upon arriving she said: "Śrī Mahārāj! Why did you do this?"
Yes, why did you do this today?
Rāvjī said: "Washerwoman! What are you doing? Why are you prancing around?"—*mhe*—
Kapūrī said: "What do you mean prancing? You've disregarded the servant's laws and honor!"
Yes, you disregarded them today
She said: "There are three names of servants in the city.—*mhe*—
In one half of the city I'm called Kapūr Candajī.—*vāh vāh*—
In one half of the city I'm called Kapūr Kākājī, in one half I'm called Kapūrḍī Dhoban.—*mhe*—
Śrī Mahārāj, there are three names of servants, aren't there?—*vāh vāh*—
But you've given me the authority,—*vāh vāh*—
So why did you forget me today?"
Yes, why didn't you inform me? How did you forget?
Rāvjī said: "Washerwoman, go together with the other washermen!—*mhe*—
You'll get your money—your share will come!"—*vāh vāh*—
She said: "I won't go like this!
Yes, why should I go like this?
Only if my rules and honor are kept will I go."
Yes, only if the very same rules and the very same honor are kept, will I go to wash clothes

"Go, hey, washerwoman, they'll remain the same!
Yes, they'll remain the very same!
What rule do you have?" *tell me!*
"Śrī Mahārāj, I used to receive all these clothes.—*mhe*—
Then I would have them washed by the city's washermen
All the royal money would go into my hands
I would pay the other washermen.
Yes, if anyone paid the washermen, it was I who did. They weren't paid by the royal court
The royal court would give me the money.—*vāh vāh*—
And, by God's grace, I would receive mules from the royal court—*mhe*—to carry the clothes on."
Yes, they aren't there either
Rāvjī said: "All right, washerwoman! You'll have the very same rules and the very same honor!"—*vāh vāh*—

The washerwoman returned home. A son-in-law stayed with her.—*mhe*—
Her son-in-law to whom her daughter Kamālī was married.—*mhe*—
Kapūrī said: "Son-in-law, go and get sixty mules from the royal court!"—*mhe*—

He ran there all confused.
Yes, he ran!
"Śrī Mahārāj, Śrī Mahārāj, my mother-in-law has ordered eight mules!"
Yes, give me eight mules
The stupid fellow forgot to ask for sixty!—*vāh vāh*—
Rāvjī Sāī said: "Hey, the washerwoman asks for much more!—*mhe*—
This son-in-law has asked for only eight. It doesn't matter, give them to him."
Yes, give them to him,
With eight mules the son-in-law reached the washerwoman
The washerwoman said: "Why did you do this?"
Yes, why did you do this? I told you to get sixty mules!
The son-in-law said: "Your father! I didn't remember the number!"
Yes, I only remembered the number eight!
Kapūrī said: "We won't get any more from the royal court!
Yes, there's no way we'll get others now
You do the following.—Somehow load the clothes onto six.—*mhe*—
And, son-in-law, you climb onto one.—*vāh vāh*—
Put me onto one
Load all the clothes onto six. *Load them onto six*
And tell the city's washermen to go on foot!
Goddammit! You go on foot!"—*vāh vāh*—
So, what did they do with six? They loaded Mīr's clothes onto them
The washerwoman climbed onto one mule. The washerwoman speaks.—*mhe*—
What news does she tell the washermen, let's see.
By saying it, know it, let's see, by saying it
I'll say it now, by Dev's grace, here you are.—*vāh vāh*—

—*gāv*—

"Now, be alert, my washermen! Brother!—*mhe*—
Devjī's cowherds will run away!
We'll capture the cows and cowherds and bring them to Rātākoṭ.—*vāh vāh*—
Then I'll have you receive a great reward from Rāvjī
I'll have you receive a great reward from Rāvjī!—*vāh vāh*—
But, by God's grace, we have to capture the cows and cowherds, hey, brother, washermen!"—*vāh vāh*—
Kānīyā Dhobī was her son-in-law—*mhe*—
The washerwoman's.—*mhe*—
Kānīyā Dhobī speaks. What news does he tell, let's see.
By saying it, know it, let's see, by saying it

—*gāv*—

By God's grace, Kānīyā Dhobī, champion amongst the washermen.—*mhe*—
He caught hold of his mule's tail:
"I'll throw down those cowherds like this, O mother-in-law—*mhe*—
Both arms full!"
Holding onto the mule's tail—*mhe*—

The washerman turned about in all the directions.—*vāh vāh*—
The washerwoman said: "Great, wonderful, O son-in-law, wonderful, O son-in-law, wonderful! *What is there lacking in you?*
You alone are enough for fifty or sixty.—*vāh vāh*—
And I'll take on a hundred or so.
Yes, I'll help you,
And these goddammed washermen of the city, they can take care of the rest afterward.
Yes, they'll do some work at least!
Let's capture those cowherds of Devjī!"—*vāh vāh*—
So, by God's grace, what did the washerwoman do?—*mhe*—
She left, and, reached the Gudaliyā Pond.—*vāh vāh*—
She spoke to the washermen:
"Hey, washermen!—*mhe*—
By God's grace, start washing half the clothes.—*vāh vāh*—
And make me a large tent with the other half
Fix up the curtains
By God's grace, they set up the curtains. And, the washerwoman saw they had made a palace for her from half the clothes.—*vāh vāh*—
The washermen began washing half the clothes
What did the washerwoman do? She went and sat down in the tent, *sir said*
She commanded the city's washermen: "Go, brother, wash clothes!"—*vāh vāh*—
At dawn, Dev Mahārāj's cowherd and cows arrived, *sir said*
The footsteps of horses sounded.—*mhe*—
The cowherds came riding on a horse.—*vāh vāh*—

Devnārāyaṇ's cows and Kapūrī Dhoban at Gudaliyā Pond.

So, the washerwoman speaks.—*mhe*—
What news does she tell the cowherds, *let's see*

—*gāv*—

"Brother, you have a fine hound on the line, O Prince!—*mhe*—
Pearls adorn your ears
Hey, your face looks like that of King Bisaldev Cauhān.—*mhe*—
Why have you arrived at my great fort Rāṇ,
O Prince?"
Yes, why have come today?
Dev Mahārāj's Guāl speaks.—*mhe*—
What news does he tell the washerwoman. *Let's see, by saying it, know it, now, by saying it*
I'll say it now, by Dev's grace, here you are.—*vāh vāh*—*jī*—*vāh vāh*—

—*gāv*—

"By God's grace, I have a fine hound on the line.—*mhe*—
And, pearls adorn my ears
I'm Ṭhākur Dev's Guāl, O Mother Washerwoman!—*mhe*—
I came grazing these cows to the great fort of Rāṇ
Washerwoman!—*mhe*—
I'm no prince and so on!"
Yes, I'm the cows' cowherd!
By God's grace, the Guāl said: "Washerwoman!—*mhe*—
Not at all am I a prince or something, by God's grace!"
The washerwoman spoke.—*mhe*—
How does she reprimand the cowherds now, let's see.
By saying it, know it, let's see, now, by saying it

—*gāv*—

"You tore down the curtain.—*mhe*—
I'm Rāvjī's confidant!
Hey, I'll go to the royal court tomorrow morning.—*mhe*—
Hey, I'll have you brought with water-bags tied to your back
Godammit! Aren't you ashamed!"
Yes, coming so close to the curtain!
Picking up a mallet—*mhe*—
And she stepped out.—*vāh vāh*—
Devjī's cows were drinking water. Kapūrī said: "Hey, washermen!—*mhe*—
Godammit, the cows are just drinking up the water!"
Yes, they'll spoil the clothes. Beat them!
By God's grace, picking up their mallets—*mhe*—
And they started beating up Devjī's cows, *said sir.*
The washerwoman beat Suremātā once with her mallet
She beat her twice with the mallet
The Guāl speaks.—*mhe*—

What does news does he tell the washerwoman.
By saying it, know it, let's see, by saying it
I'll say it now, by Bhagavān's grace, here you are

—gāv—

Kapūrī Dhoban Is Beaten by the Cowherds

"By God's grace, washerwoman, don't beat my cow with the mallet!—*mhe*—
It hurts my Kāmdhīn's body! Hey, what are you standing around, looking at, Dev's Guāls?
The woman's beating Suremātā, hey!" he said.—*mhe*—

—gāv—

By God's grace, the news was spoken by Dev's Guāl.—*mhe*—
He said: "O Mother Washerwoman! Don't beat Suremātā with the mallet.—*mhe*—
It hurts my Kāmdhīn's snout!
What are you standing around looking at, Dev's Guāls? Shave off the widow washerwoman's head!
Look, she's standing there beating the cow!"—*mhe*—
By God's grace, Berībāj Guāl wouldn't say what he was going to do, he wouldn't listen to what others said
So, he went and caught hold of the washerwoman's braid
Up to his waist he entered into the water, *said sir.*
By God's grace, the Guāls from the far end came in one swoop.—*mhe*—
By God's grace, what did he do? Berībāj Guāl caught hold of her braid and gave her a swing.—*mhe*—
"Come, Kapūrī, go Kapūrī, come Kapūrī, go Kapūrī!" *He gave her 'Go Kapūrī'*
The way acrobats fill their drums with water
Filled like that he went and put down the washerwoman on the banks of the Gudaliyā Pond
The cowherds from the other end arrived
They said: "What are you quarreling about?"
Yes, what's the noise about?
Berībāj said: "There's no quarrel!—*mhe*—
I'm just 'caressing' the washerwoman!"—*vāh vāh*—
"Well, then call us too, brother!" Berībāj said: "Water has been applied—*mhe*—
You pluck out the hairs!"
Yes, you pluck out the hairs of her head
It took no time saying it!
Not even one hair could the washerwoman catch hold of.
Yes, they pulled out all of them!
More cowherds from the other end arrived
"What are you quarreling about on the banks of the Gudlīyā Pond?"

"No, brother, I'm not quarreling at all. I'm 'caressing' the washerwoman."
"Well, then, brother, she'll be annoyed at us!"
Yes, call us too!

Berībāj said: "Her hair has been already removed—*mhe*—
You make some dents, *a few notches*"
With a knife, Dev's cowherds made dents on her head
In the meantime, more cowherds from the other side arrived
"Berībāj, what are you quarrelling and making a noise about today at the Pond?"
They said
Berībāj said: "No quarrel at all. Washerwoman came today, which is why I'm 'caressing' her."
Yes, I'm 'caressing' Washerwoman
"Well, then call us too!"
Yes, we'll do some too!
Berībāj said: "You heat up the head a little.—*vāh vāh*—
Put this ākaḍā onto it."—*vāh vāh*—
The washerwoman was beaten the way a drum is.
Yes, in the same way, the washerwoman was beaten and sat upon the bank
The chief cowherd came afterward
"Berībāj, what are you quarreling about, today at the pond?"
Berībāj said: "I'm not quarreling.—*mhe*—
I'm 'caressing' the washerwoman!"—*vāh vāh*—
The chief cowherd said: "Then she'll be annoyed with me!"
Yes, tell me something
By God's grace, the chief cowherd took a look at her head.—*mhe*—
"Hey, daughter's father! *You've done a great injustice!*
Why did you beat this creature, Berībāj!"—*mhe*—
By God's grace, the washerwoman noticed: "That cowherd is the cleverest of all."
Yes, he's smart!
The washerwoman said:—*mhe*—
What news does she tell the chief among Dev's cowherds, let's see.
By saying it, know it, by saying it, let's see, by saying it
I'll say it now, by Bhagavān's grace, let's see.—*vāh vāh sā*—

—*gāv*—

The Cowherds Gift Their Rings to Kapūrī Dhoban

"The knife's point, hey, Dev's cowherd—*mhe*—
My precious head did suffer!
I can hardly speak with this tongue!—*mhe*—
By God's grace, look, your cowherds have done this to my head!"

Yes, look, they've done this!
The washerwoman speaks. What news does she tell the chief cowherd.
By saying it, know it, let's see, by saying it
I'll say it now, by Bhagavān's grace, here you are.—*vāh vāh*—

—*gāv*—

"This tongue has come to give you pleasure
Guāl!—*mhe*—
In the tongue there is poison, *and in the tongue itself there is nectar*
By God's grace, my tongue didn't stay in its place, look, that's why my head has become like this!"—*vāh vāh*—

—*gāv*—

"By God's grace, hey, Guāl, the crow doesn't destroy anyone's wealth.—*mhe*—
And the koyal doesn't destroy anyone's gift
Whoever has nectar in the tongue, hey, Guāl, he makes the world belong to him
The way the crow speaks, isn't it.—*mhe*—
Then you throw a stone!
Yes, scare it away!
When a koyal speaks—*mhe*—
Then, look, people say she spoke sweetly.—*vāh vāh*—
If there is sweetness in the tongue—*mhe*—
Then the world becomes one's own!"—*vāh vāh*—
By God's grace, the washerwoman came close to the Guāl and showed him her head.—*mhe*—
And, she said: "Look, Guāl!" She had her veil on one side, that she struck down on the ground.—*vāh vāh*—
"Look what they did to my head."
Yes, how they've done it all
By God's grace, Berībāj was standing next to the chief Guāl. The washerwoman had struck the shoulder sash down on the ground, didn't she—*mhe*—
Right then Beribāj picked up a one-and-a-quarter-maṇ heavy boulder
The chief Guāl said: "Hey, Berībāj!"
Yes, what are you going to do with it?
Berībāj said: "Washerwoman's struck her shoulder sash down, hasn't she!"
Yes, I'll fill it
The chief Guāl said: "Listen, hey, Berībāj—*mhe*—
There are two kinds of sashes in the world.—*vāh vāh*—
There's one sash that belongs to the lord, *and there's one sash that belongs to the king*
There's no sash for throwing stones into!"—*vāh vāh*—
So, what did the chief Guāl do? Well, he had nothing else with him.—*mhe*—
And he had a ring worth one and a quarter crore on his hand.—*vāh vāh*—
In the washerwoman's sash, *yes, he took off the ring and threw it*

So, fourteen hundred and forty four Guāls, all of them—the chief Guāl threw the ring didn't he—*mhe*—
The remainder—all of them—quickly filled up the washerwoman's sash.
Yes, filled it up with rings and rings
The washerwoman places her hands on the rings, and her senses feel all right
She places her hands on her head and thinks: "Hey, this body's going to die tomorrow, who will enjoy these?"
Yes, who will enjoy this immortality?
By God's grace, the Guāls took leave from the washerwoman and departed.—*vāh vāh*—

After they went—now, the time when the washerwoman received the invitation—*mhe*—
At that time because of the Guāls, the washermen ran away on their own.—*vāh vāh*—
Kānīyo Washerman ran away.—*mhe*—
On the one side there was a jungle twelve kos wide, and on the other side there was water. *Water came*
Where could he go? *Where could he go?*
Now, there's that washerman's stone, isn't there. That high one.
Yes, made like a mare
He hid underneath it.—*vāh vāh*—
By God's grace, after Dev's Guāl left, he came out into the open.—*mhe*—
The washerwoman said: "Hey, Son-in-law, where were you?
Yes, where did you go off to?
Look, from beating the Guāls I've become crazy
Yes, "I beat them thoroughly and collected such a lot of rings," she said, "by beating them!"
I would whack them with the mallet and they would fling down the rings.—*vāh vāh*—
A whack with the mallet I'd give them—*mhe*—
The rings they would fling down!"—*vāh vāh*—
The washerman said: "Mother-in-law, stay deaf.
Yes, stay deaf
I know all about the rings."
Yes, the invitation you received, I know about all that. I saw it all!
"What did you see?" *Tell me about that!*
The son-in-law said: "Look, I saw the Guāls put you into the water.
Yes . . .
Yes, and, they pulled out your hair—*mhe*—
Struck it with daggers—*vāh vāh*—
Poured *ā̃kaḍo, and then after that heated the hair on your head*
After that the chief Guāl came, whereupon you cried, whereupon he gave you his ring."
Yes, he gave it to you

The washerwoman said: "O Son-in-law, what you told me just now, *don't tell anyone else*
When you go into the city—into Rāṇ City, don't say it!—*vāh vāh*—
There, take one ring!" *Don't say it!*
The son-in-law said: "Today I won't tell it, *I'll tell it tomorrow.*"
The washerwoman said: "There, take two rings!" *The son-in-law said: "I won't say it for two days!"*
The washerwoman said: "Take five rings!" *The son-in-law said: "I won't say it for five days, for sure!"*
"Why are you doing this?" *Why are you doing this?*
The son-in-law said: "Well, distribute the wealth. *Make it half and half*
I'll never say it!" *I won't say it*
The washerwoman said: "Son-in-law, if I distribute them here, then the rings may get spent.—*mhe*—
Let's go there to our home. *Hey, we'll make half and half over there!*
I'll call my daughter, Kamalūḍī,—*mhe*—
And give you exactly half!"—*vāh vāh*—
"Let's go!" He said. *Let's go!*
The washerwoman said: "I can't walk at all. There is that mule of ours, isn't it." *Bring it here, so that you can put me on and take me along*
The son-in-law said: "Your father! The Guāl drove off the mules."—*vāh vāh*—
The washerwoman said: "Well, in that case, Son-in-law, I can't walk!"
Yes, I can't walk, then

So, by God's grace, Kānīyā Washerman looked around.—*mhe*—
He saw the Kumahār's mare
He said: "Mother-in-law, the Kumahār's mare is standing there." *If you say so, I'll catch hold of it!*
The washerwoman said: "Bring it here."
Yes, put my life on it, and let's go
So, he put the washerwoman onto the Kumahār's mare.—*mhe*—
The washerman got on behind
He broke off a part of a swallow wart and made it into a whip
One time he hits the horse,—*mhe*—
And one time he hits the rider.
Yes, he hits Mother-in-law
The washerwoman said: "O Son-in-law, why are doing this—yesterday the Guāls beat me enough!"
Yes, why are you beating me?
The son-in-law said: "O Mother-in-law, if I don't beat the rider the horse will get angry.
Yes, he's not going to move
I'll have to give you some 'treatment'."—*vāh vāh*—
In this way, he reached the washerwoman's home.—*mhe*—

The swallow wart went into her blood, so that she went home and cried all night long.
Yes, great, hey!
By God's grace, there was a barber's home nearby.—*mhe*—
At dawn, the barber's wife came over.—*vāh vāh*—
She said: "O Aunt!—*mhe*—
Brothers, in the neighborhood you held a night-wake alone." The washerwoman said: "Barber's Wife!—*mhe*—
What should I have made a night-wake for? Yesterday I went to fill the mattress with cotton at Kamāliya's oil-presser's.
Godammit, some small stone was left inside." *A stone was left inside, that's why I cried*
The barber's wife thought: "Know your mother! Look, doesn't she have a tender body!"—*mhe*—
She said: "Don't tell me this! Tell me the way it happened!"
Yes, nobody cries that much because a pebble is pinching them!
Then she showed the barber's wife her head: "Look, barber's wife, you're the barber's wife.—*mhe*—
You do a lot of hair-braiding; do you have a solution for my head?"
Yes, tell me about that!
"O Auntie, if you had told me about that trouble at night, *I would have done something at night!*
So, by God's grace, she washed her head with water and put on cold ghī—*mhe*—
She put medicine on her head, and cooled it. *vāh vāh*—
She put wax onto her head.—*mhe*—
There's no dearth of hair at the barbers' home.
Yes, there's plenty
She brought long hair and stuck it onto the wax.—*vāh vāh*—
After sticking it on—*mhe*—
She plaited her hair with a braid, and got the washerwoman all settled.
Yes, she made a braid
"Well?" *She said: "Now I'm fine!"*
"Yes, without a braid, a woman doesn't know what to do, hey, barber's wife!"—*mhe*—
The barber's wife said: "I made one, didn't I?"
Yes, I made one now, didn't I
"Here, take these five gold coins!" *"Here you are," she said, "ah!"*

By God's grace, the barber's wife thought: "Hey, know your, know your mother, I braid the queen's hair every day!
Yes, she never even gave me a single gold coin, she gives me a copper coin!
Look, I plaited the washerwoman's hair just one day."
Yes, she gave me five gold coins!
The barber's wife had her three-year-old son in her lap.—*mhe*—
She said: "O Auntie Washerwoman, take care of my son for a little while,
I'll go and plait the queen's hair."

Yes, I'll braid the queen's hair, in the meantime keep the boy
The washerwoman said: "Give him to me!"
Yes, bring him quickly, I'll take care of your son
By God's grace, she strung the gold coins onto a rope made of mũj.—*mhe*—
Some of it she tied onto the child, *and some she put on herself*
And some she wore herself.—*vāh vāh*—
What did the barber's wife do? She left the child, and reached Rāvjī's palace
"Plait her hair." She braided her hair quickly. She said: "I'm in a rush today, madam."—*mhe*—
After plaiting her hair, she said: "Give me leave!"
Yes, give me payment
The queen said: "Brother, maid, give the barber's wife one copper coin and a bodice."
Yes, bring a copper coin and a bodice and give it to the barber's wife
The barber's wife said: "Śrī Mahārāj, it's all right, you give on behalf of the king.—*mhe*—
You are the country's ruler.—*vāh vāh*—
Today I came after plaiting your washerwoman's hair.
Yes, today, for the first time I've plaited her hair
She gave me these five gold coins.
Yes, she gave me five gold coins
You give only a copper coin!" *And you give only a copper coin—you are the country's ruler!*
The queen said: "Listen, O Barber's wife!—*mhe*—
Tell me about my rules and regulations first."
Yes, it's against the rules. I won't give you any
"Great, well, then, brother, I won't be able to plait your hair every day, now!"—*mhe*—

The barber's wife took the copper coin and bodice, and came down this lane.—*mhe*—
And the washerwoman took the child with the gold coins around his neck.
Yes . . .
She wore some on her feet, and some she put around his neck
She came down that lane.—*vāh vāh*—
By God's grace, she didn't come up against the barber's wife in that lane.—*mhe*—
She went, and by God's grace, said her greeting to the queen, *said sir.*
"Welcome, O Mother Washerwoman, welcome, O Auntie.
Who does that boy belong to?"
The washerwoman said: "Madam, I'm going to Bhairũjī's shrine at Gudaliyā Pond.—*mhe*—
Bhairũnāth gave him to me yesterday."
Yes, Bhairũjī presented him to me
The queen said: "Bhairũjī gave him to you.—*mhe*—
These gold coins?" The washerwoman said: "These gold coins, when Devjī's cowherds come, then I get plenty of them.

Yes, I beat them and get the gold coins
I've filled up the house.—*mhe*—
There are lots of rats in the house. Godammit, some of them took the coins into their holes and transported them to other people's homes."
The queen thought to herself: "Hey, know your mother!" she said: "Washerwoman!—*mhe*—
Get me a child too!"
Yes, please get me one child too!
"Śrī Mahārāj, how would you like it, madam," she said.
Yes, how would you like it?
"I'm a person who roams about in the jungle. If I go three times, I go on foot.
Yes, I get up and go however I please, but how will you go?
You are the land's ruler!"—*mhe*—
The queen said: "Brother, washerwoman, I have one daughter. I'm without a son, hey!"
Yes, get me a son, then things will be all right!
The washerwoman said: "Śrī Mahārāj, I'll get you one tomorrow!
Yes, I'll get you one all right, but you'll have to do what I say!
Prepare a maṇ-and-a-quarter prasād of molasses—*vāh vāh*—
Don't take anyone else along except the cart-driver and the ally. I'll accompany you.
Yes, don't take any other Sirdār along
So, by God's grace, I'll get you one tomorrow!"—*vāh vāh*—
"So how will I go in that case?" The washerwoman said: "I'll tell you, madam.
Yes, I'll tell you, madam!
Get a stomachache!—*vāh vāh*—
When the doctors and bhopās come, let your stomachache continue. When I come, I'll give you a wrap with Bhairū̃jī's name.—*mhe*—
Become silent then."
Yes, remain silent then!

So, the washerwoman said so much and left. The queen went and slept in the palace.
The king said: "What's happened to the queen, brother?"
Yes, it seems that the queen's stomach has started hurting
Rāvjī did whatever there was to be done with the doctors and bhopās
"Why is there this bad stomach?"
Yes, why is there this false stomach? She's wailing and crying a great deal!
By God's grace, in the meantime, the washerwoman got possessed by Bhairū̃jī.—*vāh vāh*—
She said: "What's all the commotion about in the court?" *Why is there a commotion?*
They said: "Washerwoman, the queen's stomach is hurting!"—*mhe*—
The washerwoman said: "Don't call me washerwoman!"—*vāh vāh*—

She said: "I'm Bherū̃nāth of the Gudaliyā Pond.
Yes, I'm not the washerwoman just now!
I keep the queen's stomach in my fist!
Yes, show her to me
But I demand to see the queen alone—*vāh vāh*—
A maṇ and a quarter of sweets made of molasses."
Yes, I demand!
They said: "Washerwoman, put it down, at least. Tell your Bhairū̃jī we'll deliver the sweets tomorrow." *Put it down*
"Here you are!"—*vāh vāh*—
It took no time giving the wrap and in no time the queen spoke: "Hey, Rām,
Hey, I'm feeling well again! *It took no time with the bad stomach*
In the morning there will be the offering."—*mhe*—
Rāvjī spoke. What news did he say, let's see.
By saying it, know it, by saying it, let's see
"Bring the ingredients for the sweets made of molasses, brother!"—*vāh vāh*—

—*gāv*—

"Harness the oxen of the oxen-driver.—*mhe*—
Bring the chariot with harnessed oxen
Hey, Bhairū̃nāthjī of Gudaliyā will gift a strong son!—*mhe*—
I've remained a sonless Maṇḍovar Paḍīhār
I'm without a son, brother.—*mhe*—
Look, when Bhairū̃ gives me a son tomorrow, it'll be very good." The queen goes inside.—*vāh vāh*—
They made a maṇ and a quarter of sweets from molasses. And made boiled whole wheat.
By God's grace, the washerwoman said: "I need a cart-driver, madam."—*mhe*—
The queen said this to Gāṅgā: "Gāṅgā!—*vāh vāh*—
Yoke up the pair of oxen, brother!"—*mhe*—
The cart-driver yoked the oxen and said: "Here you are sir, where should I leave it?"—*mhe*—
They said: "Leave it behind the palace."—*vāh vāh*—
Behind the palace, in a back lane, he left the oxen-cart
The washerwoman tied up the boiled wheat in a sack—*mhe*—
And placed it in the rear of the cart
She told the queen: "Come, madam. I'll go home so I can bless the son-in-law."—*mhe*—

So the queen came and sat down next to the window at the rear—*vāh vāh*—
And spoke to the cart-driver:
"Cart-driver!—*mhe*—
By God's grace, let the cart go down the lane to the washerwoman's house, brother!—*vāh vāh*—
The lane in which Karpūḍī lives.

Yes, let the cart roll!
The washerwoman stood there ready.—*mhe*—
The queen said: "O Aunt, are you ready?" "Yes, I've been standing here for ages."
Yes, I've been waiting for you!
The queen said: "Come! Sit in the cart."—*vāh vāh*—
The washerwoman said: "Hey, Śrī Mahārāj, people will see me and you.
Yes, should I sit next to you in the cart?
Won't they complain?"—*mhe*—
The queen said: "Which big people are going to see us together?
Yes, come, O Aunt!
Get going fast!"
Yes, she wants a boy!
The queen said: "Look, madam, get me one three years old!" The washerwoman said: "I told you I'll get you a boy!"
Yes, I'll get you one upon reaching there!
By God's grace, the washerwoman had told her son-in-law: "Son-in-law!—*mhe*—
Today I'll satisfy you with as many molasses sweets as you can lay hands on.
Yes, go to the Gudaliyā Pond tomorrow
You go to that Gudaliyā bank.—*mhe*—
By God's grace, there's that banyan tree, isn't there
There's that Bhairū̃jī of the banyan tree, isn't there.—*vāh vāh*—
Set yourself up as his priest."
Yes, put a mark on your forehead and so on, and become the priest!
Kānīyo Washerman hurries over there.—*mhe*—
He went there, put mark on his forehead, and so on, and became the priest on the platform
He built a fire, and began performing prayers and worship, the smart fellow!—*vāh vāh*—
So, the washerwoman said: "O Queen!—*mhe*—
Suppose the cart-driver gets hungry, will you get some other supplies?"
Yes, I'll bring them
"What should I get?" *Onions and bāṭīs*
"All right, who knows, supposing the son-in-law may come early or late?—*vāh vāh*—
Why, he'd remain hungry.—*mhe*—
So, time passed like this. The washerwoman said: "O Queen, we're sitting here—let's remember Bhairū̃jī!"
Yes, let's remember him at least!
So, the queen sat in the cart—the equal pair of the queen and the washerwoman.—*vāh vāh*—
They began worshipping without the molasses sweets.—*mhe*—

—*gāv*—

The queen says: "Son, why do you go hungry?—*mhe*—
The washerwoman says: "Cowherd's widow! Why did you take that false name?"
Yes, why did you mention it like that?
The queen said: "Look, you have to take some name in between."
Yes, you have to take a hit in between
By God's grace, singing and playing music, the region around Gudaliyā was reached, by God's grace isn't it.—*mhe*—
The washerwoman said: "O Queen, now it's not possible to go further riding in the cart.
Yes, halt this cart right here!
And give the cart-driver two bulbs of onions.—*mhe*—
And give him the bāṭīs
Yes, give them to the cart-driver
He'll eat them on his own."—*vāh vāh*—
The washerwoman brought the sack—*mhe*—
Somehow
Yes, and got it to Bhairũjī
She said: "Here you are, O Queen, pay your respects!" *Pay your respects*
The son-in-law had built a fire earlier. The fire was ready. After paying their respects—*mhe*—
And the washerwoman filled the folds of Kānīyā's dhoti.—*vāh vāh*—
She said: "I'm filling the dhoti's folds with sweetmeats of molasses.—Keep them!—*vāh vāh*—
Climb up!"
Yes, "Climb up the banyan tree!"
"What for?" The washerwoman said: "Keep a look out for what happened yesterday.
Yes, if the cowherds come, then you
Tell me; give me a signal!"
Yes, I'll run away!
So, that son-in-law sat up in the banyan tree.—*mhe*—
And the queen and the washerwoman are singing praises of Chappanjī Bhairũjī. *And worship Bhairũjī*

Both of them said: "Give the queen a son, Mahārāj, give a son!"—*vāh vāh*—
Now, in the meantime, the washerman couldn't see on one side because he was blind in one eye.—*mhe*—
And on the other side a branch of the banyan tree was in front.
He couldn't see the cowherds in the distance.—*mhe*—
Suddenly, the sound of horses' steps were heard, *and the washerman took a look*
When he took a look and heard the horses' steps, Kānīyā Washerman let go of his hands.—*vāh vāh*—*from the upper branch*
He fell down tumbling into the queen's lap.—*mhe*—
The queen was sitting below on the platform.—*vāh vāh*—

The washerwoman said: "Śrī Mahārāj gave me a three-year-old son yesterday.
Here you take one of twenty-five
With a beard and moustaches, here you are. *Take him, here you are!*
Here, you take the son.—*mhe*—
And, here take my cane, my cane got left behind yesterday in that bush, I'll get it. *I'll get it*
Tell the cowherd to throw down a gold coin every time you strike him with the cane!"
The washerwoman ran away.—*vāh vāh*—
She gave the queen the cane.—*mhe*—

The Cowherds Cut the Queen's Braid

Upon arriving, by God's grace, Berībāj Guāl came and stood near the queen:
"Why is Bhūnā's mother here today?" *Why have you come?*
The queen said: "I didn't suckle Bhūnā, did I!"—*mhe*—
So, by God's grace, the Guāl thought: "Hey, I'm talking to mother.—
Bhūnā's mother is just like my own mother, the poor thing."—*mhe*—
Coming close, the queen raised up the cane.—*vāh vāh*—
So, Dev's Guāl speaks.—*mhe*—
What news does Berībāj tell the queen, let's see.
By saying it, know it, let's see, by saying it
I'll say it now, by Bhagavān's grace.—*vāh vāh sā*

—*gāv*—

"O lowly queen of Rāv's—*mhe*—
O mother of Bhūnā, who gave you instruction
O Mother, on whose instruction have you come?"—*mhe*—
The queen thought: "Look, godammit, he didn't throw down a gold coin.
How dare he talk?"—*vāh vāh*—
Clasping both hands together she beat the Guāl again.
It took no time beating him.—*mhe*—
In a flash he caught hold of the queen's braid.—*vāh vāh*—
"Wait, people keep your . . .
Yes, a lot of people respect you like they do a mother, isn't it."

—*gāv*—

Standing there the Guāl reproached her—*mhe*—
Brother, he took hold of the queen's braid in his hands
He stood the queen up in mud
From the queen's braid he cut off a string of pearls. The Guāl removed the
String of pearls worth a lakh of rupees.—*mhe*—
He stood up the queen in mud—*vāh vāh*—
"I called you Mother, Mother, but then you hit me twice with the whip."—*mhe*—

The queen reflected to herself: "Where is there a son here?
Yes, where is there a son here and where gold coins?
Look, that widow washerwoman brought me here."
Yes, she arranged all this
The Guāl said: "Bhūnā's mother, you came on somebody's instruction,—*mhe*—
Go away.
Yes, get up now"
The chief Guāl said: "Berībāj!—*mhe*—
What are you doing?—*vāh vāh*—
Hey, Bhūnā's mother is like our mother, brother."—*vāh vāh*—
The Guāl came riding on his horse and stood on the banks of the Gudaliyā Pond
And he let go of the dog's leash.—*vāh vāh*—
So, what did the queen do. She told the cart-driver. Then the cart-driver grew angry.—*vāh vāh*—
He removed one part of the metal covering from both the wheels
"The queen didn't give me even one sweetmeat of molasses."
Yes, the queen's running away
The queen sat quickly in the cart and said: "Yes, drive on! *Drive on, Gāṅgā, she said*
Gāṅgā, move immediately, quickly!"—*vāh vāh*—
Gāṅgā put the cart on the road.—*mhe*—
The queen will be pained now.—*vāh vāh*—

—*gāv*—

The queen coaxed Gāṅgā, didn't she.—*mhe*—
Gāṅgā thought: "Hey, the queen will be pained. Her body will become sick."—*vāh vāh*—
He fixed on the metal plate again
"She is the king's queen. She's suffering."
"I'll have you married twice.—*vāh vāh*—
I'll be sweet to you, brother.—*mhe*—
I'll color your turban."
Yes, I'll do everything, but don't let me suffer
By God's grace, he placed the metal plate back on.—*mhe*—
And departed
What did the dog do? The Guāl had let go of the dog, hadn't he?—*mhe*—
A rabbit came out from inside that bush
The dog ran after the rabbit
What did the washerwoman do? She piled up the branches and leaves of the trees in a large pile. *And she got underneath the leaves and branches*

She reflected to herself: "The cowherds can't see me."
Yes, I'm not visible
What did the rabbit do? It ran off.—*mhe*—
At that time the rabbit went and sat next to the washerwoman.—*vāh vāh*—

The washerwoman said: "Godammit, O life's pain, where did you come from?"—*mhe*—

The dog came running after the rabbit. When the rabbit entered the pile of leaves and branches, the dog began circling it.

Yes, the dog began wandering all around the pile of leaves and branches

The Guāl followed.—*mhe*—

He said: "The dog won't go any further, brother.

Yes, there's something in this

By God's grace, do the following: keep standing all around the pile.—*mhe*—

And put fire to it."

Yes, put fire to it

When fire was mentioned, then the washerwoman jumped up and down.

The cowherd said: "Hey, the whole bush is shaking, it's no rabbit. It's a tremendous twelve-maṇ wild boar from the jungle, brother.

Yes, there's a wild boar moving in this

Set up the fire quickly!"—*mhe*—

The washerwoman said: "Śrī Mahārāj, I'm the one from yesterday.

Yesterday's one

Yesterday's one."

Yesterday's one!

The Guāl said: "Who? The washerwoman?"

Yes, she said, "It's me!"

"Śrī Mahārāj, I've been lying here since yesterday.

Yes, I wasn't able to walk

The poison got into my body."—*vāh vāh*—

The Guāl said: "Stay there, burn up! Hey, that's the washerwoman widow over here!

Yes, go on!

But she'll burn inside."

Yes, she'll burn up, let's go

The Guāl departed soon after

After the cowherds had left the washerwoman came out and ran off.—*mhe*—

So upon reaching the outskirts of the village she caught up with the queen. *vāh vāh*—

After catching up, the queen speaks. What news does she say to the washerwoman. Let's see. *By seeing it, know it. Let's see by saying it*

I'll see it now, by Lord Dev's grace

—*gāv*—

"Stay away, stay away, you widow washerwoman!—*mhe*—

Stay away from my chariot

I'll go to the court now.—*mhe*—

O widow, I'll make things worse for you today than they were yesterday."

The queen said that news,

Yes, to the washerwoman

The washerwoman uncovered her head and showed it to the queen. "Śrī Mahārāj—*mhe*—
Yesterday the cowherds did this. What will you do today, tell me!"
The queen said: "O widow, I'll do this to you! Why did you take me to that place!"
Yes, why did you take me along
The washerwoman said: "Śrī Mahārāj, yesterday the Guāl beat and hit me!
Yes, they were very bad
Nobody listened to me at all
Today the cowherds beat you.—*mhe*—
Tomorrow the fifty-two forts will go into battle."
Yes, tomorrow they will go into battle against the cowherds
So, what does the queen shout out aloud upon reaching in the palace, let's see.
By saying it, know it, let's see, by saying it

—*gāv*—

Kālū Mīr and Dīyājī Capture the Cows

Climbing up into the palace the queen said.—*mhe*—
She shouted shout upon shout
"Women's braids were cut off! Kālū Mīr will you go now or tomorrow
Hey, daughter's father," she said, "women's braids were cut off today,"—*mhe*—
Climbing up into the palace the queen spoke. She gave shouts upon shouts.
"Women's braids were cut off, O Hindvā Rāv.—*mhe*—
Hey, the Guāl Berībāj cut off the string of pearls from my head
Hey, Rāvji, see, Devji's Guāl cut off all the strings and necklaces of mine."—*vāh vāh*—
By God's grace Rāvjī Sāī summoned Mīr.—*vāh vāh*—
He said: "Mīr, buffaloes eat fodder.—*mhe*—
Look, you drink bubbling wine
By God's grace, yesterday the women's braids were cut off. Mīr will you go today or tomorrow?
Hey, daughter's father, he's still alive.—*vāh vāh*—
Hey, he cut off my wife's, the queen's braid, the Guāl!"
Yes, how did the Guāls become so powerful
Dīyā was sitting close by.—*mhe*—
Rāvjī speaks. What news does he say to Dīyā. *By saying it, know it, let's see by saying it*
I'll see it now, by Dev's grace

—*gāv*—

"Diyā, Rāv is calling you, come in front, brother, Dīyā
The women's braids have been cut, O daughter's father," he said.

Yes, hurry up and launch an assault
Mīr said, "Look, here you are Diyā, tobā, tobā, tobā, the invitation's come, brother!"—*mhe*—

—*gāv*—

Kālū Mīr, Dīyā, and the Ṭhākurs rode the horses.—*mhe*—
There was a great formation of elephants
Hey, brother, by God's grace, Fort Sāvar's Rāv went out to fight the cows' cowherds
By God's grace, Kālū Mīr and Dīyā got in a rage.—*mhe*—
They went and put up a tent in front of the cowherds.—*vāh vāh*—
Sometime *they would* return to Gudaliyā pond over there.—*vāh vāh*—
It became dawn. The enemy stood in front of the cows of Dev's prize. Three times they could not capture the cows.—*mhe*—
So, when the Guāl went grazing, by God's grace, Suremātā speaks.—*vāh vāh*—
What news does she say to the Guāl.
By saying it, know it, let's see by saying it
I'll say it now, by Dev's grace, let's see.—*vāh vāh*—*jī*—*vāh vāh*—

—*gāv*—

"You too move quickly," he said.—*mhe*—
The cow said, "Guāl, I won't graze what you give me today.
Yes, I won't consume what you give us to consume today
Well, if Savāī Bhoj's Medu comes grazing.—*mhe*—
Ṭhākur Dev comes grazing, then I'll eat fodder
If Medūjī comes then I'll eat fodder.—*mhe*—
If he doesn't come, and if Bhagavān comes then I will eat fodder."
The Guāl told Prince Medū, "Great, sir, this cow has turned us down."
Yes, she won't graze
The Guāl went to Aunt and said:—*mhe*—
"Hey, O Aunt, why have the cows turned us down today?"—*vāh vāh*—
Dev's Guāl speaks. What news does he tell Aunt, let's see
By saying it, know it, by saying it

—*gāv*—

"By God's grace come down, O Aunt, Dīyāji has filled his voice today.—*mhe*—
Bhairū̃ wailed during the middle of the passing night
O Aunt, every day there was quarrel and noise.—*mhe*—
Tomorrow morning the horses' armor will fall off
O Aunt!—*mhe*—
Tomorrow morning your cows will be captured.—*vāh vāh*—
Tell your Dev that I will graze the cows.
Yes, "After so many days there is another," he said, "the confusion used to be like this"
O Aunt, what you think is not the case today.—*vāh vāh*—
Every day I would come after making quarrel and noise.—*mhe*—

Today there is no question of their coming on their own."
Yes, there is no question of coming today

—*gāv*—

By God's grace, Bhoj's Medū came together with the cow's herder.—*mhe*—
"Don't graze today, O pleasant mother
Be a guest of the enemy for three days.—*mhe*—
Look, I've come bearing spears' tips
Taking out swords from their sheath
Wearing spears' tips.—*mhe*—
I won't let you stay there more than three days."
Yes, you will have to stay there for three days
The cow said: "O Bhoj's Medū, today I will not graze what you give me."—*mhe*—
The cow shakes her head in denial
"Either I will graze what Tejā's Madnu gives me—*mhe*—
Or child Dev should come and graze me
I don't desire to consume only what you give me today."
Yes, I don't desire only that from you alone
So, by God's grace, in this manner all the brothers came to the cow's cowherd.—*vāh vāh*—
All of them left after entreating her, but the cow didn't budge at all.
Yes, when she turned them down, she really turned them down
The lord of the three worlds, Bhagavān, speaks.—*mhe*—
What news does he tell the cow, let's see.
By saying it, know it, let's see, by saying it

—*gāv*—

Hey, Bhagavān, come to the cow's herders.—*mhe*—"Don't graze, O pleasant mother
For three days be a guest of the enemy, Suremātā.—*mhe*—
I'll come on the third day, after I fix on Līlā's hooves.—*mhe*—
Only that much time."
Yes, I won't even take that much time. I'll come right afterward
Suremātā speaks. How does Sure turn down Bhagavān. What news does she say to Bhagavān.
By saying it, know it, by saying it

—*gāv*—

"I won't consume what you've given me to graze today, Bhagavān," she said.—*mhe*—
The cow shakes her head to say no
"If Nevā's son Bhāṅgī grazes me—*mhe*—
Or if the Bagaṛāvats' Bhāṭ comes and grazes me
If your lineage's Bhāṭ comes . . ."
Yes, then I'll graze

By God's grace, Dev Mahārāj went and spoke to the Bhāṭ
"Hey, Bābā Bhāṭ!—*mhe*—
Suremātā has turned us down, brother!"
Yes, graze her
So, by God's grace, how does the Bhāṭ come.—*mhe*—
What news does the lineage's Bhāṭ tell Sure upon arriving, let's see. *By saying it, know it, by saying it*

—*gāv*—

Hey, the Bhāṭ came to the cow's herder.—*mhe*—
"Mother Cow, listen to what the Bhāṭ says
If the Cauhān's sons don't launch an assault for you—*mhe*—
I'll sell them off, O Mother Cow, for a cheap copper coin
Cheap as a copper coin, I'll make them—*vāh vāh*—
If they don't launch an assault.—*mhe*—
Come! *Come now*
I won't let you stay more than three days."—*vāh vāh*—
So, Bābā *Bhāṭ* told the cow news.—*mhe*—
The Guāl took out Suremātā grazing. Speak: victory to Śrī Devnārāyaṇ Bhagavān, victory

By God's grace, when the Guāl took out the cow—*mhe*—
Then Dev Māhārāj said: "Hey, brother, Guāl—*mhe*—
Come here.—*vāh vāh*—
Who knows, by God's grace, the Rāv's generals come every day,—*mhe*—who knows, one might be struck by a weapon, might be killed, then we'll remain *separated. Let's meet!*
Let's meet, brother!"—*vāh vāh*—
So, Dev Mahārāj and the cow's herder met each other.—*mhe*—
What did Dev Mahārāj do? He drew out the Guāl's essence, himself.
Yes, he had miraculous powers with which he took it all away
The Guāl said: "Well, Śrī Mahārāj? *What should I go there for now?*
What to do? My body has become more than that of a Brahman's."—*mhe*—
Dev said: "Guāl, go, don't worry. I have to take the Bagaṛāvats' revenge.
I've taken your essence.—*mhe*—
You will have three whole strikes."—*vāh vāh*—
The Guāl reflected to himself: "First, I'll kill Rāvjī.
Yes, the first strike I'll deliver to Rāvjī
Then, I'll kill King Nīmde.
Yes, I'll kill him
And, after that I'll kill Dīyājī."
Yes, with the three strikes, I'll finish off the three Sirdārs
Dev Mahārāj said: "Hey, Guāl, what you've guessed isn't going to happen.
Yes, what you've surmised isn't going to happen
If you kill them, then what am I going to take revenge on?
Yes, what will I take revenge on?

Go, Toḍā Jagamālo—*mhe*—
By God's grace, that Sirdār will die by your hands.—*vāh vāh*—
Graze, brother!"—*mhe*—
So, today, Darbār Bhagavān, waved his hand over Suremātā, and said easily: "Please move, O Mother!"—*vāh vāh*—

He pitched the tent in front of Sikrāṇī—*vāh vāh*—
So, Bhagavān's cows left. Rāvjī's generals surrounded them.—*vāh vāh*—
The arrow that Dev's Nāpo shoots falls flat.—*vāh vāh*—
And Kālū Mīr and Dīyājī began gaining victory there.—*mhe*—
So, the arrow that Nāpo shoots began falling flat.—*vāh vāh*—
By God's grace, Mīr said:
"Hey, Nāplā!—*mhe*—
Don't waste arrows today, brother!"
Yes, don't you waste arrows today!
The Guāl said: "Listen, hey, Mīr, I'm not wasting them at all. Bhagavān Hasn't given me permission today!"—*mhe*—

By God's grace, Sāḍū Mātā speaks.—*mhe*—
What news does she tell Dev's Guāl who has arrived, let's see.
By saying it, know it, let's see, by saying it
I'll say it now, by Dev's grace, let's see

"You fell asleep after staying awake at night.—*mhe*—
Guāl, your hands were folded on your chest
Hey, the cows climbed up the Hill of Goram, hey, Nephew!—*vāh vāh*—
You saw people going to Puṣkar
It was the month of Kārttik.
Yes, the drummer Sirdārs travel to Puṣkarrāj
Hey, brother, you fell asleep on the hill.—*mhe*—
The cows descended down the hill.
By God's grace, the drummer Sirdārs are on the move. You heard the drums, woke up, and ran to me.
What right does Rāvjī have, that he captures our cows?" *She said, "Go and bring them"*
The Guāl reflected to himself: "Hey, look, Aunt is scolding me."—*mhe*—
The Guāl speaks. What news does he tell Sāḍū, let's see. *By saying it, know it, by saying it, let's see*
I'll say it now, by Dev's grace, here you are!—*vāh vāh sā*—

—*gāv*—

"O Aunt, I didn't fall asleep after keeping awake at night.—*mhe*—
Nor did I place my hands on my chest

Translation

By God's grace, Aunt, I didn't fall asleep after keeping awake at night. I slew Toḍā Jagamālo, the pride of four villages
Dīyājī even threatened me with a wild horse.—*mhe*—
He brought Bagūl Siṅg all tied up in front of me
Your Bagūlīyā has been taken prisoner!—*mhe*—
Hey, the cows have been herded on to Rātākoṭ."
What did Sāḍū Mātā do? She took a look amongst the cowherds standing there
So, Bagūl Siṅg Guāl wasn't amongst the cowherds or cows
She reflected to herself:—*mhe*—
If today Bagūlīyā is not home, then neither are the cows."
Yes, aren't home!
Now Sāḍū Mātā speaks.—*vāh vāh*—
Let's see what news she says.
By saying it, know it, by saying it, let's see
I'll tell you now, by Dev's command, let's see

—*gāv*—

Sāḍū Mātā's Body Is Infused with Sat

"By God's grace, I used to give you cups of milk.—*mhe*—
I used to give you platters filled with ghī
Hey, why didn't you die saving the cows, O my ungrateful Guāl!
On top of it you've come to show your face!"—*vāh vāh*—
Who said that news? Sāḍū Mātā said it
Yes, to the Guāl
The Guāl speaks. What news does he tell Aunt, let's see
The Guāl reflected to himself:—*mhe*—
"The latter news was spoken by Aunt
Now you tell the next one!"
Yes, why hold back anything now!

—*gāv*—

"Why are you talking about dying?—*mhe*—
Aunt, dying is in God's hands!
When Uncle fell in the battlefield—*mhe*—
Then did you become a satī together with Uncle Bhoj or not?
All the Gūjar women burned, but you didn't burn!"
Yes, you didn't burn that day, did you!
By God's grace, the Guāl said that news.—*vāh vāh*—
So, it took Sāḍū Mātā time to say it—*mhe*—
But no time for sat to enter her body.

—*gāv*—

Prepare logs of sandalwood!—*mhe*—
Hey, beat the great drums in Goṭhā, brother!
After eleven years sat has entered Sāḍū Mātā!—*mhe*—
Hey, brother, it entered Aunt because of Nephew's harsh words
On account of Nephew's harsh words, Aunt became ready to burn.—*vāh vāh*—

—*gāv*—

Brother, offer bread rolls and boiled wheat to Bhairū̃.—*vāh vāh*—
Present the Bagaṛāvats' Bhāṭ with a goat
Hey, after eleven years sat entered Sāḍū—*mhe*—
Hey, brother, a fearsome thing happened on earth!
The Guāl reflected to himself:—*mhe*—
"You won't be able to,
By God's grace, when Dev Mahārāj wakes up he'll reprimand me twice over!
'Look, you turned over Suremātā to the enemy!
And, by talking harsh words, the bearer of dharam, you burnt up!' *Burnt up*
But I won't be able to stop it.
Yes, now, there's no question of my stopping it
Let's go to the Bagaṛāvats' Bhāṭ.—*mhe*—
You certainly will be able to stop it."—*vāh vāh*—
How does he go to the Bagaṛāvats' Bhāṭ.—*vāh vāh*—
How does Bhāṭ Bābā bring down Sāḍū Mātā's sat, let's see.
By saying it, know it, let's see, by saying it

—*gāv*—

Padmo rode on the tawny horse.—*mhe*—
Rāj Nirpāl also rode
Arise, O Bagaṛāvats' Bhāṭ—bring down Sāḍū Mātā's sat!
Dusting his waist garment, Bhāṭ Baṅgāl got up
"O Mother, without strength there's no rope, without string no bow
No pride without brothers.—*mhe*—
No family without sons
Without the roll of thunder, O Mother, the peacocks' Malhār melody seems
insipid
Without a husband, a bride's ornaments appear listless
Without ghī, O Mother, all edibles from wheat are tasteless
Both aunt and nephew have lost the opportunity.—*mhe*—
Now give up your lives,
It would have been good had the Guāl died protecting the cows
And if you had become a satī after Bhoj died—*vāh vāh*—
That would have been good
Now even if you burn it won't be called satī, or jāvar.
Yes, it won't be called jāvar
The cows were released after the Bagaṛāvats died.—*mhe*—
They wandered all over the country of Malwa with those cows

Rāvjī's generals came and captured those cows
Afterward their wives—*mhe*—
All committed jāvar and burnt themselves up. *"Burnt up," said sir.*
Guāl, bring the vessel that Dev Mahārāj uses for a bath, and sprinkle some water with it."—*vāh vāh*—
The Guāl brought the vessel that Dev Mahārāj used for a bath, and sprinkled Sāḍū with it
So, Sāḍū Mātā's sat came down. *Said sir.*
The Bagaṛāvats' Bhāṭ brought down Sāḍū's sat. And, by God's grace, the Guāl came to Goṭhā̃.
Speak: Victory, brother, victory to Śrī Devnārāyaṇ
Speak, brother, both small and great, everyone!

Queen Pīpalde Confronts Kālū Mīr and Dīyājī

When the Guāl came he fell asleep in the net of slumber.[132]—*vāh vāh*—
And Dev Mahārāj didn't awake.—*mhe*—
After Rāvjī's general had herded the cows into Rātākoṭ, he spoke to Rāvjī Sāī: "Śrī Mahārāj—*mhe*—
I've brought the cows!"—*vāh vāh*—
Clever Mīr said: "A clever thought has come into my mind. Do what I say!"—*vāh vāh*—
"Mīr, brother, what should we do?" *What's to be done?*
Mīr said: "When Dīyā and I rode to attack we captured the cows and the cowherds
Now we'll launch a second attack
So, in broad daylight, we'll plunder Daṛāvaṭ
And we'll cut off the heads of Devjī and Medūjī."—*vāh vāh*—
Rāvjī said: "Great, hey, Mīr, great, hey, Mīr, all hope is on you!"
So, gathering a second force, they arrived at Goṭhā.—*vāh vāh*—
They arrived in Goṭhā, but in Goṭhā nothing moved.
Yes, no sound!
Bhagavān Indra's spell was over them—all the people in the village were fast asleep.—*vāh vāh*—
So, by God's grace, Mīr said: "Hey, friend, Dīyā—*vāh vāh*—
You know when we beat the victory drums,—*mhe*—
It was then that life departed from the people.—*vāh vāh*—*They all died*
He fell down here.—*mhe*—
There is no general like Bhūṇā. And now there won't be one either!
Yes, there won't be!
If he died, then it happened here. Look, he fell here."—*vāh vāh*—
Dīyājī said: "Hey, Mīr!—*mhe*—
Don't talk about graves all day long!
Yes, don't keep repeating tomb, tomb all day long
Amongst us Hindus there's no grave, brother."—*vāh vāh*—

Mīr said: "So, Dīyā, let's return the way we came!"
Yes, should we turn back
Mīr said: "Do one more thing I suggest.—*mhe*—
What's that? There's Devjī's fort.—*vāh vāh*—
Place a mark on it!"
Yes, strike it with your spear
So, Dīyājī was an avatār of Kās.—*vāh vāh*—
And he struck the fort with arrows and spears.—*vāh vāh*—
Dev Mahārāj's fort was turned to pebbles
Queen Pīpalde came out onto the balcony.—*mhe*—
"By God's grace, the enemy has delivered a mighty blow with his spear, brother," she said.—*vāh vāh*—
Dev's wife speaks. What news does she tell Dīyā, let's see.
By saying it, know it, let's see, by saying it
I'll say it now, by Bhagavān's grace, here you are!

—*gāv*—

"Hey, Dīyā, don't strike the palace with your spear.—*mhe*—
Hey, the foundations of the palace are shaking
It'll be difficult for you to return to the quarters of Fort Sāvar—*vāh vāh*—
If Bhoj's Bhīm awakes in Goṭhā
Mahārāj Bhīm is going to awake now!
Yes, he's awakened! There'll be trouble!" Mīr said: "Tobā, tobā, tobā, tobā, tobā, tobā! Look, a woman spoke from this palace!—*vāh vāh*—
Give it another!"
Yes, give it another blow so that they know!
Dīyā was an avatār of Kās. With his spear
Yes, he struck the fort once again
The stones of Dev Mahārāj's fort began to shake again.—*vāh vāh*—

—*gāv*—

"Don't strike the palace with spears, brother!—*mhe*—
Hey, the palace is shaking
It'll be difficult for you to return to Fort Sāvar's quarters—*mhe*—
If the young Ṭhākur Dev awakes in Goṭhā
If that Dev Mahārāj wakes up—*mhe*—
Then you runaways won't find the road, brothers!"
Yes, you won't get to the road!
Mīr said: "Tobā, tobā, tobā, tobā, tobā, this woman's got a lot of spunk!"—*mhe*—
Queen Pīpalde reflected to herself:
"Seven and a half times twenty Dīyā Sardārs work in Rāv's court
But this one has struck your fort with spears.—*mhe*—
Who knows which Dīyā this one is?" *Let's find out which one he is!*
Dev's queen speaks.—*mhe*—
What does she tell Dīyā, let's see. *By saying it know it, let's see, by saying it*

—gāv—

"Which Dīyā has a black saddle for his camel?
Hey, which Dīyā is called Jodhkā's son?*—mhe—*
He on whose strength does the great Fort Rāṇ depend
Which Dīyā is the one Rāvjī Sāī is afraid of?"
Yes, which one amongst you is he, brother?
Mīr said:"Tobā, tobā, look a woman in the palace knows your name!"*—mhe—*
—Dīyā is strong all right!
Dīyā became very strong.*—vāh vāh—*
Dīyā was filled with pride.*—mhe—*
By God's grace, there was an elephant in Rāv's army.*—mhe—*
He lifted it up from beneath on the palm of his hand.
Yes, he whirled it around with the palm of his hand
Dīyājī speaks. What news does he tell Queen Pīpalde. *By saying it, know it, let's see, by saying it*
I'll say it now, by Dev's grace, here you are!

—gāv—

"My camel wears a black saddle
I am called Jodhkā's son.*—vāh vāh—*
Its on me that the great Fort Rāṇ depends
The Dīyā who Rāvjī Sāī is afraid off am I. *"I am he," he said, "I am great!"*
I am always mighty—what's so surprising about that?" Queen Pīpalde thought to herself:*—mhe—*
"Hey, Dīyā did you have to come to Daṛāvaṭ?
I'll break his pride into sixty pieces!"
Yes, I'll break it

—gāv—

"All this time, Dīyā, I considered you to be a wise man.*—mhe—*
Hey, but today you've turned out to be a big fool!
He'll break your teeth and put you back into the carriage.*—mhe—*
Hey, why did you come to the village chasing that lord!
Don't you know whose fort it is?*—vāh vāh—*
The lord broke all your four teeth.*—mhe—*
And, by God's grace, he took back the horse Bāvalī.*—vāh vāh—*
It's his village."
Yes, it's his village
Mīr said: "Friend, Dīyā, that woman in the palace has ripped up your pride
Yes, into sixty pieces!"

—gāv—

"All these days I considered you to be a great wise man.*—mhe—*
Hey, you turned out to be a great fool
Prince Uttam Rāī was killed at the pass of Sā̃khlī.*—mhe—*
In which village did you place your courage on that day?

Did you put your courage onto the village of Goṭhā that day?
Yes, tell me that
He killed Prince Uttam Rāī—*mhe*—
Bhagavān freed the horse Bāvlī."—*vāh vāh*—
Mīr spoke: "Tobā, tobā, tobā, tobā, tobā!
Yes, have you forgotten that?
The day Uttam Rāī's bride wore white."—*vāh vāh*—
Now Dīyājī speaks, let's see.—*mhe*—
What news does he tell Pīpalde. *By saying it, know it, let's see, by saying it*

—*gāv*—

"By God's grace, wake up your child husband now!—*mhe*—
Otherwise I'll come inside the palace and slay him
I've come to avenge Uttam Rāī and my ancestors.—*vāh vāh*—
O Queen, the earth will regain justice!
Do you understand why?—*vāh vāh*—
I've come because of this!
Yes, I've come for this reason!
To avenge my ancestors and to avenge Uttam Rāī."—*vāh vāh*—
Queen Pīpalde speaks. What news does she tell, let's see.
By saying it, know it, by saying it, let's see

—*gāv*—

"Don't call him a child, brother, Dīyā.—*mhe*—
Consider it your luck, that the 'child' is sleeping in the palace
It'll be difficult to get on the road to Fort Sāvar—*mhe*—
Hey, if Kālaknāthan Kān awakes in Goṭhā!
If Kānjī Mahārāj wakes up, then you runaways won't find the road!"
Mīr said: "Tobā, tobā, tobā, tobā, tobā, this woman's got the hidden assistance of a thousand or fifteen hundred Rajpūts!
Yes, she's talking very big."
By God's grace, Mīr said: "Dīyā!—*mhe*—
She's asked you everything about yourself
Why don't you ask, whose wife is she, and whose daughter is she, let's see!"
Yes, whose daughter is she? Ask this at least!

—*gāv*—

"Which king's daughter are you?—*mhe*—
Whose wife are you in Goṭhā?
Since when do you oppose me, O Queen—*mhe*—
Standing, by God's grace, inside your palace?
Who do you belong to?"
Yes, who do you belong to?
By God's grace, Queen Pīpalde spoke. What news does she tell, let's see.
By saying it, know it, by saying it, let's see

—*gāv*—

"I'm the daughter of the king of Dhār.—*mhe*—
In Goṭhā, I'm the wife of the house of Ūd Karaṇ
I'll oppose you, Dīyā, whenever—*mhe*—
Standing in my palace
I'm in my home.—*vāh vāh*—
You've come to my home, Dīyā. *You've come*
I'm at my place."
Yes, I am
Mīr said: "Dīyā, she's shattered your honor into sixty pieces!
Now, do what I say!"—*mhe*—
"What should I do?" Mīr said: "There are two elephants standing in the courtyard.—*vāh vāh*—
Have their chains removed.—*mhe*—
Sound the drums of victory, *and run for it!*
Then things will be all right!"—*vāh vāh*—
"Great, Mīr, great, have more chains cut!"—*mhe*—
So, there was one elephant given in Medū's dowry
One was given from the king of Dhār in Dev's dowry.—*vāh vāh*—
Kālū Mīr started on the elephants.—*mhe*—
Queen Pīpalde thought to herself: "Now, you won't be able to scare them
Take a look in the army, if there's a Sirdār who's an acquaintance,
He'll certainly be ashamed.—*vāh vāh*—
The elephants are sure to be left chained."
Yes, they'll remain certainly
She saw Dhyāvā's Karaṇ Siṅgjī Pũvār.—*vāh vāh*—
"Hey, Uncle Karaṇ Siṇjī's there, isn't he, where's the fear?"
Yes, what's there to fear?
Karaṇ Siṅgjı reflected to himself: "The king of Dhār's daughter is here!—*mhe*—
If she recognizes me, she'll give me a big reprimand."
He got off his horse—*mhe*—
And began wrapping his dhotī around his head.—*vāh vāh*—
In case Bāī recognizes him.
Yes, in case she recognizes him
Queen Pīpalde speaks. What news does she tell Karaṇ Siṅgjī, let's see.
By saying it, know it, let's see, by saying it

—*gāv*—

"By God's grace, don't wrap the dhotī around your head!—*mhe*—
Uncle Karaṇ Siṅgjī, don't become a stranger from being a friend
Place my elephants in safety.—*mhe*—
I'll praise you greatly to the king of Dhār
When I go to Dhār—*mhe*—
That day I'll increase your stature greatly."

By God's grace, that news was said by Queen Pīpalde.
Yes, she said it, said sir.
Dhyāvā's Karaṇ Siṅgjī spoke.—*mhe*—
What answer does he give to Bāī, let's see.
By saying it, know it, let's see, by saying it

—*gāv*—

"Today fire has flared up on water!—*mhe*—
It won't be put out by a bucket of water
Either Bāḷā Dev can put it out—*vāh vāh*—
Or another warrior or friend
Nor can I put out the fire."
Pīpalde said: "Don't worry uncle, go ahead." *Go on*
So, by God's grace, what did Mīr do?—*mhe*—
He went inside the doorway—*vāh vāh*—
And cut off both the elephants' chains, *sir said*
How does Queen Pīpalde go to Mother-in-law's mansion
What does she tell Mother-in-law upon arriving, let's see.
By saying it, know it, by saying it, let's see

—*gav*—

"The brave elephant's chains have been cut, O Mother-in-law.—*mhe*—
Afterward they say my horse was lost
There's no one left to save the elephants, O Mother-in-law.—*mhe*—
There's no father-in-law Savāī Bhoj at home
If Savāī Bhoj had been there—*mhe*—
Then on no account would have the elephants' chains been cut!
Yes, the chains wouldn't have been cut at all!
But, no, he who's suckled your milk has gone to sleep, he won't wake up now!"
Yes, he won't wake up!
Pīpalde speaks. What does she tell Sāḍū, let's see.
By saying it, know it, by saying it, let's see

—*gāv*—

"By God's grace, O Mother-in-law, at night the rain peacocks sing
Look, this uncouth Rāv has taken a liking—*mhe*—
That he has paid us two visits to my Goṭhā
The first time he came and captured my cows
Now for the second time he's come—*mhe*—
And my elephants' chains
Yes, he's cut away and taken the elephants along
But, brother, he's taken a liking!—*vāh vāh*—
By God's grace, if it's not affection, then what power sent him on two visits?"

Yes, he's made two visits
Mīr said: "Dīyā!—*mhe*—
Beat the victory drums!"—*vāh vāh*—
By God's grace, after they had cut away the elephants' chains—*mhe*—
They went out.—*vāh vāh*—
So, by God's grace, amongst them was Gā̃go Bhāṭ—*mhe*—
In that army of Rāvjī's.—*vāh vāh*—
Gā̃go Bhāṭ speaks. What news does he tell, let's see.
By saying it, know it, by saying it, let's see
Mīr said: "Hey, friend, Dīyā, Gā̃glo Bhāṭ used to praise Dev every day.—*mhe*—
Where's his Dev gone today?" *Where's he gone today?*

—*gāv*—

Sāḍū Mātā and Queen Pīpalde Awaken Devnārāyaṇ

So, by God's grace, now when that Bhā̃bhī brought back the elephants to the Bagaṛāvats' Daṛāvaṭ—*mhe*—
He said: "O Mother—*vāh vāh*—
Why did you do this?
Yes, why did you do this?
Daṛāvaṭ City was plundered in broad daylight, but Dev didn't undertake anything."
Yes, where did Dev go off to?
Sāḍū Mātā said: "Hey, brother, Dev went to sleep, and didn't wake up because of that." *Didn't wake up!*
Bāḷā Bhā̃bhī said: "Didn't you wake up Dev?"
Yes, didn't you wake him up?
Sāḍū Mātā said: "Hey, brother, I shouted out lots, *but he didn't awaken!*
Bāḷo Bhā̃bhī said:
"Listen, O Mother—*mhe*—
Human beings wake up if they are shouted at. *This Ṭhākur Dev is a Kalādhārī!*
He's not a being that will wake up through shouts.
Yes, he isn't
Don't you remember how to wake up Dev?"
Yes, have you forgotten?
Sāḍū Mātā said: "Son, when Bhagavān would fall asleep in Malwa—*mhe*—
I would wake him up.—*vāh vāh*—
After coming here that Nāpā and the Bhāṭ have been a nuisance to me.
Yes, I've forgotten how to wake up Dev Mahārāj
Hey, Son, because of worries I forgot how to wake him up."—*vāh vāh*—
"Well, O Mother, I'll tell you now:—*mhe*—
Put incense on the four posts of the bed on which the Lord is sleeping.—*mhe*—
And place one incense stick in Queen Pīpalde's hand
Burn camphor incense for Dev.—*mhe*—

With the fragrance of camphor, Bhagavān will wake up on his own." *He'll wake up right now!*
So, how do they worship him in the way Bāḷo Bhābhī told them to.—*mhe*—
How do they wake up Bhagavān Dev, let's see, now.
By saying it, know it, let's see, by saying it
I'll say it now, by Dev's grace, here you are.

—*gāv*—

The queen walked in the courtyard.—*mhe*—
Bhagavān heard the elephants' trumpeting first.—*mhe*—
"Wake up now!—*vāh vāh*—
Wash your face and rinse your mouth. Drink Suremātā's sweet milk
The milk you drink every day, drink it today!"
Yes, you drink it today!
Dev awoke and asked for water
Dev's Queen Pīpalde brought a jug.
A small jug made of gold.—*mhe*—
Dev's Queen Pīpalde waited on him.
On waking up, Dev Mahārāj twirled his moustache
He put flames on the tents in faraway Sikarāṇī.
Waking up, Dev Mahārāj cast his poison gaze!
Kālū Mīr's tent, which had been put up seven Kos away—*mhe*—
It was finished off instantly.—*vāh vāh*—
Mīr said: "Dīyā, what's happened to your tent?"
Yes, look what's happened to your tent
Dīyā said: "What's happened? Yours is burning and mine is burning!" *Mine too is burning*
Mīr said: "That means Devjī's woken up.
Yes, he's woken up, he's going to come now!
Let's go!"
Yes, let's run fast!
In the rush—what's that called—the horse's rear
The front and the rear, in the rush some Sirdārs fell down, some *didn't fall down*
They remained standing.—*vāh vāh*—
They caught hold of the horses.—*mhe*—
By God's grace, Bāḷo Bhābhī smashed up many of them
The dogs that were left behind, their faces were smashed up
Saddles would be empty. *Would be empty*
By God's grace, with five horses saved—*mhe*—
Dīyā and Kālū Mīr were defeated. And they went and sat on the losers' platform.
Yes, they went and sat there
Rāvjī said: "They've brought Devjī's head—I've seen how!" *You've brought Dev's and Medu's heads—I can see what you've brought now!*

Dīyā was defeated. Dev, the lord of the three worlds, Bhagavān, woke up. Speak: victory to Śrī Devnārāyaṇ, victory!

❁ Devnārāyaṇ Prepares to Attack Rātākoṭ ❁

Dev Mahārāj woke up.—*mhe*—
The village's inhabitants woke up.
Yes, "All of them woke up," said sir.
So these brothers, Medūjī, Madan Siṅgjī, Bhūṇājī, also woke up.—*vāh vāh*—
They didn't see the cows.—*mhe*—
They said: "Mother, the cows?"—*mhe*—
Sāḍū Mātā said: "Son, it's been three days since the cows have gone."
Yes, they've been locked up in Rātākoṭ
So, who rode out first for the cows?—*mhe*—
Savāī Bhoj's Medūjī departed.—*vāh vāh*—
By God's grace, Madan Siṅgjī rode out
Both brothers went off.—*mhe*—
At a distance of three kos further up there was a pond that had been dug by Bāghjī.—*vāh vāh*—
They set up camp at that place.—*mhe*—
"We won't go any further, brother, till all the brothers have assembled together here, then we'll go. *We'll go then, when they follow*
Let them follow."—*vāh vāh*—
So, by God's grace, what does the lord of the three worlds tell Pālā Kumahār.—*mhe*—
How is the Horse Līlā saddled up, let's see.
By saying it, know it, let's see, by saying it

—*gāv*—

Sāḍū Mātā Tries Holding Back Devnārāyaṇ

"Hey, Bhairavnāth, today my drinking bowl will certainly be filled!"
Yes, it'll be filled
Bhairavnāth said: "Now fill it up to complete satisfaction.—*vāh vāh*—
The Bagaṛāvats' son is going out to avenge the Bagaṛāvats.—*mhe*—
Be satisfied until intoxication sets in."—*vāh vāh*—
Sixty-four Jogīnīs, seventy-eight Khetarpāl.—*mhe*—
The Jogīnīs left at once to drink blood.—*vāh vāh*—
"We'll drink as much as we want there, brother!"
Yes, we'll drink today!
By God's grace, Bhagavān had summoned for the horse's saddle outside,

Hadn't he?—*mhe*—
Dev Mahārāj sat on Līlā.—*vāh vāh*—
Mother came and the horse's reins
Yes, she caught hold of
Mother Khaṭāṇī speaks.—*mhe*—
What news does she tell Bhagavān, let's see.
By saying it, know it, let's see, by saying it

—*gāv*—

Sāḍūjī stands there holding the horse's reins.—*mhe*—
"Son, if the cows have gone, let them go!—*vāh vāh*—
I'll buy some others
If you die in the battle of Rātākoṭ—*mhe*—
Then how will Mother Khaṭāṇī have her Ūd back?
Son, cows can be bought.
Yes, we could buy many
The kind of thing you are, son, hey, cannot be bought.
Yes, cannot
Let the cows go!" *Let them go!*
Dev Mahārāj said: "Mājī Sāī!—*mhe*—
Let go of the reins."—*vāh vāh*—
Mājī Sāī holds on to the reins tightly.—*mhe*—
Dev, the lord of the three worlds, speaks.—*mhe*—
What news does he tell Mājī Sāī.
By saying it, know it, let's see, by saying it

—*gāv*—

"By God's grace, let go of Līlā's reins.—*mhe*—
O Mother, Līlā is stamping his feet
Medū and Madno, brother, will be killed in the battle of Rātākoṭ.—*mhe*—
By God's grace, the battle will be won by Rāṇā, the Rāv of this fort
Will win the fight!—*mhe*—
And my brothers will be killed.—*vāh vāh*—
Let go of Līlā's reins!"
Yes, let go
Sāḍū Mātā holds on tight.—*mhe*—

—*gāv*—

By God's grace, Dev Mahārāj spoke the news:—*mhe*—
"Let go of Līlā's reins, O Mother.—*vāh vāh*—
Līlā will now cut the reins
Mother, the cows are captured in Rātākoṭ.—*mhe*—
The enemy Rāvjī will distribute them off to his eighty-four forts
Now they are at one place.—*mhe*—
And what if Rāvjī Sāī apportions them off?
Yes, when will I fight the eighty-four forts and when will I collect the cows together?

I don't have so much time!—*vāh vāh*—
Let go!"—*mhe*—
Sāḍū Mātā holds on tight.—*vāh vāh*—

—*gāv*—

"Let go of Līlā's reins.—*mhe*—
Līlā is stamping his hooves
Medū and Madno will be killed in Rātākoṭ's battle.—*mhe*—
Those brothers are my forehead's necklace of pearls
Mother, the enemy will cut down my necklace.—*vāh vāh*—
And I have a promise of three days with Suremātā.—*mhe*—
Let go, Mother!" *Let me go!*
Sāḍū Mātā said: "Son, hey, I won't let you go.
Yes, the brothers, let them go
They've gone ahead.—*mhe*—
Why should I let you go?"—*vāh vāh*—
Dev Mahārāj said: "Look, Mother, I'm not responsible if the horse rips away the reins!"—*mhe*—

—*gāv*—

"Son, I restrained the Bagaṛāvats a great deal!
Yes, I admonished them too
I made them swear on King Ajaypāl's name
But the goddess Kaṅkālī brought the horses of the sons of Bāgh—*mhe*—
And played them off to Durjan Sāl's Rāṇ!
Hey, I held back the Bagaṛāvats.
Yes, but they too were obstinate like you!
Because the Bagaṛāvats went even though I restrained them—*mhe*—
This is the result."
Dev Mahārāj reflected to himself:—*mhe*—
"Mother has always been quarrelsome.
Yes, she's quarrelsome
What mother's saying won't be done, she won't keep peace.
If I take Mother's blessings, then it'll be a good thing."

—*gāv*—

"I'll peel off the enemy Rāv's hide.—*mhe*—
With a knife I'll rip it off
Slain by Rāv, the sons of Bāgh died.—*mhe*—
Those men were something else!
By God's grace, the men killed by Rāvjī were something else!"
Yes, they were different, O Mother
Sāḍū Mātā said: "It isn't what you think, son! Whatever happens, brother—*mhe*—
I won't let you go!" *I won't let you go!*
The lord of the three worlds reflected to himself:—*mhe*—

"Hey, without Mother's blessing I won't leave!"
Yes, I'll leave only with her permission
So, by God's grace, Bhagavān was sitting on the horse Līlā.—*mhe*—
He threw down Līlā's whip
The Lord began looking this way and that
By God's grace, Sāḍū Mātā said:
"Hey, son!" *What are you looking for?*
Dev Mahārāj said: "O Mother, see the horse's whip has fallen down."
Yes, the whip slipped from my hand and fell down. If some Sirdār would come by and hand me the whip
Sāḍū Mātā said: "Son, I'm here, aren't I?"
Yes, I'll hand it to you
Dev Mahārāj said: "No, no, no!"—*mhe*—
He said: "Mother, I suckled milk from your body.—*mhe*—
I won't let you do any work with this body."
Yes, it's not my dharam to have you work
Sāḍū Mātā said: "Son, I won't let go."—*mhe*—
So, with one hand Mother took hold of the horse's reins firmly.—*mhe*—
In order to pick up the whip with other hand, she bent down
In the meantime *the reins slipped out of her hand*
Dev shouted out.—*mhe*—
With the sound of the shout there were a hundred Devs and a hundred Līlās.—*vāh vāh*—
When Mother lunged for the whip, the rein slipped out of her hand
This one said, "O Mother, give me the whip." That one said, "O Mother, give me the whip
Keep your Devjī now!
Yes, I don't need him. I'll go anyway
The other Devjīs will go to Rātākoṭ. Hold onto your Devjī, and take him back!" *Take him back*
Mother reflected to herself: "One hundred horses, and one hundred riders.
One doesn't know which is your Devjī amongst these.
Yes, which one is he, which one should I catch hold off?
If you catch hold of this one, he'll say I'm not your Devjī.
Yes
The matter won't come under control now!"—*mhe*—
She said: "Son, I've understood your miraculous power now.
Yes, I've understood now
What power does Rāvjī have, that he'll kill you?
I'll give you the whip only if—*mhe*—
The very same horse and the very same rider appears again. *Then I'll give it to you*
I won't give you the whip otherwise!" *Won't give!*
So, the Lord said: "O Mother, turn around!"—*mhe*—
In the time Mother took to look the other way, Dev Mahārāj stood there sitting on his horse alone.—*vāh vāh*—

"Give it to me, Mother!" *Give it to me*
So, how did Bhagavān have the whip delivered back from Mother.—*mhe*—
How, by God's grace, does she give permission for going to Rātākoṭ, let's see.
By saying it, know it, by saying it, let's see

— *gāv*—

"If you go now, then go straight, son.—*mhe*—
Go on the path to Rātākoṭ
Slay Rāvjī with your own hands.—*mhe*—
But don't ruin the Bagaṛāvats' old revenge
It's become old.—*mhe*—
Let it not happen, that you renew it again!"
Yes, make it new and return!
How does she give a word of care, let's see.
By saying it, know it, by saying it, let's see

—*gāv*—

"By God's grace, don't kill those Sardārs who are in service.—*mhe*—
They're doing their service out of necessity
Son, slay Rāv Paḍīhār with your hands!—*mhe*—
If not, then slay Rāv's younger brother, Nīmde. Slay Nīmde in case Rāvjī gets away.—*vāh vāh*—
We understand—*mhe*—
That if the younger ones are revenged, then the elder ones too
Yes, will be revenged
There were seventy children of the Bagaṛāvats that Nīmde—*vāh vāh*—
Dashed on a rock and killed.—*mhe*—
We think, brother that the young ones' revenge
Yes, will be taken."
Dev Mahārāj said: "O Mother who is Bījā Mehtā.
Yes, which one is he?
It's not that one who Brother Bhāṇgī brought tied to the horse's leg, is it? *Is it him?*
Sāḍū Māta said: "Exactly that one." *Its him*
Dev Mahārāj said: "I know him!" *"I know him," he said, "I won't kill him."*
"Well then, son, fare well!" *Go!*
Mother gave Dev Mahārāj permission to go.—*mhe*—
—*vāh vāh*—
She came up to the Pāras Pīplī.—*mhe*—
What news does she tell Pāras Pīplī, let's see. *By saying it, know it, let's see, by saying it*
I'll say it now, by Dev's command, let's see.

—*gāv*—

"O Pāras Pīplī in front of Goṭhā.—*mhe*—
Pīplī bring back Bāḷā Dev alive.

Yes, bring him back alive
Bring Dev back alive—*vāh vāh*—
Pīplī, who's to do right or wrong to whom?"—*mhe*—
She said: "Brother, Pāras Pīplī in front of Goṭhā—*mhe*—
Don't let there be a delay in the Rajpūts' spears
Pīplī, the Cauhāns' spears should strike the Paḍihārs—*mhe*—
The way rain pours—*mhe*—
That way Rāvjī, the enemy, should be struck with spears.—*vāh vāh*—

—*gāv*—

"Pīplī in front of Daṛāvaṭ—*mhe*—
With saffron and vermilion your leaves I'll adorn
Pīplī, bring back Bāḷak Dev alive!—*mhe*—
By God's grace, my young Ūdal has forgotten about his life
This Rāṇ City—*mhe*—
Has always been an unmarried woman
Bhagavān's going there today, *It'll be married*
By God's grace, Pīplī, who should do good or wrong to someone."—*mhe*—
So, by God's grace, Sāḍū Mātā talked to Pīplī.—*mhe*—
How did she give Dev permission to depart
Speak: Victory to Śrī Devnārāyaṇ Bhagavān, victory
Speak, brother, small and great, everyone!

Devnārāyaṇ Leaves with His Brothers

So, by God's grace, after giving Dev permission to leave, Sāḍū Mātā—*mhe*—
And, returned back, *said sir*
So, Bhūṇājī was calling singers and musicians—*mhe*—
And was distributing coins.—*vāh vāh*—
Sāḍū Mātā thought to herself: "Hey, an outrageous thing has happened!—*mhe*—
Bhūṇājī doesn't appear to have joined up with the brothers
He didn't go!"
Yes, he didn't go. He's still on Rāvjī's side!
Sāḍū Mātā speaks. What does she tell Prince Bhūṇā, let's see.
By saying it, know it, by saying it

—*gāv*—

"Son, Bhūṇā, very good of you to have songs sung.—*mhe*—
Good to have drums beaten
Hey, your kid brother has gone to the battle of Rātā Koṭ.—*mhe*—
He paid heed to Mother's words
The one who is child amongst you has gone into battle, and you are still sitting here."
Yes, still sitting here
Who said that news? Sāḍū Mātā said it.—*vāh vāh*—

Queen Pīpalde speaks. What news does she tell Bhūṇājī, let's see.
By saying it, know it, by saying it

—*gāv*—

"You shut the door very firmly—*mhe*—
O Brother-in-law, but you kept the window open
You didn't join the brothers.—*mhe*—
You kept the Paḍihār's honor
I've realized now that you are not with the brothers.—*mhe*—
By God's grace, you've eaten 'salt and water' at Rāvjī's.—*mhe*—
You keep to Rāvjī's side!"
By God's grace, Rāṇī Pīpalde said this news
Bhūṇājī speaks. What news does he tell Pīpalde, let's see.
By saying it, know it, by saying it
I'll say it now, by Dev's grace, here you are

—*gāv*—

"Pīpalde spoke nonsense, brother.—*mhe*—
Her eyes are untrustworthy, painted with lamp-black
O Mother, send Pīpalde back to her parental home.—*mhe*—
Bhūṇājī says he'll take her life!
If I do anything it'll be this—that she talks so much!"—*mhe*—
By God's grace, that news was spoken by Prince Bhūṇājī.
Pīpalde said:
"O Brother-in-law, since when did you learn how to break and kill?—*mhe*—
Didn't you feel shame saying this?
When Rāvjī killed Bhoj in the heroic field of the Rāṭhors—*mhe*—
Why didn't you take up arms?
You're prepared to kill me, why didn't you kill the enemy on that day?"—*vāh vāh*—
Bhūṇājī reflected to himself:—*mhe*—
"It seems the women have been let down."
Yes, they've been let down

—*gāv*—

"Listen now, maternal and paternal aunts!—*mhe*—
Listen, Aunt of the royal dynasty of Māṇḍal
You don't know about good and evil.—*mhe*—
By the time you know about good and evil, Bhūṇājī will have gone to Rātākoṭ
I'll go to Rātākoṭ.—*mhe*—
Then you'll *know about good and evil there*
By God's grace, I thought, O Mother—*mhe*—
That without giving away a lakh I won't clean my teeth in the morning.
Yes, I won't clean my teeth

It'll take two or three days in the battle
If I don't bring them all together in two, three days at this place
Yes, then I won't be blamed
It's because of them that I'm giving away offerings."—*vāh vāh*—
Prince Bhūṇājī took his army of eighteen thousand—*vāh vāh*—
And joined up with the brothers
By God's grace, Mother reached the Silver Square.—*mhe*—

So, now there was Nevājī's prince, Bhāṅgījī—vāh vāh—
He stayed behind asleep in the Silver Square.
Yes, he remained sleeping
Sāḍū Mātā thought to herself: "Hey, I bade all the brothers farewell—*mhe*—
But the one who is going to free the cows has stayed back here!
Yes, he's stayed back here sleeping
Because it was what his mother had said—*mhe*—
She held onto his leg and woke him up
Bhāṅgījī sat up and looked this way and that:
"O Mother—*mhe*—
I don't see your Devjī, and I don't see my brothers."
Yes, what's the matter?
Sāḍū Mātā said: "Son, don't you know?
Yes, they've gone to Rātākoṭ to free the cows
The enemy's captured the cows."—*vāh vāh*—
Bhāṅgījī said: "Mājī Sāī!—*mhe*—
There are no friends like brothers, and no enemies like brothers!
Wouldn't I have taken my father's revenge?
Yes, wouldn't I have taken revenge
They didn't wake me up—left me behind!—*mhe*—
What a thing they did, brother!"—*vāh vāh*—
Sāḍū Mātā said: "Son, at the moment the brothers have joined together at a distance of three kos—you go ahead too."
Yes, you go ahead
Bhāṅgījī said: "Mājī Sāī, all the brothers have horses.—*vāh vāh*—
I don't have a horse. How should I go? Should I go on foot?"
Yes, won't it seem stupid if I go on foot?
Mājī Sāī said: "Son, why should you go on foot? My mare Kāḷvī is here."
Here she is. Climb onto her.
Bhāṅgījī said: "Fine!"
Yes, now it's all right, Mother
Prince Bhāṅgījī went over to the mare.—*mhe*—
Mother had gone and said it.—*vāh vāh*—
To herself she thought: "Hey, a wrong thing has happened!—*mhe*—
That's Bhāṅgī!
Yes, he might go and leave the mare somewhere on the way!
He'll go and lose the mare!"—*vāh vāh*—

Mother speaks. What news does she tell Bhāṅgī, let's see.
By saying it, know it, by saying it, let's see
I'll say it now, by Dev's grace, let's see.—*vāh vāh—jī vāh vāh—*

—*gāv*—

"Son, this mare is the source of nourishment for that foal
Prince Bhāṅgī, my mare is giving birth to another foal
Devjī's horse drank milk from it.
Yes, it drank her milk
And, son, there's now another one exactly the same in her womb. *Another one*
It shouldn't happen that you go and lose the horse somewhere."
Bhāṅgījī said: "Mother, I won't sell it!
Yes, I won't sell it—only if my bhāṅg is all used up.
I'll go and pay money and free your mare.—*vāh vāh*—
If my bhāṅg is used up, then I'll leave the mare, whatever else happens, O Mother!"
Yes, whatever happens
Sāḍū Mātā said: "Hey, son, why should the money get used up? I have a lot of gold coins belonging to the Bagaṛāvats.
Yes, take plenty of them with you
Here, take the keys.—The safe is full of gold coins."—*mhe*—
By God's grace, Bhāṅgījī took the keys and went to the storeroom.—*vāh vāh*—
He tied up four bundles of gold coins
And placed them on the servants' heads
They went to the marketplace
When Bhāṅgījī's gold coins were spent in the marketplace—*mhe*—
That time three hundred bundles of bhāṅg were acquired.
Yes, the oxen brought it
In those days there were no motor cars.—*vāh vāh*—
Banjārās would bring things with oxen carts.—*mhe*—
Inspectors said: "Brothers, what's in the oxen carts?" *What's there, brother*
They said: "Śrī Mahārāj, it's bhāṅg." *Its bhāṅg*
He told the tradesmen: "Tradesmen, businessmen!—*mhe*—
I don't know how to add up and subtract
Do the calculations for me!—*mhe*—
Rāṇ City is twenty-four kos from here.
Yes, it's twenty-four kos
I'll pay up the hiring charges all together."
Yes, add up the charges to it
So, he paid the hiring charges for twenty-four kos, and after calculating three hundred bundles—*mhe*—
Paid the price.
Yes, here take this, brothers
The remaining dues he sent back to the storeroom.—*mhe*—
He came up to the oxen cart owners and said: "Alright, brothers, let's go!
Let's go!

The avatār has gone ahead of me.—*mhe*—
If you spot his tent,
Hey, brother, stop before it, don't move ahead of it.
Yes, don't move ahead. You'll finish off the bhāṅg's effect
If we go ahead of the avatār then I won't get intoxicated."
Yes, I won't get intoxicated

So, by God's grace, Bhāṅgījī consumed one and a quarter maṇ of bhāṅg—*mhe*—
And said: "Mājī Sāī—*vāh vāh*—
Now I won't leave your mare somewhere just like that
Yes, I won't leave it
Don't be afraid!—*vāh vāh*—
I won't ride—I don't like riding that much."
By God's grace, Bhāṅgījī released the mare Kāḷvī.—*mhe*—
And, Mother thought: "Then he won't climb onto the mare!"
Yes, he's going to lead it along
Bhāṅgījī reflected to himself: "The old woman's feelings are hurt."
Yes, the old woman's feelings are hurt
As Mājī Sāī was looking on—*mhe*—
Suddenly he climbed onto the standing horse.
Yes, he sat on it
By God's grace, he reflected to himself: "All the brothers have weapons.—*mhe*—
And I don't have a weapon."
Yes, no weapon at all
An oil-presser was turning a mill.—*mhe*—
He thought to himself: "Hey, by God's grace, I'll fight with this stick.—*mhe*—
And it'll be useful for both—I'll grind bhāṅg too!" *And put it on as a helmet too*
He gave the oil-presser a slap, the oil-presser fell down. He untied the oxen and circled them at some distance.—*mhe*—
With a twist—*vāh vāh*—
And he put the stick onto the oil-mill.—*mhe*—
—*vāh vāh*—
"Neither steel can hurt nor can wood
Yes, hurt
It's a superb thing!—*mhe*—
With this I'll grind my bhāṅg, *and with this*
I'll drink it! *Drink it!*
I didn't have any weapons, now I have weapons with me."—*vāh vāh*—
Bhāṇgījī was riding Kāḷvī.—*mhe*—
Dev Mahārāj saw him coming.—*vāh vāh*—
He said: "Bābā Bhāṭ, which brother is coming now?"
Yes, which one is coming?
The Bhāṭ said: "After the Bagaṛāvats died I don't see too well."—*mhe*—
Dev Mahārāj said: "By God's grace, he's carrying a mortar and pestle—*mhe*—
And has the mare Kāḷvī to ride on."
Yes, the one belonging to Mother

The Bhāṭ said, Bābā Bhāṭ said: "Bhāṅgī's come, brother!—*mhe*—
And in front there are oxen."—*vāh vāh*—
Dev Mahārāj said: "Hey, Bābā Bhāṭ, an outrageous thing has happened!—*mhe*—
It's that brother who consumes one and a quarter maṇ of bhāṅg every day
When he goes into battle—*mhe*—
That time he consumes two and a half maṇ
Yes, he does
In such inebriation, he won't be conscious of his own or the other
He'll slay Rāvjī's generals. If he sees us he'll kill us first!
Give this brother permission to return—*vāh vāh*—
So that he can protect our own fort."—*vāh vāh*—
The Bhāṭ said: "I won't give him permission today."
Yes, if anyone is to give him permission today, then you give it to him Śrī Mahārāj
Dev speaks.—*vāh vāh*—
How does he send Brother Bhāṅgī back, let's see.
By saying it, know it, let's see, by saying it
I'll say it now, by Dev's grace, here you are.

—*gāv*—

"O Elder Brother, bhāṅg stirs one up to fight.—*mhe*—
Seeing a fight, opium gets one stirred
Dev says, Bhāṅgī go back now to Daṛāvaṭ
Daṛāvaṭ town is unprotected, brother.
Yes, you go there!
No brothers have stayed on there. All of them have come along."—*vāh vāh*—
Bhāṅgījī reflected to himself: "The idiot, first he left you behind.
Yes, now I'm the weakest of all that he's making use of you
On top of it, he's telling you to return!"—*vāh vāh*—
Bhāṅgījī speaks.—*mhe*—
What news does he tell, let's see.
By saying it, know it, by saying it

—*gāv*—

"Bhāṅg definitely stirs up a fight.—*mhe*—
Seeing a fight opium stirs one up
Bhavānī cut Bhoj while he was running away.—*mhe*—
My father wielded his sword for eighty three-hour periods in the Mahābhārat
after he had offered Śakti his head
My father fought for eighty three-hour periods after giving his head.—*mhe*—
Tell me how much did this father of yours fight?"
"How much did he?" he said, "he ran away, and then Bhavānī pursued him"
Dev Mahārāj said: "Hey, Bābā Bhāṭ—*mhe*—
This brother is a very brave warrior.—*vāh vāh*—
He won't go back. *He's not going to go!*
By God's grace, there was no trusting Madan Siṅgjī—you know Tejājī's son.—
mhe—

They say that Father Tejājī ran away, brother.
Yes, he ran away
What if Madan Siṅgjī runs away?
Yes, then it'll all be run away run away!
Send him back." *Send him away*
The Bhāṭ said: "Śrī Mahārāj, you send him back!" *I won't send him*
Dev speaks. What news does he tell Tejājī's son.
By saying it, know it, let's see, by saying it
I'll say it now, by Bhagavān's grace, here . . .—*vāh vāh*—

—*gāv*—

"Of men who run away, sons who run away are born.—*mhe*—Of warriors are born warriors
Hey, by God's grace, Dev says.—*mhe*—
Now, you son of Tejā, go back to Daṛāvaṭ
They say that Tejājī would run away.—*mhe*—
If you run away too, then I'll become the 'run away run away,' brother.
We'll become 'run away run away'
Madan Siṅg!
Yes, go back!
I'll get very angry!"—*vāh vāh*—
Hey, the brother thought:
Yes, he's giving me permission isn't it
"He thinks you're a weakling."—*mhe*—
So, he speaks. What news does he answer back to Dev, let's see.
By saying it, know it, by saying it
I'll say it now, sir, by Dev's grace.—*vāh vāh*—

—*gāv*—

"It's true that of men who run away, sons who run away are born.—*mhe*—
God, only from heroes are born heroes
Bhavānī cut down Bhoj while he was running away.—*mhe*—
My father engaged in fifty-two small fights and twelve great battles
He fought fifty-two small fights—*mhe*—
and twelve great battles.
Do you know who set up the burning place for satīs?—*vāh vāh*—
My father did that for the others.—*mhe*—
My father had no promise with Śakti—*vāh vāh*—
That's why he didn't offer his head.—*mhe*—
My father didn't fight any battles with the Bagaṛāvats.—*vāh vāh*—
Hey, they say Savāī Bhoj ran away, brother—*mhe*—
Fearing his head.—*vāh vāh*—
You're Savāī Bhoj's son,
Yes, you may run away!
You go back!—*vāh vāh*—
I'll free the cows, brother!"

Yes, free them
My lord, Dev Mahārāj, laughed aloud: "Bābā Bhāṭ, brother is great warrior.—*mhe*—
He won't go back. *Not going back*
Now, do this—there's Bhūṇājī who grew up with Rāvjī.—*mhe*—
Rāvjī brought him up.—*vāh vāh*—
Hey, who knows at this point he might be on our side, who knows he may side up with Rāvjī, who knows. *Who knows?*
Send this brother back!"—*vāh vāh*—
So, by God's grace, Dev speaks. What does he tell Bhūṇā, let's see.
By saying it, know it, Bhopājī Mahārāj, by saying it
By saying it, let's see, by saying it, I'll say it now, by Dev's grace.—*vāh vāh*—

—*gāv*—

"Hey, Bhūṇā, turbans of flowing silk suit you Rajpūts.—*vāh vāh*—
Shields of fifty-two flowers suit you
Lord Bhagavān asks you.—*mhe*—
Elder Brother Bhūṇā, go back now to Daṛāvaṭ
Elder Brother Bhūṇā—*mhe*—
Go to Daṛāvaṭ, it's unprotected."—*vāh vāh*—
Bhūṇājī reflected to himself: "The idiot! It seems brother takes you to be a weakling."—*mhe*—
Bhūṇājī speaks.—*vāh vāh*—
What news does he tell Dev, let's see. *By saying it, know it, let's see, by saying it*

—*gāv*—

"We Rajputs prefer turbans of flowing silk, brother.—*mhe*—
Shields of fifty-two flowers suit us
Hey, you're sending me back, kid brother.—*mhe*—
You go to Goṭhā
When I rode out, no one rode behind me.—*mhe*—
And when you rode out—*vāh vāh*—
your mother came running after you for a kos or two.
Yes, she came running after
You prepare to return quickly,
Yes, I'll go and free the cows, you go return!
So that I'll free the cows and take revenge too.—*vāh vāh*—
You go on back!"
Yes, prepare to return!
Dev Mahārāj laughed aloud: "Bābā Bhāṭ!—*mhe*—
Brother's a great warrior!—*vāh vāh*—
He won't go back!" The Bhāṭ said: "Śrī Mahārāj, what you said today—*mhe*—
If I had told him, he would have smashed me up!"
Yes, he would finish off my lineage right here!

Dev Mahārāj said: "Well then, Bābā Bhāṭ do the following, brother.—*mhe*—
Tell all the Sirdārs to lead their horses on foot.—*mhe*—
Place all their weapons in front of Goṭhā,
And speak victory to Devjī three times.
Yes, let them say victory to Dev, victory to Dev
I'll make their backs all invulnerable—*vāh vāh*—
Neither steel will hurt nor will wood,
Yes, hurt."
The Bhāṭ gave a shout.—*mhe*—
The whole army turned about.—*vāh vāh*—
He said: "Sirdārs, put your weapons down in front of Goṭhā, and lead your horses on foot.—*mhe*—
And, say, speak victory to Devjī three times. *Say it three times*
Then all your backs will become invulnerable."—*vāh vāh*—
All the Sirdārs put down their weapons in front of Goṭhā.—*mhe*—
After getting down they saluted: Victory to Dev, victory to Dev, victory to Dev. *Victory to Dev*
Bhāṅgījī was standing there with his pestle and mortar.—*vāh vāh*—
The Bhāṭ said: "Śrī Mahārāj, it's Dev's command. Speak: Victory to Dev!"—*mhe*—
Bhāṅgījī said: "Hey, Bhāṭ, we've just marched three kos.—*vāh vāh*—
I can't bring myself to say to your Devjī, 'Victory to Devjī.' *I can't bring myself to it*
When I go to the battle of Rātākoṭ,
Yes, then I'll say it
Collect them all from me at one go.—*vāh vāh*—
I can't say 'Victory to Devjī' all day long!" *I can't do it!*
The Bhāṭ came and said: "Śrī Mahārāj, all the Sirdārs have said 'Victory to Devjī.'—*mhe*—
That Bhāṅgījī of yours avoided it."
Dev Mahārāj said: "Bābā Bhāṭ, the day I brought Brother Bhāṅgī from the Jogīs troop—*mhe*—
That day I made his back invulnerable
The back of Mother's mare is still vulnerable.
Yes, this mare's back has stayed vulnerable
The enemy Dīyā's arrow could strike the mare, hey, Bābā Bhāṭ.—*vāh vāh*—
Let the cavalry move." *Let it move now*
So, the Bagaṛāvats' sons are out to avenge the Bagaṛāvats. They departed from the pond.—*vāh vāh*—
By God's grace, Bhūṇājī turned about Bhāvar.—*mhe*—
After turning the horse about he said: "Śrī Mahārāj—*mhe*—
Move toward Rāṇ City very cautiously
According to my instructions.—*mhe*—
On each turret there are seventy cannons apiece.
Yes, put up

The fuses of seventy cannons will be lit at one go!"—*vāh vāh*—
So, they came to the Pass of Sā̃khlī.
Yes, the Pass of Sā̃khlī was in front
One horse and one rider would fit through it.
Yes, two together wouldn't fit through it
"So, as soon as we pass through, Rāvjī Sāī will light up the cannons' fuses.
The way chickens are roasted.—*mhe*—
He'll roast us that way!"
"So, then what shall we do, brother?" *What to do?*
Bhūṇājī said: "Śrī Mahārāj, the entire army will be slain at the pass."—*mhe*—
So, what would be the point!"—*vāh vāh*—
Bhā̃ṇgījī who was behind came up front.—*mhe*—
He said: "Bhāṭ, why have you stopped the army?"
Yes, why are you standing
The Bhāṭ said: "Śrī Mahārāj, the Pass of Sā̃khlī has come."—*mhe*—
"So now?" The Bhāṭ said: "What 'so now'? We won't pass through."
Won't fit through
Bhā̃ṅgījī said: "Hey, Bhāṭ, you've done battle with your tongue all your life.—*mhe*—
Your Dev knows nothing about this kind of fight.
Yes, he doesn't know anything
Which village has he ever gone to fight in?—*vāh vāh*—
Move aside. *Get on one side*
Bhā̃ṅgījī had a vow from Śaṅkar.—*mhe*—
So, with his stick he struck once on this side and once on that side—with that the mountain pass
Yes, he all broke apart
At that time Bhā̃ṅgījī broke apart the pass.—*mhe*—
And Dev Mahārāj opened wide his lotus mouth.—*vāh vāh*—
He threw in a fog. He created a fog through his yawn.
Yes, there was no telling what lay in front
At Rātākoṭ there was a outlook post.—*mhe*—
The fog came up to him. He couldn't see in the dense fog. *How could one see ahead?*
The Sā̃khlī Pass broke away.—*vāh vāh*—
My lord, Dev Mahārāj, laughed aloud:—*vāh vāh*—
"Hey, Bābā Bhāṭ!—*mhe*—
Should we send this brother back?
Yes, who would split this pass without him?
We got stuck right here.—*vāh vāh*—
That brother split apart the pass."—*mhe*—
After crossing through the pass, he said to the Bhāṭ: "Hey, brother, still there's no trusting Bhūṇā.—*vāh vāh*—
So, we'll try this trick. Bhāṭ ask Bhūṇā whether we should first destroy Rāṇ City or Rātākoṭ"

Yes, destroy
Bhūṇājī said: "Śrī Mahārāj, Rāṇ City is name of a woman—the name of a whore.—*mhe*—
Why destroy it? *We won't destroy it*
Rātākoṭ is the name of a man. Go and destroy this first. *Destroy this first!*
So, the cows will be freed.—*mhe*—
And we'll stay at that place and take revenge."—*vāh vāh*—
Great, the Rajpūt's son went and set up camp in front of Rātākoṭ
By God's grace, preparations began to be made for food and drink
Swords began to be sharpened and spears *began to be honed, sir said*
The lord of the three worlds cast his nectar gaze.—*mhe*—
Out of nothing he created armies.—*vāh vāh*—
There were only five brothers—not too many forces.
Yes, where should the forces come from?
By God's grace, the lord cast a look of mercy and created an army.—*vāh vāh*—
Wherever you looked, he placed a horse where there was a horse—*mhe*—
A rider *to a rider,*
A tent to a tent, *said sir.*
He surrounded the town—*mhe*—
Rātākoṭ.—*vāh vāh*—
Early in the morning the fog lifted
The lookout saw,
All over there were tents pitched up, all over there were horses and riders standing.—*vāh vāh*—
"Well, I'll know your mother, hey, a terrible thing happened!" *"A terrible thing has happened," he said, "death's come!"*
The lookout goes to Rāvjī's court in Rātākoṭ
Upon reaching there what news does he tell his master now.
By saying it, know it, let's see, by saying it
I'll say it now, hey, by Bhagavān's grace, brother.—*vāh vāh*—

—*gāv*—

"The lookout is calling today in Rātākoṭ.—*mhe*—
Rāvjī, listen now to what I say
The warriors' sons have come on attack.—*mhe*—
They've come together with the warriors
By God's grace, the Bagaṛāvats have come on attack.—*mhe*—
The sons of the Bagaṛāvats—of the Cauhāns have come to take revenge."—*vāh vāh*—
By God's grace, the lookout post told the news.—*mhe*—
He said: "By God's grace, the lookout post calls on Rātākoṭ.—*vāh vāh*—
"Rāvjī listen to what I say!
Hey, the heroes' sons have rode in battle—*mhe*—
Together with them have come the heroes too
Rāvjī, take a look."

Yes, take a look at least!
By God's grace, Rāvjī Sāī speaks. He tells the news to the lookout post. *By saying it, know it, by saying it, let's see*
I'll say it now, by Bhagavān's grace, I'll say it.—*vāh vāh*—

—*gāv*—

"I'll have you skinned, O Lookout of Rātākot, brother.—*mhe*—
Hey, I'll have black poison salt smeared into your hide!
Didn't you notice that much, brother, the Cauhān's son.—*mhe*—
In that army has come the mighty Bhūṇā
You didn't recognize the other one.—*mhe*—
Bhūṇājī left only yesterday."
Yes, don't you know that?
The lookout said: "Śrī Mahārāj, who do you mean? I didn't notice him."—*vāh vāh*—

—*gāv*—

"I'll have you skinned.—*mhe*—
Hey, I'll have handfuls of sand thrown in your eyes!
Didn't you see the Cauhān's son coming, brother—*mhe*—
Exulting in the brave field of those armies
Did even he remain concealed to you?"
Yes, he didn't come secretly
The lookout said: "Brother, Rāvjī, who do you mean?
Yes, I didn't see him
I didn't realize he was there."—*vāh vāh*—
By God's grace, in the meantime, Rāvjī Sāī's Gā̃go Bhāṭ arrived.—*vāh vāh*—

—*gāv*—

"Bāḷā Dev's armies have come.—*mhe*—
Marry your daughter with Tejā Rāvat's Madnā.—*mhe*—
Seat yourself and Dev on the same couch
I'll have you seated at one place together and talk.—*vāh vāh*—
—*mhe*—
But marry your daughter, brother.—*vāh vāh*—
Your elder daughter—*mhe*—
Get her married."—*vāh vāh*—
Rāvjī Sāī speaks.—*mhe*—
What news does he speak, let's see. *By saying it, know it, by saying it, let's see*
I'll say it now, by lord Dev's grace, by saying it.—*vāh vāh sā*—

—*gāv*—

By God's grace, Rāvjī spoke the news.—*mhe*—
He said: "Bhāṭ, my daughter is Madnā's dharam-sister.—*mhe*—
And Bhoj is her dharam-father
The Pass of Sā̃khlī is death's gate for me.—*mhe*—

Hey, Bhāṭ, just for a few hours don't draw up this big sin on the body
Don't take sin, brother.
Yes, don't talk like this
If I'm finished, then I'm finished!"—*mhe*—
Rāvjī said: "The Bagaṛāvats and I exchanged turbans, brother, they are my dharam-brothers.—*vāh vāh*—
So brothers of brothers are brothers, brother.—*mhe*—
Hey, daughter's father! Why should I get my daughter married, hey?"—*mhe*—
Gā̃go Bhāṭ speaks. And what news does he tell Rāvjī now.
By saying it, know it, by saying it, let's see
I'll say it now, by Bhagavān's grace

—*gāv*—

"Hey, Rāvjī, you killed off the Bagaṛāvats' children in their cradles.—*mhe*—
Because of those children, Rāvjī—*mhe*—
Did Devjī surround Rātākoṭ
You've forgotten about things past.
Yes, you've forgotten. Don't you remember at all?
Seventy children whom you took, hey—*mhe*—
That you smashed and killed.—*vāh vāh*—
Its because of them, see, that these forces have come."—*vāh vāh*—
By God's grace, that news was told to Rāvjī Sāī by Gā̃go Bhāṭ
Rāvjī Sāī speaks.—*mhe*—
What news does he say in return.
By saying it, know it, let's see, by saying it

—*gāv*—

"I killed the Bagaṛāvats' children in the cradle, Bhāṭ Gā̃glā.—*mhe*—
And how can I give any new ones, now, brother?
I can't make new ones, I killed them.—*mhe*—
A cavalry of eighteen thousand—*mhe*—
I'll set up in Rāṇ City
I have a cavalry of eighteen thousand with me.—*vāh vāh*—
Till they die in battle, no harm will come to me.—*mhe*—
If they die, *then we'll see further*
Then it'll be my turn!"—*vāh vāh*—
Gā̃go Bhāṭ speaks. What news does he tell, let's see. *By saying it, know it, by saying it, let's see*

—*gāv*—

"Hey, in the earlier battle, the heroes' Gūjar wives died.—*mhe*—
In this battle the Paḍihārs' wives will die.
Rāvjī Sāī, be prepared, it's your turn."
Yes, your turn has come now
Rāvjī Sāī said: "it's come, Gā̃go, now what? What's there to fear?—*vāh vāh*—
I'm ready to die!"—*mhe*—

—gāv—

By God's grace, who said that news? Gā̃go Bhāṭ said it.
He said: "Look, Rāvjī, in the skies lightning flashes.*—mhe—*
Hey, look, in the northern house, in the southern house there is an omen
Lay down your sword and take Badarase's name.*—mhe—*
You have no luck to fight Ṭhākur Dev
Lay down your sword, brother.*—vāh vāh—*
Whose name is Badaraso, sir? Say, who do you call Badaraso? Lay down the sword—Badaraso is the Paḍihār's lord. Who is Badaraso?—Bhagavān's name. Take Bhagavān's name! You won't win the battle against Dev!" Rāvjī Sāī and Gā̃gā Bhāṭ spoke to one another.*—mhe—*
In Dev Mahārāj's army, he said: "Sirdārs!" Dev Mahārāj said:*—mhe—*
"Hey, Bābā Bhāṭ!"*—vāh vāh—*
"Yes, Śrī Mahārāj!"*—mhe—*
Dev Mahārāj said: "Yes, now have the vessel brought out, churn color.
Yes, churn color
When Rajputs' sons battle,
Yes, then they churn color first
Churn the cauldron of color!"*—vāh vāh—*
In the army of the lord of three worlds*—mhe—*
Color began to be churned. The cauldron of color was heated up.*—vāh vāh—*
So, the lord gave the order to churn color.*—mhe—*
The Bhāṭ explained to Rāvjī
Speak: Victory to Śrī Devnārāyaṇ, victory
Speak, both great and small, everyone!

Bhāṅgījī Destroys Rātākoṭ

So, by God's grace, Bhāṅgījī spoke to the Bhāṭ:*—mhe—*
"Hey, Bābā Bhāṭ, *what's being cooked today?"*
The Bhāṭ said: "Where, Śrī Mahārāj?"
Yes, the cauldron is being heated up
"Your Devjī has ordered a cauldron, brother."*—mhe—*
The Bhāṭ said: "Śrī Mahārāj, where's something being cooked here?"
Yes, there's nothing being cooked here
The Bhāṭ said: "When is something cooked, when there's a battle?"*—vāh vāh—*
The Bhāṭ said: "Śrī Mahārāj, when Rajpūts' sons go into battle*—mhe—*they color themselves with saffron. They color with saffron. They churn color."
Yes, they are churning color
"Hey, Bhāṭ*—mhe—*
Tell your Lord Dev*—vāh vāh—*
If anyone churns saffron before me, then I'll kill him!"
Yes, I'll kill him. I'll churn saffron first

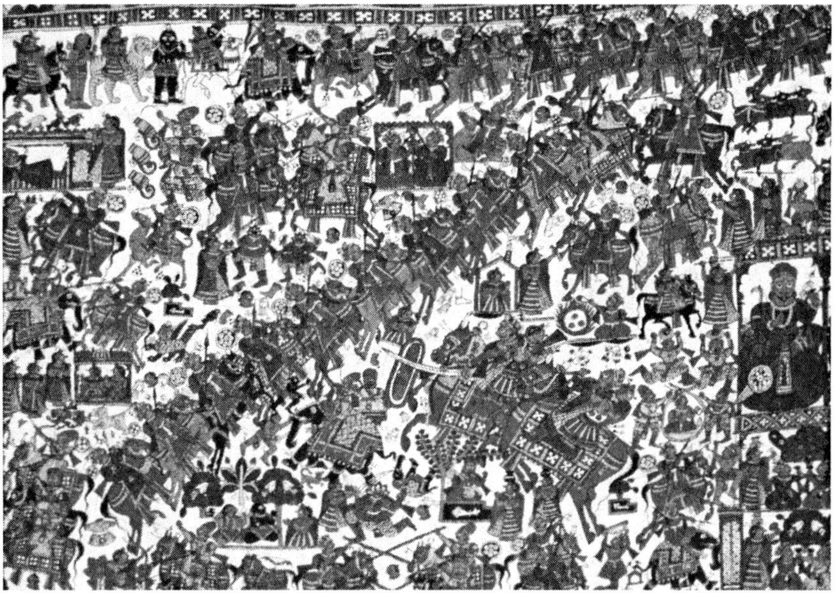

The battle of Rātākoṭ.

So, the day they left to avenge the Bagaṛāvats—*mhe*—
That day, Nevājī's son churned saffron before everyone else.—*vāh vāh*—
By God's grace, they used saffron, didn't they.—*mhe*—
Bhagavān speaks.—*vāh vāh*—
Dev speaks. What news does he tell Bhāṅgījī, let's see.
By saying it, know it, by saying it, let's see
I'll say it now, by Bhagavān's grace.—*vāh vāh—jī*

—*gāv*—

Dīyājī showered arrows on the mare.—*vāh vāh*—
So, the horse fell to one side.—*mhe*—
And Bhāṅgījī fell to one side. In the shroud of smoke and the roar of cannons—*mhe*—
By God's grace, the fuses of seventy cannons were lit simultaneously.—*vāh vāh*—
So, because of Bhagavān's power they didn't work.—*mhe*—
There was lots of smoke.
Yes, only smoke emerged
Bhāṅgījī reflected to himself: "In this smoke, hey, what happened to the mare?"
Yes, the one Mother rides—what does it know about battle?
Because she hasn't seen shrouds of smoke.—*vāh vāh*—
He brought it to the place where Dev Mahārāj's tent stood.—*vāh vāh*—
Reaching the tent, he raced the mare.
Yes, he threw the mare with great force against the tent—mhe—

Like me the Bhāṭ was sitting there with a gourd instrument around his neck.
Yes, he was sitting next to Dev Mahārāj
Dev Mahārāj said: "Bābā Bhāṭ,—*mhe*—
What made a noise?"
Yes, what made that noise against the tent?
The Bhāṭ went outside: "Śrī Mahārāj—*mhe*—
Bhāṅgījī got the mare killed!"—*vāh vāh*—
Dev Mahārāj said: "I told you didn't I.
Yes, the mare's back stayed vulnerable
Enemy Dīyā's arrow could strike her!"—*vāh vāh*—
Dev Mahārāj said: "Bābā Bhāṭ!—*mhe*—
Yes, dig a hole. Bury the mare in the ground." *Bury it in the ground*
Like me with a gourd instrument strung around his neck—*mhe*—
The Bhāṭ went away.
Yes, he departed
"Why Bhāṭ?" *Where are you going?*
The Bhāṭ said: "No, Śrī Mahārāj, you've avenged the Bagaṛāvats' deaths."
Yes, "Its been done," he said, "I've understood you!"
"Why?"—*mhe*—
The Bhāṭ said: "Up in front there's Dīyā the general.—*vāh vāh*—
He's an avatār of Kās, by God's grace." *How many horses are you going to get buried?*
"Well, then, Bābā Bhāṭ, what should we do?" *What should I do?*
The Bhāṭ said: "If this very mare, *and that very rider*
Go back to the front again—*mhe*—
Only then will the enemy Dīyā get scared."
Yes, only through deception will he fear, otherwise he won't be moved at all!
The lord of the three worlds stepped outside.—*mhe*—
He looked in the mare's direction.—*vāh vāh*—
Dev Mahārāj speaks.—*mhe*—
What news does he speak, let's see.
By saying it, know it, let's see, by saying it

—*gāv*—

"Take a look, Nāradā, does the mare have one wound or two?—*mhe*—
Take a look, Bābā Bhāṭ, does a stream of blood flow from the mare?
Great, great, hey, enemy, look you gave the mare
Yes, a hard knock!
Just one strike—enemy you didn't miss the mare's heart!"—*vāh vāh*—
The Bhāṭ said: "Śrī Mahārāj, the enemy, you're praising the enemy."
Yes, praising
Dev Mahārāj said: "Listen, hey, Bābā Bhāṭ!—*mhe*—
The wounds struck by the enemy should be praised.—*vāh vāh*—
Look, why is he an enemy? Because he's struck my mare.—*mhe*—
By God's grace, go and sprinkle some water from my jug."
Yes, the jug I use for washing, sprinkle water from it on the mare

Dev Mahārāj would rinse his mouth—*mhe*—
He got that jug and sprinkled the mare with it
So, the mare sprang up—*vāh vāh*—
Three paces high and landed at one place. *It stood there*
Bhāṅgījī said: "Look, Elder Brother Bhāṭ, over there the mare fell down.
Yes, look over here, it's started jumping around!
Because it's come here in the wilderness it's started jumping around now.—*vāh vāh*—
I thought I could take Devjī's horse this time—*mhe*—
But that horse kicks around, brother.
Yes, who knows, he might throw me off
If he throws me off in the battle, then people will kill me right there.—*mhe*—
This mare of Mother is good to ride on."
Yes, I'll take this one—only then will things work
"Take this one!"—*vāh vāh*—
So, Bhagavān brought the mare back to life
Bhāṅgījī got prepared again
Speak: Victory to Śrī Devnārāyaṇ Mahārāj, victory.

Bhāṅgījī climbed onto the mare Kāḷvī—*vāh vāh*—
got ready again to do battle again.—*mhe*—
Dev Mahārāj speaks. What words of caution does he say, now.
By saying it, know it, let's see, by saying it

—*gāv*—

Bhāṅgījī killed off generals right there with his club. He whirled the club.—*mhe*—
Hey, Rām, great and mighty generals ran away!—*vāh vāh*—
Bhāṅgījī brought the herds of cows in front of Dev's tent.
Yes, he took the cows in front, said sir.
"Here, Śrī Mahārāj, take your cows."
Yes, "take them," he said, "I've freed all of them!"
"Hey, I'll take them all right, but where's the Bagaṛāvats' revenge?—*mhe*—
Who has it been left behind inside of?"—*vāh vāh*—
Bhāṅgījī said: "I don't know. I didn't see Rāvjī Sāī.
Yes, I didn't see Rāvjī
I saw him running away."—*vāh vāh*—
Medūjī and Madan Siṅgjī said: "Let's go quickly!"
Yes, ride out soon!
Climbing onto their horses, they rode out. They told Dev: "You ride out too!"—*mhe*—

The Five Brothers Ride after Rāvjī and Kill Him

Dev Mahārāj said: "I won't ride out."
Yes, I won't ride out behind a runaway

Bhūṇājī said: "He won't ride out—it's not a question of his father, brother!
Yes, it's not his father
It's the revenge of our fathers—let us ride out." *Let us ride out—we'll catch him now*
The four brothers rode after Rāvjī.—*vāh vāh*—
When the horses' hooves sounded—*mhe*—
Rāvjī reflected to himself: "Let me ride my horse too."—*vāh vāh*—
Rāvjī got out of the ker tree and rode on his horse.—*vāh vāh*—
He didn't stay hiding any longer.—*mhe*—
So, Dev Mahārāj, the lord of the three worlds, Bhagavān, pointed the horse's reins downward.
Yes, he pointed them into the underworld
By God's grace, the horse got ahead of Rāvjī.—*vāh vāh*—
In front of Rāvjī—*mhe*—
It got to that place.—*vāh vāh*—
He got in front and Rāvjī got afraid. He stopped immediately.
Yes, he stopped
Bhūṇājī was ahead. When Rāvjī stopped—*mhe*—
He slung a bow around Rāvjī's neck—right here—from behind
"Throw the enemy in front." *Throw . . .*
Bhūṇājī slung the bow around his neck.—*mhe*—
And Dev struck him with a lance.—*vāh vāh*—
Both brothers were together. The other brothers stood behind.—*mhe*—
They threw Ravjī down.
Yes, Rāvjī died right there

Devnārāyaṇ Revives Rāvjī and Instructs Him to Establish Udaipur

By God's grace, when Rāvjī died—*mhe*—
The Bagaṛāvats' Bhāṭ came running along and began tearing open his stomach.
Yes, he jumped on Rāvjī's stomach
They said: "Hey, Bhāṭ, don't tear open his stomach!"—*vāh vāh*—
The Bhāṭ said: "You don't realize.—*mhe*—
The Bagaṛāvats' revenge is inside his stomach.—*vāh vāh*—
After tearing open his stomach I'll fill it up with stones." *I'll fill stones in it*
So, Bhūṇājī was standing nearby. Tears started flowing from Bhūṇā's eyes.
Yes, tears flowed from his eyes
Dev Mahārāj, who was standing in front, noticed: "Bhūṇā!—*mhe*—
After killing the enemy, everyone is happy." *And why do you cry?*
Bhūṇājī said: "Śrī Mahārāj, he is the enemy, *he's no friend*
But he took care of me—he raised me.
Yes, he took good care of me!
He was my father!—*mhe*—
That's why I'm sad. There's no other reason. *No other matter*

He's no friend!—*mhe*—
He's an enemy!"—*vāh vāh*—
Dev Mahārāj said: "Bhūṇā, did he take such good care of you?" Bhūṇā said: "Yes, Mahārāj!" *He kept me well!*
Dev Mahārāj said: "Then, brother, the Bagaṛavats' and my revenge has been completed."
Yes, we've taken it
He said: "It's taken since he's dead.—*mhe*—
I'll join on his head.—*vāh vāh*—
I'll revive him." *I'll revive him*
So, Bābā Rāvjī's severed head Bhūṇājī—*mhe*—
Cleaned of dust.—*vāh vāh*—
He stuck it on again.—*mhe*—
He said: "There you are, Mahārāj, I've stuck it on." *Stuck it back on*
Dev Mahārāj cast a look of mercy.—*mhe*—
Rāvjī came alive again abruptly
Dev Mahārāj said:
"Brother, the Rāv of Rāṇ City is finished as of today.
Yes, it's gone
And that title of Rāv
Yes, that too is gone
Brother, listen, so many days you were called Maṇḍovar.—*mhe*—
And, which Paḍihār-Maṇḍovar. *Maṇḍovar Paḍihār*
From today onward, the title of Maṇḍovar is finished.—*mhe*—
And by God's grace, the town that Rāṇājī will establish will be called Udaipūr after my name.
Yes, he'll establish Udaipūr
And he'll be called Sīsodiyā Rāṇā, brother.—*vāh vāh*—
I stuck his head on and revived him, didn't I!"—*mhe*—
So, the day Bhagavān stuck on his head and revived him—*vāh vāh*—
from that day the title of Sīsodiyā Rāṇā came to be.—*mhe*—
And, the town Udaipūr that Rāṇājī established was called after the name of Dev.
Yes, establish it on my name. It's your name, and the name of the village is mine
"It's mine, brother."—*vāh vāh*—
So, Rāṇājī got the title of Sīsodiyā.
By God's grace, Rāṇājī came to Udaipūr *and established it*
The Bagaṛāvats' revenge was taken completely.—*vāh vāh*—
Dev Mahārāj's cows were freed. Speak: Victory to Śrī Dev, victory, victory, victory, brother.

So, after the lord of three worlds freed the cows—*mhe*—
The brothers all returned home.—*vāh vāh*—

—*gāv*—

Devnārāyaṇ Departs to Baikuṇṭh

Devnārāyaṇ Tells Queen Pīpalde about Their Worship

By God's grace, Sāḍū Mātā caringly cooked white rice for Bhagavān
And she made rice pudding from the cows' milk for Bhagavān. She fed him well: "Come, be seated Mahārāj!"—*vāh vāh*—*"Eat!"*
Hey, on Mālāsarī—the small Mathurā—Bhagavān sat down. Then look he's going to Indra's throne.—*vāh vāh*—
She fed Bhagavān caringly with rice.—*vāh vāh*—
And did Bhagavān's āratī.—*mhe*—
Dev Mahārāj spoke to the queen—spoke to Pīpalde: "Here, brother, Queen Pīpalde, now I don't have any time to stay."
Yes, "I'm going to Indra's throne," he said, "it's time"
Queen Pīpalde said: "Śrī Mahārāj!—*mhe*—
You'll go to Indra's throne. Who'll take care of me afterward?
Yes, what will happen to me?
The world knows you!"
Yes, I come after you. Who should know me?
Dev Mahārāj said: "Queen Pīpalde!—*mhe*—
By God's grace, look, the name will be mine—*vāh vāh*—
But the worship will be yours—and we'll be united."
Yes, we'll be united for ever
He said: "A temple will be constructed."
There is a temple of Dev Mahārāj over there, sir—mhe—
So at that place bricks will be worshipped.
Yes, it'll be for bricks
When one goes into a temple there are bricks—the Syām of bricks. So, the worship will be yours—on a woman's name. The worship of bricks is on Queen Pīpalde's name. And our temple—whose is it? Its Devjī's. *Devjī's*
So, over there it's not Devjī worship, but it is Pīpalde's worship.

Queen Pīpalde Desires Children

Queen Pīpalde said: "No, Mahārāj, I don't like it.—*mhe*—
Who shall I beget children with?" So, by God's grace, Bhagavān, broke off two fruits and gave them to Queen Pīpalde
"Here, you'll have children from these." *You'll have children from these*
So, Bhagavān would come at four in the morning, play a game of caupaḍ with Pīpalde—*mhe*—
And return to his abode. *vāh vāh*—
And Bhagavān said: "I'll meet you every day for a few minutes. I'll play a game of caupaḍ that you've laid out.—*vāh vāh*—

But this rule must be kept—*mhe*—
Bring cow dung from a young cow and smear the floor with it.
Yes, smear the floor
As long as it takes to dry,
Yes, I'll stay that long with you
That's all I promise!"—*vāh vāh*—
In the evening Queen Pīpalde would bring cow dung from a young cow and would smear it beneath the bed.—*vāh vāh*—
Dev Mahārāj would come, talk a little, play a game of caupaḍ—*mhe*—
This went on for six months. So, Sāḍū Mātā, bearer of dharam, spoke to Pīpalde:—*mhe*—
"Queen Pīpalde, it's been six months since my Dev went to Indra's throne.—*vāh vāh*—
The jewelry on your arms is still on. And in the palace the oil lamp burns late at night.
Yes, it burns just like always
I didn't ask at all for a day or two."—*mhe*—
Pīpalde said: "Śrī Dev Mahārāj, Dev Mahārāj comes to my palace every day."
Yes, your son comes every day
Sāḍū Mātā said: "How can I believe that? I suckled him! He doesn't give me an appearance!" *He doesn't visit me. He goes to you*
Sāḍū Mātā said: "Tell me in what manner does he come?"
Queen Pīpalde said: "Sir, I smear the floor under the bed. As long as that remains moist—*mhe*—
He talks to me."
Yes, then he leaves
Sāḍū Mātā said: "Well, do this tomorrow, child.—*mhe*—
We have plenty of cows' ghī. Mix the cow dung with ghī
Yes, and give a smear
When that dries then Bhagavān
Yes, will return!"
The next day Queen Pīpalde mixed ghī and smeared the floor under the bed with cow dung.—*vāh vāh*—
When the time came Dev Mahārāj arrived with his celestial chariot.—*mhe*—
Now when he was about to leave at the same time, the chariot didn't move from that place. *It remained there*
Dev Mahārāj said: "Pīpalde, what's happened?"
Queen Pīpalde said: "Mahārāj, what do I know? You tell me!" *You tell me!*
Dev Mahārāj said: "No, something else has happened!—*mhe*—
The deal was that when the cow dung dries up. He took a look underneath—it was sticky in front.
Yes, it was moist as ever
He said: "Queen Pīpalde!—*mhe*—
Who did that smear today?"
Yes, who did it?
Queen Pīpalde said: "Your mother did, sir!" *Mother did*

"Well then, great, brother!" he said.—*vāh vāh*—
When morning came, Pīpalde went and told her mother-in-law:
"Here, sir, take him, there's your son, meet him!"
Yes, is it him or another?
Sāḍū Mātā came and fell at Bhagavān's feet.—*vāh vāh*—
"Come, O Mother," he said. *Come*
She said: "You did an outrageous thing, hey, brother!—*mhe*—
I suckled you—but me you didn't pay a visit. And, your wife, with her you talk every day!"
Yes, you meet her every day!
Dev Mahārāj said: "Mājī Sāī, I made a mistake all these days.—*mhe*—
Now I won't leave you and go anywhere."—*vāh vāh*—
So, by God's grace, Bhagavān met Sāḍū,—*mhe*—
And his four brothers again. *Brothers . . .*
And Dev Mahārāj—Pīpalde served Dev Mahārāj.—*mhe*—
Two children were born.—*vāh vāh*—
Dev Mahārāj said: "Here, brother, Pīpalde, if you want to keep the lineage,
This boy and girl are yours
Take care of them!"—*vāh vāh*—

Bīlā and Bīlī Establish Devnārāyaṇ's Worship

And Bhagavān gets hold of his chariot.—*mhe*—
"Sit down in the chariot."

Bīlī and Bīlā worshipping Devnārāyaṇ's bricks.

Yes, get together
Indra's fairies arrive—they are written on the paṛ.
Yes, it is
Indra's fairies have prepared the carriage and are flying in the sky
Queen Pīpalde said: "Mahārāj, its your concern and the concern of this boy and girl!"
So, the lord of the three worlds, flew the chariot.—*mhe*—
How does he take the cows, Sāḍū Mātā, the brothers in their bodies to Baikuṇṭh. *He took them, said sir.*
So, he arrived at Indra's throne. Bhagavān begot Bīlā and Bīlī
He avenged the Bagaṛāvats, he sorted out all the matters of the Bagaṛāvats.—*vāh vāh*—
That day he promised: "I'll straighten out your past matters!"—*vāh vāh*—
So, the Bagaṛāvats—the twenty-four brothers' past was resolved. Speak: victory to Śrī Devnārāyaṇ Bhagavān, victory!
From this place onward Dev Mahārāj's daughter began doing Bhagavān's sevā, and a quarrel began between Bīlā and her.—*vāh vāh*—
So, Bīlā and Bīlī spoke to one another. Speak: Victory to Śrī Devnārāyaṇ Bhagavān, victory!

Line Drawing of Paṛ

55 54 53 52 51 50 49 48 47 46 45 44 43 42 41 40
19 18 17 16 15 14 13 12 11 10 9 8 7 6 5 4 3 2 1

L

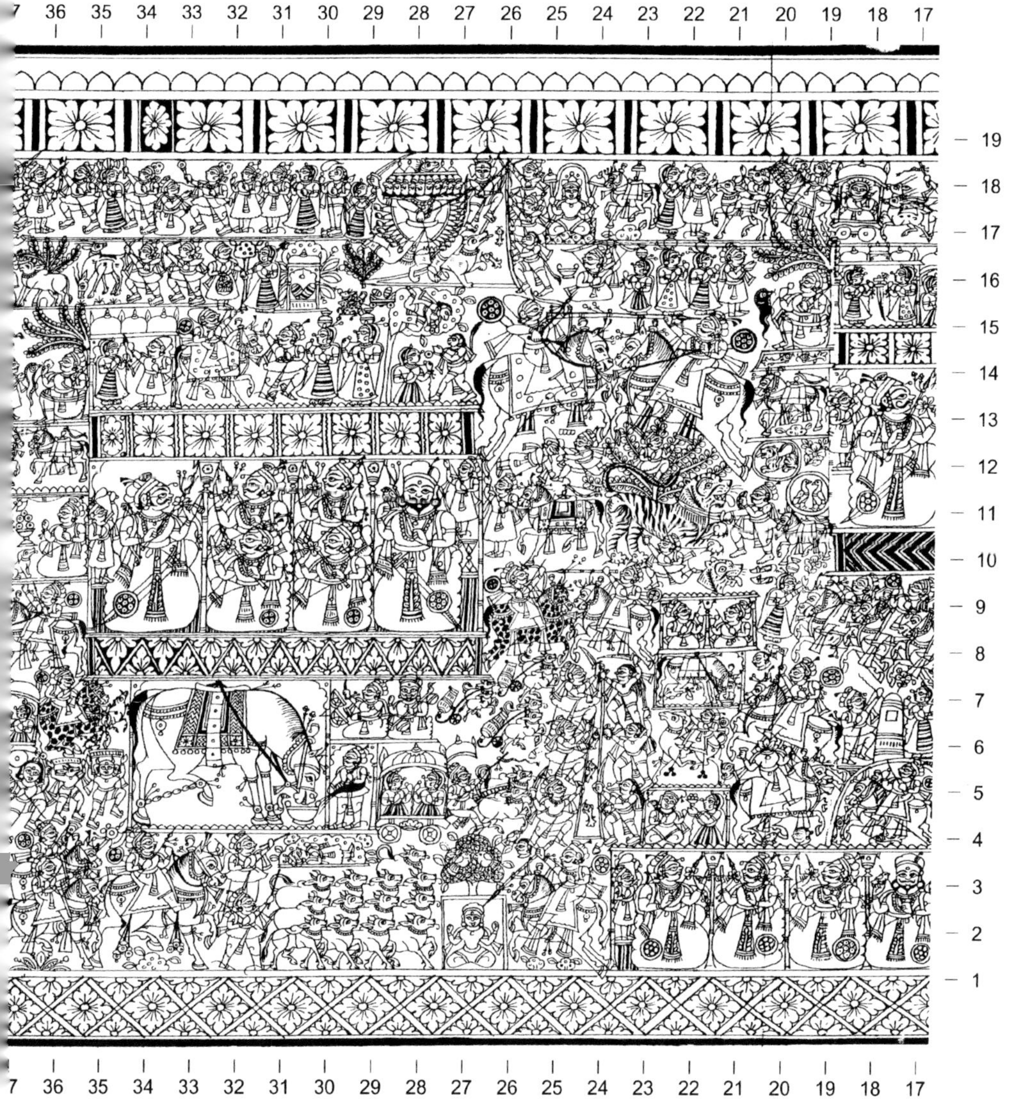
36 35 34 33 32 31 30 29 28 27 26 25 24 23 22 21 20 19 18 17
19 18 17 16 15 14 13 12 11 10 9 8 7 6 5 4 3 2 1

L

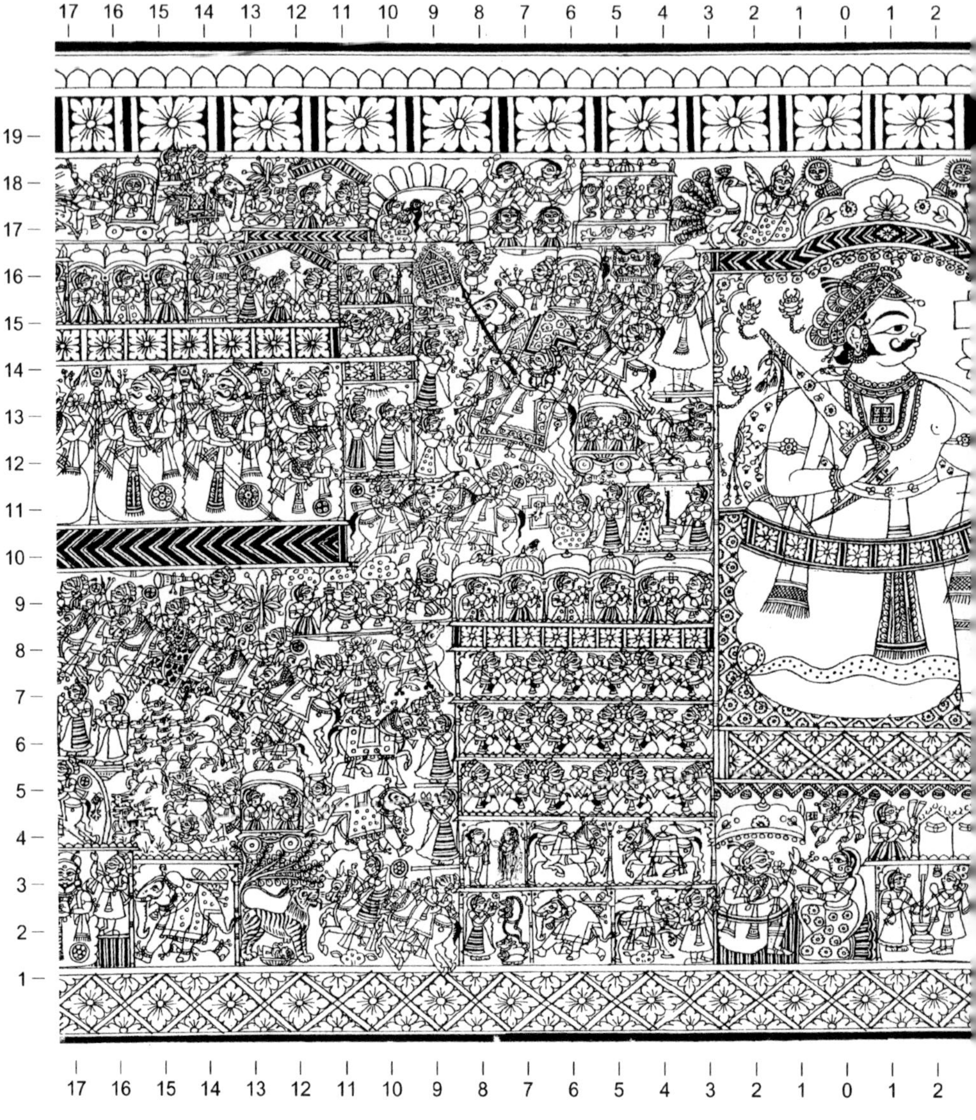

17
16
15
14
13
12
11
10
9
8
7
6
5
4
3
2
1
0
1
2
19
18
17
16
15
14
13
12
11
10
9
8
7
6
5
4
3
2
1

M

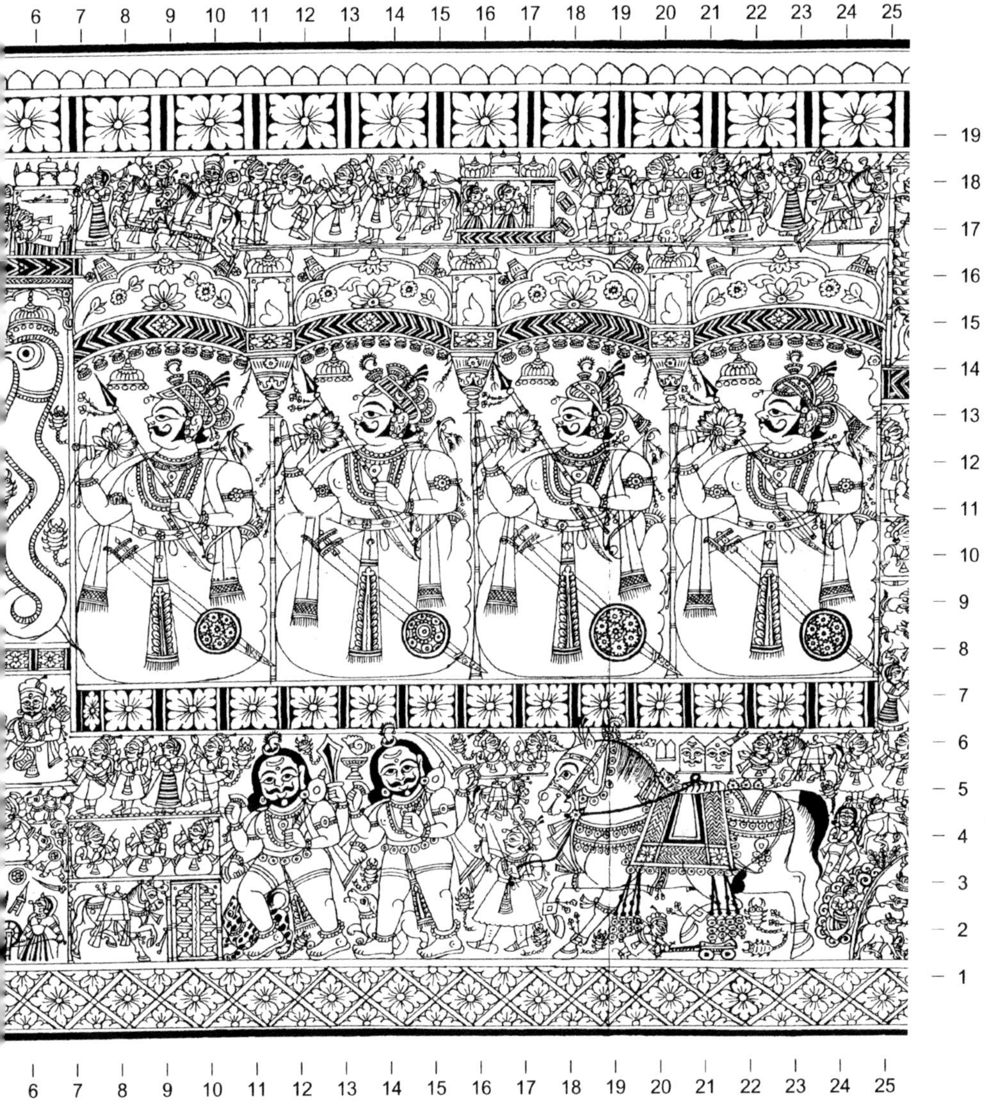

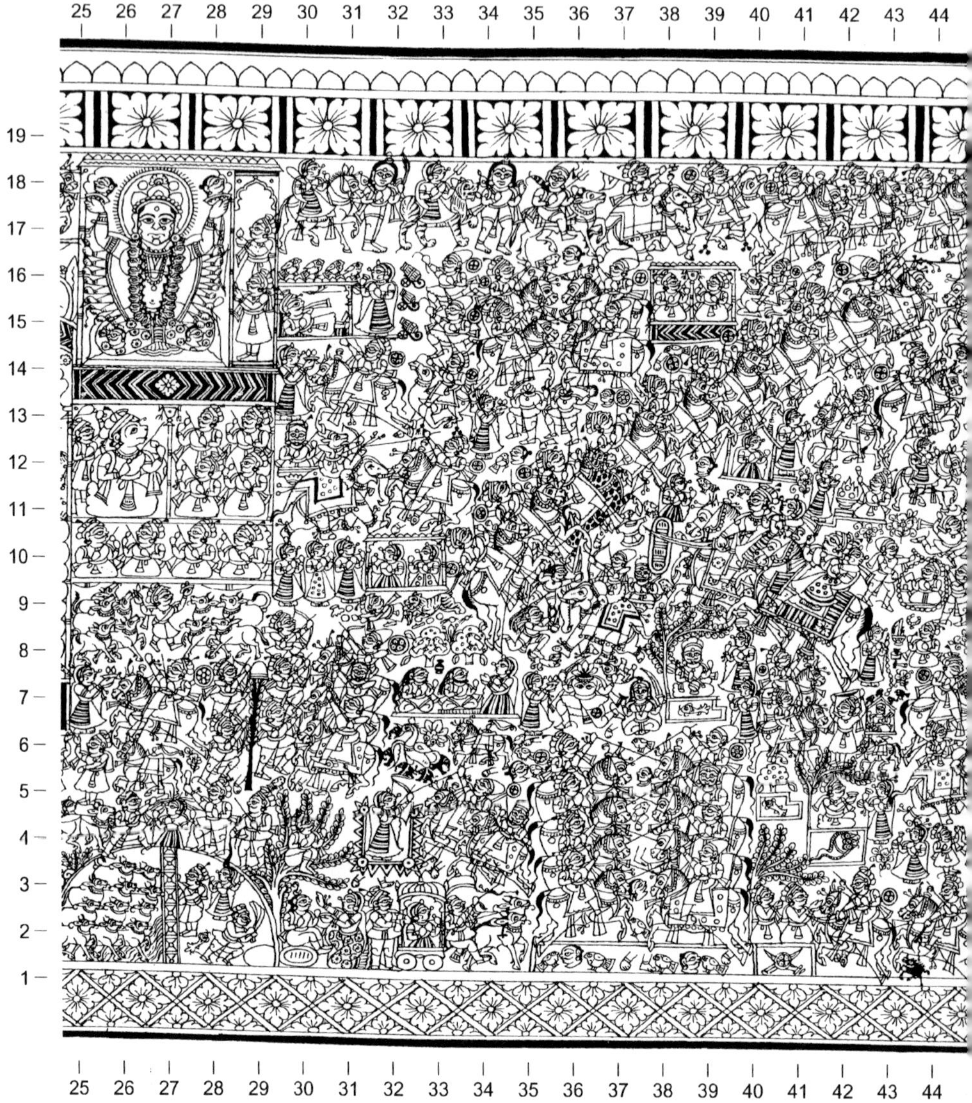
25 26 27 28 29 30 31 32 33 34 35 36 37 38 39 40 41 42 43 44
19 18 17 16 15 14 13 12 11 10 9 8 7 6 5 4 3 2 1

R

48 49 50 51 52 53 54 55
19 18 17 16 15 14 13 12 11 10 9 8 7 6 5 4 3 2 1
48 49 50 51 52 53 54 55

R

Notes

Preface

1. This is the name of the first part of the narrative, dealing with the lives of 24 brothers collectively called the Bagaṛāvats.

2. The lack of the enzyme G6PD; also called "favism."

3. See Said (1978), Inden (1990).

4. See Berg and Fuchs (1993).

5. She goes on to point out that from a Western academic perspective (referring here to an observation made by the sociologist Louis Dumont) the very adherence to membership of the researcher's own society is a contradiction in terms: "A sociology that has its roots in the Indian tradition stands in danger of compromising the values of modernity and rationality . . . Are these native social anthropologists to be regarded as native spokesmen? Do they earn membership of the anthropological community on condition that they renounce (not simply transcend) all forms of knowledge acquired through membership of the society of which they now write?" (40).

6. *ibid* (1993:2).

7. Superintendent of police.

8. See Raheja and Gold 1994: xv.

9. The "first" part dealing with the Bagaṛāvats was recorded in 1994.

10. Barthes (1987a: 84–97).

1. Introduction

1. The philosopher of language George W. Grace, for example, distinguishes between the "mapping" and the "reality-construction" view of language. In the "mapping" view the basic epistemological premise is that "there is a common world out there and our languages are analogous to the maps of this world. Thus this common world is represented or "mapped" (with greater or lesser distortion) by all languages." In the reality-construction view "the imperfectness of our access to the knowledge of the real world assumes central importance. . . . [O]ur sensory data are regarded as falling seriously short of constituting an adequate picture of the real world . . . all we can do is to theorize about reality, or to put it more precisely still, to construct models of it. These models are our constructed realities, and they are reflected in the languages we speak" (1987: 6).

2. See Valdés (1991: 26) on Ricoeur: "since the idea of literature Ricoeur holds is that of a tradition of texts with a maximum capacity to induce the redescription of the world in the reader, it follows that the game we play as readers of and commentators on literature is that of world-making."

3. This state of affairs is particularly reflected in Indological studies even today.

4. See, for example, Blackburn, Claus, Fluekiger, and Wadley (1989), Malik (1993a), Miller (1994), Singh (1993), Smith (1991). Blackburn furthermore classifies the narrative under the category of so-called martial epics in India that emphasize "group solidarity" and are "concerned with power, social obligation, and social unity; they turn on themes of revenge, regaining lost land, or restoring lost rights. . . . Martial epics celebrate external—often military or political—conflict and a warrior ethic" (1989: 5).

5. A synopsis of the contents of the narrative is offered in chapter 4.

6. See Binford (1976), Blackburn, Claus, Fluekiger, and Wadley (1989), Gold (1992), Lapoint (1978), Smith (1991).

7. Śrī Hukamārām Bhopā was accompanied by Śrī Moṭārām in 1991 and by his nephew Śrī Kiṣnārām in 1994.

8. The narrative is performed in front of a painted scroll depicting Devnārāyaṇ together with hundreds of other items such as courts, towns, individual characters, deities, animals, birds, trees, water reservoirs, weapons, musical instruments, and so on and on. An extensive audiovisual documentation of the contents of the scroll, and techniques of painting was undertaken in the presence of the foremost painter of the paṛ-painting tradition, Śrī Śrīlāl Jośī.

9. These and other locations are part of a "sacred geography" that is exemplified through the narrative as well as the paṛ. Thus the visual and the verbal narratives both represent a "map" of places and locations occurring within the "universe" of the cult.

10. For example, Pollock (1991: 17) while discussing interpretations of the Rāmāyaṇa points out that these are structured by a "historically effected consciousness" (*wirkungsgeschichtliches Bewußtsein*) similar to that shaping the interpretation of other non-Indian "classical" epics, for example of ancient Greece.

11. See, for example, Blackburn, Claus, Fluekiger, and Wadley (1989), Malik (1993a), Miller (1994), Singh (1993), Smith (1991).

12. For a discussion of "caste purāṇas" and the problems related to their study, see Das (1977).

13. As Das (1977: 13), in the context of the analysis of "caste purāṇas," points out, "Indologists and social historians alike have used texts of this kind for purposes of historical reconstruction. . . . While this approach may have some utility, it is much more profitable to try and explain the structure of these texts in their entirety. To see confused history in these texts is to misinterpret the *rationale* of the documents. . . . After all the authors of these texts were not necessarily interested in providing an objective history (of the groups)."

14. It should be clear that the majority of these terms—including the term "religion"—are more "etic" rather than "emic" in their content. Here too, as in the case of the terms outlined in the passage at the beginning of this section, there is a necessity to locate corresponding categories while understanding their meaning, as far as possible, from within the tradition.

15. This position is somewhat different from the one, for example, taken by Sontheimer (1989). While examining the oral traditions of the Dhangars in Maharashtra, he writes that "the myths of the Dhangars are relatively concrete in their setting and contents, and often correspond to verifiable occurrences. . . . Many of the situations referred to in the legends and stories, but also in casual statements . . . reflect typical events that have occurred again

and again in the history of the Dhangars and of the many groups related to them—and perhaps also generally in the history of the Deccan" (viii–ix).

16. As an example of how community history and sacred power are interconnected I refer later to a locally printed version of the narrative. In this version of the narrative there is a reference to the past within the time frame of yugas. This time frame supports the idea of a beginning of the cult in a long-gone, ancient epoch. By establishing the identity of Devnārāyaṇ and Rāma on the one hand and the Gujars and Gopāls on the other, in the past, the sacred significance of both the deity and the community are established in the present.

17. See Ortner 1990 and chapter 5.

18. By using the term *dialogue* I do not intend to imply a harmonious arrangement of utterances (or for that matter "texts" or "social interaction") but the *polyphonic* nature of all thought, speech, and action. As Bakhtin (1986: 91–92) observes: "Each utterance refutes, affirms, supplements, and relies on the others. . . . The utterance is filled with *dialogic overtones*. . . . After all, our thought itself—philosophical, scientific, and artistic—is born and shaped in the *process of interaction and struggle* with others' thought" (emphasis added).

19. Parcyo is cognate with Hindi *paricay*, which can mean "proof" or "testimony," "introduction," or in religious contexts also "hagiography."

2. Verbal Narrative

1. Cited in Kersenboom (1995: 5).

2. There is no doubting the fact that performances are held for a number of reasons, such as the fulfilment of individual vows or during religious festivals. However, the binding feature of all performances beyond individual or group motivations is the celebration of the deity's presence. Without this the fulfilment of vows and other religious observances do not make sense.

3. Thus as Kersenboom (1995: 16) with reference to the "Tamil text" observes: "While the nature of the Western text is static, an object of analytical abstraction, and takes the form of a document, the Tamil text is organic in nature, a process of synthetic absorption, living a reality of performance. The application of both differs as well: while the document adds to a database that eventually will produce the ultimate interpretation as truth, the performance offers a becoming, an embodiment of life, here and now. These extremes are substantiated in their material representations."

4. Thiel-Horstmann (1985) provides a complete documentation of the *jāgraṇ* in the context of worship conducted by the north Indian bhakti sect, the Dādūpanth. In her preface she notes that the jāgraṇ is temporally speaking, the most extended form of worship that occurs in front of the community. During the course of a jāgraṇ a number of texts are either sung or declaimed. The purpose of these texts is to "awaken" the devotee, and to motivate him or her to be free of *saṃsāra* (ocean of existence). She also notes that the documentation in published form denies the reader many other components of the night-wake such as "die musikalisch-ästhetischen Freuden der Veranstaltung, ihre zeitliche Geschlossenheit, das Milieu des *satsaṅga* und den verdienstlosen Triumph einer doch glücklich überstandenen Nachtwache" (10). Again, the implication here is that the texts are embedded in a larger aesthetic, "performative" situation in which their meaning unfolds, thereby motivating singers and listeners.

5. Since my intention here is to provide an understanding of the "concept" of performance, I do not describe the performance itself in great detail. The main features are summarized hereafter. A complete documentation of a single night's performance would,

as Thiel-Horstmann's study (mentioned in the preceding note) shows, entail a monograph in itself. For details on the performance situation of Devnārāyaṇ, see further Miller (1980, 1994).

6. See Mair (1988: 102), and Miller (1994).

7. Similarly Smith (1991: 17), writing on the related "picture story-telling" tradition of Pābūjī, points out that: "the use of the phrase 'reading the paṛ' is a valuable indication of the way in which *bhopos* conceptualize their work. They do not speak of 'singing an epic'; they refer not to singing or narrative but to performance, and their term for performance invokes the cloth-painting. . . . We approach Pābūjī through his paṛ, and we approach the paṛ through the *bhopo's* 'reading' of it."

8. Miles (1985: 34) distinguishes between religious images that are either iconic, representational, impressionistic, or abstract. According to her, of these four types, iconic images are "most denotative . . . that is, organized according to traditional depiction whose every detail . . . may be 'read' by the worshipper in terms of a particular content of scriptural or historic significance. . . . The interpreter of images, like the interpreter of texts, must determine the denotation of the image as a preliminary step to suggesting the spectrum of meanings it was likely to have had for the different members of its historical community."

9. Thus even to claim that these images are strongly denotative in the sense of being icons would be to fall short of their meaning.

10. On the other hand the written word represents an abstraction or distancing from the real world: "With its connection to existential events broken, an alphabetically written word becomes a set of abstract symbols in static, quasi-permanent space rather than a dynamic event. The context, which is so important to oral communication . . . tends to recede greatly into the tacit or even unconscious background" (9). In this connection see also the important work of Ong (1982).

11. Mūrtis are, strictly speaking, not "images" of a deity; they are a concrete manifestation of a deity and its divine power.

12. Bolle (1969: 127) points out that: "unless one understands the primacy of the *place*, the nature of the sacred in most of Hinduism remains incomprehensible, and the plurality and variety of gods continues to form an unsolvable puzzle. *God is universal because he is there*."

13. It is interesting to note that the notion of "speaking/reading" and "writing" should relate to visual images in a predominantly oral tradition. The orality of the narrative does not allow for a notion of reading and writing connected to the written word, that is, to the symbolic manifestation of language in script. Since there are no symbols to place language "inside," reading and writing are used with reference to visual "text." It is, of course, surprising that concepts of reading and writing at all emerge in such a context. In other words we would have to understand that reading and writing as concepts are not possessions of senders and receivers of "Schriftsprache" alone. Naturally the occurrence of such terms could also be attributed to the fact that we are not dealing here with a primary oral culture but with one that exists in relationship to written culture.

14. This is very similar to the oral poetry of the Hāṭkar Dhangars of Maharashtra, who begin compositions (*ovīs*) with "sumbarāna māṇḍilā" or "sumbārana devācā" ("the remembrance is set," "the remembrance of God") (Sontheimer 1989: 9). The oral narrative of Devnārāyaṇ involves memory in two senses. One sense, of course, is that in which the singer himself sings from "memory" (although this is not what singers claim; more frequently a singer talks of being "inspired" or "energized" by Sarasvatī or Devnārāyaṇ). The other sense is that in which the singer is involved in re-creating and reexpressing the past in the present. When concerned with the meaning of the narrative it is also imperative

to look into the latter aspect of "memory" and "remembrance," although from the point of view of oral transmission the first sense of memory is equally important. Memory in the sense of the re-creation of history brings us squarely onto one of the central concerns of the narrative, namely, a discourse on historicity.

15. The aniconic representation of Devnārāyaṇ in the form of a row of large upright bricks is taken up in more detail in chapter 3.

16. The question that needs to be asked here is why a religious event requires such an elaborate "performance" context. Supposing we were to take the notion of prakāś (presence, light, radiance) as the central feature around which all the other performative elements are organized. Since the purpose of a performance is, from the singers' and the audience's point of view, to bring forth, make possible, the prakāś of Devnārāyaṇ, we need to understand how and why the entire range of audiovisual and other sensory experience created by the "transmission media" are geared toward bringing forth prakāś, and toward expressing the audience's devotion toward Devnārāyaṇ. We would have to understand that the narrative performance, which is about Devnārāyaṇ, and his ancestors, is linked to different sensory elements and lives within the framework of the deity's presence.

17. Kersenboom (1995: 19, 94).

18. From the verb *gāvṇo*, "to sing."

19. This term is discussed in more detail hereafter.

20. These may involve humans, gods, demons, animals, and even trees.

21. On discourse and conversational analysis, see also Goodwin (1981), Gumperz (1982), Wardough (1985).

22. In the following sections, under the headings "Repetition," "Dialogue," and "Reported Speech," I examine the "conversational" nature of the narrative both from the point of view of its internal structure and the exchange between the two singers.

23. Cited in Tannen (1994: 20).

24. Notwithstanding the common occurrence of repetition in oral forms of poetry, Finnegan concludes, however, that "the exact significance of repetition in oral poetry is not, therefore, clear" (132).

25. These sections have been placed in italics in the following examples for the lead *and* the second singer's phrases. The second singer's lines are given in parenthesis.

26. See translation on p. 119, lines 23–33.

27. This system of terse, compact verse followed by a commentary reminds one of Indian philosophical and literary schools, which reproduce texts verse by verse, each of which is followed by a longer, detailed commentary. The distinction between such philosophical and literary commentaries and the oral narrative of Devnārāyaṇ lies of course in the fact that in the latter case the narrative (also) progresses in the arthāv sections, which themselves anticipate the next gāv, and so on.

28. This becomes easier to comprehend when actually listening to the second singer's spoken style of repeating the first singer's lines.

29. The relationship between language and utterance is comparable to the distinction between *langue* and *parole* made by Ferdinand Saussure. Thus "the language, thought of as an abstract pattern or scheme, and speech (to adopt the usual, somewhat unsatisfactory, translation of *parole*) or individual uses of language on particular occasions" (Turner 1987: 14).

30. See the preceding section.

31. This notion is also found in other narrative traditions of Rajasthan (Pābūjī etc.). In fact it would be worthwhile to examine the notion of speaker and respondent in other performative traditions relating not only to narratives but also to music and dance. A comparative study would perhaps reveal the centrality of "dialogue" in Indian expressive

traditions and the arts. It may also reveal something about the way in which "reality" is constructed.

32. This results in a kind of "inner" intertextuality. There exists, therefore, also at the level of text (qua the notion of an inter/intratext) a notion of dialogue—of telling and responding—that interrelates the first and second singer's texts with each other.

33. On reported speech and code-switching see, for example, Gumperz (1982).

34. Listening in this sense is distinguishable from Bakhtin's notion of dialogic response. Whereas listening is certainly a crucial element of all dialogue, it is not manifest in the form of a response. It is the *pretext,* so to speak, of speech—the attentive field within which all speech arises. On the idea and consequences of listening, see Fuimara (1990) and Malik (1995).

35. These passages appear in more detail again in chapter 5 where they are discussed in the context of Devnārāyaṇ's history and Gujar history.

3. Visual Narrative

1. Mitchell (1986: 31). Mitchell continues to point out that the distinction made here between image and its material representation rests on a fear of idolatry and "image-worship" in a literal sense.

2. The distinction between visual and verbal text is reflected in the deep cleavage between painting and poetry that runs through Western art history and literary criticism. In the tradition of Devnārāyaṇ, verbal and visual text are not disconnected, separate spheres of expression. In the last section of this chapter I discuss the way they are interconnected.

3. Mitchell refers here to the petroglyphs of Northwest Native American "Indians."

4. The significance of cloth or textile is also evident in the bond between the community of weavers called Bhā̃bhī and Devnārāyaṇ. This connection is apparent, for example, in the story of Devnārāyaṇ's grandfather, Bāgh Siṃh and his Brahman caretaker, who "accidentally" marries a Bhā̃bhī girl, whose descendants become the priests of the Bhā̃bhī community called Garuḍ. (See the synposis of the narrative in chapter 4, and Malik 1996. See also the story of Lālo Bhā̃bhī hereafter.

5. Smith (1991: 8) refers to the scroll of Pābūjī as a "portable temple."

6. In most cases Devnārāyaṇ is shown with his brother Bhūṇājī, and sometimes with his mother, Sāḍū Mātā.

7. In particular his father, Savāī Bhoj.

8. These forms of mobile and immobile worship are reminiscent of the concepts of the *sthāvara* and *jaṅgama* of Vīraśaivism. Here *sthāvara* represents the established and immovable and *jaṅgama* the moving or moveable: " 'sthāvara' is that which stands, a piece of property, a thing inanimate. Jaṅgama is moving, moveable, anything given to going and coming. Especially in Vīraśaiva religion, a Jaṅgama is a religious man who has renounced world and home, moving from village to village, representing god to the devoted, a god incarnate. Sthāvara could mean any static symbol or idea of god, a temple, or a liṅga worshipped in a temple. Thus the two words carry a contrast between two opposed conceptions of god and of worship" (Ramanujan 1973: 20). In contrast to the Vīraśaiva tradition, in the case of Devnārāyaṇ it is the scroll and the brick(s) in the temple that respectively embody Devnārāyaṇ. The emphasis here, therefore, is on the deity who is manifest in both places rather than in the person of the bhopā. Moreover, it is interesting that the status of the bhopās is opposite that of the jaṅgama and sthāvara. Whereas in the Vīraśaiva tradition it is the mobile jaṅgama who has renounced the world to incorporate God, and to move from place to place, in the Devnārāyaṇ tradition it is the *bhekdhārī*

bhopā, or the bhopā who tends the shrines and temples, who has renounced the world and taken a vow of celibacy. The paṛdhārī bhopā, or the bhopā who performs in front of the paṛ, is on the other hand also called the ghardhāri or householder bhopā. For the story relating the origins of these two institutions of bhopās, see hereafter.

9. Hofstadter (1980: 709).

10. *Bidyā* could also be translated as knowledge.

11. Devnārāyaṇ is considered to be no more than 11 years old when he accomplishes his task on earth. His four elder brothers are also taken to be only a few years older than this.

12. The self-referential interrelationship between visual narrative, verbal narrative, and religious cult is potently expressed in the fact that the image of the bricks is represented on the paṛ as well. Thus the verbal narrative and the paṛ both refer to this manifestation of Devnārāyaṇ's power, while at the same time themselves being the result of that same power.

13. "Kṛṣṇa of Bricks."

14. The shrine of Demālī is considered to be Devnārāyaṇ's first place of worship. It was established prior to his departure to Baikuṇṭh. The first priest to perform *sevā* here was his son Bīlā. See hereafter for the story of the origins of two kinds of priests or bhopās.

15. A son and a daughter. Whereas Devnārāyaṇ's daughter Bīlī recognizes and acknowledges his divinity, his son is rebellious to the point of going through a great deal of physical suffering before assenting to his father's authority.

16. A knee-length outer garment worn by men. Bhopās wear this regularly during performances of the narrative. This item of their costume is supposed to represent Devnārāyaṇ. See hereafter for more details on other features of their costume.

17. Devnārāyaṇ is often referred to in this way, suggesting his royal character.

18. In reality paṛ painters are not Brahmans but derive their name from a lineage of artisans or craftsmen (*śilpī*) called Jośī.

19. The reference here is to the Bagaṛāvats' genealogist, Chochū Bhāṭ, who witnessed all the events of their lives and of Devnārāyaṇ's.

20. The book of records kept by a genealogist (Hindi: *bahī*).

21. Chochū Bhāṭ is frequently referred to as *nāradī bhāṭ*, implying his "trickster" qualities. The name also reflects an affinity between Devnārāyaṇ and Chochū Bhāṭ, and their puranic counterparts, Nārāyaṇa and Nārada.

22. The significance of Devnārāyaṇ's marriage to Rāṇī Pīpalde, and to his other two wives in the narrative, is discussed in more detail in chapter 7.

23. These two forms of representation also allude to the different ways Devnārāyaṇ is conceived: formless and untainted (*nirākār, nirañjan*) on the one hand and a regal deity (*darbār, ṭhākur*) with all the attributes of a king on the other.

24. Although cloth as a material is more susceptible to decay than brick or stone, it is still a strong constituent of rituals and metaphors of connectedness and continuity. This is evident in rituals of tying fabrics together (as in marriage ceremonies in India); in the use of threads in initiation rites; in the widespread understanding of textile and fabric as being family heirlooms and, therefore, a source of wealth; or, for that matter, in the usage of terms related to weaving, thread, fabric and so on to describe the *interwovenness* of society. On the cultural, economic, and political significance of cloth, see, for example, Weiner and Schneider (1989).

25. It is interesting to note that the bhopās are identified or even named in terms of the different kinds of cloth they wear and bear.

26. Even though this story involves the winning over of Baidnāth Bābā in the form of contest, it must not be overlooked that Bīlā himself has, till the point of being healed,

resisted acknowledging the authority and divinity of his father. In fact, Bīlā's leprosy is Devnārāyaṇ's answer to his defiance. Only after a considerable amount of physical suffering does Bīlā finally submit to his father's wish that he become a bhopā.

27. Paradoxically this event is not in any way related to a shrine or temple as one might have thought, since bhekdhārī bhopās are usually in charge of temples, while paṛdhārī bhopās journey from village to village.

28. Udojī is a name of Devnārāyaṇ.

29. See the synopsis of the narrative in chapter 4.

30. It must be noted that the semiotic understanding of the symbol goes further than its common meaning. Thus, for example, C. S. Peirce places symbol within a threefold arrangement that, together with icon and index, defines all signs: "For Peirce, the world of signs is fully described by the trio of icon, symbol, and index—signs, that is by resemblance or analogy, by convention (words and other arbitrary signs), and by 'causal' or 'existential' connection (a trace that signals its cause; a pointing finger)" (Mitchell 1987: 56). In terms of time, the symbol, as the third aspect of all signs, encompasses the potentiality of the future. The other two aspects, namely icon and index, represent past and present experience. See Kersenboom (1995: 49).

31. Not only is the paṛ as a whole a sign, its individual images and scenes are also signs that refer to the past that is recreated in the present.

32. This is true for the work of J. D. Smith and J. C. Miller. Bahadur Singh also brings the temporal dimension of the paṛ into play.

33. The epigraph to this section is from Mitchell (1986: 95).

34. Other paintings are of course also visual narratives. The point here is of emphasis: the *message* of the paṛ involves, on one important level, a story in the literal sense of the word.

35. See the section entitled "Performance," in which I point out that the scroll is "decoded" through the verbal narrative.

36. In a broader context, these limitations are common to the scientific description of any living, experienced phenomenon.

37. The duration can vary according to circumstances.

38. See Hofstadter (1980: 127). This can be observed, for example, in spoken language, when a speaker moves through a series of different but associated thoughts before returning to the original idea with which he or she began.

39. The phrase "picture story-telling" is of course not a very accurate description of what the narrative tradition of Devnārāyaṇ is about. As I have shown above, we are not dealing here just with pictures, or just with a story that is illustrated through a visual counterpart.

40. See Mair (1988) for an extensive discussion of various traditions in South Asia, and elsewhere.

41. An extensive description and analysis of the epic of Pābūjī with reference to its performance modes can be found in Smith (1991).

42. Smith makes an interesting remark regarding the ambiguity of scenes and figures. At one point during a performance of Pābūjī, the singer Parbū Bhopo reaches a section that features a gardener. But since there is no gardener in the scene he is pointing to, Parbū "simply points to the nearest male figure, which happens to be one of the attendants who stand behind the large central figure of Pābūjī to fan him. Iconographically, this man cannot be a gardener . . . in terms of scenic organization he cannot have anything to do with the girls in the garden . . . but for a second or two he nevertheless becomes a gardener. The logic of the paṛ, like any other logic, can be and is manipulated for gain by those who are expert in it" (63). The question here is whether what Smith considers a "ma-

nipulation of logic" is a sufficient explanation for the occurrence of the changeable identity of the figure in question. Such cases of implicit "ambiguity" may arise from an understanding of transformations and are an all-pervasive feature of many aspects of South Asian culture, society, and religion. But underlying many examples of "ambiguity" there seems to be a notion or even experience of "sameness" that is radically different from a rigid, fixed, unitary notion of identity. Like the elasticity of space that Smith talks about, "identity" too, thus, appears to be elastic. It may very well be that it is because of this inherent elasticity that scenes and characters may be substituted for one another and have multiple meanings and multiple identities. Perhaps the fact that Parbū Bhopo chooses to transform an anonymous figure momentarily into a gardener does not lie in the *manipulation* of a fixed logic but in a tacit understanding of transformations, flexible identities, and an "elastic logic."

43. This presentation is based in part on extensive discussions with one of the foremost living exponents of paṛ painting, Śrī Śrīlāl Jośī.

44. Some of the deities depicted on the paṛ are, for example, Gaṇeśa, Sarasvatī, Varāha, Narasiṃha, Kṛṣṇa, Rāmā, Bhairū̃, and Bhavānī. The different kinds of trees include the baḍ, khejaṛī, nīm, ām, kelā, pīpal, imlī, aśok, and kalpavṛkṣa.

45. Of course it should not be forgotten that "natural" environment is not a neutral category: it too is replete with cultural interpretations and symbols. I take up the cultural and religious significance of natural markers depicted on the paṛ and corresponding events occurring in the narrative in more detail in the chapters focusing on the content of the narrative.

46. It is important to remember that the left of the paṛ is on Devnārāyaṇ's *right*, and conversely, the right of the paṛ, on his *left*.

47. In the following passages some of the places and persons mentioned are referred to by means of coordinates marked on the pen drawing of the paṛ (following translation). The paṛ has been divided into a left half (L) and a right half (R). Devnārāyaṇ occupies the middle of the drawing. Thus, for example, the coordinates L 9, 18 refer to the number 9 on the left horizontal axis and the number 18 on the vertical axis. The coordinates R 6, 15 refer to the number 6 on the right half of the horizontal axis and the number 15 on the vertical axis, and so on.

48. *Ammī kī nazar*, literally: "nectar gaze."

49. *Jahar kī nazar*, literally: "poison gaze."

50. Goṭhā and Daṛāvat are used interchangeably as the name of Devnārāyaṇ's birthplace. Kheḍā Causlā is the capital of the Bagaṛāvats, which Devnārāyaṇ reestablishes.

51. The dividing line between allies and foes is not always clear-cut or final. Allies may turn into foes at some point. The progression of the narrative determines whether a particular scene thereby portrays allies or enemies.

52. Nevājī is Savāī Bhoj's impetuous and daring younger brother. He is the father of Bhāṅgījī, who singlehandedly destroys Rāṇ City later.

53. The other source of sacred power issues from Devnārāyaṇ himself, and his divine acts.

4. Textual Narrative

1. Brahmā's performance of a *yajña* is also the central theme of the eulogistic work on the origins of the pilgrim town called in Sanskrit the *Puṣkara-Māhātmya*. See Malik (1993b).

2. On Śiva as an Aghori in the Bagaṛāvat, see Singh (1993: 415).

3. A close parallel to this motif is also found in the *Puṣkara-Māhātmya*, where Brahmā's ritual activity is disrupted by Śiva. Appearing in the form of a naked, skull-bearing ascetic, here he magically lets his impure "begging-bowl" replicate itself to the extent that the entire sacrificial awning is inundated with polluting human skulls. See Malik (1993b: 69–74; 284–288). Śiva's interference with Brahmā's sacrifice echoes the ancient myth of Śiva and Dakṣa's rivalry. In the myth, Śiva, after having been excluded from Dakṣa's sacrifice, proceeds to destroy it and to kill Dakṣa.

4. In one variant, Hari Rām is supposed to be a Gujar who is later given the title "Siṃh" from King Bisaldev because of his selfless act of slaying the maneating lion. See also Malik (1993a: 381)

5. On the paṛ Hari Rām is shown carrying the lion's head facing the lake of Pushkar at L 52–55, 6–7.

6. This incident and the one following it in which Rūpnāth's body turns into gold, are typical of the large corpus of legends extolling Nāth Yogīs' miraculous powers. See Gold (1992).

7. See also Singh (1993: 414).

8. The mare, in fact, is a manifestation of Śakti. The cow is none other than Kāmadhenū, the "wish-fulfilling" cow. The elephant, too, is a form of the Goddess. For variants on this, see Singh (1993: 414).

9. Banyā is the name of a caste of merchants and traders known for their dealings with trade and commerce and money.

10. See L 7–8, 3–4, on the paṛ.

11. Rāṇā is a title carried by the Rajput chiefs of Mewar.

12. The Rāṇā is supposedly 120 years old!

13. See L 9, 17, on the paṛ.

14. "Playing dice" is a euphemism for sexual activity. See Gold (1992: 99 n. 66).

15. The number 52 denotes the vast extent of the Rāṇā's military dominion. The number is used elsewhere also in order to convey greatness. See, for example, the "fifty-two" ghāṭs of Pushkar (Malik 1993b: 7) or the "fifty-two" forts of the epic hero Pābūjī's kingdom of Koḷū (Smith 1991: 289).

16. See R 24–29, 14–18, on the paṛ.

17. The symbolism of this event can be compared with images of the womb and birth, fertility and victory, found in the myth of Indra, who slays the serpent demon Vṛtra and splits open the "mountains' bellies," freeing the waters (Ṛg Veda 1.32.1).

18. Written or printed texts in general may also match the oral-visual narrative with respect to entailing the possibility of endless interpretations issuing out of the interactive situation between the reader and the text.

19. Although this may sound quite obvious, the representation of oral narratives as *texts* is rarely, let alone briefly, problematized in studies on South Asian culture and religion, and this is especially true for Indological research.

20. Under the term 'signifiance' Barthes understands that aspect of a narrative that is not "a finished, closed product, but a production in progress, 'plugged in' to other texts, other codes (this is the intertextual), and thereby articulated with society and history in ways which are not determinist but citational" (135).

21. Barthes is apparently citing Nietzsche here.

22. See Blackburn, Claus, Fluekiger, and Wadley (1989), Smith (1991), Singh (1993), Malik (1993), Miller (1994).

23. I am using the term *epic* here not to limit the description of the text of Devnārāyaṇ but to be able to place it in a particular academic discussion relevant to this enquiry. The

category of *epic* is a point of departure that must be taken into account before developing an alternative understanding of the text.

24. This concern pervades the scholarly analysis of other genres as well (for example, māhātmyas and purāṇas). The problems that arise here are limited not to questions of scholarly "method" but more radically to the politicization of the past, for example, in the context of the historicity texts and the pursuit of the location of corresponding archaeological sites, and so on.

25. For example, Kothari (1989), Smith (1991).

26. For example, in the *Rāmāyaṇa* it is Rāma who, by accepting his banishment, is in favor of daiva, and Lakṣmaṇa who, by being against it, is in favor of pauruṣa.

27. Gadamer (1953: 300, 307), cited in Pollock (1991: 17).

28. See, for example, also Vatsyayan's (1995: 3) discussion on the issue of authorship and historicity with regard to Bharata and the Nāṭyaśāstra: "One can continue to discuss the perennial problems of dating and exact locations, even the historicity of many authors, writers, theoreticians . . . The application of inappropriate yardsticks for comprehending a tradition has sometimes caused confusion and misconception. . . . As a result, often 'where' and 'when' have been the end of the investigation rather than the 'what' and 'why' of the text, work of art, or theory."

29. This list is neither meant to be exhaustive nor essentializing.

30. For a discussion of the meanings and different understandings of the term, see Plett (1991).

31. See also chapter 2, for a discussion of "conversational discourse" in the context of the oral narrative structure of the verbal narrative.

32. Kristeva (1969: 36), cited in Mai (1991: 40). Mai (40) observes that Kristeva's idea of intertextuality "resembles very closely a sociological theory of literature. The important difference is that Kristeva no longer conceives of society/history as something *outside* the text, some objective entity over and against the text, but partaking of the same textuality as literature."

33. Ramanujan (1989: 189). Ramanujan adds that within the range of reflexive interrelationships it is possible to determine different sets of texts such as pretexts, subtexts, cotexts, countertexts, and metatexts. Cotexts are "responsive," in the sense that "text A responds to text B in ways that define both A and B." Countertexts are "reflexive," in the sense that "text A reflects on text B, relates itself to it directly or inversely"; metatexts are "self-reflexive" because here "a text reflects on itself or its kind" (188).

34. The notion of an "original"—whether constructed by scholars or by "tradition"—is of course completely arbitrary.

35. This is the name of a fictitious, composite animal. See R 25,4, on the paṛ.

36. Trans. O'Flaherty (1982: 220); *Bhāgavata Purāṇa* 10.8.2145; see also *Mahābhārata* 3.1867 (cited in O'Flaherty).

37. I am grateful to David Shulman for pointing out that the passages are not simpler in cosmological terms than the puranic one.

38. This scene again is reminiscent of the encounter between Nāpā Guāl and Sāḍū Mātā during the opening section of the narrative. Here too, Nāpā does not believe Sāḍū when she says that she has a "pact" with Bhagavān that he will manifest as her son. Even after his birth Nāpā is not convinced of his divinity. Only after the infant Devnārāyaṇ revives two slain Rajput confederates of the Bagaṛāvats does Nāpā begin to believe in his divine powers. See chapter 7.

39. See the subsection entitled "Devī and Devnārāyaṇ," this chapter.

40. *Bhāgavata Purāṇa* trans. O'Flaherty (1982: 22). In contrast to Yaśodā, Sāḍū Mātā is

aware of her son's divinity from the very beginning. There is no web of māyā spread over her perceptions; the distinction between māyā and knowledge is not drawn, even though Devnārāyaṇ continuously "proves" his divinity to other individuals.

41. *Bhāgavata Purāṇa*, trans. O'Flaherty (1982: 221).

42. See the oral story of the Dhangar shepherd who, naively following the instructions of a Brahman, almost drowns and thereby "forces" God to reveal himself to him. Sontheimer (1993: 148).

43. Other motifs are discussed in more detail in chapter 7.

44. See Smith (1991: 908).

45. See, for example, (Thiel-)Horstmann (1993) and Sontheimer (1994).

46. See Sontheimer (1994), Erndl (1993), Binford (1976), Roghair (1982). The various avatāras of the epic of Pābūjī have already been listed (Smith 1991).

47. These are obvious links made in the written text; more subtle links to the *Mahābhārata* are perceptible in the oral telling. Thus, while Devnārāyaṇ is explicitly called Dharamrāj, his brothers have correspondences with the other four Paṇḍavas. Bhāṅgī: Bhīma; Bhūṇā: Arjuna; Medū/Madnā: Nakula/Sahadeva.

48. See R, 42, 4–5, on the paṛ, Savāī Bhoj is depicted sitting under a khejaṛī tree. His alter ego, Śeṣa, is shown in the square beneath him, which represents a water reservoir.

49. See also Pābūjī's mare Kesar Kālamī, which is a manifestation of Śakti.

50. The source of this information is the paṛ. It is not mentioned in the version of the recorded narrative presented here. See L 54, 7, on the paṛ.

51. The depiction of deities is continued to the right of the scene depicting Laṅkā. Sitting in crosslegged posture with his horse facing him is Rāmdevjī, followed by Yama riding a buffalo. After this come the chariots of the sun and the moon.

52. In contemporary folk religious cults, "transgressive" figures like Bhairava or a whole range of other demonic figures occupy the peripheries of religious or sacred enclosures such as temples and shrines. The "impure," "aggressive," "wild," "bloodthirsty," "rapacious" nature of demonic figures relegates them to the status of "bodyguards," "doorguards," "warrior attendants," and the like. Invariably there is a myth explaining the encounter between the deity and his or her "guardian." The encounter usually involves a clash of powers wherein the "demon" looses, only to be converted into the deity's most trusty assistant or devotee after his defeat or even slaying. In Devnārāyaṇ's case there is no such narrative that explains the occurrence of his "impure," sword-wielding, dog-riding *aṅgarakṣakas* Kālā and Gorā Bherū̃. And in terms of iconography or even temple topography, Kālā and Gora Bherū̃ are not so distant from the god, as is the case in other examples. It is true that they are his attendants and bodyguards, performing a number of deeds that Devnārāyaṇ does not himself perform, but there is no tale of submission or conversion involved here. Nor do they feature in any overt way as Devnārāyaṇ's steadfast devotees. (Chochū Bhāṭ comes much closer to the ideal figure of a transgressive, tricksterlike character who nevertheless extols the god's greatness to the highest degree: he is supposed to be the composer of the narrative.) The most explicit contrast between Devnārāyaṇ and Kālā and Gorā Bherū̃ is on the level of ritual offerings. Whereas Devnārāyaṇ accepts only vegetarian and nonalcoholic offerings, Bherū̃ receives nonvegetarian offerings and *dārū*. And while possession (*bhāv āvṅo*) does not play any role during jāgraṇs for Devnārāyaṇ, since he does not "possess" his devotees, there is regular possession through Bherū̃, although this happens at other locations that are wholly dedicated to him. The kind of possession that occurs here is mainly of an oracular kind that is not part of any "performative" situation. The contrast between Devnārāyaṇ and Bherū̃ is partially repeated in the contrast between Devnārāyaṇ and his father, Savāī Bhoj, who, as befits a warrior (*jhū̃jhār*), receives daily offerings of dārū (locally made liquor).

53. Other deities in Rajasthan are also referred to in this way. See German: "Herr," Spanish: "Señor."

54. On the conception of the deity as king in folk cults, see Sontheimer (1993a, b), Fuller (1992), Brückner (1995).

55. The phrase *ād jugād* can also refer to a thing that is ancient or belonging to tradition.

56. Alternately, this is also a Gujar lineage title. On the overlap between Gujar and Rajput lineage names, see also chapter 5.

57. The *agni-kula* origin myth of the Cahamānas is supposed to have been current in the fourteenth century, with reference to the Cahamānas of Mount Abu, who appeared as a new warrior race after the solar and lunar dynasties were destroyed. On the emergence of Rajput lineages in medieval Rajasthan, see Chattopadhyaya (1992).

58. See, for example, *Devī-Māhātmya* 2.8–2.10: "Having heard these words of the gods, the slayer of Madhu (Viṣṇu) became angry, and Śiva too, with furrowed brows and twisted faces. Then from Viṣṇu's face, which was filled with rage, came forth a great fiery splendor (*tejas*). (And also from the faces) of Brahmā and Śiva. And from the bodies of the other gods, Indra and the others, came forth a great fiery splendor, and it became unified in one place. An exceedingly fiery mass like a flaming mountain did the gods see there, filling the firmament with flames. That peerless splendor, born from the bodies of all the gods, unified and pervading the triple world with its lustre, became a woman." Trans. Coburn (1991: 40).

59. *Mānava Dharma Śāstra* 7.36, 1011, trans. G. Bühler, "The laws of Manu" is cited in Coburn (1982: 160).

60. Nevājī is Savāī Bhoj's brave, impetuous younger brother. He is Bhāṅgījī's father.

61. The motif of possessing the triple-world by repeating a seemingly trivial action three times is also found in the myth of the three steps of Viṣṇu's dwarf incarnation, and in the story of Kṛṣṇa who is stopped from eating three handfuls of rice that his impoverished childhood friend Sudāma has brought for him as a gift. In the latter case it is not Kṛṣṇa but Sudāma who would have unknowingly benefited from the god's action.

62. "Filled with divine knowledge," "knowledgeable like the gods."

63. See the section on Sāḍū Mātā in chapter 6.

64. *Sakalp*, Skt. *saṃkalpa*: "an offering," "the intention to offer," or "a promise."

65. Skt. *saṃkalpa* a solemn vow or determination to perform any ritual observance; declaration of purpose. Thus, for example, in the *Antyeṣṭipaddhati* of Nārāyaṇabhaṭṭa, which deals with rites to be performed for the deceased, saṃkalpa is one of the ceremonies performed during the course of the entire ritual: "Der *saṃkalpa* ist die Absichtserklärung des Vollziehers, einen Ritus zu vollziehen. Diese Absichtserklärung bekundet er, indem er nach der *deśa-kāla-smṛti* vor dem Beginn eines Ritus erklärt: 'Ich werde den Ritus N. N. vollziehen, damit N. N. [oder ich, N. N.] aus dem *gotra* N. N. die Früchte erlangt, die in den *śāstras*, in der *śruti*, in der *smṛti* und in den *purāṇas* beschrieben sind.' Erst nach dem *saṃkalpa* kann ein Ritus vollzogen werden. Unter bestimmten Umständen wird nur der *saṃkalpa* gesagt, der Ritus selbst aber erst später vollzogen" (Müller 1992: 41). Müller adds that the preceding description is general, whereas otherwise a concrete result is usually mentioned that is to be attained through the performance of the rite.

66. See Beck (1981).

67. See Hiltebeitel (1989).

68. *yajñabhāgam ahaṃ bhoktum icchāmī tvat-prasādataḥ / yathā makheṣu sarveṣu pūjyo 'haṃ syāṃ tathā kuru / tvat pādasevaṃ na tyakṣye yāvat sūryaḥ pravartate / evaṃ varadvayaṃ dehī yadi deyo varo mama* (*Kālikā-Purāṇa* 60.104–105).

69. *yajñabhāgāḥ surebhyastu kalpitā vai pṛthak pṛthak / bhāgo na vidyate cānyo yaṃ dāsyāmī*

tavādhunā / kintu tvayi mayā siddhe nihate mahiṣāsur / naiva tyakṣyasi matpādam satataṃ nātra saṃśayaḥ (*Kālikā-Purāṇa* 60.106–107).

70. See narrative on pp. 85–86.

71. It is possible to interpret the overt theme of marrying the queen as an underlying tussle for obtaining the spiritual and political favor of the Goddess. In this case, however, she ultimately belongs only the those who give up their lives to her in an act of voluntary self-sacrifice. Moreover, the Bagaṛāvat's deaths provide a continuation of a motif from the beginning of the narrative when the 24 Ṛṣis offer their own bodies to satisfy Śiva's hunger.

72. This is evident in Nevājī's choice to distribute their wealth for social purposes rather than hoard it as the eldest brother, Tejājī, suggests.

73. While the brothers' lives express a kind of fierce or radical *ugra bhakti*, Sāḍū Mātā's devotion toward Bhagavān expresses a kind of *vātsalya bhakti*, characterized by their mother-child relationship.

74. Taken together, these motifs form a complex nexus of "sacrificial" values and actions.

75. *Mahābhārata*, book 6 (*Bhīṣma Parvan*), chapter 23, beginning of Gītā. The *Durgā Stotra* is inserted at the end of chapter 22.

76. A mirror image of this is provided by the final battle scene in the *Mahābhārata*, in which Arjuna envisions Kṛṣṇa "swallowing" the Pāṇḍava's enemies, the Kauravas and their armies.

77. The destructive imagery of battles and armed confrontation is also expressed on the right half of the paṛ. See the last section of chapter 3.

78. See chapter 7.

5. Historical Narrative

1. The epigraph is from Ohnuki-Tierney (1990: 3).

2. The singers come from different regions of Rajasthan. They also tell the story in different dialects.

3. Examples are provided in chapter 2.

4. These points are dealt with in greater detail in chapter 6.

5. Utānpād, Devahutī, Kardam, Prīyavrat, Barhismatī, Āgnidhra, and so on.

6. Jambū, Plakṣa, Puṣkara, and so on.

7. "Śrī Aṇandārāmjī, village Bistārī, Jātī Gurjar, Got Phāgaṇā, Father Jagārāmjī, Mother Pārvatī, Daughter of Rūpār Koli (and) Bholūjī Kaṃvararāmjī, Sister of Nandājī, Tehsīl Hiṇḍoti, Jilā Būndī (Rāj). In the protection (at the feet of) Śrī Satguru Śrī Mahārāj Kiśandāsjī Rāmeśvar, Śrī Rāmnārāyaṇ Gurjar Bihāḍā, Got Lītryā, Father Baradu Rāmjī, Mother Phūmā, village Jāgolāī, Sister of Kālūjī Gedā, Teh(sil) Jahājpur, Jilā Bhivāḍāī (Rāj.). In the protection of Śrī Satguru Mahāraj Śrī Aṇaṇdārāmjī (of village) Bistārī (and) Hālā Phāguṇā is a maintainer of the *dharam* of Viṣṇu and (belongs) to the Bairāg Panth. There are 4 *sampradāya* of Bairāg. 1. Rāmāvat, 2. Nīmāvat, 3. Biṣṇu Svāmī, 4. Madhvācāryajī. [There are] 52 gateways. We are disciples of the Rāmāvat *sampradāya*. There are 7 *akhāḍās* of the Bairāg. Khākī, Nirbāṇī, Nirmoī, Parlamya, Santokī, Jaṅgam [*sic*], Prāsaṃam.

We belong to the Rām Jaygam [*sic*] *akhāḍā*. There are two paths [to the] Rām Jaygam, Nirpatī and Parbatī, Godāvarī, Parkamā, Ajodhyā, Dharmśālā āsaṇ Śrī Dākor, Mūjya Khāk, Cauk Urad, Kuṇḍ Tilak, Siddhi Siṅghāsaṇ, Kirīt Mukuṭ, Gotra Vaitra, Kambādevī, Dvār, Śravaṇṛṣi Viṣvāmītrajī Vasiṣṭhamunī, Capaḍās the pair of sūt, Koṭval Śrī Hanumān."

8. See Sontheimer (1993b) for a detailed account of three Maharashtrian dieties,

Birobā, Mhaskobā, and Khaṇḍobā, in terms of the history of the groups behind the cults of the deities. For a discussion of the social and ritual status of Gujars in Uttar Pradesh, see Raheja (1988).

9. "Poetry," or a poem usually consisting of four lines with 31 syllables per line.

10. This is similar to the invocatory passage at the beginning of the oral narrative.

11. *Tū baḍadā̃ kī bhārī?*

12. The term used here is *najar*, which can mean "gaze" or also gift.

13. These are the names of the four *agni-kula* Rajput clans ("fire-clan," Rajputs who originated from a ritual fire).

14. See Westphal-Hellbusch (1975) for an ethnographic study of pastoral and farmer communities in northwestern India.

15. In the *Bhāgavata Purāṇa* there is a similar episode involving the sage Atri and his wife, Anasūyā. After performing severe penance, the couple are visited by the three gods mentioned earlier. The couple's wish to be blessed with progeny exactly like the "Lord of the World" is the same as Suvāī Manu and Satrūpā's desire to have a child like Pārbṛhm Parameśvar born to them: "He contemplated (and prayed in his mind): 'I take shelter under him who alone is the Lord of the World. May he bless me with progeny just like himself.' (20) Seeing that the three worlds were being distressed by the fire produced by the fuel of (the sage's) breath-control (prāṇāyāma) and issuing from the head of the sage, the three Lords (of the world, Brahmā, Viṣṇu, and Śiva) went to the hermitage of the sage. (21–22) . . . With his mind concentrated on them and with folded palms he praised, in sweet words of deep significance, the three gods who are the supreme-most in the world. (25) You are (obviously the celebrated gods) Brahmā, Viṣṇu and Śiva who in every yuga (kalpa) assume forms with the help of the *guṇas* (attributes) of māyā. . . . (27) In this hermitage, I have concentrated (contemplated) only on one glorious Lord by various means, with a desire to get a child. It is a great surprise to me how (all of) you who are beyond the range of the mind of bodied beings have come here. Be pleased to tell me the mystery (28)" (*Bhāgavata Purāṇa* 4.1. 20, 21–22, 25, 27, 28; trans. Tagare [1976: 423]).

16. *Aur merī taraṅgā nirākār se phaṭphaṭ.*

17. In Sanskrit sources Garuḍa's brother's name is Aruṇa.

18. In the *Kathāsaritsāgara* Garuḍa, on his way to acquire *amṛta* from the devas, alights briefly on a branch of the *kalpavṛkṣa* in order to eat a gigantic elephant and tortoise. The branch sags under his weight, "but Garuḍa held it in his beak out of respect for the *Vālakhilyas* who were practising austerities there. Afraid that if he dropped the branch human beings would be crushed, Garuḍa took the advice of his father and placed it down in an uninhabited place. Laṅkā was built on that branch and the ground here is therefore wooden" (Sattar 1994: 55).

19. *Kos ūpar adhak-pramāṇ dakhjyo.*

20. *Mār legā kālan ek kī coṭ.*

21. *Baḍā pracit ho jāvegā.*

22. *Nau garah = nava graha.*

23. *nau peḍiyā ke pīṇd.*

24. In the Vālmīki Rāmāyaṇa, Narāntaka is the name of one of Rāvaṇa's generals who dies in the battle against Rāma.

25. Rāvaṇa's origins otherwise go back to Viśravas, the grandson of Brahmā and son of Pulastya who marries Kaikasī, the daughter of Sumālī.

26. Judging from the chronology of events, this paragraph describing Rāvaṇa's birth from Bisvejī should appear before the previous one.

27. The damming of waters and the captivity of cows, of course, echoes an ancient motif found already in the Ṛg Veda (1.32) in the story of Indra's killing of Vṛtra. This

motif or rather myth was one of the central myths of the Indo-European warrior class: "In this was told how the first warrior, whose name was 'Third' (**Trito*), conducted the first cattle raid. . . . Here it is related that cattle originally belonging to the Indo-Europeans . . . were stolen by a monstrous three-headed serpent . . . who was a non-Indo-European, an aborigine living in land entered by I-E invaders. Following this theft, it fell to 'Third' to recover the stolen cattle, and he began his quest by seeking the aid of a warrior deity to whom he offered libations of intoxicating drinks. . . . Having won the god's assistance, and himself fortified by the same intoxicating drinks, 'Third' set forth, found the 'Serpent,' slew him, and released the cattle which had been imprisoned by the monster" (Lincoln 1991: 10).

28. Translation of pp. 2–7 of the printed text (*Bagaṛāvat Bhārat* n.d.).

29. Bhārat refers to the great battle; Devnārāyaṇ's birth is described on p. 88 of the printed text (*Bagaṛāvat Bhārat* n.d.).

30. Or: in the family; see earlier.

31. For an extensive discussion of these terms and their position within systems of Hindu mythology and religious thought, see Bailey (1983).

32. See also Raheja (1988: 22–23) on the overlap of Gujar and Rajput clan names.

33. On the political and historical discourse that the figure and narrative of Rāma has offered and continues to offer, see, for example, Pollock (1993).

34. Similarly, in another telling of the opening episodes of the Bagaṛāvat that deals with the previous existence of the 24 brothers, Sītā is born from the blood of 24 sages. The sages deposit their blood in a jar in lieu of a tax that Rāvaṇa has demanded from them. Realizing that the jar filled with blood spells his doom, Rāvaṇa has it buried in a field on the boundaries of King Janaka's kingdom. It is out of that jar that Sītā later appears. For a translation of this story, see Malik (1996). See also the Kannada *Adbhuta Rāmāyaṇa*, in which Sītā is born after Maṇḍodarī has unknowingly drunk the blood of ṛṣis (Aithal 1987: 1–2). For many other tellings of the Rāma story see, for example, Ramanujan (1991), Richman (1991), and Thiel-Horstmann (1991).

35. Taken as a whole, the narrative tradition of Devārāyaṇ entails distinct sets of reworkings of the avatāra concept. While the oral telling both replicates and refashions the avatāras of Kṛṣṇa and Devī, the printed telling draws on the Rāma avatāra to produce its own narrative.

36. Ramanujan (1991: 44) distinguishes between three kinds of translation: iconic, indexical, and symbolic.

37. The connection between Hanumān and the Gujars is significant because they both share qualities of strength, vigor, warriorhood, and devotion. While Hanumān is both beast and god, Gaupāl Gujar is human, but born of a god's seed from a sacred animal. For a discussion of Hanumān's characterization in Vālmīki's *Rāmāyaṇa*, see Goldman and Sutherland Goldman (1994).

38. This is true also for the two parts of the narrative whose different yet interconnected religious ideologies I have discussed in chapter 4.

39. See especially the following section "Another History."

40. See the story of Sāḍū Mātā's birth in chapter 6.

41. See chapter 5, the section dealing with Sāḍū Mātā's role in the narrative.

42. For details of Devnārāyaṇ's birth, see also chapter 7.

43. Ramanujan (1991: 45), drawing on C. S. Peirce's work, explains indexicality as follows: "Very often, although Text 2 stands in an iconic relationship to Text 1 in terms of basic elements such as plot, it is filled with local detail, folklore, poetic traditions, imagery, and so forth. . . . We may call such a text *indexical*: the text is embedded in a

locale, a context, refers to it, even signifies it, and would not make much sense without it."

44. This is also partially true for the printed text, which, however, rewrites Devnārāyaṇ's birth with exact astronomical dates, the ritual ceremonies of Brahmans, and the song and dance of Gandharvas, Caraṇas, and Apsaras.

45. The narrative is thus about multiple deaths, making it difficult in terms of a hypothesis about the "deified dead" (see references to S. H. Blackburn's work in chapter 4), to identify a single "death" that could have formed the historical basis of the story.

46. See synopsis, and Singh (1993). See also L 39, 16–17, on the paṛ.

47. Ortner (1990: 60). Although Ortner uses the concept specifically in the context of social and ritual activity, I am introducing it here to understand the structure and workings of the narrative text of Devnārāyaṇ. Moreover, I consider the idea of a "cultural schema" as a possible alternative to notions such as "great" and "little" or "classical" and "folk," which may suggest a hierarchical ordering of culture. This is not to deny the fact that cultural symbols are pervasively used to create power relations and hierarchies in society. The critique implicit in the idea of "cultural schemas" is directed against a particular *intellectual* or *academic* conceptualization of culture.

48. An understanding of such concepts in these terms suggests an alternative to the notions of "cultural ownership" that categories like "great," "little," "high," "low," "classical," or "folk" tend to invoke. Similarly, Sells (1994: 4) while discussing apophasis in the work of five mystical writers from "separate religious traditions . . . of the west," points out that it is "profitable to see these traditions as competing within a partially shared intellectual and symbolic world, defining themselves in conversation with one another and against one another." See also Ramanujan (1989).

49. Tod (vol. 2, p. 564). See also Harlan (1992: 30).

50. Uday Siṃh, who was a descendant of the famous Rajput chieftain and founder of Chitor Bappa Rāval, ascended the throne of Chitor in 1542. He later established the city of Udaipur.

51. Sections of the episode of Devnārāyaṇ's revival of the slain Jogīs are structurally similar to the episode involving Chochū Bhāṭ and Bhūṇā on the banks of Puṣkara. (See the section on Chochū Bhāṭ in chapter 6.) The intention here is again to provide testimony of Devnārāyaṇ's powers. Similar to the incident at Puṣkara Lake, Devnārāyaṇ, in the episode involving the Jogīs, is "absent" and is called on by a person—in this case his own mother, Sāḍū Mātā—to both save her dignity and life and to prove his divinity to someone who is a "disbeliever." The episode is equally important because it deals with the—albiet accidental—recovery of Bhāṅgījī, the son of the most brave and impetuous Bagaṛāvats, Nevājī. Bhāṅgījī has been adopted from birth by the Bagaṛāvats guru, Bābā Rūpnāth. He has grown up as a Jogī ignorant of his family and real origins. A maidservant of Sāḍū Mātā is the first to spot him while she was fetching water from a well:

> There was a banyan tree above the well—*mhe*—
> Half of the Jogīs were sitting beneath the banyan tree playing caupaḍ—*vāh vāh*—
> The other half of the Jogīs were sitting on the well's steps
> *Yes, they were on the steps*
> Nevājī's son Bhāṅgījī was sitting in the midst of those Jogīs like a lord
> *Yes, he was sitting in their midst like a master*
> Upon seeing the Jogī's face—*mhe*—the maidservant swooned on that spot—*vāh vāh*—

[Instead of collecting water, she returns to Sāḍū Mātā and tells her:]

"In the middle of the well there's a twisted banyan tree—*mhe*—
O Mother, as I went down there, I saw a group of Jogīs
I saw one Jogī—*vāh vāh*—
With the face of our brother-in-law, Nevā
Nevājī features—*mhe*—
And the Jogīs features were identical, O Mother!"

[Sāḍū Mātā is enraged at the maidservant's claim and the possibility that anyone of the Bagaṛāvats' offspring would join up with the Jogīs:] "The Bagaṛāvats were hardly such a feeble family that one of them would join the Jogīs."

This statement, once again, expresses a perspective on the hierarchy of power. Not only is there friction between Devnārāyaṇ, the Bagaṛāvats, their followers, and the regents of temporal power, namely the Rajputs, but also between the former and the holders of ascetic power, namely the Nāth Jogīs. As with the relationship to the Rajputs, shades of ambivalence are at work here, too.

52. A person of the Damāmī community (a caste of drummer-genealogists attached to Rajput ruling houses and clans) once remarked that " 'real' [*aslī*] Rajputs do not listen to this story because of the killings and losses [*mār-kāṭ*] their community is subjected to."

53. See section on Chochū Bhāṭ in chapter 6.

6. Social Narrative

1. The metaphor of different communities "commingling" is also found in the epic of Pābūjī. In a scene from the culminating battle, Pābūjī requests the Goddess to mix the blood of different warriors (Bhīl, Rebārī, and Rajput) so that these communities may participate together in his cult. See Smith (1991: 450)

2. I am using this term in a qualified sense to set apart the authority of mortal kings in the narrative from that of the explicitly divine king, Devnārāyaṇ. Traditionally speaking, of course, there are mergers between "secular" and divine kingship. See Gonda (1954) and Heesterman (1957, 1985).

3. According to Komal Kothari (personal communication, 1997), the rivalry between Gujars and Rajputs is in reality about a conflict between different forms of economy or subsistence. Kothari suggests that the entire region of Rajasthan may be divided into three main ecological and "economic" zones, each with a different type of narrative tradition. Roughly speaking, these zones are the millet (*bājrā*) growing area in the western part of Rajasthan; the sorghum (*jovār*) growing area in the eastern part; and the maize (*makkī*) growing area in the south. In the western zone there is a predominance of cattle breeding; the eastern zone is charactarized by cattle herding, and the southern zone by hunter-gatherer communities inhabiting forests. Each of these ecological and economic areas have produced narratives that articulate themes connected to the vicissitudes of living in those regions. For example, (epic) narratives from the western zone center on incidents related to cattle raids, the protection of cattle, and clashes arising from the theft of cows. In the eastern region, the (epic) narratives focus on conflicts arising between grazers and agriculturalists, and in the southern zone, "epic-cycle" stories invariably seem to thematize the encroachments of the settled, agricultural people into the forest, which is the living space of the Bhīls and Mīnās. Following the pattern in the eastern zone, the culminating sections of the narrative make it evident that the conflict toward which Devnārāyaṇ and his four cousins are heading against the Rāṇā is also one between cattle-herders and land-

owners. Devnārāyaṇ is portrayed as the chief of a herd of 980,000 cattle and buffaloes. The Rāṇā is referred to as the sovereign of 52 forts, together with a vast quantity of villages and agricultural property. One of the "military" strategies that Devnārāyaṇ uses to weaken the Rāṇā is to destroy his produce by releasing the gigantic herd of cattle into his fields.

4. In order to shorten them I have summarized the passages from the original telling by combining the voices of the singer Śrī Hukamārām and his partner Śrī Moṭārām. The effect provided by this fusion is that the text reads as continual prose and has syntactically "complete" sentences instead of the syntactically truncated but verbally complete "utterances" of the oral rendering. See Malik (1999: 159–162).

5. The double-gourd stringed instrument used by bhopās during recitations of the narrative.

6. A term used for Rajpūt warriors.

7. "White One."

8. A mythical flower.

9. A weight approximately equivalent to ¼ kilogram.

10. Approximately 1 kilogram.

11. Around 40 kilograms.

12. See Malik (1999: 163–164).

13. Steps leading down to the lake of Puṣkara.

14. The text is unclear here.

15. The annual fair held in Puṣkara during the month of Kārttika.

16. An animal resembling a mongoose only larger and poisonous.

17. *Bak-bak.* The phrase also suggests a nonsensical, raving, or incoherent kind of laughter. See Śiva's wild laughter (*aṭahāsa*).

18. See Shulman (1990) for an excellent crosscultural study of south Indian clowns and their intricate relationships to kings; On Tēnāli Rāma see pp. 180–200.

19. While the figures of Chochū Bhāṭ and Sāḍū Mātā are both defined by devotion toward Devnārāyaṇ, Sāḍū Mātā sees the troublemaking, trickster-like qualities of the former as a threat to her own relationship with her son. The conflict between mother and bard is described in chapter 7.

20. See chapters 4 and 7.

21. For details, see chapter 4, synopsis of the Bagaṛāvat Bhārat.

22. At this Śrī Hukamārām Bhopā comments: "Look, now the Gujars come into [the story]. Otherwise [till now] they were Rajputs, what! Understood!"

23. Again Śrī Hukamārām Bhopā comments: "This story is about here, nowhere else—about Nāg Pahāḍ (the chain of hills running between Puṣkara and Ajmer."

24. Today there is also a considerable Gujar population living in Ajmer and its surrounding villages.

25. The *Mahābhārata* also contains a number of examples of "cross-marriages," resulting, for example, in the births of Bhīṣma, Karṇa, and the five Paṇḍavas, who are all born of pairings between deities and humans. See van Buitenen (1973: xix–xxi).

26. Later the Gujars are "joined forces" with by potters, leatherworkers, and cowherds in general. Together they form a "subaltern" troop ranked together against the more powerful armies of the Rāṇā and his generals. It is significant that the destruction of the Rāṇā's fort is led by the strongest but most awkward "warrior" figure, Bhāṅgī, whose weapons themselves speak for their "nonmartial," domestic character: the mortar from an oil press as his club, the wooden wheel of an oxen-cart as his shield, and the stone pestle from the oil press as his helmet! Here again, as in the earlier instance of the encounter between Chochū Bhāṭ and King Nīmde, the downfall of the mighty Rāṇā is precipitated

by a relatively marginal figure. While the Bhāṭ is a physical weakling who relies on his wit and the magical support of Devnārāyaṇ, Bhāṅgī is bumbling and slow on the intellectual uptake but monstrously strong physically. However, neither of the two represent typical warrior-like personalities that might be deemed appropriate for a confrontation with the vast military forces of the Rāṇā.

27. While this section involves a discussion on images of women, these are not necessarily images of women drawn by themselves, even though there may be some mutually shared perspectives. Whatever the source of the images presented here, the picture created does not always support the commonly held description of women as submissive and voiceless. Moreover, as Gold (Raheja and Gold 1994: 71) observes in her study of Rajasthani women's songs, perspectives on gender are shared by both men and women: "both visions coexist and are available to both sexes. Men can and do partake at times of . . . female-generated visions . . . even as women often articulate perfectly and subscribe behaviourally to the prevalent set of values . . . heuristically described as having male orientations and origins."

28. See also Appadurai, Korom, and Mills (1991).

29. The meaning of Devnārāyaṇ's three marriages is discussed in chapter 7.

30. See, for example, also Gold (Raheja and Gold 1994: 164–181), who, while writing about the exceptional case of a Rajput woman's worship of Devnārāyaṇ, frequently refers to devotees of the god as constituting a "mixed-caste" group.

31. This is in continuation of the story presented in chapter 4 in the section "Devī as Avatāra."

32. That is, when he is cremated.

33. To worship or sing devotional songs.

34. Another telling of Sāḍū Mātā's birth also connects her origins to the powers of ascetics. Here she is portrayed as being in her previous life a frog, which sacrifices itself in order to save the lives of ṛṣis and sādhus who are engaged in performing a complex fire ritual. During the ceremony a poisonous snake is accidently dropped by a bird of prey from the sky into the cauldron of boiling rice pudding being prepared for the officiants. When the frog sees the snake fall into the cauldron, it decides to float on the surface of its contents so as to warn the sages and mendicants not to consume the poisoned pudding. When they see the scalded, dead frog in the cauldron they pour out its contents, only to find the snake at the bottom. Realizing that the frog has sacrificed its life for the sake of theirs, they decide to bring it back to life in the shape of a girl, whom they name Sāḍū.

35. See also chapter 4, section entitled "Devī as Avatāra."

36. On the fulfilment of vows for the engenderment and protection of sons in a folk-religious context, see Feldhaus's detailed study of the significance of rivers and water in Maharashtra (1995: 118–145).

37. The implication is that she is infused with the moral and spiritual quality of sat, which can lead to the self-combustive act of sati (see Harlan 1992, 1994). The fact that she has not committed sati like the other wives of the Bagaṛāvats is, in subsequent sections of the narrative, called into question at times. On one such occasion she is charged by the energy of sat and is almost on the verge of self-immolation when she is "cooled" down by Devnārāyaṇ. By carrying the power of sat within her, Sāḍū Mātā, in a sense, has put the potential for becoming a sati on "hold."

38. Queen Jaimatī, in fact, embodies the figure of a "murderous," "virgin" bride. See Shulman (1976).

39. The word "continuum" is used here to emphasize the interconnected rather than dichotomous ways that women are represented in the narrative. Similarly, Sax (1997) in the context of the Pāṇḍav Līlā in Garhwal, writes, "the wild goddesses are seen as rep-

resenting raw female power (*śakti*), autonomous and dangerously out of control, while the domestic goddesses, tamed by their male consorts, are more dependably auspicious and benevolent. . . . The problem with the debate over split goddesses is that it is all too often represented as a choice between competing essentialisms. . . . Here is where a perspectival approach can help: goddesses (and women, too) are sometimes fierce and sometimes peaceful, depending on the goddess's actions and the perspective of the worshipper. Women (and goddesses, too) are sometimes fierce and sometimes peaceful, sometimes angry and sometimes benign."

40. An interesting ethnographic parallel to this is provided by Gold's (Raheja and Gold 1994: 168) description of the worship of Devnārāyaṇ by a Rajput woman, Sobhag Kanvar. Her devotion to Devnārāyaṇ results in a conflict over the constrictions of *purdah*, or the rules of decorum and propriety expected of Rajput women. But, as Gold points out, Sobhag Kanvar is able to sustain her devotion (bhakti) to Devnārāyaṇ while at the same time "stretching the meaning" of purdah. Sāḍū Mātā represents the extreme case of a woman's denial of social restrictions in order to fulfil her religious sentiments.

41. Other more ambivalent aspects of Sāḍū Mātā's personality are discussed in greater detail in chapter 7.

42. See Ramanujan (1986) on the distinction between inner and outer realms (*akam* and *puram*) in Tamil poetry. The movement between these realms is also reflected in the episodes featuring Chochū Bhāṭ discussed earlier. Here "outer" religiopolitical satire is juxtaposed with "inner" issues of divine proof and devotion to God.

7. Divine Testimony

1. See chapter 2.

2. Parcyo is cognate with Hindi *paricay*: acquaintance; knowledge, experience; information, data.

3. This individual parcyo is not mentioned in the main narrative but belongs to the series of stories connected to it.

4. Tej Siṃh, the eldest of the Bagaṛāvats and the son of Bāgh Siṃh's Banyā wife, is the only brother who is not fated to be killed by the goddess. See also the section on Sāḍū Mātā in chapter 6.

5. By taking Sāḍū Mātā into captivity, the Rāṇā feels he will be able to even out the Bagaṛāvat's "capture" of his wife, Queen Jaimatī.

6. See the section on Sāḍū Mātā in chapter 6.

7. See the central image of Devnārāyaṇ on the paṛ, and the opening invocatory sections of the narrative.

8. Here Malwa is, like Bengal, in other folk narratives in northern India, being identified as a faraway place where magic and sorcery flourish. See Gold (1992).

9. The Kacchavāhā Rajputs reigned over the important princely state of Jaipur in Rajasthan.

10. This is in contrast to similar stories of revival in which a deity restores the founder of a kingdom and later becomes the ruling family's *kuldevī* or *kulsvāminī*. See, for example, Harlan (1992: 55, 102) on the founding myths of the Kacchavāhā Rajputs of Jaipur.

11. See chapter 5.

12. Raglan (1934: 212–231) sets up a motif list for the lives of Indo-European (and non-Indo-European) heroes. Some of the salient features of his list are (1) the mother is a royal virgin; (2) the father is king; (3) the father is related to the mother; (4) the circumstances of conception are unusual; (5) the child is reputed to be the son of God; (6) there

is an attempt to kill him at birth; (7) the hero is spirited away; (8) he is reared by foster parents in a far country; (9) there are no details of his childhood; (10) he goes to his future kingdom; (11) he is victor over a king, giant dragon, or wild beast; he (12) he marries a princess; (13) he becomes a king; and so on. However, Raglan's list cannot be taken to supply the narrative structure of certain myths; it is rather a sketch of character components of a predefined notion of the "hero." It thus inadvertently determines who or what may be considered a hero, thereby making the search for a hero a tautologous undertaking.

13. These are mixtures of jaggery and chickpea flour, and grass and oats, respectively, roasted in clarified butter.

14. See the following subsection.

15. This motif is also found, for example, in the myth of the goddess Reṇukā, the mother of Viṣṇu's incarnation as Paraśurāma. The ability to carry water in a pot of unburnt clay rests in the powers that arise from Reṇukā's purity and chastity as a devoted wife of her husband Ṛṣi Jamadagni.

16. Pūtanā's body emits a sweet-smelling odor when it is burnt. She reaches heaven because of her contact with Kṛṣṇa.

17. See also the stories about the fox and about the sandpipers.

18. Sāḍū Mātā's mare and her foal.

19. This is also expressed on the paṛ, which shows the figure of Devnārāyaṇ with the bhāṭ reverentially positioned at his feet. See paṛ, R 6, 7.

20. The central figure of Devnārāyaṇ is surrounded by three or four scorpions.

21. Cited in Zoller (forthcoming).

22. Zoller *ibid.*

23. At one point in the narrative Sāḍū Mātā even calls Devnārāyaṇ "Bhīm." See hereafter.

24. In textile illustrations from Gujarat composed by Garoda "Brahmans," the scene depicting Bhīma and the banyan tree shows Bhīma's body half light and half dark. See Fischer, Jain, and Shah (1982: 241). This depiction has an even more direct association with Bherū̃, who is split into a dark (*kālā*) and light (*gorā*) Bherū̃: "The fourteenth panel depicts the scene of the game amli-pipli played between the Pandavas and the Kauravas. One day Bhīma decided on revenge. Being gigantic in stature, he held the entire tree in his embrace and shook it so violently that many of the Kauravas fell on the ground and were injured. Half of Bhīma's body was made from vajra, and it is always shown painted with a silver pigment." Jain (1980).

25. Ujjain is also the town that features in the stories about the famous renunciate King Bhartharī, who later becomes a Nāth Yogi. King Bhartharī is frequently identified with the Sanskrit poet Bhartrihari, who is "renowned for three sets of eloquent verse on worldly life, erotic passion, and renunciation" (Gold 1992: 60). Bharthari is also identified as being King Vikramāditya's elder brother, to whom he hands over the throne after deciding to renounce the world (61). In the story of Bharthari, the founding of Ujjain or Dhār Nagar is caused "by the grace of Nāth gurus and the acts of a haughty donkey who is Bharthari's progenitor, Gandaraph Syan, cursed by his father to enter a donkey womb" (60). The donkey, who belongs to a potter, promises that he will beautify the king's city on the condition that the princess marry him. To the donkey king and the princess is born "Bhartari Panvar of Dhar Nagar." The surname Panvar (Parmār, Pũvār), which is a lineage or *kul* name of Sūryavaṃśī Rajputs, suggests that Bharthari is, in fact, an "ancestor" of Pīpalde, who is the daughter of Jaisalrāj Pũvār.

26. The motif of sleep occurs elsewhere as well. In a place called Soniyānā (in Bhilwara/ Chitor District) Devnārāyaṇ falls asleep for six months and can be awakened only when a conch shell is blown into his ear. This long duration of sleep also corresponds to the

god's rest period during the four months of the rainy season, or *caūmāsā* (eleventh Āsāḍha to eleventh Kārttika), after which he is, like many other deities, awakened. This period of slumber has direct parallels to Viṣṇu's periodical sleep. According to Gonda (1954: 89), "the god is said to fall asleep at the end of every yuga or age of the world. . . . Viṣṇu is the pradhānapuruṣa—or Supreme Soul, who at the termination of such a long period not only burns the world but, as the earth becomes flooded with water, also sleeps upon the serpent Śeṣa. When, finally, his creative junction is stirred, he awakes. . . . As long as Viṣṇu sleeps, that is as long as the annual rains, it is said, the world sleeps . . . during the god's annual sleep, his functions, like those of man when he is asleep (ŚB. 10, 5, 2, 15) cease.

27. See chapter 6, "Images of Women."

28. See Malik (1993b).

29. See Sontheimer (1994).

30. See Miller (1994: 720) These lines and the ones cited below them are not found in Śrī Hukmārāṃ Bhopā's telling of the narrative.

31. See also his encounter with Pārvatī's lion described later.

32. See Sontheimer (1994) on the categories of the vana and kṣetra.

33. This is nicely brought to expression in Jaisalrāj Pūvār's reaction to Pīpalde's wish to marry Devnārāyaṇ: "The king said: "Look, Pīpalde, that's the road going to Malwa. / —*vāh vāh*—So the people of Marwar,—*mhe*— / they travel along this road every day . . . / Lots of cowherds journey along here—*vāh vāh*— / I'll hardly get my daughter married to a cowherd." Pīpalde's answer is equally significant: [She] said: "Father, he's not a cowherd! / —He's believed to be an avatār."

34. See the paṛ, L 16–19, 3–7.

35. The fire or fire-place (*dhūnī*) of the Nāths is kept perpetually burning.

36. See Gold (1992).

37. He means the capital city of Kheḍā Causlā.

38. See the paṛ, L 39–42, 8–9.

39. That is, the king of Ajmer.

40. Prior to Devnārāyaṇ, Medu, the eldest of the brothers, and natural heir to the throne, also attempts to undertake the journey through the forest but retreats after being confronted by Pārvatī's lion.

41. See the illustration on the paṛ, L 20, 12–13.

42. The last item falls closest to fertility, and the element earth. The number of elements is actually five: wind, water, fire, earth, and ether. (Skt.: *pañca-bhūta*).

43. See, for example, the myth of Durgā and the buffalo-demon Mahiśāsura.

44. Bā̃vlī Ghoḍī is a manifestation of the goddess Cā̃vaṇḍā (Skt.: Cāmuṇḍā). See Coburn (1991) for myths of the Goddess. See also the mythology of Pābūjī's mare Kesar Kālamī which is also an incarnation of the goddess (Smith 1991).

45. See the illustration on the paṛ (L 30–34, 4–7) showing the mare in chains being given liquor to drink by Chochū Bhāṭ.

46. Badnor is the name of the territory that once belonged to the Bagaṛāvats. See also sections of the printed text that identify Savāī Bhoj's home in Badnor.

47. Chochū Bhāṭ refers to his master as being a prince born under an ill-fated constellation.

48. The two suns are of course the sun in the sky and Devnārāyaṇ.

49. See the paṛ, L 20–26, 12–16.

50. It is important to note that Devnārāyaṇ not only breaks Dīyājī's teeth but kills his son, Uttam Rai, who, after hearing of his father's humiliation, in a rage attacks the god at the Pass of Sā̃khlī.

51. That such ties can also carry a feeling of intimacy is poignantly expressed in the

brother-sister relationship between Bhūṇā and the Rāṇā's daughter, Tārāde. When Bhūṇā decides to leave his foster home and return to his ancestral lands, Tārāde asks him:

> "Dear Bhūṇā you're going to your country.—*mhe*—
> Brother, there's no one protecting me who I can call Brother
> When you go to your country, who'll wrap silk cloth from the Deccan
> around me at Sā̃j's wedding?
> There is your niece, Sā̃jā̃ Bāī.—*mhe*—
> Who'll come in her wedding, brother?"

Later, when Bhūṇā is finally about to leave, she says:

> "Once we used to swing in the cradle.—*mhe*—
> Dear Bhūṇā, we suckled together
> Hey, we didn't know about jāt-pā̃t for so many days.—*mhe*—
> Today we found out.—*vāh vāh*—
> You're a Gūjar, I'm a Rajpūt
> Bhūṇā you're a Gūjar.—*mhe*—
> I'm a Rajpūt, brother.—*vāh vāh*—
> But so many days we suckled together and swung together.—*mhe*—
> It didn't come to our attention."

52. This is not Chochū Bhāṭ but a bhāṭ from the Rāṇā's court who is accompanying Bhūṇā. Bārahaṭh is a title given to a bhāṭ.

53. Salūṇ was Sāḍū Mātā's younger sister, who was married to Savāī Bhoj's brother, Bārāvat. See chapter 6, for the story of the birth of Sāḍū Mātā and Salūṇ.

54. The bangles on her arm signify the fact that Salūṇ is not a widow; this is because she has committed satī. Many satī memorials, especially in Maharashtra and Rajasthan, feature just an arm with bangles on it. See Sontheimer and Settar (1982); see also the illustration on the paṛ, R 21–22, 6.

55. *Jam* literally means Yama, but can also imply a strong, demon- or giant-like person.

56. In the battle of Rātākoṭ, it is primarily Bhāṅgī who, armed with a pestle as club, cart-wheel as shield, mortar as helmet, and his immense strength, destroys the enemy forces.

57. Devnārāyaṇ and Bhūṇā's meeting is also depicted on stone and clay slabs. Here the brothers face each other on their horses. The upright figure of Rājā Bāsak runs between them.

58. In order to mark his foster nephew in some way, the Rāṇā's brother-in-law slices off Bhūṇā's little finger and calls him Prince Khāṇḍerāv thereafter.

59. See chapter 6 regarding the incident featuring Chochū Bhāṭ and Bhūṇā on the steps of Puṣkara.

60. This is, of course, only partially true, since Medu is also initially angered, claiming to be the real chief of the herds and lands, because he is the eldest of the five brothers.

61. See, for example, Daniel's superb study (1984) on the construction of personhood in Tamil Nadu.

Translation

1. Chapter 2 provides an extensive description of oral structure of the narrative, along with an explanation of these expressions.

2. The transcription of the oral rendering in Mārvāṛī does not involve changes of this

kind. There the two voices have been set off through the use of round brackets. For the complete original language text printed in Devanagari, see Malik (2003).

3. Again, these have been reproduced in full in the transcription of the narrative.

4. The preliminary section of the narrative, containing an invocation of different deities, has not been included in the translation. These passages are discussed in detail in chapter 2. Similarly, the translation of the fifth and fourteenth sections of the sixth "chapter" of the narrative are included in chapter 6 and not here. See Malik (1999: 154–162; 163–164).

5. This is a reference to the very beginning of the narrative, in which Savāī Bhoj receives a golden image from the ascetic Rūpnāth. See the summary of first part of the narrative in chapter 4. See also Malik (1993a) and Singh (1993).

6. The place where a woman immolates herself after her husband's death.

7. *Jī kīyo.*

8. Paternal aunt.

9. *Bikharālrūp.*

10. *Sāī* is a term of respect.

11. The month of Māgh, that is, January–February.

12. *Tap.*

13. *Rākas.*

14. *Nirā lagyoḍī hai.*

15. This refers to the thirteenth day after the cremation ceremony for a deceased person has been performed. In certain traditions it marks the end of the period of pollution generated by death.

16. Paternal uncle. Refers to Sāḍū Mātā's husband, Savāī Bhoj.

17. That is, the infant or child Devnārāyaṇ.

18. Shoulder sash or pouch used by mendicants.

19. A game of dice.

20. *Tẽhrvī pīyā̃le.*

21. *Āpo āp.*

22. That is, in Malwa, a region in the state of Madhya Pradesh.

23. Here we encounter the idea that Sāḍū Mātā is an ascetic or a sorceress.

24. This a reference to Rāṇī Jaimatī, on account of whom the Bagaṛāvats and the Rāṇā went to battle.

25. *Darbār*—a frequent epithet of Devnārāyaṇ.

26. A mixture of molasses and chickpea flour roasted or fried in clarified butter.

27. A kind of grass or mixture of oats roasted in clarified butter mixed in molasses.

28. Offering in the form of money or kind, given to ritual officiants.

29. That is, to Causle Kheḍā.

30. A woman belonging to the Gūjar community.

31. Mahādevī.

32. *Dān.*

33. Allusion to the cremation and death ceremonies.

34. The bīṇ, or double-gourd instrument played by bhopās.

35. *Sā* is a term of address denoting respect, like "sir."

36. *Goḍālakaḍī,* a severe form of punishment.

37. A sign of royalty.

38. A name for Sāḍū Mātā.

39. The Bhāṭ.

40. *Bhojāī*: elder brother's wife.

41. *Lākh ṭakās*: a lakh of coins. Someone with great authority.

42. Stable-boy, saddler.
43. "Vomit his remains out."
44. Ritual offerings consisting of one and a quarter maṇ of different substances.
45. *Dhāpayoḍī*: satisfied.
46. Sāḍū Mātā.
47. Dhār is the name of a town in Madhya Pradesh; on the outskirts of a town cows are assembled before taking them to graze.
48. Usually sticks of dry bamboo are used. "Green bamboo" suggests that preparations should be made quickly, without further delay.
49. *Nāgḍīyā*, can also denote a wicked or immoral person.
50. The sun.
51. Or: bhāṅg.
52. The 24 brothers.
53. *Dūd*: "milk," meaning lineage or family.
54. *Keḍā*: descendant.
55. *Bīr khet*: "warrior-field" = battlefield.
56. Nevā's wife and Bhāṅgījī's mother.
57. *Dhūnī*: sacred fire-place used by mendicants.
58. The rites of cremation and subsequent ceremonies.
59. An epithet of Devnārāyaṇ.
60. A mythical flower.
61. The name of Savāī Bhoj's horse.
62. This is a reference to the Goddess's bowl from which she drinks blood.
63. Indra's.
64. Literally: "bathing."
65. This refers to Devnārāyaṇ.
66. *Bhāṇjo*, sister's son.
67. In other words: without being taught a lesson.
68. *Lāljī*: husband's younger brother.
69. Prince Medū.
70. An ornamental mark of religious or royal investiture.
71. *Akal ghaṇī ho jāy śarīr.*
72. Father's younger brother, father's elder brother, mother's sister's husband.
73. Literally: send your valor off to the village.
74. Literally "someone with moustaches."
75. Śrī Hukmārām Bhopā seems to have mixed up days and months in this sentence.
76. The amount of time Devnārāyaṇ has on earth.
77. An owl-like species of bird.
78. An epithet of Devnārāyaṇ.
79. *Darbār kavū̃ darpaṇ kī nai boltā hai kā̃c nai.*
80. Place where ash was kept for cleaning pots and pans.
81. This is the name of a detergent commonly used in India today. The singer used this modern term to make things easier for me to understand.
82. That is, they have smallpox.
83. Merchants and traders.
84. Śrī Hukmārām made a mistake here, since Khāṇḍerāv is the name given to Bhūṇā by the Rāṇā. Śrī Moṭārām corrected the slip in the next line by saying that it is Nīmde, the Rāṇā's younger brother's cavalry.
85. For a continuation of this passage, see the section on Chochū Bhāṭ in chapter 6.

86. This reply is based on a misunderstanding on Śrī Moṭārām's part, since Bhūṇājī is not putting a question to the Bhāṭ.

87. That is, the Bhāṭ.

88. That is, Sāḍū Mātā.

89. The local Rajasthani name for Puṣkar.

90. That is, Rāvjī.

91. A kind of insect.

92. The singer is referring to himself.

93. A mythical bird that can carry off five elephants.

94. Name of a bird or composite animal.

95. The name of an owl-like bird associated with omens.

96. *Hāthī hāthī*: elephants, elephants.

97. *Phī̃parā phoḍīyā̃.*

98. *Bhak ko ṭheṭh ko hī bhūko hai.*

99. *Pañctīrthīyā̃.*

100. The eleventh day during the bright half of the lunar cycle in the month of Kārttik.

101. The singer is referring to himself.

102. A meal prepared from vegetables.

103. Moṭārām mistakenly mentions Dev here as part of the *hũkāro*.

104. For a continuation of this passage, see the section on Chochū Bhāṭ in chapter 6.

105. A person of the low-ranked, untouchable "sweeper" caste.

106. That is, Dev's court.

107. *Dharam ko bāp.*

108. *Pāp kaṭ jāyī*: "evil" will be removed.

109. That is, he calmed down.

110. A ceremony during a wedding in which the bride's or bridegroom's maternal uncle presents his niece or nephew with gifts of money, ornaments, or clothes.

111. A term identical to *bhāt*. See the preceding note.

112. Long-sleeved blouse worn by widows.

113. *Cūḍ*, that is, bangles worn by a married woman.

114. The black mare.

115. She became a satī.

116. A demon, giant, or Yama, the god of death.

117. God, the Creator.

118. Vṛndāvan.

119. The sandpiper or lapwing.

120. The celestial cow Surabhī; cows in general.

121. *Ghaḍanā*, i.e., to mold from clay.

122. A kind of grass.

123. *Pārbrahm.*

124. That is, a military drummer.

125. The sun.

126. A large army.

127. A small, low, square table.

128. Powder (usually red) used by people during the Holi festival.

129. Or: because the Five Patels said so, I was leaving.

130. A liquid prepared from yoghurt and wheat.

131. Or: keep vows of the eleventh and twelfth?

132. *Nīñdaḍā kā jāl.*

Glossary

Ād: Name of king who is first in a genealogy of Cauhān kings, at the end of which Savāī Bhoj and Devnārāyaṇ appear. The genealogy is recited on different occasions by Chochū Bhāṭ.

Ād Sagat: Great or first Goddess.

Agra: City in which the Taj Mahal is built.

Ajaypāl: Legendary ancestor of equally legendary Cauhān king Bisaldev. Ajaypāl supposedly founded the city of Ajmer.

Ajmer: Famous Sufi pilgrimage center near Pushkar.

Ākhā Tīj: Festival of swings celebrated in the month of Baisākh (April–May) on the third day of the bright half of the lunar cycle.

Āḷā Rāvat: One of the 24 Bagaṛāvats.

Amarāv: King, general, high-ranking person.

Āmbesar: Name of a well near Daṛāvaṭ.

Āmo and Nīmo: Sāḍū Mātā's brothers who accompany her on the way to Malwa.

Amṛt: Nectar or ambrosia of the gods.

Āṇandrāmjī: Gatekeeper at Pātū Kaḷālī's mansion.

Ann/Anndev: Nourishment, grain, food; lord of nourishment or food.

Aṛadū: Main market place or bazaar.

Āratī: A prayer or hymn of praise performed with lamps in front of a deity or person.

Arjan: Arjun, younger brother of Bhīma, the strongest of the five Pāṇḍāva brothers.

Āsīn: Township *Āsīnd* in the vicinity of Bhilwara city in Bhilwara district on the banks of the Khārī river.

Avadhūt: Yogi, ascetic, renouncer; especially an ascetic of the Nāth Panth.

Āvar-Sāvar: Territory under the jurisdiction of Dīyājī Jodhkā.

Avatār: Incarnation, especially of Lord Viṣṇu.

Badnor: Capital of the Bagaṛāvats.

Bagaṛāvats: The 24 brothers who are the heroes of the narrative called the Bagaṛāvat Bhārat. The most famous are Savāī Bhoj and Nevājī.

Bāgh Siṃh: Father of the 24 Bagaṛāvats, man-lion with head of a lion and body of a man.

Bāgoṭ: Territory belonging to Bhūṇājī's father Bārāvat.

Bāījī: Term of endearment used for "sister."
Baikuṇṭh: Lord Viṣṇu's heavenly abode.
Bālā Dev: The infant or child Devnārāyaṇ.
Bāndarvāḍā: Territory belonging to Rāvji's younger brother, Nīmde.
Bandrāban: Vṛndāvan, the forest in which Kṛṣṇa lived. Devnārāyaṇ is often referred to as the king of Bandrāban.
Banīyā: Shopkeeper, merchant, trader.
Banjāra/Binjarā: Cattle-keeping pastoralist.
Bārāvat: Bhūṇājī's father; one of the 24 Bagaṛāvats.
Bārahaṭh: A title given to a cāraṇ or royal bard.
Bāsak: Serpent king of the underworld.
Baṭūṭ: Territory in the district of Ajmer held under the jurisdiction of Devnārāyaṇ's brother Medu.
Bā̃vlī ghoḍī: Savāī Bhoj's mare.
Berībāj Bagūl Siṅg: Cowherd who defends the capture of Devnārāyaṇ's cows.
Bhā̃bhī: Person belonging to the community of leather-workers and weavers.
Bhādvā: Lunar month from mid-August to mid-September.
Bhagavān: Lord/God; frequent address for Devnārāyaṇ.
Bhairū̃jī/Bhairavnāth/Bherū̃nāth: Kālā and Gorā Bhairū̃, assistants/guardians of Devnārāyaṇ.
Bhāṅg: Narcotic drink made from hemp leaves.
Bhāṅgījī: Devnārāyaṇ's elder brother, the son of Nevājī. He compares with Bhīmā in having enormous strength as well as a gargantuan appetite, especially for opium and bhāṅg.
Bhārat: Lengthy martial narrative.
Bhāṭ: Person belonging to the community of bards and genealogists.
Bhāṭaṇī: Female member of the community of bards and genealogists; a Bhāṭ's wife.
Bhāṭṭī: Rajput clan ruling over Jaisalmer.
Bhavānī: The goddess of battle; the Goddess Durgā.
Bhīl: A "tribal" community living in southern Rajasthan and Malwa.
Bhīlmal: Capital of the Bhīl king.
Bhojī/Bhojāī: Elder brother's wife; sister-in-law.
Bholānāth: Address for Lord Śiva.
Bhopā: Generic term for singer or priest in Rajasthan.
Bhū̃āl: Kingdom belonging to Queen Jaimatī's father.
Bhūṇājī: Bārāvat's son; Bhūnājī was adopted by Rāvjī and brought up under the name of Khāṇḍerāv.
Bhuvājī: Father's sister, paternal aunt.
Bhuvānī: Owl-like bird associated with omens.
Bījā Mehtā: A village headman in the service of Rāvjī.
Bīlā and Bīlī: Devnārāyaṇ's son and daughter.
Bīṇ: Double-gourd stringed instrument used by bhopās.
Bijorī Kā̃jarī: Clan goddess of the Bagaṛāvats.
Bisaldev: Legendary ruler of Ajmer.
Bor ghoḍī: Bārāvat's mare.
Cā̃dan: "Silver" Square; a particularly fine marketplace.

Chochū Bhāṭ: The Bagaṛāvats' genealogist and bard.
Cāmal: Name of a stretch of ravines in Madhya Pradesh famous for being the hideout of many dreaded dacoits.
Cāmpānehrī: Village in the district of Bhilwara.
Cāṇdārūṇ: Territory ruled over by Sāṇkhlā Sirdār, who cut off Bhūṇājī's little finger when he was adopted by Rāvjī.
Caṇḍī: The goddess Pārvatī, Lord Śiva's wife.
Cāraṇ: Person belonging to the community of bards, singers, and genealogists.
Caudharī: Village headman; a person belonging to the Jāṭ community.
Cauhān: The Rajput (and Gujar) ruling clan to which Devnārāyaṇ and his brothers belong.
Caupaḍ: A game of dice played on a cross-shaped piece of cloth or board.
Causle Kheḍā/Causlā Kheḍā: Capital of Devnārāyaṇ's kingdom.
Cāvaṇḍā: The goddess Cāmuṇḍā.
Cā̃vṭī: Devnārāyaṇ's second wife; daughter of the demon of Fort Gājanā.
Crore: A number equalling ten million.
Daṛāvaṭ: Place of Devnārāyaṇ's childhood.
Deḷū Bhāṭanī: Chochū Bhāṭ's mother.
Demālī: Hillside shrine marking the first place of Devnārāyaṇ's worship.
Devlī: Memorial stone, small shrine.
Dharamrāj Devjī: An epithet of Devnārāyaṇ.
Dhobī/Dhoban: A man or a woman belonging to the community of clothes-washers.
Dīyājī Jodhkā: A general in the service of Rāvjī.
Dūdiyā Talāv: A pond on the way to Malwa. Devnārāyaṇ is supposed to have stopped drinking his mother's milk at this place.
Durjan Sāl: Seldom-used address for Rāvjī.
Dūtī: Messenger-woman or sorceress.
Dvārkā: Lord Kṛṣṇa's capital in Saurashtra.
Gajmaṅgalā: An elephant belonging to the Bagaṛāvats that was captured by Rāvjī.
Gaṇeś/Guṇeś: Lord Ganeśa; term for elephants in general.
Goḍī Mālāgarī Rāg: A particular rāga, or Indian musical melody.
Goṭhā: Place of Devnārāyaṇ's childhood (see Darāvaṭ).
Guāl: A cowherd.
Gudaliyā: Pond on the borders of Rāvjī's kingdom.
Gūjar: The pastoral and farming community into which Devnārāyaṇ was born.
Gūjrī: A woman belonging to the Gujar community.
Harirāmjī: Bāgh Siṃh's father; Devnārāyaṇ's great-grandfather.
Hīrāgar: A maidservant.
Ind: Indra, king of the gods.
Jagīśyo: A fictional name given by Chochū Bhāṭ to himself.
Jaldev: Lord of water.
Jam: Yama, the god of death; a demon or giant.
Jāsā: Father of Nirpāl, a cowherd in the service of Devnārāyaṇ.
Jāṭ: A farming and cattle-breeding community.
Jaymaṅgalā: Elephant belonging to the Bagaṛāvats that was captured by Rāvjī.

Jogīṇī: Lower ranked demonic female deities or witches.

Kacchāvā: Kacchavāhā Rajputs; name of a clan that ruled over the kingdom of Jaipur.

Kālīyode: Pond frequented by Devnārāyaṇ's cows.

Kālū Mīr: A Paṭhān general in the service of Rāvjī.

Kāḷvī: Sāḍū Mātā's mare.

Kapurḍī/Kapurī Dhoban: Washerwoman in the service of Rāvjī.

Kārttik: Auspicious lunar month in October–November during which a number of festivals are held.

Kās: Kaṃsa—Kṛṣṇa's maternal uncle, who tries to kill the latter while he is an infant; a particularly evil or wicked person.

Khanār: A territory in Afghanistan whose king kept Rāvjī in captivity.

Khāṇḍerāv: Name given to Bhūṇājī after his adoption by Rāvjī.

Khārī: A river that flows past Āsīnd in the district of Bhilwara.

Khejaḍā: The sāmī tree.

Kos: A distance of about 3.2 kilometers.

Koṭ: A fort or citadel.

Kuldevī: Family or clan goddess.

Kuldevī Āsāvarī: Clan goddess of the Bagaṛāvats.

Kumahār: Person belonging to the community of potters.

Lakh: Number equalling one hundred thousand.

Lenuḍī Kumahārī: An acquaintance of Chochū Bhāṭ belonging to the potter community.

Līla/Līlāgar: Devnārāyaṇ's horse.

Madnā/Madan Siṅg: Tejājī's son; Devnārāyaṇ's eldest brother.

Mahābhārat: A story of epic dimensions; a great battle.

Māh: The lunar month of Māgh (January–February).

Mahājan: Person belonging to the trader or merchant community.

Mālāgar: The region of Malwa.

Mālāsarī: The hilltop where Devnārāyaṇ arises from the underworld to take incarnation.

Malhār: Name of a rāga, or Indian musical melody.

Maṇ: A weight equalling about 40 kilograms.

Māṇḍal: Lake situated halfway between Āsīnd and Bhilwara.

Maṇḍovar: City ruled over by a Paḍihār king.

Maṅgānā: Elephant belonging to Rāvjī that is slain by Bhūṇājī.

Medū: Devnārāyaṇ's elder brother who was adopted by the king of Ajmer.

Nāg: A serpent deity; snake, cobra.

Nagaur: Capital of the district of Nagaur in Rajasthan.

Nāgkanyā: Devnārāyaṇ's wife; daughter of the serpent king of the underworld.

Nāglī: Nevājī's cow.

Nāpā: Cowherd chieftain in the service of Devnārāyaṇ.

Nāradī Bhāṭ: Address for Chochū Bhāṭ associating him with Nārada Muni.

Nāth: An ascetic belonging to the Nāth Panth.

Nausar: A pass on the Arāvalli hill range between Ajmer and Pushkar.

Netūjī: Nevājī's wife and Bhāṅgījī's mother.

Nevājī: The bravest and most impetuous of the Bagaṛāvats.
Nīm: The margosa tree.
Nīmde: Rāvjī's younger brother.
Nolke Bāg: Garden located on the outskirts of Rāṇ City.
Pālāsānī: Stable-boy.
Pālī: Capital of the district of Pali.
Pāras Pīplī: Name of a particular pīpal tree *(ficus religiosa)*.
Paṭel: Village headman.
Pātū Kaḷālī: Name of the owner of the liquor shop frequented by the Bagaṛāvats.
Paṛ: "Cloth"; cloth scroll from Rajasthan on which a narrative is depicted.
Pavan: Lord of air/wind.
Phep: A mythic flower.
Phūlrīyo: Chochū Bhāṭ's horse.
Pilodā: Fort belonging to the Dhārapatī king.
Pīpalde: Devnārāyaṇ's wife; daughter of the king of Dhār.
Puṣkar: Pilgrimage town and sacred lake situated near Ajmer; "Old Puṣkar": another lake on the vicinity of the town.
Puṭiyā: A bird that sleeps with its feet pointing upward.
Rābaṛī: A meal prepared with millet or wheat flour and buttermilk.
Rākhī: A protective talisman consisting of a rosette tied around the wrist with a thread.
Rāṭhor: A Rajput ruling clan.
Rāṇ Śahar: Rāvjī's city; Rāṇ City.
Rāv/Rāṇā: Title of Rajput ruler; the ruler of Rātākoṭ; enemy of the Bagaṛāvats and Devnārāyaṇ.
Rūpnāth: The Bagaṛāvats' guru; adopted Bhāṅgījī after their deaths.
Sāḍū Mātā/Māt Khaṭānī: Devnārāyaṇ's mother and Savāī Bhoj's wife.
Sālagrām: An aniconical image of Viṣṇu in the form of a naturally found smooth, rounded black stone containing ammonites.
Sāṅkhlī: Name of a hill pass.
Salūṇ: Bhūṇājī's mother's name; Sāḍū Mātā's sister.
Saprā: A river flowing through Rajasthan and Madhya Pradesh.
Sarvāḍ: Territory given to Kālū Mīr to oversee by Rāvjī.
Sat: Truth, honor, virtue; the force of virtue that enters a woman about to commit the act of sati.
Sati: Act of self-immolation by women; a woman who has committed the act of self-immolation.
Sativaḍā: Place where a women commits sati.
Savāī Bhoj: One of the principal characters of the narrative; Devnārāyaṇ's father, Saḍū Mātā's husband, and Queen Jaimatī's lover.
Savāmaṇi: A feast consisting of one and a quarter maṇ of foods, celebrated in honor of Devnārāyaṇ, usually as a consequence of a vow being fulfilled.
Sāvan: The lunar month falling in July–August.
Siddhi: Mystical or magical power obtained through yogic meditational practices; supernatural power of a Yogi.
Sikarānī: A place near Bhilwara.

Sindhbāḍā: Location inhabited by the Jogīṇīs who devour Chochū Bhāṭ.

Sisodīyā: A Rajput clan whose rulers established the city of Udaipur.

Sudābāī: A sacred pool within the boundaries of Puṣkar that has healing properties for people suffering from spirit possession.

Surbīṇ: See *bīṇ*.

Suremātā: The divine or celestial cow.

Tārāde: Rāvjī's daughter; Bhūṇājī's foster sister.

Tejājī: The eldest of the 24 Bagaṛāvats.

Ṭīm Talāv: A pond where Dīyājī and Devnārāyaṇ confront each other during the latter's recovery of Bā̃vlī ghoḍī.

Ṭī̃ṭoḍī: Sandpiper or lapwing.

Ṭoḍā Solaṅkī: Rāvjī's son-in-law who belongs to the Solaṅkī Rajput ruling clan.

Ṭhumrī: A kind of song sung with two voices.

Toraṇ: An emblem struck down by the bridegroom before entering the bride's home.

Ūd, Ūdkaraṇ, Ūdojī: Epithets of Devnārāyaṇ that associate him with the rising sun, auspiciousness, and prosperity.

Ūsrī Talāv: Name of pond where Devnārāyaṇ beheads King Bisaldev's buffaloes.

Wazir: Vizier; a minister.

Yogi: An ascetic or renouncer; a member of the Nāth Panth.

Bibliography

Aithal, P. 1987. The Rāmāyaṇa in Kannada literature. *South Asian Digest of Regional Writing* 12: 1–12.

Allen, W. S. 1957. Some phonological characteristics of Rājasthānī. *Bulletin of the School of Oriental and African Studies*. 20: 5–11.

Allen, W. S. 1960. Notes on the Rājasthānī verb. *Indian Linguistics*. 21: 4–13.

Appadurai, A., F. Korom, and M. Mills (eds.). 1991. *Gender, genre, and power in South Asian expressive traditions*. Philadelphia: University of Pennsylvania Press.

Bagaṛāvat Bhārat n.d Ajmer: Phūlcand Book Seller.

Bailey, G. 1983. *The mythology of Brahmā*. Delhi: Oxford University Press.

Bakhtin, M. M. 1986. The problem of speech genres. In *Speech genres and other late essays*. Trans. V. W. McGee. Austin: University of Texas Press.

Barthes, R. 1987a. Textual analysis of a tale of Poe. In Young (1987).

Barthes, R. 1987b. Theory of the text. In Young (1987).

Beck, B.E.F. 1981. The goddess and the demon: A local south Indian festival and its wider context. *Puruṣārtha* 5: 83–136.

Behl, K. C. 1980. *Ādhunik rājasthānī kā saṃracanātmak vyākaraṇ*. Jodhpur: Rājasthānī Śodh Saṃsthān Caupāsanī.

Berg, E., and M. Fuchs (eds.). 1993. *Kultur, Soziale Praxis, Text: Die Krise der ethnographischen Repräsentation*. Frankfurt: Suhrkkamp.

Binford, M. R. 1976. Mixing in the colour of Ram of Ranuja. In *Hinduism: New essays in the history of religions*. Ed. B. L. Smith. Leiden: Brill.

Blackburn, S. H. 1985. Death and deification: Folk cults in Hinduism. *History of Religions*, 24: 255–274.

Blackburn, S. H., P. J. Claus, J. B. Fluckiger, and S. B. Wadley (eds.). 1989. *Oral epics in India*. Berkeley: University of California Press.

Bolle, K. W. 1969. Speaking of a place. In *Myths and Symbols: Studies in honour of Mircea Eliade*. Ed. C. H. Long and J. Kitagawa. Chicago: University of Chicago Press.

Breckenridge, C. and P. van der Veer. 1993. *Orientalism and the postcolonial predicament*. Philadelphia: University of Pennsylvania Press.

Brückner, H. 1995. *Fürstliche Feste*. Wiesbaden: Harrasowitz.

Brückner, H., L. Lutze, and A. Malik (eds.). 1993. *Flags of fame: Studies in South Asian folk culture*. Delhi: Manohar.

Chattopadhyaya, B. D. 1992. The emergence of the Rajputs as historical process in early medieval Rajasthan. In *The Idea of Rajasthan*. Ed. K. Schomer, J. L. Erdman, D. O. Lodrick, and L. J. Rudolf. Delhi: Manohar.

Coburn, T. 1982. Consort of none, Śakti of all: The vision of the Devī-Māhātmya. In Hawley and Wulff (1982).
Coburn, T. 1991. *Encountering the Goddess.* Albany: SUNY Press.
Daniel, E. V. 1984. *Fluid signs: Being a person the Tamil way.* Berkeley: University of California Press.
Das, V. 1977. *Structure and cognition.* Delhi: Oxford University Press.
Das, V. 1995. *Critical events: An anthropological perspective on contemporary India.* Delhi: Oxford University Press.
Erndl, K. 1993. *Victory to the mother.* New York: Oxford University Press.
Feldhaus, A. 1995. *Water and womanhood.* New York: Oxford University Press.
Finnegan, R. 1977. *Oral Poetry: Its nature, significance and social context.* Cambridge: Cambridge University Press.
Finnegan, R. 1992. *Oral traditions and the verbal arts.* London: Routledge.
Fischer, E., J. Jain, and H. Shah (eds.). 1982. *Tempeltücher für die Göttin.* Zürich: Rietberg Museum.
Fuimara, G. C. 1990. *The other side of language: A philosophy of listening.* London: Routledge.
Fuller, C. J. 1992. *The camphor flame: Popular Hinduism and society in India.* Princeton: Princeton University Press.
Gadamer, H. G. 1993. *Truth and method.* Trans. J. Weisenheimer and D. G. Marshall. Continuum.
Gold, A. G. 1992. *A carnival of parting.* Berkeley: University of California Press.
Goldman, R., and S. Sutherland Goldman. 1994. Vālmīkī's Hanumān: Characterization and occluded divinity in the *Rāmāyaṇa. Journal of Vaiṣṇava Studies* 2: 32–54.
Gonda, J. 1954. *Aspects of early Viṣṇuism.* Utrecht: N.V.A. Oostoek's Uitgevers Mij.
Goodwin, C. 1981. *Conversational organization.* New York: Academic Press.
Grace, G. W. 1987. *The linguistic construction of reality.* London: Routledge.
Grierson, G. A. 1908/1968. Rājasthānī. In *Linguistic survey of India.* Vol. 9, part 2. Delhi: Motilal Banarasidass.
Gumperz, J. 1982. *Discourse strategies.* Cambridge: University of Cambridge Press.
Harlan, L. 1992. *Religion and Rajput women.* Berkeley: University of California Press.
Harlan, L. 1994. Perfection and devotion: Sati tradition in Rajasthan. In *Sati: The blessing and the curse.* Ed. J. S. Hawley. New York: Oxford University Press.
Hawley, J. H., and D. M. Wulff (eds.). 1982. *The divine consort: Rādhā and the goddesses of India.* Boston: Beacon Press.
Heesterman, J. C. 1957. *The ancient Indian royal consecration.* The Hague: Mouton.
Heesterman, J. C. 1985. The conundrum of the king's authority. In *The inner conflict of tradition.* J. C. Heesterman. Chicago: University of Chicago Press.
Henige, D. P. 1974. *The chronology of oral tradition: Quest for a chimera.* Oxford: Clarendon Press.
Hiltebeitel, A. (ed.). 1989. *Criminal gods and demon devotees.* Albany: SUNY Press.
Hiltebeitel, A. 1990. *The ritual of battle.* Albany: SUNY Press.
Hiltebeitel, A. 1995. Religious studies and Indian epic texts. *Religious Studies Review* 21: 26–32.
Hiltebeitel, A. 1999. *Rethinking India's oral and classical epics.* Chicago: University of Chicago Press.
Hofstadter, D. R. 1980. *Gödel, Escher, Bach: A metaphorical fugue on minds and machines in the spirit of Lewis Carroll.* Harmondsworth, England: Penguin Books.
Inden, R. 1990. *Imagining India.* Oxford: Blackwell.
Jain, J. 1980. The painted scrolls of the Garoda picture-showmen of Gujarat. *National Center for the Performing Arts Quarterly Journal* 9,3: 3–33.

Jardine, M. 1996. Sight, sound, and epistemology: The experiential sources of ethical concepts. *Journal of the American Academy of Religion* 64: 1–26.
Kersenboom, S. 1995. *Word, sound, image.* Oxford: Berg.
Kothari, K. 1989. Performers, gods, and heroes in the oral epics of Rajasthan. In Blackburn, Claus, Fluekiger, and Wadley (1989).
Lalas, S. n.d. *Rājasthānī Sabad Kos.* Four vols. in 9 parts. Jodhpur: Caupāsanī Śikśā Samiti.
Lapoint, E. C. 1978. The epic of Guga: A north Indian oral tradition. In *American Studies in the anthropology of India.* Ed. S. Vatuk. Delhi: Manohar.
Leshnik, L. S., and G. D. Sontheimer (eds.). 1975. *Pastoralists and nomads in South Asia.* Wiesbaden: Harrasowitz.
Lincoln, B. 1991. *Death, war, and sacrifice.* Chicago: University of Chicago Press.
Lord, A. B. 1960. *The singer of tales.* Cambridge, Mass.: Harvard University Press.
Magier, D. 1992. The language of the bard. Appendix to Gold (1992).
Mai, H.-P. 1991. Bypassing intertextuality: Hermeneutics, textual practice, hypertext. In Plett (1991).
Mair, V. 1988. *Painting and performance.* Honolulu: University of Hawaii Press.
Malik, A. 1993a. Avatāra, avenger, and king: Narrative themes in the oral epic of Devnārāyaṇ. In Brückner, Lutze, and Malik (1993).
Malik, A. 1993b. *Das Puṣkara-Māhātmya: Ein religionswissenschaftlicher Beitrag zum Wallfahrtsbegriff in Indien.* Stuttgart: Franz Steiner.
Malik, A. 1996. Brahmās Heirat mit dem Hirtenmädchen Gāyatrī: Zwei Legenden über die Entstehung Puṣkaras. In *Nānāvidhaikatā: Festschrift für Hermann Berger.* Ed. D. Kapp. Wiesbaden: Harrasowitz.
Malik, A. 1999. Powers of the timid: Aspects of humour in the Rajasthani oral epic of Devnārāyaṇ. In *Of clowns and gods, Brahmans and Babus: Humour in South Asian Literatures.* Ed. Ch. Oesterheld and C. P. Zoller. Delhi: Manohar.
Malik, A. 2003. *Śrī Devnārāyaṇ Kathā: An oral narrative of Marwar.* (Introduction in Hindi and English; text in Rajasthani.) New Delhi: South Asia Institute.
Malik, S. C. 1995. *Reconceptualizing the sciences and the humanities: An integral approach.* Delhi: Manohar.
Miles, M. R. 1985. *Image as insight.* Boston: Beacon Press.
Miller, J. C. 1980. Current investigations in the genre of Rajasthani paṛ painting recitations. In *Early Hindī devotional literature in current research.* Ed. W. M. Callewaert. New Delhi: Impex India.
Miller, J. C. 1994. *The twenty-four brothers and Lord Devnārāyaṇ: The story and performance of a folk epic of Rajasthan.* Ph.D diss., University of Pennsylvania.
Mitchell, W.J.T. 1986. *Iconology: Image, text, ideology.* Chicago: University of Chicago Press.
Müller, K. W. 1992. *Das brahmanische Totenritual.* Stuttgart: Franz Steiner.
Narayana Rao, V., D. Shulman, and S. Subrahmanyam. 2001. *Textures of time: Writing history in South India 1600–1800.* Delhi: Permanent Black.
O'Flaherty, W. 1982. *Hindu myths.* Harmondsworth, England: Penguin Books.
Ohnuki-Tierney, E. (ed.). 1990. *Culture through time.* Stanford: Stanford University Press.
Ong, W. 1982. *Orality and literacy.* London: Methuen.
Ortner, S. 1990. Patterns of history: Cultural schemas in the founding of Sherpa religion. In Ohnuki-Tierney (1990).
Piatigorsky, A. 1985. Some phenomenological observations on Indian religion. In *Indian religion.* Ed. R. Burghart and A. Cantlie. London: Curzon Press.
Plett, H. F. (ed.). 1991. *Intertexuality.* Berlin: de Gruyter.

Pollock, S. I. 1991. *The Rāmāyaṇa of Vālmīki.* Vol. 3. Princeton: Princeton University Press.
Pollock, S. I. 1993. Rāmāyaṇa and political imagination in India. *Journal of Asian Studies* 52: 261–297.
Raglan, Lord. 1934. The hero of tradition. *Folklore* 45: 212–231.
Raheja, G. G. 1988. *The poison in the gift.* Chicago: University of Chicago Press.
Raheja, G. G., and A. G. Gold. 1994. *Listen to the heron's words: Reimagining gender and kinship in North India.* Berkeley: University of California Press.
Ramanujan, A. K. 1973. *Speaking of Śiva.* Harmondsworth, England: Penguin Books.
Ramanujan, A. K. 1985. *Poems of love and war.* New York: Columbia University Press.
Ramanujan, A. K. 1989. Where mirrors are windows: Towards an anthology of reflections. *History of Religions* 28: 187–216.
Ramanujan, A. K. 1991. Three hundred Rāmāyaṇas: Five examples and three thoughts on translation. In Richman (1991).
Richman, P. (ed.). 1991. *Many Rāmāyaṇas.* Berkeley: University of California Press.
Ricoeur, P. 1981. *Hermeneutics and the human sciences: Essays on Language, action and interpretation.* Cambridge: Cambridge University Press.
Roghair, G. 1982. *The epic of Palṇāḍu.* New York: Oxford University Press.
Saha, P. K. 1995. Translating Indian literary texts into English. In *Literary India: Comparative studies in aesthetics, colonialism, and culture.* Ed. P. C. Hogan and L. Pandit. Albany: SUNY Press.
Said, E. 1978. *Orientalism.* New York: Pantheon.
Sakariya, A. B., and B. Sakariya 1977/1982/1984. *Rājasthānī Hindī Sabad Kos.* Jaypur: Pañcśil Prakāśan.
Sattar, A. 1994. *Tales from the Kathāsaritsāgara.* New Delhi: Penguin Books India.
Sax, W. 1996. Draupadi and Kunti in the Pandavlila. In *The wild goddess in South Asia.* Ed. A. Michaels, C. Vogelsanger, and A. Wilke. Zürich: Studia Religiosa Helvetica, Vol. 1.
Sax, W. Forthcoming. Gender and the representation of violence in Pandav Lila.
Sells, M. A. 1994. *Mystical languages of unsaying.* Chicago: University of Chicago Press.
Shulman, D. D. 1976. The murderous bride: Tamil versions of the myth of Devī and the buffalo-demon. *History of Religions* 16: 120–146.
Shulman, D. D. 1989. Introductory chapter. In *Hinduism reconsidered.* Ed. G. D. Sontheimer and H. Kulke. Delhi: Manohar Publishers.
Shulman, D. D. 1990. *The king and the clown in South Indian myth and poetry.* Princeton: Princeton University Press.
Singh, B. 1993. The episode of the golden Śiva image. In Brückner, Lutze, and Malik (1993).
Singh, K. 1995. The painted epic: Narrative in the Rajasthani Phad. In *Indian painting.* Ed. B. N. Goswamy. New Delhi: Lalit Kala Akademie.
Smith, J. D. 1976. *The Vīsaldevarāsa: A restoration of the text.* Cambridge: Cambridge University Press.
Smith, J. D. 1991. *The epic of Pābūjī.* Cambridge: Cambridge University Press.
Smith, J. D. 1992. *Epic Rajasthani. Indo-Iranian Journal* 35: 251–269.
Soifer, D. A. 1991. *The myths of Narasiṃha and Vāmana.* Albany: SUNY Press.
Sontheimer, G. D. 1989. The myth of the god and his two wives. In *Living texts in India.* Ed. M. Thiel-Horstmann and R. Barz. Wiesbaden: Harrassowitz.
Sontheimer, G. D. 1993a. King Khaṇḍobā's royal hunt. In Brückner, Lutze and Malik (1993).
Sontheimer, G. D. 1993b. *Pastoral deities in western India.* Trans. A. Feldhaus. Delhi: Oxford University Press.

Sontheimer, G. D. 1994. The *vana* and the *kṣetra*. In *Religion and society in eastern India*. Ed. G. C. Tripathi and H. Kulke. Delhi: Manohar.
Sontheimer, G. D., and S. Settar (eds.). 1982. *Memorial stones*. New Delhi: South Asia Institute.
Srinivas, M. N. 1952. *Religion and society amongst the Coorgs of south India*. Oxford: Oxford University Press.
Tagare, G. V. 1976. *The Bhāgavata Purāṇa*. Part 2. Delhi: Motilal Banarsidass.
Tannen, D. 1994. *Talking voices: Repetition, dialogue, and imagery in conversational discourse*. Cambridge: Cambridge University Press.
Thiel-Horstmann, M. 1985. *Nächtliches Wachen*. Bonn: Indica et Tibetica Verlag.
(Thiel-)Horstmann, M. 1993. Hochkulturliche Rezeption lokaler Gottheiten nach dem avatāra-Konzept: Ausgewählte Typen. In *Die anderen Götter*. Ed. C. Mallebrein. Köln: Braus.
Thiel-Horstmann, M. (ed.). 1991. *Rāmāyaṇa and Rāmāyaṇas*. Wiesbaden: Harrassowitz.
Tod, J. 1829/1957. *Annals and antiquities of Rajasthan*. London: Routledge and Kegan Paul.
Turner, G. W. 1987. *Stylistics*. Harmondsworth, England: Penguin Books.
Valdés, M. J. 1991. *A Ricoeur reader: Reflection and imagination*. Toronto: University of Toronto Press.
Van Buitenen, J.A.B. 1973. *The Mahābhārata*. Book 1. Chicago: University of Chicago Press.
Vatsyayan, K. 1995. *Bharata: The Nāṭyaśāstra*. New Delhi: Lalit Kala Akademie.
Vaudeville, C. 1975. The cowherd-god in ancient India. In Leshnik and Sontheimer (1975).
Wardough, R. 1985. *How conversation works*. Oxford: Blackwell.
Weiner, A. B., and J. Schneider (eds.). 1989. *Cloth and the human experience*. Washington, D.C.: Smithsonian Institution Press.
Westphal-Hellbusch, S. 1975. Changes in the meaning of ethnic names as exemplified by the Jat, Rabari, Bharvad and Charan in Northwestern India. In Leshnik and Sontheimer (1975).
Young, R. (ed.). 1987. *Untying the text: A post-structuralist reader*. London: Routledge and Kegan Paul.
Zoller, C. P. Forthcoming. Bhīma und der Baum und Hundert Gegner.

Index

Abhīras, 89, 151, 154
Agni, 106, 107
Ajmer, 5, 52–53, 56, 64, 94, 125–127, 159, 161, 198, 228–231, 233–236, 238–239, 241, 258, 309
Ākhā tīj, 226–227
Āmo-nīmo, 126, 142, 187
Arjun(a), 88, 146, 148, 156, 225
Arthāv, 19, 20, 28–29, 31, 174
Audience, 33–34, 36
Aurangdīb, 44
Avatār(a), 7, 55, 70–71, 77–80, 83–84, 90–92, 96, 98, 101–103, 107–110, 114, 132, 139, 142, 150, 154, 163
and kingship, 81–84
Ayodhya, 100

Bāgā, 14, 40–41
Bagaṛāvat Bhārat, 55, 87, 94
Bagaṛāvats, 5, 36, 51–52, 54–59, 61–64, 79, 85, 86, 89, 101, 108, 111, 118–120, 124–125, 127, 130, 133, 138–139, 143, 147–149, 152, 156, 163, 177–180, 182–183, 191–192, 213, 218, 224, 229, 232, 235–236, 245, 273, 275, 277, 302
Bāgh Siṃh, 45, 53, 57–58, 79, 80, 86, 109–110, 125, 129–130, 140–141, 218
Baidnāth Bābā, 41–43
Baikunṭh, 9, 39, 45, 65, 96
Bakhtin, M. M., 31–32, 73–74, 170
Balī-dāna, 7, 88
Banyā, 125, 129, 132, 136
Banyan tree, 144–147, 151, 160
Barthes, R., 66–67, 74
Bā̃vli Ghoḍī, 53, 136, 162, 229, 259, 268, 270
Bhā̃bhis, 38, 43, 45, 93
Bhāgavata Purāna, 76–77, 94, 142
Bhairū̃jī/Bhairavnāth/Bherū̃nāth, 18, 22, 80, 82, 118–119, 121–125, 144–145, 147, 150, 177, 193, 195, 199, 200–201, 220, 230, 402–403, 413, 415, 428, 445–449, 468, 516n.52
Bhakti, 7, 77, 88, 91, 125, 130, 133
Bhāṇgījī, 64, 102, 112, 114–115, 118, 147, 152, 157–158, 165, 212–217, 221–223, 281, 319, 344, 364, 366, 377–378, 397–399, 401–402, 475–478, 481–482, 486, 488–489
Bharthari, 5
Bhavānī, 54, 62–63, 77–78, 80, 84–85, 88–89, 109, 117, 128, 133–134, 153, 273, 367, 376
Bhilwara, 5, 40, 53
Bhīm(a), 145–147, 156, 225
Bhomiyo, 70
Bhopā, 13, 16, 18, 38, 42
Bhopā, ochre-clad, 41–42
Bhopā, scroll-bearing, 41–42
Bhopā, Śrī Aṇandārām, 93–94
Bhopā, Śrī Hukmārām, 5, 12, 26, 27, 41, 93, 127, 136, 173, 506n.7
Bhuṇājī, 53, 64, 101, 112–113, 118–120, 122–123, 126, 136, 147, 163–165, 168–169, 213, 276, 279–280, 282, 285, 286, 299–301, 305–327, 329–339, 341–364, 366, 369–382, 473–475, 480, 482, 484, 490
Bīlā, 40–41, 53, 65, 149, 494, 495, 511n.14, n.26
Bīlī, 40, 53, 65, 149, 150, 494–495
Bīn, 14, 41, 118
Blackburn, S. H., 69, 71
Brahmā, 35, 56, 88, 96, 151, 154–155, 513n.1
Brahmans, 125, 129, 140–143, 150, 184, 187–189, 208, 210, 233–234

Caste purāṇa, 6
Cauhān Rajputs, 83–84, 103, 195, 210, 235, 309–310
Causle Kheḍā, 52–54, 64, 83, 119, 122–123, 136–137, 144, 156–157, 159, 219, 221, 224–228
Cā̃vṭī, 40–41, 52, 150–151, 207
Chitor, 5

Chochu Bhāṭ, 8, 23, 26, 35 40, 64, 79, 82–83, 118–125, 136, 143–150, 159–165, 168, 192–200, 202–203, 208–210, 226–227, 230, 279, 288, 302
Coburn, T., 84, 88
Commensality, 127
Conversation, 3, 21, 30
Cosmogonic myth, 102
Cultural schemas, 109–110

Dāna, 86
Daṛāvat, 52, 140–142, 165, 168, 184, 187, 216, 238–239, 242, 270, 279, 360, 363–364, 368, 380, 478–480
Darbār, 13, 82, 195
Death, 69, 108–110
Demālī, 5,40, 42, 44, 53
Devī, 84, 87–89
Devī-Māhātmya, 84–85
Dhār, 52, 136, 149, 151–152, 205, 207–208
Dharma, 68, 81, 84, 102, 143, 178, 190
Dialogue, 8, 30, 507n.18, 509n.31
Dice game, 64, 108, 133, 138, 145, 147
Divine testimony, 7
Dīyājī Jodhkā, 53, 79, 90, 136, 157, 160, 162–163, 177, 228–229, 237, 246, 255–257, 260, 262–269, 287, 297, 312–317, 320, 337, 339–340, 404–420, 422, 426–429, 432, 453–454, 457, 460–464, 467, 487, 488
Draupadi, 148
Durgā, 18, 79–80, 84–85, 89, 153
Durgā Stotra, 88
Dutī, 187

Emptiness, 142
Epic, 3, 5, 7, 28, 34, 66, 67–68, 143
Epic map, 49, 51

Finnegan, R., 18–19, 22
Franke, O., 48

Gaḍgājanā, 52
Gajmaṅgal elephant, 179
Garhwal, 145–146, 148
Gāv, 20, 27–28, 32, 34, 47, 174
Gold, A. G., 116, 128
Golden image, 138, 158, 177
Gonda, J., 81
Gopi Chand, 5
Goṭhā, 52, 179, 183, 192, 195–196, 220–221, 229, 231, 463–465
Great Tradition, 71
Gudalīyā Talāv, 53
Gugājī, 5
Gujars, 93–96, 103–104, 107, 110, 115, 117, 125–127, 130, 151, 177, 188

Hanumān, 61, 71, 80, 106–107
Hermeneutics, 4, 10
Hiltebeitel, A., 68, 72, 88
Historiography, 72, 92, 111
History
counter, 8, 92, 93, 111, 117
oral, 92
subaltern, 8

Image, 15, 37
Indexicality, 108
Indra, 78, 102, 495
Interpretations, 4
Intertexuality, 73–74, 140, 169–170
Iṭh, 18, 38, 40, 492
Itihāsa, 72

Jāgraṇ, 12–13, 507n.4
Jardine, M., 16
Jhũjhār, 54
Jogīṇī, 22, 122–123, 136, 144–145, 147–149, 151, 197–201, 253
Jogis, 114–115, 131, 210–217, 221–222

Kacchāvā Rajputs, 139, 178–179, 182
Kālikā Purāṇa, 87
Kali Yuga, 56, 64, 103–104, 107–108
Kālu Mīr Paṭhān, 53, 177, 257, 263, 297–298, 312–313, 316, 320, 337–339, 346–347, 353, 391–392, 404, 407–420, 422, 426–427, 429, 432–434, 453–454, 457, 460–467
Kapurī Dhoban, 434–440, 447
Kaṛī, 20–21
Kārttik(a), 12–13, 123, 199
Kāśī, 184–185
Kauravas, 145–148
Kersenboom, S., 10–11
Khaṇḍobā, 78, 151, 154–155
Khārī river, 54, 61, 63, 156, 163, 179, 213, 218, 355, 361–362
Kheḍā Causlā. *See* Causle Kheḍā
King Bisaldev, 53, 56, 126–127
King Nīmde, 118–124, 162, 177, 286, 300, 303–307, 393, 405–406, 415, 423, 472
Kinship, 51, 125, 163
Kothari, K., 70
Kṛṣṇa, 76–78, 80, 88–89, 98, 103, 137, 140, 142, 152–153, 163
Kṛṣṇadevarāya, 125
Kṣetra, 151–153
Kṣetra, 151–153
Kumahārs, 93, 185, 306
Kunti, 145–149
Kūrma avatāra, 80

Lakṣmaṇa, 70–71, 79–80, 101, 104
Lakṣmī, 153
Lālo Bhā̃bhī, 43–44
Lekh, 15–16
Lenuḍī Kumahārī, 283–287
Leper, 85, 227

Leprosy, 41–42, 149
Lessing, G. E., 46
Līlāgar, 82–83, 142–144, 159, 188–189, 199, 224, 229, 230, 233–236, 249, 268–269, 377, 379–380, 399, 468–469, 471
Līlā Sevrī, 56–57, 79, 127, 129–130
Listening, 33
Lord, A. B., 72

Madnājī, 64, 147, 165, 168, 198, 213, 229, 316, 364–365, 468, 470
Mahābhārata, 6, 63, 68, 81, 88, 132, 138, 145, 147–149, 163, 177, 229, 238
Mahiṣāsura, 84–85, 87
Mair, V., 48,
Mālāsarī, 5, 51–52, 65, 102, 108, 131–132, 140, 179–182, 362, 492
Malwa, 5, 50, 52, 64, 101, 140, 142–144, 149–150, 158, 181, 187, 190–192, 203, 219–220, 240, 253, 525n.8
Māṇḍal's monument, 217, 221, 223–224
Marriage
  metaphor of, 128–130, 134
  mixed, 125, 129
Maternal realm, 143–144
Mathura, 120, 232
Matysa avatāra, 80
Medūjī, 53, 64, 102, 147 165, 168, 198, 239–248, 362, 364–365, 468, 470
Memory, 18–19
Mhe, use of, 25–26
Miller, J., 49–51, 152
Mitchell, W. J. T., 38, 45–46
Murukaṉ, 151, 154–155

Nāg Kanyā, 40–41, 145, 149, 151, 210, 203
Nāg Pahāḍ, 56–57
Nāpā Guāl, 138–139, 158, 179, 181–182
Narasiṃha, 78, 80
Nāths, 212, 214–216, 218–220
Nectar gaze, 42, 52, 114, 139, 149
Nevājī, 53, 59, 85, 114, 152, 212–216, 219, 229, 301, 305, 367–368
Nivṛtti, 103
Nolkhā Bāg, 54

Ohnuki-Tierney, E., 92, 111
Ong, W., 3
Opium, 120–122
Oral-visual composition, 46–48, 65
Orientalism, 11
Ortner, S., 109

Pābūjī, 5, 48–49, 69–71, 136, 508n.7, 512n.42, 522n.1
Pāṇḍavas, 146–148
Paṛ, 5, 12–13, 15–16, 19, 38, 45–51, 79–80, 82, 139
  cosmology of, 50–51
Paraśurāma, 80
Parcyo, 7, 9, 90, 123, 136–137, 154
Paṛ vā̃cṇo, 12, 15, 37
Pārvatī, 80, 105, 138, 151, 160–162, 246–247, 249, 250, 255
Pātāñjali, 49
Patel, 126–127
Paternal realm, 144
Pātu Kaḷālī, 54, 290–302, 314
Performance, 6, 11, 15
Performers, 6
Personhood, concept of, 108
Petroglyph, 38
Piatigorsky, A., 11
Picture story-telling, 48
Pīpalde, 40, 52, 64, 114, 128, 14–153, 155, 205, 208, 209, 244, 245, 280, 315, 377, 462, 464–467, 474, 492–494
Pīpal tree, 146–147
Place, 93
Plett, H. F., 74
Poison breath, 52, 139
Prakāś, 5, 12, 16, 509n.16
Pravṛtti, 103
Pujā, 39–40
Purāṇa, 34, 68–69, 73, 94
Pushkar/Puṣkar/Puṣkara, 5, 42, 53, 56–57, 80, 82, 123–124, 151, 154, 158, 316–317, 320–322, 330–334, 423
Putanā, 142

Raheja, G. G., 116, 128
Rājā Bāsak, 52, 59, 61, 64, 82, 85, 87, 108, 138–139, 141, 145, 147, 181, 201–202
Rajasthan, 5, 50, 78, 92–93, 111, 115, 118, 522n.3
Rajput, 125, 127, 12–130, 139–140, 148, 155, 163–164, 221–222
Rām(a), 35–36, 70, 76, 79–80, 96–99, 102
Ramanujan, A. K., 73, 75, 169
Rāmāyaṇa, 6, 68, 104
Rāmdevjī, 5, 78
Rāṇ City, 5, 52, 54, 59, 87, 103, 113, 118, 137, 142, 183–184, 186, 224, 277, 279, 286, 296, 302, 304, 307, 332, 357, 370, 374, 391
Rāṇī Jaimatī, 53–54, 60, 62–63, 79–80, 117, 128, 133–134, 138, 147, 150, 152–153
Rātākoṭ, 54, 122–113, 127, 163, 238, 269, 366, 471, 481–483, 486
Rāvan(a), 36, 71, 79–80, 100–101, 103
Rāvjī/Rāṇā, 59, 62–664, 79, 85, 87, 89–90, 93, 102, 109, 111–114, 117–118, 123, 127, 133–134, 137–141, 150, 162–164, 177–184, 186–187, 196, 227–228, 245, 272, 274–277, 296–298, 309–310, 316–317, 320–321, 332, 342, 345–346, 348–354, 392–393, 404–405, 430, 432–436, 484–484, 489–490
Recursion, 47
Rejoinder, 30–31
Remembrance, 8, 17–18

Repetition, 8, 22–24
allo-, 24
function of, 28–29
Reported speech, 8, 31–34, 36
Ricoeur, P., 3, 10
Rupnāth, 57–58, 64, 79–80, 109–110, 138, 152, 157–158, 215, 217, 220

Sāḍu Mātā, 5, 52–53, 60–61, 64, 86, 101–103, 108, 110, 114, 117, 126, 128, 130–131, 133–134, 138–144, 147–150, 152–153, 157–158, 168, 177–181, 183–190, 193–194, 196–197, 204, 209, 211–214, 216–218, 220–221, 223–224, 226, 240–243, 248, 280, 285–286, 360, 362–364, 377–381, 385–386, 388–401, 458–460, 466, 468–476, 492–494, 524n.34
Ṣakalp/saṃkalpa, 86, 131–133, 147
Śakti, 61, 75–76, 79, 87, 273, 479
Saluṇ, 126, 356, 362
Samcār, 21, 27
Ṣandpipers, 165–167
Śāradā, 18, 20, 95
Sarasvatī, 18, 20, 95
Sat, 35
Satarupā, 35–36, 96–98, 100–104, 107–108, 110
Satī, 54, 64, 133, 163–164, 179
Satīvāḍā, 177, 179
Satya yuga, 55, 79, 103, 107–108, 110
Savāī Bhoj, 53, 58, 64, 79–80, 83–85, 103, 110, 10, 125, 128, 132–134, 138, 148, 150, 153, 157–158, 162, 178–179, 181, 218–219, 225, 228, 248, 258, 260, 263, 272, 274, 326, 337, 339, 340, 342, 342, 361–362, 365, 479
Sāvar, 162
Sax, W. S., 148–149
Self-reference, 38
Śeṣ(a), 79 80, 101, 104, 141, 185
Shulman, D. D., 72, 141, 170
Siṃvarno, 18–19
Sindhan Rajputs, 114–115, 222
Sindhbāḍā, 22, 136, 144–145, 149, 151, 159, 197–200
Singh, K., 49–50
Sisodiya Rajputs, 111, 113–114, 140, 491
Sītā, 80, 101, 123–124
Śītalā Mātā, 80
Śiva/Śaṅkar, 35, 56, 78, 80, 89, 97, 99, 104, 105–106, 109, 114, 138, 151, 160, 177, 180, 191, 210, 216, 247, 249–251, 482
Smith, J. D., 49–51, 69–70, 136
Smṛti, 19
Soifer, D. A., 78, 89–90
Sontheimer, G. D., 151–153, 155
Space, 45–47, 49–50
Ṣpeech genre, 8, 21, 30
Śrauta Sutras, 102
Śrī, 153
Srinivas, M. N., 141
Śruti, 19
Strange loop, 39
Sumiran, 18–19
Suremātā, 75–77, 79, 194, 229, 422–426, 438–439, 455–457, 467, 470
Śurpanakhā, 71
Suvāī Manu, 35–36, 96–98, 100–103, 110
Symbolic translation, 104

Tannen, D., 21, 23, 28–29, 32–33
Tapas/tap, 64, 108
Tejājī, 5, 59, 86, 132, 138, 177, 191, 213, 225, 243, 316, 479
Tejas, 81, 84
Tenāli Rāma, 125
Time, 46–47, 93
cyclical, 109–110
linear, 92, 110
Ṭīṭoḍī, 165–167, 371–374
Tyāga, 88

Udaipur, 113–114, 118, 140, 491
Uncertainty, 171
Utterance, 21,23, 30, 32, 35, 73, 137

Vāh vāh, use of, 25–26
Valdes, M. J., 4
Vāmana, 78, 80
Vana, 151–153
Varāha, 79–80
Vartā, 27–28
Vatsyayana, K., 73
Vaudeville, C., 89
Verbal narrative, 46–47, 80–81, 139, 170
Viṣṇu, 35, 52, 77–81, 83, 85, 87–89, 95–97, 107, 147, 153
Visual narrative, 6, 37, 46, 170

Wilderness, 151, 153, 155
Women, representation of, 128, 134

Yajña, 95, 102–103, 109, 154

Zoller, C. P., 147